Economics and Discrimination
Volume II

The International Library of Critical Writings in Economics

Series Editor: Mark Blaug

Professor Emeritus, University of London
Professor Emeritus, University of Buckingham
Visiting Professor, University of Exeter

This series is an essential reference source for students, researchers and lecturers in economics. It presents by theme an authoritative selection of the most important articles across the entire spectrum of economics. Each volume has been prepared by a leading specialist who has written an authoritative introduction to the literature included.

A full list of published and future titles in this series is printed at the end of this volume.

Economics and Discrimination Volume II

Edited by

William Darity, Jr

Cary C. Boshamer Professor of Economics
University of North Carolina at Chapel Hill, US

THE INTERNATIONAL LIBRARY OF CRITICAL WRITINGS IN ECONOMICS

An Elgar Reference Collection
Aldershot, UK • Brookfield, US

Published by
Edward Elgar Publishing Limited
Gower House
Croft Road
Aldershot
Hants GU11 3HR
UK

Edward Elgar Publishing Company
Old Post Road
Brookfield
Vermont 05036
US

British Library Cataloguing in Publication Data
Economics and Discrimination. –
(International Library of Critical
Writings in Economics; Vol. 57)
I. Darity, William II. Series
331.133

Library of Congress Cataloguing in Publication Data
Economics and discrimination / edited by William Darity Jr.
p. cm. — (The international library of critical writings in economics ; 57) (An Elgar reference collection)
Includes bibliographical references and index.
1. Discrimination in employment. 2. Equal pay for equal work.
3. Employment (Economic theory) I. Darity, William A., 1953–
II. Series. III. Series: An Elgar reference collection.
HD4903.E26 1995
331.13′3—dc20 95–13443
CIP

ISBN 1 85278 790 2 (2 volume set)

Printed in Great Britain by Galliard (Printers) Ltd, Great Yarmouth

Contents

Acknowledgements ix

An introduction to both volumes appears in Volume I

PART I INDIRECT TESTS OF THE PRESENCE OF ECONOMIC DISCRIMINATION

1. Ronald Oaxaca (1973), 'Male-Female Wage Differentials in Urban Labor Markets', *International Economic Review*, **14** (3), October, 693–709 3
2. Alan S. Blinder (1973), 'Wage Discrimination: Reduced Form and Structural Estimates', *Journal of Human Resources*, **VIII** (4), Fall, 436–55 20
3. Alan S. Blinder (1974), 'The Decomposition of Inequality', *Toward An Economic Theory of Income Distribution*, Chapter 5, Cambridge: MIT Press, 119–41 and references 40
4. Francine D. Blau and Marianne A. Ferber (1987), 'Discrimination: Empirical Evidence from the United States', *American Economic Review*, **77** (2), May, 316–20 65
5. Bennett Harrison (1972), 'Education and Underemployment in the Urban Ghetto', *American Economic Review*, **62**, December, 796–812 70
6. George J. Borjas (1983), 'The Substitutability of Black, Hispanic, and White Labor', *Economic Inquiry*, **XXI** (1), January, 93–106 87
7. Michael Firth (1981), 'Racial Discrimination in the British Labor Market', *Industrial and Labor Relations Review*, **34** (2), January, 265–72 101
8. J.B. Knight and M.D. McGrath (1977), 'An Analysis of Racial Wage Discrimination in South Africa', *Oxford Bulletin of Economics and Statistics*, **39** (4), November, 245–71 109
9. J.B. Knight and R.H. Sabot (1982), 'Labor Market Discrimination in a Poor Urban Economy', *Journal of Development Studies*, **19** (1), October, 67–87 137
10. Biswajit Banerjee and J.B. Knight (1985), 'Caste Discrimination in the Indian Urban Labour Market', *Journal of Development Economics*, **17**, April, 277–307 158
11. Reynolds Farley (1990), 'Blacks, Hispanics, and White Ethnic Groups: Are Blacks Uniquely Disadvantaged?', *American Economic Review*, **80** (2), May, 237–41 189
12. James P. Smith (1984), 'Race and Human Capital', *American Economic Review*, **74** (4), September, 685–98 194

13. Dave M. O'Neill (1970), 'The Effect of Discrimination on Earnings: Evidence from Military Test Score Results', *Journal of Human Resources*, **V** (4), Fall, 475–86 208
14. June O'Neill (1990), 'The Role of Human Capital in Earnings Differences Between Black and White Men', *Journal of Economic Perspectives*, **4** (4), Fall, 25–45 220
15. Jeremiah Cotton (1988), 'On the Decomposition of Wage Differentials', *Review of Economics and Statistics*, **LXX** (2), May, 236–43 241

PART II DIRECT TESTS OF THE PRESENCE OF ECONOMIC DISCRIMINATION

16. Roger Jowell and Patricia Prescott-Clarke (1970), 'Racial Discrimination and White-collar Workers in Britain', *Race: A Journal of Race and Group Relations*, **XI** (4), April, 397–417 251
17. Neil McIntosh and David J. Smith (1974), *The Extent of Racial Discrimination*, **Vol.XL** (547), London: PEP, September, 1–55 272
18. John Yinger (1986), 'Measuring Racial Discrimination with Fair Housing Audits: Caught in the Act', *American Economic Review*, **76** (5), December, 881–93 325
19. Peter A. Riach and Judith Rich (1991–2), 'Measuring Discrimination by Direct Experimental Methods: Seeking Gunsmoke', *Journal of Post Keynesian Economics*, **14** (2), Winter, 143–50 338
20. Ronald B. Mincy (1993), 'The Urban Institute Audit Studies: Their Research and Policy Context', in Michael Fix and Raymond J. Struyk (eds), *Clear and Convincing Evidence: Measurement of Discrimination in America*, Chapter 4, Washington: Urban Institute Press, 165–86 346
21. Michael Fix, George C. Galster and Raymond J. Struyk (1993), 'An Overview of Auditing for Discrimination', in Michael Fix and Raymond J. Struyk (eds), *Clear and Convincing Evidence: Measurement of Discrimination in America*, Chapter 1, Washington: Urban Institute Press, 1–67 369

PART III IDENTIFYING WINNERS AND LOSERS FROM DISCRIMINATION

22. John E. Roemer (1979), 'Divide and Conquer: Microfoundations of a Marxian Theory of Wage Discrimination', *Bell Journal of Economics*, **10** (2), Autumn, 695–705 439
23. Michael Reich (1981), 'White Workers are Hurt by Racism: Econometric Evidence', in *Racial Inequality: A Political-Economic Analysis*, Chapter 7, Princeton: Princeton University Press, 268–304 450

24. Steven Shulman (1990), 'Racial Inequality and White Employment: An Interpretation and Test of the Bargaining Power Hypothesis', *Review of Black Political Economy*, **18** (3), Winter, 5–20 487

PART IV ASSESSING ANTIDISCRIMINATION MEASURES

25. S. Dex and P.J. Sloane (1988), 'Detecting and Removing Discrimination Under Equal Opportunities Policies', *Journal of Economic Surveys*, **2** (1), 1–27 505
26. Augustin Kwasi Fosu (1992), 'Occupational Mobility of Black Women, 1958–1981: The Impact of Post-1964 Antidiscrimination Measures', *Industrial and Labor Relations Review*, **45** (2), January, 281–94 532
27. Charles Brown (1984), 'Black-White Earnings Ratios Since the Civil Rights Act of 1964: The Importance of Labor Market Dropouts', *Quarterly Journal of Economics*, **XCIX** (1), February, 31–44 546
28. Jonathan S. Leonard (1984), 'Employment and Occupational Advance Under Affirmative Action', *Review of Economics and Statistics*, **LXVI** (3), August, 377–85 560
29. James J. Heckman and Brook S. Payner (1989), 'Determining the Impact of Federal Antidiscrimination Policy on the Economic Status of Blacks: A Study of South Carolina', *American Economic Review*, **79** (1), March, 138–77 569
30. Jomo K.S. and Ishak Shari (1986), *Development Policies and Income Inequality in Peninsular Malaysia*, Chapters 1–2, Kuala Lumpur: Institute of Advanced Studies, 3–22 and references 609

Name Index 631

Acknowledgements

The editor and publishers wish to thank the following who have kindly given permission for the use of copyright material.

American Economic Association for articles: Bennett Harrison (1972), 'Education and Underemployment in the Urban Ghetto', *American Economic Review*, **62**, December, 796–812; James P. Smith (1984), 'Race and Human Capital', *American Economic Review*, **74** (4), September, 685–98; John Yinger (1986), 'Measuring Racial Discrimination with Fair Housing Audits: Caught in the Act', *American Economic Review*, **76** (5), December, 881–93; Francine D. Blau and Marianne A. Ferber (1987), 'Discrimination: Empirical Evidence from the United States', *American Economic Review*, **77** (2), May, 316–20; James J. Heckman and Brook S. Payner (1989), 'Determining the Impact of Federal Antidiscrimination Policy on the Economic Status of Blacks: A Study of South Carolina', *American Economic Review*, **79** (1), March, 138–77; Reynolds Farley (1990), 'Blacks, Hispanics, and White Ethnic Groups: Are Blacks Uniquely Disadvantaged?', *American Economic Review*, **80** (2), May, 237–41; June O'Neill (1990), 'The Role of Human Capital in Earnings Differences Between Black and White Men', *Journal of Economic Perspectives*, **4** (4), Fall, 25–45.

Basil Blackwell Ltd for articles: J.B. Knight and M.D. McGrath (1977), 'An Analysis of Racial Wage Discrimination in South Africa', *Oxford Bulletin of Economics and Statistics*, **39** (4), November, 245–71; S. Dex and P.J. Sloane (1988), 'Detecting and Removing Discrimination Under Equal Opportunities Policies', *Journal of Economic Surveys*, **2** (1), 1–27.

Elsevier Science Publishers B.V. for articles: Jonathan S. Leonard (1984), 'Employment and Occupational Advance Under Affirmative Action', *Review of Economics and Statistics*, **LXVI** (3), August, 377–85; Biswajit Banerjee and J.B. Knight (1985), 'Caste Discrimination in the Indian Urban Labour Market', *Journal of Development Economics*, **17**, April, 277–307; Jeremiah Cotton (1988), 'On the Decomposition of Wage Differentials', *Review of Economics and Statistics*, **LXX** (2), May, 236–43.

Frank Cass & Co. Ltd for article: J.B. Knight and R.H. Sabot (1982), 'Labor Market Discrimination in a Poor Urban Economy', *Journal of Development Studies*, **19** (1), October, 67–87.

Industrial and Labor Relations Review for articles: Michael Firth (1981), 'Racial Discrimination in the British Labor Market', *Industrial and Labor Relations Review*, **34** (2), January, 265–72; Augustin Kwasi Fosu (1992), 'Occupational Mobility of Black Women, 1958-81: The Impact of Post-1964 Antidiscrimination Measures', *Industrial and Labor Relations Review*, **45** (2), January, 281–94.

Institute of Advanced Studies, Kuala Lumpur for excerpt: Jomo K.S. and Ishak Shari (1986), *Development Policies and Income Inequality in Peninsular Malaysia*, Chapters 1–2, 3–22.

Institute of Race Relations for article: Roger Jowell and Patricia Prescott-Clarke (1970), 'Racial Discrimination and White-collar Workers in Britain', *Race: A Journal of Race and Group Relations*, **XI** (4), April, 397–417.

International Economic Review for article: Ronald Oaxaca (1973), 'Male-Female Wage Differentials in Urban Labor Markets', *International Economic Review*, **14** (3), October, 693–709.

M.E. Sharpe, Inc. for article: Peter A. Riach and Judith Rich (1991–2), 'Measuring Discrimination by Direct Experimental Methods: Seeking Gunsmoke', *Journal of Post Keynesian Economics*, **14** (2), Winter, 143–50.

M.I.T. Press for excerpt: Alan S. Blinder (1974), 'The Decomposition of Inequality', *Toward an Economic Theory of Income Distribution*, Chapter 5, 119–41.

M.I.T. Press Journals for article: Charles Brown (1984), 'Black-White Earnings Ratios Since the Civil Rights Act of 1964: The Importance of Labor Market Dropouts', *Quarterly Journal of Economics*, **XCIX** (1), February, 31–44.

Policy Studies Institute for article: Neil McIntosh and David J. Smith (1974), *The Extent of Racial Discrimination*, **XL** (547), September, 1–55.

Princeton University Press for excerpt: Michael Reich (1981), 'White Workers are Hurt by Racism: Econometric Evidence', *Racial Inequality: A Political-Economic Analysis*, Chapter 7, 268–304.

RAND for article: John E. Roemer (1979), 'Divide and Conquer: Microfoundations of a Marxian Theory of Wage Discrimination', *Bell Journal of Economics*, **10** (2), Autumn, 695–705.

Transaction Publishers for article: Steven Shulman (1990), 'Racial Inequality and White Employment: An Interpretation and Test of the Bargaining Power Hypothesis', *Review of Black Political Economy*, **18** (3), Winter, 5–20.

University of Wisconsin Press for articles: Dave M. O'Neill (1970), 'The Effect of Discrimination on Earnings: Evidence from Military Test Score Results', *Journal of Human Resources*, **V** (4), Fall, 475–86; Alan S. Blinder (1973), 'Wage Discrimination: Reduced Form and Structural Estimates', *Journal of Human Resources*, **VIII** (4), Fall, 436–55.

Urban Institute Press for excerpts: Michael Fix, George C. Galster and Raymond J. Struyk (1993), 'An Overview of Auditing for Discrimination', in Michael Fix and Raymond J. Struyk (eds), *Clear and Convincing Evidence: Measurement of Discrimination in America*, Chapter 1, 1–67; Ronald B. Mincy (1993), 'The Urban Institute Audit Studies:Their Research and Policy Context', in Michael Fix and Raymond J. Struyk (eds), *Clear and Convincing Evidence: Measurement of Discrimination in America*, Chapter 4, 165–86.

Western Economic Association International for article: George J. Borjas (1983), 'The Substitutability of Black, Hispanic, and White Labor', *Economic Inquiry*, **XXI** (1), January, 93–106.

Every effort has been made to trace all the copyright holders but if any have been inadvertently overlooked the publishers will be pleased to make the necessary arrangement at the first opportunity.

In addition the publishers wish to thank the Library of the London School of Economics and Political Science, the Marshall Library of Economics, Cambridge University and the Photographic Unit of the University of London Library for their assistance in obtaining these articles.

Part I
Indirect Tests of the Presence of Economic Discrimination

[1]

INTERNATIONAL ECONOMIC REVIEW
Vol. 14, No. 3, October, 1973

MALE-FEMALE WAGE DIFFERENTIALS IN URBAN LABOR MARKETS*

BY RONALD OAXACA[1]

CULTURE, TRADITION, AND OVERT DISCRIMINATION tend to make restrictive the terms by which women may participate in the labor force. These influences combine to generate an unfavorable occupational distribution of female workers vis-à-vis male workers and to create pay differences between males and females within the same occupation. The result is a chronic earnings gap between male and female full-time, year-round workers. Unfortunately, explanations at this level of generality are mainly descriptive. It is the purpose of this paper to estimate the average extent of discrimination against female workers in the United States and to provide a quantitative assessment of the sources of male-female wage differentials.

1. INTRODUCTION

In his study of sex differentials from the 1950 U. S. Census, Sanborn [13] found the female/male annual income ratio to be .58 which implies a male-female wage differential (as a proportion of the female wage) of .72. Sanborn's stated objective was to consider discrimination only in the context of equal pay for equal work and not to deal with discrimination stemming from occupational barriers. Using both male and female adjustment weights, Sanborn adjusted the income ratio for occupational distribution, annual hours of work, education, urbanness, race, turnover, absenteeism, and work experience. In his attempt to approximate equal work, Sanborn controlled for 262 detailed occupations. These adjustments brought the income ratio up to .87—.88. The residual difference was therefore .13 and thus about 18% of the original differential. As an estimate of the upper limits of the effects of discrimination it is rather low, but this is not surprising in view of the aspect of discrimination under study.

Using data from the 1960 U. S. Census, Fuchs [6] calculated the hourly earnings of females relative to males to be .60 which implies a male-female wage differential of .66. Fuchs does not believe that inherent differences in physical strength account for the sizeable pay difference simply because jobs requiring heavy labor are in a minority in the present day occupational structure. He contended that role differentiation stemming from social attitudes and discrimination affects the determinants of earnings. The earnings ratio was raised to .66

* Manuscript received May 1, 1972; revised November 13, 1972.

[1] The author wishes to thank Orley Ashenfelter, Daniel Hamermesh, Albert Rees, Sherwin Rosen, and a referee for comments on an earlier version of this paper. Naturally, the responsibility of any remaining errors lies with the author. Financial assistance for this study was provided by the U.S. Department of Labor, Manpower Administration, under the provisions of Title 1 of the Manpower Development and Training Act, Public Law 87-415, as amended.

after adjustments for color, schooling, age, city size, marital status, class of worker, and length of trip to work. This adjusted ratio implies a residual differential of .51, which is 77% of the original differential. From the results of his regressions of hourly earnings across occupations, Fuchs concluded that nearly all of the wage differential could be explained away if one chooses sufficiently narrow occupational categories. As Fuchs observed, this merely casts the problem interms of why occupational distributions are so different between males and females.

In Cohen's study of sex differentials [5], an annual difference of $5,000 for full-time employed males and females was calculated from a 1969 working conditions survey. Cohen adjusted the difference in pay by excluding those under the age of 22 and over 64, the self-employed, persons without a steady job, and professionals. He also adjusted for differences in annual hours worked, fringe benefits, absenteeism, seniority, education, and unionization. The income difference was reduced to $2,550 or 51% of the original difference. Cohen attributed this large residual to the concentration of women in lower paying jobs.

The Malkiels' study [9] of professional workers revealed male-female wage differentials that ranged from .48 to .51 for the years 1966, 1969–1971. Adjustment for differences in schooling and experience yielded residual differentials varying between 37% to 49% of the original wage differentials. For one of the years the unexplained residual was reduced to only 3% of the original wage difference by adjusting for differences in schooling, experience, job level, critical area of study, and publications. This clearly indicates that unequal pay for equal work is not a significant source of discrimination. The problem of discrimination centers around the assignment of job levels. The Malkiels found that 53% of the male-female difference in job levels could not be explained by differences in personal characteristics.

2. A MEASURE OF DISCRIMINATION

Discrimination against females can be said to exist whenever the relative wage of males exceeds the relative wage that would have prevailed if males and females were paid according to the same criteria. We can formalize this notion by proposing the concept of a discrimination coefficient (D) as a measure of discrimination:

$$D = \frac{W_m/W_f - (W_m/W_f)^0}{(W_m/W_f)^0}; \tag{1}$$

where

(W_m/W_f) = the observed male-female wage ratio;

and

$(W_m/W_f)^0$ = the male-female wage ratio in the absence of discrimination.

An equivalent expression in natural logarithms is

$$\ln(D+1) = \ln(W_m/W_f) - \ln(W_m/W_f)^0 . \tag{2}$$

Assuming that employers in a nondiscriminating labor market adhere to the principle of cost minimization, we have

$$\left(\frac{W_m}{W_f}\right)^0 = \frac{MP_m}{MP_f};$$

where MP_m and MP_f are the marginal products of males and females, respectively.

In [2] Becker defined the market discrimination coefficient as the percentage wage differential between two types of perfectly substitutable labor. For those cases in which the two factors were not necessarily perfect substitutes, Becker defined the discrimination coefficient as the simple difference between the observed wage ratio and the wage ratio in the absence of discrimination. The discrimination coefficient defined by (1) is simply Becker's generalized measure divided by the wage ratio in the absence of discrimination. The generalized measures admit perfect substitutes as a special case and thus afford more flexibility for empirical work.

3. ESTIMATION PROCEDURES

Since $(W_m/W_f)^0$ is unknown, the estimation of D is equivalent to estimating $(W_m/W_f)^0$. On the basis of either of two assumptions, we can estimate the male-female wage ratio that would exist in the absence of discrimination: If there were no discrimination, 1) the wage structure currently faced by females would also apply to males; or 2) the wage structure currently faced by males would also apply to females. Assumption one (two) says that females (males) would on average receive in the absence of discrimination the same wages as they presently receive, but that discrimination takes the form of males (females) receiving more (less) than a nondiscriminating labor market would award them.

Ordinary least squares estimation of a wage equation for any given group of workers provides an estimate of the wage structure applicable to that group. The wage equation to be estimated separately for each race-sex group has the semi-log functional form

$$\ln(W_i) = Z_i'\beta + u_i , \qquad i = 1, \ldots, n \tag{3}$$

where

W_i = the hourly wage rate of the i-th worker,
Z_i' = a vector of individual characteristics,
β = a vector of coefficients,
u_i = a disturbance term.

When the male-female wage differential is expressed in natural logarithms, the formulation of the discrimination coefficient in (2) and our alternative assumptions about which wage structure would prevail in the absence of discrimination together imply that the wage differential can be decomposed into the effects of discrimination and the effects of differences in individual characteristics.

Let

$$G = \frac{\bar{W}_m - \bar{W}_f}{\bar{W}_f},$$

then

$$\ln(G+1) = \ln(\bar{W}_m) - \ln(\bar{W}_f) \tag{4}$$

where $\bar{W}_m$ and $\bar{W}_f$ are the average hourly wages for males and females, respectively.[2] From the properties of ordinary least squares estimation, we have

$$\ln(\bar{W}_m) = \bar{Z}_m'\hat{\beta}_m \tag{5}$$

$$\ln(\bar{W}_f) = \bar{Z}_f'\hat{\beta}_f \tag{6}$$

where

$\bar{Z}_m'$ and $\bar{Z}_f'$ = the vectors of mean values of the regressors for males and females, respectively.

$\hat{\beta}_m$ and $\hat{\beta}_f$ = the corresponding vectors of estimated coefficients.

Upon substitution of (5) and (6) into (4), we obtain

$$\ln(G+1) = \bar{Z}_m'\hat{\beta}_m - \bar{Z}_f'\hat{\beta}_f. \tag{7}$$

If we let

$$\Delta\bar{Z}' = \bar{Z}_m' - \bar{Z}_f' \tag{8}$$

$$\Delta\hat{\beta} = \hat{\beta}_f - \hat{\beta}_m \tag{9}$$

and substitute $\hat{\beta}_m = \hat{\beta}_f - \Delta\hat{\beta}$ in (7), then the male-female wage differential can be written as

$$\ln(G+1) = \Delta\bar{Z}'\hat{\beta}_f - \bar{Z}_m'\Delta\hat{\beta}. \tag{10}$$

On the basis of equation (2) and the assumption that the current female wage structure would apply to both males and females in a nondiscriminating labor market, it can be shown that

$$\ln\left(\widehat{\frac{W_m}{W_f}}\right)^0 = \Delta\bar{Z}'\hat{\beta}_f \tag{11}$$

$$\ln(\widehat{D+1}) = -\bar{Z}_m'\Delta\hat{\beta}. \tag{12}$$

Thus expressions (11) and (12) represent the decomposition of the wage differential into the estimated effects of differences in individual characteristics and the estimated effects of discrimination, respectively.

An alternative decomposition of the wage differential is obtained by substi-

[2] These wage figures are computed as geometric means, i.e.,

$$\bar{W} = \exp\left\{\left[\sum_{i=1}^{n} \ln(W_i)\right]/n\right\}.$$

tuting $\hat{\beta}_f = \Delta\hat{\beta} + \hat{\beta}_m$ in (7):

$$(13) \qquad \ln (G + 1) = \Delta\bar{Z}'\hat{\beta}_m - \bar{Z}_f'\Delta\hat{\beta} .$$

On the basis of (2) and the assumption that the current male wage structure would apply to both males and females in the absence of discrimination, it can be shown that

$$(14) \qquad \ln \left(\widehat{\frac{W_m}{W_f}}\right)^0 = \Delta\bar{Z}'\hat{\beta}_m$$

$$(15) \qquad \ln (\widehat{D + 1}) = -\bar{Z}_f'\Delta\hat{\beta} .$$

Our method of estimating the effects of discrimination involves the familiar index number problem. Therefore, the separate estimates obtained from using both the male and female regression weights establish a range of possible values.

4. SPECIFICATION OF THE CONTROL VARIABLES

In accordance with the post-schooling investment model of human capital formation as developed in [8] and [10], a quadratic experience variable is included in the wage equations. The corresponding coefficients measure the combined effects of the average rate of return to on-the-job training, the initial proportion of time allocated to OJT, and the length of the investment horizon.

Since data on the actual number of years of work experience for a large sample of workers are generally unavailable, we define a proxy for actual work experience:

$$(16) \qquad X_i = A_i - E_i - 6$$

where

X_i = potential experience,
A_i = the age of the i-th individual,
E_i = the number of years of schooling completed by the i-th individual.

When work experience is acquired without interruption after the completion of formal schooling, potential and actual experience coincide. Potential experience is a reasonable proxy for actual experience in the case of males since males on average exhibit a strong attachment to the labor force. However, potential experience overstates the actual years of work experience of females to the extent that many female workers have left the labor force for some period in the past due to their household and childbearing activities. The difficulty this presents for estimation is of course the errors in variables problem. It is not clear what the net effect would be on our estimates of discrimination. It seems reasonable to suppose that the potential experience-wage profile would be flatter than the actual experience-wage profile. If the estimator of the coefficient on the linear experience term were biased downward for females, then $-\Delta\hat{\beta}$ would be biased upward in this instance. Consequently, there would be a bias toward finding discrimination.[3]

As a rough attempt to handle the problem of lost experience, we have controlled for the number of children (C) born to the female. The linear children variable reflects the cost of lost experience due to child care, including the costs from the depreciation of skills during the periods of absence from the labor force. Accordingly, we expect the estimated coefficient ($\hat{\beta}_c$) to have a negative sign. There is some difficulty associated with the introduction of this variable since it is obviously correlated with the proxy experience variable; however, in the absence of data on actual work experience, the use of the children variable seems justified.[4]

The remaining control variables are briefly described:

Education: years of schooling completed (linear and quadratic terms);

Class of Worker: dummy variables for union membership (privately employed wage and salary worker), government employed, and self-employed with non-union private wage and salary workers as the reference group;

Industry: dummy variables for U.S. Census two digit industries with retail trade as the reference group;

Occupation: dummy variables for U.S. Census two digit occupations with sales workers as the reference group;

Health Problems: dummy variable = 1 if the individual reports health problems that affect the kind or amount of work he or she can perform, and '0' otherwise;

Part-Time: dummy variable = 1 if the individual works less than thirty-five hours a week, and '0' otherwise;

Migration: a) dummy variable = 1 if the individual has maintained a residence more than fifty miles from his or her current address since the age of seventeen, and '0' otherwise, b) *YRSM*: number of years since the individual last migrated (linear and quadratic terms);

Marital Status: dummy variables for spouse present, spouse absent, widowed, and divorced (or separated) with never married individuals as the reference group;

Size of Urban Area: dummy variables for residence in Standard Metropolitan Statistical Areas less than 250,000 (SMSA<250), greater than or equal to 250,000 but less than 500,000 (SMSA 250–500), greater than or equal to 500,000 but less than 750,000 (SMSA 500–750), and greater than or equal to 750,000 (SMSA 750+) with urban, non-SMSA's as the reference group; and

Region: dummy variables for U.S. Census regions North East, North Central, and West with South as the reference group.[5]

One difficulty with the present formulation of the wage equation is that it controls for what many would consider to be major sources of discrimination

[3] These considerations also apply to wage models that specify an age variable in lieu of experience.

[4] The consequences of omitting this variable are discussed in footnote 6.

[5] The rationale for including most of these variables in a wage regression is fairly well known; nevertheless a more detailed discussion is given in [11].

against women. By controlling for broadly defined occupation, we eliminate some of the effects of occupational barriers as sources of discrimination. As a result, we are likely to underestimate the effects of discrimination. Therefore, we estimate another set of equations that do not control for occupation, industry, and class of worker. We shall refer to this set of regressions as the personal characteristics wage regressions, and to the original set as the full-scale wage regressions.

It is clear that the magnitude of the estimated effects of discrimination crucially depends upon the choice of control variables for the wage regressions. A researcher's choice of control variables implicitly reveals his or her attitude toward what constitutes discrimination in the labor market. If it were possible to control for virtually all sources of variation in wages, one could pretty well eliminate labor market discrimination as a significant factor in determining wage differentials by sex (or race). This is because $\Delta\hat{\beta}$, and therefore $\ln(D+1)$, would be very small. The result is that whatever the wage differential observed, it is completely justified on the grounds of alleged productivity differences. The other extreme is to control for virtually nothing and thereby minimize the role of productivity differences, $\Delta\bar{Z}$. This is tantamount to declaring at the outset that the two labor inputs are near perfect substitutes and therefore attributing virtually all of the observed wage differential to labor market discrimination, i.e., relatively high values of $\Delta\hat{\beta}$.

In reference to the type of regression approach we have adopted, it is impractical to control for detailed occupation. When we control for broadly defined two digit categories, we are not assuming that the conditions of equal work are met. Although the full-scale wage regressions eliminate male-female differences in broad occupational attachment as possible sources of discrimination, they can still reflect job and pay discrimination within each two digit category. The personal characteristics wage equations were specified with the intention of examining the issue of equal pay for roughly similar personal characteristics and not just for equal work.

5. EMPIRICAL RESULTS

The data for the study are from the 1967 Survey of Economic Opportunity. The particular subsample used for this study consists of the intersection of the following sets: those individuals who show an hourly wage for the week preceding the survey; adults sixteen years or older; those who live in urban areas; and those who report their race as either White or Negro.

The regression coefficients corresponding to the full-scale and personal characteristics wage equations are presented in Tables 1 and 2, respectively. Coefficients were not estimated in the following cases: 1) the particular characteristic served as the base group; 2) there were no observations in a particular cell: 3) the same observations were found in another cell; or 4) the regressor was left out on the basis of poor results from earlier regressions. The joint tests of significance for $\Delta\hat{\beta}$ in both the full-scale and personal characteristics wage regressions

TABLE 1

FULL-SCALE WAGE REGRESSIONS[a]

Variable	Whites			Blacks		
	Male	Female	Δβ	Male	Female	Δβ
Constant	.0365 (.77)	−.1024 (−1.34)	−.1389 (−1.60)	.0953 (1.71)	−.3851* (−6.35)	−.4804* (−5.85)
Experience						
Experience	.0176* (13.89)	.0138* (8.19)	−.0038 (−1.88)	.0117* (7.73)	.0067* (4.38)	−.0050* (−2.29)
Experience**2	−.000288* (−12.22)	−.000248* (−7.31)	.000040 (.98)	−.000204* (−7.59)	−.000122* (−4.33)	.000082* (2.11)
Education						
Education	.0082 (1.27)	−.0118 (−.98)	−.0200 (−1.53)	−.0308* (−4.60)	−.0175* (−1.98)	.0133 (1.19)
Education**2	.00169* (5.92)	.00194* (3.53)	.00025 (.42)	.00300* (8.23)	.00245* (5.26)	−.00055 (−.93)
Class of Worker						
Union	.1113* (9.39)	.1500* (6.70)	.0387 (1.59)	.2129* (14.15)	.0719* (3.11)	−.1410* (−5.14)
Nonunion Private Wage and Salary	—	—	—	—	—	—
Government	.0646* (3.15)	.1445* (5.89)	.0799* (2.54)	.1328* (5.44)	.1263* (5.19)	−.0065 (−.19)
Self-Employed	−.1290* (3.51)	.1137 (1.22)	.2427* (2.54)	−.0128 (−.15)	−.3437* (−2.67)	−.3309* (−2.15)
Industry						
Agriculture	.1285 (1.81)	.2847 (1.09)	.1562 (.61)	−.0067 (−.08)	−.0190 (−.21)	−.0123 (−1.18)
Mining	.3604* (6.83)	.4112* (2.02)	.0508 (.26)	.0697 (.40)	—	—
Construction	.2997* (13.72)	.2444* (3.80)	−.0553 (−.86)	.2729* (10.54)	.0395 (.22)	−.2334 (−1.30)
Manufacturing-Durable	.2398* (13.76)	.2562* (8.39)	.0164 (.48)	.2101* (9.15)	.2590* (6.46)	.0489 (1.06)
Manufacturing-Non Durable	.2086* (11.03)	.1968* (6.60)	−0.118 (−.35)	.1679* (6.85)	.2305* (6.46)	.0626 (1.45)
Transportation	.2332* (9.81)	.3154* (5.54)	.0822 (1.40)	.2182* (7.39)	.5463* (5.73)	.3281* (3.32)
Communications	.2370* (5.62)	.2290* (4.56)	−.0080 (−.12)	.1555 (1.78)	.2657* (3.71)	.1102 (.98)
Utilities	.2414* (7.32)	.2451* (2.83)	.0087 (.04)	.1433* (3.45)	.7026* (2.76)	.5593* (2.19)
Wholesale Trade	.2039* (8.45)	.1979* (4.74)	−.0060 (−.13)	.1204* (3.76)	.3065* (4.34)	.1861* (2.41)
Retail Trade	—	—	—	—	—	—
Finance	.2224* (8.25)	.1761* (5.65)	−.0463 (−1.14)	.0184 (.47)	.1593* (3.22)	.1409* (2.25)

(*Continued on next page*)

TABLE 1

(CONTINUED)

Variable	Whites			Blacks		
	Male	Female	Δβ	Male	Female	Δβ
Business and Repair Services	.1385* (4.44)	.1525* (3.24)	.0140 (.26)	.0766* (2.10)	.1326* (2.31)	.0560 (.83)
Personal Services	−.0618 (−1.71)	−.0183 (−.50)	.0435 (.85)	−.1055* (−3.22)	.0118 (.40)	.1173* (2.65)
Recreation	.0488 (.97)	.1527* (1.97)	.1039 (1.16)	.0020 (.04)	.1019 (1.29)	.0999 (1.05)
Professional Services	−.0629* (−2.53)	.0528* (2.01)	.1157* (3.24)	.0633* (2.13)	.1181* (4.45)	.0548 (1.38)
Public Administration	.1970* (6.58)	.2165* (4.86)	.0195 (.37)	.2374* (6.75)	.2170* (5.61)	−.0204 (−.39)
Occupation						
Professional Workers	.1563* (6.62)	.3736* (10.25)	.2173* (5.16)	.2144* (4.62)	.4631* (10.80)	.2487* (3.43)
Managers	.1822* (8.27)	.2759* (6.85)	.0937* (2.12)	.0810 (1.49)	.2792* (3.53)	.1982* (2.07)
Clerical Workers	−.0639* (−2.68)	.1665* (6.03)	.2304* (6.41)	.0208 (.54)	.1509* (4.50)	.1301* (2.55)
Sales Workers	—	—	—	—	—	—
Craftsmen	.0275 (1.28)	.0932 (1.31)	.0657 (.93)	.0733* (1.99)	.1297* (1.97)	.0564 (.75)
Operatives	−.1064* (−4.92)	.0128 (.37)	.1192* (3.00)	−.0271 (−.77)	.0236 (.62)	.0507 (.98)
Private Household Workers	−.1900 (−1.03)	−.3060* (−5.46)	−.1160 (−.58)	−.0458 (−.28)	−.1432* (−3.58)	−.0974 (−.58)
Service Workers	−.1358* (−5.19)	−.0219 (−.72)	.1139* (2.89)	−.0998 (−2.84)	−.0164 (−.53)	.0834 (1.78)
Farm Laborers	−.4570* (−5.38)	.1579 (.43)	.6149 (1.71)	−.1421 (−1.36)	—	—
Laborers	−.1540* (−5.59)	−.0166 (−.15)	.1374 (1.29)	−.0637 (−1.77)	.0317 (.37)	.0954 (1.03)
Health Problems	−.1001* (−6.08)	−.0710* (−2.70)	.0291 (.97)	−.0811* (−3.79)	−.0270 (−1.31)	.0541 (1.82)
Part-Time	−.1874* (−9.14)	−.0445* (−2.64)	.1429* (5.37)	−.1117* (−4.80)	.0034 (.21)	.1151* (4.04)
Migration						
Migration	−.0356* (−2.48)	−.1073* (−5.03)	−.0717* (−2.87)	.0052 (.44)	−.0361 (−1.94)	−.0413 (−1.88)
YRSM	.0072* (4.22)	.0087* (3.33)	.0015 (.48)	—	.0025* (2.73)	—
YRSM**2	−.000140* (−3.08)	−.000147* (−2.14)	−.000007 (−.10)	—	—	—
Marital Status						
Spouse Present	.1841* (11.88)	.0883* (4.51)	−.0958* (−3.91)	.1211* (6.43)	.0995* (5.13)	−.0216 (−.80)

(Continued on next page)

TABLE 1

(CONTINUED)

Variable	Whites			Blacks		
	Male	Female	$\Delta\beta$	Male	Female	$\Delta\beta$
Spouse Absent	.1124 (1.72)	.0852 (1.39)	−.0272 (−.30)	.0446 (.79)	.1050* (2.38)	.0604 (.84)
Widowed	.1030* (2.37)	.0687* (2.21)	−.0343 (−.64)	.0920* (2.13)	.0980* (3.47)	.0060 (.12)
Divorced	.0793* (2.74)	.0933* (3.38)	.0140 (.35)	.0396 (1.53)	.0607* (2.72)	.0211 (.62)
Single, Never Married	—	—	—	—	—	—
Children	—	−.0198* (−4.51)	—	—	−.0007 (−.24)	—
Size of Urban Area						
Urban, Non SMSA	—	—	—	—	—	—
SMSA<250	.0332* (1.98)	.0920* (3.86)	.0588* (2.07)	.0523 (1.54)	.1458* (4.19)	.0935 (1.93)
SMSA 250–500	.0727* (3.89)	.0956* (3.65)	.0229 (.73)	.1098* (2.83)	.1833* (4.61)	.0735 (1.32)
SMSA 500–750	.1411* (7.30)	.1524* (5.46)	.0113 (.34)	.1349* (3.55)	.1816* (4.46)	.0467 (.84)
SMSA 750+	.1745* (12.57)	.2186* (11.21)	.0441 (1.89)	.2079* (6.46)	.3643* (10.92)	.1564* (3.38)
Region						
North East	.0738* (5.63)	.0882* (4.69)	.0144 (.64)	.1366* (7.86)	.1724* (9.24)	.0358 (1.41)
North Central	.0749* (5.85)	.0646* (3.52)	−.0103 (−.47)	.1479* (9.37)	.1376* (8.00)	−.0103 (−.44)
South	—	—	—	—	—	—
West	.1200* (8.51)	.1389* (6.83)	.0189 (.79)	.2452* (12.48)	.2612* (12.07)	.0160 (.55)
F Statistic for Joint Test of Significance	128.31*	50.88*	13.28*	71.96*	97.14*	9.93*
R^2	.43	.33		.46	.56	
Standard Error of Estimate	.40	.45		.35	.36	
Number of Observations	8,123	4,962		3,897	3,502	

[a] '*t*' values in parentheses.

* Significant at the 5% level.

reveal that the wage structure for males and females are significantly different with respecct to the regressors common to both groups.

The average logarithms of the hourly wages (and the corresponding geometric mean wages) computed from our sample are as follows: 1.0806 ($2.95) for white males, .6499 ($1.92) for white females, .7721 ($2.16) for black males, and .3732 ($1.45) for black females. The values of the wage differentials in logarithmic terms, ln $(G + 1)$, are .4307 for whites and .3989 for blacks. To facilitate com-

TABLE 2

PERSONAL CHARACTERISTICS WAGE REGRESSIONS[a]

Variable	Whites			Blacks		
	Male	Female	Δβ	Male	Female	Δβ
Constant	−.0681*	.0894	.1575	.1472*	−.2325*	−.3797*
	(−2.03)	(.94)	(1.87)	(2.44)	(−3.75)	(−4.65)
Experience						
Experience	.0222*	.0182*	−.0039	.0195*	.0066*	−.0129*
	(16.51)	(10.20)	(−1.81)	(12.03)	(4.02)	(−5.53)
Experience**2	−.000354*	−.000349*	.000005	−.000340*	−.000133*	.000207*
	(−14.19)	(−9.69)	(.13)	(−11.69)	(−4.26)	(4.86)
Education						
Education	.0342*	−.0394*	−.0736*	−.0434*	−.0660*	−.0226
	(5.24)	(−3.30)	(−5.63)	(−6.16)	(−7.12)	(−1.95)
Education**2	.00097*	.00450*	.00353*	.00417*	.00685*	.00268*
	(3.51)	(8.63)	(6.24)	(11.46)	(15.35)	(4.68)
Health Problems	−.1325*	−.1097*	.0228	−.1275*	−.0638*	.0637
	(−7.57)	(−3.89)	(.71)	(−5.41)	(−2.75)	(1.92)
Part-Time	−.3154*	−.1560*	.1594*	−.1908*	−.1139*	.0769*
	(−14.84)	(−9.09)	(5.81)	(−7.57)	(−6.73)	(2.52)
Migration						
Migration	−.0316*	−.1262*	−.0946*	.0125	−.0726*	−.0851*
	(−2.05)	(−5.54)	(−3.56)	(.96)	(−3.48)	(−3.49)
YRSM	.0073*	.0107*	.0034	—	.0034*	—
	(3.98)	(3.81)	(1.05)		(3.24)	
YRSM**2	−.000140*	−.000169*	−.000029*	—	—	—
	(−2.91)	(−2.29)	(−.34)			
Marital Status						
Spouse Present	.2514*	.1246*	−.1268*	.1584*	.0986*	−.0598*
	(15.44)	(5.96)	(−4.90)	(7.66)	(4.53)	(−1.99)
Spouse Absent	.1189	.0706	−.0483	.0975	.0964	−.0011
	(1.71)	(1.07)	(−.51)	(1.56)	(1.94)	(−.01)
Widowed	.1389*	.0804*	−.0585	.1648*	.0754*	−.0894
	(3.00)	(2.41)	(−1.01)	(3.46)	(2.38)	(−1.55)
Divorced	.1027*	.1064*	.0037	.0511	.0618*	.0107
	(3.34)	(3.61)	(.09)	(1.78)	(2.46)	(.28)
Single, Never Married	—	—	—	—	—	—
Children	—	−.0295*	—	—	−.0025	—
		(−6.31)			(−.80)	
Size of Urban Area						
Urban, Non SMSA	—	—	—	—	—	—
SMSA<250	.0412*	.1080*	.0668*	.0667	.1415*	.0748
	(2.30)	(4.23)	(2.20)	(1.78)	(3.60)	(1.38)
SMSA 250–500	.0845*	.1154*	.0309	.1103*	.1879*	.0776
	(4.26)	(4.11)	(.92)	(2.57)	(4.20)	(1.25)
SMSA 500–750	.1739*	.1721*	−.0018	.1821*	.1769*	−.0052
	(8.47)	(5.77)	(−.05)	(4.34)	(3.86)	(−.08)

(Continued on next page)

TABLE 2

(CONTINUED)

Variable	Whites Male	Whites Female	Whites $\Delta\beta$	Blacks Male	Blacks Female	Blacks $\Delta\beta$
SMSA 750+	.1972* (13.45)	.2543* (12.27)	.0571* (2.31)	.7452* (6.95)	.3888* (10.39)	.1436* (2.80)
Region						
North East	.0655* (4.73)	.1129* (5.69)	.0474* (2.01)	.1704* (8.97)	.2268* (11.07)	.0564* (2.02)
North Central	.0790* (5.91)	.0685* (3.52)	−.0105 (−.46)	.2255* (13.56)	.1996* (10.57)	−.0259 (−1.03)
South	—	—	—	—	—	—
West	.1111* (7.49)	.1174* (5.43)	.0063 (.25)	.2889* (13.44)	.3027* (12.56)	.0138 (.43)
F Statistic for Joint Test of Significance	213.29*	67.51*	45.05*	103.93*	132.01*	58.14*
R^2	.34	.22		.33	.43	
Standard Error of Estimate	.43	.49		.39	.40	
Number of Observations	8,123	4,962		3,897	3,502	

[a] *t* values in parentheses.
* Significant at the 5% level.

parison of our results with those of other studies, the wage differential *G* is also calculated. The value of *G* is .54 for whites and .49 for blacks.

The effects of discrimination are approximated by the residual left after subtracting the effects of differences in individual characteristics from the overall wage differential. The calculations based on the full-scale wage regressions are presented in Table 3. As a simple average of the two estimates obtained, discrimination accounts for 58.4% of the logarithmic wage differential for whites and 55.6% for blacks. The average value of the discrimination coefficient is .29 for whites and .25 for blacks. Table 4 presents the effects of discrimination calculated from the personal characteristics wage regressions. Predictably, the estimated effects of discrimination are larger than those reported in Table 3: Discrimination accounts for approximately 77.7% of the wage diffferential for whites and 93.6% for blacks. The averaged estimates of the discrimination coefficient are .40 and .45 for whites and blacks, respectively. Under both sets of regressions and for both races, sex differences in the distribution of part-time employment and marital status significantly contributed to a narrowing of the wage differential. It is evident from Tables 1 and 2 that workers with spouse present tend to earn more than others even after controlling for other factors. A smaller proportion of women workers fall into the category of spouse present, and therefore this difference reduces the wage differential due to discrimination. The difference probably reflects the competing activities of production in the home. In the case of whites, the effects of childbearing also narrow

TABLE 3

THE EFFECTS OF DISCRIMINATION ESTIMATED FROM THE FULL-SCALE WAGE REGRESSIONS

Item	Whites				Blacks			
	Female Regression Weights		Male Regression Weights		Female Regression Weights		Male Regression Weights	
	(1)[a]	(2)[b]	(3)[c]	(4)[b]	(5)[a]	(6)[b]	(7)[c]	(8)[b]
Wage differential	.4307	100.0%	.4307	100.0%	.3989	100.0%	.3989	100.0%
Adjustment for sex differences in								
Experience	−.0056	−1.3	−.0074	−1.7	−.0009	−0.2	−.0017	−0.4
Education	−.0051	−1.2	−.0037	−0.9	+.0170	+4.3	+.0140	+3.5
Class of Worker	−.0218	−5.1	−.0144	−3.3	−.0120	−3.0	−.0418	−10.5
Industry	−.0745	−17.3	−.0901	−20.9	−.0995	−24.9	−.1170	−29.3
Occupation	−.0059	−1.4	−.0338	−7.8	−.0451	−11.3	.0090	−2.3
Health Problems	+.0012	+0.3	+.0017	+0.4	−.0006	−0.2	−.0019	−0.5
Part-time	−.0065	−1.5	−.0273	−6.3	+.0006	+0.2	−.0184	−4.6
Migration	+.0030	+0.7	+.0001	0.0	+.0013	+0.3	−.0002	0.0
Marital Status	−.0078	−1.8	−.0271	−6.3	−.0070	−1.8	−.0157	−3.9
Children	−.0309	−7.2	.0000	0.0	−.0015	−0.4	.0000	0.0
Size of Urban Area	−.0015	−0.3	−.0012	−0.3	−.0030	−0.8	−.0022	−0.6
Region	+.0002	0.0	.0000	0.0	−.0045	−1.1	−.0050	−1.3
	$\ln(\widehat{D+1}) = .2755$ ($\hat{D} = .32$)	63.9%	$\ln(\widehat{D+1}) = .2275$ ($\hat{D} = .25$)	52.9%	$\ln(\widehat{D+1}) = .2437$ ($\hat{D} = .27$)	61.1%	$\ln(\widehat{D+1}) = .2000$ ($\hat{D} = .22$)	50.1%

[a] The adjustment for the j-th variable using female regression weights is $-\hat{\beta}_{fj}\Delta\bar{Z}_j$, and therefore the sum is $-\Delta\bar{Z}'\hat{\beta}_f$. This implies
$\ln(\widehat{D+1}) = \ln(G+1) - \Delta\bar{Z}'\hat{\beta}_f = -\bar{Z}_m{}'\Delta\hat{\beta}$.

[b] Each adjustment is expressed as a percentage of the wage differential.

[c] The adjustment for the j-th variable using male regression weights is $-\hat{\beta}_{mj}\Delta\bar{Z}_j$, and therefore the sum is $-\Delta\bar{Z}'\hat{\beta}_m$. This implies
$\ln(\widehat{D+1}) = \ln(G+1) - \Delta\bar{Z}'\hat{\beta}_m = -\bar{Z}_f{}'\Delta\hat{\beta}$.

TABLE 4

THE EFFECTS OF DISCRIMINATION ESTIMATED FROM THE PERSONAL CHARACTERISTICS WAGE REGRESSIONS

Item	Whites				Blacks			
	Female Regression Weights		Male Regression Weights		Female Regression Weights		Male Regression Weights	
	(1)[a]	(2)[b]	(3)[c]	(4)[b]	(1)[a]	(2)[b]	(3)[c]	(4)[b]
Wage differential	.4307	100.0%	.4307	100.0%	.3989	100.0%	.3989	100.0%
Adjusment for sex differences in								
Experience	−.0072	−1.7	−.0094	−2.1	−.0007	−0.2	−.0028	−0.7
Education	−.0122	−2.8	−.0008	−0.2	+.0351	+8.8	+.0190	+4.8
Health Problems	+.0018	+0.4	+.0022	+0.5	−.0015	−0.4	−.0030	−0.8
Part-Time	−.0227	−5.3	−.0459	−10.7	−.0187	−4.7	−.0314	−7.9
Migration	+.0033	+0.8	−.0002	0.0	+.0024	+0.6	−.0004	−0.1
Marital Status	−.0143	−3.3	−.0380	−8.8	−.0086	−2.2	−.0167	−4.2
Children	−.0460	−10.7	.0000	0.0	−.0052	−1.3	.0000	0.0
Size of Urban Area	−.0017	−0.4	−.0012	−0.3	−.0033	−0.8	−.0029	−0.7
Region	+.0003	+0.1	−.0001	0.0	−.0058	−1.5	−.0069	−1.7
	$\ln(\widehat{D+1})=.3320$ ($\hat{D}=.39$)	77.1%	$\ln(\widehat{D+1})=.3373$ ($\hat{D}=.40$)	78.4%	$\ln(\widehat{D+1})=.3913$ ($\hat{D}=.48$)	98.5%	$\ln(\widehat{D+1})=.3538$ ($\hat{D}=.42$)	88.7%

[a] The adjustment for the j-th variable using female regression weights is $-\hat{\beta}_{fj}\Delta Z_j$, and therefore the sum is $-\Delta Z'\hat{\beta}_f$. This implies $\ln(\widehat{D+1}) = \ln(G+1) - \Delta Z'\hat{\beta}_f = -Z_m'\Delta\hat{\beta}$.

[b] Each adjustment is expressed as a percentage of the wage differential.

[c] The adjustment for the j-th variable using male regression weights is $-\hat{\beta}_{mj}\Delta Z_j$, and therefore the sum is $-\Delta Z'\hat{\beta}_m$. This implies $\ln(\widehat{D+1}) = \ln(G+1) - \Delta Z'\hat{\beta}_m = -Z_f'\Delta\hat{\beta}$.

the differential. Differences in the mean years of schooling completed widens the differential for blacks because black females complete on average almost a full year more of schooling than black males. It is clear from Table 3 that sex differences in the distributions by class of worker, industry, and occupation significantly narrow the wage differential even though industry and occupation are represented by highly aggregated categories.

Space limitations permit discussion of only a few selected aspects of the regression coefficients reported in Tables 1 and 2. The estimated experience coefficients under both sets of regressions imply that for the same rate of return to OJT, males invest more initially and for a longer period. If both sexes invest the same initially, then the pattern of differences in the coefficients imply that males earn a higher rate of return and invest for a longer period than females. The coefficients on the children variable indicate that each child lowers the white female wage by 2 or 3% but has a negligible effect on the black female wage.[6] This may suggest that black females do not stay out of the labor force as long as white females for each child born.[7] Our results are consistent with those studies of labor supply, such as [3] and [4], that find that the presence of children inhibits the labor force participation of white females significantly more than for black females. Perhaps some form of extended family arrangement in black communities provides a ready source of child care for working mothers. It may also be that lost experience and acquired skills are not very important in the kinds of jobs black females typically hold. For example, 52% of the black

[6] The personal characteristics wage equations were also estimated without the children variable. Generally, the positive coefficients were reduced in magnitude and the negative coefficients became larger in absolute value. Consequently, $-\Delta\hat{\beta}$ was biased upward, which implies a larger estimated effect of discrimination.

[7] The cost of children in terms of their effect on the hourly wage can be translated into an equivalent number of years of potential experience; 1) Set the estimated female experience profile minus the children term equal to zero; and 2) Solve the resulting quadratic for the negative root. Let R_1 be the negative root of

$$\hat{\beta}_2 X^2 + \hat{\beta}_1 X - \hat{\beta}_c C = 0 .$$

The absolute value $|R_1|$ is an estimate of the equivalent number of years of experience. The mean number of children per white female was 1.6. Using the coefficients from the personal characteristics wage regressions, we evaluated $|R_1|$ at $C = 1.6$. The value of $|R_1|$ was approximately 2.5 years. As an estimate of the number of years of experience lost to child care, 2.5 years seems low. Yet this may be a reasonable estimate when one considers that ours is a sample of employed females. A sample from the total population of adult females would include mothers not in the labor force. The years of actual work experience lost would be higher for such a sample. Since we are interested in the average years of lost experience for all employed females, the estimate of 1.6 children per female was computed using the total number of females. However the sample includes women who have never had chidren. Thus the mean number of children per mother and the estimate of their lost experience would be higher. The average ages of white males and females in our sample were 39.5 and 38.9 years, respectively. The average difference in potential experience was 0.6 years. When 0.6 is added to the estimated 2.5 years. we have a total estimated male-female experience difference of 3.1 years. In the Malkiels' study [9, (24)] the difference in actual work experience was 2.9 years in 1971 for males and females whose average ages were 40.8 and 38.9 years, respectively. Another independent source [14, (94)] shows that the difference in years of employment covered by Social Security was 3.2 years in 1960 between males and females in the 35-39 age group.

females in our sample held private household and service worker jobs whereas only 16% of the white females held these jobs.

6. CONCLUDING REMARKS

As in other studies we find the sex differential to be quite large. We are in agreement with other researchers that unequal pay for equal work does not account for very much of the male-female wage differential. Rather it is the concentration of women in lower paying jobs that produces such large differentials. Our results suggest that a substantial proportion of the male-female wage differential is attributable to the effects of discrimination.

The effects of discrimination are estimated as the residual left after adjusting the sex differential for differences in various characteristics. This methodological technique is found in other studies as well and may take the form of regression analysis or standardization analysis. There are some difficulties with this general approach which should be mentioned. Could it be that the wage structures for males and females would differ even in the absence of discrimination? For example, male-female differences in the coefficients of the experience variable suggest that the rate of return to OJT may be higher for males, and/or females invest less in OJT. One might argue that even in the absence of discrimination females may plan on a shorter working life and hence invest less than men. The result would be a difference in the parameters of the experience variables, yet these differences contribute to the effects of discrimination under our analysis. In defense of this approach it should be pointed out that occupational barriers against women deny them the opportunities to invest to the same extent as men. Also, the short work life expectancy of women may represent a rational response to anticipated discrimination in the labor market. The issue becomes one of how much of the male-female difference in the coefficients is due to discrimination.

Another difficulty with the residual approach is that it does not take into account the effects of the feedback from labor market discrimination on the male-female differences in the selected individual characteristics. The differences could reflect the adaptation of women to the biases of the labor market; yet under the residual approach all differences in the characteristics contribute to a reduction of the wage differential attributable to discrimination. The problem becomes one of how much of the observed differences in individual characteristics would exist in the absence of discrimination.

These very difficult problems have not been dealt with in this study, but they are clearly important in terms of policy prescriptions for narrowing the male-female wage differential.

University of Massachusetts, Amherst, U. S. A.

REFERENCES

[1] ASHENFELTER, ORLEY, "Racial Discrimination and Trade Unionism," *Journal of Political Economy*, LXXX (May/June, 1972), 435–464.
[2] BECKER, GARY S., *The Economics of Discrimination* (Chicago: University of Chicago Press, 1957).
[3] BOWEN, WILLIAM G., AND T. A. FINEGAN, *The Economics of Labor Force Participation* (Princeton: Princeton University Press, 1969).
[4] CAIN, GLEN G., *Married Women in the Labor Force: An Economic Analysis* (Chicago: University of Chicago Press, 1966).
[5] COHEN, MALCOM S., "Sex Differences in Compensation," *Journal of Human Resources*, VI (Fall, 1971), 434–447.
[6] FUCHS, VICTOR R., "Differences in Hourly Earnings Between Men and Women," *Monthly Labor Review*, XCIV (May, 1971), 9–15.
[7] GWARTNEY, JAMES, "Discrimination and Income Differentials, *American Economic Review*, LX (June, 1970), 396–408.
[8] JOHNSON, THOMAS, "Returns from Investment in Human Capital," *American Economic Review*, LX (September, 1970), 546–559.
[9] MALKIEL, BURTON G., AND JUDITH A. MALKIEL, "Male-Female Pay Differentials in Professional Employment," Working Paper No. 35, Industrial Relations Section, Princeton University.
[10] MINCER, JACOB, "The Distribution of Labor Incomes: A Survey with Special Reference to the Human Capital Approach," *Journal of Economic Literature*, VIII (March, 1970), 1–26.
[11] OAXACA, RONALD L., *Male-Female Wage Differentials in Urban Labor Markets*, unpublished Ph. D. dissertation, Department of Economics, Princeton University, (1971).
[12] REES, ALBERT, AND GEORGE P. SHULTZ, *Workers and Wages in an Urban Labor Market* (Chicago: Chicago University Press, 1970).
[13] SANBORN, HENRY, "Pay Differences Between Men and Women," *Industrial and Labor Relations Review*, XVII (July, 1964), 534–550.
[14] U. S. SOCIAL SECURITY ADMINISTRATION, OFFICE OF RESEARCH AND STATISTICS, *Workers Under Social Security, 1960: Annual and Work History Statistics* (Washington, D. C.: U. S. Government Printing Office, 1968).

[2]

WAGE DISCRIMINATION: REDUCED FORM AND STRUCTURAL ESTIMATES*

ALAN S. BLINDER

ABSTRACT

Regressions explaining the wage rates of white males, black males, and white females are used to analyze the white-black wage differential among men and the male-female wage differential among whites. A distinction is drawn between reduced form and structural wage equations, and both are estimated. They are shown to have very different implications for analyzing the white-black and male-female wage differentials. When the two sets of estimates are synthesized, they jointly imply that 70 percent of the overall race differential and 100 percent of the overall sex differential are ultimately attributable to discrimination of various sorts.

It is well known that, in the American economy, whites earn much higher wages than blacks and males earn substantially higher wages than females. In view of the important role which inequality in wages plays in explaining overall inequality of incomes,[1] it seems likely that the white-black and male-female wage differentials are major contributors to the unequal distribution of income in the United States. An understanding of these differentials, therefore, is vitally important where questions of income redistribution are concerned.

The author is Assistant Professor of Economics, Princeton University.

* I owe a great deal to Robert E. Hall who furnished me with the data, assisted with computational problems, and commented astutely on an earlier draft. I am also indebted to Orley Ashenfelter, Yoram Ben-Porath, Nicholas Barr, Ronald Oaxaca, Ray Fair, A. P. Thirlwall, and a referee for their helpful comments. Partial support under National Science Foundation Grant GS 32003X is gratefully acknowledged. [Manuscript received August 1972; accepted December 1972.]

1 Other research I have done suggests that roughly half of total income inequality, as measured by the Gini ratio, is attributable to unequal wage rates. See [2].

It is known that part of each wage differential is due to differences in "objective" characteristics such as education and work experience, while part remains even when white-black and male-female differences in these traits are controlled for. However, the quantitative dimensions of the various causes of unequal wages are not well known. How much of the white-black wage differential is attributable to the superior education of the whites? How much of the male-female differential is due to the fact that men have easier access to the high-paying occupations? It is questions such as these which this paper seeks to answer.

Section I below outlines the techniques I shall use to decompose the two wage differentials into their component causes, a simple technique which is of quite general applicability. Section II discusses the unique features of the data source upon which this study is based. The distinction between reduced form and structural estimation, which is almost always ignored in micro wage equations of the kind employed here, is drawn, and methods for estimating each equation are discussed. Sections III and IV report the results of applying these procedures to the wage differentials between white males and black males, and between white males and white females, respectively.[2] An Appendix provides the regression estimates upon which the results in Sections III and IV are based.

The main findings of this study are two: First, while the overall white-black and male-female differentials are strikingly similar is size, decomposition shows that the qualitative nature of race and sex differentials differ quite radically. Second, whether we use structural or reduced form estimates of the wage equation greatly colors our view of the wage differentials. For example, when we use the structural equations, the regressions suggest that about 60 percent of the white-black wage differential is due to the whites' superior endowments of various characteristics, leaving 40 percent to be attributed to discrimination of various kinds. By contrast, the reduced form estimates attribute only about 30 percent of the raw differential to objective traits and 70 percent to discrimination.

I. THE DECOMPOSITION OF WAGE DIFFERENTIALS

The most common way to study the dispersion in individual wages or incomes is to estimate a regression like:

$$(1) \qquad Y_i = \beta_o + \sum_{j=1}^{n} \beta_j X_{ji} + u_i$$

where Y_i is the level or natural logarithm of earnings, income, or wage rate,

2 Due to the small sample sizes, no attempt was made to compare black males with black females or white females with black females.

and $X_{1i}, \ldots, X_{ni}$ are n observable characteristics used to explain Y. If we are particularly interested in comparing two demographic groups (such as whites and blacks), it makes sense to estimate an equation like (1) for each group:

$$(2) \qquad Y_i^H = \beta_o^H + \sum_{j=1}^{n} \beta_j^H X_{ji}^H + u_i^H$$

$$(3) \qquad Y_i^L = \beta_o^L + \sum_{j=1}^{n} \beta_j^L X_{ji}^L + u_i^L$$

where the H superscript indicates the high-wage group (always white males in this study) and the L superscript indicates the low-wage group (alternatively, white females and black males in this study).

Given (2) and (3), it is a simple matter to compute the portion of the differential explained by the regression: $\Sigma_j \beta_j^H \bar{X}_j^H - \Sigma_j \beta_j^L \bar{X}_j^L$ and the amount which is captured by the shift coefficient, $\beta_o^H - \beta_o^L$. The latter is typically attributed to discrimination (see, for example [14], ch. 5). However, we can carry our breakdown farther than this. The explained part of the differential comes from both differences in the coefficients, β_j^H and β_j^L, and differences in the average characteristics, $\bar{X}^H$ and $\bar{X}^L$. In particular:

$$(4) \quad \sum_j \beta_j^H \bar{X}_j^H - \sum_j \beta_j^L \bar{X}_j^L = \sum_j \beta_j^H (\bar{X}_j^H - \bar{X}_j^L) + \sum_j \bar{X}_j^L (\beta_j^H - \beta_j^L)$$

Here the first sum is the value of the advantage in endowments possessed by the high-wage group *as evaluated by the high-wage group's wage equation*.[3] The second sum is the difference between how the high-wage equation *would value* the characteristics of the low-wage group and how the low-wage equation *actually values* them. For brevity, I shall say that the first sum is "attributable to the endowments," while the second is "attributable to the coefficients." Note that the latter sum, which exists only because the

3 Any such breakdown of wage differentials runs into obvious index-number problems. For example, I could equally well have evaluated the differences in endowments by using the low-wage equation, i.e., by calculating

$$\Sigma_j \beta_j^L (\bar{X}_j^H - \bar{X}_j^L)$$

There is obviously no "right" and "wrong" answer here. My reason for adopting the alternative procedure is that the above formulation leaves as a residual:

$$(\bar{Y}^H - \bar{Y}^L) - \Sigma_j \beta_j^L (\bar{X}_j^H - \bar{X}_j^L)$$
$$= \beta_o^H - \beta_o^L + \Sigma_j \bar{X}_j^L (\beta_j^H - \beta_j^L) + \Sigma_j (\bar{X}_j^H - \bar{X}_j^L)(\beta_j^H - \beta_j)$$

While we obviously could label the first two terms as "attributable to the coefficients," the interaction term has no obvious interpretation. The breakdown which I employ in the text, while in no sense theoretically "superior" to this, at least has the advantage that each term has a ready economic interpretation.

market evaluates differently the identical bundle of traits if possessed by members of different demographic groups, is a reflection of discrimination as much as the shift coefficient is.

In summary, the measures we shall use in Sections III and IV below are:

R = raw differential

$$= \beta_o^H + \Sigma_j \beta_j^H \overline{X}_j^H - (\beta_o^L + \Sigma_j \beta_j^L \overline{X}_j^L) = E + C + U$$

E = portion of differential attributable to differing endowments

$$= \Sigma_j \beta_j^H(\overline{X}_j^H - \overline{X}_j^L)$$

C = portion of differential attributable to differing coefficients

$$= \Sigma_j \overline{X}_j^L(\beta_j^H - \beta_j^L)$$

U = unexplained portion of the differential $= \beta_o^H - \beta_o^L$

D = portion of the differential attributable to discrimination $= C + U$

II. DATA AND ESTIMATION TECHNIQUES[4]

The data bank on which the present study is based is the Michigan Survey Research Center's "Panel Study of Income Dynamics."[5] This unique data source has several important advantages over most competing data sources. First, because income variables include many diverse sources of nonlabor income and because earnings variables confound differences in wage rates with differences in labor supply (which are themselves functions of wages), it is imperative that studies such as the present one use actual wage rates as the dependent variable.[6] Most survey data generated by the Bureau of the Census lack such a measure, which probably explains the paucity of empirical wage equations until very recently. The Survey of Economic Opportunity (SEO) has, however, provided the micro data for a number of recent regression studies of individual wages (see, for example, [9, 4, 11, 10]).

4 For more details on the precise definitions of the variables employed here, and a more thorough discussion of estimation problems, see the longer paper [1] upon which the present paper is based. It is available upon request.

5 For information on the survey techniques, collection, and processing of the data, see [13].

6 For example, use of earnings data instead of wage rates can seriously bias estimates of the real rates of return to education. Suppose, for example, that wages depend on education and labor supply depends on wages. Then, estimating the effect of education on *earnings* will over- or underestimate the impact on *wage rates* according as the labor supply curve is normal or backward-bending.

The Michigan data have only a minimal advantage over the SEO in this respect: the latter calculates the average wage earned in the week previous to the survey, while the former computes the average wage over the preceding year (1967). A more important advantage is that the Michigan data provide a rich set of variables pertaining to the individual's family background. These enable us to estimate a meaningful reduced-form equation which explains the wage rate only on the basis of characteristics which are truly exogenous to the individual (such as his father's education). The SEO is a much poorer source of family background data.[7] A third advantage of the Michigan data is its superior treatment of union membership—an important determinant of earnings. The SEO follows Census procedures in asking only *nongovernment* workers whether or not they are members of a union; thus government workers must be either eliminated or treated as nonmembers. Since government employees generally earn higher wages than private nonunion workers, the latter procedure would bias downward the estimated union-nonunion differential.[8] The Michigan survey asked the union membership question of every household head. Finally, the SRC tape offers data on the length of time each individual has worked for his present employer, thus giving us a direct measure of at least one part of the individual's total work experience.

Of course, there are some serious shortcomings of these data as compared, say, with the SEO. Most important is the small sample size, which makes the standard errors regrettably large in many cases. While the R^2s from my wage equations are quite comparable to those obtained with the SEO, the standard errors of individual coefficients are far larger. For this reason the inferences drawn in Sections III and IV are very tentative.[9] Finally, the Michigan tape lacks information on the industry of employment, a variable often deemed to be an important determinant of wages.[10]

To sharpen the estimates, I have selected a subsample from the SRC tape for use in my wage regressions. First, to eliminate household heads who may still be acquiring formal education, I dropped from the sample all households whose heads were younger than age 25. Also dropped from

7 Recent work by Samuel Bowles suggests that this may be a serious omission, but Bowles's work utilizes income as the dependent variable. See [5].

8 My thanks to Orley Ashenfelter for pointing this out to me. This may be one reason why the studies cited above [9, 4, 11, 10] all find smaller union-nonunion differentials than those reported here.

9 However, the procedures used to analyze the sex and race wage differentials automatically give lower weight to the coefficients with larger standard errors. So the analysis in Sections III and IV below may be more accurate than the regression coefficients given in the Appendix.

10 Like many other data banks, the SRC panel study also lacks an ability variable. However, some recent work by Gintis [7] and Griliches and Mason [8] suggests that this may not be an important omission.

consideration were household heads who were neither black nor white or who did not work for money in 1967.

I have argued above that the proper dependent variable in equations (2) and (3) is the hourly wage rate.[11] But what of the independent variables? This, of course, depends on one's (tacit or explicit) model of microeconomic wage determination. Most previous studies have been content to list certain obvious correlates of wages and estimate the resulting regression by ordinary least squares. But correlation does not imply causation, and if we are interested in the latter, we ought to specify a more precise model. The structural model which underlies the present study is the following:

$$\log w = f(Ed, Occ, J, M, V, T, Z) + u_1 \quad (5)$$
$$Ed = g(Occ, V, B, Z) + u_2 \quad (6)$$
$$Occ = h(Ed, J, V, B, Z) + u_3 \quad (7)$$
$$J = k(Occ, V, M, B, Z) + u_4 \quad (8)$$
$$M = l(Ed, Occ, V, B, Z) + u_5 \quad (9)$$
$$V = m(Ed, Occ, J, B, Z) + u_6 \quad (10)$$
$$T = n(Ed, Occ, J, M, V, Z) + u_7 \quad (11)$$

where w is the hourly wage; Ed is a vector of six educational dummy variables; Occ is a set of eight dummies for occupation; J is a dummy for vocational training; M is 1 for members of unions and 0 otherwise; V is 1 for veterans and 0 otherwise; T is a set of six dummies for tenure on the present job; B is a set of 13 family-background variables; Z is a set of other exogenous variables; and f, g, h, k, l, m, and n are all linear functions. In this model, w, Ed, Occ, J, M, V, and T are taken to be endogenous, while B and Z are exogenous. The elements of Z which enter the wage equation with nonzero coefficients are age, health, residence, and local labor market conditions.

While every reader can doubtless quarrel with some detail of this specification, the two most important features are relatively noncontroversial. Presumably, no one would wish to exclude from the structural wage equation any of the variables which I have included (though other investigators have added variables to the above list). The dichotomization of variables into endogenous and exogenous sets may require some comment, however, as it is rather novel in this context. In the intuitive model I have in mind, each individual is presented with endowments of human and nonhuman capitals and at some point in his life-cycle, jointly decides how far he wishes to pursue his formal education and to what occupational strata he aspires. Thus Ed and Occ, the two chief determinants of the wage rate, are endogenous and simultaneously determined. This seems very much in the

11 Like most other investigators, I have actually used the natural logarithm of the wage rate as the dependent variable.

spirit of the human-capital-theory approach to wage differences. Union membership is endogenous because each worker may opt for a "union job" at his discretion and because unions themselves may be selective about whom they admit.[12] Similar remarks hold for veteran status: some men volunteer, while others are selected by a not-quite-random process.

Once this simultaneous-equations viewpoint is adopted, the estimation problem seems quite straightforward: Ideally, equations (5) through (11) should be estimated as a simultaneous system by two-stage least squares or some similar technique. Unfortunately, this is not possible because, as the reader can verify, the wage equation is underidentified. The only variables omitted from (5) are the family-background variables, B. And this identification problem is by no means restricted to my particular model. Almost any specification of a micro wage equation will have difficulty excluding enough variables to identify the coefficients since these excluded variables (family background in my model) must be included in some other equation of the system. That is, they must be important determinants of education or occupation, etc., but have no direct impact on wage rates.

What can be done about this problem? In this study I have adopted two second-best procedures. The first is to estimate the reduced-form wage equation:

$$\log w = F(B, Z) + v_1 \quad (12)$$

instead of equation (5), by ordinary least squares. This is rigorously correct, and not without interest if we are concerned with the "ultimate causes" of wage differentials rather than the mechanisms through which these causes operate. Still, we would like to get a look inside the "black box," that is, to get some structural information about equation (5). To do this we need another, rather restrictive, assumption—that the error terms in equations (6) through (11) are all uncorrelated with u_1. As the reader may readily verify, if $E(u_1u_2) = E(u_1u_3) = E(u_1u_4) = E(u_1u_5) = E(u_1u_6) = E(u_1u_7) = 0$, then the system is block recursive and ordinary least squares is the best linear unbiased estimator of equation (5).

In summary, we present two wage-equation estimates. The reduced-form estimates—which are always unbiased—are obtained by ordinary least squares estimation of equation (12). The structural estimates—which are biased unless the error terms are uncorrelated—are obtained by ordinary least squares on equation (5). Very roughly speaking, the structural estimates can be thought of as the conditional expectation of (the log of) the wage, given the individual's present socioeconomic condition; and the reduced form can be thought of as the conditional expectation of (the log of) the wage, given the circumstances of his birth.

---

12 I have presented and discussed the results of estimating equation (9), the equation for union membership, in [3].

III. ANALYSIS OF THE WHITE-BLACK WAGE DIFFERENTIAL FOR MALES

This section breaks down the raw differential between white males and black males into its component parts, using the procedures outlined in Section I above.[13] The regression coefficients upon which the following tables are based are provided in the Appendix.

Table 1 decomposes the overall 50.5 percent wage advantage of whites in the manner implied by the structural estimates. One striking re-

13 One question not considered in Section I was the choice of the control group. For example, if a person can fall into one of eight mutually exclusive and exhaustive occupational categories, then we have eight possible ways to choose seven dummy variables to enter into the regression. My choices for the control group are all indicated in the Appendix. But a question arises as to whether a different choice of the control group would have altered my decompositions of the wage differentials.

While it is difficult to prove that this holds in an arbitrary regression using a set of K qualitative variables with n_k classes in each, one can show that in the simplest case of a *single dichotomous* classificatory variable, the choice of the control group does not matter. *Proof*: In this simple case, equations (2) and (3) become:

$$(2') \qquad Y_i^H = \beta_o^H + \beta_1^H X_{1i}^H + U_i^H$$

$$(3') \qquad Y_i^L = \beta_o^L + \beta_1^L X_{1i}^L + U_i^L$$

if group 2 is the control group. Under the alternative choice they would be:

$$(2'') \qquad Y_i^H = b_o^H + \beta_2^H X_{2i}^H + V_i^H$$

$$(3'') \qquad Y_i^L = b_o^L + \beta_2^L X_{2i}^L + V_i^L$$

My procedure is to divide the overall differential, $\bar{Y}^H - \bar{Y}^L$, into $E_1 = \hat{\beta}_1^H(\bar{X}_1^H - \bar{X}_1^L)$ and $\bar{Y}^H - \bar{Y}^L - E_1$. Using the other group as control, we would want instead $E_2 = \hat{\beta}_2^H(\bar{X}_2^H - \bar{X}_2^L)$. But since $X_{1i} + X_{2i} = 1$ for all i we have:

$$\bar{X}_2^H - \bar{X}_2^L = -(\bar{X}_1^H - \bar{X}_1^L)$$

And from the standard formula for the estimated slope coefficients, we can show:

$$\hat{\beta}_2^H = \hat{\beta}_1^H$$

So $E_2 = E_1$, and our dichotomization of the wage differential is the same for either choice of the control group.

TABLE 1

STRUCTURAL ANALYSIS OF THE WHITE-BLACK WAGE DIFFERENTIAL FOR MALES

Causal Factor	Amount Attributable	Amount Attributable to Endowments	Amount Attributable to Coefficients
Age	5.1%	−0.7%	5.8%
Region of residence	−3.6	5.1	−8.7
Education	19.8	14.5	5.3
Vocational training	2.1	0.2	1.8
Occupation	1.4	10.3	−8.9
Union membership	−5.7	−0.4	−5.3
Veteran status	−2.0	0.5	−2.5
Health	−0.6	−0.5	−0.1
Local labor market conditions	−0.7	−0.1	−0.6
Geographical mobility	0.9	0.5	0.5
Seasonal employment	−1.7	0.3	−2.0
Length of time on job	−36.2	0.7	−36.9
Subtotal	−21.1%	$E = +30.7\%$	$C = -51.5\%$
Shift coefficient	$U = +71.9\%$		
Total	$R = +50.8\%$		$D = C + U = 20.4\%$

Notes: A + sign indicates advantage for whites; a − sign indicates advantage for blacks. Components may not add to totals due to rounding.

sult is that the regression (ignoring the constant) actually accounts for a 21.1 percent differential *in favor of blacks.* That is to say, if black males kept their current socioeconomic traits (including their less advantageous distributions of education and occupation), and kept the same wage equation as they now have but were given the shift coefficient of the whites, they would earn 21.1 percent more than white males. The table also shows that a 30.7 percent differential (about 60 percent of the total) can be attributed to blacks' inferior endowments, in the sense that black wages would average 30.7 percent less than white wages if the former were given the entire white wage equation. Closer examination reveals that the main reason why the regression calls for higher wages for blacks is that they gain more by having seniority in their present jobs. The regression coefficients in the Appendix further show that just about all of this difference is accounted for by the large gain in wages which accrues to black males from being in an occupation where tenure on the job is applicable (as opposed to the self-employed who were the control group). If this were ignored, the regression (ignoring the constant) would predict a 15.8 percent advantage for whites, a rather small difference.

Foremost among the factors contributing to the white male wage advantage is education, and the breakdown shows that most of this is due to the fact that whites have more education rather than to the higher rates of return on education which whites also receive. The other main advantage for white men is the more concave age-wage profile, a fact that has been noted in many studies of age-earnings profiles as well. Whites apparently gain more than blacks from experience in the labor force, and therefore they exhibit a more pronounced life-cycle pattern of wages.

Aside from tenure on the job, the most important factors favoring black males are union membership and geographical distribution across regions of the country. While blacks and whites are about equally likely to be union members, blacks gain much more from being in a union. The regression coefficients show an average union-nonunion differential of 39 percent for black males and 23 percent for white males. Both of these are larger than the differentials which have been estimated from the SEO (see [9, 4, 11, 10]). How much of this discrepancy is due to the superior data on union membership (see above), how much is due to omission of relevant variables fom the regression, and how much is due to the absence of interaction terms which allow the union-nonunion differential to vary across occupations[14] is an open question. However, the fact that Stafford's estimates [12], which used Survey Research Center data, are among the highest obtained to date lends some credence to the notion that differences in the conceptual basis of the data may well be the reason for the high differentials. As to the regional distribution, the fact that blacks are more heavily concentrated in the South (a disadvantage) is more than balanced by their higher coefficients for each region (as compared to the North Central region which is the control group).

Interestingly, the distribution of workers across occupations—at least at this relatively coarse level of disaggregation—contributed only negligibly to the white-black differential. This would appear to fly in the face of casual empirical observation, but in fact it does not. Decomposition of the meagre 1.4 percent occupational differential in favor of whites reveals that the superior white occupational distribution actually accounts for a substantial 10.3 percent wage advantage, most of which is neutralized by higher co-

14 Boskin [4], p. 470, suggests that ignoring the interactions between occupation and union membership (i.e., that union-nonunion differentials differ across occupations) results in a serious *overestimate* of the *average* union-nonunion differential. However, as Orley Ashenfelter points out to me, his reasoning is flawed. The figures in his Table 2 for union differentials in each occupation ignore the geographical area-union interactions which also appear in his regressions. That is, to his estimated union-nonunion differentials for each occupation in Table 2 one should add the average (over all regions) of the union differential in that occupation. That would (almost) always result in higher union differentials than he presents. Indeed, it is difficult to see how a weighted average of the union-nonunion differentials (weighted by occupation) could differ much from the overall average differential in the sample.

TABLE 2
REDUCED FORM ANALYSIS OF THE WHITE-BLACK WAGE DIFFERENTIAL FOR MALES

Causal Factor	Amount Attributable	Amount Attributable to Endowments	Amount Attributable to Coefficients
Age	83.6%	−1.1%	84.7%
Region of residence	−0.8	8.8	−9.6
Parents' income	5.6	0.5	5.1
Father's educaion	12.3	3.6	8.7
Place where grew up	16.2	−0.7	16.9
Number of siblings	−6.6	1.2	−7.7
Health	−0.9	−1.0	0.1
Local labor market conditions	−6.4	0.3	−6.6
Geographical mobility	6.8	2.9	3.9
Seasonal employment	−2.5	0.8	−3.4
Subtotal	+107.4%	$E = +15.2\%$	$C = +92.2\%$
Shift coefficient	$U = -56.7\%$		
Total	$R = +50.7\%$		$D = C + U = 35.5\%$

Notes: A + sign indicates advantage for whites; a − sign indicates advantage for blacks. Components may not add to totals due to rounding.

efficients for occupational advancement for blacks.

Table 2 portrays a similar decomposition based on the reduced-form estimates. The results are strikingly different. When wages are explained by circumstances of birth and other exogenous characteristics, the shift coefficient (56.7 percent) now favors black men. The regression itself, apart from the constant, actually accounts for a 107.4 percent wage differential in favor of whites, and most of this comes from a superior wage equation rather than from superior endowments.

The dominant factor favoring whites is, of course, the age-wage profile. As white males mature from age 25 to age 46, wage rates rise steadily due to past investments in human capital and to experience. After that, wages decline with age as training becomes obsolete and physical conditions deteriorate. Blacks also show a concave age profile, but it is much less steep. Table 2 shows that these differing age profiles account for nearly 80 percent of the explained white-black wage differential, and almost all of the part attributable to the regression coefficients.

Not surprisingly, the other major factors favoring whites are almost all family-background indices: parents' income, father's educational attainment, and the place where the individual was brought up (whether on a farm, in a city, or in the South). What is surprising is that most of the advantage for whites comes from the coefficients rather than from the endowments. Whites' superior endowments of these three characteristics can explain only a 3.4 percent differential in their favor, while a 30.7 differential is explicable by the whites' more favorable coefficients. Blacks generally gain less by having an educated father, lose more by coming from a poor family, gain less by being born in an urban area, and so on. The only family-background variable favoring blacks is the number of siblings. While the sizes of black and white families are not very different, blacks actually reap gains from having brothers and sisters, while whites suffer wage reductions.

Note that since $D = 35.5$ percent and $R = 50.7$ percent in Table 2, the reduced form attributes about 70 percent (that is, .355/.507) of the raw white-black wage differential for men to the various dimensions of discrimination, including discrimination in education and occupation. By contrast, the structural equation, which measured only discrimination in wage rates, attributed only about 40 percent to discrimination (D/R = .204/.508 in Table 1). Thus, we might tentatively break down the raw differential as follows: 30 percent to blacks' inferior endowments of exogenous variables (the ratio E/R in Table 2); 40 percent to outright discrimination in rates of pay (the ratio D/R in Table 1); and 30 percent to discrimination in achieving the other endogenous variables (such as education, occupation).

It is perhaps of some interest to compare these crude results to Duncan's attempt to break down the black-white *income* differential for adult males.[15] Using a somewhat different specification and different statistical methods, but a decomposition technique which is almost the same as mine, he attributed 26.6 percent of the differential to family-background variables,[16] 35.6 percent to divergent attainments of education and occupational status which could not be predicted by family background, and the remaining 37.8 pecent to discrimination in income. This seems remarkably comparable to my rough 30-30-40 percent breakdown,[17] especially in view of the many differences between the two studies.

IV. ANALYSIS OF THE MALE-FEMALE WAGE DIFFERENTIAL FOR WHITES

Table 3 utilizes the structural regressions to decompose the 45.6 percent raw wage differential for white males over white females. The nature of this differential is seen to be radically different from the structural race differ-

15 Duncan [6], pp. 84–110. Specifically, his sample was black versus *nonblack* males aged 25–64 years who were in the experienced labor force and whose fathers did not work on farms.

16 This groups "number of siblings" with the family-background variables, as I do. Duncan takes this to be an endogenous variable instead.

17 Of course, I have many exogenous variables aside from family background and more endogenous variables than just education and occupation.

TABLE 3

STRUCTURAL ANALYSIS OF THE MALE-FEMALE WAGE DIFFERENTIAL FOR WHITES

Causal Factor	Amount Attributable	Amount Attributable to Endowments	Amount Attributable to Coefficients
Age	87.5%	0.2%	87.3%
Region of residence	−0.9	0.2	−1.1
Education	21.3	−0.4	21.7
Vocational training	−3.5	−0.1	−3.4
Occupation	−4.1	5.1	−9.1
Union membership	3.3	3.9	−0.6
Veteran status	1.6	1.6	0
Health	2.0	0.0	1.9
Local labor market conditions	12.2	0.1	12.1
Geographical mobility	−0.9	0.5	−1.3
Seasonal employment	0.1	0.0	0.1
Length of time on job	−4.7	4.7	−9.4
Subtotal	113.8%	$E = 15.7\%$	$C = 98.1\%$
Shift coefficient	$U = -68.0\%$		
Total	$R = 45.8\%$		$D = C + U = 30.1\%$

Notes: A + sign indicates an advantage for males; a − sign indicates an advantage for females. Numbers may not add to totals due to rounding.

ential. The independent variables account for a 113.8 percent differential in favor of males on the basis of "objective" characteristics, leaving a 68 percent advantage for white *females* to the unexplained shift coefficient. Breaking down the explained 113.8 percent further shows that only 15.7 percent is due to inferior endowments, while 98.1 percent comes from different coefficients in the two wage equations.

By far the largest part of the differential is accounted for by the age-wage profile. This is in marked contrast to the structural differential between the races, where age profiles were not terribly important. In our estimates, white women exhibit an almost flat (in fact, slightly convex) age-wage profile—that is, their wages do not show any tendency to rise over the life cycle, whereas wages for white men certainly do. Thus, the failure of women *in the same education-occupation category* to rise on the economic ladder over their working lives is seen to be the single largest cause of the male-female differential among whites.

There are two further factors which place men at a distinct advantage: education and conditions in the local labor market. In each case, the sexes barely differ in their endowments; it is the coefficients that matter. Men earn much larger wage increments for advancing to higher educational levels, and they are much less sensitive to local labor market conditions.[18]

Notably absent from this list of factors explaining the male-female differential is occupation. It has been widely held that the main way in which women are discriminated against in labor markets is not in rates of pay, but by being relegated to lower positions on the occupational ladder than their qualifications would merit (see, for example, [16, 15]). Yet Table 3 shows occupational factors as contributing a 4.1 percent wage advantage to white women. On closer examination, however, the apparent conflict disappears. It is indeed true that men have a superior distribution across occupations (accounting for a 5.1 percent wage advantage for men), but the regressions show that this is more than balanced by the greater gains reaped by women when they enter certain occupations (accounting for a 9.1 percent differential for women). Furthermore, part of the disparity in age-wage profiles mentioned above is surely a reflection of the failure of women to rise to the higher occupational strata *within* any of the broad occupational groupings.

Table 4 shows that endowments count for even less (essentially zero) and discrimination for even more when reduced-form estimates are applied to the sex differential. In fact, there are hardly any differences between the reduced form endowments of white men and white women.

Once again the age profile dominates all other considerations, and it now accounts for the entire wage difference between the sexes. Embodied in this reduced-form age-wage profile, of course, are any age-related differences in the attainment of the other endogenous variables, such as occupation, union membership, and job experience. Most of the family-background variables operate in favor of the females, and most of their impact comes through the coefficients. (Obviously, white women are born in about the same places to the same kinds of parents and in families of about the same size as are white men.) The regression coefficients show that white women gain more from having educated fathers and from being brought up in a city or in the South, and actually benefit (while men lose) from having poor parents and being raised on a farm. Other than age, the main advantage accruing to white men is their reduced sensitivity to local labor market conditions.

In summary, the regressions attribute none of the observed male-female wage differential for whites to differences in their endowments of exogenous variables (E is about 0 in Table 4), about two-thirds to outright discrimination in labor markets (the ratio D/R in Table 3), and about one-third of the differential to discrimination in attaining other endogenous variables such as occupational status and job seniority.

18 This last remark ought to be discounted heavily since our dummy variables are very imperfect indices of local labor market conditions.

TABLE 4

REDUCED FORM ANALYSIS OF MALE-FEMALE WAGE DIFFERENTIAL FOR WHITES

Causal Factor	Amount Attributable	Amount Attributable to Endowments	Amount Attributable to Coefficients
Age	132.5%	1.0%	131.5%
Region of residence	4.8	0.4	4.4
Parents' income	−5.4	−0.7	−4.7
Father's education	−9.5	−1.0	−8.5
Place of birth	−14.8	−2.6	−12.2
Number of siblings	3.4	−0.1	3.5
Health	0.6	−0.1	0.6
Local labor market conditions	15.5	0.0	15.5
Geographical mobility	4.1	2.8	1.3
Seasonal employment	0.6	0.1	0.6
Subtotal	131.7%	$E = -0.3\%$	$C = 132.0\%$
Shift coefficient	$U = 86.2\%$		
Total	$R = 45.4\%$	$D = C + U = 45.8\%$	

Notes: A + sign indicates an advantage for males; a − sign indicates an advantage for females. Numbers may not add to totals due to rounding.

REFERENCES

1. A. S. Blinder. "Estimating a Micro Wage Equation: Pitfalls and Some Provisional Estimates." Princeton University Econometric Research Program, Research Memorandum No. 131, November 1971.
2. ———. *Towards an Economic Theory of Income Distribution*. Cambridge, Mass.: MIT Press, forthcoming 1974.
3. ———. "Who Joins Unions?" Princeton University Industrial Relations Section, Working Paper No. 36, February 1972.
4. M. J. Boskin. "Unions and Relative Real Wages." *American Economic Review* 62 (June 1972): 466–72.
5. S. Bowles. "Schooling and Inequality from Generation to Generation." *Journal of Political Economy* 80:2 (May-June 1972): S219–51.
6. O. D. Duncan. "Inheritance of Poverty or Inheritance of Race?" In *On Understanding Poverty*, ed. D. P. Moynihan. New York: Basic Books, 1968.
7. H. Gintis. "Education, Technology and the Characteristics of Worker Productivity." *American Economic Review* 61 (May 1971): 269–79.
8. Z. Griliches and W. M. Mason. "Education, Income and Ability." *Journal of Political Economy* 80:2 (May-June 1972): S74–103.
9. R. E. Hall. "Wages, Income and Hours of Work in the U.S. Labor Force." In *Labor Supply and Income Maintenance*, eds. G. Cain and H. Watts. Chicago: Markham, 1973.

10. M. D. Hurd. "Changes in Wage Rates Between 1959 and 1967." *Review of Economics and Statistics* (May 1971): 189–99.
11. R. Oaxaca. "Sex Discrimination in Wages." In *Discrimination in Labor Markets,* eds. O. Ashenfelter and A. Rees. Princeton, N.J.: Princeton University Press, forthcoming 1973.
12. F. Stafford. "Concentration and Labor Earnings: Comment." *American Economic Review* 58 (March 1968): 174–80.
13. Survey Research Center, University of Michigan. *A Panel Study of Income Dynamics: Study Design, Procedures, Available Data: 1968–1970 Interviewing Years (Waves I–III).* Ann Arbor: The Center, 1970.
14. L. C. Thurow. *Poverty and Discrimination.* Washington: Brookings Institution, 1969.
15. F. B. Weisskoff. " 'Women's Place' in the Labor Market." *American Economic Review* 62 (May 1972): 161–66.
16. H. Zellner. "Discrimination Against Women, Occupational Segregation and the Relative Wage." *American Economic Review* 62 (May 1972): 157–160.

APPENDIX

Tables A-1 and A-2 list, respectively, the structural and reduced-form wage regressions upon which the analysis in Sections III and IV is based. Coefficients are presented only for white males, black males, and white females. Results from estimating wage equations for black females and for the pooled sample, with race and sex entering as dummy variables only, are reported in the expanded version of this paper.[19]

19 See fn. 4 in the text.

TABLE A-1

STRUCTURAL COEFFICIENTS (Standard Errors)
(Dependent Variable: Natural Log of Wage)

Independent Variable	White Males	Black Males	White Females
Constant	4.86	4.14	5.54
	(.20)	(.45)	(.64)
Age	.0271	.0296	−.0110
	(.0078)	(.0195)	(.0240)
$(Age)^2$	−.00029	−.00038	.00009
	(.00008)	(.00022)	(.00026)
Region			
Northeast	.061	.144	.109
	(.038)	(.107)	(.108)
North Central	0	0	0

TABLE A-1 (*Continued*)

Independent Variable	White Males	Black Males	White Females
South	−.107	−.013	−.090
	(.038)	(.088)	(.106)
West	−.011	.189	−.006
	(.042)	(.117)	(.113)
Local labor market			
Low unemployment	−.024	.014	−.246
	(.031)	(.054)	(.098)
High unemployment	−.095	−.168	−.255
	(.051)	(.097)	(.151)
Low wage	.010	−.207	.231
	(.041)	(.068)	(.122)
High wage	.073	.315	.203
	(.046)	(.109)	(.136)
Geographical mobility			
Moved for job	.025	−.056	.032
	(.030)	(.070)	(.100)
Refused to move for job	.016	.088	.230
	(.043)	(.083)	(.162)
Health impediments			
Obvious disfigurement	−.119	.004	−.183
	(.053)	(.103)	(.131)
Some work limitation	−.081	−.227	−.189
	(.038)	(.082)	(.135)
Sick recently	−.013	.049	−.030
	(.050)	(.074)	(.140)
Education			
0–5 years	0	0	0
6–8 years	.075	−.015	.179
	(.065)	(.065)	(.227)
9–11 years	.133	.175	.247
	(.043)	(.063)	(.128)
12 years	.084	.110	.022
	(.040)	(.075)	(.109)
Some college	.155	.012	.187
	(.042)	(.115)	(.119)
College graduate	.212	.136	−.109
	(.059)	(.259)	(.180)
Advanced degree	.164	.248	.241
	(.070)	(.323)	(.218)
Occupation			
Professional, technical	.049	.159	.130
	(.053)	(.174)	(.332)

TABLE A-1 (*Continued*)

Independent Variable	White Males	Black Males	White Females
Managers, officials, proprietors	.124	.567	.133
	(.049)	(.344)	(.354)
Self-employed businessmen	–.395	–.019	–.290
	(.069)	(.214)	(.412)
Clerical, sales	–.085	.011	–.024
	(.049)	(.115)	(.305)
Craftsmen	0	0	0
Operatives	–.162	–.193	.014
	(.040)	(.067)	(.309)
Laborers, service, farmhands	–.333	–.123	–.263
	(.053)	(.067)	(.305)
Farm managers	–.719	–1.051	—
	(.076)	(.213)	
Union member	.228	.393	.276
	(.032)	(.056)	(.122)
Veteran	.029	.099	—
	(.028)	(.053)	
Seasonal employment	–.050	.050	–.055
	(.038)	(.057)	(.107)
Vocational training	.031	–.069	.147
	(.032)	(.061)	(.085)
Tenure on the job			
Self-employed	0	0	0
Less than 6 months	–.085	.393	–.027
	(.065)	(.139)	(.237)
6–18 months	.025	–.103	.047
	(.069)	(.101)	(.146)
10–42 months	.020	.122	–.075
	(.060)	(.089)	(.129)
4–9 years	.056	.020	.189
	(.045)	(.073)	(.119)
10–20 years	.078	–.001	.024
	(.041)	(.068)	(.110)
Over 20 years	.081	.082	.125
	(.044)	(.081)	(.151)
R^2	.498	.467	.449
s.e.	.437	.466	.465
N	1239	467	194

Note: The coefficients for education and tenure-on-the-job variables are *increments* from advancing from one category to the next higher one.

TABLE A-2
REDUCED FORM COEFFICIENTS (Standard Errors)
(Dependent Variable: Natural Log of Wage)

Variable	White Males	Black Males	White Females
Constant	4.75	5.32	5.62
	(.22)	(.45)	(.59)
Age	.0427	.0110	–.0160
	(.0093)	(.0200)	(.0250)
$(Age)^2$	–.00047	–.0002	.00014
	(.00010)	(.0002)	(.00027)
Region			
Northeast	.080	.130	–.007
	(.050)	(.119)	(.117)
North Central	0	0	0
South	–.205	–.099	–.235
	(.065)	(.101)	(.158)
West	–.024	.198	–.104
	(.053)	(.124)	(.120)
Local labor market			
Low unemployment	.015	.150	–.249
	(.040)	(.060)	(.102)
High unemployment	–.087	–.082	–.319
	(.060)	(.104)	(.159)
Low wage	.018	–.226	.369
	(.050)	(.077)	(.132)
High wage	.159	.400	.165
	(.057)	(.118)	(.141)
Geographical mobility			
Moved for job	.144	–.109	.034
	(.036)	(.074)	(.105)
Refused to move for job	.134	.059	.218
	(.053)	(.088)	(.167)
Health impediments			
Obvious disfigurement	–.201	–.018	–.189
	(.066)	(.111)	(.131)
Some work limitation	–.176	–.216	–.231
	(.048)	(.090)	(.138)
Sick recently	–.028	–.018	–.053
	(.062)	(.080)	(.149)
Seasonal employment	–.136	.032	–.177
	(.046)	(.063)	(.110)
Siblings			
Number if ≦ 7	–.003	.013	–.012
	(.009)	(.013)	(.023)

TABLE A-2 (*Continued*)

Variable	White Males	Black Males	White Females
Eight or more	−.071	.050	−.153
	(.059)	(.074)	(.157)
Father's education			
0–5 years	0	0	0
6–8 years	.090	−.015	.166
	(.055)	(.061)	(.153)
9–11 years	.163	−.055	.161
	(.067)	(.125)	(.160)
12 years	−.015	.109	−.012
	(.080)	(.171)	(.186)
Some college	−.143	.303	.178
	(.095)	(.392)	(.244)
College graduate	.228	.016	.282
	(.125)	(.410)	(.276)
Advanced degree	.082	—	−.874
	(.176)		(.356)
Parents' economic status			
Poor	−.012	−.075	.136
	(.036)	(.075)	(.092)
Rich	.060	.033	.041
	(.054)	(.107)	(.111)
Place where grew up			
In the South	.045	−.177	.070
	(.059)	(.090)	(.155)
On a farm	−.214	−.112	.063
	(.040)	(.064)	(.107)
In a city	.099	−.017	.222
	(.040)	(.060)	(.093)
R^2	.200	.329	.335
s.e.	.550	.516	.500
N	1239	467	194

Note: Coefficients for father's education indicate *incremental* impact of advancing to next highest educational category.

[3]

The Decomposition of Inequality

...a man...can stare stupidly at phenomena; but in the absence of imagination they will not connect themselves together in any rational way.

C.S. Peirce

As has been stated earlier, the strength of the simulation method lies in its ability to answer the kinds of counterfactual questions that do not admit readily to statistical treatment. How unequal would the income distribution be if inherited wealth were distributed equally? How unequal would it be if everyone had the same taste for leisure?

Now that it has been established that a theoretical model of a perfectly functioning capitalist economy can indeed produce the degree of inequality observed in the real world, it is appropriate to consider the *quantitative* dimensions of the various causes of inequality. Among the more obvious sources of dispersion in incomes, the following seem relevant to all capitalist societies:

1. unequal inherited wealth; or, in fact
2. the existence of inherited wealth at all, even if equal;
3. dispersion in wage rates caused by
(a) unequal abilities
(b) unequal education and training;
4. dispersion in tastes, especially in relative liking of leisure versus consumption goods;
5. unequal rates of return on wealth. Owing to transactions indivisibilities and the advantages of risk pooling through diversification, there are probably considerable increasing returns to wealth-holding by an individual.[1]

1. Evidence for this is provided by Projector, Weiss, and Thoresen [1969, p. 111], who report a Gini ratio for property income of 0.93 for the United States in 1962, as compared to the Gini ratio for net worth of 0.76 reported by Projector and Weiss [1966, p. 30].

And of special relevance to the United States, it seems appropriate to add:

6. racial and sexual discrimination in employment and wages;
7. uneven incidence of unemployment;
8. the effects of monopolies and monopsonies, especially the more powerful trade unions.

The ultimate positive study of the U.S. income distribution would culminate in a breakdown of, say, the total Gini coefficient of lifetime income into that part accounted for by each of these eight causes, and perhaps others. This is a very important question for social policy. The implications for both social stability and the quality of life are very different in an economy where most of the observed inequality is due to differences in tastes, abilities, and stage in the life cycle, as opposed to an economy where most of the inequality is caused by inherited wealth, discrimination, and monopoly power. While this breakdown is terribly important, it is impossible to make empirically. Nature does not provide the econometrician with the controlled experiments he needs. Too many things have changed in the United States since 1900 for time series analysis of income inequality, even were a long enough time series available, to explain the observed movements in inequality.[2] Similar difficulties beset cross-section studies across nations; and this is compounded by the noncomparability of income distribution statistics from different countries.

Simulation, it would appear, is the *only* way this important question can be answered. The present study takes only a few strides towards this goal. The model is quite well equipped to deal with some of the causes of inequality, but not so well equipped for others. For example, it can—as will shortly be shown—determine the disequalizing effects of inherited wealth and dispersion in wages. But it cannot, until a satisfactory model of the education-ability-wages nexus is provided, decompose the effect of wage dispersion into the part due to ability (which, presumably, is "good" or at least tolerable) and the part due to unequal opportunities (which, presumably, is "bad"). The model, as it stands, can cope adequately with the effects of differences in tastes, but has not considered the impact of different rates of return. This factor could conceivably be added, but I have not attempted that here. Turning to those aspects uniquely important to the American economy, by using *actual* observed wage rates, the

2. For a heroic attempt in this direction, see Chiswick and Mincer [1972, pp. S51–S52].

model automatically accounts for *that part of the impact of discrimination and unionization that operates through wage rates*. However, it does not come to grips with the direct effects (if any) of these phenomena on hours of work, and fails completely to consider the incidence of unemployment.[3]

Nevertheless, owing to the extreme importance of the question, it is worth providing even a partial answer. In Section 5.1, therefore, I begin this task by breaking down the observed Gini coefficient of $K_0 + M$ in each regime into the parts attributable to each of the following five causes:

1. the tax system;
2. differences in tastes;
3. the existence of inherited wealth at all;
4. the unequal distribution of inherited wealth;
5. the dispersion in wage rates.

This is done in two different ways. First, starting always from the standard case, I investigate the responses of the Gini coefficient to certain hypothetical changes (for example, an equalization of all tastes). Second, starting from an imaginary economy of identical individuals, I add first one and then another cause of inequality and observe how the Gini ratio "grows."

In Section 5.2 I delve somewhat more deeply into the factor that seems to account for the most inequality—the dispersion in wage rates. Here, since a satisfactory model is yet to be developed, my approach is crudely empirical. Making use of a cross-section study of individual wages, I estimate the effect on overall income inequality of obliterating alternatively black-white, male-female, and union-nonunion wage differentials.

The last section raises a question which is important both in its own right and because it contributes to an assessment of the "goodness of fit" of the entire simulation apparatus. For the first time in the book a population of people of all ages—rather than an age cohort—is considered, and the distribution of *annual*—rather than lifetime—income is simulated. The results turn out to be remarkably close to the actual American income distribution and enable me to estimate the fraction of the inequality observed in U.S. data which is simply attributable to people being at different stages in their life cycles.

3. On the latter, see Solow [1951].

5.1 The Causes of Inequality in Lifetime Incomes

5.1.1 The Egalitarian Society (Regime I)

Table 5.1 indicates the impact on the Gini coefficient for K_0+M of each of several hypothetical changes in the economic environment of the egalitarian society. In each case, I have simulated the standard case of subsection 4.4.1 with only one modification. In line 1, both tax rates are set to zero. In lines 2–4 the variance of each taste parameter is, in turn, set to zero while the mean remains the same. Line 5 combines lines 2–4 by giving all individuals identical tastes. Line 6 alters the distribution of inherited wealth by giving each family the mean inheritance, $5,754; and line 7 takes the more radical step of equalizing all inherited wealth at zero. Finally, line 8 shows the effect of a hypothetical equalization of all wage rates.

The results in Table 5.1 point overwhelmingly in one direction, suggesting that equalizing the distribution of wages is the only way to effect a substantial redistribution of income. The proportional tax system, as one would expect, has almost no effect on inequality. (The potential effects of certain explicitly redistributive tax systems will be considered in the next chapter.) Of the three taste parameters, only ξ, the taste for leisure versus consumption, seems to have any significant effect on inequality. Considering the extreme dispersion given to the parameter b,[4] it is rather surprising that it contributes so little to

TABLE 5.1 IMPACTS ON GINI RATIO IN THE EGALITARIAN SOCIETY

Change from Standard Case	Effect on Gini Ratio		
(1) Remove proportional taxes	−0.000		
(2) Equalize labor-leisure tastes (ξ)	−0.024	or	−8.3%
(3) Equalize taste for bequests (b)	−0.001	or	−0.2%
(4) Equalize time preferences (ρ)	+0.000	or	+0.1%
(5) Equalize all tastes	−0.026	or	−8.7%
(6) Equalize inheritances at $5,754	−0.010	or	−3.5%
(7) Equalize inheritances at zero	−0.006	or	−2.0%
(8) Equalize wage rates	−0.161	or	−54.6%

Note: A change of "+0.000" means an increase in the Gini ratio of less than 0.0005. Conversely, a change of "−0.000" means a decrease in the Gini ratio of less than −0.0005.

4. The reader will recall that $E(b)=\sigma(b)=0.25$.

inequality. Chance variations in ρ, in fact, have a negligible *equalizing* effect. It should be noted however, that equalization of ξ has more impact when ρ and b are also equalized (compare lines 2 and 5).

Lines 6 and 7 contain the most startling information of all. Line 6, for example, simulates a quite radical reform of the inheritance laws whereby all bequests would be confiscated by the government and redistributed equally among all consumer units. Yet it appears that even such an extremely egalitarian policy would improve the Gini ratio by only 3.5%. Line 7 points out that if, instead of redistributing the bequests in equal amounts, the government merely commandeered all estates (this is *not* a balanced-budget policy), the equalizing effects would be cut almost in half. Because of the work disincentive provided by inheritance, it appears that, once a policy of equal inheritance for all has been decided upon, a large inheritance level is preferable to a zero level.[5] The reader should realize that this conclusion—that a radical reform of inheritance policies can accomplish comparatively little income redistribution—has been reached starting from an extremely unequal distribution of K_0. The Gini ratio of K_0 is 0.938; the top 1% of households receives almost 55% of all inherited wealth while the bottom 80% receives less than 1%. Yet even a completely equal division of this inheritance pool would lower the Gini ratio of lifetime incomes by only 0.01.

Of course, it can still be objected that such a conclusion might not stand up in a model which included some truly fabulous fortunes, that is, if J. Paul Getty were included in the sample of 400 persons. This is a difficult question to answer since the expected number of, say, million-dollar inheritances in a sample of 400 is zero. For example, according to federal estate tax returns—and this already covers only about the top 2.5% of all estates[6]—only 3.3% of the returns filed in 1969 were for gross estates over $1 million.[7] Based on this one might hazard the guess that about 0.083% (2.5%×3.3%) of all estates exceeded $1 million, that is, about one in 1,200. So a much larger sample size is needed to replicate adequately the extreme upper tail of the inheritance distribution.

As a weak test of the importance of giant fortunes, I resimulated the standard case of the egalitarian society with the highest inheritance raised from $479,000 to $4,790,000. Note that this certainly

5. This assumes that the goal is to minimize inequality. Another goal, for example, to maximize aggregate labor supply, would lead to a very different optimal inheritance level.

6. According to R.J. Lampman [1962, p. 11].

7. U.S. Internal Revenue Service [1972, Table 8, p. 20].

gives an overestimate of the importance of large fortunes. The resulting distribution of K_0 is absurdly unequal: the Gini ratio is 0.962, and 1/4 of 1% of the population receives 72 1/2% of all inherited wealth. A further indication is that the sample correlation between K_0 and $K_0 + M$ rises to a phenomenal +0.965, implying that a simple regression of lifetime incomes on inherited wealth in this economy would explain 93% of the variance of the former. Surely no modern economy has ever been so inegalitarian as this. The result of the stimulation is that the Gini ratio rises dramatically to 0.350. Comparing this with previous outcomes suggests that abolition of inheritance in such a regime would lower the Gini ratio by a substantial 0.055. This, in turn, suggests that experimentation with a much larger synthetic sample including some very large fortunes might be worthwhile.

Finally, line 8 reveals the one place the state may have real leverage if it desires to affect the income distribution. Something like 55% of all the observed inequality appears to be caused by unequal wage rates. This suggests that one way to achieve an equalization of income may be through some sort of wage subsidy program—an idea that is tested in the following chapter.

Table 5.2 considers the same set of questions from the opposite point of view; that is, instead of *decomposing* the inequality I *build it up* from zero. In the hypothetical world upon which most economic theory is based, where all individuals have the same tastes, same inheritance, and same wage rates, there would be no inequality of

TABLE 5.2 DERIVATION OF THE GINI RATIO IN THE EGALITARIAN SOCIETY

Type of Economy	Gini Ratio
All persons identical	0.000
Different tastes No inheritances Equal wages	0.121
Different tastes Actual K_0 distribution Equal wages	0.134
Standard case	0.295

incomes. Adding to this world dispersion in tastes (as in the standard case), results in a Gini ratio of 0.121 which is about 41% of the total inequality. If, keeping wages the same, I then superimpose the actual American distribution of inherited wealth, the Gini ratio rises to only 0.134, an additional 4.4% of the ultimate total. This corroborates the relatively small role assigned to inheritance by Table 5.1, and leaves almost 55% to be accounted for by wage dispersion.[8]

One might tentatively conclude for the egalitarian society that, in round numbers—

1. about 40% of the observed lifetime inequality is due to differences in tastes, and thus "desirable." However, with the other inequalities already present, equalization of tastes would decrease overall inequality by less than 10%.
2. about 4 to 5% of observed inequality is caused by unequal inheritances.
3. about 55% of the inequality is directly attributable to differences in wage rates. I defer to the next section the question of how much of this 55% can be attributed to race and sex discrimination or to unionism, and how much is left to other factors (like genetic and acquired ability).

5.1.2 The Other Regimes

With the method by now clear, I shall quickly review the simulation results for the other regimes. Tables 5.3 and 5.4 contain the same information as Tables 5.1 and 5.2 for the two possible versions of inequality of opportunity (Regime II). Basically, they corroborate the ideas obtained from the previous tables. Again, disparities in wages dominate all other causes of inequality. With moderate correlation between w_0 and K_0 (Regime IIa) equalization of tastes is a somewhat stronger equalizing factor than it was in Regime I; but with very high correlation tastes have about the same impact as they did there. Line 1 strongly suggests that removal of the two taxes would cause a slight increase in inequality. The reason is the previously cited high income elasticity of bequests, which lends some mild progressivity to even a proportional estate tax.

Tables 5.5 and 5.6 repeat this same information for the four possible versions of the programmed society (Regime III). The reader

8. Due to interaction effects, the derivation of the Gini ratio presented in Table 5.2, as well as in Tables 5.4, 5.6 and 5.8 to follow, is somewhat sensitive to the *order* in which the various causes of inequality are added. Rather than bore the reader with every possible permutation, I have settled upon one particular order selected to reflect declining degrees of exogeneity (from tastes to inheritances to wages).

TABLE 5.3 IMPACTS ON GINI RATIO UNDER INEQUALITY OF OPPORTUNITY

Change from Standard Case	Effects on Gini Ratio in	
	Regime IIa	Regime IIb
(1) Remove proportional taxes	+0.001	+0.002
(2) Equalize labor-leisure tastes	−0.026	−0.023
(3) Equalize taste for bequests	−0.001	−0.001
(4) Equalize time preferences	+0.000	−0.000
(5) Equalize all tastes	−0.028	−0.025
(6) Equalize inheritances at $5,754	−0.016[a]	−0.015[a]
(7) Equalize inheritances at zero	−0.011[a]	−0.011[a]
(8) Equalize wage rates	−0.166	−0.168

[a]This case is indistinguishable from Regime I.

TABLE 5.4 DERIVATION OF THE GINI RATIO UNDER INEQUALITY OF OPPORTUNITY

Type of Economy	Gini Ratio in	
	Regime IIa	Regime IIb
All persons identical	0.000	0.000
Different tastes	0.121[a]	0.121[a]
Unequal inheritance	0.134	0.132
Unequal wage rates	0.300	0.300

[a]This case is indistinguishable from Regime I.

will recall that IIIa signifies moderate negative correlation between ξ and w_0 and K_0; IIIb represents strong negative correlation; and IIIc and IIId capture the effects of unlikely positive correlations. The results reported in these tables are about as expected. Once again, dispersion in wages dominates all other causes. Inequality in wages causes more inequality in income when the taste for leisure is negatively correlated wth wages, and less inequality when the taste for leisure is positively correlated. Similarly, equalizing tastes would be a far stronger egalitarian change in Regimes IIIa and IIIb (as compared to Regime I), but would of course be disequalizing in Regimes IIIc and IIId. Using Table 5.5 and 5.6 to break down the causes of inequality in Regime IIIa as I did for Regime I, I might hazard the guess that —

1. 36% (0.120) is due to taste dispersion; but with interactions present a complete equalization of tastes would reduce inequality only about 19%;
2. 4% (0.015) is due to inheritance;
3. 48% (0.061) is due to wage dispersion;
4. 12% (0.037) is due to correlation of tastes with wages and inheritance.

Finally, Tables 5.7 and 5.8 report the same information for the stratified society, the regimes that combine positive correlation between w_0 and K_0 with negative correlation between ξ and endowments. The same general picture emerges. Wage dispersion is far and away the most important single cause of inequality, though in regimes where the correlation between endowments and ξ is extreme differences in tastes are also quite significant. The proportional tax system now turns out to be a slight disequalizer[9] (though never by very much); and equal inheritances are considerably better than no inheritances at all. Using Regime IVa as the most plausible version, and continuing my heroic "guesstimates," I might surmise that inequality is caused—

1. 35% (0.121) by differences in tastes;
2. 5% (0.018) by unequal inherited wealth;
3. 47% (0.161) by dispersion in wage rates;
4. 13% (0.042) by the intercorrelations among K_0, w_0, and ξ.

In retrospect, the four most plausible regimes (I, IIa, IIIa, IVa) agree rather more closely than might have been expected. All point to

9. The reason, I suppose, is that income taxation reduces M proportionately for each family, but does not affect K_0. Thus it appears slightly disequalizing. Of course, including the effect of the inheritance tax on K_0 might upset this conclusion.

TABLE 5.5 IMPACTS ON GINI RATIO IN THE PROGRAMMED SOCIETY

Change from Standard Case	Effects on Gini Ratio under Regime—			
	IIIa	IIIb	IIIc	IIId
(1) Remove proportional taxes	−0.001	−0.002	+0.001	+0.004
(2) Equalize labor-leisure tastes	−0.063[a]	−0.099[a]	+0.018[a]	+0.064[a]
(3) Equalize taste for bequests	−0.001	−0.001	−0.001	−0.001
(4) Equalize time preferences	+0.001	+0.001	+0.001	+0.000
(5) Equalize all tastes	−0.064[a]	−0.100[a]	+0.017[a]	+0.063[a]
(6) Equalize inheritances at $5,754	−0.011	−0.013	−0.010	−0.012
(7) Equalize inheritances at zero	−0.007	−0.009	−0.006	−0.007
(8) Equalize wage rates	−0.198	−0.228	−0.122	−0.083

[a]This case is indistinguishable from Regime I.

TABLE 5.6 DERIVATION OF GINI RATIO IN THE PROGRAMMED SOCIETY

Type of Economy	Gini Ratio in Regime—			
	IIIa	IIIb	IIIc	IIId
All persons identical	0.000	0.000	0.000	0.000
Different tastes	0.120	0.122	0.120	0.114
Unequal inheritances	0.135	0.142	0.131	0.124
Unequal wage rates	0.333	0.369	0.252	0.206

the relative unimportance of inherited wealth in the overall picture, attribute around 40% of total inequality to differing tastes, and underscore the overriding importance of unequal wages.

5.2 Wage Dispersion and Income Inequality

As indicated earlier, I do not believe that a satisfactory model of wage dispersion has as yet been devised. In view of the results just obtained, this leaves size distribution theory in a rather awkward position, not unlike the proverbial *Hamlet* without the Prince of Denmark. Of course, I have not written the Prince out of the play; he simply has yet to make his appearance.

Until a rigorous model of the inequality in wage rates is developed, one can either close the story with the simple statement that the (unexplained) wage distribution is the primary determinant of the income distribution; or one can attempt to make some crude empiri-

TABLE 5.7 IMPACTS ON GINI RATIO IN THE STRATIFIED SOCIETY

Change from Standard Case	Effect on Gini Ratio under Regime			
	IVa	IVb	IVc	IVd
(1) Remove proportional taxes	−0.000	−0.002	−0.001	−0.002
(2) Equalize labor-leisure tastes	−0.068[a]	−0.111[a]	−0.078[b]	−0.116[b]
(3) Equalize taste for bequests	−0.001	−0.001	−0.001	−0.001
(4) Equalize time preferences	+0.001	+0.001	+0.001	+0.001
(5) Equalize all tastes	−0.070[a]	−0.113[a]	−0.079[b]	−0.117[a]
(6) Equalize inheritances at $5,754	−0.017	−0.020	−0.021	−0.023
(7) Equalize inheritances at zero	−0.013	−0.015	−0.016	−0.019
(8) Equalize wage rates	−0.203	−0.234	−0.210	−0.237

[a]This case is indistinguishable from Regime IIa.
[b]This case is indistinguishable from Regime IIb.

TABLE 5.8 DERIVATION OF GINI RATIO IN THE STRATIFIED SOCIETY

Type of Economy	Gini Ratio under Regime—			
	IVa	IVb	IVc	IVd
All persons identical	0.000	0.000	0.000	0.000
Different tastes	0.121	0.126	0.123	0.127
Unequal inheritances	0.139	0.151	0.144	0.155
Unequal wage rates	0.342	0.385	0.354	0.392

cal guesses regarding one or the other of the many causes of wage inequality. The present section follows the second course.

5.2.1 The Method

Specifically, I seek to develop estimates of the *quantitative* importance for income inequality of the following three phenomena: discrimination against blacks, discrimination against females, and union-nonunion wage differentials. The method of inquiry is as follows. In some previous empirical work [Blinder, 1971, 1973a], I have developed regression equations to explain individual wage rates on the basis of socioeconomic characteristics. More precisely, I have estimated regressions of the form

$$\log w_i = \alpha \cdot X_i + \beta_1 R_i + \beta_2 S_i + \beta_3 U_i + e_i, \tag{5.1}$$

where w_i is the wage rate of individual i, X_i is a vector of characteristics of the individual which are being controlled for, R_i (race) is a dummy variable equal to unity for blacks and zero for whites, S_i (sex) is a dummy equal to one for males and zero for females, U_i (union) is a dummy equal to unity for union members and zero for nonmembers, the vector α and the scalars β_1, β_2, β_3 are constants, and e_i is a stochastic error. Under this specification, for example, β_1 can be interpreted as the *percentage* reduction in wages attributable to being black, all other things held equal.

Such a regression enables me to correct for the pure effect of black skin, or female gender, or lack of a union card on wage rates in one of two ways. Taking union differentials as an example, I can either multiply all nonunion wage rates by a factor $1+\beta_3$ to put them on a par with union wages; or I can divide all the union wages by $1+\beta_3$. What I would like to know, of course, is what the wage distribution *would look like* in the absence of unions. The first procedure essentially assumes that current union wages would remain the same and all nonunion wages would rise by $100\beta_3\%$ if the unions were to disappear all at once. The second procedure adopts the opposing extreme assumption; namely that union wages would fall by $100\beta_3\%$ while nonunion wages would be unaffected. Presumably, the actual effect of the abolition of unions would be somewhere in between these two extremes; union wages would fall somewhat and nonunion wages would rise. So looking at the effect on the income distribution in both ways supplies bounds on the true effect of unionism on income distribution. If these bounds are rather tight, as they typically turn out to be, the procedures will at least have given an unambiguous estimate of the effect of the unions.

In applying this method to estimate the effects of race, sex, and union membership on wages, a question of obvious importance is, What variables shall be controlled for? That is, what variables belong in the vector X_i? For example, in isolating the effect of racial discrimination on wages, should one control for education and occupation? Surely a black and a white with different educational credentials will earn different wages even in the absence of discrimination. This argues that education, occupation, and the like should be controlled for. But it is equally clear historically that some of the discrimination against blacks has taken the form of denial of access to education and/or relegation to inferior occupations. And this argues against controlling for education and occupation.

In Blinder [1971, 1973a] I argued that it is important to distinguish between *structural* and *reduced-form* wage equations. If one believes, as I do, that education and occupation have a *direct* impact on wage rates, then they should appear in the vector X_i in the structural equation. By contrast, certain other variables which may affect wages only *indirectly*—for example, family background, which may influence schooling and other things but which presumably has no direct effect on wages—ought to be excluded from X_i in the structure. The reduced-form wage equation, of course, would include all variables that influence wage rates either directly or indirectly *and that are exogenous to the individual.* Thus, such obvious determinants of wages as education, occupation, and union membership ought not to appear in the reduced form, while variables like family background should. Thus, in the papers just cited, I estimated both structural and reduced-form wage equations. For present purposes, equation (5.1) adequately represents the structure, while the reduced form is

$$\log w_i = a \cdot Z_i + b_1 R_i + b_2 S_i + v_i, \tag{5.2}$$

where Z_i is some vector different from (though partially overlapping with) X_i, and v_i is a stochastic error. Note that union membership, an endogenous variable in my formulation, appears only in the structural equation; so I have only one estimate of the union impact on wages. However, since race and sex presumably influence wages both directly and indirectly (via educational attainment and the like), (5.1) and (5.2) each provide a separate estimate of the extent of race and sex discrimination. For example, β_1 is an estimate of the direct discrimination against blacks in wages, while b_1 includes also the monetary equivalent of discrimination in education, occupational assignments and union membership.

5.2.2 The Effect of Racial Discrimination on Inequality

Consider first the results on the race differential obtained from the structure. The point estimate of β_1 is -0.223 (with standard error 0.028),[10] indicating that, other things equal, black wages average only 77.7% of those of whites. Therefore, to simulate the end of *direct discrimination in wages only*, I first multiply the wage of every white person in the sample[11] by 0.777 in order to obliterate the race differential. The result[12] is a decline in the Gini ratio of income

10. The empirical estimates cited here and below are from Blinder [1971].

11. As the wages are actual data drawn from the Survey Research Center [1970] data, the race, sex, and union affiliation of each individual are known.

12. All experiments reported in this section were performed using the standard case of the egalitarian society (Regime I).

$(K_0 + M)$ from 0.295 to 0.286. The alternative procedure is to divide every black wage by 0.777, and this leads to a Gini ratio of 0.283.

The two estimates agree quite well, and suggest that racial discrimination, while indubitably an urgent social problem on other grounds, is simply not a major contributor to inequality in the overall income distribution. To me, at least, this is an unexpected finding, but the explanation is not hard to find. It is well known that there is substantial inequality between the races; but those familiar with American income distribution statistics also know that the inequality *among blacks* is far greater than the inequality *among whites*. This is evidenced in my sample of 400 individuals by Gini ratios for lifetime income of 0.255 within the subset of 282 whites and 0.343 among the 118 blacks. So obliterating the racial wage differential does two things to the overall distribution. Eliminating racial inequality clearly has an equalizing effect. But increasing the fraction of total income going to blacks puts more weight on the group with the more dispersed income distribution, and this is clearly disequalizing. The net result of these two factors is the trivial equalization uncovered by the simulations.

Of course, overt wage discrimination has not been the only obstacle in the way of economic progress for blacks. The coefficient b_1 of race in the reduced form equation is -0.353 (with standard error 0.032), suggesting that when discrimination in education, occupational attainment, and union membership are included the average black earns only 64.7% as much as the average white. When all white wages are multiplied by 0.647, the simulated Gini ratio for income falls to 0.288; and when black wages are divided by 0.647, the resulting concentration ratio is 0.282. Again the two procedures lead to roughly the same conclusion—that eliminating racial discrimination entirely would not make the U.S. income distribution very much more equal.[13]

5.2.3 The Effect of Sex Discrimination on Inequality

The procedure used to assess the significance of sex discrimination as a determinant of income inequality is identical. In the structural equation, the point estimate of β_2 is 0.339 (with standard error 0.031). This means that, holding education, occupation, and many other things equal, males on average earn 33.9% more than females. To simulate the effect of eliminating sex discrimination in wages, then,

13. It would, of course, eradicate the close asociation between skin color and position in the income distribution, a goal that is highly desirable in its own right.

the wage rates of all females are increased by 33.9%. The Gini ratio for lifetime incomes in this experiment falls to 0.293, an almost imperceptible drop from the 0.295 when there is sex discrimination. Adopting the alternative of reducing all male wages by 33.9% leads to a concentration ratio of 0.297, which is actually higher than in the absence of discrimination. The conclusion appears to be that sex discrimination does not lead to any noticeable increase in inequality in the overall income distribution. The reason is the same as in the case of blacks. While obliterating the sex differential in wages is equalizing, placing more weight on the more unequal female income distribution is disequalizing.[14]

Use of the reduced form coefficient b_3 suggests that raising the wage of the average female up to the level of the average male would actually make the overall income distribution more unequal. The point estimate of b_3 is 0.462 (with standard error 0.031), and when all female wages are increased 46.2%, the Gini ratio rises to 0.297. When, instead, all male wages are reduced 46.2%, the corresponding ratio is 0.302. As should be clear by now, the reason for this unexpected result is the increased weight that is attached to the more unequal female distribution.

5.2.4 The Effect of Unions on Inequality

As explained in subsection 5.2.1 above, the dummy variable for union membership appears only in the structure, and therefore I have just one estimate of the union-nonunion wage differential. In equation (5.1), the point estimate of β_3 is 0.292 (with standard error 0.026). Using this to raise average nonunion wages to equality with union rates results in a decline in the Gini ratio for lifetime income to 0.280, suggesting a moderate equalization. However, when I reduce union wages 29.2% instead, the concentration ratio falls only to 0.290, a negligible decline from the 0.295 of the standard case. The explanation for the small equalization is what we have by now come to expect: nonunion workers have a much more disperse income disribution than union workers.[15] The large difference between the two procedures is due, I suppose, to the fact that inheritances (which are highly unequally distributed) bulk comparatively larger in the simulation in which union wages are reduced.

14. In the sample, the concentration ratio among the 276 men is 0.274, while among the 134 women it is 0.329.

15. The concentration ratios in the sample are 0.212 for the 134 union members and 0.323 for the 266 nonmembers.

One important caveat should be entered as an epilogue to the results on discrimination and unions just mentioned. In each case I conduct a thought experiment whereby race or sex or union wage differentials are eliminated by magic. Nothing is said about how this program might be effected, and, indeed, I have no intention of discussing such weighty issues here. It is clear, however, that *some* mechanism for eliminating the average race or sex or union pay differential—other than waving a magic wand—would have to be devised. And it would be a strange coincidence indeed if *every* black or female or non-union member benefited by precisely the same percentage. Social policies that, for example, concentrate the gains from ending racial discrimination in the lower tail of the black income distribution would *both* eradicate racial differences *and* equalize the distribution among blacks. It is quite conceivable that such policies might have far more substantial impacts on overall income inequality than has been indicated here. What is suggested is that their equalizing effects would not be much stronger than those of a program to aid families in the lower tail of the *white* distribution.

5.3 The Distribution of Annual Income

I turn now to a question raised several times during the course of this book but as yet unanswered. In the preceding sections of this chapter, I have tentatively attributed the total inequality in *lifetime* incomes to its various causes. However, the observed income distribution is generally for a far shorter accounting period, typically one year. When considering such a distribution, there is an additional cause of dispersion which does not appear in lifetime distributions: the fact that different households are at different stages in their life cycles. Some young households which will ultimately be among the rich in lifetime income appear poor, since the breadwinner is just starting his career (or, perhaps, is still in school). Other older households, which have not adequately provided for their retirement years, have an income standard far below their lifetime average. Also, owing to the two qualitatively different life cycles in leisure and labor outlined in Chapter 3 (increasing leisure versus decreasing leisure), even people of the same age, same labor-leisure tastes, and same endowments may have different incomes if their rates of subjective time discounting are different.

So in order to test the realism of the simulation model—and in particular to discover which regime most closely resembles the U.S.

economy— it is necessary to consider the distribution of annual income in a population composed of diverse age cohorts.

The model of microeconomic behavior developed in Chapters 2 and 3 is quite capable of generating an individual's income at a particular age. So, it would appear, all that is necessary is to superimpose an age distribution for the population and grind out a simulated income distribution. In fact, a few adjustments in the data are also required.

Consider first the age distribution. I was fortunate to have access to the aforementioned Survey Research Center (SRC) tape of 4,460 families which includes, among other things, both the wage rates and ages of the household heads. Since it was felt that a much larger sample was required to simulate a continuous distribution of people of varying ages (whereas only 400 sufficed for a single age cohort), all families on the tape with heads at least 18 years of age (the assumed age of economic birth) and younger than 73 (the assumed age of death) were included in the sample. There were 3,612 such households, and this was arbitrarily truncated to 3,600 for convenience. For each household, the "age" was defined as the actual age of the head minus 18 years. Thus the age variable ran from zero to 54, and reproduced exactly the age distribution in the SRC sample.

The relevant wage variable for each household was not similarly observable since the variable of interest in the theoretical model is *not* the current wage but rather w_0, the wage at economic age zero. In view of the assumption of a constant rate of growth of wage rates m, each current wage rate $w(A)$, where A is the economic age of the individual, was transformed into a hypothetical initial wage rate by the relation $w_0 = e^{-mA}w(A)$. After this alteration, the 3,600 wage observations were entered as the w_0 distribution for the simulation.

The distribution of inherited wealth represented a real problem. On the supposition that the present distribution of inherited wealth is a steady state—an assumption made for lack of contradicting data[16]— the distribution of K_0 used in the sample of 400 was employed again. That is, there were assumed to be nine individuals inheriting each of the K_0 values used in the sample of 400. Since there is a background rate of growth of wealth in the economy, this may introduce some systematic errors (making older people appear richer than they actually are); but it was thought that such errors were not likely to be serious.

16. For what it is worth, Robert Gallman [1969] has constructed an estimate of the wealth distribution in the United States in 1860 which is not too different from the wealth distribution in 1960.

Finally, a distribution of taste parameters—that is, a triple (ξ,b,ρ) —was generated from independent normal distributions as explained in subsection 4.1.3. Since the annual sample of 3,600 is so much larger than the lifetime sample of 400, it was thought that sampling variances would be small enough to be ignored. Owing to the high computational cost of dealing with such a large sample, no runs were made to estimate these sampling variances.

Table 5.9 presents the simulated income distribution for the standard case in the egalitarian society. The estimated Gini coefficient for this distribution is 0.425; the coefficient of variation is 0.941. Average income per household (after tax) is \$5,644; the largest is \$54,303 while the smallest is −\$1,876. This distribution has an uncanny resemblance to actual published data on the U.S. income distribution during the 1960s.

There is some ambiguity as to which factual distribution this simulated distribution should be compared with. Though another

TABLE 5.9 SIMULATED DISTRIBUTION OF ANNUAL INCOME: THE EGALITARIAN SOCIETY

Population Group		Approximate Income Range	Relative Share
Lowest	10%	\$ −1,900 – \$ 1,400	1.52%
Second	10%	1,400 – 2,100	3.12
Third	10%	2,100 – 2,700	4.27
Fourth	10%	2,700 – 3,500	5.48
Fifth	10%	3,500 – 4,300	6.83
Sixth	10%	4,300 – 5,200	8.35
Seventh	10%	5,200 – 6,400	10.27
Eighth	10%	6,400 – 8,100	12.71
Ninth	10%	8,100 – 11,000	16.54
Highest	10%	11,000 – 54,300	30.93
Top	5%	14,400 – 54,300	19.98
Top	1%	27,000 – 54,300	6.70
Gini concentration ratio			0.425
Coefficient of variation			0.941

investigator might make a different choice, it seems to me that distributions over households, or spending units, or some such concept offer the most relevant comparisons. Table 5.10 summarizes some actual U.S. income distributions which appear conceptually comparable to the simulation results. (The source for each distribution is explained in the notes to the table.) Though they refer to different years and slightly diifferent concepts of income and of the recipient unit, the distributions are reasonably similar to one another. Comparing these authentic data with the simulated distribution in Table 5.9 reveals an astonishing similarity. The three annual distributions (columns 1–3 of Table 5.10) have nearly the same Gini ratio as the simulated distribution.[17] Among the averages of annual distributions (included to average out year-to-year fluctuations in the data and, hopefully, reduce sampling variation), the CPS data (column 4) exhibit very slightly less inequality than the simulated data; the latter seem to assign too much income to the upper and lower tails. Comparing the simulation to the average OBE distribution (column 5), I would again appear to slightly overestimate inequality, though the shares of particular fractiles match extraordinarily well; only for the ninth decile and the upper 1% are the errors substantial.

As the reader by now has probably come to expect, the distribution of annual incomes in Regime IIa[18] does not differ very much from Regime I, while the distribution under Regime IVa[19] is notably less equal. These two distributions are given in Table 5.11. The figures for Regime IVa confirm the previous impression that such a regime is more inegalitarian than the U.S. economy has been for a long while.

5.4 Recapitulation

Appending these last results to the previous breakdown of the overall Gini coefficient for lifetime incomes, and using Regimes I and IIa as the paradigm cases, I am led to the following (very approximate) attribution of the total observed inequality (a Gini ratio of 0.43) in annual incomes.

1. About 30% (or 0.13) of the Gini ratio appears to be caused by

17. Budd's Gini ratios are calculated by a different method. See his paper.

18. The actual correlation between w_0 and K_0 in the annual simulation is 0.24 as opposed to 0.26 in the lifetime distribution.

19. The actual correlation of ξ with w_0 is -0.41, and with K_0 is -0.21 in the annual experiment, as compared to -0.40 and -0.22, respectively, in the lifetime experiments.

TABLE 5.10 SOME ACTUAL U.S. INCOME DISTRIBUTIONS

Population Group		(1)	(2)	(3)	(4)	(5)
Lowest	10%	0.94%	1.34%	1%	0.81%	1.39%
Second	10%	2.72	3.22	3	2.63	3.32
Third	10%	4.43	4.77	4	4.37	4.87
Fourth	10%	6.10	6.12	6	6.14	6.20
Fifth	10%	7.76	7.43	7	7.80	7.45
Sixth	10%	9.48	8.80	9	9.54	8.75
Seventh	10%	11.29	10.39	11	11.34	10.26
Eighth	10%	13.37	12.34	13	13.45	12.10
Ninth	10%	16.20	15.53	16	16.35	15.11
Highest	10%	27.72	30.17	30	27.61	30.93
Top	5%	17.50	19.80	20	17.34	20.44
Top	1%	6.01	7.50	NA	5.89	8.04
Gini Ratio		0.416	0.417	0.43	0.418	0.415

Notes:

NA: not available

(1): 1967 Current Population Survey (CPS) distribution for families and unrelated individuals (pooled), as computed by Budd [1970, Table 4, p. 253].

(2): 1961 Office of Business Economics (OBE) distribution for families and unattached individuals (pooled), from Budd [1970, Table 4, p. 253].

(3): 1963 Survey of Financial Characteristics of Consumers (Federal Reserve) distribution for consumer units, as reported by Projector, Weiss and Thoresen [1969, Table 4, p. 128].

(4): Average of nine annual distributions, 1960–68, CPS families and unrelated individuals (pooled), computed from Budd [1970, Table 4, p. 253].

(5): Average of five distributions: 1947, 1950, 1955, 1960, 1961, OBE families and unattached individuals, computed from Budd [1970, Table 4, p. 253].

TABLE 5.11 SIMULATED DISTRIBUTION OF ANNUAL INCOME: REGIMES IIa AND IVa

Population Group		Share in Regime IIa	Share in Regime IVa
Lowest	10%	1.41%	1.15%
Second	10%	3.20	2.57
Third	10%	4.30	3.49
Fourth	10%	5.38	4.41
Fifth	10%	6.67	5.54
Sixth	10%	8.19	6.84
Seventh	10%	9.94	8.46
Eighth	10%	12.36	10.65
Ninth	10%	16.11	14.18
Highest	10%	32.46	42.72
Top	5%	21.74	32.79
Top	1%	8.21	18.20
Gini concentration ratio		0.436	0.523
Coefficient of variation		1.064	2.366

life-cycle influences, and disappears when the lifetime is taken as the unit of account.

2. About 28% (or 0.12) is due to differences in tastes. This part, of course, is highly conjectural since I have no idea if the constructed distributions of taste parameters are either too disperse or too concentrated. Like the portion attributable to the life cycle, this part of observed inequality is not only tolerable, but actually desirable in a society that prides itself in respecting individual preferences.

3. Only about 2% (or 0.01) is attributable to the unequal distribution of inherited wealth. Presumably none of this would be tolerated in a strictly egalitarian society. But it appears that even radical reforms of current inheritance procedures would not alter the basic inequality of incomes very dramatically.

4. Almost 40% (or 0.17) is attributable to the distribution of wage rates, including any correlation wages might have with inherited

wealth. This is the area that seems to be pinpointed for further research.

There are a number of distinct reasons why wages differ; and the attribution of the total dispersion in wages among these causes has great bearing on social policies towards redistribution. Among the more important causes are—

a. innate ability of individuals, which is transmitted genetically by the parents. Presumably only the most radical of redistributionists would want to eliminate this cause of wage dispersion.

b. unequal educational attainment. This, in turn, may result from differing abilities, inequality of opportunity, and differences in tastes. To the extent that the first and/or the last prevail, one may be quite satisfied with the resulting inequality. However if, as some previous studies indicate, unequal opportunity is at the root of the inequality in educational attainment, the policy prescription is clear.

c. discrimination in wage rates. The distribution of wages fed into the model included wages of blacks and whites, and of males and females. While the simulations suggested that very little of the total dispersion is attributable to race and sex discrimination, further studies are necessary to either buttress or overturn this conclusion. Again, this is presumably one source of inequality which is not tolerable in a society such as ours.

d. unions and other departures from competitive labor market conditions. The question of unions is a vexing one. According to the folklore, if there is at least some monopsony power, unionization shifts distributive shares in favor of labor and against capital, and this should be equalizing. At the same time, unions tend to drive the wages of highly paid hourly employees up closer to parity with salaried workers (which is equalizing), while forcing down the wages received by the lower paid sectors of the labor force (which is disequalizing). A consensus—supported by no facts that I know of—seems to have evolved around the point of view that "...the direct effect of unionism upon the distribution of personal incomes is...minor."[20] Of course, this is a consensus based on casual empiricism, and therefore not terribly persuasive. My simulations really consider only the disequalizing aspect, and conclude that it is probably of minor significance.

It is clear that there is much more work, both empirical and theoretical, to be done on explaining the dispersion in wage rates.

20. Hildebrand [1952-1953, p. 385]. See also Rees [1962, pp. 96-99] for a casual guess that the effect of unions is slightly disequalizing.

Fifty-five years ago, Joseph Schumpeter wrote: "The great idea of investigating the relationship between wage differences and differences in ability opens a vast perspective. The new trail is steep and stony, but it must be followed".[21] So far, it must be admitted, economists have not traveled very far along this path. The simulation results reported here suggest that the payoff to such research, in terms of increasing our understanding of the income distribution, may be quite high indeed.

21. Quoted by Staehle [1943, p. 77].

References

Blinder, Alan S., 1971.
"Estimating a Micro Wage Equation: Pitfalls and Some Provisional Estimates," *Research Memorandum No. 131*, Princeton: Econometric Research Program.

———, 1973a.
"Wage Discrimination: Reduced Form and Structural Estimates," *Journal of Human Resources* 8: 436–455.

Budd, Edward C., 1970.
"Postwar Changes in the Size Distribution of Income in the U.S.," *American Economic Review, Papers and Proceedings* 60: 247–260.

Chiswick, Barry R. and Jacob Mincer, 1972.
"Time-Series Changes in Personal Income Inequality in the United States from 1939, with Projections to 1985," *Journal of Political Economy* 80 (Supplement): S34–S66.

Gallman, Robert E., 1969.
"Trends in the Size Distribution of Wealth in the Nineteenth Century: Some Speculations," in L. Soltow (ed.), *Six Papers on the Size Distribution of Wealth and Income*. New York: Columbia University Press for NBER.

Hildebrand, George H., 1952–1953.
"American Unionism, Social Stratification, and Power," *American Journal of Sociology* 58: 381–390.

Lampman, Robert J., 1962.
The Share of Top Wealth-Holders in National Wealth, 1922–56. Princeton, N.J.: Princeton University Press for NBER.

Projector, Dorothy S. and Gertrude S. Weiss, 1966.
Survey of Financial Characteristics of Consumers. Washington: Board of Governors of the Federal Reserve System.

Projector, Dorothy S., Gertrude S. Weiss, and Erling T. Thoresen, 1969.
"Composition of Income as Shown by the Survey of Financial Characteristics of Consumers," in L. Soltow (ed.), *Six Papers on the Size Distribution of Wealth and Income*. New York: Columbia University Press for NBER.

Rees, Albert, 1962.
The Economics of Trade Unions. Chicago: University of Chicago Press.

Solow, Robert M., 1951.
On the Dynamics of the Income Distribution, Unpublished Ph.D. dissertation. Harvard University.

Staehle, Hans, 1943.
"Ability, Wages and Income," *Review of Economics and Statistics* 25: 77–87.

Survey Research Center, 1970.
A Panel Study of Income Dynamics: Study Design, Procedures, Available Data, 1968–1970 Interviewing Years (Waves I–III). Ann Arbor: Survey Research Center.

U.S. Internal Revenue Service, 1972.
Statistics of Income – 1969: Estate Tax Returns. Washington: U.S. Government Printing Office.

[4]

Discrimination: Empirical Evidence from the United States

By Francine D. Blau and Marianne A. Ferber*

The study of discrimination received a major impetus in the 1960's when increasing social attention focused upon race and gender differentials in market outcomes. Gary Becker's *The Economics of Discrimination* (1957) strongly influenced empirical research by providing a definition of wage discrimination and suggesting a specific way in which it might operate. During the following years new theories were developed and refined in an attempt to explain why there appears to be continued discrimination in spite of market forces presumably operating against it. Similarly, a large amount of empirical work has been done to determine whether and how much discrimination actually exists, and to a lesser extent to test the implications of the various theories. Even so, the hope expressed by Becker in the preface of the second edition (1971) that our understanding of discrimination would increase so rapidly that the materials in his book would become obsolete before another decade began has clearly not been fulfilled. Here, we review what has been learned in the intervening years and suggest some fruitful directions for future research.[1] The focus of this paper, like that of most of the empirical research in this area, is on determining the extent of discrimination rather than on testing alternative models of discrimination.

I. Evidence from Econometric Studies

Becker defined the market discrimination coefficient as the difference between the ratio of two groups' wage rates with and without discrimination. Since it is assumed that, in the absence of discrimination, the members of each group would be paid in accordance with their productivities, wage discrimination may also be defined as pay differences between two groups that are not accounted for by productivity differences. Such a definition of discrimination implies, however, that any wage differences associated with productivity differences which are themselves caused by discrimination should be included in the discrimination coefficient.

In the late 1960's and early 1970's, a widely used method of empirically measuring discrimination was developed. In this approach, separate wage or earnings regressions are estimated for the members of each group, say blacks and whites. The portion of the pay differential due to differences in the returns to a given set of characteristics (i.e., differences in coefficients, including the constant term) is then used as an estimate of discrimination (for further explanation, see Alan Blinder, 1973; Glen Cain). Specifically, let U_r = the unadjusted wage ratio; A_r = the adjusted wage ratio of black to white wages if the two groups had equal values of the explanatory variables; and U_x = the unexplained portion of the wage differential or the estimate of discrimination, then

$$(1)\quad U_r = \sum_i B_{ib}\bar{X}_{ib} \Big/ \sum_i B_{iw}\bar{X}_{iw}$$

$$(2)\quad A_r = \sum_i B_{ib}\bar{X}_{iw} \Big/ \sum_i B_{iw}\bar{X}_{iw}$$

$$(3)\quad U_x = (1-A_r)/(1-U_r)$$

$$= \left[\sum_i \bar{X}_{iw}(B_{iw}-B_{ib})\right] \Big/ \left(\sum_i B_{iw}\bar{X}_{iw} - \sum_i B_{ib}\bar{X}_{ib}\right)$$

where B_i and $\bar{X}_i$ are, respectively, the coefficient and mean of the ith variable in an OLS

*Professor of Economics and Labor and Industrial Relations, and Professor of Economics, respectively, University of Illinois-Urbana, Champaign, IL 61820.
We are grateful for the comments and suggestions of Barbara Bergmann, Charles Brown, Barry Chiswick, Claudia Goldin, Daniel Hamermesh, Lawrence Kahn, Barbara Reskin, and Robin Williams.

[1] For more detailed reviews, see Blau (1984), Glen Cain (forthcoming), William Darity (1982), and Janice Madden (1985).

wage (earnings) regression and the subscripts b and w denote blacks and whites, respectively. It should be noted that (3) is essentially an index number formulation. The estimate of discrimination will depend upon the weights chosen and the use of any particular set of weights, such as the $\bar{X}_{iw}$ above, is arbitrary.

In evaluating the findings of such studies, it is important to bear in mind that, apart from the index number problem, (3) may yield either an over- or an underestimate of the true extent of labor market discrimination. On the one hand, conventional data sources do not allow for the measurement of all productivity-related characteristics. The concern is generally that if, on average, whites (males) are more highly qualified with respect to these omitted variables, labor market discrimination will be overestimated.[2] On the other hand, differences with respect to some productivity-related characteristics may reflect the indirect effects of discrimination (Blinder). For example, employers may discriminate against blacks (women) in access to training programs or in hiring for particular occupations. Further, if one takes into account the endogeneity of choice variables, we see that labor market discrimination may adversely affect the human capital investment decisions and labor market behavior of groups experiencing discrimination. Thus, such characteristics as education and training, actual labor market experience, and tenure may potentially be impacted by feedback effects. Measured labor market discrimination is likely to be underestimated to the extent that factors representing other dimensions of discrimination are controlled for.

The difficulties posed by these biases may be illustrated by a consideration of whether it is appropriate to include controls for occupation in analyses of discrimination. Their use tends to add considerably to the explanatory power of regressions (see below), though exactly how much depends on the precise form and amount of detail of the categories employed. If it is believed that individuals freely choose occupations according to their talents, tastes, and plans for labor force participation, differences in rewards for different types of work are appropriately included in the "explained" part of the earnings gap. If, on the other hand, occupational differences are caused by labor market discrimination and the adverse feedback effects it generates, occupational variables should be excluded. In the not implausible case that both discrimination and choice play a role, neither procedure will be unbiased. Indeed, what is called for is a two-equation model that explicitly treats occupation as endogenous.[3] Nonetheless, it is likely that specifications which exclude occupations (and other similar variables) yield an upper-bound estimate of discrimination and those which include such variables yield a lower bound.

With these issues in mind, we review the findings of the studies summarized in Table 1. It may be seen that, by the conventional measure, labor market discrimination has a substantial negative effect on the earnings of women and blacks.[4] Mean estimates of adjusted earnings ratios range from .62 to .81 for women and .67 to .81 for blacks, depending on specification. The mean unexplained portion of the gross differential ranges from 51 to 87 percent for women and from 39 to 66 percent for blacks. Table 1 also indicates the impact of alternative specifications. In the case of both gender and race differentials, the estimate of discrimination is considerably higher when a control for occupation is omitted.

The improved conceptualization of the role of labor market experience in explaining the gender differential (Jacob Mincer and

[2] Recently it has been suggested that the bias produced by imperfect measures of productivity could be eliminated by using a "reverse regression," in which the wage is the independent variable and an index of qualifications is the dependent variable. However, it appears that this method is not clearly superior and may be as much subject to bias as the traditional approach (Arthur Goldberger, 1984).

[3] Alternatively, a reduced form may be estimated in which occupational variables are excluded, but the underlying exogenous variables which determine them (for example, socioeconomic background) are included (Blinder).

[4] See Cain for a review of the findings for other minorities.

TABLE 1—SUMMARY OF CROSS-SECTIONAL STUDIES OF GENDER AND RACE DIFFERENTIALS

Control for			Means		
Occupation	Actual Experience	N[b]	U_r	A_r[c]	U_x
I. Gender (Women/Men)[a]					
No	No	8	.56	.62	.87
			(.13)	(.12)	(.10)
No	Yes	2	.65	.81	.56
			(.01)	(.01)	(.01)
Yes	No	6	.57	.70	.66
			(.14)	(.14)	(.10)
Yes	Yes	6	.59	.79	.51
			(.17)	(.12)	(.15)
II. Race (Black Men/White Men)	Hours of Work[d]				
No	No	4	.49	.67	.66
			(.04)	(.07)	(.16)
No	Yes	6	.60	.81	.47
			(.12)	(.11)	(.18)
Yes	Yes	1	.49	.80	.39

Source: Compiled with some additional calculations and small corrections from the studies summarized in Cain. Cain's table is in turn based on that presented in Donald Treiman and Heidi Hartmann (1981).

Note: Standard deviations are shown in parentheses.

[a]Includes results for all (black and white) or white workers. In the studies which present separate results for blacks and whites, U_r, A_r, and U_x tend to be higher for blacks than whites.

[b]The included studies were published between 1964 and 1981. Studies may be counted more than once if results are presented for different specifications or years. Citations of the studies are available upon request from the authors.

[c]Generally obtained by applying the findings for U_x based on regressions in which log earnings is the dependent variable to the observed earnings ratio (U_r).

[d]A study is included in this category if there is an explicit control for hours of work (annual, weekly, full-time/part-time) or if hours are implicitly controlled for by employing the wage rate as the dependent variable.

Solomon Polachek, 1974), as well as the more recent availability of appropriate information, mark a significant advance in our understanding of the causes of earnings differences by sex. As may be seen in Table 1, inclusion of actual (as opposed to potential) labor market experience considerably lowers the estimate of discrimination. It is important to note, however, that feedback effects have not been adequately taken into account by these studies (Blau, 1984). This suggests that, at least with regard to this consideration, labor market discrimination has been underestimated.

In the case of race differentials, it may reasonably be argued that discrimination has lowered the hours worked by black relative to white men (Cain). Blacks face substantially higher rates of unemployment and involuntary part-time employment. Their annual hours may also have been reduced by labor market discrimination in that it decreases the opportunity cost of temporary labor force withdrawals. Table 1 illustrates the substantial positive impact on the estimate of discrimination of omitting a control for hours worked.

In light of such sensitivity of the magnitude of discrimination to plausible alternative specifications of the underlying regression equations, and the fact that neither productivity nor discrimination itself is directly observable, some skepticism has arisen about the adequacy of this technique for measuring discrimination. Concern focuses on the possibility noted above that unmeasured nondiscriminatory factors could account for some or all of these differences. In the case of women, the traditional division of labor in the family may lower their motivation, commitment, and effort. For blacks, the poorer education they received, even when years of schooling are held constant, might be responsible in part for their lesser success. It is, however, likely that some unmeasured factors could work in the opposite direction.[5] Moreover, it is impressive that substantial unexplained race and sex pay differentials remain even in the most conservative estimates.

The conclusion from the cross-sectional studies that labor market discrimination plays an important role has been challenged recently by researchers using time-series data.

[5]For example, there is some evidence that, all else equal, the labor force group is more selective of those with higher wage offers among women (relative to men) and among black (relative to white) males (Blau and Andrea Beller, 1986). The issue of selectivity bias has been of particular concern in time-series studies (for example, Charles Brown, 1982; James Smith and Michael Ward, 1984).

Their studies show that the earnings gap between blacks and whites (James Smith and Finis Welch, 1986), as well as between women and men (June O'Neill, 1985; Smith and Michael Ward, 1984), has been narrowing, while relative human capital endowments of the relevant groups were changing correspondingly. Though the argument that the two developments were related is entirely convincing, it is not necessarily the case that the increase in human capital accounted for *all* of the observed improvement. There have been studies which suggest that equal opportunity legislation played a part (for example, Andrea Beller, 1979; Charles Brown, 1982). Further, a perceived decline in labor market discrimination may have helped to induce the very increase in human capital upon which these studies focus.

II. Other Sources of Evidence

Additional evidence of the importance of labor market discrimination is embodied in the significant number of court cases where individual employers have been found guilty of employment discrimination or have reached out-of-court settlements with the plaintiffs. Although these are at best "case studies," the number of such instances strongly suggests that they are more than isolated incidents. While the statistical techniques used to support legal charges of discrimination are quite similar to those reviewed above (demonstrating the wide impact of this approach), the argument of important omitted variables is less compelling in this context where it should be possible for firms to document the nondiscriminatory criteria which resulted in the observed race (sex) difference, if indeed such criteria exist.

Finally, it may be instructive to consider the direct evidence of discriminatory attitudes that has been accumulated by other social scientists. This research strikes us as particularly interesting in what is suggests about the nature of such attitudes. For example, a number of studies have found that both female and male college students gave identical papers higher ratings on such dimensions as value, persuasiveness, profundity, writing style and competence when respondents believed the author to be male rather than female. Similar findings have been obtained in studies requiring both women and men to evaluate the resumés of applicants for employment (for a review, see Virginia O'Leary and Ranald Hansen, 1982). Moreover, beliefs regarding sex differences in average ability and productivity-related behavior appear to be quite prevalent among managers (Benson Rosen and T. H. Jerdee, 1978).

Of course, the existence of such discriminatory attitudes does not prove that people act on them. It is, however, reasonable to suppose that employers who perceive the performance of members of a particular group as inferior would treat them accordingly without realizing that this might be costly for them. Some evidence in this regard is Ferber and Michele Teiman's (1980) finding that the acceptance rate for papers authored by women relative to those authored by men was higher in economics journals with double-blind refereeing than in those which had not adopted this practice.

III. Conclusions

A review of empirical studies suggests that even when fairly refined measures of productivity-related characteristics are held constant, blacks and women earn less than whites and men. We are inclined to accept this as evidence of labor market discrimination, although it is not possible at this point to determine the precise magnitude of the discriminatory wage effect. Future research could shed greater light on the process of discrimination if more effort were devoted to empirically testing various models of discrimination, and if it were recognized that a number of causes of discrimination may interact and reinforce each other. Our understanding of discrimination would also be enhanced if more were known about the mechanisms by which these outcomes are produced. Considerably more work is needed to understand fully the causes of race/sex differences in occupations, including the precise role played by discrimination in recruitment, hiring, job assignment, and promotion. The puzzling persistence of large racial differences in unemployment rates is also much in need of further research. Finally, estimation of feedback effects is an extremely important area which has been neglected in previous work.

In both conventional studies testing for discrimination and in those focusing on the other issues outlined above, we believe that researchers need to continue to explore all possibilities for getting more and better data on qualifications, performance and personnel practices, including information on individual enterprises where better measures of some of these variables may be obtained. Such information might be complemented by data on perceptions and attitudes from direct surveys of employers and workers as well as from experiments. Even with improved methods and better data it may be no easier to make progress towards consensus in the future than it has been in the past. In view of the pressing policy relevance of this research, however, it is as important as ever to continue trying.

REFERENCES

Becker, Gary S., *The Economics of Discrimination*, Chicago: University of Chicago Press, 1957; 2nd ed., 1971.

Beller, Andrea H., "The Impact of Equal Employment Opportunity Laws on the Male/Female Earnings Differential," in C. B. Lloyd et. al., eds., *Women in the Labor Market*, New York: Columbia University Press, 1979, 304–30.

Blau, Francine D., "Discrimination Against Women: Theory and Evidence," in W. A. Darity, Jr., ed., *Labor Economics: Modern Views*, Boston: Kluwer-Nijhoff, 1984, 53–89.

______ **and Beller, Andrea H.**, "Trends in Earnings Differentials by Sex: 1971–1981," paper presented at the American Statistical Association Meetings, Chicago, 1986.

Blinder, Alan S., "Wage Discrimination: Reduced Form and Structural Estimates," *Journal of Human Resources*, Fall 1973, *8*, 436–55.

Brown, Charles, "The Federal Attack on Labor Market Discrimination: The Mouse That Roared?," *Research in Labor Economics*, Vol. 5, 1982, 33–68.

Cain, Glen G., "The Economic Analysis of Labor Market Discrimination: A Survey," in O. Ashenfelter and R. Layard, eds., *Handbook of Labor Economics*, Amsterdam: North-Holland Press, forthcoming 1987.

Darity, William A., Jr., "The Human Capital Approach to Black-White Earnings Inequality: Some Unsettled Questions," *Journal of Human Resources*, Winter 1982, *17*, 72–93.

Ferber, Marianne A. and Teiman, Michele, "Are Women at a Disadvantage in Publishing Journal Articles?," *Eastern Economic Journal*, August-October 1980, *6*, 189–94.

Goldberger, Arthur, "Reverse Regression and Salary Discrimination," *Journal of Human Resources*, Summer 1984, *19*, 293–318.

Madden, Janice, "The Persistence of Pay Differentials: The Economics of Sex Discrimination," *Women and Work*, Vol. 1, 1985, 76–114.

Mincer, Jacob and Polachek, Solomon W., "Family Investments in Human Capital: Earnings of Women," *Journal of Political Economy*, March/April 1974, *82*, S76–S108.

O'Leary, Virginia E. and Hansen, Ranald D., "Trying Hurts Women, Helps Men: The Meaning of Effort," in H. Bernardin, ed., *Women in the Work Force*, New York: Praeger, 1982, 100–23.

O'Neill, June, "The Trend in the Male-Female Wage Gap in the United States," *Journal of Labor Economics*, January 1985, *3*, S91–S116.

Rosen, Benson and T. H. Jerdee, "Perceived Sex Differences in Managerially Relevant Behavior," *Sex Roles*, December 1978, *4*, 837–43.

Smith, James P. and Ward, Michael P., *Women's Wages and Work in the Twentieth Century*, Santa Monica: Rand Corporation, 1984.

______ **and Welch, Finis R.**, *Closing the Gap, Forty Years of Economic Progress for Blacks*, Santa Monica: Rand Corporation, 1986.

Treiman, Donald J. and Hartmann, Heidi I., *Women, Work, and Wages: Equal Pay for Jobs of Equal Value*, Washington: National Academy Press, 1981.

[5]

Education and Underemployment in the Urban Ghetto

By BENNETT HARRISON*

With the recent availability of several government generated microdata files, it has become possible to develop rigorous quantitative measures of ghetto economic activity, to complement the qualitative impressions contained in the literatures of urban sociology and social psychology.[1] More importantly, analysts are now able to undertake econometric investigations of the structure of ghetto poverty.[2]

The first of these sources, produced by the U.S. Department of Labor, was the 1966 ten ghetto Urban Employment Survey (*UES*). The 37,330 individual person records in the *UES* were assembled from interviews conducted in November 1966. These data facilitated the estimation of ghetto income and unemployment rates, and the comparison of these (and other) statistics with similar indicators for the cities and metropolitan areas of which these ghettos were a part. In general, as the figures in Table 1 illustrate, the jobs to which ghetto workers have access were found to be of poor quality and paid wages which were substandard by a number of widely accepted benchmarks. Occupation by occupation, the median wage rates of ghetto workers averaged only 40–60 percent of the 1966 annual average wage rates in the corresponding metropolitan area. Given the extent of low-wage work in the slums, it is perhaps not too surprising that so many ghetto men leave (or do not form) families so that mother and children will be eligible for welfare—what amounts to a desperately needed second income. Broken homes in the ghetto may sometimes represent a rational response to the need for multiple incomes. Yet the median incomes of female-headed *UES* households (including welfare receipts), added to the median individual incomes of "unattached" adult males, still sum to less than $4,000. In 1966, ghetto families with both parents present received only about $3,500 in gross income. As the data in Table 1 indicate, this is some $2,500 below the benchmark established by the Department of Labor as a minimum family budget just adequate to sustain an urban family of four in a cheap, rented apartment, with an eight-year-old automobile, and subsisting on a diet consisting largely of dried beans.[3]

* Associate professor of economics and urban studies, Massachusetts Institute of Technology. This paper is based upon my Pennsylvania Ph.D. thesis. I would like to acknowledge receipt of dissertation fellowships from the Office of Economic Research, Economic Development Administration, U.S. Department of Commerce; and from the Manpower Administration, U.S. Department of Labor. Additional support was provided by the Bureau of Business and Economic Research of the University of Maryland, and by the University's Computer Science Center. Constructive criticism of earlier drafts and materials was contributed by Barbara Bergmann, Norman Glickman, Lawrence Klein, Stephan Michelson, William Milligan, Mancur Olson, Thomas Vietorisz, and several anonymous referees. Marianne Russek provided programming assistance. Elisabeth McDonnell supplied the diagrams. An earlier paper with the same title, reporting on intermediate results of the thesis-in-progress, appeared in David Gordon (1971b).

[1] I refer, for example, to the work of Claude Brown, Kenneth Clark, Elliot Liebow, and Malcolm X.

[2] For some examples, see Peter Doeringer, Gordon, Harrison (1972b), and Thomas Vietorisz and Harrison (1970).

[3] See U.S. Bureau of Labor Statistics. For comparative purposes, it should be noted that the income estimates in Table 1 refer to the year preceding November 1966, while the *BLS* budgets refer to March 1967. For an extended discussion of the relevance of the *BLS* cross-section urban budgets as normative benchmarks against which to judge various income distributions, see Vietorisz and Harrison (1971).

TABLE 1—INCOME, UNEMPLOYMENT, AND SUBEMPLOYMENT IN TEN URBAN GHETTOS

Ghetto and City	Unemployment Rate Ghetto[a]	Unemployment Rate *SMSA*	Ghetto Subem-ployment Rate[a]	Median Individual Weekly Wage[a]	Median Annual Family Income[a]	*BLS* Lower Level Family Budget[b]
Roxbury (Boston)	6.5	2.9[a]	24.2	$74	$4224	$6251
Central Harlem (New York City)	8.3		28.6	73	3566	
East Harlem (New York City)	9.1	3.7[a]	33.1	67	3641	6021
Bedford-Stuyvesant (New York City)	6.3		27.6	73	4736	
North Philadelphia	9.1	3.7[a]	34.2	65	3392	5898
North Side (St. Louis)	12.5	4.4[a]	38.9	66	3544	6002
Slums of San Antonio	7.8	4.2[b]	47.4	55	2876	n.a.
Mission-Fillmore (San Francisco)	11.4	5.4[a]	24.6	74	4200	6571
Salt River Bed (Phoenix)	12.5	3.3[b]	41.7	57	2520	n.a.
Slums of New Orleans	9.5	3.3[b]	45.3	58	3045	n.a.

Source: Computations from unpublished 1966 *UES* data files and *BLS* worksheets.
[a] November 1966
[b] March 1967

In conducting the 1966 *UES*, the Department of Labor's survey researchers recognized the inability of the conventional measure of unemployment to capture the full force of labor market failure in the ghetto.[4] As the first step toward a remedy, a new index number called the "subemployment rate" was constructed, consisting of the sum of those who are actually unemployed, those working part-time but seeking full-time work, heads of households under 65 years of age earning less than $60 a week full-time, nonheads under 65 years of age earning less than $56 a week full-time, half the number of male nonparticipants aged 20–64 (on the grounds that they have given up looking not because they do not want to work but because of the "conviction—whether right or wrong—that they can't find a job"), and half of the "unfound males."[5]

Among the ten ghettos surveyed by the Department of Labor in 1966 and listed in Table 1, the highest subemployment rate was found in the predominantly Mexican-American slum areas of San Antonio; nearly one out of every two ghetto residents was unemployed or underemployed. The lowest subemployment rate in the sample was 24.2 percent in Boston's Roxbury-South End neighborhoods. Clearly, the problem of underemployment reflected in this indicator lies at the very core of the "urban crisis."

[4] "The traditional unemployment measure counts as working the person who is working only part-time, although he is trying to find full-time work; gives no consideration to the amount of earnings; omits those who are not "actively looking for work"—even though the reason for this is their conviction (whether right or wrong) that they can't find a job, at least one they want; and omits the "undercount" factor—those who are known to be present in the community but who do not show up at all under the present survey methods" U.S. Department of Labor (1967, p. 5).

[5] Highly imperfect and even arbitrary in its weights (if not in its definitions), the index nevertheless represents an extremely important first step toward the measurement of *underemployment* in the United States. Indeed, in all countries—rich and poor alike—the study and the reporting of underemployment as a measure of the *quality* of working life is bound to become increasingly important to the formation of public policy.

From July 1968 through June 1970, the Urban Employment Survey Group of the Department of Labor, together with the Census Bureau, engaged in continuous interviewing of about 3,500 households in each of six central city ghetto areas and two nonghetto "control" areas. The results of these 1969 and 1970 *UES*s are being published gradually by the regional *BLS* offices.

In March 1966, the Census Bureau conducted a Survey of Economic Opportunity (*SEO*) for the Office of Economic Opportunity, with an overall sample size of about 30,000 households (nearly 4,000 adult workers in the sample resided in the central city poverty areas of the twelve largest Standard Metropolitan Statistical Areas (*SMSA*)). About 75 percent of the sample were reinterviewed in March 1967. A large (and growing) number of doctoral dissertations are making use of the *SEO*, the editing of which was performed on contract by the Brookings Institution.

Finally, the *UES* questionnaire was appended to the decennial Census long-form in sixty areas in 1970. When this file is assembled, it will represent by far the largest data source on urban poverty areas ever available.

A wide variety of quantitative studies of the ghetto economy are now possible. One question of considerable theoretical and policy interest is the extent to which the underemployment of ghetto residents is attributable to inadequate human capital formation among the ghetto labor force. This is the particular research issue addressed in the following pages.

I. Education, Training, and the Urban Ghetto

Neoclassical theories of unemployment and poverty are oriented almost entirely toward the "supply side." Thus, according to Lester Thurow, the originators of the antipoverty program decided that "poverty was to be eliminated by raising everyone's marginal product to the level where [they] would be able to earn an acceptable income. Education and training programs were to be the principal means for raising marginal products . . . increasing workers' human capital could eliminate poverty . . . " (pp. 91–92).

During the first half of the 1960's, many economists—and most policy makers—supported the contention that public education (and, to a somewhat lesser extent, institutional training) were probably the most effective instruments for combatting poverty.[6]

However, more recent empirical research—much of it using microdata—strongly challenges the conventional wisdom which links nonwhite poverty in particular to inadequate human capital (this literature is surveyed in Harrison (1971b)). The marginal efficiency of nonwhite educational quantity and (in some of the studies) quality has been found to be relatively modest in studies by Ivar Berg, Barbara Bergmann and Gerolyn Lyle, Stephan Michelson (1968), Bradley Schiller, and Randall Weiss. The relative ineffectiveness of various kinds of government training is documented by Berg, Harrison (1972b, chs. 1 and 6), Earl Main, Thomas Ribich, and the U.S. General Accounting Office.

None of these studies has explicitly examined the human capital of *ghetto* residents, however. The poverty areas of our central cities, and the more compact "hardcore" ghetto communities within them, contain families of many races and ethnic origins: Blacks, Puerto Ricans, Chicanos, some American Indians, and substantial numbers of poor whites. There is new evidence that ghetto workers—and Blacks in particular—*are* investing in themselves through the mechanism of

[6] For a comprehensive review of the literature, see Harrison (1972b), ch. 1.

TABLE 2—EDUCATIONAL ATTAINMENT OF NEGRO AND WHITE GHETTO RESIDENTS
November 1966

	All Persons Age 20 and Over			Persons Age 20–24 Only		
Ghetto	Sample Size	Median Years Completed[a]	Percent With 12 Or More Years	Sample Size	Median Years Completed[a]	Percent With 12 Or More Years
Negroes						
Roxbury (Boston)	1897	11.5±0.2	45.4	282	12.2±0.3	57.1
Central Harlem (New York City)	2501	11.4±0.2	45.2	214	12.3±0.4	69.2
East Harlem (New York City)	689	10.7±0.4	38.0	85	11.7±0.7	47.1
Bedford-Stuyvesant (New York City)	2711	11.7±0.2	47.3	338	12.3±0.3	64.5
North Philadelphia	2414	10.5±0.2	33.8	271	12.1±1.0	53.5
North Side (St. Louis)	2791	9.7±0.2	29.7	280	12.1±0.4	52.9
Slums of San Antonio	320	11.1±0.6	43.4	31	12.7±0.8	80.6
Mission-Fillmore (San Francisco)	720	12.1±0.3	52.5	113	12.5±0.4	71.7
Salt River Bed (Phoenix)	661	9.0±0.4	23.6	53	11.9±0.9	49.1
Slums of New Orleans	2047	8.8±0.2	23.1	266	11.9±0.5	49.2
Whites[b]						
Roxbury (Boston)	858	11.1±0.3	42.8	85	12.3±0.8	61.2
Central Harlem (New York City)	139	10.8±1.0	46.0	17	12.4±2.4	76.5
East Harlem (New York City)	796	10.3±0.4	38.3	91	12.4±0.6	67.0
Bedford-Stuyvesant (New York City)	196	11.4±0.7	46.4	9	11.2±1.6	44.4
North Philadelphia	199	11.7±0.9	48.2	17	12.3±0.9	64.7
North Side (St. Louis)	226	8.8±0.7	27.0	14	12.2±1.4	57.1
Slums of San Antonio	157	11.5±0.8	47.8	15	12.0±2.6	53.3
Mission-Fillmore (San Francisco)	881	12.1±0.3	54.3	123	12.9±0.6	79.7
Salt River Bed (Phoenix)	570	9.2±0.4	28.4	41	12.1±1.0	53.7
Slums of New Orleans	593	9.4±0.4	35.2	55	12.3±1.1	63.6

Source: Computations from unpublished 1966 *UES* data files
[a] 95 percent confidence intervals shown
[b] Excludes Mexican-Americans, Puerto Ricans, and other Spanish-surnamed persons

public education. In fact, Blacks in the urban slums have achieved levels of schooling comparable to those of whites in the same neighborhoods, as shown by the overlapping confidence intervals between the two portions of Table 2, which is constructed from 1966 *UES* materials. Moreover, ghetto Blacks seem to have achieved about the national nonwhite average for years of school completed.[7] In fact, the gap between the national average school completion rates of young whites and blacks has itself nearly disappeared. By 1970, the interracial difference in median years of schooling for persons under 35 years of age was only .4 (U.S. Department of Commerce, table 65).

Data on institutional training in the ghetto areas of New York City are displayed in Table 3, together with compara-

[7] A third of the nonwhite workers living in the poverty areas of the nation's twelve largest cities in March 1966, had completed at least twelve years of school, according to my calculations from the 1966 *SEO* tapes. About 38 percent of the Blacks living in the ten *UES* areas (identified in Table 2) had attained at least that level of schooling by November 1966. For the nation as a whole in 1966, only about 28 percent of the nonwhites aged 25 or more were high school graduates. While no 1966 national statistics on the educational attainment of younger Blacks have been published, Table 2 shows that, at least in the ghetto, younger Blacks do better than the racial average; they *are* staying in school longer. Nationally, the rate of high school completion for Black adults aged 20 and over is therefore probably somewhat greater than 28 percent. It is the similarity of these national and ghetto estimates which is reported in the text.

TABLE 3—PROPORTION OF LABOR FORCE HAVING COMPLETED IN-SCHOOL VOCATIONAL TRAINING OR INSTITUTIONAL TRAINING, BY RACE, SEX, AND RESIDENCE
July 1968–June 1969
(in percent)

	Whites		Blacks	
	Men	Women	Men	Women
Completed in-school vocational training				
New York City ghettos[a]	5	15	11	12
Detroit nonghetto[b]	16	28	16	22
Completed institutional training				
New York City ghettos[a]	22	20	24	17
Detroit nonghetto[b]	41	34	36	20

Source: David Gordon, (1971a) Appendix C, based upon 1969 *UES*.
[a] $N = 2{,}651$ individuals aged 16–54 and out of school. Sample areas include Harlem, Bedford-Stuyvesant, and the South Bronx.
[b] $N = 3{,}899$ individuals aged 16–54 and out of school.

tive figures for nonghetto Detroit. In every case, the incidence of program completion among ghetto dwellers during fiscal year 1969 was lower than for workers residing in the nonghetto control area. *Within* the ghetto, however, Black men compared quite favorably with their white neighbors in terms of the incidence of completion of training programs.

Have ghetto dwellers been able to translate this acquired human capital into improved economic status? Are the interracial differences in the marginal efficiency of human capital as significant *within* the ghetto as they are in the nation as a whole? Has ghetto underemployment been relieved by increased education and training? These are the specific questions to which we now turn our attention.

II. Returns to Human Capital in the Ghetto

The Quality of Education

Before considering my own thesis results on eighteen urban ghettos, a word is in order concerning the devilishly difficult problem of accounting for interracial differences in the quality of education. To some extent, the discussion has been mooted by Randall Weiss' demonstration of the (rather remarkable) insensitivity of white-nonwhite income differentials to educational "quality" adjustments using the Coleman scores. Moreover, my "controlling" for residence probably includes some adjustment for quality, to the extent that inner city neighbors attend the same (or similar) schools. Finally, it is reasonable to assume that poor white urban adults educated elsewhere (for example, in the rural South or in Appalachia) received relatively low quality schooling. For these reasons, the models employed in my study make no attempt to control for possible variations in educational returns attributable to differences in the quality of education. In this, I am following a precedent set by Gary Becker, who assumed that whites and Negroes of equivalent age and sex were equally productive at the margin.

Within racial groups, the implications of not adjusting the data for educational quality are fairly easy to assess. Following Weiss, we may assume that the "quality of schooling, grades, individual ability and motivation, and *parents'* income, education, and occupation [are] probably . . . correlated positively with years of school [such that] estimates of the increase in earnings associated with an additional year of school will [in the absence of controls for the above factors] be biased upward" (p. 152). It follows that my intraracial estimates of the marginal returns to education are, if anything, too high.[8]

Human Capital and Underemployment in the Central City Poverty Areas of Twelve SMSAs[9]

The wage and employment-determination process which informs these studies of the ghetto labor force is based upon the work of Otis Dudley Duncan and his associates.[10] A fundamentally recursive process is assumed, according to which education, occupational "assignment," and employment (i.e., the practice of an occupation) occur sequentially, with education reentering the system at each "step" because of its convenience to employers as a seemingly inexpensive (although perhaps unreliable) indicator of potential productivities. Wage bargaining, which depends upon the relative economic power of labor and capital, occurs *after* individuals have been "assigned" to occupations. Since economic power varies among industries, the industry attachment of a worker is an important determinant of his or her wage (industry is also a sensible—if crude—proxy for the complementary capital structures with which workers cooperate). The validity of the recursive hypothesis (confirmed by tests on the residuals of the wage and unemployment equations) permits the use of single-equation methods of estimation. Thus, *OLS* was used throughout.

It has been suggested that controlling for industry eliminates one important source of interpersonal wage variation. If serious, this would tend to bias the "pay-

[8] While we are on the subject of bias in the intraracial regressions, there are two further observations to make, both favorable to the conclusions of this paper. First, Ivar Berg observes that "the basic assumption of the theory of human capital" (i.e., that education and productivity are positiveiy correlated) usually goes untested in most human capital studies—including my own. If earnings are roughly proportional to productivity, then any model which assumes a positive correlation between education and productivity may impart an upward bias to the estimates of the monetary returns to that education. Berg (ch. 5) himself has identified industries in which (he estimates) education and productivity are, if anything, inversely related. Second, Barbara Bergmann believes that the results reported in this paper may be biased upward vis-à-vis appropriate time series estimates. The differences in pay between a (well-educated) Black professional and less-educated Blacks may depend a good deal on the relative scarcity of educated Blacks. Increasing the number of Black professionals by increasing the number of educated Blacks —over time—might reduce the differential between the pay of Blacks with different amounts of education. The result is that a cross-section model predicting income from schooling may exaggerate the effect of improving Black educational achievement on Black income.

[9] From the 61,517 persons aged 14 or more who are described in the March 1966 *SEO*, I selected for analysis those 3,756 persons living in the central city poverty areas of the twelve largest *SMSA*s: Baltimore, Chicago, Cleveland, Detroit, Houston, Los Angeles, New York, Philadelphia, Pittsburgh, St. Louis, San Francisco, and Washington, D.C. These are the only areas which are individually identifiable on the current edition of the *SEO* tapes (while the 1967 file is more recent, only the 1966 file contains data on training program participation). For technical documentation and the definition of "poverty area" as employed in the *SEO*, see J. R. Wetzel and Susan Holland.

In order to permit comparisons among wage rates in the twelve different cities, it was necessary to construct a cross-section inter-city deflator. The "fixed market bundle" data for such an index was obtained from the *BLS* Lower Level Family Income Schedule for March 1967 (see Bureau of Labor Statistics, bulletin 1570-5; data for the relevant cities are not available for any earlier date). While the size of the sample may appear to be more than adequate, the specification of analytic models using categorical variables rapidly exhausts observations. For individual cities, there are many categories (e.g., "13-15 years of school," "employment in state government," "completion within the last five years of an on-the-job training program") whose cells are empty or nearly so. For this reason, the data from the twelve *SMSA*s have been pooled. Whenever this was done, however, inter-city variations were captured (at least to some extent) by city dummies.

[10] Compare Duncan's methodological exposition and the monograph by Duncan and Peter Blau.

off" coefficients downward. This is, of course, an empirical question. My fifteen industry categories appear to be sufficiently highly aggregated such that there is as much wage and unemployment variation within these major industry groups as there is among them. For example, a model containing education-industry interaction terms was fitted; nearly all of these terms were statistically insignificant. Regressions of earnings and unemployment on age, race, sex, and schooling, using a completely different data source this time, yielded substantially similar estimates of the payoff to education, even though (in this case) industry was not specified (see the following section). Nevertheless, it must be admitted that the inclusion of industry *may* have imparted some degree of downward bias to the results. The aforementioned experimental evidence suggests, however, that it is unlikely to be serious enough to offset the upward biases discussed in footnote 8.

Several different micromodels were specified for each of the two racial groups indentifiable in the *SEO*: "whites" (including a small proportion of Spanish-Americans) and "nonwhites" (of whom about 94 percent are Negroes). Multiple regression models with a linear, continuous specification of "education" (measured by years of school completed) indicated that white workers in the twelve central city "ghettos" earn on the average more than twice as much in weekly wages per extra year of school completed as nonwhites from the same neighborhoods. Interaction models showed that the nonwhite payoff varies very much more than the white payoff—from city to city, across the sexes, and by age. Similar contrasts were obtained from models with unemployment specified as the measure of payoff, i.e.,

$$u = \left[1 - \frac{\text{weeks worked in 1965}}{\text{weeks in the labor force in 1965}}\right] \times 100$$

The white slope estimate greatly exceeded the nonwhite coefficient in the simple linear analysis, but (again using interaction models) there was considerably more intercity and interage variation about the nonwhite slope than about the white slope, just as before. This same contrast was also found to obtain for two other measures of the returns to schooling: annual wage income of the worker and his or her occupational status.[11]

Perhaps the most interesting of the models developed to study the returns to schooling enjoyed by current ghetto residents were those specifying discontinuous educational steps, designed to capture the discrete effects (if any) of the possession of educational credentials, such as a high school diploma. Let us examine these nonlinear (but additive) models carefully. For each of the two racial groups, four models were estimated:

$$(1) \quad \phi = \beta_0 + \sum_{i=1}^{6} \beta_i E_i + \sum_{i=7}^{14} \beta_i T_{i-6} + \beta_{15} S + \beta_{16} A + \sum_{i=17}^{28} \beta_i C_{i-16} + \epsilon$$

$$(2) \quad w = \beta_0 + \sum_{i=1}^{6} \beta_i E_i + \sum_{i=7}^{16} \beta_i T_{i-6} + \beta_{17} S + \beta_{18} A + \sum_{i=19}^{33} \beta_i I_{i-18} + \sum_{i=31}^{45} \beta_i C_{i-33} + \beta_{46} F + \epsilon$$

[11] These status calculations employ an ordinal prestige scale which assigns a rank of 0-100 to each of 308 Census occupational titles. This index was developed by the National Opinion Research Corporation (*NORC*) and Otis Dudley Duncan. The properties of the index and a description of the methodology by which it was created are also presented in my dissertation (see Harrison (1972b), Appendix One).

(3) $$Y = \beta_0 + \sum_{i=1}^{6} \beta_i E_i + \sum_{i=7}^{16} \beta_i T_{i-6} + \beta_{17} S + \beta_{18} A + \sum_{i=19}^{33} \beta_i I_{i-18} + \sum_{i=31}^{45} \beta_i C_{i-33} + \beta_{46} F + \epsilon$$

(4) $$u = \beta_0 + \sum_{i=1}^{6} \beta_i E_i + \sum_{i=7}^{16} \beta_i T_{i-6} + \beta_{17} S + \beta_{18} A + \sum_{i=19}^{33} \beta_i I_{i-18} + \sum_{i=31}^{45} \beta_i C_{i-33} + \beta_{46} F + \epsilon$$

where

ϕ = Duncan—*NORC* ordinal status score ($0 \leq \phi \leq 100$), based upon occupation in March 1966

w = individual weekly earnings in March 1966

Y = individual annual earnings in 1965

$$u = \left[1 - \frac{\text{weeks worked in 1965}}{\text{weeks in the labor force in 1965}}\right] \times 100$$

$E_1 = E_{0\text{–}7\text{ years}}$ = 1 if individual completed less than 8 years of school; 0 otherwise

$E_2 = E_{8\text{ years}}$ = 1 if individual completed exactly 8 years of school; 0 otherwise

$E_3 = E_{9\text{–}11\text{ years}}$ = 1 if individual completed some but not all high school; 0 otherwise

$E_4 = E_{12\text{ years}}$ = 1 if individual completed high school; 0 otherwise

$E_5 = E_{13\text{–}15\text{ years}}$ = 1 if individual completed some but not all college; 0 otherwise

$E_6 = E_{16^+\text{ years}}$ = 1 if individual completed at least 4 years of college; 0 otherwise

T_1 = 1 if individual completed a private institutional training program since 1956; 0 otherwise

T_2 = 1 if individual started but did not complete such a program; 0 otherwise

T_3 = 1 if individual completed an apprenticeship since 1956; 0 otherwise

T_4 = 1 if individual started but did not complete an apprenticeship; 0 otherwise

T_5 = 1 if individual completed an on-the-job training (*OJT*) program of at least 6 weeks duration since 1956; 0 otherwise

T_6 = 1 if individual started but did not complete such a program; 0 otherwise

T_7 = 1 if individual completed an armed forces vocational program since 1956; 0 otherwise

T_8 = 1 if individual started but did not complete such a program; 0 otherwise

T_9 = 1 if individual completed a government training program, e.g., *MDTA* training, Job Corps; 0 otherwise

T_{10} = 1 if individual started but did not complete such a program; 0 otherwise

S = 1 if individual is male; 0 otherwise

A = individual's age (in years)

$\{I_i\}, i=1, \ldots, 15$
- 1 = construction industry
- 2 = durable goods manufacture
- 3 = nondurable goods manufacture
- 4 = transportation
- 5 = communication
- 6 = utilities, sanitation
- 7 = wholesale trade
- 8 = retail trade
- 9 = finance, insurance, real estate
- 10 = business and repair services
- 11 = personal services
- 12 = entertainment, recreation
- 13 = professional services
- 14 = federal government
- 15 = state or local government

$\{C_i\}, i=1, \ldots, 12$
- 1 = Baltimore
- 2 = Chicago
- 3 = Cleveland
- 4 = Detroit
- 5 = Houston
- 6 = Los Angeles
- 7 = New York
- 8 = Philadelphia
- 9 = Pittsburgh
- 10 = St. Louis
- 11 = San Francisco
- 12 = Washington, D.C.

$$F = \begin{cases} 1 & \text{if individual worked at least 35 hours/week for at least half of the weeks he or she worked in 1965} \\ 0 & \text{otherwise} \end{cases}$$

In all runs, (E_1), (I_1), and (C_7) were deleted to avoid singularity. The absence of the industry and OJT dummies and the "full-time/part-time" variable F from model (1) is motivated by the previously described assumption (following Duncan) that occupational "assignment" precedes actual employment in a specific job in a specific industry.[12]

The estimated education parameters for all eight regressions are displayed in Table 4.[13] For each of the four measures of payoff for each racial group, the table lists the level of the marginal impact of each of the mutually exclusive and exhaustive education classes, and the intraracial differences between successive levels. The weekly wage and annual unemployment *differences* are displayed as step-functions in Figures 1 and 2 (only those steps—i.e., differences—which are significantly different from zero at the .10 level have been graphed). Finally, for each of the payoff variables, Table 4 shows the differences between the white and nonwhite returns at each level of education. Notice that the great majority of these interracial differences are statistically significant.

Let us first consider the weekly wage indicator. According to Table 4 and Figure 1, the weekly wage of white high school graduates in the pooled set of twelve poverty areas is nearly \$25 higher than that of whites who never entered high school. For nonwhites, the difference is only \$8.33. High school, therefore, has three times as high a marginal payoff for ghetto whites as for ghetto nonwhites.[14] On the assumptions of a forty-year working life, a rectangular lifetime earnings

[12] The variables displayed surprisingly mild multicollinearity. For all but 34 of the 1225 simple correlation coefficients (r) associated with the 50 variables (x) in the analysis, $r_{x_i x_j} < R_k$, where R_k represents the multiple correlation coefficient of the kth regression ($K=1, \ldots, 8$). (See Donald Farrar and Robert Glauber, p. 98). Even among the 60 human capital variables ($E_1, \ldots, E_6$; $T_1, \ldots, T_{10}$) there was little intercorrelation. In fact, only 29 of the 60 simple correlation coefficients r_{ET} were themselves significant at the .05 level, and in *no* case was $r_{ET} \geq R_k$.

[13] Unfortunately, the training variables in the *SEO* proved to be rather weak. There were too few observations (particularly of persons having completed training) to permit much confidence about the results. Nevertheless, for what it is worth, very few of the training coefficients in any of the regressions were significant at the .05 level.

[14] A 95 percent confidence interval on the interracial difference of \$16.55 is \$2.35-\$30.25.

TABLE 4—MARGINAL RETURNS TO WHITE AND NONWHITE EDUCATION IN THE CENTRAL CITY POVERTY AREAS OF TWELVE *SMSA*'s, March 1966

Measure of Payoff	Years of School Completed 8	9–11	12	13–15	16+	R^2	F	Sample Size
Occupational Status (rank order)								
Whites								
Levels	+2.8	+3.7	+15.8[a]	+24.1[a]	+37.9[a]	.203	16.24	821
Differences		+0.9	+12.1[b]	+ 8.3[b]	+13.8[b]			
Nonwhites								
Levels	+1.7	+2.9[a]	+10.2[a]	+17.4[a]	+40.4[a]	.309	32.19	2935
Differences		+1.2	+ 7.3[b]	+ 7.2[b]	+23.0[b]			
Absolute difference between white and nonwhite levels	1.1	0.8	5.6[d]	6.7[d]	2.5[e]			
Weekly Wages (dollars)								
Whites								
Levels	+2.47	+14.80	+24.88[a]	+16.99[a]	+61.36[a]	.287	9.68	821
Differences		+12.33[b]	+10.08[c]	− 7.89	+44.37[b]			
Nonwhites								
Levels	+2.33	+1.00	+8.33[a]	+14.39[a]	+41.36[a]	.361	45.80	2935
Differences		−1.33	+7.33[c]	+ 6.06[c]	+26.97[b]			
Absolute difference between white and nonwhite levels	0.14	13.80[e]	16.55[e]	2.60	20.00[b]			
Annual Unemployment (percent)								
Whites								
Levels	+0.4	+0.5	−3.5[a]	−4.9[a]	−5.4[a]	.135	4.36	821
Differences		+0.1	−4.0[b]	−1.4[c]	−0.5[c]			
Nonwhites								
Levels	−0.6	+0.3	−0.4[a]	−1.9	−1.1	.231	23.54	2935
Differences		+0.9	−0.7[c]	−1.5	+0.8			
Absolute difference between white and nonwhite levels	1.0	0.8	3.1[e]	3.0[e]	4.3[d]			
Annual Wages (dollars)								
Whites								
Levels	+313.66[a]	+378.20[a]	+694.46[a]	+1016.03[a]	+3228.02[a]	.277	8.31	821
Differences		+ 64.54[c]	+316.26[b]	+ 321.57[b]	+2211.99[b]			
Nonwhites								
Levels	+115.99	+184.24	+300.21[a]	+ 849.07[a]	+1514.35[a]	.425	51.41	2935
Differences		+ 68.25	+117.97[c]	+ 539.86[b]	+ 674.28[b]			
Absolute difference between white and nonwhite levels	147.67	193.96[e]	394.25[d]	175.96[e]	1713.67[d]			

Source: Calculations from unpublished 1966 *SEO* data files.

[a] Regression coefficient is significant at the .05 level.

[b] Difference is significant at the .05 level (the standard error of the difference between two coefficients β_i and β_j within a regression is estimated by $\sqrt{\text{Var}_i+\text{Var}_j-2\text{ Cov}_{ij}}$).

[c] Difference is significant at the .10 level.

[d] Difference is significant at the .05 level (determined by pooling the racial samples, adding education-race interaction terms for each education class, and conducting t-tests on the coefficients associated with each of these education-race dummies).

[e] Difference is significant at the .10 level.

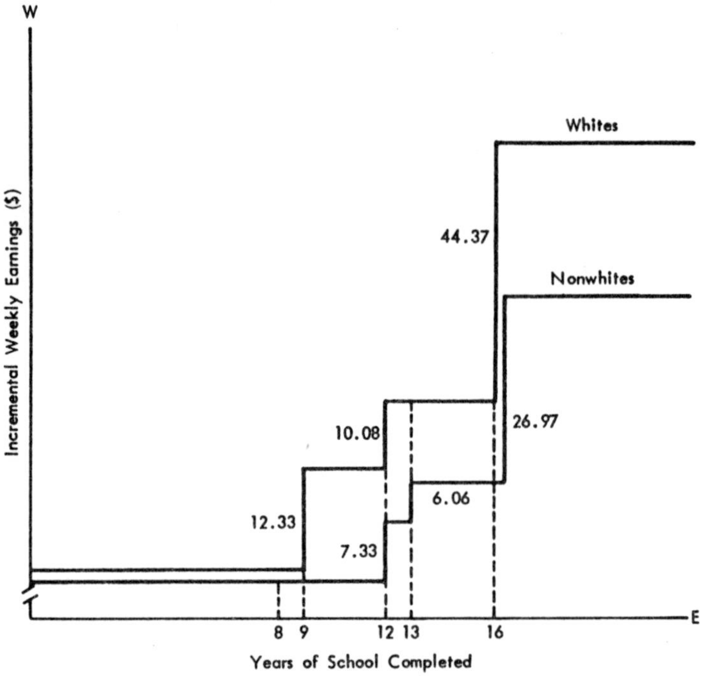

FIGURE 1. INCREMENTAL WEEKLY EARNINGS ASSOCIATED WITH EDUCATION-CENTRAL CITY POVERTY AREAS IN TWELVE *SMSAs*: MARCH 1966

distribution,[15] and a 6 percent rate of time preference, the present value of the lifetime return to completion of high school is nearly $19,000 for whites but only $6,000 for nonwhites. Clearly, education has a very high opportunity cost for nonwhites living in the urban ghetto. There are any number of (largely illegal) activities out "on the street" which are capable of returning at least $6,000 in a single year.[16]

For whites, the risk of unemployment falls with years of school completed. Over the interval 9–12 years inclusive, the expectation of joblessness falls by 4.0 percent (see Figure 2). For white college graduates, it falls an additional 1.9 percent. For nonwhites, on the other hand, the average effect of education on unemployment, while statistically significant, is numerically inconsequential. A white college graduate from the slums can expect to be involuntarily out of work nearly three weeks less per year than a white high school drop-out who also lives in one of the urban ghettos in the sample. But the nonwhite college graduate faces only a 0.7 percent lower risk of unemployment than the high school dropout. And that effect is attributable to the high school, not the college, diploma (8.3 per cent of the non-

[15] This is, of course, an unrealistic assumption; age-earnings profiles are known to be hill-shaped. But for the immediate purpose, it is also an inexpensive assumption, and it facilitiates computation. Actually, there is some evidence (presented in Harrison (1972b) ch. 2) that a rectangular model gives a tolerably good approximation if one is interested only in the present values computed from an early age.

[16] By assuming equivalent (and *continuous*) earnings periods for both races, I am surely understating the racial earnings "gap" since nonwhite employment and labor force participation rates are well known to be significantly lower over time than the rates for white workers.

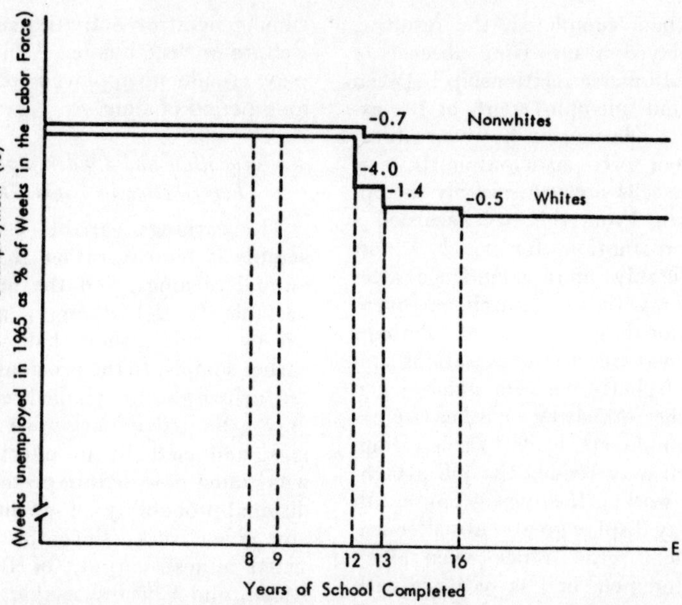

FIGURE 2. INCREMENTAL UNEMPLOYMENT RATES ASSOCIATED WITH EDUCATION-CENTRAL CITY POVERTY AREAS IN TWELVE *SMSA*s: MARCH 1966

white ghetto sample completed at least some college).

That the annual earnings variable shows the same relative behavior as the other payoff measures, and that education clearly *is* positively associated with occupational status, suggests the following hypothesis: Education facilitates the entry of both white and nonwhite ghetto workers into new occupations, and (at least for whites) leads to greater interoccupational mobility. Moreover, by national standards, these variations represent a "move up" into higher status positions. But this finding only confirms that the effects of racial discrimination pervade even these poorest neighborhoods in the urban economy, for, even though they share many similar problems associated with their common environment, ghetto residents diverge significantly by race insofar as their labor force status is concerned. Education may help members of both races to move into what are nationally considered to be more prestigious positions. But, once there, the nonwhites find themselves underemployed again: receiving earnings which are hardly above the levels enjoyed in the previous position, and facing the same expectations of unemployment as before. For ghetto whites, on the other hand, the occupational mobility facilitated by education is translated into substantially higher earnings and significantly lower risks of joblessness.

Probably the most dramatic of these findings concerns the virtual absence for nonwhites of any relationship between education and unemployment, after the effects of age, sex, industry, city, training experience, and full-time/part-time status have been removed. In an earlier study of the Harlem economy (Vietorisz and Harrison (1970)), it was found that when we stratified both unemployment and labor force participation rates by age, sex, and years of school completed, the resulting tables displayed a surprising absence of the expected inverse relationship between education and unemployment, or the expected direct relationship between education and labor force participation. In fact, many of the cells showed precisely the opposite effects. From this, we hazarded a tentative explanation, for which I now feel considerably more confidence after completing my thesis research on seventeen additional ghetto areas. Perhaps education increases the expectations and standards of ghetto workers which, when unmet by discriminating or otherwise exploitative employers, leads to frustration. This in turn may reduce the job attachment of the worker. If presently employed, he or she may display greater absenteeism, more frequent recalcitrance when given orders by foremen, or less patience with what is perceived as racist behavior on the part of coworkers.[17] If the ghetto worker is not presently employed, then—although he is indeed searching for work—the change in his standards or expectations may lead him to increase his reservation wage. If the offered positions do not meet his standards, then he will reject the job and search further, or turn to other income-generating activities such as public welfare or "the hustle."[18] In this way, he may remain unemployed for a relatively long period of time.

Education and Underemployment in Ten Ghettos in Eight SMSAs[19]

The earnings variable used with this sample is hourly, rather than weekly or annual earnings, and the unemployment variable (a 0–1 dummy) refers to the survey week rather than, as with the earlier sample, to the previous year. In the ten urban ghettos studied, education has only a limited impact upon hourly earnings, and virtually no effect at all upon what must now be interpreted as the conditional probability of unemployment in any given week (since this sample consisted almost entirely of Black, Puerto Rican, and Chicano workers, white/nonwhite differences were not studied at all).

A number of different earnings models yielded estimated returns of from 3 to 9 cents per hour for each additional year of schooling and, over the interval of 9–12 years of schooling inclusive, an average return of 15 cents. Workers with at least some college received, on the average, only 20 cents more per hour than high school graduates who went directly to work and did not go to college. One model was designed to test for the existence of an upper limit to hourly wages and salaries in the ghetto, irrespective of education, i.e., the upper asymptote e^a in the function

$$w = e^{a-bE^{-1}}$$

[17] Harold Sheppard's famous studies of "workers with the 'blues' " have shown that "the greater a person's education achievements, as measured by years of school, the greater are his life and job aspirations," and the greater his discontent if he fails to achieve those goals (1971, p. 28). In their study of Boston labor market institutions, Doeringer and his colleagues found that ghetto job-seekers were systematically placed in jobs similar (in wage and working conditions) to those which they had just left. This lack of upward mobility in the placement system probably contributes to the poor work habits (such as tardiness and high quit rates) which then frighten off other and perhaps genuinely concerned businessmen. Doeringer hypothesizes that "the availability of alternative low wage job opportunities and the unattractiveness of such low wage work interact to discourage the formation of strong ties to particular employers . . . for wage rates higher than the 'prevailing' ghetto wage, disadvantaged workers are more likely to be stable employees than other workers" (pp. 10–11).

[18] The functional similarities and complementarities between these "irregular" activities and the low-wage jobs which make up what some economists call the "secondary labor market" are explored in Daniel Fusfeld, Harrison (1972b, ch. 5), and U.S. Department of Labor (1968, pp. 94–99).

[19] The *UES* areas in this sample are identified in Table 1. Usable records on 37,330 individuals aged 14 and over were available. The wage data were again adjusted to control for intercity variations in the cost of living.

Such limits were indeed found, ranging from a low of $1.56 per hour in San Antonio's Chicano *barrios* to a high of $2.04 per hour in the Bedford-Stuyvesant ghetto of New York City. *No* amount of education would lead us to expect a Bedford-Stuyvesant worker of having an hourly wage of more than $2.04. All ten asymptotes were statistically significant. Interestingly, Doeringer had identified the same threshhold in his own studies of urban poverty in Boston. While Boston's antipoverty agency set up neighborhood employment centers in the slums to recruit ghetto workers for Boston industry, "many of these jobs pay only $2.00 an hour or less" (p. 9). Thus, says Doeringer, "the main benefits of the system have come from prompt referrals to jobs similar to those already available to the ghetto community" (p. 17).

III. Minority Economic Opportunity Outside the Ghetto[20]

It has been suggested that a sample of ghetto residents is inherently biased, since those for whom education has "paid off" will presumably have moved out, leaving us with a sample skewed toward the "failures." A very recent (and decidedly unofficial) finding of the Bureau of Labor Statistics' Urban Employment Survey Group provides us with some direct evidence that the ghetto samples are probably not biased, at least not because of selective outmigration. Of 7,200 ghetto families in six cities who were to be reinterviewed by the *BLS* over a twelve-month period in 1968–69 (a period of exceptionally high mobility nationally), only 900 had moved from one residence to another. And of these 900 families, only 60 had moved out of the ghetto; all of the rest were either intraghetto moves (750) or involuntary relocations, for example, to jail or into the armed forces (90). In other words, the rate of family outmigration from the urban ghetto, only two years after the date of the surveys we are analyzing, was less than 1 percent. According to Anthony Downs, p. 36, "normal population turnover causes about 20 percent of the residents of the average U.S. neighborhood to move out each year."[21]

This same question about selective outmigration motivated the extension of my researches to urban workers living outside of the ghettos, (a) in nonpoverty central city neighborhoods, and (b) in suburban communities (the source of this intrametropolitan data is, again, the 1966 *SEO*). The results of these studies seem to validate the earlier findings. More important, they cast considerable doubt on the validity of widely held assumptions about the intrametropolitan spatial distribution of poverty and discrimination.

In terms of average economic opportunity—measured by weekly earnings, annual unemployment, and occupational status—the white levels improve monotonically with "distance" from the core, while nonwhite opportunity increases somewhat with "move" from the ghetto to the nonpoverty central city, but falls again with the further move out to the suburban ring.[22] (See Table 5 where only the male figures are tabulated.) When 95 percent confidence intervals are constructed around these means or medians,

[20] For a more extensive "inside-outside" comparison, using *SEO* data, see Harrison (1972a), (1972b, ch. 4).

[21] In 1969–70, 25 percent of all Black households in America changed residence (U.S. Department of Commerce, Table 9). In the *UES* sample, as indicated in the text, only 900 of 7,200 households (13 percent) changed residences in 1968–69. It may be worth noting that, unencumbered by the obstacle of purely racial discrimination, the "leakage" of highly motivated and able ghetto whites is at least as likely as the loss of similarly equipped Blacks. If so, then the results reported in this paper imply that even the *least* able ghetto whites receive a significantly higher return to schooling than do ghetto Blacks.

[22] The reader is to be reminded that we are in fact dealing with a 1965 cross-section.

TABLE 5—INDICATORS OF RELATIVE ECONOMIC OPPORTUNITY IN TWELVE *SMSA*s, BY RACE AND LOCATION OF RESIDENCE

March 1966
(95% confidence intervals shown)

Residential location	Sample Size	Median weekly male earnings	Mean male unemployment rates	Median male occupational status[a]	Incremental return to high school (both sexes)[b]	Incremental return to college (both sexes)[c]
Central city povery areas						
whites	821	\$93.33±5.76	8.8%±1.8	19.4±2.0	\$24.88	\$36.48
nonwhites	2935	78.19±2.36	10.4 ±1.2	14.7±0.9	8.83	33.03
Rest of central city						
whites	2125	123.67±4.88	3.9 ±0.8	36.8±1.4	9.16	51.62
nonwhites	1565	99.87±4.16	5.3 ±1.2	16.7±1.6	[d]	53.50
Suburban ring						
whites	3163	133.58±4.68	3.5 ±0.6	40.7±1.1	32.80	65.32
nonwhites	845	96.12±5.32	8.8 ±1.9	15.7±1.8	[d]	38.87

Source: Calculations from unpublished 1966 *SEO* data files.

[a] Measured by a scoring procedure which assigns an ordinal rank of 0–100 to each of the 308 occupational titles on the *SEO* tapes.

[b] Measured relative to a person who never attended high school at all. Each of the component "steps" is statistically significant at the .05 level. Estimated by multiple regression, controlling for age, sex, industry, city of residence, and training program experience.

[c] Measured relative to a high school graduate who never attended college at all.

[d] Statistically insignificant at the .05 level.

the contrast is even more dramatic. For whites, employment opportunity definitely rises (or at least does not fall) as we move from the innermost to the outermost sample areas. For nonwhites, however, the three descriptors of employment opportunity show relatively little sensitivity to intrametropolitan residential location. Nonwhite earnings are significantly higher outside the ghetto than inside, but—once "outside"—there is no significant difference between the median levels associated with central city as against suburban residence. Nonwhite unemployment rates in the ghetto and in the suburbs are not statistically different from one another, and may be only slightly lower in the nonpoverty central city. Finally, the indicator of occupational status for nonwhite men is totally insensitive to residential location.

Nor are the marginal weekly wage returns to nonwhite education significantly greater in the suburbs than in the ghetto. Indeed, the high school diploma as a terminal credential is less valuable to an outside nonwhite than to a nonwhite residing within the ghetto. This controversial empirical result was predicted several years ago by Stephan Michelson (1969), in a behavioral model suggesting that, unless a Black high school student is certain that he will complete college, he may be better off (in terms of his lifetime income) by dropping out of the educational system before finishing high school.

IV. Conclusions

Do these findings suggest that public investment in ghetto schools should be cut back? I believe not. In Michelson's words: "Equal education should be a goal in itself, not diminished for its failure to produce income for nonwhites" (1968, pp. 8–28). Continued education should be an important objective of all those concerned with improvement in the lives of ghetto residents. Certainly any final judgment should be withheld pending the availability of true longitudinal data (indeed, Finis Welch has discovered evidence that Black-white income differences may be shrinking over time, although not necessarily in the ghetto).

Nevertheless, as a short-run antipoverty policy instrument, education without a supply of jobs which utilize and reward the capabilities of ghetto workers is unlikely to have much impact. The prevalence of ghetto unemployment, involuntary part-time employment, and substandard wages, in conjunction with these new findings on nonwhite educational attainment and the recent studies of the relatively modest technical skills required for the "average" performance of an extremely broad range of "typically urban" jobs,[23] strongly suggests that existing urban labor markets under-utilize ghetto workers and do not permit these individuals to realize their potential productivities. If this interpretation is correct, then the remedy must be sought in opening up *new* urban job markets to the ghetto poor, markets whose jobs are physically accessible to ghetto residents, whose availability is made known to them, and whose entry level wages and promotional possibilities will in fact lead to a significant improvement in their levels of living.[24]

In other words, the findings reported in this paper seem to call rather convincingly for a change in emphasis away from concentration on the alleged defects of the ghetto poor themselves toward the investigation of defects in the market system which constrains the poor from realizing their potential. Without a direct transformation and augmentation of the demand for their labor, significant improvement in the economic situation of ghetto dwellers is unlikely.[25] Attempts to change the worker himself—whether to remedy his personal "defects" or to move him to a "better" environment—have not worked up until now, and the several new micro-data sources explored in this study provide little if any evidence to support the belief that such attempts will be sufficient in the future.

REFERENCES

G. Becker, *The Economics of Discrimination*, Chicago 1957.

I. Berg, *Education and Jobs: The Great Training Robbery*, New York 1970.

B. R. Bergmann and G. Lyle, "The Occupational Standing of Negroes by Areas and Industries," *J. Hum. Resources*, fall 1971, *6*, 411–33.

P. Blau and O. D. Duncan, *The American Occupational Structure*, New York 1967.

P. B. Doeringer, "Ghetto Labor Markets—Problems and Programs," Program on Regional and Urban Economics, Disc. Paper No. 35, Harvard Univ., 1968.

A. Downs, "Alternative Futures for the American Ghetto," in A. Downs, ed., *Urban Prob-*

[23] Compare Berg, Charlotte Fremon, and Harrison (1972b) ch. 1.

[24] Federally supported and widely publicized attempts to open up *existing* urban labor markets to minorities have not been particularly successful. In the construction industry, for example, ". . . the Philadelphia Plan, which would compel the hiring of members of minority groups on federal projects totaling $500,000 or more . . . has not begun to produce even minimal gains toward its modest goal of breaking the color barrier in six construction trades. As a result, the Department of Labor is moving to sue a number of contractors" (New York Times, p. 1). The only other significant minority hiring effort currently underway is the Job Opportunities in the Business Sector (*JOBS*) program being implemented by the National Alliance of Businessmen with Labor Department subsidies. Recently completed studies by the Senate Subcommittee on Employment, Manpower and Poverty and by the U.S. General Accounting Office suggest that "many (*JOBS*) employers are . . . taking federal money for hiring people in low-paying jobs that require little or no training" and that, in any case, "many of the larger firms . . . have had to lay off many of the trainees they took on in 1968 and 1969" (Washington Evening Star, p. A-20). These programs are discussed at length in Harrison (1972b), (ch. 1, 6) and the U.S. Senate report.

[25] This conclusion constitutes one of the strongest arguments for a program of public service jobs for the disadvantaged. See Harrison (1971a) and Sheppard (1969).

lems and Prospects, Chicago 1970.

O. D. Duncan, "A Socioeconomic Index for all Occupations," in A. J. Reiss, Jr., ed., *Occupations and Social Status*, Glencoe 1961.

D. E. Farrar and R. R. Glauber, "Multicollinearity in Regression Analysis: The Problem Revisited," *Rev. Econ. Statist.*, Feb. 1967, *49*, 92–107.

C. Fremon, "The Occupational Patterns in Urban Employment Change, 1965–67," Urban Institute Paper No. 113–32, Washington, Jan. 1970.

D. Fusfeld, "The Basic Economics of the Urban and Racial Crisis," in *Conference Papers of the Union for Radical Political Economics*, Ann Arbor 1968; reprinted in the *Rev. Black Polit. Econ.*, spring-summer 1970, *1*, 58–83.

D. M. Gordon, (1971a) "Class, Productivity, and the Ghetto," unpublished doctoral dissertation, Harvard Univ. 1971.

———, (1971b), *Problems in Political Economy: An Urban Perspective*, Lexington 1971.

B. Harrison, (1971a), "Public Employment and Urban Poverty," Urban Institute Paper No. 113–43, Washington, June 1971.

———, (1971b), "Human Capital, Black Poverty, and 'Radical' Economics," *Ind. Rel.*, Oct. 1971, *10*, 277–86.

———, (1972a), "The Intrametropolitan Distribution of Minority Economic Welfare," *J. Reg. Sci.*, Apr. 1972, *12*, 23–43.

———, (1972b), *Education, Training, and the Urban Ghetto*, Baltimore 1972.

E. Main, "A Nationwide Evaluation of M.D.T.A. Institutional Job Training," *J. Hum. Resources*, spring 1968, *3*, 159–70.

S. Michelson, "Incomes of Racial Minorities," unpublished doctoral dissertation, Stanford Univ. 1968.

———, "Rational Income Decisions of Negroes and Everybody Else," *Ind. Labor Relat. Rev.*, Oct. 1969, *23*, 15–28.

T. Ribich, *Education and Poverty*, Washington 1968.

B. Schiller, "Class Discrimination Versus Racial Discrimination," *Rev. Econ. Statist.*, Aug. 1971, *53*, 263–69.

H. L. Sheppard, *The Nature of the Job Problem and the Role of New Public Service Employment*, Kalamazoo 1969.

———, "Discontented Blue-Collar Workers," *Mon. Labor Rev.*, Apr. 1971, *94*, 25–32.

L. Thurow, "Raising Incomes Through Manpower Training Programs," in A. H. Pascal, ed., *Contributions to the Analysis of Urban Problems*, Santa Monica 1968.

T. Vietorisz and B. Harrison, *The Economic Development of Harlem*, New York 1970.

——— and ———, "Ghetto Development, Community Corporations, and Public Policy," *Rev. Black Polit. Econ.*, fall 1971, *2*, 28–43.

R. Weiss, "The Effect of Education on the Earnings of Blacks and Whites," *Rev. Econ. Statist.*, May 1970, *52*, 150–159.

F. Welch, "Black-White Differences in Returns to Schooling," paper delivered to the Princeton Conference on the Economics of Discrimination, mimeo. Sept. 1971.

J. R. Wetzel and S. B. Holland, "Poverty Areas of Our Major Cities," *Mon. Labor Rev.*, Oct. 1966, *89*, 1105–10.

New York Times, July 20, 1970.

U.S. Bureau of the Census, *Current Population Reports*, Series P-23, No. 38, "The Social and Economic Status of Negroes in the United States, 1970," Washington 1971.

U.S. Department of Labor, "A Sharper Look at Unemployment in U.S. Cities and Slums," Washington 1967.

———, *Manpower Report of the President: 1968*, Washington 1968.

U.S. Bureau of Labor Statistics, "1966 Urban Employment Survey," computer tapes and mimeographed worksheets.

———, "Three Standards of Living for an Urban Family of Four Persons: Spring, 1967," Bull. 1570–5, Washington 1967.

U.S. General Accounting Office, "Improvements Needed in Contracting for On-the-Job Training Under the Manpower Development and Training Act of 1962," Washington 1968.

U.S. Office of Economic Opportunity, "1966 Survey of Economic Opportunity," computer tapes and mimeographed codebooks.

U.S. Senate, Committee on Labor and Public Welfare, *The J.O.B.S. Program*, Washington 1970.

Washington Evening Star, Apr. 29, 1970.

[6]

THE SUBSTITUTABILITY OF BLACK, HISPANIC, AND WHITE LABOR

GEORGE J. BORJAS*

This paper analyzes the extent of labor market competition among blacks, hispanics, and whites in the United States. The specification of a generalized Leontief production function leads to an empirically tractable system of input demand functions. The estimation of the demand system, using the 1976 Survey of Income and Education, reveals that (a) blacks and hispanics are complementary inputs; (b) hispanics and whites may also be complements; and (c) blacks and whites are not complements and may be substitutes.

I. INTRODUCTION

The economic status of minorities in the United States has been an important area of research in the last twenty-five years.[1] Most of this research has concentrated on documenting the economic status and progress of blacks in the U.S. labor market. Researchers have paid little attention to the labor market experiences of other minority groups. However, major changes in immigration laws as well as political and economic upheavals in various Spanish-speaking countries have led to a substantial increase in the number of individuals of hispanic descent living in the U.S.

The initial work on the analysis of hispanics in the U.S. labor market has concentrated on two issues: (a) the rate of economic progress of hispanic immigrants; and (b) the measurement of wage differentials between hispanics and non-hispanics.[2] This paper extends previous research by focusing on the question of how the black and hispanic minorities have interacted with each other and with white workers in the labor market.[3] In other words, this paper attempts to explore the degree of substitutability or complementarity among the various types of workers. This kind of analysis may be used to answer several important questions. For instance, has the emergence of the hispanic minority hampered the economic progress of black workers? Conversely, have the job opportunities available to hispanics worsened because of the existence of a large pool of (presumably) substitutable black workers? More generally, what are the substitution possibilities among the various types of labor?

These questions are easily analyzed in the context of multifactor production functions, where the various factors of production are black, hispanic and white labor. The recent development of multifactor production functions (and the dual cost functions) which are empirically tractable has led to the discovery of important empirical results about production technologies.[4] The analysis in this paper provides new

*Professor of Economics, University of California, Santa Barbara. I am grateful to Daniel Hamermesh and Marta Tienda for helpful comments, to Wei Jang Huang for skillful research assistance, and to the Department of Labor for research support.

1. Of course, the interest began with the publication of Becker's (1957) seminal work.

2. See, for example, Borjas (1982), Chiswick (1978), and Reimers (1980).

3. Throughout the paper, all workers who are not hispanic or black will be called "white" workers.

4. See, for example, Berndt and Christensen (1973), the studies in Fuss and McFadden (1978), and Grant and Hamermesh (1981). An excellent survey of empirical results on the substitution possibilities among various types of labor is given by Hamermesh and Grant (1979).

insights into the relationships among black, hispanic, and white labor. For example, the empirical evidence unambiguously rejects the hypothesis that blacks and hispanics or hispanics and whites are easily substitutable.

Section II presents the theoretical framework. An econometrically simple system of equations describing the wage determination process in a labor market is derived using a generalized Leontief production function. Sections III and IV present the empirical results using individual data from the 1976 Survey of Income and Education. Finally, section V summarizes the results of the study.

II. FRAMEWORK

Suppose there are three inputs in the short-run aggregate production function in a given labor market (*e.g.*, SMSA): black labor (L_b), hispanic labor (L_h), and white, non-hispanic labor (L_w). If the production function, $g(L_b, L_h, L_w)$, exhibits the usual neoclassical properties and is linearly homogeneous, it is well known that the necessary conditions for profit-maximization are:

$$(1) \qquad r_i = g_i(p_b, p_h, p_w), \quad (i = b, h, w),$$

where r_i = wage rate of input i, $g_i = \partial g(L_b, L_h, L_w)/\partial L_i$, $p_i = L_i/(L_b + L_h + L_w)$, and the price of the output is taken as the numeraire. Equation (1), of course, has the interpretation that type i workers are paid the value of their marginal productivity. It is clear from these profit-maximizing conditions that even in the absence of discriminatory behavior by firms, workers, or consumers, the productivity of, say, black labor depends not only on the *relative* number of black workers, but on the *relative* numbers of the other groups as well. Therefore, the degree of substitutability among the various types of labor will be an important determinant of wage levels in the local labor market.

The determination of wage rates depends not only on the demand functions in (1), but also on the relative supply of the groups to the local labor market. Initially it will be assumed that the relative supplies of black, hispanic, and white workers are perfectly inelastic. This assumption helps to simplify the presentation of the model and the estimation of the production function parameters. In the long-run type-i workers likely migrate to the labor markets where they expect to do relatively well. The analysis in section IV will incorporate the role of the endogenous migration decision into the model.

Given the assumption of perfectly inelastic relative labor supplies, the demand system in (1) describes the wage determination process in the particular labor market. It is then relatively simple to predict what will happen to wage rates when relative supplies shift exogenously. For example, it has been argued that the emergence of the hispanic minority (say, through immigration) has been a major obstacle to black economic progress in the U.S. This argument, of course, implicitly assumes that hispanic workers and black workers are highly substitutable. Thus the increase in the relative supply of hispanics lowers the marginal productivity of blacks.[5]

5. Note, however, that since $p_b + p_h + p_w = 1$, the increase in the relative supply of hispanics must be compensated by a fall in the relative supply of the other inputs. The discussion in the text implicitly assumes that p_b is held constant and p_w falls.

The measurement of the actual extent of substitutability or complementarity requires further specification of the production technology's structure. A useful functional form for the aggregate production function in the local labor market is the generalized Leontief production function:

$$g(L_b, L_h, L_w) = \sum_j \sum_i \gamma_{ij} (L_i L_j)^{1/2}, \quad (i, j = b, h, w), \tag{2}$$

where the technology parameters are restricted so that $\gamma_{ij} = \gamma_{ji}$.[6]

The functional form given by (2) can be viewed as a second-order approximation to a concave, neoclassical production function with constant returns to scale. Its usefulness follows from the fact that the wage determination equations are linear in the technology parameters γ_{ij}. In particular, the profit-maximizing hypothesis leads to:

$$r_b = \gamma_{bb} + \gamma_{bh} \left(\frac{p_h}{p_b} \right)^{1/2} + \gamma_{bw} \left(\frac{p_w}{p_b} \right)^{1/2} \tag{3a}$$

$$r_h = \gamma_{hh} + \gamma_{bh} \left(\frac{p_b}{p_h} \right)^{1/2} + \gamma_{hw} \left(\frac{p_w}{p_h} \right)^{1/2} \tag{3b}$$

$$r_w = \gamma_{ww} + \gamma_{hw} \left(\frac{p_h}{p_w} \right)^{1/2} + \gamma_{bw} \left(\frac{p_b}{p_w} \right)^{1/2} \tag{3c}$$

Three important properties should be noted about equations (3). First, they can be easily estimated using least squares given data on the wage rates and relative proportions of the various groups. Secondly, the production technology imposes a set of cross-equation restrictions. In particular, if γ_{ij}^n is the estimate of the technology parameter γ_{ij} in the nth equation ($n = b, h, w$), then the cross-equation restrictions are given by:

$$\gamma_{bh}^b = \gamma_{bh}^h, \quad \gamma_{bw}^b = \gamma_{bw}^w, \quad \text{and} \quad \gamma_{hw}^h = \gamma_{hw}^w. \tag{4}$$

By estimating (3) both unconstrained and with the symmetry constraints in (4), a likelihood ratio test can be made on the validity of the symmetry restrictions. Finally, by ignoring the role of capital in the production process, a strong separability between capital and the various labor inputs is implicitly assumed. This assumption may be justified empirically since serious problems exist with current measurements of the capital stock. In any case, section IV extends the analysis by introducing rough measures of capital into the model. It will be seen that these results imply that the separability assumptions in (3) serve as a useful approximation.

6. See Diewert (1971) for a discussion of the properties of this production function and for its derivation from the dual cost function.

An important motivation for estimating (3) is to obtain a measure of the degree of substitution among the various inputs. Define the Hicks partial elasticity of complementarity between factors L_i and L_j as[7]

$$c_{ij} = \frac{g\, g_{ij}}{g_i g_j}. \tag{5}$$

The Hicks elasticity of complementarity measures the effect on the relative price of factor i of a change in the relative quantity of that factor, holding marginal cost and the quantities of other factors constant. Since the present focus is on the effects of changes in the quantities of inputs on relative factor prices, the elasticity of complementary (rather than the dual and better known elasticity of substitution) is the natural measure to quantify these effects.[8] Note that the sign of the c_{ij} depends on the cross-partial g_{ij} from the production function. Therefore, the elasticity of complementarity will be positive (negative) if the inputs are complements (substitutes).

The elasticity of complementarity implied by (2) can be shown to be

$$c_{ij} = \frac{\gamma_{ij}\, \bar{r}}{2 r_i r_j (p_i p_j)^{1/2}}, \quad i \neq j, \tag{6a}$$

$$c_{ii} = \frac{(\gamma_{ii} - r_i)\, \bar{r}}{2 p_i r_i^2}, \quad i = j, \tag{6b}$$

where $\bar{r} = p_b r_b + p_h r_h + p_w r_w$. Equations (3) and (6) demonstrate that the generalized Leontief production technology leads to an econometrically simple system of wage equations which can be used to obtain insights into the production relationships among various labor inputs.

III. EMPIRICAL ANALYSIS

The empirical analysis is conducted on the 1976 Survey of Income and Education (SIE), a large intercensal survey compiled by the Bureau of the Census. The SIE is useful for present purposes because it contains detailed information on socioeconomic characteristics at the individual level, not usually found in census data, and also because the sample design ensured a sufficiently large number of both black and hispanic workers. The empirical analysis is restricted to male individuals aged 18-64 who reported positive annual earnings in 1975, positive hours worked per week in 1975, and positive weeks worked during the 1975 calendar year. These restrictions resulted in a sample of 3089 individuals of hispanic origin and a sample of 3890 black men. These samples contain all the observations in the SIE for blacks and hispanics which satisfied the sample restrictions. Since the SIE is a very large survey, the analysis of white men is restricted to a 5 percent random sample of 3844 men from all "white" observations which satisfy the sample selection rules.[9]

7. The elasticity of complementarity is introduced in Hicks (1970). The dual relationship between the elasticities of substitution and complementarity is discussed in Sato and Koizumi (1973).

8. Recall that the elasticity of substitution measures the effect of a change in the relative price of factor i on the relative quantity of that factor, holding output and the prices of other factors constant.

9. The "white" men sample contains native-born men whose race is reported as white and who are not of hispanic origin.

TABLE 1

Summary Statistics

	Blacks	Hispanics	Whites
Average Education	11.135	10.351	12.663
Average Age	37.247	35.059	37.328
Average Wage Rate	4.905	4.656	5.732
% Immigrants	—	36.3	—
Industry:			
% Agriculture	1.9	6.0	3.2
% Mining	.5	3.2	2.1
% Construction	7.7	11.0	10.3
% Durable Goods	18.2	15.8	16.9
% Nondurable Goods	8.9	10.2	9.3
% Transportation	11.0	7.8	9.0
% Wholesale Trade	3.5	3.8	5.8
% Retail Trade	10.9	13.3	14.5
% Finance	3.8	2.7	4.1
% Business Services	3.8	4.4	3.9
% Private Household	.5	.2	.3
% Personal Services	2.6	2.9	1.6
% Entertainment	1.4	1.6	1.0
% Professional	13.3	9.2	11.3
% Public Administration	12.1	7.8	7.0
Occupation:			
% Professional	8.5	9.1	15.6
% Managers	5.2	6.2	15.0
% Sales	1.9	2.6	6.6
% Clerical	9.6	5.7	5.9
% Craft	15.9	22.3	23.0
% Operatives (exc. Transport)	16.8	17.4	11.0
% Transport Operatives	10.2	6.6	5.7
% Nonfarm Laborers	13.4	11.8	6.8
% Private Household	.1	.03	.03
% Other Service	17.1	13.8	7.8
% Farmers	.1	.2	.9
% Farm Laborers	1.4	4.4	1.6
No. of Observations	3890	3089	3844

Table 1 presents summary statistics for each of the three samples. The average 1975 wage rate varies widely among the three samples. The white wage rate of \$5.73 exceeds the black wage by nearly 80 cents, and the hispanic wage rate by over \$1. Clearly a fraction of these wage differentials is due to differences in skill and other observable socioeconomic characteristics. For example, educational attainment is, on the average, lowest for hispanics and relatively low (compared to whites) for blacks.

Table 1 presents the proportion of each of the groups employed in broadly defined industries and occupations. The differences in employment by industry among the samples are notable. For example, black males have a much greater percentage of workers in the public sector than either hispanics or whites. On the other hand, blacks are under-represented in the agriculture and construction industries. The occupation characteristics reveal similar dispersion among the three groups. For example, blacks are less likely to be found in craft occupations, but more likely to be employed in clerical and service jobs. Although these statistics are only suggestive, they do provide an "institutional" background for the empirical results presented below.

The system of equations derived in (3) gives the determination of wage levels in a particular labor market. To apply this model to the micro data available in the SIE, it is necessary to control for individual differences in productive skills. It is insightful to view individual ℓ's wage as being determined by both the geographic wage level given by (3), r_i, and by an individual specific fixed effect, $f_{i\ell}$. This fixed effect measures the individual's deviation in productive skills from the average type i individual in the local labor market. The simplest estimating equation is obtained by assuming that the individual's wage, $r_{i\ell}$, is determined by an additive fixed effect, hence $r_{i\ell} = r_i + f_{i\ell}$. That is, the demand system in (3) determines the "basic" wage level, and the additive fixed effect captures individual differences in effective labor supply. This additivity means that the individual's stock of productive skills is valued independently of the racial/ethnic composition of the local labor market.[10] Further, the definition of $f_{i\ell}$ implies that it has zero mean so that the demand system in (3) determines the average wage level of type i individuals in the local labor market.

If it is assumed that the individual fixed effects can be approximated by a vector of socioeconomic variables, the empirical specification of (3) is given by:

$$r_b = x_b\alpha_b + \gamma_{bb} + \gamma_{bh}\left(\frac{p_h}{p_b}\right)^{1/2} + \gamma_{bw}\left(\frac{p_w}{p_b}\right)^{1/2} + \epsilon_b; \tag{7a}$$

$$r_h = x_h\alpha_h + \gamma_{hh} + \gamma_{bh}\left(\frac{p_b}{p_h}\right)^{1/2} + \gamma_{hw}\left(\frac{p_w}{p_h}\right)^{1/2} + \epsilon_h; \tag{7b}$$

$$r_w = x_w\alpha_w + \gamma_{ww} + \gamma_{hw}\left(\frac{p_h}{p_w}\right)^{1/2} + \gamma_{bw}\left(\frac{p_b}{p_w}\right)^{1/2} + \epsilon_w, \tag{7c}$$

10. A more general specification of the individual fixed effect would assume $r_{i\ell} = r_i f_{i\ell}$. This multiplicative specification, which allows variations in the value of the individual's effective labor supply according to the ethnic composition of the local labor market, leads to similar empirical results as the simpler, additive specification.

where x_i is a vector of skill characteristics.[11] The empirical definition of p_i is the proportion of the working age population ($14 \leq$ age ≤ 64) in the individual's "local" labor market which belongs to group *i*. The local labor market is defined to be the SMSA for individuals residing in metropolitan areas. All individuals residing in non-metropolitan areas *within* a given state are assumed to be living in the same non-metropolitan labor market. Given these operational definitions, the variables p_b, p_h, and p_w were calculated for each labor market using the entire SIE sample.[12]

TABLE 2

Unconstrained Wage Equations*

	BLACKS		HISPANICS		WHITES	
Variable	**Coeff.**	**t**	**Coeff.**	**t**	**Coeff.**	**t**
CONSTANT	–.2079	(–.55)	1.0363	(1.74)	–1.9118	(–4.22)
EDUC	.2716	(9.12)	.1810	(7.34)	.3822	(14.76)
EXPER	.1643	(7.86)	.1373	(7.07)	.1924	(10.09)
EXPER^2	–.0024	(–5.80)	–.0020	(–5.17)	–.0029	(–7.48)
VETERAN	–.0208	(–.13)	.2602	(1.56)	.1544	(1.13)
SMSA	.6622	(3.93)	.2362	(1.53)	.6792	(4.84)
MARRIED	.3047	(1.50)	.4003	(2.04)	.5411	(2.94)
SEPARATED	–.1288	(–.49)	.6916	(2.25)	.3831	(1.28)
HEALTH	–.4660	(–1.92)	.3332	(1.29)	–.2118	(–1.00)
IMMIGRANT	—	—	–1.0470	(–3.94)	—	—
YSM	—	—	.0596	(4.63)	—	—
$(p_h/p_b)^{1/2}$	.0240	(.15)	—	—	—	—
$(p_w/p_b)^{1/2}$	.0074	(.15)	—	—	—	—
$(p_b/p_h)^{1/2}$	—	—	.1462	(1.74)	—	—
$(p_w/p_h)^{1/2}$	—	—	.0431	(1.73)	—	—
$(p_b/p_w)^{1/2}$	—	—	—	—	1.1716	(3.23)
$(p_h/p_w)^{1/2}$	—	—	—	—	.0258	(.06)
R^2	.075		.139		.206	
No. of Observations	3890		3089		3844	

*Key to Variables: *EDUC* = years of schooling; *EXPER* = *Age* – *EDUC* – 6; *VETERAN* = 1 if veteran; SMSA = 1 if resides in SMSA; *MARRIED* = 1 if married, spouse present; *SEPARATED* = 1 if separated or divorced; *HEALTH* = 1 if health limits work activity; *IMMIGRANT* = 1 if immigrant; *YSM* = years since migration (if immigrant). All regressions include a vector of industry dummies at the level of aggregation indicated in table 1. The hispanic regression also includes a vector of dummy variables indicating nationality (*i.e.*, whether Mexican, Puerto Rican, Cuban, Central or South American, or "other").

11. It should be noted that the specification of the earnings functions generated by the generalized Leontief production function is quite different from the specification suggested by the human capital model [see Mincer (1974)]. However, the human capital earnings function is derived without taking into account the profit-maximizing objectives of firms. It is far from clear whether the log-linear specification of the human capital earnings equation would remain if the objectives of the firm were modeled explicitly.

12. That is, the estimates of p_i are based on *all* the observations in the Census version of the SIE.

The vector x_i is composed of the standard variables (*e.g.*, education, experience) used in human capital studies. It also includes a vector of industry dummies to control for wage differentials arising from differences in job environments. Further, to the extent that the capital/labor ratio differs across industries, the industry dummies partially control for the omitted capital variables. It should be noted that the deletion of the industry vector from the regressions did not qualitatively affect any of the results discussed below.

In this section the system of equations given in (7) is estimated using ordinary least squares. Table 2 presents the estimated wage equations for each of the three samples.[13] In general, the coefficients of the socioeconomic characteristics have the expected signs in all samples. In the hispanic sample, the variables *IMMIGRANT* (= 1 if immigrant) and *YSM* (years since migration) show the strong effect on wage rates of the immigration and assimilation experience. In particular, the wage rate of recent hispanic immigrants is about $1 less than that of hispanic non-immigrants. After 18 years, however, the immigrants reach parity with the native hispanics.[14]

The coefficients of interest for the study are the ones which indicate the degree to which the relative number of blacks, hispanics, and whites affect the wage rates of each of the groups. Table 2 reveals that *none* of the cross effects are negative. This result indicates that there is no evidence of substitutability among the three groups.

TABLE 3

Symmetry-Constrained Technology Coefficients*

Technology Parameter	Estimate	Elasticity of Complementarity
γ_{bh}	.1099 (1.49)	.1579
γ_{bw}	.0083 (.20)	.0026
γ_{hw}	.0497 (2.08)	.0234
γ_{bb}	4.8281 (47.29)	–.0742
γ_{hh}	4.3587 (53.53)	–.6346
γ_{ww}	5.7226 (287.98)	–.0010

*The estimated coefficients are from regressions which hold constant the same variables as table 2. The t-ratios are given in parentheses.

13. Since the earnings functions are estimated in the sample of working men, the deletion of non-working individuals could lead to selectivity biases in the estimates of the wage equations. However, most of the working-age men in the samples do participate in the labor force, hence the importance of these biases is likely to be minimal.

14. A detailed discussion of the effect of immigration on hispanic wage rates is contained in Borjas (1982).

Before discussing these coefficients in detail it is instructive to test for the cross-equation symmetry restrictions given in (4). The demand system was re-estimated after imposing these restrictions, and the estimated technology coefficients are presented in table 3. The likelihood ratio test for the validity of the symmetry conditions yielded an F statistic of 2.32, below the critical value at conventional significance levels.[15] Since the data is consistent with the symmetry conditions imposed by the theory, the discussion of the coefficients will be limited to the constrained estimates in table 3.[16]

The estimate of γ_{bh}, the parameter measuring the substitution possibilities between blacks and hispanics, is .110 and approaches statistical significance. The fact that it is positive reveals that there is no evidence that blacks and hispanics are substitutes in the labor market. The elasticity of complementarity implied by this estimate is approximately .16. The implications of this magnitude can be understood by comparing it to the elasticity of complementarity between men aged 20-34 and women estimated by Freeman (1979). This elasticity is .17. Thus the empirical results in table 3 indicate the same extent of complementarity between blacks and hispanics as between younger men and women.

The results in table 3 also show that black and white labor are neither complements nor substitutes. This finding should prove useful to researchers trying to measure the extent of racial wage discrimination in the labor market. It is usually assumed in these studies that blacks and white are (perfect) substitutes. The results in table 3 indicate that measures of wage discrimination based on the assumption of perfect substitution may be seriously biased since black and white labor are not, on the average, substitutable inputs.

Finally the estimate of γ_{hw}, the parameter measuring the relationship between hispanic and white labor, is .050 and significant. The implied elasticity of complementarity is .023. The positive sign of γ_{hw} indicates the existence of complementarity between hispanic and white labor. Again, the empirical results show that hispanic (white) labor has not been hurt by the presence of whites (hispanics) in the local labor market. In fact, their wage rates have increased slightly.

Table 3 also presents estimates of the own-elasticities of complementarity.[17] Although these elasticities are negative (as predicted by theory) only the hispanic elasticity has a magnitude comparable to that found for other groups in previous studies (see, for example, Grant and Hamermesh, 1981).

It is important to emphasize the substantive implications of these results. The estimation of the derived demand functions implied by the generalized Leontief technology leads to the finding that *none* of the three types of labor has been hurt by competition from other types of workers. In fact, there is evidence that due to complementarity in production both blacks and whites have been helped by the presence of hispanics in the U.S. labor market.

15. The critical value for $F(3, \infty)$ at a 5 percent level of significance is 2.60.

16. It is also important to note that a test of the hypothesis $\gamma_{bh} = \gamma_{bw} = \gamma_{hw} = 0$ is rejected by the data (the F statistic is 4.68). This result implies that (3) does not degenerate to a linear production function.

17. Calculation of γ_{ii} (and c_{ii}) requires the use of the maintained assumption that the individual fixed effects have zero mean in each of the samples.

IV. EXTENSIONS OF EMPIRICAL ANALYSIS

A. *Endogenous Supply*

The empirical analysis in the previous section was based on the assumption that, from the individual's perspective, the relative employment rates given by $(p_i/p_j)^{1/2}$ $(i \neq j)$ in (7) were exogenous. It is possible, however, that over time migration patterns respond to regional wage differentials creating some correlation between the employment variables and the disturbances ϵ_i in (7). A simple solution to this econometric problem is to obtain instruments for these variables, and then re-estimate the wage determination system.

The instruments are obtained by first regressing $(p_i/p_j)^{1/2}$ $(i \neq j)$ in the relevant sample on a set of exogenous variables affecting migration decisions and then using the predicted values in the wage determination equations. The independent variables in the first stage include both individual and area characteristics. These variables are designed to measure both the individual's incentives to migrate and the attractiveness of the area to ethnic and racial minorities.[18]

TABLE 4

Employment Coefficients in Wage Equations*
(Using Instruments for Relative Employment Variables)

	BLACKS		HISPANICS		WHITES	
Variables	Coeff.	t	Coeff.	t	Coeff.	t
$(p_h/p_b)^{1/2}$	.8181	(1.64)	—	—	—	—
$(p_w/p_b)^{1/2}$	-.3116	(-2.59)	—	—	—	—
$(p_b/p_h)^{1/2}$	—	—	.4008	(1.70)	—	—
$(p_w/p_h)^{1/2}$	—	—	.0669	(.90)	—	—
$(p_b/p_w)^{1/2}$	—	—	—	—	2.4799	(3.51)
$(p_h/p_w)^{1/2}$	—	—	—	—	4.1858	(3.46)
No. of Observations	3890		3089		3844	

*These regressions hold constant the same variables as table 2.

18. The individual characteristics are education, age, whether the wife works, and in the hispanic sample whether immigrant and years since immigration. The area characteristics are the unemployment rate of white, non-hispanics in the SMSA; the proportion of males in government jobs; the median education of males aged 25 and over; the percent of individuals living in public housing divided by the percent of individuals (in the SMSA) defined to be below the 1976 poverty line; the percent of individuals receiving public assistance divided by the percent of individuals (in the SMSA) below the 1976 poverty line; the percent of individuals in blue collar jobs; and the percent of males who have worked in the past five years. All area characteristics are calculated from the complete version of the SIE.

The second stage in the econometric procedure is to estimate the system in (7) using the predicted values for the relative employment variables in each of the samples. The (unconstrained) coefficients of the relevant variables are presented in table 4. The estimated parameters of the production function are generally statistically stronger than the estimates in section III. The major discrepancy from the earlier results is the technological relationship between black and white labor. The coefficient γ_{bw} in the black equation is significantly negative, while the coefficient in the white equation is significantly positive. Moreover, the imposition of symmetry significantly reduces the explanatory power of the model. The likelihood ratio test for symmetry leads to an F statistic of 7.9, which is well above the critical value at accepted confidence levels. Note, however, that the theoretical restriction of symmetry is a necessary condition for the derivation of the demand system in (3). This fact suggests that the estimated wage regressions can be interpreted in terms of the theoretical model *only if* the symmetry conditions are imposed. Table 5 presents the estimated technology coefficients and the elasticities of complementarity after the theoretical restriction of symmetry has been imposed.

TABLE 5

Symmetry-Constrained Employment Effects*
(Using Instruments for Relative Employment Variables)

Technology Parameter	Estimate	Elasticity of Complementarity
γ_{bh}	.4048 (1.90)	.5813
γ_{bw}	−.2025 (−2.36)	−.0639
γ_{hw}	.0751 (1.05)	.0353
γ_{bb}	4.9080 (27.09)	.0030
γ_{hh}	3.9799 (18.21)	−1.4472
γ_{ww}	5.7667 (232.68)	.0036

*The estimated coefficients are from regressions which hold constant the same variables as table 2. The t-ratios are given in parentheses.

Even though the symmetry restrictions are rejected by the data, it is important to note that both the unconstrained (table 4) and the constrained (table 5) regressions lead to results that are qualitatively similar to those of section III for black/hispanic and hispanic/white comparisons. For instance, tables 4 and 5 provide strong evidence that blacks and hispanics are complements in production. In fact, the constrained γ_{bh} is .405 and more significant than the parameter estimated in section III using ordinary least squares. The implied elasticity of complementarity is .581 (as compared to a section III estimate of .158). Similarly, the results in tables 4 and 5 indicate that γ_{hw} is positive although in the constrained regression it is insignificant. The results in section III indicated that hispanics and whites are complements. Again, the data show weak evidence of complementarity between hispanics and whites. The results are not as conclusive in the black/white comparison. The unconstrained regressions show that the sign of γ_{bw} depends on which equation is being estimated. In the constrained regression, γ_{bw} is negative and significant. If we accept the theoretical restriction of symmetry, therefore, the results indicate that blacks and whites are substitutable inputs.[19]

B. *The Role of Capital*

The empirical analysis has been conducted under the assumption of strong separability between capital and the various labor inputs. If this assumption is relaxed, the wage determination equation in the labor market is given by:

$$r_i = \gamma_{ii} + \gamma_{ij}\left(\frac{p_j}{p_i}\right)^{1/2} + \gamma_{iv}\left(\frac{p_v}{p_i}\right)^{1/2} + \gamma_{ik}\left(\frac{k}{p_i}\right)^{1/2}, \quad (i, j, v = b, h, w) \tag{8}$$

where k is the labor market's capital/labor ratio.

TABLE 6

Selected Technology Coefficients Accounting for Capital*

	METHOD OF ESTIMATION	
	OLS Estimate	Instrumental Variable Estimate
γ_{bh}	.1356	.3886
	(1.76)	(1.82)
γ_{bw}	.0071	−.2072
	(.15)	(−2.39)
γ_{hw}	.0679	.0705
	(2.45)	(.98)
γ_{bk}	−.0301	.1048
	(−.15)	(.59)
γ_{hk}	−.0308	.0154
	(−1.34)	(.88)
γ_{wk}	.1150	.1216
	(.23)	(.24)

*The estimated coefficients are from regressions which hold constant the same variables as table 2. The t-ratios are given in parentheses.

19. Note also that the use of instrumental variables leads to a more negative own elasticity of complementarity for hispanics, but to positive (and very close to zero) own elasticities for blacks and whites.

Obviously, the estimation of (8) requires data on k across SMSAs. The difficulty of constructing measurements of capital even for manufacturing industries is well known in the literature. If the analysis is conducted over all industries, as is done in this paper, the measurement problem becomes much more severe. Some preliminary tests on the importance of the capital variable in (8) can be conducted with the aid of two simplifying assumptions, however. In particular, assume that the labor market's capital stock is closely approximated by the capital stock in the manufacturing sector. Secondly, following Berndt and Christensen (1973), assume that the flows of expenditures on capital equipment are proportional to the capital stock. These assumptions allow the use of the geographic series on new capital expenditures available in the 1977 Census of Manufactures (U.S. Department of Commerce, 1981).

Table 6 presents the technological coefficients obtained from the symmetry-constrained wage equations in (8). The first column gives the ordinary least squares estimates, while the second column presents the results using instruments for the employment variables. The main result from this exercise is that the γ_{ik} are insignificantly different from zero. The assumption of strong separability between capital and the various labor inputs used in the previous section is, therefore, not rejected by the rough data available on capital. Note also that the inclusion of the capital variables, if anything, reinforces the previous results concerning the technological relationships among blacks, hispanics, and whites.

V. SUMMARY

This paper attempts to measure the degree of substitution or complementarity among black, hispanic, and white workers. Using the generalized Leontief production function, it is shown that the estimation of linear wage equations leads to a useful interpretation of the coefficients in terms of the underlying production technology. The empirical results from the 1976 Survey of Income and Education imply that (a) blacks and hispanics are complementary inputs; (b) hispanics and whites also may be complements; and (c) there is weak evidence that blacks and whites may be substitutes.

The implications of these results for labor market analysis are not trivial. Nevertheless, the research should be expanded in several directions. First, the hispanic sample has been treated as a homogeneous group when, in fact, strong differences by nationality are likely to exist. Since 61 percent of the hispanic sample is composed of men of Mexican origin, the results in this paper are likely to reflect this sample composition. The use of larger data sets should allow the researcher to study substitution possibilities among the other hispanic groups (Cubans, Puerto Ricans, etc.) with blacks and native whites. Second, the data should be disaggregated to allow for differences between immigrants and natives. Any economic discussion of immigration must confront the interaction of immigrant labor with native labor. Third, the empirical results using the production function framework can be complemented with detailed case studies analyzing the types of jobs held by the groups in question. Finally, the individual's decision to migrate across regions of the U.S. in response to wage differentials could be modeled explicitly if internal migration data were available. These research questions can serve the useful purpose of pushing forward the basically descriptive empirical literature on racial and ethnic differences in the labor market.

REFERENCES

Becker, Gary S., *The Economics of Discrimination*, University of Chicago Press, Chicago, 1957.

Berndt, Ernst R., and Christensen, Laurits R., "The Translog Function and the Substitution of Equipment, Structures, and Labor in U.S. Manufacturing 1929-68," *Journal of Econometrics*, March 1973, *1*, 81-114.

Borjas, George J., "The Earnings of Male Hispanic Immigrants in the United States," *Industrial and Labor Relations Review*, April 1982, *35*, 343-353.

Chiswick, Barry R., "The Effect of Americanization on the Earnings of Foreign-Born Men," *Journal of Political Economy*, October 1978, *86*, 897-922.

Diewert, W. E., "An Application of the Shephard Duality Theorem: A Generalized Leontief Production Function," *Journal of Political Economy*, May/June 1971, *79*, 481-507.

Freeman, Richard B., "The Effect of Demographic Factors on Age-Earnings Profiles," *Journal of Human Resources*, Summer 1979, *14*, 289-318.

Fuss, Melvyn and McFadden, Daniel, eds., *Production Economics: A Dual Approach to Theory and Applications*, Vols. 1 and 2, North Holland Publishing Company, Amsterdam, 1978.

Grant, James H. and Hamermesh, Daniel S., "Labor Market Competition Among Youths, White Women and Others," *Review of Economics and Statistics*, August 1981, *63*, 354-360.

Hamermesh, Daniel S., and Grant, James H., "Econometric Studies of Labor-Labor Substitution and their Implications for Policy," *Journal of Human Resources*, Fall 1979, *14*, 518-542.

Hicks, John, "Elasticity of Substitution Again: Substitutes and Complements," *Oxford Economic Papers*, November 1970, *22*, 289-296.

Mincer, Jacob, *Schooling, Experience, and Earnings*, Columbia University Press, New York, 1974.

Reimers, Cordelia, "Sources of the Wage Gap Between Hispanics and Other White Americans," mimeograph, Princeton University, 1980.

Sato, Ryuzo and Koizumi, Tetsunori, "On the Elasticities of Substitution and Complementarity," *Oxford Economic Papers*, March 1973, *25*, 44-56.

U.S. Department of Commerce, *1977 Census of Manufactures: General Summary*, Washington, 1981.

[7]

RACIAL DISCRIMINATION IN THE BRITISH LABOR MARKET

MICHAEL FIRTH*

This paper reports the results of a study of racial discrimination in the British job market for accountants and financial executives. The research design involved sending letters from fictitious applicants in response to job advertisements in the press. The applicants represented seven different nationalities, although all had identical qualifications and work experience. An analysis of the responses to these applications shows that considerable racial discrimination remains in the British labor market several years after the adoption of the Race Relations Act of 1968.

GREAT BRITAIN has a growing nonwhite population and the integration of these ethnic minorities with the indigenous white population is not without sociological and economic problems. One major problem area has been that of racial discrimination in the labor market, one aspect of which is the focal point of this paper: racial discrimination in the hiring of professionals.

Previous research has shown that there is indeed discrimination in the British job market. In 1970, for example, Jowell and Prescott-Clarke reported significant discrimination against minority races in white-collar jobs.[1] In 1973 McIntosh and Smith reported significant discrimination against minority races in both manual and professional jobs.[2] These two studies showed that nonwhite job applicants, even though possessing identical or superior qualifications, had a much poorer chance of getting specific jobs than did their white counterparts.[3]

Other studies have shown that nonwhites in the U.K. often receive substantially lower salaries than whites with similar or lesser

*Michael Firth is in the Department of Accountancy of Victoria University of Wellington, New Zealand.

[1]Roger Jowell and Patricia Prescott-Clarke, "Racial Discrimination and White Collar Workers in Britain," *Race*, Vol. 11, No. 4 (April 1970), pp. 397–417.

[2]Neil McIntosh and David J. Smith, "The Extent of Racial Discrimination," *P.E.P. Broadsheet*, No. 547 (1974).

Both these studies—Jowell and Prescott-Clarke's and McIntosh and Smith's—reported that significant racial discrimination also existed in the housing market, although there had been a substantial improvement since 1967. This improvement was attributed primarily to the Race Relations Act of 1968, but McIntosh and Smith found that the act's impact on job discrimination had been far smaller.

[3]In contrast, a similar U.S. study recently concluded that among a group of fictitious job applicants discriminated against by U.S. companies, whites were discriminated against slightly more often than were blacks. See Jerry M. Newman, "Discrimination in Recruitment: An Empirical Analysis," *Industrial and Labor Relations Review*, Vol. 32, No. 1 (October 1978), pp. 15–23; see also Shelby McIntyre, Dennis J. Moberg, and Barry Z. Posner, "Discrimination in Recruitment: An Empirical Analysis—Comment," *Industrial and Labor Relations Review*, Vol. 33, No. 4 (July 1980), pp. 543–47 and Jerry M. Newman, "Reply," same issue, pp. 547–50.

Industrial and Labor Relations Review, Vol. 34, No. 2 (January 1981).
0019-7939/81/3402-0265$01.00

qualifications. Among individuals in certain age groups with an economics degree, for example, the salaries of nonwhites were found to be, on average, only half the salaries of white British subjects.[4] Similar results have been obtained in the United States,[5] although some American studies have found that the salaries of nonwhites in certain occupations have more than caught up with those of whites.[6]

The Race Relations Act of 1968 produced a legal definition of racial discrimination under which court cases could be brought in the United Kingdom. This act states that job selection should be based on qualifications and experience, the race of applicants receiving no consideration whatsoever. The act also established the Race Relations Board, which is empowered to investigate complaints of racial discrimination and to initiate legal proceedings where necessary. In spite of these measures, however, racial discrimination in employment is still considered to be a significant problem in Britain.[7]

The present study was designed to update earlier research by examining the success of fictitious applicants of various nationalities in passing the first screening stage in the accounting and financial management job market. This profession was chosen for several reasons: (a) Limited research funds required a choice between an in-depth investigation of a specific job area and more superficial coverage of a wide number of job areas. The former strategy was selected, focusing on accountancy, which contains a large segment of the professional job market in the U.K. (more than 100,000 professionally qualified accountants plus many unqualified personnel). (b) Accountancy is an easily identifiable subgroup of the professional job market with professional examinations that are universally recognized. This factor made it practicable to control the qualifications and experience variables. (c) The demand for accountants is very high in the U.K. Therefore, the number of job vacancy advertisements was high, as was the probability that an applicant would be "successful."

The research design follows that used in the earlier studies of Jowell and Prescott-Clarke and of Smith and McIntosh. The results should indicate whether there has been any substantial change in the incidence of racial discrimination since those studies were conducted in the late 1960s and early 1970s.

Research Design

The basic research design involved sending letters of application in response to job advertisements appearing in the British press. The letters were sent by a number of "different" people, one of whom was a British white and the others of other nationalities and races. The qualifications and experience of these job applicants for each individual job vacancy were virtually identical, the only major difference between them being nationality and race.

For each job seven applications were sent, one each from a (fictitious) British white, Australian, French, African, Indian, Pakistani, and West Indian. Each immigrant's application included a statement of the form, "I was born in Calcutta, India in 1947 and I arrived in Britain in 1959, after completing my primary schooling." The applicants also stated that they now had permanent residence in Britain and, hence, would have no problem working in Britain. The names of the applicants were also a guide to their country of origin.

The Australian and French nationals were included to identify discrimination between British-born whites and other whites who have English as their mother tongue (Australians) or have a foreign lan-

[4] C. Selby Smith, "Racial Discrimination by British Employers," *Race*, Vol. 12, No. 2 (October 1970), pp. 201–06.

[5] See, for example, James D. Gwartney and James E. Long, "The Relative Earnings of Blacks and Other Minorities," *Industrial and Labor Relations Review*, Vol. 31, No. 3 (April 1978), pp. 336–46.

[6] Richard B. Freeman, "The New Job Market for Black Academicians," *Industrial and Labor Relations Review*, Vol. 30, No. 2 (January 1977), pp. 161–74; Nancy M. Gordon, Thomas E. Morton, and Ina C. Braden, "Faculty Salaries: Is There Discrimination by Sex, Race and Discipline?" *American Economic Review*, Vol. 64, No. 3 (June 1974), pp. 419–27.

[7] See Jowell and Prescott-Clarke, "Racial Discrimination and White Collar Workers in Britain," and McIntosh and Smith, "The Extent of Racial Discrimination."

guage as their mother tongue (French). This factor was expected to allow assessment of the impact of discrimination due to race, nationality, and language.

Jowell and Prescott-Clarke used Australians and Cypriots (white, non-English speaking) in their research design, together with British, Asians, and West Indians.[8] They found no discrimination between British and Australians, equal discrimination against Cypriots and West Indians, and by far the most discrimination against Asians. McIntosh and Smith used five different nationalities as job applicants: British, Italian, West Indian, Indian, and Pakistani.[9] They found West Indians, Indians, and Pakistanis about equally discriminated against as compared to the British. The Italians were found to be significantly less successful than the British but significantly more successful than the nonwhite immigrants. These two studies have indicated that there is some prejudice against foreign white nationals whose mother tongue is not English (even though the applicant had a good command of the English language), but a much larger degree of discrimination against nonwhite races (even though they are British Commonwealth subjects and even though some have English as their mother tongue).

The advertised jobs in accountancy and financial management that were responded to in this study can be organized into five types:

Articled clerks (trainee chartered accountants). These jobs are for university graduates, or school leavers with good examination results, who plan to train to become chartered accountants. (Chartered accountants are the British equivalent of American certified public accountants.)

Unqualified personnel. These are entry level accounting jobs for persons who do not have formal qualifications. Individuals who hold these jobs do not belong to any of the major professional groups of accountants.

Qualified accountants working for professional accounting firms.[10] These are jobs in firms of professional accountants, available primarily to recently qualified accountants (in the age range of 22–30 years).

Qualified accountants working in industry. These jobs cover a wide range of experience requirements, starting salaries, and work (ranging from pure accounting to general management).

Financial jobs. These are senior jobs in commerce and financial institutions (such as corporate finance work in a merchant bank or portfolio management in a stockbroker firm) often based in London. These jobs require professional accounting qualifications and, in the case of more senior positions, specific prior job experience.

The job advertisements for articled clerks were taken from the annual *Directory of Opportunities for Graduates,* which annually lists firms of chartered accountants who wish to recruit articled clerks. Most of the major firms of chartered accountants are listed in this publication. Some advertisements for articled clerks, however, appeared in the financial press listed below.

The advertisements for the other job types were taken from the following daily, weekly, and monthly publications: *Financial Times; Daily Telegraph; Accountancy Age; Accountants Weekly; The Accountant; Sunday Times; Accountancy;* and *The Accountant's Magazine.* The employers advertising vacancies for articled clerks and qualified personnel to work for professional accounting practices, were often seeking a number of candidates, while the others tended to seek only one.

Seven applications were sent for each specific job. The qualifications and work experience in all seven were virtually identical, except for slight differences made to avoid the recipient's becoming suspicious.

[8]Jowell and Prescott-Clarke, "Racial Discrimination and White Collar Workers in Britain."

[9]McIntosh and Smith, "The Extent of Racial Discrimination."

[10]These will be mainly chartered accountants. There are two other major professional bodies of accountants in the U.K., these being cost and management accountants, and certified accountants; the former tend to be employed exclusively in industry, while the latter are employed mainly in industry but also in professional accounting firms.

In cases that explicitly or implicitly required it, the applicants mentioned that they had a professional accounting qualification (as a chartered accountant or cost and management accountant, for example).

All seven applicants also were given virtually identical background variables, including such items as age, marital status, number of children, and location of residence. In order not to arouse suspicion, slight differences were included in the letters, randomized across the applicants. All the letters gave broad details of the applicants' past experience but excluded specific names of employers. Work experience was frequently mentioned in the form "three years as a company chief accountant in a medium size engineering company." No references or specific salary levels were given in any of the application letters. (It was reasoned that past and present salaries might well be an important factor in obtaining a job but that to have given all applicants the same salary level would have raised suspicion.) The grammatical structure in all the letters implied that all applicants were fluent in English and the style of all letters for each job was similar. Both the content and style of the letters were determined in consultation with a group of personnel officers who were interested in the study, and special consideration was given to ensuring that the background variables of the applicants were very similar.

With the job applicants' qualifications and experience identical, the success rate of the different applicants was expected to be very similar absent racial or national discrimination. (We defined success as being sent an application form or offered an interview.) Were the success rate of, say, British whites to be significantly higher than, say, West Indians, when measured over a large number of job applications, this would be *prima facie* evidence of discrimination. Of course, the study only tests for discrimination at the initial screening stage. There is no guarantee that, even if nonwhite applicants are sent application forms or offered interviews, they will not be discriminated against at the next stage of the selection process. (This latter aspect awaits future study, but the research design will be faced with a severe problem of controlling all the relevant variables.[11])

The testing for this study was carried out in the last three months of 1977 and the first three months of 1978—the traditional months for recruiting articled clerks. Application letters were given an address in the region of the job so that the recipient would not be deterred from pursuing an applicant for fear the latter would have to move his home if offered the job. All seven letters for each specific job were mailed within one day of one another so as to avoid the confounding variable of first letters received being given preference in the job-screening process. Prior consultation with personnel officers had established that accounting vacancies typically draw many responses and thus the arrival of the seven letters used in the research was not expected to lead to an employer receiving a suspiciously large number of applications. Applications were sent for a total of 282 jobs. The response is summarized below.

Table 1. Success Rates of Job Applicants by Nationality.[a]

1	*2*	*3*
Nationality	*Number of Successes*	*Percentage Success Rate*
Great Britain	240	85
Australia	211	75
France	192	68
Africa	150	53
India	124	44
Pakistan	123	44
West Indies	136	48

[a] There were 282 applications for each nationality.

Results

The number of successful outcomes to job applications for each nationality and race and the successful applications as percent-

[11]See McIntosh and Smith, "The Extent of Racial Discrimination." They tested discrimination at the interview stage for manual jobs by using a team of white and nonwhite actors; their results indicated a significant level of racial discrimination in manual jobs. Their paper also discusses the problems in using this research approach.

Table 2. Comparison of Responses by Pairs of Nationalities.

1 Nationality[a]	2 Both failed	3 Col. 2 as a % of 282	4 At least one applicant succeeded	5 Both succeeded	6 Col. 5 as a % of Col. 4	7 Discrimination against second named nationality	8 Col. 7 as a % of Col. 4	9 Discrimination against first named nationality	10 Col. 9 as a % of Col. 4
B-Au	37	13	245	206	84	34	14	5	2
B-F	37	13	245	187	76	53	22	5	2
B-Af	35	12	247	143	58	97	39	7	3
B-I	41	15	241	123	51	117	49	1	1
B-P	41	15	241	122	51	118	49	1	1
B-WI	38	13	244	132	54	108	44	4	2
Au-F	67	24	215	190	88	21	10	4	2
Au-Af	64	23	218	143	66	68	31	7	3
Au-I	71	25	211	124	59	87	41	0	0
Au-P	70	25	212	122	58	89	42	1	1
Au-WI	68	24	214	133	62	78	36	3	1
F-Af	79	28	203	137	67	55	27	11	5
F-I	88	31	194	120	62	72	37	2	1
F-P	86	30	196	117	60	75	38	4	2
F-WI	84	30	198	128	65	64	32	6	3

[a] Comparisons are made between each of the three white nationalities and each other nationality:

B = British
Au = Australian
F = French
Af = African
I = Indian
P = Pakistani
WI = West Indian

ages of total applications made are shown in Table 1, columns two and three, respectively. While being "successful" in the sense of being sent an application form or being granted an interview in no way means the applicant will actually get the job, the act of not being given an application form or not being granted an interview means the applicant has absolutely no chance of being fully successful. Thus, "successful" in this sense means the applicant has passed through the first stage of the screening process and still has some chance of getting the job.[12]

The figures from Table 1 show that British whites have a much greater chance of obtaining a job (in that they get through the initial screening selection) than other whites, and a considerably greater chance than nonwhites. Among white applicants, the French did not have as much success as the English-speaking applicants from the Commonwealth country of Australia. While the success rate depended partly on nationality, the race of the applicant had a greater impact.

In order to examine the extent of discrimination in more detail, the success rate of the three white nationalities was compared with the success rate of the other nationalities. (See Table 2.) The table shows:

(1) the two nationalities being compared (column 1).

[12] Of course, a distinction should also be made between being granted an interview and being given an application form; the former is a much clearer indicator of employer interest, while the latter may in many cases imply little or no screening (application forms being sent out automatically to all who write after the job advertisement). Additional analyses were therefore made where success was defined (1) as being granted an interview and (2) as being sent a formal application form. The results of these additional tests produced similar discrimination findings to those reported in Tables 1 and 2. These additional results are available from the author on request.

(2) the number of cases in which both nationalities failed to get interviews or application forms (column 2). In 37 cases, for example, both British and Australian applicants had no success. These cases provide no evidence for or against discrimination.

(3) the number of cases in which both nationalities failed as a percentage of the total number of applications (282) (column 3).

(4) the number of cases in which at least one nationality had success (column 4). For example, in 245 cases out of 282 an interview or application form was given to a British or Australian applicant or both. These cases can be used to assess the level of discrimination.

(5) the number of cases in which both nationalities had success in their applications (column 5). This figure is then expressed (in column 6) as a percentage of the figure appearing in column 4, giving the percentage of cases in which no discrimination was apparent (each applicant received a favorable response). For example, in 84 percent of the cases British and Australian applicants both received favorable responses; in the remaining 16 percent there was discrimination, either against Australians or against Britons (columns 7 to 10).

(6) the number of cases in which the first nationality had positive replies from job applications while the second nationality had negative replies (column 7). In 34 instances, for example, the British applicants had a positive reply while the Australians had a negative reply. This is treated as discrimination against the Australians as they had virtually identical qualifications and experience as the British and yet received negative responses. Column 8 expresses column 7 as a percentage of column 4.

(7) the absolute and percentage discrimination against the first nationality in favor of the second named (columns 9 and 10). In five instances, it can be seen, Australians received positive replies while the British did not.

The data in Table 2 corroborate the results from Table 1: in the labor market tested, British employers discriminate to some extent against foreign whites and considerably against nonwhites. (There were a few instances of the British applicants being discriminated against, but these instances were rare.) Australians are treated favorably, the French slightly less favorably, and nonwhites least favorably (and about equally among themselves). When the results from Table 2 were disaggregated by the five job types, similar patterns of discrimination evolved (the results of these additional analyses are available from the author on request).

The data show that the race of an applicant is a significant factor in gaining employment in the accounting job market in Great Britain; it was hypothesized, however, that race may be of special importance for certain situations, such as with specific job types or jobs located in specific geographical areas. In order to analyze the importance of the job variables in the success rates of various nationalities and races, Analysis of Variance (ANOVA) tests were conducted. The variables extracted from each job were job type, salary level (where the salary was stated), location of job, and whether or not the employing firm was a multinational. Job type and salary level were thought to reflect, to some extent, the seniority of the position, which could, in turn, have an impact on the success rate of minority-race applicants (because it could be hypothesized that minority race groups would have a greater relative difficulty in obtaining more senior jobs). The location of the job could be important because certain areas (such as the West Country) do not have large nonwhite race populations and thus they might exhibit more prejudice. In addition, it could also be hypothesized that multinational firms or those with international affiliates might discriminate less against nonwhites because they are more used to employing different races and because their nonwhite employees could be relocated to the firm's operations overseas after experience in the U.K. This may be an important factor, because many developing nations require local branches of the international accounting firms to be staffed by their own nationals. Hence, British accounting firms may employ foreigners with a view to their eventually moving abroad.

The specific make-up of the variables used in the ANOVA was as follows: (1) Race and nationality (seven types): British-white; Australian; French; African; Indian; Pakistani; and West Indian. (2) Job type (five types): articled clerks; unqualified personnel; professional practice; industry; and financial. (3) Salary levels (five levels): ≤ £3,000; £3,001 to £5,000; £5,001 to £8,000; £8,001 to £10,000; and > £10,000. Since some advertisements stated no salary levels, this variable was examined in a separately run ANOVA covering only those jobs that had included them. (4) Location of job (seven locations): London and Home Counties; Midlands; North West; Scotland; Wales; West Country; and Yorkshire and North East. (5) Firm (two categories): multinational; and nonmultinational. The dependent variable was the applicant's success or failure.

The results of the ANOVA test showed that only the race and nationality variable ($F = 8.61$, $p < .001$) had a significant impact on the success rates of applicants. The other main effect variables had no significant association with success rates (at the $p < .10$ level). Additionally, none of the interactive effects was statistically significant.

Thus the ANOVA results show that the race of an applicant is an important factor in obtaining employment in the accountancy job market, but that the level of racial discrimination occurs evenly across various types of accounting jobs. The variables of job type, salary levels, location of job, and the type of firm worked for did not appear to be significant in explaining job success rates.

Discussion

The results of the study have shown that racial discrimination still exists in the British job market. Of the seven nationalities represented among the fictitious job applicants, the white Britons had the greatest success in obtaining favorable responses. Following the British in order of success came Australians (white, English-speaking), French (white, foreign language), and then nonwhite races (both English-speaking and non-English-speaking). The results also revealed that racial discrimination appeared to be evenly spread across various types of jobs. These results for 1977 – 78 are very similar to the earlier studies of Jowell and Prescott-Clarke in the late 1960s and McIntosh and Smith in 1973.[13] Thus there appears to have been no noticeable change in British employers' attitudes as regards employing nonwhites. The results from the study do contrast, however, with Newman's research in the United States, which indicated some discrimination against whites.[14] This contrast may be due in part to differences in the research design,[15] in part to the affirmative action obligation imposed on many American employers,[16] and in part to differences in employer attitudes.

In order to find out what the stated views of employers are as regards employing nonwhite minority races, a short questionnaire was sent to those involved in the study. The questionnaire asked:

> If two applicants, one a British white, the other a non-white minority race immigrant, applied for a job in your firm and they had identical qualifications and experience, would they stand an equal chance of getting the job (and of getting an application form, and an interview)? How would you choose between them? Have you ever been placed in this position?[17]

---

[13]Jowell and Prescott-Clarke, "Racial Discrimination and White Collar Workers in Britain," and McIntosh and Smith, "The Extent of Racial Discrimination."

[14]Newman, "Discrimination in Recruitment: An Empirical Analysis," pp. 15 – 23.

[15]Among the major differences in the research designs were (1) the present study sent in applications for advertised positions whereas Newman sent unsolicited applications, a difference which resulted in a higher percentage of "success" responses to the applicants in the present study; (2) applicants' ages, education, and so forth were changed for each advertised job in this study so as to meet the specified requirements, whereas Newman's research involved sending a standard letter (all of Newman's applicants were approximately 23 years old) and thus his results could be specific to the standard set of applicants' characteristics; (3) no photograph was utilized in this study, in contrast to Newman's practice of attaching a photo to each application, and hence the problem of physical attractiveness does not arise in this study.

[16]The Race Relations Act of 1968 does not impose an obligation of affirmative action on British employers.

[17]The questionnaire also posed other questions. These are of lesser importance to the current study and so they are not discussed here.

The questionnaires were sent out several months after the job applications were mailed in, so that the employer would not connect the occurrences. Also, the questionnaire did not refer to the prior job applications. The responses to the questionnaire totalled 167 out of a total of 282, a response rate of 59 percent. The responses of those employers replying late were found to be similar to those who replied very quickly and this gives one indication that there may not be a significant amount of nonresponse bias.[18]

Virtually all respondents said they would treat British whites and nonwhites equally when coming to job decisions. Of 147 respondents, 119 said they had been in positions in which a choice had to be made between white and nonwhite applicants. (Some stated that differences nearly always occurred in qualifications and experience, two major criteria used in the selection process.) Chi-square tests were conducted to compare the actual decisions of employers and their stated views (that a minority-race applicant of equal academic ability and equal experience as a British white stood a 50–50 chance of getting the job or progressing to the next stage of the selection process). The tests showed that the respondents' stated views were not matched by their decisions in practice; similar conclusions have been reached in the United States.[19]

Conclusions

The research study set out to assess how prevalent racial discrimination is in the British labor market for accountants and financial management. The results show there is a significant amount of discrimination in all the various segments of the accounting job market at the initial screening stage, and thus there appears to have been little improvement in the discrimination situation since the early 1970s. The study also found that the stated viewpoints of employers did not correspond to their decisions in practice. Clearly there is a considerable way to go before nonwhite minority races can be said to compete equally with British whites in the professional job market.

[18]Abraham O. Oppenheim, *Questionnaire Design and Attitude Measurement* (London: Heinemann, 1966).

[19]Jerry M. Newman and Frank Krzystofiak, "Self-Reports Versus Unobtrusive Measures: Balancing Method Variance and Ethical Concerns in Employment Discrimination Research," *Journal of Applied Psychology*, Vol. 64, No. 1 (February 1979), pp. 82–83.

[8]

OXFORD BULLETIN
of
ECONOMICS *and* STATISTICS

Volume 39 *November 1977* *No. 4*

AN ANALYSIS OF RACIAL WAGE DISCRIMINATION IN SOUTH AFRICA*

By J. B. KNIGHT and M. D. MCGRATH

1. INTRODUCTION

This paper examines a particular aspect of earnings structure in South Africa, that of racial wage discrimination. We define racial wage discrimination as a difference in earnings among people of different races but of equal productivity as determined by their endowments of such economic characteristics as ability and human capital. Wage discrimination can exist either within an occupation or between occupations, in the sense that different occupations, each racially specific but involving the same levels of ability and human capital, may receive different wages. The major part of the racial earnings disparities is not to be explained in terms of our definition of wage discrimination. Nevertheless, wage discrimination merits separate study because racial overlapping in occupations and in the possession of education is of growing importance in the South African labour market, and because wage discrimination poses interesting theoretical problems which have attracted the attention of economic theorists.[1] Do the economic theories of wage discrimination which have been developed in the United States have relevance for the South African case? There is also a growing literature on labour market segmentation and the lack of competition between groups of workers as an explanation of wage disparities.[2] What light do these segmentation theories throw on wage discrimination in South Africa?

2. WAGE DISCRIMINATION IN PERSPECTIVE

Wage discrimination in South Africa must be seen in perspective. The ratio of White to African personal per capita income in 1970 was 14 to 1, whereas the

* The research for this paper was done during Michael McGrath's visit to the Institute in 1976. We are grateful to Sean Archer, Gavin Maasdorp, Richard Porter, Lawrence Schlemmer and Arnt Spandau for their comments.

[1] Recently surveyed by Ray Marshall, 'The economics of racial discrimination: a survey', *Journal of Economic Literature*, September 1974.

[2] Recently surveyed by Glen G. Cain, 'The challenge of segmented labor market theories to orthodox theory: a survey', *Journal of Economic Literature*, December 1976.

ratio of White to African average earnings from employment was 7 to 1.[3] Thus wage discrimination in the modern sector at the very most can explain only half of the difference in racial per capita income. The other half is due mainly to discrimination against Africans in access to modern sector employment, the unequal racial distribution of income from wealth and entrepreneurship, and the higher dependency ratio among Africans. Africans have access only to those modern sector jobs left vacant after the Non-Africans have been employed. This is the result of the land policies which confine many Africans in the over-crowded reserves, the controls which restrict their movement to and residence in the urban areas, and the policies which impede Africans from acquiring knowledge and skills appropriate for modern sector employment. There are institutional constraints on the accumulation of capital by Africans (e.g. the prohibition of freehold in the main urban areas) and African entrepreneurs face various obstacles imposed by government (e.g. on the location of businesses).

Ideally we should divide the racial difference in average earnings in the modern sector into that part which is due to wage discrimination and that due to racial inequality in productive economic characteristics. Limitations of data prevent such an exercise, although a simple attempt is made to standardize for education. However, for reasons of both data and economics, much of the analysis is cast in terms of occupations.

There are enormous racial differences in occupational structure. Table 1 gives employment in selective occupations, drawn from the 1975 Manpower Survey, in order to indicate the extent of racial separation and overlapping in occupations. We see that Whites dominate the 'managerial, executive and administrative' and 'professional, semi-professional and technical' occupations. Africans and 'other races' (Asians and Coloureds) in the latter category are largely school teachers and nurses: there are very few with other professional qualifications and even in technician and technical assistant grades Whites predominate. Artisan jobs are largely a Non-African preserve, and Africans are to be found as 'unqualified artisans' or 'artisan aides'. There is a considerable overlapping of the races in the 'skilled and semi-skilled operator' grade and in such jobs as heavy lorry driver. Blacks have made inroads into shop assistant work, but only into the lowest clerical grades. In the category 'labourer' there were over a million Africans but less than 11,000 Whites.

In occupational distribution, as in many other respects, Asian and Coloured people occupy an intermediate position between Whites and Africans. For our purposes the most relevant distinction is sometimes between Whites and others (whom we shall refer to as Blacks) and sometimes between Africans and others (whom we shall refer to as Non-Africans), but generally the analysis is simplified by concentrating on the two main and most disparate groups, Africans and Whites.

Two main forms of discrimination contribute to the unequal racial distribution of occupations: an educational and an occupational colour bar. Inequality of access

[3] The statistics are drawn from M. D. McGrath, 'Income and Material Inequality in South Africa', in L. Schlemmer and E. Webster (eds), *Change, Reform and Economic Growth in South Africa*, Ravan Press, 1977.

TABLE 1

Racial Distribution by Occupation, 1975 (000)

	African	*White*	*Other*	*White as percentage of total*
Managerial, executive and administrative	3.8	124.9	4.2	94
Professional, semi-professional and technical	118.1	243.3	43.4	60
of which:				
qualified engineer	0	15.0	0	100
medical doctor	0.1	8.9	0.7	92
registered nurse, midwife	19.3	17.6	4.1	43
school teacher (excl. vocational)	75.0	54.9	29.5	34
technician, technologist	2.4	45.8	1.8	92
technical assistant	1.9	10.5	1.5	76
priest	3.3	5.5	0.1	62
Clerical	74.6	409.7	79.6	73
of which:				
typist, stenographer, telephonist	1.1	64.9	3.7	93
general clerk, clerical assistant	20.7	76.2	11.2	70
Skilled and semi-skilled operator	484.4	88.0	237.5	11
Foreman, supervisor, overseer	11.7	43.5	8.1	69
Artisan	8.2	176.3	43.6	77
Handiman, including artisan hand or mate, unindentured artisan	42.1	6.8	9.3	12
Shop and counter assistant	18.6	78.6	28.4	63
Driver: heavy and extra heavy lorry, tanker	38.1	11.1	13.4	18
Labourer	1095.0	10.9	129.6	1
All occupations	2749.9	1458.3	707.8	30

Source: Department of Labour, *Manpower Survey No. 11. All Industries and Occupations, April 1975.*

Note: The survey covers all employees outside agriculture and domestic service. Various occupations ill-defined in terms of skill, e.g. mineworker, are not listed in the table.

TABLE 2

Racial Distribution of Education in the Urban Male Economically Active Population, 1970 (per cent)

Education level	*African*	*White*	*Other*	*All races*
0–6 years	73.8	1.8	38.6	48.8
	(87.7)	(1.0)	(11.3)	*(100)*
7–8 years	18.8	16.0	37.3	20.6
	(52.7)	(21.7)	(25.6)	*(100)*
9–10 years	5.1	33.7	16.1	14.6
	(20.2)	(64.2)	(15.6)	*(100)*
11–12 years	1.9	32.3	5.5	10.9
	(10.4)	(82.5)	(2.4)	*(100)*
Post-Secondary	0.4	16.2	2.4	5.1
	(4.3)	(89.0)	(6.7)	*(100)*
All Levels	*100*	*100*	*100*	*100*
	(57.9)	(27.9)	(14.2)	*(100)*

Source: Department of Statistics, *Population Census 1970, Level of Education,* Report 02-05-07.

Notes: Figures in parenthesis show the proportion of the row totals accounted for by each race, and those not in parenthesis show the proportion of the column totals accounted for by each level of education.

Included in post-secondary education are people with diplomas who have not obtained full secondary education.

to education is shown in Table 2. Over 90 per cent of urban male Africans had completed less than 8 years of schooling (a full primary course), whereas over 80 per cent of equivalent Whites had completed more than that level. Whites constituted some 85 per cent of the group who had completed a full secondary education or gone even further. There are also qualitative differences in the standards of education received, with White schools generally having lower pupil-teacher ratios and better qualified teachers. The occupational colour bar is enforced through social custom and convention, White trade union collective bargaining, public sector employment policies and statutory job reservation.

The segmentation of the labour market into two non-competing groups—probably at its height in the early 1960s—led one of the authors to formulate a theory of wages in South Africa along the following lines.[4] The labour force is divided into two separate factors of production, skilled labour, entirely White, and unskilled labour, entirely Black. The Black wage is determined by the supply curve of labour in Black agriculture, assumed to be perfectly elastic at a subsistence level over the relevant range. Skilled White labour, on the other hand, is in perfectly inelastic supply and fully employed. There is scope for substitution between the two factors. The equilibrium employment condition (the amount of Black labour which is combined with the fully employed White labour force) is that the marginal rate of substitution between the two factors equals the ratio of the White wage rate to the constant Black wage rate. The White wage can be seen both as a reward for higher productivity at the margin and as a scarcity rent secured from the White monopoly of skills. Capital accumulation and technical progress are shown to benefit White labour by raising wages and Black labour by increasing employment. Within the institutional and political framework which keeps Black labour unskilled and plentiful and White Labour skilled and scarce, the market mechanism acts as a malevolent Invisible Hand to produce increasing racial inequality of income.

The rapid growth of the South African economy after the early 1960's increased the crucial shortage of educated and skilled labour. The expansion of Black education was also accelerated. Consequently, the colour bar moved upwards in the hierarchy of occupations and tended to disintegrate as Black and White increasingly competed in the semi-skilled, skilled and lower white collar jobs. It is this process of Black job advancement and increasing inter-racial job competition which makes the assumption of complete segmentation in the 1964 model less adequate and calls for an analysis of wage discrimination.

3. Theories of Discrimination and Segmentation

Models of economic discrimination grew out of attempts by theorists to analyse racial income differences in the United States. They perceived a need to explain the existence, in competitive markets, of wage differences between workers of different race but of equal productivity. The main division in approach has been

[4] J. B. Knight, 'A theory of income distribution in South Africa', Bulletin, November 1964.

between those who use a neo-classical framework and those who stress market imperfections and segmentation, and collusive and collective behaviour.

In the neo-classical approach, the wage difference is explained by assuming that there are racially specific characteristics—not productivity—which are valued in the market, and that the values placed on these characteristics are determined by a 'taste for discrimination'. There is diversity within the neo-classical camp, and the following account draws mainly on the formulations by Kenneth Arrow.[5] Three types of discrimination can be distinguished: discrimination by employers, by employees and by consumers.

First, consider an employer with a taste for discrimination against Black and in favour of White workers. In equilibrium the marginal product of Black labour exceeds its wage by an amount equal to the psychic cost of employing Black labour, and similarly the marginal product of White labour is less than its wage. Since the two kinds of worker are perfect substitutes in production, their marginal products are the same. The White wage must therefore be above marginal product and the Black wage below it. Discrimination by employees is illustrated by assuming White foremen working with both White and Black production workers but preferring Whites. The more Blacks are employed the greater the wage necessary to attract and retain White foremen: the cost of employing Black labour exceeds the Black wage. Since the marginal products of Black and White production workers must be the same, a wage difference is created in favour of Whites. Discrimination by consumers in the purchase of personalised services reduces the value of services provided by Blacks in relation to those produced by Whites. A racial gap in the incomes of factors is therefore created, which can be reduced only if there is scope for unprejudiced intermediaries to buy standardised products from Black suppliers and sell to the public.

These models of discrimination have been criticised on various grounds. Arrow recognised that wage discrimination is their short run rather than their long run prediction.[6] Given competitive product markets and the existence of sufficient non-discriminating employers, the expansion of non-discriminating enterprises will tend to drive out those which discriminate and to equalise wages. If it is White workers in competition with Blacks who are prejudiced and need to be paid more as compensation for sharing jobs with Blacks, employers have an incentive to replace White workers. The result will be segregation of the races in White and Black plants, and the elimination of wage discrimination. The existence of non-discriminatory foremen also tends to produce segregation and wage equalisation. Some explanation must be found for the failure of these long run predictions. One possibility is to withdraw the assumption of competition in the product market; discriminatory firms may then be able to satisfy their prejudices and accept a lower return on their capital. Another way out is to relax the assumption that adjustments can be made costlessly. If there are costs of altering the racial

[5] In particular, Kenneth J. Arrow, 'Models of job discrimination', in Anthony H. Pascal (ed.) *Racial Discrimination in Economic Life*, 1972, and 'The theory of discrimination', in O. Ashenfelter and A. Rees (eds.), *Discrimination in Labor Markets*, 1974.

[6] Kenneth Arrow, 'Models of job discrimination', *op. cit.*, pp. 89–93.

composition of the labour force (i.e. of hiring and firing labour), adjustments need not occur to the extent predicted and wage differences may persist.[7]

A second strand of criticism questions the motive generally assumed for discriminatory behaviour, i.e. aversion to the physical proximity of Black workers. Alternative motives have been suggested: that the aversion is social and reflects a concern for status,[8] that the racial loyalty of White employers engenders a concern to increase the share in income of the White group as a whole,[9] or that the envy or malice of White employers towards Black workers produces a desire to reduce the Black share of wage income.[10] In each case the previous type of analysis holds, in that the cost to employers of hiring Black labour exceeds the Black wage.

In only one case does the neo-classical model explain wage discrimination as resulting from the self-interested pursuit of income: that is the use of race as a screening device when information is imperfect.[11] When they must incur a cost before the productivity of an individual can be determined, employers may use race as a criterion for hiring if they believe that Whites and Blacks have different distributions of the imperfectly observable economic characteristics. Black workers wishing to be hired must accept a lower wage in order to offset the perceived lower probability of their having the desired economic characteristics. Unless the employers' beliefs are correct, discriminating firms are again liable to be driven out of competitive product markets by non-discriminating firms. If the probabilities are indeed different, then it is true that Blacks can be paid less than Whites of equal efficiency: an employer need not pay more than his Black employee would be paid by employers without information on his personal efficiency.

The dividing line between an economic and a social explanation of screening is not clear-cut, for two reasons. If employers' beliefs about productivity are false, their persistence requires explanation. It might be explained by the theory of 'cognitive dissonance', i.e. if individuals act in a discriminating manner they will be willing to entertain beliefs which justify their actions. Beliefs may be correct because they are self-fulfilling, i.e. potentially efficient Blacks may not be given the necessary on-the-job training, or their lower wages may adversely affect their productivity, or the low expectations of or lack of interest by employers may deter Black workers from acquiring the characteristics (e.g. steadiness, punctuality, responsiveness and initiative) which employers value.

Theories of labour market segmentation differ from these theories of discrimination in that they place emphasis on competition for jobs rather than competition for wages, on the reasons why workers do not compete rather than the consequences of their competing, on group rather than individual interests and behaviour, and on the institutional framework within which market forces operate. There are three relevant aspects: 'job competition', 'internal labour markets' and 'crowding'.

[7] *Ibid.*, pp. 90–2, 95–6.

[8] Kenneth Arrow, 'Models of job discrimination', *op. cit.*, p. 89.

[9] Anne O. Krueger, 'The economics of discrimination', *Journal of Political Economy*, October 1963.

[10] Marcus Alexis, 'A theory of labor market discrimination with interdependent utilities', *American Economic Review*, May 1973, pp. 297–8.

[11] Kenneth Arrow ,'Models of job discrimination', *op. cit.*, pp. 96–8.

According to the job competition theory, workers are not paid wages based on such economic characteristics as education and ability.[12] The wage is linked to the job, and custom and views of fairness are relevant to its determination. Informal training is more important than formal education in providing relevant skills. To reduce training costs, employers use observable characteristics such as formal education and race as screening devices to order the job queue and to select people for on-the-job training. The distribution of job opportunities determines the distribution of earnings, while screening characteristics determine the order of access. Blacks and Whites of equal productive potential may achieve different actual productivity and pay if the Blacks are assigned to jobs which are lower in the hierarchy of skill and pay. An increase in the education of Black people need not raise their earnings if they are discriminated against in the job queue.

Swinton takes the notion of job competition further by attempting to explain why racial preference is shown in the job queue.[13] Discrimination is seen to arise out of the collective attempt by workers in the dominant group to increase their collective income. The separate group identities which exist independently of economic discrimination in some societies help to produce 'we' and 'they' thinking and the solidarity necessary for collective racial discrimination in the labour market. The dominant group of workers (here assumed to be White) ensure that they receive preference in the queue for the prized jobs. They achieve this through a variety of industrial actions which impose a cost on employers unless, either formally or informally, they agree to co-operate. The employer has a profit incentive to co-operate if the cost of retaliation by White workers exceeds the cost imposed by discrimination. Discrimination will break down if and when there is a change in the relative economic power of the two groups of workers.

An internal labour market can be the means by which job competition is regulated. An internal labour market, as opposed to the external labour market of conventional theory, is said to exist where the pricing and allocation of services is governed by a set of administrative rules and procedures.[14] The internal market—normally within an enterprise—is linked to the external market only at limited points of entry and exit. Wage structure is administratively determined, with greater emphasis on internal relationships, governed by such factors as custom and job evaluation, than on external relationships. Workers have employment continuity and security, rewards for seniority, preference in promotion, and protection from external competition. For management, promotional ladders and seniority rules reduce labour turnover and provide information on employee performance, thus cutting the cost of training. The internal labour market may indeed be seen as the employers' institutional response to the problem of securing and retaining the benefits of specific training. On the other hand, there is a strong element of custom and practice, and this may become formalised through collective bargaining.

The institutional framework of the internal labour market can be used by

[12] Lester C. Thurow, ***Generating Inequality***, 1975, chs. 4–5.

[13] David H. Swinton, 'A labor force competition theory of discrimination in the labor market', ***American Economic Review, Papers and Proceedings***, February 1977.

[14] Peter B. Doeringer and Michael J. Piore, ***Internal Labor Markets and Manpower Analysis***, 1971, chs. 2–4, 7.

prejudiced workers to keep out Blacks; the same result may occur through the employer's use, as a screening device in recruitment, of race or employee contacts. In these circumstances, White employees can be protected from the undercutting threatened by Black job-seekers with a supply price lower than the White wage. Whites may also have the power to restrict the internal promotion of Blacks of equal efficiency into the higher-paid occupations. On the other hand, the security which an internal labour market provides could also make White workers more amenable to accepting and training Black workers.

The term 'crowding' was used by Edgeworth in examining sexual inequality in pay for equal work.[15] He explained the failure of employers to substitute female labour for dearer male labour by the restriction of competition: men were better organised than women and exercised pressure on employers to their own advantage. The pressure of male trade unions was largely responsible for the crowding of women into a comparatively few occupations. These pressures included outright exclusion, the prevention of training, and an insistence on equal pay in cases where women were less efficient workers than men.

The theory of crowding has also been applied to racial wage discrimination.[16] White workers have the power to monopolise the high-skill, and possibly certain other occupations, so crowding Black workers into the remaining low-skill occupations and depressing wages in them. A by-product of this process is that the transfer earnings of the few Black workers who find employment in the reserved occupations may be low. Provided that there is no competition among employers for these Black workers, an employer needs to pay them no more than their transfer price from occupations dominated by Blacks. This can give rise to racial wage discrimination within an occupation.

The path is now clear for an evaluation of these theories in the South African context. Our procedure is as follows: we examine the extent and nature of wage discrimination in the private sector, in the public sector, and in relation to educational attainment; then we study the interests of different groups and the institutional framework within which these are pursued; finally, we draw together the various strands to produce a realistic theory of wage discrimination in South Africa.

IV. Wage Discrimination in the Private Sector

A detailed and accurate source of information on wage and occupational structures is the evidence which British companies were required to produce to the House of Commons in 1973 on the employment practices in their South African subsidiaries and associates.[17] Tables 3–5 illustrate different types. Table 3 relating to a large chemical plant, is an example of complete lack of overlap in

[15] F. Y. Edgeworth, 'Equal pay to men and women for equal work', *Economic Journal*, December 1922.

[16] Barbara R. Bergmann, 'The effect on white incomes of discrimination in employment', *Journal of Political Economy*, March/April 1971.

[17] Fifth Report from the Expenditure Committee, Session 1973–74, *Wages and Conditions of African Workers Employed by British Firms in South Africa*, H.M.S.O., January 1974; also *Minutes of Evidence*, Vols. 1–4. One of the authors acted as Specialist Adviser to the Committee in this Inquiry.

TABLE 3

Average Wages and Employment by Grade and Race, Chemical Plant

	Unskilled		*Semi-skilled*					*Skilled*						
Grade	*Y*	*Z*	*P*	*Q*	*R*	*S*	*T*	*G*	*H*	*I*	*J*	*Arti-sans*	*K*	*Total*
Employment														
Africans	1646	1503	819	547	291	67	32	—	—	—	—	—	—	4905
Whites	—	—	—	—	—	—	—	22	113	212	134	113	231	825
***Average Basic Wage** (R per month):*														
Africans	71	80	89	102	133	148	177	—	—	—	—	—	—	86
Whites	—	—	—	—	—	—	—	331	342	358	381	559	408	400

Source: Expenditure Committee, *Wages and Conditions of African Workers Employed by British Firms in South Africa*, p. 75.

Notes: The data relates only to the Modderfontein factory of AE and CI, an associate of I.C.I. There are no Asian and Coloured employees. A dash (—) indicates none in this grade.

TABLE 4

Average Earnings by Grade and Race, Manufacturing Conglomerate

Grade	*W1*	*W2*	*W3*	*W4*	*S1/W5*	*S2/W6*	*S3/W7*	*S4/W8*	*S5*	*S6*	*S7*	*Manag-erial*	*Total*
Employment:													
Africans	994	1290	562	241	186	143	109	58	15	43	3	1	3645
Whites	—	—	—	—	—	17	133	292	351	187	273	463	1716
Asians and Coloureds	21	77	35	39	58	82	113	44	17	21	2	—	509
Average Earnings (R per month):													
Africans	91	107	121	138	152	166	195	197	257	305	345	*	119
Whites	—	—	—	—	—	173	198	241	324	367	414	*	315
Asians and Coloureds	91	104	115	138	149	180	199	233	264	277	352	—	170

Source: Expenditure Committee, *op. cit.*, p. 77.

Notes: The data refer to the operations of Unilever South Africa.
A dash (—) indicates none in this grade.

* Indicates no figure proviced. Earnings of the managerial grade are excluded from the total.

TABLE 5

Average Earnings and Employment by Grade and Race, Industrial Gas Company

Grade	1	2	3	4	5	6	7	A1	A2	B3	B4	C5 and above	Total
Employment:													
Africans	285	714	588	214	92	92	1	7	—	3	—	—	1993
Whites	—	—	—	—	—	—	—	741	209	557	188	209	1904
Asians and Coloureds	7	54	37	39	57	52	16	32	1	—	—	—	295
Average earnings (R per month)													
Africans	72	78	91	106	128	142	179	162	—	228	—	—	90
Whites	—	—	—	—	—	—	—	216	302	375	488	*	309
Asians and Coloureds	67	78	92	119	149	163	175	197	349	—	—	—	133

Source: Expenditure Committee, *op. cit.*, p. 76.

Notes: The data relate to the operations of African Oxygen, a subsidiary of British Oxygen.

* Indicates figure not provided. The average earnings exclude the top grade C5 and above.
A dash (—) indicates none in this grade.

occupation. In 1973 a rigid colour bar existed between the semi-skilled grade T and the skilled grade G. Corresponding to the colour bar there was a sharp discontinuity in the wage scale. The average basic wage of the lowest grade of White worker was nearly double that of the highest grade of African worker. This gap in pay appeared to result from the African exclusion by law from the registered trade union which negotiated on pay and ensured that skilled jobs required union membership. Under questioning the company admitted that the pay difference at the racial dividing line was not warranted by the difference in job content.[18] Here wage discrimination occurred between occupations. This example of occupational separation was typical of firms facing powerful White trade unions, as in mining.[19]

An example of racial overlap in occupations without wage discrimination is provided by Table 4, which refers to a conglomerate manufacturing soaps, detergents, toilet preparations, etc. The data on average earnings in the overlapping grades support the company's claim that it pursues a policy of 'the rate for the job'.[20] The company's introduction of a non-racial wage structure based on principles of job evaluation had been facilitated by the absence of unionisation among White employees.[21] Among the firms claiming to pay 'the rate for the job' irrespective of race were a banking group (with respect to bank clerks) and a manufacturer of cans and metal products which claimed that a selection of skilled jobs (e.g. machine setter, storeman, timekeeper, clerk, technician) were open equally to White and Black employees on the same scales of pay.[22]

A third type of firm has some racial overlapping in occupations but unequal pay. A company manufacturing gas and gas equipment was among the leaders in the promotion of Africans: only 50 per cent of African employees could be classified as unskilled, 45 per cent were semi-skilled, and 5 per cent were skilled (Table 5).[23] Nevertheless, there was little overlap between Whites and Blacks, because the colour bar had moved to higher jobs as Blacks advanced. In the grade A1 (unsophisticated clerical positions) White pay averaged a third more than that of Africans. The company explained that the gap had been much greater three years before, and also that the Africans had been in the grade for a relatively short time.[24]

In a large chain of retail shops the pay of White, Coloured and African salesmen averaged R260, R220 and R103 per month respectively.[25] The company claimed that salesmen were remunerated irrespective of race, and that the differences in pay were due to differences in productivity, i.e. response to sales opportunities. However, it acknowledged a reluctance on the part of White customers to be served by African salesmen.[26] The restriction of African salesmen

[18] *Minutes of Evidence*, Vol. I, Q830–34.

[19] For instance, Consolidated Gold Fields. *Ibid.*, Vol. I, pp. 206–34, esp. pp. 220–1.

[20] *Ibid.*, Vol. I, p. 151.

[21] *Ibid.*, Vol. I, Q303, Q371.

[22] *Ibid.*, Vol. I, pp. 554–72, esp. p. 555 and Q1589 (Barclays Bank); and pp. 188–205, esp. p. 193 (Metal Box).

[23] Grades 1–2 can be classified as unskilled, grades 3–5 as semi-skilled, and grades 6 and above as skilled.

[24] *Ibid.*, Vol. II, p. 709, Q2132.

[25] Lewis Stores, a subsidiary of Great Universal Stores. *Ibid.*, Vol. II, p. 830.

[26] *Ibid.*, Vol. II, Q2589 and 2602.

to the shops serving less prosperous areas no doubt meant that on average they had less sales opportunities to which to respond. An engineering company employed White and African crane operators at R269 and R142 per month respectively in the same factory.[27] Another employed White setters and erectors at about R300 per month and African setters and erectors at under R100.[28] An insurance company employed service clerks in the same office at an average monthly pay of R245 in the case of Whites, R198 in the case of Coloureds and Asians, and R135 in the case of Africans.[29]

The evidence of companies replying to the House of Commons Committee provided numerous such instances of significant racial wage differences in an occupation. However, two qualifications must be made. First, the occupations in which the races overlapped accounted for only a small proportion of the labour force. Secondly, although it is reasonable to doubt whether a difference in efficiency could account for all of the racial differences in pay, variation in the degree of education, skill, experience and responsibility may well have existed within an occupational category. Probably more pervasive than wage discrimination within an occupation, but more difficult to identify and measure, were racial wage differences across occupations which could not be wholly explained in terms of job content, i.e. the economic characteristics required of job-holders.

The problem of disentangling pay differences arising from differences in job content from those arising from wage discrimination might be solved by detailed job evaluation. In the absence of job evaluation it is possible only to give reasons for suspecting wage discrimination. Take the case of qualified and unqualified artisans. Apprenticeship is generally confined to membership of a registered trade union, from which Africans are excluded by law, so that the scope for Africans to acquire artisan skills except through experience on-the-job is very limited. Moreover, in some negotiated Industrial Council Agreements—which are given the force of law—the performance of artisan jobs is confined to membership of a recognised union. It is customary for the Non-African (mainly White) artisans to have African 'artisan assistants'. The gap in pay between an artisan and an artisan assistant is generally very great. For instance, in a glass producing company the minimum rate for a White artisan was R325 per month, whereas an African plumber's mate got R128, yet the company acknowledged under questioning that 'after a few years he is a very good plumber'.[30] In an engineering firm the average basic rate for the category 'fitter' was R103 per month in the case of Africans and R380 in the case of Whites.[31] One company—a rural pulpmill fortunate in having its own Industrial Council agreement—was said to provide formal artisan training for Africans and to pay the rate for the job.[32] However, this is the exception and not the rule: Africans are normally prevented *de jure*, if not always *de facto*, from becoming full artisans.

[27] A subsidiary of Taylor Woodrow. *Ibid.*, Vol. IV, p. 747.
[28] A subsidiary of Acrow Engineers. *Ibid.*, Vol. II, pp. 896–9.
[29] A subsidiary of Commercial Union. *Ibid.*, Vol. IV, p. 504.
[30] Subsidiary of Pilkington Brothers. *Ibid.*, Vol. II, pp. 776–7, 782, Q2443.
[31] Affiliate of the George Cohen 600 Group. *Ibid.*, Vol. III, p. 133.
[32] Subsidiary of Courtaulds. *Ibid.*, Vol. I, Q152.

A detailed study in 1972 by Spandau of a brewery employing some 1400 workers suggests that the racial differences in pay found in the factory could not be justified by differences in job content.[33] African wages varied from R56 to R143 a month. Production workers doing repetitive work (e.g. handling materials) received less than process operators, formally trained and responsible for the monitoring of processes. The highest paid Africans were those whose skills were least specific to the firm (e.g. heavy duty lorry drivers and clerks). Only three of the hourly rated jobs were filled by Whites (and only by them): artisan fitter, linesman (controlling production on the line and supervising some 30 workers), and shift supervisor (controlling the linesmen). Their pay ranged from R472 to R585 per month. The most interesting comparisons are of jobs at the interface between the races. The interface in the bottling and canning lines was between the White linesman and the African leading hand (who exercises authority over the workers on the line). The job of heavy duty lorry driver had recently been Africanised and that of linesman was Africanised after the survey had taken place.

There are reasons to doubt whether these racial wage differences were entirely due to differences in efficiency. First, it is implausible that the firm could previously have been able to hire Whites as heavy duty lorry drivers at the African rate of R143 a month, or that it would be necessary to continue to pay the White rate for linesmen once the job was Africanised. Secondly, the following figures suggest that the racial wage differences do not correspond to differences in job content:

	Race	*Wage (R per month)*	*Job score*	*German wage*[34]
Unloader	African	56	1.13	347
Heavy duty lorry driver	African	143	3.60	377
Leading hand	African	95	4.67	412
Linesman	White	472	4.53	429
Shift supervisor	White	585	4.80	611

The 'job score', based on techniques of job evaluation, shows the job of leading hand as no less demanding than that of linesman, and the wages for the two jobs in a German factory as very little different, even granted the much higher pay for unskilled jobs (e.g. unloader) and thus the much more compact wage structure in the German case. Thirdly, Spandau produced evidence of very inadequate communication across the racial divide, and suggested that White linesmen were poor supervisors of African process workers. It would be difficult, therefore, to argue that African replacements would be less efficient than the White supervisors.

V. Wage discrimination in the Public Sector

The public sector is the dominant employer of well-educated Blacks. In 1970 it employed 74 per cent of Africans in professional, technical, administrative and

[33] Arnt Spandau, 'A study in the Dual labour market in a South African plant', (mimeo), to be published as 'Residence and workplace in dynamic tension: a study in the dual labor market of a South African plant' in Alan A. Brown and Egon Neuberger (eds.), *Internal Migrations: A Comparative Perspective.*

[34] Converted to rands at the official exchange rate.

managerial occupations. This sector was less dominant at the clerical level, accounting for 24 per cent of African employees.[35]

The most overt cases of wage discrimination are to be found in the public sector, where for many years it has been the enshrined principle. A three-tier salary structure, applying in descending order to Whites, Asians and Coloureds, and Africans is found over a broad spectrum of skills. Traditional government thinking on this principle is perhaps reflected in the following ministerial response to a plea for higher salaries for African teachers: "The Bantu teacher . . . must learn not to feel above his community with a consequent desire to become integrated with the life of the European community. Present salary scales are quite adequate . . .'[36]

TABLE 6

Maximum Salaries by Race in Certain Public Sector Posts[a]

(Actual salary per month and salary expressed as a percentage of the White salary)

Post	*White*	*African*		*Other races*		*Date*
	Rands	*Rands*	(%)	*Rands*	(%)	
Medical						
Medical specialist	1155	920	80	1035	90	1977
Intern	470	330	70	390	83	1977
Pharmacist	675	455	67	560	83	1977
Nursing sister	400	270	67	330	83	1977
Student nurse	235	135	57	190	81	1977
Police						
Captain	610	440	72	510	84	1977
Lieutenant	555	390	70	455	82	1977
Constable	410	210	51	260	63	1977
Teaching						
University professor	1150	735	85	1110	96	1974
	1265	1170	92	1265	100	1977
University lecturer	765	645	84	700	92	1974
	840	770	92	810	96	1977
High school principal	975	440	45	825	85	1974
Secondary school teacher	585	295	50	410	70	1974
Primary school teacher[b]	525	210	40	365	70	1974

Sources: Medical: *Hansard No. 2*, 1977, pp. 102, 163. Police: *Hansard No. 6*, 1977, pp. 566–8, and *Estimates of Expenditure 1977–8*, R.P. 2/77, section 32/7. Teaching: IRR 75, p. 261; *Hansard No. 4*, 1977, pp. 49–50; *Hansard No. 6*, 1977, pp. 527–30, 577; Province of Natal, *Estimates of Expenditure*, N.P. 2/75, pp. 49/50; *Bantu Education Journal*, 1974, pp. 29, 35.

[a] The salary data refer only to maxima on the scale, they ignore the length of the scale and exclude fringe benefits such as housing subsidies, and they are rounded to the nearest R5.

[b] Primary school teachers have equivalent jobs but different qualifications. The salaries compared are those for junior certificate education plus a professional qualification in the case of Africans and matriculation plus a three-year qualification in other cases: the predominant scale for each race is used. Data are not available for school teachers after 1974.

The three-tier structure of salaries is illustrated forcefully by Table 6, which shows the maximum salary for each race in certain public sector occupations. African salaries are considerably lower than those of Whites in the same post, and the salaries of other races are generally intermediate. There is a pronounced

[35] Department of Statistics, *Population Census 1970. Occupations*, Report No. 02-05-04, Table D4. Public enterprises are excluded from the public sector.

[36] Statement by Dr. H. F. Verwoerd, then Minister of Native Affairs, reported in Institute of Race Relations, *A Survey of Race Relations in South Africa 1953/54*, p. 99. Hereafter the annual surveys of this Institute will be referred to as I.R.R. 1953/54, etc.

tendency for Black salaries in relation to White salaries to be higher in higher income posts, i.e. wage discrimination is reduced as the level of education required in a post increases. Thus African university professors and medical specialists are seen to receive respectively 92 and 80 per cent of the pay of their White counterparts, whereas African primary school teachers and police constables receive respectively 40 and 51 per cent. The tendency for relative wage discrimination to fall as White pay rises applies not only as between occupations but also quite commonly within the experience-related salary scales.

Part of the explanation for the difference in salary scales may be that the level of education required to obtain a post is higher for Whites. For instance, in primary school teaching most Africans have had two years less of formal education than most Whites, and Black police constables can begin service with two years less of schooling than White constables. Even if this additional education is highly valued, it is unlikely to explain why Africans receive no more than half the pay of Whites in these occupations. In posts requiring professional qualifications such as university teacher and doctor, the level of education required is the same for each race. Educational differences in the lower posts therefore partly explain the inverse relationship. Since the budgetary cost of reducing wage discrimination is less at the higher than at the lower levels which contain many more Black employees, finance may also enter into the explanation.

It is a declared government policy objective that, in the provision of public services, each race group should be served by members of the same group. Consequently in these occupations Blacks have greater upward mobility than in the private sector. However, in practice Whites still hold many of the senior posts and, because Blacks receive relatively fewer public services, proportionally fewer public service jobs are open to Blacks than to Whites in relation to population numbers. The public sector in South Africa has traditionally provided job security and a 'civilized living standard' to those Whites of low ability who could command only very low pay in the private sector. In recent years, under pressure of manpower shortage, the public sector enterprises have advanced Blacks into semi-skilled and artisan jobs, but not at the same rates of pay. For example, the South African Railways have been forced to employ Blacks as shunters, but in 1972 White shunters received a basic monthly wage on the scale R160–200, Africans R90–100, and other races R110–120.[37]

In the 1970s the government moved towards acceptance of the principle of 'equal pay for equal work'. This culminated in an announcement by the Prime Minister in 1977 that the racial differences in all public sector salary scales would be gradually and systematically eliminated.[38] Action has so far been concentrated on the highest posts, e.g. senior civil servants. The change in policy reflects a growing government concern to promote Black élite formation. Market pressures could also have operated in that the recent expansion of Black posts in the public sector may have generated a shortage in some professional occupations. However,

[37] Blacks are called 'train marshallers' but it is implausible that the minor differences in job content can explain the wage differences.

[38] *House of Assembly Debates* (*Hansard*), 1977, No. 12, p. 5640.

TABLE 7

Average Income of Male Employees by Level of Education Completed, 1970
(Rands per month)

	Whites R	Africans R	Africans as % Whites	Other Races R	Other Races as % Whites
No education—standard 6	225	53	24	64	28
Standards 7–8	255	67	26	115	45
Standards 9–10	315	87	28	160	51
Degree or diploma	510	102	20	*	*

* An open-ended size interval is crucial.

Sources: Africans: Bureau of Market Research, *Income and Expenditure Patterns of Non-White Urban Households*, Report Nos. 27.1, 27.14, 27.2, 27.15.

Others: South African Department of Statistics, *Population Census 1970, Level of Education*, Report No. 02-05-07, Tables A5, B5 and C5.

Notes: Being taken from two sources, the data are not strictly comparable. Income includes income from sources other than employment. African income is the weighted average in single and multiple person households in Johannesburg and Pretoria.

both these explanations are more persuasive in relation to the higher posts than to the lower.

VI. Wage Discrimination in Relation to Education

Of the various personal characteristics which determine efficiency, data are available on only one, formal education. Table 7 suggests very considerable racial income discrimination among people of the same educational level. However, this conclusion must be qualified in various ways. First, the data on income include income derived from sources other than employment: this tends to exaggerate the differences in earnings from employment. Secondly, the number of years of education is a poor indicator of education received. 'Bantu education' is notorious for its low quality, high pupil-teacher ratios, overcrowded classrooms, poorly qualified teachers not fluent in the medium of instruction, and rote learning.[39] Thirdly, it is possible that Whites have more experience, on-the-job training, fluency in the official languages, self-confidence and initiative, and that these characteristics contribute to the wage differences. Nevertheless, the income differences shown in the table are enormous, and they are very likely to reflect an element of wage discrimination. The inverse relationship between wage discrimination and income level, found in the public sector salary scales, is apparent in Table 7 except for the case of Africans with degrees.

Further light can be thrown on racial income differences by level of education by examining the employment opportunities open to educated Africans. Some evidence is available from a 1972 sample survey of nearly 500 urban African men and women who left secondary school between 1966 and 1971.[40] The sample was restricted to people who had written junior certificate (standard 8)—an educational

[39] Muriel Horrell, *Bantu Education to 1968*, South African Institute of Race Relations, 1968, pp. 150–6.

[40] Ann Perry, *African Secondary School Leavers: Employment Experiences and Attitudes to Employment*, South African Institute of Race Relations, 1974.

level normally regarded as the minimum for White school leavers—and 80 per cent of the sample had no more than junior certificate.[41] Some 25 per cent were unemployed and looking for work at the time of the survey; many of these had aspirations which were high in relation to opportunities. Of those who were employed, 14 per cent were teachers, 34 per cent clerical or routine white collar, 23 per cent skilled or semi-skilled manual or service workers, and 20 per cent were in unskilled work.[42] In the case of men, the median monthly pay in unskilled jobs was R44, in teaching and clerical jobs R58 and R62, and in skilled manual and driving R66 and R70 respectively.[43] Nevertheless, over half of the men aspired to a teaching or other professional job (suggesting that they perceived better lifetime prospects).[44] Nearly 90 per cent of the women aspired either to teaching or nursing jobs; and they saw very little opportunity for using their education except in these two occupations.[45] Another survey of Africans with at least junior certificate presented a similar picture: there was very limited access to skilled manual or to other than a few, low-grade white collar jobs.[46]

The 1970 census suggests a distinction between those whose highest schooling is a full secondary education (standard 10) and those with less (standards 8 and 9). In the former group 72 per cent of economically active Africans were in what roughly corresponds to the non-manual occupations (31 per cent were teachers, 24 per cent clerks and 11 per cent nurses); in the latter group, only 39 per cent were (13 per cent were teachers, 13 per cent clerks and 11 per cent nurses).[47] This helps to explain why over half the 1972 survey respondents had plans for further study, the majority giving an economic reason.[48] Nevertheless, it is clear that African secondary school leavers have a limited range of employment openings in which their education is of much value to them.

VII. White Worker and Employer Attitudes and Actions

Wage discrimination in South Africa cannot be understood without studying the attitudes and behaviour of the actors in the labour market. The interests of individuals and groups, the political and institutional framework which provides some actors individually or collectively with the power to pursue their interests, and the methods by which they are pursued, must each be examined.

We begin with the interests and powers of White workers. The basic determinant of the distribution of political power in South Africa is the fact that the franchise is exclusively White. This gives workers of the White race disproportionate influence in the framing of labour laws and policies. Only Non-Africans

[41] *Ibid.*, p. 8.
[42] *Ibid.*, p. 12.
[43] *Ibid.*, p. 52.
[44] *Ibid.*, p. 58.
[45] *Ibid.*, p. 58.
[46] M. Hubbard and V. Qunta, 'Education for Underemployment', South African Institute of Race Relations, 1975 (mimeo). The survey was conducted in Cape Town in 1973/4.
[47] Department of Statistics, *Population Census 1970. Occupations*, Report No. 02-05-11, Table D3. Persons with post-school diplomas are included. We define non-manual occupations as 'professional, technical and related worker', 'administrative and managerial worker' and 'clerical and related worker'.
[48] Ann Perry, *op. cit.*, pp. 21, 26.

can be members of legally recognized trade unions, and most White manual workers are unionized. Collective bargaining between employers and registered unions—on wages and conditions and on the designation of 'closed shop' grades or occupations —is carried on in Industrial Councils, and their agreements are given legal force in the industry. African trade unions, by contrast, enjoy almost no legal rights and are weak in membership. White workers see four main reasons to fear Black workers, concerning wage levels, jobs, status and power. Consider each in turn.[49]

White workers are accustomed to a relatively high standard of living, and they are concerned to defend their established wages against the competition of Blacks willing to work for lower pay. White wages could be determined either institutionally or by the market: as the result either of trade union power or of scarcity. If wages are determined competitively, White wages are driven down by market forces on the entry of Blacks to an occupation. To protect their wages White workers have an interest in erecting and maintaining barriers to Black entry, whether they be barriers to education or training, or statutory or customary job reservation.

If wages are determined institutionally, White workers may be able to protect their wage levels in the face of Black entry to an occupation. However, Black competition then brings another threat, that of displacement through wage undercutting. White workers therefore have an interest in maintaining not only their own wages but also those of their Black competitors. By insisting on 'the rate for the job', and also setting that rate, White workers may be able to protect both their wage levels and their jobs. The rate for the job has been the consistent policy of part of the White trade union movement, and it is embodied in industrial legislation, e.g. that governing the determinations of the Wage Board.

The other form of response to the threat of displacement is racial job reservation. The most notable example was the Rand Rebellion of 1922, arising from an attempt by the mine-owners to replace White miners with cheaper Black labour, after which the statutory colour bar was more firmly entrenched in the mining industry. In the post-war period, low-calibre Whites have retained semi-skilled jobs by applying political pressures: government has responded by means of statutory job reservation in the private sector and administrative job reservation in the public sector. Racial job reservation achieved through collective bargaining normally takes the form of closed shop agreements. The persistent full employment of Whites in the post-war period has reduced fears of displacement. When Blacks have taken over White jobs, this has been possible because Whites have found more attractive work.

White workers often perceive a social stigma attached to work performed by Black workers. They are generally unwilling to perform work entailing the same occupational status as Blacks, particularly if such work is performed in close proximity or if it is visible to the public. The importance of proximity is social and not physical: there is no general dislike of working with subordinate Blacks.

With the growth of employment and unionisation of Blacks, Whites may fear

[49] This account draws on Wolfgang H. Thomas (ed.), *Labour Perspectives on South Africa*, 1974, especially the chapter by Jeffrey Lever.

the loss of their power as workers. They may fear that Blacks organized in separate unions will collude with employers to work against the interests of White workers, or that Blacks may come to dominate mixed unions and pursue policies inimical to Whites, e.g. on the level at which the rate for the job is set. It is not obvious that the interests of Black workers in a union would differ from those of their White colleagues, but there could be some conflict of interest on such issues as wage structure and the use of union power for political ends. However, Blacks have not yet posed a serious threat to White worker power.

The South African trade union movement can be divided into three groups of roughly equal membership, the South African Confederation of Labour (SACL) on the right, unaffiliated unions in the centre, and the Trade Union Council of South Africa (TUCSA) on the left. The SACL draws its support from White workers largely in the public sector. It pursues a 'separationist' strategy: its unions are racially exclusive, and it attempts to eliminate racial competition by allocating different jobs to different races. Its most important weapon has been the colour bar, and it has relied on the support of government in securing job reservation. TUCSA officially follows a 'unionist' strategy, i.e. it accepts multiracial unionism and pursues the principle of the rate for the job irrespective of race in order to protect the interests of established workers. In this it has the support of Black as well as White members of mixed trade unions: it is only the Black would-be entrants who suffer. The distinction between the policies of the SACL and TUCSA can be exaggerated. The pressing shortage of White manpower, on the one hand, and the inadequacy of protection afforded by the rate for the job, on the other, have produced many hybrid responses.

We take the main objective of employers to be the pursuit of profit. Therefore they can be expected to favour the removal of the artificial barriers which raise White earnings, to press for the advancement of Blacks into White jobs, and for the payment of the rate for the job at a level determined by market forces and not by the White trade unions. A contrary, Marxist argument is that employers, in the pursuit of profit, use job discrimination to create divisions within the working class, and so weaken the bargaining power of labour or forestall the long run threat to the capitalist system. It is not implausible that employers as a group benefit from the division of the working class, i.e. their loss as a result of the power of White workers may be offset by their gain from the powerlessness of Black workers. However, it is implausible that an individual employer will on that account choose to maintain the privileges of his own White employees.

Our interpretation is supported by the claims of employers including many affiliates of British companies,[50] that it is in their interest to promote Blacks, and to press for that as hard as possible. The extreme shortage of skilled manpower in recent years has no doubt contributed to this view. The evidence to the House of Commons inquiry did not suggest that management in British affiliates regard Africans as inferior workers. Indeed, when asked, two companies asserted that, for the grades in which Africans and Whites performed the same jobs, the standard

[50] House of Commons, *op. cit.*, pp. 83–4.

of African labour is higher than that of White.[51] This result is to be expected because these overlapping grades contain the most successful Africans and the least successful Whites. A recent study of employers revealed that, of the firms which had replaced Whites with Blacks, 55 per cent claimed to have experienced an increase in productivity in the relevant operations and only 10 per cent claimed a decrease.[52]

Two qualifications are in order. The first stems from the enforced migrant labour system, by which about half the African urban employees are unsettled migrants.[53] Because migrants have less opportunity to acquire skills and employers less incentive to train them, they are at a disadvantage in competing with other workers. Secondly, it is more likely that Africans are no less efficient than Whites in manual jobs, such as semi-skilled operator or supervisor, than in white-collar jobs, for which the quality of education and command of the official languages are important.

Employers' freedom of action is of course limited by various constraints imposed by White workers, by government, and by customers. They are faced by e.g. negotiated closed shop agreements restricting certain occupations to Whites or Non-Africans, and—although statutory job reservation now occurs on only a very limited scale, potentially affecting 2.3 per cent of the labour force[54]—by the fear that job reservation will be introduced if their White employees complain. It was a common feeling among witnesses before the House of Commons Committee that management had to carry White workers with them on African advancement, and that to proceed very rapidly would be counterproductive. The cost of producing separate offices, cloakrooms and canteens, as required by law, could deter the replacement of Whites, especially in the case of office work. The prejudice of White consumers against being served by Black salespeople, and against the provision of certain other non-menial services by Blacks, has impeded employers from advancing Blacks into these positions.

This picture of profit-maximizing managers constrained only by circumstances beyond their control is too simple. Virtually all employers and managers in South Africa are of the White race. Even in multinational companies the majority of managerial staff normally are White South Africans. While the good relationship which often exists between management and White workers is likely to be based on rational economic calculation by management, there may also be an element of racial sympathy and fellow-feeling. Management, too, may perceive a threat to White status if Black and White do the same work for the same pay. In the words of a businessman: '. . . by a combination of national policy and business apathy we provide (Africans) with the sort of environment which produces low productivity—and then we rationalize the situation by saying that they are lazy, can't learn, won't accept responsibility and all that rot'.[55] The attitudes and stereotypes held

[51] Unilever and G.E.C., in *Minutes of Evidence*, Vol. I, Q297 and Q425.
[52] L. Schlemmer and M. Boulanger, 'Race and employment patterns among larger employers in Durban: a brief profile' (mimeo), p. 11, published in L. Schlemmer and E. Webster (eds), *op. cit.*, 1977.
[53] See Francis Wilson, *Migrant Labour in South Africa*, 1972, esp. Ch. 9.
[54] I.R.R. 1976, p. 285.
[55] D. A. Etheredge, 'Wages, Productivity and Opportunity', South African Institute of Race Relations, 1973 (mimeo).

by employers can be self-fulfilling through the response which they elicit from Black employees. Some African workers may therefore be less efficient than Whites precisely because less is expected of them; and some may never be given an opportunity to disprove managerial stereotypes. Firms differ in the extent to which they pursue effective policies to promote Blacks.

It is frequently the case that both White workers and employers favour the payment of the rate for the job, and disagree only on its level. However, for those industries in which White workers have combined for the overt exclusion of Africans from certain jobs, the very process of bargaining between employers and trade unions on African advancement can increase wage discrimination. 'Productivity agreements' are negotiated, by which Africans are promoted into jobs previously performed by Whites and the affected Whites are compensated with promotion or 'job enrichment' involving higher pay. Pay in the Africanized jobs is often reduced immediately, especially if there is 'job dilution' or 'fragmentation', but otherwise gradually with inflation. For these reasons, the elimination of wage discrimination—through the achievement of a non-racial wage scale based on job evaluation—is improbable in such industries as gold mining.

VIII. A Theory of Wage Discrimination

Are the neo-classical theories of wage discrimination relevant to the South African case? It was argued above that a 'taste for discrimination' in the form of physical aversion is unimportant. More important is the concern of Whites about the loss of status which results from the sharing of an occupation with Blacks. While it would be foolish to deny that many Whites possess some form of racial prejudice, we suggest that their pursuit of economic self-interest may well be the main cause of discrimination. Even if employers regard Blacks as no less able than Whites, they may still be willing to restrict Black access to jobs. The main reason is the power of White workers, whether through informal pressures or formalized collective bargaining, and the need for employers to keep on good terms with their White employees. Thus the exercise of power by Whites to exclude Blacks from jobs or from training often has the acquiescence of employers. For these reasons it is possible for Blacks of equal productive potential to be paid less than Whites without the Whites being replaced. The similarity with the neo-classical models is that there is a sense in which the cost to employers of hiring Black labour exceeds its wage. However, the reason is different: it is the collective action of White workers which imposes the cost on employers and not a 'taste for discrimination'. Moreover, the 'cost' generally takes the form of straightforward prohibition.

Because of the implicit threat to their jobs, White workers do not think in terms of the higher wage necessary to compensate them for working with Blacks. On the contrary, it was in order to prevent undercutting by Blacks that the trade union policy of the rate for the job evolved. Given racial equality of wages for a job, within a firm or Industrial Council, White workers rely on racial solidarity or perceptions of Black inferiority on the part of employers, and on employers' use of race as a screening device, to provide security of employment.

Where there is wage discrimination initiated by White workers, the long run prediction is racial segregation by plant and the elimination of wage discrimination. Firms which are located in the 'African Homelands' or in declared 'Border Areas' are not subject to racial employment regulations, and in practice there is normally no impediment to the promotion of able Africans in these areas. The theory therefore predicts that wage discrimination would cause wholly Africanized plants to be established in the Homeland areas. However, the incentive so provided for decentralization is frequently offset by the disadvantages of decentralized location, e.g. transport costs and the higher cost of employing non-replaceable Whites. Racial specialization by plant has not occurred on any significant scale.

Whereas the neo-classical theories of wage discrimination have limited application, the segmentation theories provide insights to the South African labour market. It is only by means of job discrimination that wage discrimination can be explained. The job competition model is relevant: White workers take precedence in the job queue and in access to on-the-job training. Through selection for jobs and subsequent training on-the-job, some White workers have higher productivity than Black workers who were initially of the same productive potential. However, we need not accept that wages are determined in the way that Thurow has claimed —by a mixture of bargaining and sociology—rather than by the forces of demand and institutionally determined supply.

The internal labour market concept is also relevant: given the formalized or informal power of White workers, a set of administrative rules—reflecting a compromise between employers and White employees—is commonly established. This offers the White workers preferential access to jobs and it makes Black advancement into previously White jobs a matter not for the market but for negotiation. On the other hand, most African workers form the supply side of an external labour market in which, owing to the lack of job security and the impediments to effective unionisation, employers are able to harness market forces. However, there is one piece of evidence which tells against an internal/external labour market distinction by race, in so far as labour turnover can be taken as the distinguishing characteristic. Considering 'productive and related workers' in manufacturing in 1974, we find that a higher proportion of White than of African employees (61 per cent compared with 48 per cent) were discharged or resigned during the year.[56] It is great shortage more frequently than an internal labour market which provides high pay and sure employment for skilled manual Whites.

The most fruitful concept for explaining wage discrimination in South Africa is that of 'crowding'. This can be used not only to explain why Whites are generally skilled and high-paid, and Blacks generally unskilled and low-paid, as in the theory of non-competing groups outlined above;[57] it can also explain why Blacks are paid less than Whites of the same ability and human capital.

The clearest and most important cases of wage discrimination are to be found in the public sector. It occurs in the public sector because the government does not have profit objectives, and its need to reduce costs does not override political

[56] Department of Statistics, *Bulletin of Statistics*, March 1976, Table 2.8.1.
[57] See p. 248.

objectives. The government provides job security and a 'civilized living standard' for the unskilled minority of Whites. It also discriminates on pay in occupations requiring certain levels of education and qualification. This is easiest done in those occupations for which it is virtually a monopsonist in the employment of Blacks, e.g. nursing, medical practice, administration, and teaching. Both private prejudice and public policy are responsible: it is not customary for Black nurses, teachers or doctors to serve Whites, and it is prohibited within the state sector. In this way the market for their services is separated, and they cannot compete with their White colleagues.

The opportunity cost for Whites in these occupations is higher than that for Blacks. They are able to earn a scarcity rent wherever there is substantial competition between the private and the public sectors, as in the case of White doctors and administrators. Where there is no competition among employers within an occupation, there are still opportunities in other occupations. Even where skills are fairly specific, recruitment to an occupation is sensitive to income. Thus the state monopsonist cannot maintain the supply of White teachers unless it pays them at least the earnings—adjusted for non-pecuniary differences—received by other Whites with the same education.

The state employs the vast majority of Blacks with education. Their opportunities for private sector employment in any occupation requiring education are expanding but still very limited. Here social custom and practice—which in the case of non-manual employment are more important than collective bargaining—operate to exclude Blacks. Custom and practice are fortified by the government's administrative rule that no Black shall supervise a White and by the laws requiring racially separate facilities. The effective lack of competition from the private sector means that the government needs to pay Black nurses, teachers and administrators little more than the earnings of uneducated Black workers in order to retain their services. In order to recruit, it needs to pay only this sum plus compensation for the private cost of education and training.

The degree of racial wage discrimination is likely to reflect the extent of racial differences in transfer earnings. The greater are opportunities for educated Blacks outside the public sector, the less scope is there for public sector wage discrimination. This may help to explain why the percentage rate of wage discrimination is lower for the higher posts in the public sector. The fact that Coloured and Asian people are less subject to occupational discrimination than are Africans may explain why the degree of wage discrimination is less for these other races, e.g. as revealed in Table 7.

The private firm employing educated Black labour may well find that it can meet its needs by paying only slightly more than the public sector does. However, institutional constraints prevent the large-scale substitution of Black for White workers and the equalization of Black and White pay which the individual pursuit of profit would then imply. As Blacks take over the more skilled manual jobs formerly held by Whites, so the previous artificial scarcity in a job gives way to an abundance of trainable—and eventually of trained—labour. Even if the replacement labour is no less well-trained and equally efficient, market forces, which previously raised the wage in response to the scarcity of labour, now tend to depress it in response to abundance.

The distinction between general and specific skills, which has been touched on at different points, deserves more thorough treatment. Because general skills possess a market value, it is a competitive market prediction that employees both benefit from and pay for general training. Specific skills are of value to only one employer, and hence he can be expected to derive the benefits and bear the costs of specific training. However, in so far as training costs are a function of labour turnover and turnover is a function of the wage, the employer has an incentive to reduce turnover by sharing some of the benefits of specific training with employees. The excess supply of recruits thus induced enables him also to pass on part of the costs. The precise sharing of the costs and benefits depends, for example, on the relations between turnover and wages and between turnover and training costs, and on attitudes to risk.[58]

The distinction between general and specific skills is relevant to racial wage discrimination in two ways. First, it is possible that Whites, with their greater formal education and choice of jobs, tend to have more general skills than do Blacks of similar skill level. That would be consistent with the labour turnover figures cited above. For instance, the training and certificate of a White artisan make his skill more marketable than that of his African 'artisan assistant' who has learned on the job. Part of the difference in pay between the two may thus be due to the greater share of the product of skill which the White is able to command. Secondly, the employee share of the benefit even from specific training may be lower for Africans than for other races. There are bureaucratic controls which restrict the mobility of Africans between employers, particularly in the case of workers recruited in the reserves on annual contracts. In so far as African workers are 'tied in' to an employer, the employer has less need to share the benefits of specific training. Although less important than 'crowding', this may help to explain the different transfer earnings for Whites and Africans of similar productivity.

Some of the arguments above may be stated and elaborated in a partial equilibrium framework by reference to Fig. 1, which shows the wage rate (w) for a certain category of educated manpower (or quality of labour) and White and Black labour with that level of education (L_w and L_b respectively). The crucial assumption is that the demand curves for White and Black labour (D_w and D_b) can be separated, i.e. that certain jobs are restricted to Whites only, thus preventing Black labour from being substituted for White. Market forces produce an equilibrium in the White labour market at a, the intersection of D_w and S_w. If White labour can be substituted for Black (even though the reverse possibility is assumed away), the equilibrium value of w_w imposes an upper limit to the demand curve for Black labour. Blacks have a lower supply price than Whites: the horizontal section of S_b' is below that of S_w. Two Black supply curves are shown, S_b (if supply is limited) and S_b' (if supply is unlimited over the relevant range); M_b (corresponding to S_b) is the marginal cost curve facing a monopsonist. Given S_b', equilibrium is

[58] Gary S. Becker, *Human Capital*, second edition, 1975, Ch. II,1.

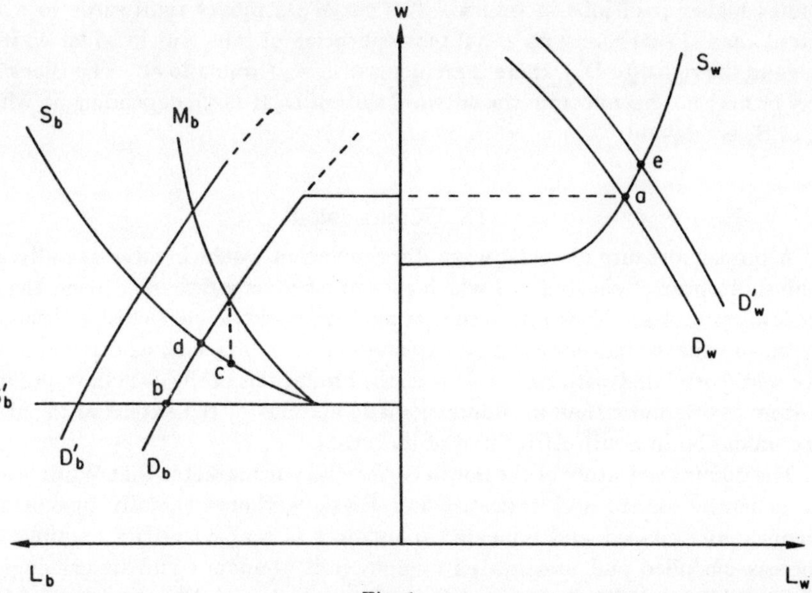

Fig. 1

at b; given S_b, equilibrium is at c (if the employer is a monopsonist) or at d (if there is competition for labour). At c and d, educated Blacks can earn a scarcity rent; at b, the wage equals their transfer earnings. If S_b becomes perfectly inelastic when it ceases to be horizontal, the government monopsonist need pay no more than the wage corresponding to b.

In practice there may be elements in the market for educated Black labour corresponding to all four points a, b, c and d. Where government possesses a virtual monopsony, as in the case of nurses, the Black wage corresponds to that at b or at c. Where the monopsony is less complete, as in the case of various clerical posts, the wage may be depicted at b or at d. The forces underlying wage determination at point a are not normally found in the public sector, which is the predominant employer of educated Blacks. Now consider the private sector. Where a white-collar private sector union insists on the rate for the job, as in the case of bank clerks, Black workers receive a wage corresponding to a, but their entry is thereby controlled. However, while point a may apply to a specific occupation involving a particular educational level, it is unlikely to apply to an educational level as a whole. We have argued that the process of crowding produces wage discrimination between occupations. The private sector Black wage for the given educational level is therefore likely in most cases to be determined by the forces corresponding to points b or d.

The effect of economic growth in moving the colour bar up the hierarchy of jobs can also be illustrated in Fig. 1. Growth increases the demand for White labour, so tending to raise the competitively determined wage. However, employers may negotiate the transfer to Blacks of previously reserved jobs, offering incumbent

Whites higher paid jobs in return. The curve D_w moves rightwards to a lesser extent than if there were no racial reclassification of jobs, but in so far as it does move to the right (to D'_w), there is an increase in w_w (from a to e). The Black wage may or may not benefit from the outward shift of D_b (to D'_b), depending on whether S_b or S'_b is relevant.

IX. Conclusion

A proper measure of racial wage discrimination would involve a multivariate analysis to predict earnings, in which race appears as a dummy among the independent variables. However, even that analysis could be inconclusive if there was reason to believe that unmeasured explanatory variables such as drive and initiative were correlated with race. As it is, the limitations of the data have prevented us from giving more than an impressionistic account of the extent of racial wage discrimination in South Africa and of its causes.

The dominant feature of the South African labour market is that White workers are generally skilled and educated and Black workers generally unskilled and uneducated. Skilled and educated manpower is scarce and its earnings high, whereas unskilled and uneducated manpower is abundant and its earnings low. Where Whites and Blacks perform the same type of work the protection of White jobs against Black undercutting permits wage discrimination in both the public sector (where the wage discrimination is overt) and the private sector (where it may be concealed by differences in job title). If Blacks are assigned to jobs with lower productivity and pay than their education and ability warrant, that is wage discrimination no less for being disguised. Private sector wage discrimination within a job is not widely found at the level of the firm or negotiating unit, because of the security which equal pay offers White workers. By preventing wage discrimination within an occupation, White workers achieve occupational discrimination and hence the possibility of wage discrimination between occupations. There is often a big wage gap between the jobs performed by Whites and those performed only by Blacks. As Blacks of no less efficiency take over a job completely from Whites, so the move from scarcity to abundance of labour tends to depress the wage for the job. The small proportion of Whites who are unskilled are assured of public sector employment at a wage above the market rate or are protected against competition by statutory or bargained job reservation. The small proportion of Blacks who are educated are employed mainly in the public sector at a wage reflecting their low transfer earnings, and are generally unable to compete directly with educated Whites.

Our chosen subject is wage discrimination and yet much of the paper has been concerned with job discrimination. There is no inconsistency: why people with the same economic characteristics receive different income is a theoretically interesting and socially important question, but the answer has involved our studying differential access to jobs. The theories of labour market segmentation provide valuable insights. In particular, wage discrimination is seen to result from the exclusion from certain jobs of Blacks whose economic characteristics are appropriate, and their 'crowding' into others for which the demand is limited in relation to supply. It follows from the crowding explanation that the current rapid expansion of Black education need not improve the racial distribution of income unless employment opportunities are also expanded.

Many of the models of economic discrimination developed to analyse racial income differences in the United States have limited application to South Africa, based as they are on a 'taste for discrimination'. There is a case for regarding discrimination as endogenous to the labour market. There are instances in which race is used as a screening device by employers, and here prejudice may be entwined with the profit motive. However, the most plausible reason for discrimination in the South African case lies in the possibility of White workers raising their incomes by means of job discrimination, and in their power to do so through various forms of collective action.[59] There is no economic incentive for individual workers to break away from the White coalition. Economic discrimination in South Africa is deeply rooted in the economic interests of White workers and is not merely the result of moral deviation or irrational racial prejudice. In establishing these results we have had to go beyond the conventional boundaries of economics to examine motives, institutions and collective behaviour.

It is a common view among observers that there is some move towards the acceptance of the principle of equal pay for equal work in the private sector.[60] Pressure for a reduction in wage discrimination comes from three sources. Economic pressure—acute shortage of Whites for various jobs—can force Whites to accept Black competition, and they then choose to protect themselves by insisting on the rate for the job. There are perhaps 1000 foreign-owned firms operating in South Africa. Pressure emanating from abroad has recently had some impact on the labour policies of these producers. For instance, the British government has laid down a Code of Practice which incorporates the following guideline: 'A company's wage structure should be determined independently of race, according to principles of job evaluation'.[61] There can also be a political response from the group being discriminated against. This, or the threat of it, may help to explain the evolving policy of Black élite formation and the tendency during the 1970s to reduce wage discrimination in the public sector. That trend can be seen as part of a response to the changing balance of power.

Institute of Economics and Statistics,
University of Oxford.
University of Natal.

[59] This reason for discrimination is not necessarily confined to South Africa. An account of trade union practices in the United States reveals similar—albeit increasingly disguised—forms of job discrimination by some unions. See Herbert Hill, 'Comment' in Ashenfelter and Rees, *op. cit.*, pp. 113–23.

[60] See, for instance, Wolfgang Thomas, *op. cit.*, pp. 89, 117; House of Commons, *Minutes of Evidence*, Vol. I, p. 160.

[61] House of Commons, *op. cit.*, p. 101.

[9]

Labor Market Discrimination in a Poor Urban Economy

by J. B. Knight and R. H. Sabot***

Labor market discrimination by sex and by race in a poor urban economy is analyzed using a survey of manufacturing employees in Tanzania. There are large differences in mean wages by both sex and race. Using techniques previously applied to developed countries, it is found that, whereas the sex difference in mean wages can be explained mainly in terms of sex differences in personal characteristics, the race difference is mainly the result of wage and job discrimination. An attempt is made to explain the results, which run counter to common presuppositions about discrimination.

I. INTRODUCTION

Distinguishing between differences in earnings which can be justified on efficiency grounds and those which, by misallocating labor, are inefficient is relevant to the debate, hotly contested in many developing countries, over wages policy. According to this distinction, government interventions to alter the earnings structure on equity grounds may either improve or worsen allocative efficiency. By labor market discrimination it is generally meant that some workers are paid more than others with the same endowment of productive economic characteristics by virtue of some non-economic personal characteristic. The existence of discrimination implies that governments have an opportunity simultaneously to improve the distribution of income and the efficiency with which labor is allocated. The perceived injustice of discrimination has spurred the growth of civil rights movements and of remedial government legislation in the industrialized social democracies. Discrimination is thus an important political issue irrespective of the costs it imposes or its implications for the distribution of income. Despite the policy relevance of the phenomenon in poor countries, discrimination has been more intensively studied in rich countries, largely because of the lack of appropriate data.

In this paper we apply to detailed data from Tanzania what in the rich countries have come to be the conventional tools of analysis of discrimination. The data set we use was generated by a 1971 establishment-based survey of some 1,000 randomly selected workers in Tanzania's manufacturing sector, specially designed by one of the authors to avoid the deficiencies in the usual labor force data in poor countries which preclude detailed analysis of

* Institute of Economics and Statistics, University of Oxford.
** Development Research Department, The World Bank, Washington, D.C.

wage structures and of what they reveal about the determinants of wages and the functioning of labor markets.[1]

Our concern is with discrimination by sex and by race. Our results are surprising. They run counter to two common presumptions about discrimination. One is that development can be expected to bring changes in attitudes and institutions which diminish arbitrary disadvantages inflicted on women by sex discrimination in the labor market: such discrimination is found to be far smaller in Tanzania than in the United States. The other presumption is that racial discrimination is practised either by a majority group with power against a minority lacking such power or in some instances such as South Africa by a minority against a relatively powerless majority: we find evidence for Tanzania of discrimination in favor of the non-African minority group with apparently limited power.

Section II outlines the methods we employ to analyze labor market discrimination in Tanzania. Section III assesses the extent of sex discrimination and Section IV the extent of race discrimination. In Section V we draw out some of the implications of our findings.

II. THE METHOD

Our aim is to decompose the difference in mean wages between males and females or between Africans and non-Africans into the component 'explained' by differences in economic characteristics between the two groups and the 'unexplained' component which can be regarded as reflecting the extent of labor market discrimination. Within the unexplained component we attempt to distinguish wage and job discrimination. The distinction is relevant where occupation is itself one of the variables determining earnings. Wage discrimination occurs if, even within occupations, group differences in mean personal characteristics cannot entirely explain group differences in mean earnings. Job discrimination occurs if, for non-economic reasons, the different sexes or races have unequal access to the higher-paying occupations.

Our procedure for measuring discrimination follows that conventionally used in industrialized countries.[2] The standard technique for measuring discrimination when two groups differ in their personal characteristics and in the function relating these characteristics to earnings is to compare their actual mean wages with their mean wages if all were paid according to the same 'earnings structure', that is, the same constant term and set of coefficients on the independent variables.

Assume that the mean wage of men is $\bar{w}_m$ and that of women $\bar{w}_f$ (we could equally use $\bar{w}_a$ and $\bar{w}_n$, denoting Africans and non-Africans respectively). Assume that the mean wage of men is determined by the earnings function

$$\bar{w}_m = f_m(\bar{x}_m) \tag{1}$$

where x_m is a vector of characteristics applicable to men and $\bar{x}_m$ denotes their mean values; there is a corresponding expression for women. The mean wage which women would receive if they were paid according to the male wage is $f_m(\bar{x}_f)$.

The gross difference in mean wages (G) between men and women can be divided into the part 'explained' by different personal characteristics ($\bar{w}_m - f_m(\bar{x}_f)$), and the unexplained part ($f_m(\bar{x}_f) - \bar{w}_f$), reflecting differences in the constant terms and coefficients of the regression equations for men and women:

$$G = \bar{w}_m - \bar{w}_f = (\bar{w}_m - f_m(\bar{x}_f)) + (f_m(\bar{x}_f) - \bar{w}_f) = E + D \text{ respectively} \quad (2)$$

where E is the explained and D the unexplained part of the gross difference. The estimation of the wage received by men if they are paid according to the female wage structure permits a corresponding decomposition.

That part of G which is due to labor market discrimination is in turn decomposable into the parts attributable to wage and job discrimination.[3] The choice of occupation can influence the wage a worker receives: occupation may be one of the personal characteristics included among the independent variables in the earnings function. The finding of significant coefficients on dummy variables representing occupation would not affect the analysis if the determinants of occupational attainment were the same for men and women. However, job discrimination may cause men and women who otherwise have the same characteristics to work in different occupations. Thus for men the sample proportion in occupation i is given by

$$p_{im} = g_m(\bar{x}_m). \quad (3)$$

The probability of women attaining occupation i if their occupational attainment was determined in the same way as that of men would be $g_m(\bar{x}_f)$.

The gross difference in mean wages can be decomposed as follows:

$$\begin{aligned}
\bar{w}_m - \bar{w}_f &= \sum_i (p_{im}\bar{w}_{im} - p_{if}\bar{w}_{if}) \\
&= \sum_i (p_{im} f_{im}(\bar{x}_{im}) - p_{if} f_{if}(\bar{x}_{if})) \\
&= \sum_i p_{if}(f_{im}(\bar{x}_{im}) - f_{if}(\bar{x}_{if})) \\
&\quad + \sum_i f_{im}(\bar{x}_{im})(p_{im} - p_{if}) \qquad (4a) \\
&= W + J \text{ respectively} \\
&= \sum_i p_{if}(f_{im}(\bar{x}_{if}) - f_{if}(\bar{x}_{if})) \\
&\quad + \sum_i p_{if}(f_{im}(\bar{x}_{im}) - f_{im}(\bar{x}_{if})) \\
&\quad + \sum_i f_{im}(\bar{x}_{im})(p_{im} - g_m(\bar{x}_f)) \\
&\quad + \sum_i f_{im}(\bar{x}_{im})(g_m(\bar{x}_f) - p_{if}) \qquad (4b) \\
&= WD + WE + JE + JD \text{ respectively.}
\end{aligned}$$

WD represents wage discrimination, since it isolates the effect of sex differences in wage structure. WE is the part explained by differences in personal characteristics, since both wage structure and job proportions are being held constant. JE and JD together show the contribution of occupation to G. JE is the explained part, reflecting differences in occupational attainment which are due to differences in personal characteristics: the male occupational attainment function is applied to both men and women. JD represents job discrimination since it isolates the effect of sex differences in occupational attainment which cannot be explained by group differences in personal characteristics. The alternative decomposition of G introduces $\sum_i p_{im}(f_{if}(\bar{x}_{if}))$ instead of $\sum_i p_{if}(f_{im}(\bar{x}_{im}))$ to derive (4'a) and (4'b), not shown.

III. DISCRIMINATION BY SEX

Female manufacturing workers are a rather select group in Tanzania. While 15 per cent of all urban adult males are employed in manufacturing, only 1.6 per cent of females are so engaged. This difference is largely a result of the lower participation rate of urban women and the under-representation of female labor force participants in wage employment.[4] Women wage-earners are not only under-represented but also subject to a higher degree of selectivity by level of education. Despite the markedly lower educational attainment of the female than of the male population and labor force, male and female wage-earners have roughly equivalent levels of education. This applies as well to the manufacturing segment of the wage sector: male manufacturing employees have, on average, 4.0 years of formal schooling and females 3.9 years. When the equivalence of the educational levels of males and females is set alongside the difference in mean earnings between them, the comparison is suggestive of discrimination. The mean monthly wage of female employees in our manufacturing sample is 276 shillings; the mean for males is 379 sh., that is, 37 per cent above that for females.

The mean values for males and females of the independent variables included in the earnings functions that will serve as the basis for our assessment of wage discrimination suggest that women are at a disadvantage in their occupational distribution. Whereas 34 per cent of male workers are in supervisory or skilled occupations, only four per cent of female workers are in these occupations; no fewer than 58 per cent of women are unskilled (see Table 3). Again, given the evidence of educational attainment, the differences in occupational distributions reinforce the impression of labor market discrimination. Qualifying this impression, however, are some other sex differences in personal characteristics. More men (13 per cent) have had formal training than women workers (four per cent). The proportion of men aged 35 or older is higher than that of women (21 versus 7 per cent) and, in part reflecting the age distribution, men have greater seniority in the firm (6.1 versus 3.8 years) and considerably more experience in previous wage employment (3.0 versus 0.5 years) than women.

To what extent is the sex structure of wages the result of differences between men and women in personal characteristics other than education, and to what extent is it the product of discrimination? When an earnings function for the sample as a whole with the natural logarithm of monthly wages (Z) as the dependent variable and a full set of independent variables including dummy variables for different occupations is estimated, the coefficient on the dummy variable denoting male sex (S1)[5] is slightly positive

(.042) but insignificant, being smaller than its standard error. This preliminary result suggests that in Tanzania's manufacturing sector, men and women with the same personal economic characteristics and type of job receive roughly the same pay. However, the coefficients on the independent variables in the whole sample earnings function are constrained to be the same for both males and females. This may result in an underestimate of the independent impact of sex on wages if, for instance, the returns to education are higher for males. Estimates of separate earnings functions for males and females are presented in Table 1. A comparison of regressions a and c suggests that coefficients do indeed vary with sex. The coefficients on

TABLE 1

EARNINGS FUNCTIONS FOR MALES AND FEMALES

Independent Variable	Coefficient: Males a	Males b	Females c	Females d
Non-African race (T2)	0.594**	0.711**	0.488**	0.834**
Years of education (E)	0.053**	0.078**	0.030*	0.049**
Years of current employment (L1)	0.029**	0.035**	0.029	0.013
Years of previous employment (L4)	0.028**	0.030**	0.089*	0.096**
Formal training, 3 months or less (F1)	0.069	0.089	0.037	0.054
Formal training, more than 3 months (F2)	0.131*	0.191**	-0.097	-0.092
Age 15-19 (A1)	-0.255**	-0.331**	-0.003	-0.018
Age 35-49 (A3)	0.158**	0.168	0.422**	0.415*
Age 50 or more (A4)	-0.005	-0.008	x	x
Regular employment status (R2)	0.359**	0.392**	0.523	0.213
Supervisory (O1)	0.601**	-	x	-
Clerical (O2)	0.480**	-	0.697**	-
Headman/skilled (O3)	0.238**	-	0.270	-
Semi-skilled (O4)	0.029	-	0.057	-
Constant term	4.681	4.633	4.911	4.849
R^2	0.591	0.533	0.742	0.628
S.E.E.	0.393	0.418	0.268	0.321
F	78.3	85.1	16.7	13.3
N	803.	810	72.	74.
Dependent mean (Z)	5.710	5.707	5.422	5.428

Notes: * Indicates in this, and in subsequent, tables that the coefficient is significant at the 5 per cent level.

** Indicates in this, and in subsequent, tables that the coefficient is significant at the 1 per cent level.

x Indicates in this, and in subsequent, tables that the coefficient could not be computed.

The base sub-categories of the dummy variables in this, and in subsequent, tables are T1 (African race), S2 (female sex), O5 (unskilled occupation), F3 (no formal training), R1 (casual employment status) and A2 (age 20-34).

education, formal training and seniority are significant only for men. The impression that, in marked contrast to men, women are not rewarded for accumulating human capital, is nevertheless misleading. No fewer than 78 per cent of women are in unskilled or semi-skilled manual jobs. As the returns to education (for both males and females) are insignificant for semi-skilled and unskilled workers,[6] it is not surprising to discover that for women as a group the returns to education are low. Regression c indicates that the coefficient on the clerical occupation dummy is positive, large and significant: on average, women in clerical jobs earn 101 per cent more than unskilled women.[7] Furthermore, the partial correlation coefficient between the education and clerical occupation variables is high, 0.43. Women reap returns to education mainly in the form of access to clerical jobs; these account for 18 per cent of female employees. Estimates of the earning functions without the occupation dummy variables (regressions b and d) confirm that in regression c the clerical occupation variable captures the returns to education. In regression d the coefficient on education is positive and significant: on average each additional year of education adds 4.9 per cent to a female employee's earnings.[8] Although women do earn returns to their human capital, differences in rates of return nevertheless persist in regressions b and d.

Table 2 presents the contributions to the gross difference (G) that are made by differences in personal characteristics (E) and by sex discrimination (D). These are estimated on alternative assumptions, namely, that the male 'earnings structure' applies to females (corresponding to equation (2)) and that the female structure applies to males. The method of decomposing G is to estimate E as the sum of the product of coefficients and the sex difference in the average values of characteristics and to estimate D as the residual.[9] As is to be expected, personal characteristics explain a somewhat higher percentage of G when the results are based on regressions which include occupation dummies among the independent variables than when based on regressions excluding occupation. Nevertheless, the largest single contribution to E is made not by the occupation variables but by the experience variables; the contribution of education is slight. The most important finding of the table is that the contribution of personal characteristics is overwhelming, and that of discrimination slight. The estimates of D based on the male earnings structure represent five or 17 per cent of G; indeed, the estimates based on the female structure show the contribution of discrimination to be negative! The results based on the male coefficients are more reliable, however: the female regressions contain under 80 observations and their results are sensitive to the values of insignificant coefficients on the occupation dummy variables. We conclude from this exercise that sex discrimination in Tanzania is negligible.

Our findings are at odds with the findings of an important role for sex discrimination in analogous studies for the United States. For instance, Oaxaca estimated that the proportion of the gross difference in mean wages attributable to sex discrimination was 74 per cent for whites and 92 per cent for blacks (54 and 45 per cent respectively including occupation).[9a]

The inclusion of occupational dummy variables produces significant coefficients. There is also a marked difference in occupational distribution between men and women (Table 3). The view that women are 'crowded' into inferior jobs, and that this is the cause of their wage disadvantage, has a long history in various countries.[10] These considerations raise two questions: To what extent is G due to occupational differences (JE + JD in equation 4)? To what extent is it due to occupational discrimination (JD alone) rather than occupational differences which can be explained by differences in group mean characteristics (JE)?

In answering the first question we use the relation based on (4a):

$$JD + JE = \sum_i f_{im}(\bar{x}_{im})(p_{im} - p_{if}).$$

We apply the mean wage of men to the proportions of men and of women respectively in each occupation. The mean wage of males using female occupational weights is 338 sh. The resulting estimate of JD + JE (derived in Table 3) implies that different job proportions explain 42 per cent of G. The alternative decomposition of G indicates that different job proportions explain only 22 per cent of G.

The separation of JE and JD requires an estimate of $g_m(\bar{x}_f)$, that is, what the distribution of female occupations would be if it were determined according to the male occupational attainment function. A function must be estimated to predict the occupational attainment of men on the basis of their personal characteristics, which in turn involves earnings functions stratified by occupation and the application of a multinomial logit model.[11] We adopt a similar approach but data constraints necessitate a cruder method: our sample is too small to permit the estimation of regressions for sub-samples stratified by both occupation and sex. Education and occupation are highly correlated in Tanzania,[12] but the educational attainment of male and female employees in our sample is almost equal, despite the marked difference in their occupational distributions. The main sex difference in personal characteristics lies in the extent of employment experience. This difference can be taken into account in measuring $g_m(\bar{x}_f)$. We estimate the proportions of men and of women in the five occupations, stratifying by five experience groups, and then apply the male experience-specific occupational proportions to females in order to obtain an estimate of the female occupational distribution in the absence of job discrimination (column $g_m(\bar{x}_f)$ of Table 3).[13] Two estimates of JD can be made, according to (4b) and (4′b); they represent 23 and 10 per cent of G respectively. Even the higher percentage amounts to only 28 sh. per month. Our estimates of JD suggest that job discrimination by sex in Tanzania is not an important problem.

There is another indication that the influence of sex differences in occupational attainment on the gross difference in mean earnings is minor. If it were major, we would expect the exclusion of the occupation variables from the earnings function to increase the significance of the sex dummy variable. When the earnings function for the sample as a whole is re-estimated with the dummy variables denoting occupation excluded, the coefficient on sex remains very small (.055) and insignificant, that is, males do not earn a premium even if there is no standardization for occupation.

TABLE

THE EFFECTS OF DISCRIMINATION AND PERSONAL CHARACTERISTICS

	Natural logarithms (sh.p.m.)
Mean wage, male ($\bar{w}_m$)	5.710
Mean wage, female ($\bar{w}_f$)	5.422
Gross difference in mean wages ($\bar{w}_m - \bar{w}_f$)	0.288

Wage structure:	Male		Female	
Occupation dummies:	Included	Excluded	Included	Excluded
Contribution of personal characteristics (E): $f_i(\bar{x}_m - \bar{x}_f)$	0.273	0.232	0.391	0.295
of which, due to:				
experience (L1, L4)	0.136	0.155	0.288	0.271
education	0.008	0.011	0.004	0.007
occupation (01-04)	0.054	-	0.028	-
other variables	0.075	0.066	0.071	0.017
Residual contribution of sex discrimination (D): $f_m(\bar{x}_i) - f_f(\bar{x}_i)$	0.015	0.056	-0.107	-0.007

Notes: 1. The absolute values of mean wages are geometric means; they differ from the arithmetic means ($\bar{w}_m$ = 378.7, $\bar{w}_f$ = 276.3) but their ratios are very similar.

2. Using the male wage structure, the contribution of personal characteristics is $f_m(\bar{x}_m - \bar{x}_f)$ and the corresponding residual contribution of sex discrimination is $f_m(\bar{x}_f)-f_f(\bar{x}_f)$.

2

ON THE GROSS DIFFERENCE IN MEAN WAGES BETWEEN MEN AND WOMEN

Absolute Values							
Sh.p.m.				As percentage of gross difference in mean wages (G)			
301.9							
226.3							
75.6				100.0			
Male		Female		Male		Female	
Included	Excluded	Included	Excluded	Included	Excluded	Included	Excluded
72.2	62.6	109.7	77.8	95.5	82.8	145.1	102.9
38.4	43.4	75.6	70.5	50.8	57.4	100.0	93.3
2.4	3.4	0.5	1.6	3.0	4.5	0.7	2.1
15.9	-	6.5	-	21.0	-	8.6	-
21.8	19.3	16.7	3.9	28.8	25.5	22.1	5.2
3.4	13.0	-34.1	-2.2	4.5	17.2	-45.1	-2.9

3. The contributions of particular personal characteristics (aggregated into the 2 experience variables, education, the 4 occupation dummy variables, and the remaining variables) sum to more (less) than the absolute value of E in the case of male (female) structure, because the divergence from $\bar{w}_m$ ($\bar{w}_f$) produced by each is measured in isolation.

TABLE 3

THE EFFECTS OF OCCUPATIONAL DIFFERENCES AND JOB DISCRIMINATION BY SEX

Occupation	Mean wage (sh.)		Occupational Distribution		
	Men	Women	Men	Women	Women, male structure
	($\bar{w}_{im}$)	($\bar{w}_{if}$)	(P_{im})	(P_{if})	($g_m(\bar{x}_f)$)
Supervisory	981	763	4	0	1
Clerical	783	609	11	18	12
Skilled	427	274	31	4	27
Semi-skilled	263	229	33	21	36
Unskilled	219	173	21	57	24
Total	390	267	100	100	100

Note: As there are no women in the supervisory occupation, we assume that the sex ratio applying to clerical workers would apply also to supervisory workers.

The following results are obtained from the table: G = 123; J = 52, JD = 28, JE = 24 (from (4)); J = 27, JD = 12, JE = 15 (from (4')).

It is possible that sex differences in the personal characteristics of our sample may themselves be the result of sex discrimination. The main differences in the average values of characteristics concern current and previous employment experience, age, and training. The occupations which women attain affect the amount of human capital that they can accumulate in employment. Exclusion of women from the more skilled manual and supervisory jobs might explain why a smaller proportion of women than of men receive formal training. Lack of reward for employment experience could deter women from staying with an employer or even in wage employment. The response of employers in their hiring and promotion decisions would in turn contribute to a 'vicious circle'. It is difficult to assess the relative importance of the effects of discrimination and the effects of non-discriminatory social factors, such as child-rearing, in explaining why women are at a disadvantage in possession of these productive characteristics. It is not clear that the coefficients on employment experience are lower for women. The coefficient on previous employment experience is actually higher for them, and that on current employment experience is the same when standardized for occupation, and lower for women when occupation is excluded from the independent variables (Table 1). This similarity and the remarkable youthfulness of female employees (18 per cent being under 20 and 93 per cent under 35) suggest that the difference in employment experience is either a life-cycle phenomenon or it reflects the recent entry of women to manufacturing employment.[14] If the difference in employment experience is the result of sex discrimination, it must stem from unequal access to manufacturing employment in the 1960s.

IV. DISCRIMINATION BY RACE

Eight per cent of the sample were non-African, who—Europeans being excluded from the survey—were almost all Asians. During the colonial period Asians occupied the middle rung of the clearly demarcated racial hierarchy in Tanzania. The mean wage in 1971 of 994 sh. for non-Africans is more than three times that of Africans (321 sh.), indicating that, at least in the manufacturing sector, Asians have perpetuated their economic advantage. Is this dramatic difference in earnings, like that between males and females, to be explained by differences between the two groups in personal economic characteristics? The shift in the distribution of power between the sexes is not nearly so marked as the change in the racial balance of political and economic power that Independence brought. This suggests that Africans are less likely to be the victims of labor market discrimination than women.

Certainly non-Africans are better endowed with human capital than Africans. While there was little difference between the two in length of employment experience (non-Africans averaged 9.2 and Africans 8.8 years), non-Africans averaged more than twice as much schooling (8.3 versus 3.6 years), and a higher proportion of non-Africans had received formal training (17 versus 12 per cent). The difference in education was reflected in the occupational distributions: nearly 60 per cent of non-Africans were in the supervisory and clerical occupations, while over 60 per cent of Africans were semi-skilled or unskilled workers (see Table 6).

When we estimate a full-sample regression equation, controlling for these differences in characteristics between Africans and non-Africans on the assumption that the coefficients on independent variables do not vary with race, contrary to expectations the wage differential associated with race is neither reversed nor eliminated. The premium received by non-Africans is reduced but remains surprisingly large. The coefficient on the non-African race variable (T2)[15] indicates that the earnings of non-Africans with the same characteristics as Africans are nevertheless 87 per cent higher. The coefficient is highly significant, and the race variable is the first to enter a stepwise regression, that is, it explains more of the variation in earnings (just over a quarter) than any other variable. Apparently the color of a worker's skin is a better predictor of his wage level than his educational attainment or employment experience.

This striking result is not simply the consequence of inappropriate aggregation. Differences between Africans and non-Africans in returns to human capital are found when the earnings function is estimated separately for each ethnic group (Table 4), but the advantage is not clearly with

TABLE 4

EARNINGS FUNCTIONS FOR AFRICANS AND NON-AFRICANS

Independent Variable	Coefficient			
	Africans		Non-Africans	
	a	b	c	d
Male sex (S1)	0.039	0.057	x	0.035
Years of education (E)	0.045**	0.071**	0.091**	0.110**
Years of current employment (L1)	0.030**	0.036**	0.017	0.019
Years of previous employment (L4)	0.022**	0.030**	0.040**	0.043**
Regular employment status (R2)	0.287**	0.335**	0.694*	0.599*
Age 15-19 (A1)	-0.143**	-0.217**	-0.464*	-0.435*
Age 35-49 (A3)	0.147**	0.158**	0.258	0.224
Age 50 or more (A4)	-0.017	-0.031	-0.046	-0.003
Formal training, 3 months or less (F1)	0.050	0.059	0.065	0.288
Formal training, more than 3 months (F2)	0.128*	0.185**	0.037	0.158
Supervisory (01)	0.652**	-	0.833*	-
Clerical (02)	0.526**	-	0.451	-
Headman/skilled (03)	0.249**	-	0.474	-
Semi-skilled (04)	0.026	-	0.147	-
Constant term	4.724	4.645	4.632	4.907
$\bar{R}^2$	0.478	0.391	0.544	0.527
S.E.E.	0.379	0.410	0.436	0.444
F	53.4	51.1	7.82	9.91
N	861.	861.	81.	81.
Dependent mean (Z)	5.602	5.602	6.721	6.721

Africans. Whereas the constant term and the coefficients on current employment experience and formal training are higher for Africans, the coefficient on years of education is more than twice, and that on previous employment experience nearly twice, as large for non-Africans.

The procedure for decomposing the race G into its E and D components is directly analogous to that used in the case of sex. When the African wage structure is used, D is found to be 69 (with the occupation variables included in the regressions) or 78 (with occupation excluded) per cent of G (Table 5). Occupation (in the former case) and education (in the latter) are the single most important contributors to E. When estimated from the non-African wage structure, the contribution of D is much smaller (24 and 33 per cent of G respectively); but these results are less reliable, being based on only 81 observations and sensitive to a number of non-significant coefficients. Yet even when the non-African structure is used, the absolute size of D is very large in relation to the mean wage of Africans. The exercise implies that labor market discrimination based on race is an important phenomenon in Tanzania.

Comparison of these results with the results of the analysis of sex discrimination is instructive. Using in each case the coefficients of the larger group, the means of the two estimates (including and excluding occupation variables) indicate that D as a proportion of G is 11 per cent for sex and 74 per cent for race. In addition, G is only 76 sh. for sex and 559 sh. for race. Thus the mean absolute value of D for race is 50 times that for sex: after differences in personal characteristics are accounted for, men earn 8 sh. more whereas non-Africans earn over 400 sh. more.

We next examine the extent to which differences in occupational distribution account for the racial gap in mean wages, and the extent to which such differences are due to job discrimination. One indication that job discrimination may be important is provided by the earnings functions for the sample as a whole. The omission of the occupation dummies alters the coefficient representing race: the premium for non-Africans rises from 87 to 110 per cent, and the statistical significance of the race coefficient increases, indicating that the influence on earnings of race is more important across than within occupations.

Our estimates of the effects of race differences in occupational distribution are made using the same method as in the case of sex differences, and are reported in Table 6. The estimate of JE + JD amounts to 33 per cent of G using one set of weights and to 13 per cent using the other. Occupation clearly plays some role in explaining why Asians fare better than Africans. Unlike males and females, Asians and Africans differ markedly in educational attainment. These differences in education should be taken into account in measuring $g_n(\bar{x}_a)$. Thus we estimate the proportions of Africans and non-Africans in the 5 occupations, stratifying by 4 education levels, and then apply the non-African education-specific occupational proportions to Africans in order to obtain an estimate of the African occupational distribution in the absence of job discrimination (column $g_n(\bar{x}_a)$ of Table 6). The two estimates of JD represent only six and 11 per cent of G respectively. These are likely to be overestimates of the effect of job discrimination because no standardization was made for group differences in the other productive characteristics, in which non-Africans were at a (slight) advantage. Wage discrimination by race is more important than job discrimination.

In Tanzania a minority, ostensibly without power, appears to be the beneficiary of discriminatory practices. The oddity of this phenomenon compels us to ask the questions: Is the net wage differential in fact due to unmeasured differential productivity, that is, is it the result of our using inadequate proxy measures for productivity? Alternatively, if we find the evidence of discrimination persuasive, do non-Africans actually possess more power to discriminate than a superficial assessment would suggest?[16]

There are reasons why the productivity of Asians may have been underestimated in the empirical analysis. The education, experience and training variables included in the earnings function are only proxies for the productivity of a worker, reflecting inputs to, not output from, the skill formation process. Racial differences in the quality of education may account for part of the unexplained differential. We have no measure of

TABLE

THE EFFECTS OF DISCRIMINATION AND PERSONAL CHARACTERISTICS ON THE

	Natural logarithms (sh.p.m.)			
Mean wage, Non-African ($\bar{w}_n$)	6.721			
Mean wage, African ($\bar{w}_a$)	5.602			
Gross difference in mean wages ($\bar{w}_n - \bar{w}_a$)	1.119			

Wage structure:	African		Non-African	
Occupation dummies:	Included	Excluded	Included	Excluded
Contribution of personal characteristics (E): $f_i(\bar{x}_n - \bar{x}_a)$	0.491	0.368	0.715	0.604
of which, due to:				
experience (L1, L4)	0.002	0.007	0.038	0.040
education	0.202	0.335	0.429	0.519
occupation (01-04)	0.254	-	0.206	-
other variables	0.023	0.026	0.042	0.045
Residual contribution of race discrimination (D): $f_n(\bar{x}_i) - f_a(\bar{x}_i)$	0.628	0.751	0.404	0.515

Notes: 1. The absolute values of mean wages are geometric means; they differ from the arithmetic means ($\bar{w}_n$ = 994.4, $\bar{w}_a$ = 321.2) but their ratios are very similar.

2. Using African wage structure, the contribution of personal characteristics is $f_a(\bar{x}_a - \bar{x}_n)$ and the corresponding residual contribution of race discrimination is $f_a(\bar{x}_n)-f_n(\bar{x}_n)$.

5

GROSS DIFFERENCE IN MEAN WAGES BETWEEN AFRICANS AND NON-AFRICANS

Absolute Values							
Sh.p.m.				As percentage of gross difference in mean wages (G)			
829.6							
271.0							
558.6				100.0			
African		Non-African		African		Non-African	
Included	Excluded	Included	Excluded	Included	Excluded	Included	Excluded
171.8	120.5	423.8	376.0	30.8	21.6	75.9	67.3
0.5	1.9	30.9	32.5	0.0	0.3	5.5	5.8
64.0	107.8	289.4	335.9	11.4	19.3	51.8	60.1
78.3	-	154.4	-	14.0	-	27.6	-
6.3	7.1	34.1	36.4	1.1	1.3	6.1	6.5
386.8	438.1	134.8	182.6	69.2	78.4	24.1	32.7

3. The contribution of particular personal characteristics (aggregated into the 2 experience variables, education the 4 occupation dummy variables, and the remaining variables) sum to more (less) than the absolute value of E in the case of non-African (African) structure, because the divergence from w_n (w_a) produced by each is measured in isolation.

TABLE 6

THE EFFECTS OF OCCUPATIONAL DIFFERENCES AND JOB DISCRIMINATION BY RACE

Occupation	Mean Wage		Occupational Distribution		
	Non-Africans	Africans	Non-Africans	Africans	Africans, non-African structure
	$(\bar{w}_{in})$	$(\bar{w}_{ia})$	(p_{in})	(p_{ia})	$(g_n(\bar{x}_a))$
Supervisory	1538	884	7	13	3
Clerical	1107	570	52	8	17
Skilled	841	382	31	28	55
Semi-skilled	595	253	9	34	17
Unskilled	185	210	1	27	9
Total	1001	323	100	100	100

The following results are obtained from the table: G = 678; J = 225, JD = 39, JE = 186 (from (4)); J = 87, JD = 72, JE = 15 (from 4')).

'ability' among the independent variables. Whereas the most able non-Africans are unlikely to be excluded from the sample, the most able Africans may well have been drawn into the public services, in which preference is shown for citizens. We have no independent measure of such qualities as personal drive, acumen and ambition; these are characteristics which are culturally influenced and which insecure minority groups often possess disproportionately.

If employers pay some workers more than others simply on account of their non-economic characteristics, they can be said to be indulging their prejudices or their 'taste for discrimination'.[17] If the marginal products of African and non-African workers are equal, the wage difference represents the psychic value which employers place on their prejudice; profits are not being maximized. In theory such discrimination should be a temporary phenomenon: non-discriminating enterprises should drive out those which discriminate and should equalize wages. However, product markets in Tanzanian manufacturing are generally not competitive and entrepreneurship is scarce. The cost to discriminating firms of satisfying their prejudices may simply be a lower return on their capital. Discrimination is not necessarily the result of prejudice. Where employers lack the information needed to measure personal productivity, they may find it profitable to use race as a statistical screening device in setting pay.[18] It is then sufficient that employers believe that Asians are more likely to possess such unmeasured productive characteristics for Asians as a group to be paid more.

Alternative stratifications of the sample into sub-samples, and the estimation of separate regressions which include race among the independent variables, help us to choose between these competing hypotheses.[19] A markedly higher proportion of parents of Asian workers are educated and work in white-collar occupations. Any advantage to Asian workers conferred by this difference in family background is more likely to be reflected in superior performance in white-collar than in blue-collar occupations where strength and manual dexterity are more important determinants of productivity. If otherwise undetected racial differences in productivity were the explanation, we would expect the coefficient on the race variable to be higher in high- than in low-level occupations. The neo-classical theory of discrimination predicts the opposite relationship. Assuming that employers' taste for discrimination is equally strong in all occupations, it is easily shown that the size of the premiums paid to the preferred group in various occupations are determined solely by the relative supply of that group. In any given occupation the greater the supply of the preferred group as a proportion of the total supply of qualified workers, the lower the premium paid. This is because in each occupation some employers will have a stronger taste for discrimination than others. In those occupations where the beneficiaries are least abundant they will tend to be employed by those with the strongest discriminatory taste; where they are more abundant some will be employed by those with weaker tastes for discrimination, and hence will receive a smaller premium.

Table 7 shows the coefficients on the race variable declining as occupational level increases. This relationship contradicts the prediction based on the hypothesis that the premium is simply a reward for higher productivity.

TABLE 7

COEFFICIENTS ON THE RACE VARIABLE IN OCCUPATION-SPECIFIC EARNINGS FUNCTIONS

Occupation	Observations	Non-Africans as percentage of total	Coefficient on race dummy
White collar	147	32	0.45**
Skilled	277	9	0.60**
Semi-skilled	350	2	0.69**

Note: These results are taken from equations which contain all the personal independent variables. The occupational category 'unskilled' is excluded because it contains only one non-African.

The table also shows the proportion of non-Africans in each occupation: there is a negative relationship between this proportion and the premium. This is consistent with the prediction of the neo-classical model of discrimination. The white-collar category has the highest proportion of non-African workers and the lowest ratio of non-African to African wages.

Asian ownership of manufacturing enterprises may dispel the image of a powerless group benefiting from discrimination. Asian entrepreneurs were among the first to invest in manufacturing enterprises, and while with nationalization and increased foreign investment, they controlled less than they had done before Independence, they retained a substantial portion of the private sector in 1971. Was it in this sector that discrimination was concentrated? The estimation of three separate earnings functions for firms whose ownership is 'wholly local and private', 'foreign and private' and 'mixed local and foreign, government and private', permits us to answer this question (Table 8). Asian owners of manufacturing enterprises are found in the first category; the coefficient on the race variable is markedly higher in the equation for this category than in those for the other categories. Asians working in wholly local and private firms receive a premium of 139 per cent while the premiums in the other two categories are 55 and 30 per cent. It is certainly suggestive of racial favoritism: Asians are paid the highest premiums in firms owned by Asians. This finding does not entirely resolve the anomaly of a powerless group as the beneficiary of discrimination. The coefficients on the race variable are also significant in the earnings functions estimated for employees of 'foreign and private' firms and of 'mixed local and foreign, government and private' firms. In other words, while discrimination is marked in Asian-owned firms, Asians still receive substantial wage premiums in firms owned by foreigners or jointly by foreigners and the Tanzanian government. The difference between the premiums found in local private firms and in these other firm categories can be regarded as the minimum measure of discrimination.

TABLE 8

COEFFICIENTS ON THE RACE VARIABLE IN EARNINGS FUNCTIONS DISAGGREGATED BY FIRM OWNERSHIP

Ownership category	Observations	Non-Africans as percentage of total	Coefficient on race dummy
Wholly local and private	218	12	0.87**
Foreign and private	209	7	0.44**
Mixed local and foreign; government and private	161	12	0.26**

Note: These results are taken from equations containing all the personal independent variables.

V. CONCLUSIONS

Our analysis of labor market discrimination in Tanzania has confounded expectations. In Tanzania, as in every other country for which we have seen evidence, the mean wage of males is substantially in excess of the mean wage of females. In marked contrast to the other, almost exclusively industrialized, countries where these sex differentials have been subjected to rigorous analysis, in Tanzania the premium paid to males is explained almost entirely by differences between males and females in economic characteristics. Men and women with the same level of education, employment experience, formal training and other personal characteristics receive roughly the same pay.

The mean wage of non-Africans in Tanzania is much higher than that of Africans. Given the vigor with which the governments of East Africa have attempted to redress the racial inequities of the colonial era, we expected to find this differential entirely accounted for by the markedly higher level of education and training attained by Asians. In fact, decomposition of the gross difference in mean wages reveals that only a small part is so explained. After standardizing for differences in economic characteristics, non-Africans are found to earn a net premium in excess of the mean wage of Africans. Moreover, our attempt to discover whether this premium is simply due to underestimation of the productive characteristics of non-Africans adds to the evidence that non-Africans are the beneficiaries of discrimination. They earn the largest premiums in the (manual) occupations where unmeasured human capital is likely to have the least impact on productivity, but where their numbers are fewest, and hence their likelihood of finding an employer with a 'taste' for non-Africans is greatest. The anomaly of a powerless minority benefiting from discriminatory behavior is resolved in part by the finding that the premium earned by Asians is markedly higher for local private firms, in which Asian ownership and management are concentrated.

We can only speculate as to why, contrary to expectations, female wage earners in Tanzania are not subject to discrimination while non-Africans are the beneficiaries of such discrimination. The explanation may lie in the difference between women and non-Africans, collectively, in their wage employment experience. Female participation in urban wage employment on a significant scale is a post-Independence phenomenon, whereas non-Africans have occupied a privileged position ever since an urban wage labor force emerged in Tanzania. While the government is avowedly opposed to both sex and race discrimination, it may have proved easier to prevent the emergence of sex discrimination than to erode the longstanding advantages of non-Africans. One aspect of our analysis does suggest that sex discrimination may yet become a problem. In our sample there are no women in high-level technical or managerial positions. Because of the relatively high wages paid to clerical workers this occupational segregation did not explain much of the difference in mean wages between males and females. However, if such segregation persists as the supply of educated females increases, crowding of females into clerical positions may result. This, in turn, could depress the relative wage of this occupation; consequently, men may begin to earn more than women with the same economic characteristics.

The problem of sex discrimination in Tanzania may not be as small nor the problem of race discrimination as large as our results imply. Firstly, the under-representation of females in urban wage employment may, in part, be the result of discriminatory hiring practices. The higher educational attainment of the male than the female population may similarly reflect discriminatory practices within the educational system. Discrimination in access to schooling and to wage employment have, however, been beyond our purview. Secondly, our evidence of racial discrimination is suggestive rather than conclusive. Unmeasured differences in economic characteristics, possibly in quality of education and stemming from culture, may yet be part of the story.

final version received April 1982

NOTES

1. A detailed description of the data base and sampling procedures is available in Knight and Sabot [*1980*].
2. See Blinder [*1973*], Oaxaca [*1973a, 1973b*], Malkiel and Malkiel [*1973*], and Brown, Moon and Zoloth [*1980*]. For an application to a developing country using a similar methodology see Birdsall [*1980*].
3. Brown, Moon and Zoloth [*1980*], and Birdsall [*1980*].
4. While 86 per cent of urban males are labor force participants only 29 per cent of females participate. Some 68 per cent of male labor force participants are wage employees; the proportion of female participants so engaged is only 37 per cent. See Knight and Sabot [*1980*].
5. Female sex (S2) is the base sub-category.
6. Knight and Sabot [*1980*].
7. Because the dummy variable enters the equation in dichotomous form, the coefficient must be adjusted to obtain its percentage effect. See Halvorsen and Palmquist [*1980*].
8. The case against the inclusion of occupation as an explanatory variable in earnings function analysis is that it biases downwards the coefficient on education which is normally a determinant of occupation. However, the coefficients on occupation may represent the influence of institutional wage determination or occupation-specific human capital acquired on-the-job.
9. All the independent variables representing personal characteristics, and not only the productive economic characteristics, are included as part of E, because our object is to isolate the contribution of discrimination attributable solely to sex.

9a. Oaxaca [*1973a: 146–7*].

10. See, for instance, Edgeworth [*1922*].
11. Brown, Moon and Zoloth [*1980*]. The probability that an individual will enter a particular occupation was treated as a function of factors affecting the demand for and supply of labor, such as education, training, experience, stability of employment, and job preference.
12. Knight and Sabot [*1980*].
13. This standardization for years of employment experience eliminates the effects of skill acquisition on-the-job and the advantages in access to jobs which earlier cohorts of labor market entrants possessed over later cohorts in a loosening labor market. See Knight and Sabot [*1981*].
14. Preliminary results of a corresponding survey conducted in 1980 by a team including the authors favor the latter interpretation: the attrition rate over the decade was only slightly higher for women than for men and the average length of female employment experience doubled to 8.8 years.
15. African race (T1) is the base sub-category.
16. Differences in the supply prices of Africans and non-Africans would provide a third possible explanation of the net wage differential if non-Africans were foreigners. However, almost all of the non-Africans in the sample were of Asian extraction and generally long-established residents of Tanzania.
17. Becker [*1971*]; Arrow [*1974*].

18. Arrow [*1974*]; Phelps [*1973*].
19. Constraints imposed by sample size prevent us from conducting a decomposition analysis for the sub-samples. However, the consistency of the sign and significance of the coefficient on the race dummy variable with the findings of the decomposition analysis in the sample as a whole suggests that the race dummy can be used as a rough measure of the extent of discrimination in the sub-samples.

REFERENCES

Arrow, K. J., 1974, 'The Theory of Discrimination', in Orley Ashenfelter and Albert Rees (eds), *Discrimination of Labor Markets*, Princeton, N.J.: Princeton University Press.

Becker, Gary S., 1971, *The Economics of Discrimination*, second edition, Chicago: University of Chicago Press.

Birdsall, Nancy, 1980, 'Male–Female Pay Differentials: Brazilian Schoolteachers', mimeo, The World Bank, Washington, D.C.

Blinder, Alan S., 1973, 'Wage Discrimination: Reduced Form and Structural Estimates', *Journal of Human Resources*, Fall, 436–55.

Brown, Randall S., Marilyn Moon, and Barbara S. Zoloth, 1980, 'Incorporating Occupational Attainment in Studies of Male–Female Earnings Differentials', *Journal of Human Resources*, Winter, 3–28.

Edgeworth, F. Y., 1922, 'Equal Pay to Men and Women for Equal Work', *Economic Journal*, 4, December, 431–57.

Halvorsen, Robert and Raymond Palmquist, 1980, 'The Interpretation of Dummy Variables in Semilogarithmic Equations', *American Economic Review*, 3: 474–5.

Knight, J. B. and R. H. Sabot, 1980, 'Why Wages Differ: A Study of Tanzania's Manufacturing Sector', mimeo, The World Bank, Washington, D.C.

Knight, J. B. and R. H. Sabot, 1981, 'The Returns to Education: Increasing with Experience or Decreasing with Expansion?', *Oxford Bulletin of Economics and Statistics*, 43, February, 51–72.

Malkiel, Burton G. and Judith A. Malkiel, 1973, 'Male–Female Pay Differentials in Professional Employment', *American Economic Review*, 4: 693–705.

Oaxaca, Ronald, 1973a, 'Sex Discrimination in Wages', in Orley Ashenfelter and Albert Rees (eds.), *Discrimination in Labor Markets*, Princeton, N.J.: Princeton University Press.

Oaxaca, Ronald, 1973b, 'Male–Female Differentials in Urban Labor Markets', *International Economic Review*, 3, October, 693–709.

Phelps, E. S., 1973, 'The Statistical Theory of Racism and Sexism', *American Economic Review*, 4, September, 659–61.

[10]

Journal of Development Economics 17 (1985) 277–307. North-Holland

CASTE DISCRIMINATION IN THE INDIAN URBAN LABOUR MARKET*

Biswajit BANERJEE

International Monetary Fund, Washington, DC 20431, USA

J.B. KNIGHT

University of Oxford, Oxford OX1 3UL, UK

Received April 1983, final version received August 1983

This, the pioneering quantitative analysis of caste in the Indian urban labour market, examines the age-old problem of caste in the light of discrimination theory and government policy. Using a survey of workers in Delhi, the gross wage difference between 'scheduled' (untouchable) and 'non-scheduled' caste is decomposed into its 'explained' and 'discrimination' components and, from a model of occupational choice, into wage- and job-discrimination. Discrimination is found to exist, and to operate at least in part through the traditional mechanism, *viz.* assignment to jobs, with the scheduled castes entering poorly-paid 'dead-end' jobs. It is assisted by methods of recruitment based on contacts, prevalent in the manual occupations, which also cause past discrimination to carry over to the present. Its practice serves the economic interests of those who exercise a taste for discrimination.

1. Introduction

There is now an extensive theoretical literature on the economics of discrimination in the labour market.[1] Most of the empirical analysis is concerned with discrimination by race or sex in developed countries.[2] There is as yet little applied work on discrimination in developing countries.[3] The analysis of caste in India has been the preserve of social scientists other than economists.[4]

Yet the possibility of labour market discrimination based on caste poses interesting questions for economists. Does discrimination exist? Does it take

*The survey which provides the data base for this paper was financed by a grant (RF71078, allocation no. 16) from the Rockefeller Foundation, and was conducted by the first author when he was visiting the Institute of Economic Growth, Delhi, during 1974–76. The paper was completed at the Institute of Economics and Statistics, Oxford, before he moved to the International Monetary Fund. We are grateful to Gordon Hughes for his help with the estimation of the logit model. We acknowledge the assistance of a referee; but we alone are responsible for the views expressed.

[1]Notable contributions include Becker (1971) and Arrow (1974).

[2]Surveyed by Marshall (1974) and Cain (1976).

[3]But see Birdsall and Fox (1981), Knight and McGrath (1977), and Knight and Sabot (1982).

[4]For instance, Berreman (1979), Béteille (1969), Cox (1959) and Wadhawa (1975).

the form of 'wage discrimination' or 'job discrimination', i.e., unequal pay for workers with the same economic characteristics even within the same job, or unequal pay for workers with the same economic characteristics which results from their being employed in different jobs? How might such discrimination be explained? Are there some segments of the labour market in which we would particularly expect to find discrimination? What are the policy implications?

Section 2 gives a brief account of the historical and institutional basis of caste discrimination in India insofar as it is relevant to our analysis. Section 3 provides a statement of the techniques of analysis to be used, and section 4 describes briefly the labour market survey to which they will be applied. Section 5 examines the extent of wage discrimination and job discrimination by caste, and attempts to pinpoint the phenomenon by occupation and sector. Section 6 offers an interpretation of the results, and section 7 concludes.

2. Caste in India

The problem of caste in India is an age-old one. Life in the traditional Indian village was based on caste. Some of the upper castes owned or controlled the land, and possessed the power. The middle and lower castes — the artisans and untouchables — provided services for the dominant castes, in return for which they received an assured livelihood through payments in kind. Under the *jajmani* system, each caste had a traditional occupation, regarded as its sacred duty. The caste structure was thus a labour structure, fixing the supply of any kind of labour through heredity; such occupational mobility as occurred was collective rather than individual.[5]

The lowest castes (the Harijans) occupied the lowliest jobs such as agricultural labourer and sweeper. There was also a religious and a social basis to their condition. The notion of untouchability separated the Harijans from the main body of Hindus. Their landlessness and their abject poverty, together with the justification provided by religion, in turn contributed to their social ostracism. The Harijans normally could not use the public well in the village nor enter the shops and houses of higher castes, nor attend school, nor take part in religious services, nor attend village festivals; they lived separately from other castes.

Those who promulgated the Constitution after Indian Independence were determined to provide a framework which would help to rid India of caste discrimination and, in particular, of untouchability. Article 17 of the Constitution abolishes untouchability and its practice in any form, and makes it an

[5]Cox (1959, ch. 5).

offence to enforce any disability arising from untouchability. The Constitution is impressive and unusual in specifically making provision for reverse discrimination. It lays down that the scheduled castes should receive preferential treatment in recruitment to employment in public administration (art. 335) and, in this respect, permits the reservation of posts for scheduled castes [art. 16(4)]. The Constitution forbids discrimination in admission to education [art. 29(2)], and further stipulates (art. 46): 'The State shall promote with special care the educational and economic interests of the (scheduled castes) and shall protect them from social injustice and all forms of exploitation.' The castes subsequently scheduled by government for favourable treatment corresponded to the Harijans; they constituted 14.6 percent of the Indian population in 1971.

A legislative programme and administrative machinery were established to implement the safeguards for scheduled castes enshrined in the Constitution. 12.5 percent (15 percent after 1970) of vacancies in the public services which were filled by direct recruitment through open competition were reserved for scheduled castes, and $16\frac{2}{3}$ percent of the vacancies filled by direct recruitment other than through open competition. In 1963 the Government extended the reservation of public service posts to posts filled on the basis of promotion in classes III and IV (and class II after 1968). Relaxation of recruitment standards was permitted, and dereservation of posts was made difficult. The percentage of scheduled caste members in central government employment was as follows:[6]

	Class	1951	1960	1970	1979
Senior administrative	I	0.6	1.2	2.4	4.8
Other administrative	II	0.8	2.4	3.8	7.4
Clerical	III	3.2	7.2	9.9	12.6
Attendants, peons	IV[7]	9.4	17.2	22.3	19.3

The relative importance of the scheduled castes increased in each class over the decades but, given that they represented 14.6 percent of the population in 1971, they were still greatly under-represented in all but the lowliest class of public service employment. The reservation policy has been extended beyond the public services to other parts of the public sector in an *ad hoc* way.

Government provides free primary education to all throughout India; at the secondary level, scheduled castes are exempted from tuition fees in government and aided schools, and pre- and post-matriculation scholarships are available to them. From 1962 onwards the Government required 15 percent of the places in technical institutions to be reserved for the scheduled

[6]Commissioner for Scheduled Castes and Scheduled Tribes (various years).
[7]Excluding sweepers.

castes, and permitted them relaxed entry conditions. Despite the policy of reverse discrimination, the enrolment of scheduled caste children in primary and middle (standards I–VIII) and post-middle (standard IX and above) education represented only 10.4 and 7.7 percent of total enrolment, respectively, in 1973–74.[8] Owing to the lack of qualified candidates or lax implementation of the reservation policy, scheduled caste enrolment in medical, engineering and agricultural colleges was well below the reserved number of places in 1969.[9] The educational attainment of scheduled caste members improved after Independence, but remained below that of the population as a whole. Scheduled caste members as a percentage of the total population in each educational category changed as follows between 1961 and 1971:[10]

	1961	1971
Illiterate or literate without education	15.7	16.7
Primary and middle	5.3	7.1
Matriculate and above	2.0	3.2
All educational levels	14.7	14.6

At the social level, also, progress was slow. The Committee on Untouchability, having taken evidence in villages throughout India, reported in 1969: 'In spite of all efforts the scheduled castes continue to suffer from various social disabilities... To our utter dismay the Committee found that untouchability is still being practised in virulent form all over India.'[11] The Indian village, at least, remains very much a caste society.

The persistence of caste may be due to the fact that the caste system represents a voluntary stable equilibrium, justified by religion and based on consensus, not coercion. The lower castes have not questioned the system. Although they suffer from the restrictions imposed upon them, their response — feelings of envy in relation to immediately superior castes and of pride in relation to inferior castes — does not threaten the social order.[12]

The urbanization accompanying economic development tended to weaken the caste system. Some of the traditional caste occupations became redundant or required fewer workers, and villagers commuted or migrated to the towns to work. In the urban areas — where the scheduled castes made up 8.8 percent of the population in 1971 — the caste system became less rigid owing to the greater anonymity, and the diminishing correlation between

[8]Commissioner for Scheduled Castes and Scheduled Tribes (1973–74, p. 75).

[9]Department of Social Welfare (1969, pp. 207–208).

[10]Taken from the Census Reports of 1961 and 1971; corresponding data are not available for 1951.

[11]Department of Social Welfare (1969, p. 15).

[12]This argument is developed by Cox (1959, chs. 1–2) and supported by Moffat (1975).

occupational or economic stratification and the traditional ranking of the castes. Social discrimination against the scheduled castes is generally deemed to be less powerful in the towns and cities than in the villages.[13] Nevertheless, the greater economic and social mobility of the scheduled castes in the urban areas has not been achieved without resistance. Caste riots — such as the Gujarat riots of 1981 — reflect the hostility of the middle castes with whom the scheduled castes compete. A study of the Gujarat riots argues that they occurred mainly in urban areas and that they were directed against the upwardly mobile members of the scheduled castes, i.e., those with relatively good education and jobs.[14] It was not clear, however, whether the scheduled castes were perceived to be competing for jobs from which they were traditionally excluded, or to be competing unfairly for jobs owing to the reservation policy. Resentment of preferential treatment may reinforce prejudice against the scheduled castes.[15]

Economic discrimination against the scheduled castes operates powerfully in the rural areas and it predominantly takes the form of discrimination 'prior to the market', i.e., in access to land, property and education. In this paper our interest is much narrower: we are concerned with discrimination in the cities and 'within the market'. We pose the question: is there caste discrimination in the urban labour market after standardizing for the economic characteristics of workers? But in order to explain our affirmative answer, such discrimination must be seen in the broader context.

3. The method

We decompose the difference in mean wages between scheduled and non-scheduled castes into the component 'explained' by differences in economic characteristics between the two groups and the 'unexplained' component, which can be regarded as reflecting the extent of labour market discrimination. We use the standard technique for measuring discrimination when two groups differ in their personal characteristics and in the function relating these characteristics to earnings.[16] It can be explained as follows.

Assume that the mean wage of scheduled castes (S) is $\bar{w}_s$ and that of non-scheduled castes (N) is $\bar{w}_n$. Assume that the mean wage of S is determined by the earnings function

$$\bar{w}_s = f_s(\bar{x}_s), \tag{1}$$

where x_s is a vector of characteristics applicable to S and $\bar{x}_s$ denotes their

[13] For instance, Berreman (1979, ch. 10), Cox (1959, pp. 22, 70, 439).
[14] Bose (1981).
[15] Dushkin (1979).
[16] Blinder (1973) and Oaxaca (1973a, b) are pioneering examples.

mean values; similarly for N. The mean wage which the N group would receive if they were paid according to the S earnings function is $f_s(\bar{x}_n)$.

The gross difference in mean wages (G) between S and N can be divided into the part 'explained' by different personal characteristics (E) and the unexplained part (D), reflecting differences in 'wage structure', i.e., in the constant terms and coefficients of the regression equations for the two caste groups:

$$\begin{aligned} G=\bar{w}_n-\bar{w}_s &= (\bar{w}_n-f_n(\bar{x}_s))+(f_n(\bar{x}_s)-\bar{w}_s) \\ &= f_n(\bar{x}_n-\bar{x}_s)+(f_n(\bar{x}_s)-f_s(\bar{x}_s)) \\ &= E+D, \end{aligned} \tag{2}$$

respectively. Similarly, the estimation of the wage received by the N group if they are paid according to the S wage structure permits the decomposition, into $D+E$, respectively,

$$G=(f_n(\bar{x}_n)-f_s(\bar{x}_n))+f_s(\bar{x}_n-\bar{x}_s). \tag{3}$$

The term D is assumed to represent that part of the wage difference which is due to discrimination.

The choice of occupation can influence the wage a worker receives, either because occupational wages are influenced by institutional factors or because they represent human capital acquired in the job. Where this is the case, a distinction can be made between wage and job discrimination. The finding of significant coefficients on dummy variables representing occupation in the earnings function would not complicate matters if the determinants of occupational attainment were the same for the two caste groups. However, job discrimination may cause persons of different castes who otherwise have the same characteristics to work in different occupations. If we incorporate a separate model of occupational attainment into the analysis of wage differentials, the gross difference in mean wages can be decomposed as follows:[17]

$$\begin{aligned} \bar{w}_n-\bar{w}_s &= \sum_i (p_{in}\bar{w}_{in}-p_{is}\bar{w}_{is}) \\ &= \sum_i (p_{in}f_{in}(\bar{x}_{in})-p_{is}f_{is}(\bar{x}_{is})) \\ &= \sum_i p_{is}(f_{in}(\bar{x}_{in})-f_{is}(\bar{x}_{is}))+\sum_i f_{in}(\bar{x}_{in})(p_{in}-p_{is}) \\ &= W+J, \end{aligned} \tag{4a}$$

[17]In line with Brown, Moon and Zoloth (1980).

respectively. p_{in} and p_{is} represent the sample proportions of non-scheduled caste and scheduled caste workers respectively, W represents that part of the gross difference in wages which is due to wage differences within occupations, and J that part which is due to differences in occupational composition. Both W and J contain an 'explained' and an 'unexplained' component. Denoting $\hat{p}_{is}$ as the proportion of scheduled caste workers in the sample who would be in occupation i if scheduled castes faced the same occupational structure as non-scheduled castes, G can be further decomposed as follows:

$$\bar{w}_n - \bar{w}_s = \sum_i p_{is}(f_{in}(\bar{x}_{in} - \bar{x}_{is})) + \sum_i p_{is}(f_{in}(\bar{x}_{is}) - f_{is}(\bar{x}_{is}))$$

$$+ \sum_i \bar{w}_{in}(p_{in} - \hat{p}_{is}) + \sum_i \bar{w}_{in}(\hat{p}_{is} - p_{is})$$

$$= WE + WD + JE + JD, \tag{4b}$$

respectively. WE is the part explained by differences in personal characteristics since both wage structure and job proportions are being held constant. WD represents wage discrimination, since it isolates the effect of caste differences in wage structure within occupations. Now consider the contribution of occupation to G. JE is the 'explained' part, reflecting differences in occupational attainment which are due to differences in personal characteristics: the N occupational attainment function is applied to both N and S. JD represents job discrimination since it isolates the effect of caste differences in occupational attainment which cannot be explained by group differences in personal characteristics. An alternative decomposition of G is possible [(5a) and (5b), not shown], weighting the wage components (W) by the occupational proportions for N instead of S, and the job components (J) by the occupational mean earnings for S instead of N.

For the standard exercise of measuring the extent of discrimination by means of eqs. (2) and (3), we estimate an OLS earnings function with the logarithm of wages as the dependent variable. To distinguish wage and job discrimination using eqs. (4a) and (4b), we estimate the determinants of occupational attainment by means of multinomial logit analysis.

4. The data

The empirical basis of this paper is a survey conducted in Delhi by one of the authors from October 1975 to April 1976. As the primary objective of this survey was to test the empirical validity of economic models of migration, detailed data were collected only from migrant heads of households.[18] At the first stage of the survey 10,000 heads of households were

[18] Results of prior analyses of the survey data and details of sampling procedure are contained in Banerjee (1981).

enumerated in 76 census blocks — representing 1.14 percent of the total number of census blocks into which the city was divided — which were selected by weighted stratified random sampling. At the second stage no sampling was involved, and all heads of households who satisfied the following criteria were interviewed in detail: (i) male, (ii) born outside Delhi, (iii) age on arrival in Delhi being 14 years or more, (iv) came to Delhi in 1965 or later, and (v) came after securing employment or in search of employment. The last criterion eliminates migrants who were transferred to Delhi by their employers, and those who had come as dependents and students. A total of 1,615 migrant heads of households, of whom 1,408 had come from rural areas, were interviewed in the second stage.

The questionnaire included questions on socio-economic backgrounds of migrants, and their urban employment and income history. Respondents were asked their caste affiliation, and for the purpose of this analysis we classified them as scheduled and non-scheduled castes using the list of scheduled castes contained in the 1961 Census reports for Delhi. Given the practice of 'Sanskritization'[19] — the tendency among those in the lower levels of the caste hierarchy to emulate the ways of the upper castes and reduce the social distance between them — it is possible that some scheduled caste migrants concealed their true caste affiliation and claimed to be of a higher caste which belonged to the non-scheduled caste spectrum.[20]

Establishing the accuracy of an individual's response on caste affiliation is an extremely difficult task, particularly in a large-scale survey in an urban environment. For this reason and to avoid the risk of terminating the interview or losing the rapport of the respondent, no attempt was made during the fieldwork to probe the issue of caste affiliation. Twenty-nine percent of the migrants from rural areas and 13 percent of the urban migrants in the sample claimed to be (members of) castes which fell in the scheduled caste group. These percentages are almost twice as high as those in the areas from which the migrants originate. This is a reflection of scheduled castes having a higher propensity to migrate, and also suggests that mis-reporting of caste affiliation was low. However, scheduled castes reporting to be non-scheduled would generally produce a downward bias in the standardized caste differential in earnings, and correction for mis-reporting would thus strengthen, rather than weaken, any evidence of discrimination against scheduled castes. Even if the mis-reporting were concentrated among the highest wage-earners in the scheduled caste group, whereas this might raise the observed mean wage of the non-scheduled relative to the scheduled castes, such mis-reporting could raise the standardized differential only if the relatively high wages of these workers were due to lack of discrimination

[19]See Srinivas (1962, pp. 42–62).

[20]Mis-reporting of caste which did not result in mis-classification as between the scheduled and non-scheduled caste-groups would clearly not affect the findings in this paper.

against them and not to their possession of productive characteristics. Insofar as those who mis-reported in the survey also 'passed' as non-scheduled in the labour market, mis-reporting would not produce bias if the estimate was of discrimination conditional upon the caste information of employers.

The focus throughout this paper is on migrants from rural areas employed in the wage sector of the labour market.[21] Members of the scheduled castes from rural areas have already been exposed to caste prejudice and discrimination in their place of origin. This is likely to influence their attitudes and expectations in the urban environment. The response of scheduled castes who have been born and brought up in the city may be different. Estimating caste discrimination among urban natives and comparing the results with those obtained for migrants would be of value, but the data base does not permit us to carry out such an exercise or to make formal statistical corrections for any sample selection bias. However, an examination of occupational distribution by residential status and caste based on the more limited data collected in the first stage of the survey does not suggest that the findings for rural migrants cannot be generalized to the entire urban labour market: though there are significant differences in the occupational distributions of urban natives and rural migrants, caste differentials in occupational attainment among urban natives are remarkably similar in qualitative terms to those observed among rural migrants.

The analysis also omits the unemployed — defined as those who had not worked at all during the week preceding the day of enumeration. This should not bias our findings in any way as only 0.8 percent of the scheduled castes and 1.2 percent of the non-scheduled castes reported being unemployed.

The monthly earnings of salaried employees include the basic wage, allowances and bonuses before tax. For those who were paid daily wages or worked on a piece-rate basis, monthly earnings are calculated on the assumption that they worked for 25 days at the wage rate indicated by them.[22] No account is taken of earnings from overtime work.

Occupation is classified into six broad groups: professional, clerical, production, service, skilled and unskilled workers. Professional workers include also managerial, executive and administrative workers, and clerical and production workers are the same as those classified under these headings in India's *National Classification of Occupations.* Service workers consist of policemen and security guards (*chowkidars*), and skilled workers include motor vehicle drivers and skilled construction workers. Unskilled workers comprise all other occupational groups, including shop and sales assistants,

[21]We exclude from the analysis cooks and domestic servants, for the practical reason that free board and lodging are important elements in their remuneration, and we have no obvious criterion for evaluating remuneration in kind.

[22]An overwhelming majority of wage employees indicated that they had worked on all working days during the week preceding the interview day.

sweepers, loaders, unskilled construction workers, and 'labourers not classified elsewhere'.

5. Empirical results

The average monthly earnings of scheduled castes and non-scheduled castes in 1976 were Rs. 272 and Rs. 337, respectively. A part of this difference of Rs. 65 per month, which is statistically significant at the 1 percent level, could be attributed to differences between the two groups of workers in several characteristics that are associated with earnings (table 1). The two groups are similar in their mean age at time of arrival in the city, in the average length of urban experience, and in their distribution between the formal and informal sectors. However, the non-scheduled castes are at an advantage in three main respects: in the average number of years of education they possess, in the proportion who are salaried, as opposed to daily-wage workers, and in their occupational distribution. The notable occupational difference is that the proportion in unskilled manual jobs is greater by 13 percentage points for scheduled than for non-scheduled caste workers, and the proportion in white-collar jobs — professional and clerical work — is lower by 9 percentage points.

Table 1

Mean values of earnings and characteristics of all migrants and of scheduled and non-scheduled caste migrants in Delhi, 1975–76.

Variables	Entire sample	Scheduled castes	Non-scheduled castes
Monthly earnings (Y)	317.32	271.94	337.14
$\ln Y(W)$	5.5891	5.4710	5.6406
Years of education	5.4996	3.8923	6.2017
$(\text{Education})^2$	53.0117	37.2824	59.8831
Age on arrival	22.7030	22.7129	22.6987
$(\text{Age on arrival})^2$	564.9339	569.6192	562.8872
Urban experience	5.7365	6.0098	5.6171
$(\text{Urban experience})^2$	44.0008	47.4712	42.4847
Professional workers	0.0637	0.0443	0.0721
Clerical workers	0.1408	0.0944	0.1611
Production workers	0.3982	0.3451	0.4214
Service workers	0.0529	0.0442	0.0567
Skilled workers	0.0484	0.0826	0.0335
Unskilled workers	0.2960	0.3894	0.2552
Salaried employees	0.7274	0.6431	0.7642
Formal sector employees	0.6762	0.6608	0.6830
(N)	(1115)	(339)	(776)

5.1. Earnings function analysis

As the earnings function is best viewed as a reduced form equation, i.e., the outcome of an interaction of the forces of demand and supply, there is no theoretical justification for restricting the independent variables in the estimated equations to the conventional human capital variables. The additional variables measure sector of employment, employment status, and occupation. It is generally claimed that urban labour markets in developing countries are characterized by dualism. Minimum wage legislation and its implementation, and efforts by large firms to promote stability of labour and reduce turnover may raise wages above the supply price of labour. Accordingly, we introduce a dummy variable to indicate employment in the formal sector, i.e., in government and public sector establishments, and in privately owned establishments employing more than twenty workers. A distinction is made between salaried workers and workers employed on a daily-wage basis, because establishments, including those in the formal sector, often pay different rates to these two groups even when they perform the same job. Occupation is introduced in the earnings function as a set of five dummy variables, with professional workers being the omitted group. The classification is based as far as possible on skill level: a justification for including occupation dummy variables in the earnings function is that they are a way of identifying occupation-specific skills acquired in the job.

The sample consists of migrants who have arrived at the city at different points in their life cycles. Some have come at an early age at the beginning of their careers after a short spell in the rural labour force or soon after finishing school or college, while others have come with many years of work experience in the rural area behind them. Individuals who are alike in every respect, including their period of urban work experience, except for the stage of the life-cycle at which they came to the city may not have the same level of earnings. We therefore include age on arrival in the city as an explanatory variable. It can be interpreted as a crude proxy for pre-migration experience in the rural area or for qualities such as trainability, responsibility and job performance potential: qualities which may be associated with age.

The estimated earnings functions for the entire sample and separately for the two caste groups are presented in table 2. The dependent variable is the natural logarithm of monthly earnings. Let us first consider an equation for the entire sample [column (1)]. The coefficients for the two education regressors indicate that the gross return to education becomes positive after 2.3 years of education, and that it increases with the level of education. An additional year of education adds 2.4 percent to earnings when evaluated at five years of education, 6.9 percent at ten years, and 11.4 percent at fifteen years. Both pre-migration 'experience' and experience in the city have significant positive but diminishing effects on earnings, but as might be expected the effect of the latter variable is stronger. An additional year spent

Table 2

Regression analysis of earnings for the entire sample and for scheduled and non-scheduled castes.[a]

	Entire sample			Scheduled caste interaction terms	Scheduled castes	Non-scheduled castes
Sample	(1)	(2)	(3)	(4)	(5)	(6)
Education	−0.02095	−0.02539	−0.02908	0.02232	−0.00675	−0.02908
	(0.00729)[b]	(0.00737)[b]	(0.00881)[b]	(0.01636)	(0.01299)	(0.00902)[b]
$(\text{Education})^2$	0.00449	0.00473	0.00507	−0.00228	0.00279	0.00507
	(0.00061)[b]	(0.00061)[b]	(0.00071)[b]	(0.00142)	(0.00116)[c]	(0.00073)[b]
Age on arrival	0.04407	0.04364	0.04460	−0.00012	0.04449	0.04460
	(0.00746)[b]	(0.00743)[b]	(0.00953)[b]	(0.01526)	(0.01123)[b]	(0.00976)[b]
$(\text{Age on arrival})^2$	−0.00065	−0.00065	−0.00063	−0.00009	−0.00071	−0.00063
	(0.00013)[b]	(0.00013)[b]	(0.00016)[b]	(0.00025)	(0.00018)[b]	(0.00017)[b]
Urban experience	0.07109	0.07210	0.09756	−0.07024	0.02732	0.09756
	(0.01068)[b]	(0.01063)	(0.01357)[b]	(0.02211)[b]	(0.01644)[d]	(0.01389)[b]
$(\text{Urban experience})^2$	−0.00247	−0.00251	−0.00414	0.00421	0.00007	−0.00414
	(0.00084)[b]	(0.00084)[b]	(0.00109)[b]	(0.00170)[c]	(0.00123)	(0.00112)[b]
Clerical workers	−0.39019	−0.38719	−0.36794	−0.00452	−0.37246	−0.36794
	(0.05734)[b]	(0.05708)[b]	(0.06563)[b]	(0.13257)	(0.10851)[b]	(0.06719)[b]
Production workers	−0.50264	−0.50331	−0.45674	−0.19598	−0.65272	−0.45674
	(0.06060)[b]	(0.06032)[b]	(0.06878)[b]	(0.14204)	(0.11708)[b]	(0.07041)[b]
Service workers	−0.53471	−0.53425	−0.48073	−0.24008	−0.72081	−0.48073
	(0.07335)[b]	(0.07301)[b]	(0.08311)[b]	(0.17327)	(0.14324)[b]	(0.08508)[b]
Skilled workers	−0.28493	−0.26587	−0.24445	−0.13180	−0.37625	−0.24445
	(0.07699)[b]	(0.07685)[b]	(0.09587)[c]	(0.17101)	(0.13342)[b]	(0.09814)[c]
Unskilled workers	−0.70618	−0.69853	−0.65519	−0.16549	−0.82068	−0.65519
	(0.06193)[b]	(0.06168)[b]	(0.07079)[b]	(0.14464)	(0.11883)[b]	(0.07247)[b]
Salaried employees	0.13079	0.12310	0.06983	0.13237	0.20220	0.06983
	(0.02581)[b]	(0.02579)[b]	(0.03252)[c]	(0.05316)[c]	(0.03962)[b]	(0.03329)[c]
Formal sector employees	0.08266	0.08525	0.11972	−0.12794	−0.00822	0.11972
	(0.02393)[b]	(0.02383)[b]	(0.02856)[b]	(0.05235)[c]	(0.04134)	(0.02924)[b]
Scheduled castes		−0.08063				
		(0.02407)[b]				
Constant	4.88838	4.92862	4.80501	0.33546	5.14047	4.80501
	(0.12716)[b]	(0.12715)[b]	(0.15647)[b]	(0.27240)	(0.21007)[b]	(0.16017)[b]
R^2	0.57464	0.57894	0.59090		0.56062	0.58939
$\bar{R}^2$	0.56962	0.57358	0.58074		0.54305	0.58239
F	114.41509	108.03038	58.15027		31.89873	84.13770
Residual sum of squares	137.54110	136.15223	132.28316		35.10569	97.17747
(N)	(1115)	(1115)	(1115)		(339)	(776)

[a]The dependent variable is the natural logarithm of monthly earnings. The table shows the coefficients of the independent variables, with the standard errors in parentheses beneath. Columns (3) and (4) refer to the same regression equation, with column (3) showing the coefficients on the independent variables and column (4) the coefficients on the scheduled caste interaction terms.

[b]Significant at the 1 percent level, using a two-tailed test.

[c]Significant at the 5 percent level.

[d]Significant at the 10 percent level.

in the rural area adds 1.5 percent to earnings when evaluated at the mean age on arrival (twenty-two years), while an additional year of urban experience adds 4.1 percent to earnings when evaluated at six years of urban residence.

The coefficients for all the occupation dummies are significant, and their ordering is consistent with *a priori* expectations. Compared to professional workers the earnings of clerical workers, production workers and unskilled workers are lower by 32 percent, 40 percent and 50 percent, respectively. Skilled workers have slightly higher earnings than clerical workers, and service workers earn marginally less than production workers. The coefficients for salaried worker and formal sector dummies are both positive and significant. *Ceteris paribus*, salaried workers earn 14.0 percent more than those who are paid on a daily-wage basis, and employment in the formal sector is associated with 8.6 percent higher earnings than informal sector employment.

When the earnings function is re-estimated [column (2)] with membership of the scheduled castes included as a dummy variable (membership of the non-scheduled castes being the base sub-category), that coefficient is negative and significant at the 1 percent level: membership of the scheduled castes reduces pay by 7.7 percent. However, this method of estimating the impact of caste on earnings is appropriate on condition that the earnings functions for the two caste-groups differ only with respect to the constant term. To determine whether there are significant differences in coefficients on the other explanatory variables between the two caste-groups, we estimate a regression equation for the full sample with the same independent variables as that in column (1) but with the addition of a set of intercept and slope dummy variables representing the products of each of these independent variables and the dummy variable for scheduled castes. Column (3) thus shows the constant term and coefficients for the non-scheduled castes, and column (4) the difference which membership of the scheduled castes makes to each of these terms. These results are equivalent to those in columns (5) and (6), which present separate earnings functions for scheduled and non-scheduled castes, respectively. The former method provides significance tests of the caste differences in each coefficient, whereas the latter provides a significance test for the two sets of coefficients. The Chow test yields an F ratio of 3.09 (critical value: $F_{0.01}=2.07$): the earnings functions for the two caste-groups are significantly different at the 1 percent level.

The coefficients on education, age on arrival, occupation and intercept for scheduled caste workers are not significantly different from comparable coefficients for non-scheduled caste workers. There are significant caste differences in the coefficients on urban experience, employment status and sector of employment. One of these effects favours scheduled castes, and two favour non-scheduled castes. Among scheduled caste workers, salaried employees earn, *ceteris paribus*, 22.4 percent more than daily wage earners, while among non-scheduled castes this differential is only 7.2 percent. However, among non-scheduled castes the earnings of formal sector workers are 12.7 percent higher than those in the informal sector, but among scheduled caste workers the formal–informal sector distinction does not appear to be a meaningful one. The coefficient on the formal sector dummy is not statistically significant in the earnings function for scheduled castes. The third, and most striking, difference is that the earnings–urban experience profile for scheduled caste workers is flatter than that for non-scheduled castes. An additional year of urban experience increases earnings by 2.8 percent for scheduled castes and 4.8 percent for non-scheduled castes, when evaluated at six years of residence in the city.

5.2. Simple decomposition analysis

The significant difference in the earnings functions for scheduled and non-scheduled castes indicates that the observed earnings differential between these two caste-groups cannot be explained entirely in terms of differences in characteristics. Following the procedure outlined in section 3, we decompose the observed difference into two components: that due to differences in characteristics (E) and that due to differences in earnings function (D); we also indicate the contribution of individual groups of variables to the difference in earnings. It is assumed in the decomposition that the earnings function for non-scheduled castes also applies to scheduled castes (the upper part of table 3), and alternatively that the earnings function for scheduled castes also applies to non-scheduled castes (the middle part of the table). These two sets of estimates provide the upper and lower extremes of a range of values: intermediate estimates (presented in the lower part of the table) are calculated as the geometric mean of the two sets of independent estimates.

When expressed in terms of natural logarithms, the gross earnings difference between scheduled castes and non-scheduled castes is 17 percent. Less than one-half of this is accounted for by differences in characteristics, if the wage structure of non-scheduled castes is used. If the wage structure for scheduled castes is used, the difference in characteristics explains slightly less than two-thirds. Virtually the entire effect of differences in characteristics can be attributed to education and occupation. The mean value of the earnings difference arising from differences in earnings functions is 0.07. The lower rate of return to urban experience for the scheduled castes gives rise to an earnings difference (0.22) which actually exceeds the gross difference in earnings (0.17). The differential return to formal sector employment in favour of the non-scheduled castes is offset in its effect by their lower return to salaried employment. The impact of the differences in the coefficients of the occupation dummies (0.15) and the constant term (−0.34) work in opposite

Table 3

Decomposition of difference in earnings between caste groups.[a]

Independent variable	Earnings difference due to: Characteristics (E)	Earnings function (D)
A		
Education	0.0474	−0.0019
Age on arrival	0.0036	0.0481
Urban experience	−0.0177	0.2223
Occupation	0.0345	0.1540
Salaried employment	0.0085	−0.0851
Formal sector employment	0.0027	0.0845
Constant term		−0.3355
All variables	0.0790	0.0864[b]
B		
Education	0.0475	−0.0020
Age on arrival	0.0041	0.0475
Urban experience	−0.0111	0.2157
Occupation	0.0450	0.1436
Salaried employment	0.0245	−0.1012
Formal sector employment	−0.0002	0.0874
Constant term		−0.3355
All variables	0.1098	0.0555[b]
C		
Education	0.0474	−0.0019
Age on arrival	0.0038	0.0478
Urban experience	−0.0140	0.2190
Occupation	0.0394	0.1487
Salaried employment	0.0144	−0.0928
Formal sector employment	0.0000[c]	0.0859
Constant term		−0.3355
All variables	0.0931	0.0692[b]

[a]The decomposition in the upper part, *A*, of the table is based on eq. (2), and that in the middle, part *B*, on eq. (3). The lower part, *C*, is the geometric mean of the estimates in *A* and *B*.

[b]The calculated figures for *E* and *D* do not add up exactly to the gross earnings difference because of rounding.

[c]Set to zero because the two sets of figures above have the opposite sign.

directions and appear to be high, but, as indicated above, these differences are not statistically significant.

5.3. Multinomial logit estimation of occupational choice

So far we have regarded that part of the gross earnings difference which is due to differences in earnings functions as the measure of discrimination, and that due to differences in characteristics as being 'explained' in the sense that they are economically justified. This approach ignores the potential discriminatory nature of differences in characteristics. While it is possible that the different educational and occupational distributions of scheduled and non-scheduled castes are the result of differences in 'tastes', e.g., in attitudes and aspirations, differential access to education and discrimination in hiring cannot be ruled out. Moreover, if tastes are responsible, they may have been conditioned by past experience of discrimination both prior to and within the market.[23] In order to take into account the possibility of 'unexplained' differences in characteristics, in section 3 we proposed an approach that incorporates into the analysis a separate model of occupational attainment. The exercise involves predicting the occupational distribution of one caste-group assuming that it is determined in the same way as that of the other caste-group, and estimating within-occupation earnings functions.

We analyze occupational attainment within the framework of a multinominal logit model. If there are N occupation groups, the probability that an individual i characterized by the vector $x^i=(1,x_2^i,\ldots,x_h^i)$ of the independent variables will be found in the jth occupation group is given by

$$P_j^i=\exp\beta_j'x^i \Big/ \sum_{k=1}^{N}\exp\beta_k'x^i,$$

where β_k is the vector of h coefficients corresponding to the kth occupation group. The total number of parameters to be estimated is $h(N-1)$, since coefficients for each element of x are determined only up to an arbitrary normalization. In our estimated model we set the coefficients for skilled workers to zero for the purpose of normalization. The parameters of the model are estimated by the maximum likelihood method. We are constrained by the nature of the data set to restrict the independent variables to education, age on arrival, urban experience, and, for the model based on the entire sample only, caste.[24]

The maximum likelihood estimates of the model based on observations for the entire sample are presented in the upper part of table 4. These indicate

[23]Béteille (1974, p. 65).

[24]Marital status and region of origin could not be included because for at least one of the alternatives these variables had no variance or were collinear.

Table 4

Coefficients and asymptotic standard errors for the multinomial logit model of occupational attainment.

	Independent variable				
Occupation	Constant	Education	Age on arrival	Urban experience	Scheduled caste dummy
A. Entire sample					
Professional	−11.28825	0.89585	0.10771	0.06264	−0.69613
	(1.49681)[a]	(0.08564)[a]	(0.03403)[a]	(0.07176)	(0.51049)
Clerical	−2.18749	0.38627	0.01579	0.06888	−1.00754
	(0.85573)[b]	(0.04930)[a]	(0.02354)	(0.05204)	(0.36373)[a]
Production	4.29213	−0.02169	−0.04951	−0.09496	−1.07198
	(0.65432)	(0.03775)	(0.01886)[b]	(0.04411)[b]	(0.30376)[a]
Unskilled	3.53073	−0.07701	−0.03038	−0.07812	−0.56551
	(0.65278)[a]	(0.03859)[b]	(0.01855)	(0.04450)[c]	(0.30581)[c]
Service	−1.10017	0.06719	0.02892	0.08782	−1.10387
	(0.86103)	(0.04916)	(0.02253)	(0.05799)	(0.41784)[a]
Log likelihood		−1331.152			
(*N*)		(1112)			
B. Non-scheduled caste workers					
Professional	−11.32318	0.92390	0.07365	0.14487	
	(1.74704)[a]	(0.10458)[a]	(0.04050)[c]	(0.09233)	
Clerical	−1.79233	0.35283	−0.00042	0.12562	
	(1.04347)[c]	(0.06239)[a]	(0.02871)	(0.06989)[c]	
Production	4.32412	−0.02589	−0.06316	−0.03820	
	(0.88463)[a]	(0.05215)	(0.02538)[b]	(0.06332)	
Unskilled	3.46289	−0.05353	−0.04612	−0.01715	
	(0.90073)[a]	(0.05339)	(0.02579)[c]	(0.06462)	
Service	−1.34307	0.08993	0.01999	0.14489	
	(1.10904)	(0.06366)	(0.02940)	(0.07737)[c]	
Log likelihood	−929.029				
(*N*)	(773)				

[a]Significant at the 1 percent level, using a two-tailed test.
[b]Significant at the 5 percent level.
[c]Significant at the 10 percent level.

that there is differential access to certain occupations according to caste. The coefficient for the scheduled caste dummy is significantly different from zero in all occupation groups except professional workers. By ranking the coefficients of a given variable by size, we can see the relative impact of that variable on probabilities of being in specific occupations. Thus, it is less likely, *ceteris paribus*, that a scheduled caste worker will be a service worker, production worker or a clerical worker than an unskilled worker, the coefficients for the first three occupations being more negative.

Education enables workers to enter better paying occupations. The coefficients on education indicate that the higher is the level of education the greater is the likelihood of being in professional and clerical jobs, and the lower is the likelihood of being engaged in unskilled work. The coefficients of age on arrival and urban experience have to be interpreted with some care. They suggest that, compared to migrants in other occupational groups, professional workers tend to be older and production workers younger at the time of their arrival in the city. This is not surprising as migrants entering professional jobs may have come to the city after several years of experience in a similar activity in the rural area, and employers of production workers are likely to prefer younger men because on-the-job training is important. Production workers and unskilled workers have been in the city for a shorter period than those in other occupation groups. This could be a reflection of three factors at work: (a) in recent years job opportunities have arisen in larger numbers in these two occupation groups, (b) individuals are able to move to other occupation groups over time, and (c) the incidence of return migration is higher among those who enter production and unskilled occupations.

5.4. *Job discrimination versus wage discrimination*

To measure the impact of occupational discrimination on occupational distribution and ultimately on wages, we estimate a separate model of occupational attainment for non-scheduled caste workers. Employing these estimates, shown in the lower part of table 4, we obtain the predicted distributions for scheduled ($\hat{P}_s$) and non-scheduled ($\hat{P}_n$) castes as follows: substitute the sample data for each caste group into the estimated model, producing for each individual a vector of predicted probabilities of belonging to each of the six occupations; and calculate the mean of the predicted probabilities for each occupation after summing over observations. For non-scheduled castes this estimation procedure yields a predicted distribution which is identical to their actual sample distribution, i.e., $\hat{P}_n = P_n$. The difference in the predicted distributions, $(P_n - \hat{P}_s)$, is the 'explained' component due to differences in characteristics, and the residual difference, $(\hat{P}_s - P_s)$, is the 'unexplained' component due to differential access or discrimination. The exercise shows that, except for professional and clerical workers, the residual component accounts for the major part of the observed differences (table 5). For production workers the residual difference (0.11) is actually greater than the observed difference (0.08). If there were no differential access to occupation by caste, the proportion in production occupations would be higher for scheduled than for non-scheduled castes.

Table 5

Full decomposition of gross earnings difference between scheduled and non-scheduled caste workers.

Occupation	Observed occupational distribution		Predicted occupational distribution		Observed difference	Explained difference	Residual difference
	P_n (1)	P_s (2)	$\hat{P}_n$ (3)	$\hat{P}_s$ (4)	$P_n - P_s$ (5)	$P_n - \hat{P}_s$ (6)	$\hat{P}_s - P_s$ (7)
Professional workers	0.0721	0.0443	0.0721	0.0427	0.0278	0.0294	−0.0016
Clerical workers	0.1611	0.0944	0.1611	0.1110	0.0667	0.0501	0.0166
Production workers	0.4214	0.3451	0.4214	0.4556	0.0763	−0.0342	0.1105
Unskilled workers	0.2552	0.3894	0.2552	0.2970	−0.1342	−0.0418	−0.0924
Service workers	0.0567	0.0442	0.0567	0.0574	0.0125	−0.0007	0.0132
Skilled workers	0.0335	0.0826	0.0335	0.0363	−0.0491	−0.0028	−0.0463
	$G = \ln Y_n - \ln Y_s$ (8)	$E = f_n(\bar{x}_n - \bar{x}_s)$ (9)	$D = \bar{x}_s(f_n - f_s)$ (10)	$P_s \times E$ (11)	$P_s \times D$ (12)	$(P_n - \hat{P}_s) \times \ln Y_n$ (13)	$(\hat{P}_s - P_s) \times \ln Y_n$ (14)
Professional workers	0.2607	0.1329	0.1278	0.0059	0.0057	0.1988	−0.0108
Clerical workers	−0.1154	−0.0438	−0.0716	−0.0041	−0.0068	0.2954	0.0979
Production workers	0.1235	0.0174	0.1061	0.0060	0.0366	−0.1895	0.6122
Unskilled workers	0.0922	0.0039	0.0883	0.0015	0.0344	−0.2226	−0.4921
Service workers	0.3296	0.1154	0.2142	0.0051	0.0095	−0.0040	0.0751
Skilled workers	0.0240	−0.1275	0.1515	−0.0105	0.0125	−0.0161	−0.2654
Total				0.0039 *WE*	0.0919 *WD*	0.0620 *JE*	0.0169 *JD*

Within-occupation earnings functions are needed to complete the decomposition based on the full model outlined in section 3. The dependent variable and the independent variables, with the obvious exception of the occupation dummies, are the same as those which appear in the earnings functions presented in table 2. The regressions confirm that returns to education and experience vary substantially between different occupational groups. For each occupational group we decompose the actual earnings difference into the 'explained' (E) and 'unexplained' (D) components, assuming that the earnings functions for non-scheduled castes also apply to scheduled castes. The results are presented in columns (8) to (10) of table 5. Among clerical workers the mean earnings of scheduled castes are greater than those of non-scheduled castes, and scheduled castes have a more favourable earnings structure. In all other occupational groups the earnings functions favour non-scheduled castes. With the exception of professional workers, 'unexplained' differences account for the bulk of the gross difference in earnings.

The final calculations of the decomposition exercise [columns (11) and (14) of table 5] involve using the figures for 'explained' and 'unexplained' components of differences in earnings within occupations, and in occupational distributions, in the manner indicated by eq. (4b) in section 3. They leave no doubt that the actual earnings difference between the two caste-groups is indeed largely the result of discrimination. Of the gross earnings difference (G) of 17 percent, the explained wage difference (WE) accounts for 0.39 percentage points, the explained occupational difference (JE) for 6.20 percentage points, wage discrimination (WD) for 9.19 percentage points, and occupational discrimination (JD) for 1.69 percentage points.[25] Thus, discrimination accounts for two-thirds of the gross earnings difference, with wage discrimination being considerably more important than job discrimination.

5.5. Pinpointing discrimination by occupation and sector

The within-occupation earnings function analysis can assist our understanding of the discrimination we have observed. The gross earnings difference between scheduled and non-scheduled castes ($\ln Y_n - \ln Y_s$) is significant at the 5 percent level or better only among production, unskilled and service workers. In these three occupations the two caste-groups also differ significantly in their mean level of education. Despite the large share of the 'unexplained' difference in earnings in all occupations, the Chow test reveals that earnings functions for scheduled and non-scheduled castes are signifi-

[25]As in the exercise presented in table 3, these components do not add up exactly to the gross earnings difference between the two caste-groups because of rounding.

cantly different only among production workers and service workers.[26] However, there is a contrary indication that caste may be important for unskilled workers. When an equation is estimated for all unskilled workers with a dummy variable for scheduled caste membership included in the list of independent variables, that coefficient is negative and significant at the 5 percent level. The coefficient indicates an earnings differential of 7.8 percent between the two caste-groups, which is slightly less than the 'unexplained' difference obtained in the decomposition exercise. A similar exercise for professional, clerical, and skilled workers confirms that caste does not play an important role in the determination of earnings in these occupations.

The sub-sample of service workers is too small for detailed analysis; that of production workers is considerably larger: 444 workers of whom 117 are scheduled castes. We therefore examine the source of wage discrimination in this occupation in some detail. The earnings functions for production workers are presented, separately for the two caste-groups, in table 6. Scheduled and non-scheduled castes differ significantly in three respects. First, the urban experience variables are statistically significant for non-scheduled castes but not for scheduled castes. An additional year of urban experience adds 6.6 percent to earnings of non-scheduled castes, when evaluated at five years of residence in the city. Secondly, for scheduled caste workers the coefficient on formal sector employment has an unexpected negative sign and is significant at the 1 percent level. *Ceteris paribus*, scheduled castes employed in the formal sector have 11.4 percent lower earnings than those in the informal sector. In contrast, among non-scheduled castes formal sector employees earn 11.4 percent more than informal sector employees. Finally, among scheduled castes salaried workers earn 21.1 percent more than those who are paid on a daily-wage basis, but among non-scheduled castes daily-wage employees are not at a disadvantage.

The finding on the coefficient of formal sector employment for scheduled caste workers suggests that caste discrimination may be a formal sector phenomenon. This is confirmed by the earnings functions estimated separately for the formal and informal sectors (table 7). The coefficient for the scheduled caste dummy in the equation for all production workers in the informal sector is not statistically significant. A Chow test shows that informal sector earnings functions estimated separately for the two caste groups are also not significantly different (computed $F=1.52<$critical $F_{0.05}=2.01$). On the other hand, in the equation for the formal sector, the coefficient for scheduled caste membership is negative and significant at the 1 percent level. *Ceteris paribus*, among formal sector production workers, scheduled castes have 17.3 percent lower earnings than non-scheduled castes.

[26]The computed F ratios are 3.38 for production workers and 2.14 for service workers.

Table 6

Regression analysis of earnings of all production workers and by caste.[a]

Independent variable	All production workers	Scheduled castes	Non-scheduled castes
Education[b]	0.01785	0.01972	0.01592
	(0.00433)[c]	(0.00741)[c]	(0.00521)[c]
Age on arrival	0.06996	0.05122	0.07129
	(0.01489)[c]	(0.02190)[d]	(0.01966)[c]
(Age on arrival)^2	−0.00116	−0.00087	−0.00114
	(0.00027)[c]	(0.00038)[d]	(0.00037)[c]
Urban experience	0.09070	0.02402	0.12348
	(0.01685)[c]	(0.03017)	(0.01980)[c]
(Urban experience)^2	−0.00358	0.00054	−0.00573
	(0.00136)[c]	(0.00247)	(0.00159)[c]
Salaried workers	0.09111	0.19160	0.03629
	(0.03770)[d]	(0.06267)[c]	(0.04566)
Formal sector workers	0.04190	−0.12063	0.10778
	(0.03681)	(0.06094)[d]	(0.04456)[d]
Constant	4.06599	4.47770	3.96814
	(0.20079)[c]	(0.30454)[c]	(0.25850)[c]
R^2	0.23444	0.23798	0.27400
$\bar{R}^2$	0.22215	0.18904	0.25807
F	19.07360[c]	4.86287[c]	17.19881[c]
SEE	0.36023	0.31708	0.36397
(N)	(444)	(117)	(327)
Residual sum of squares	56.57729	10.95878	42.25905

[a]Figures in parentheses are standard errors.
[b]Education was entered linearly because in the quadratic specification both the linear and squared term become insignificant.
[c]Significant at the 1 percent level, using a two-tailed test.
[d]Significant at the 5 percent level.

Table 7

Selected results in earnings functions for production workers in the formal and informal sectors, and in the public and private sub-sectors of the formal sector.[a]

	Entire sample		Formal sector	
	Formal sector	Informal sector	Public	Private
Coefficient on scheduled caste dummy (standard error)	−0.19339 (0.05315)	0.02016 (0.05827)	−0.33680 (0.13646)	−0.16392 (0.05484)
$\bar{R}^2$	0.24795	0.20104	0.55617	0.19367
(N)	(287)	(157)	(40)	(247)
Computed F ratio to test for equality of coefficients for scheduled and and non-scheduled castes	2.63325	1.52155	[b]	2.70678

[a]The dependent variable is again natural logarithm of earnings. Other variables included in the equation, but not reported, are as in table 6.
[b]Separate equations could not be estimated for the two caste-groups, as only seven observations belonged to scheduled castes.

Over four-fifths (86 percent) of production workers in the formal sector are employed in privately owned establishments. Caste discrimination clearly takes place in these. An interesting question, therefore, given the public sector reservation policy, is whether wage discrimination also exists in public sector establishments. Regressions are estimated separately for public sector and the private formal sector (table 7). The coefficient for the scheduled caste dummy is negative and significant at the 1 percent level in both the estimated equations, and the coefficient for public sector (−0.34) is twice that for the private formal sector (−0.16). However, we cannot place too much weight on this finding as only seven of the forty production workers in the public sector are members of the scheduled castes.

6. Interpretation

Caste differs from sex and race in that it is less readily identified. This means that caste discrimination is less likely to be found in the city than in the village, and that the caste of a worker is unlikely to be known to a customer, and possibly not even to an employer, in the city.[27] Whether the caste of a worker is known to the employer depends partly on whether the worker wishes to disclose it, in order to take advantage of the reservation policy, or to conceal it, in order to avoid discrimination. It also depends on the method of application. For instance, caste is likely to be revealed where hiring takes place through contacts of the same caste. These considerations will help to explain the incidence of discrimination which we observed.

In attempting to explain our results, we recognise that they are not necessarily due to discrimination against the scheduled castes. It is possible that certain personal economic characteristics not measured in the survey — for instance, 'drive, determination and doggedness' or other attitudes which are likely to be negatively associated with a 'culture of poverty' — are correlated with caste. The caste variable in the earnings function may be acting simply as a proxy for unidentified productivity differences. Consistent with this explanation was our finding that, in the case of the scheduled castes only, salaried status made a significant difference to the pay of production workers. This may be because scheduled caste workers paid on a daily basis — which included all piece workers — were less effective than others at piece work. It could, however, be due to the exclusion of daily paid scheduled caste workers from the lucrative piece-rate jobs.

It is similarly possible that profit-maximising employers use caste as a screening device for differences in productivity in the absence of perfect

[27]In the rural context, Srinivas (1969, pp. 90–91) notes that when a non-scheduled low caste person became wealthy he tended to follow it up by Sanskritizing his style of life and ritual and claimed to be of higher caste, but similar mobility was extremely difficult for untouchable castes who became wealthy by local standards. Sociologists expressing a view to us on this unresearched question expect that some dissembling does occur in the urban context.

information.[28] When they incur a training cost before the productivity of the individual can be determined, employers may use caste as a criterion for hiring if they believe that the two caste-groups have different distributions of the imperfectly observable economic characteristics. Scheduled caste workers wishing to be hired must accept a lower wage in order to offset the perceived lower probability of their having the desired economic characteristics. Provided that the scheduled caste-group is indeed less efficient on average, someone from that group can be paid less than others of equal efficiency from the non-scheduled group: he need be paid no more than he would receive from employers without information on his personal efficiency.

Although we do not expect unmeasured productivity differences to provide a full explanation for our results, the possibility of such differences nevertheless qualifies the analysis below. This qualification is weakened by the lack of a clear-cut dividing line between economic and discriminatory explanations of screening. Employers' beliefs about caste differences in productivity may be correct only because they are self-fulfilling, i.e., potentially efficient scheduled caste workers may not be given the necessary on-the-job training, or their lower wages may adversely affect their productivity, or the low expectations of or lack of interest by employers may deter scheduled caste workers from acquiring the characteristics (e.g., steadiness, punctuality, responsiveness and initiative) which employers value.

According to the neo-classical theory of labour market discrimination, wage differences arise among equally productive workers because group-specific characteristics are valued in the market, and the values placed on these characteristics are determined by a 'taste for discrimination' exercised by employers, employees or consumers.[29] Scheduled and non-scheduled castes receive different pay even in the same jobs because of the psychic cost attached to the presence of scheduled caste employees. According to the segmented labour market explanations of discrimination, wage differences arise because group differences in political or economic power produce unequal access to earning opportunities.[30] The scheduled castes are at a disadvantage in pay because they are allocated to less well-paid jobs.

It might therefore appear that, with our estimate of wage discrimination five times that of job discrimination (table 5), the neo-classical explanation is the more important. But such a conclusion would be too simple. The relative importance of wage and job discrimination depends on the degree of occupational disaggregation. If job discrimination occurs within as well as between the broad occupational skill categories used in the decomposition

[28] Arrow (1973), and Aigner and Cain (1977) who argue that screening based on correctly perceived group differences in mean productivity cannot be regarded as discrimination.

[29] Arrow (1973) examines each case. See also Becker (1971), Marshall (1974) and Knight and Sabot (1982).

[30] Bonacich (1979), Cain (1976), Darity (1982), Knight and McGrath (1977), Marshall (1974) and Swinton (1977).

analysis, part of the measured wage discrimination is in fact attributable to job discrimination. Other evidence on the competing explanations must therefore be examined.

Given the extent of social discrimination found by the Committee on Untouchables,[31] a 'taste for discrimination' on grounds of caste could plausibly be assumed to exist in the urban labour market. However, the neo-classical theory of discrimination is unsatisfactory in three respects. First, it overlooks the mechanism by which a taste for discrimination is likely to be exercised. Secondly, it is a prediction of the theory that discrimination does not continue in the long run: competition should eliminate wage differences by driving out the discriminators or producing segregated firms.[32] For the theory to hold, it must be the case that caste prejudice is too pervasive, or competition in the product market too weak, for discrimination to be eliminated in India. Thirdly, in simply postulating a taste for discrimination, the theory fails to delve into the economic basis for that taste and the economic interests which it consciously or unconsciously serves.

It is in the allocation of workers to jobs that discrimination is most likely to be practised. An employer would have no aversion to employing an untouchable provided that he worked in an untouchable's job. The village customer might dislike being served by a scheduled caste shop assistant but he would be unlikely to complain if the more menial jobs in the shop were performed by the scheduled castes. Non-scheduled caste employees in a firm might object to the scheduled castes being employed in work of higher or equal status, but they would have no objection to the scheduled castes doing work of lower status. Given the size and significance of the occupation coefficients obtained in the earnings function analysis, discrimination in access to occupation groups is potentially an important cause of caste differences in earnings. The scheduled castes were at some disadvantage in getting access to all but professional, skilled manual, and unskilled occupations. They were at a particular disadvantage in entering production jobs and were as a result — in relation to their characteristics — disproportionately confined to unskilled jobs.

Even discrimination within occupation groups may arise because of caste differences in access to specific occupations. For the sample as a whole, and within the occupation group 'production worker', the significantly lower return to urban experience for scheduled castes could reflect their confinement to 'dead-end' jobs. For instance, scheduled caste workers may tend to be machine helpers whereas non-scheduled castes may tend to be machine operators. Thus, even if the reservation policy assists entry to an occu-

[31] Department of Social Welfare (1969, p. 15).

[32] Arrow (1973), Marshall (1974) and Stiglitz (1973). Similarly, if screening by employers is based on false beliefs, discriminating firms are liable to be driven out by non-discriminating firms.

pational category, subsequent promotion to more responsible or supervisory jobs within that category may be impeded by discrimination. Our measure of *JD* is therefore likely to understate the effects of job discrimination.

Even in the absence of discrimination in the present, discrimination in the past could be responsible for our results. Historical patterns of employment may influence the scheduled castes' choice of occupations: because their expectations and aspirations are lower, they accept lower status jobs and lower pay. This interpretation is consistent with the view expressed that the scheduled castes have generally accepted their economic lot and their place in society without protest.[33]

The occupation-specific earnings functions provide helpful clues to the causes of the wage differences found between the two caste-groups. There was no significant difference in earnings functions between the caste-groups in the professional and clerical occupations. Indeed, the earnings functions for clerks actually favoured the scheduled castes. There was evidence of discrimination in some of the other categories, being clearest in the case of production workers. Here discrimination was observed in the formal but not in the informal sector, and no less in public than in private employment. Discrimination is found in the formal sector and not in the informal sector perhaps because formal sector jobs are prized jobs, and hence resistance to hiring scheduled castes is greater. Or it could be that non-scheduled castes have historically monopolized this sector, with its prized jobs, and scheduled castes have not been able to break their way in.

There are three possible explanations for the distinction found between the manual and non-manual occupations, each of which suggests that the disadvantages of the scheduled castes will not be easily removed. First, the explanation may lie in a difference in recruitment patterns. Non-manual jobs are filled mainly through open advertisements and manual jobs mainly through contacts. Virtually all professional workers and two-thirds of the clerical workers had responded to advertisements in newspapers or obtained information from the employment exchange. In contrast, 58 percent of production workers, 53 percent of skilled workers, 47 percent of unskilled workers and 31 percent of service workers reported that they had obtained their jobs through relatives or covillagers.[34] Contacts are almost invariably from within the same caste-group,[35] and the job secured through contacts is rarely better than that of the contact.[36] Scheduled caste workers may be at a

[33]For instance, in Cox (1959, chs. 1–2) and Fukutake (1967, p. 41).

[34]For a more detailed discussion of the role of contacts, see Banerjee (1981). There was no significant difference in the importance of contacts as between scheduled and non-scheduled castes.

[35]Banerjee (1983).

[36]In general prospective candidates hear about the same job that their contact is engaged in, and this tendency increases inversely with the status and skill of the contact's job. See Banerjee (1981).

disadvantage because they lack contacts in the occupations sought. In these circumstances it is apparent why, even after the elimination of discrimination, the scheduled castes attempting to rise above unskilled manual jobs could be trapped in a vicious circle. Reverse discrimination is required to overcome the discrimination of the past. Scheduled caste workers recruited through contacts are also more prone to discrimination because they are less able to conceal their caste affiliation.

A second possible explanation lies in differing expectations. It is plausible that the relative expectations of scheduled caste members are lower, the lower their level of education, i.e., education brings with it a growth in self-confidence and assertiveness. If that were the case, we would expect to observe discrimination more in manual than in non-manual occupations.

Finally, the government reservation policy may have been more successful within the clerical, professional and service occupations. The policy may more readily be applied, and be observed to apply, when jobs are filled through open advertisement than when, as in the case of manual jobs, they are filled through personal recommendations. The fact that 60 percent of non-manual employees, and only 21 percent of manual employees were in the public sector also means that the government reservation policy had more leverage in the non-manual labour market.

Finally, we consider whether a 'taste for discrimination' is an adequate explanation of the discriminatory practices which we have observed. The relation between caste and class is recognised as a central question in Indian sociology.[37] Whatever the answer, it is clear than an effect of caste prejudice in the labour market and more generally is to promote the economic interests of some groups and to harm those of others. The caste system is thus functional to the generation and maintenance of economic inequalities. Job discrimination produces caste differences in the price of labour and therefore in incomes.[38] It can be expected that these economic interests contribute to the preservation of the caste system.

Support for an economic interpretation of caste discrimination in the labour market comes from a detailed historical study of the Bombay cotton mills: 'The exclusion of untouchables from weaving jobs may well have operated as a device to preserve the monopoly of particularly well-paying jobs for all Muslims and clean-caste Hindus against all untouchables more than it constituted a carryover of traditional ritual barriers into the factories.'[39] Further support is to be found in a study of scheduled caste shoemakers in Agra, whose occupation has been undermined by the develop-

[37]See, for instance, Dumont (1966).

[38]The interpretation of racial discrimination as a means of splitting the labour market into high- and low-priced labour and of preventing displacement of high- by low-priced workers is stressed by Bonacich (1979).

[39]Morris (1965, p. 201).

ment of shoe factories. The status of factory owner and middleman is traditionally ascribed to and exclusively occupied by upper castes. Through their support for each other, business skills and control of the shoe market, 'upper caste Punjabis resist any incursion on their occupational monopoly by the low caste Jatavs'.[40]

Being generally accepted by all castes, the system is more subtle and stable than systems of discrimination in which one group more overtly exercises power over another in the pursuit of its economic interests.[41] Nevertheless, the caste riots referred to in section 2 — which were riots by non-scheduled against scheduled castes — suggest that those who benefit from the caste system would not meekly accept a perceived threat to their interests.

7. Conclusion

In this, the pioneering quantitative analysis of caste discrimination in the urban labour market of India, we found that caste discrimination continued to exist long after the Indian government had introduced its policy of reverse discrimination. The conventional exercise for measuring the extent of discrimination 'within the market' indicated that it accounted for nearly half of the gross earnings difference between scheduled and non-scheduled castes. We were able to pry into the reasons for this discrimination by examining the precise ways in which the earnings functions for the two caste-groups differed. Our occupational attainment function permitted a distinction to be made between wage and job discrimination, and the occupation-specific earnings functions — by enabling us to pinpoint discrimination — provided clues to its causes.

Our results might reflect unmeasured caste differences in labour productivity: an omitted variables or screening explanation cannot be wholly ruled out, although even this may contain a self-fulfilling element of prejudice. Nevertheless, the strength of caste prejudice observed in rural India suggests that discriminatory preferences might well have an influence in the urban labour market. Discrimination appears to operate at least in part through the traditional mechanism, *viz.* the assignment of workers to occupations, with scheduled caste workers disproportionately represented in poorly-paid 'dead-end' jobs. Even if discrimination were no longer practised, the effects of past discrimination could carry over to the present, for instance in the choice of occupation. This may help to explain why discrimination is greatest in the operative jobs, in which contacts are important for recruitment, and not in white collar jobs, recruitment to which involves more formal methods. The economic function which the system performs for the favoured castes

[40]Lynch (1969, p. 39).

[41]See, for instance, Knight and McGrath (1977) and Bonacich (1979, esp. pp. 42–45) on racial discrimination in the South African labour market.

suggests that their 'taste for discrimination' is based, consciously or unconsciously, on economic self-interest, so making prejudice more difficult to eradicate.

In the absence of direct evidence on earnings and occupation according to caste for other major Indian cities, it is difficult to know how far our findings can be generalized for urban India. However, a study of factory workers in Poona conducted in 1957 found that backward castes were hardly represented at all among supervisors and clerks, and that they had significantly lower mean wages in all factories.[42] When standardized for education, caste differentials in mean earnings were most striking among illiterates and matriculates. Evidence on other aspects of labour markets suggests that labour market conditions elsewhere are likely to be similar to those in Delhi. Studies for Bombay and for Calcutta found that within the overall industrial or occupational structure there was a significant degree of specialization by workers from different places of origin.[43] Joshi and Joshi (1976) attributed this concentration to the importance of informal networks of contacts in placing people in employment. The importance of contacts in the recruitment process was also observed in Ahmedabad.[44] These results are relevant because differential access to jobs is potentially an important cause of caste differences in earnings.

It is not easy to evaluate the affirmative action on untouchability that the Indian government has taken since Independence, because we cannot be sure what would have happened in its absence. Our results for non-manual workers nevertheless provide some justification for the decision made to renew the legislation favouring scheduled castes in access to public sector education and jobs, when it elapsed in 1980. Yet our results for manual workers suggest that, especially where employers recruit by means of informal contacts, caste discrimination in the labour market for migrants is alive and well and living in Delhi impervious to such policy.

[42] Lambert (1963).
[43] Joshi and Joshi (1976, pp. 132–134, 166–167), Morris (1965, pp. 132–143), Lubell (1973, p. 31).
[44] Papola (1977, pp. 148–149, 153–155).

References

Aigner, Dennis, J. and Glen G. Cain, 1977, Statistical theories of discrimination in labor markets, Industrial and Labor Relations Review 30, no. 2, 175–187.

Arrow, Kenneth J., 1973, The theory of discrimination, in: O. Ashenfelter and A. Rees, eds., Discrimination in labor markets (Princeton University Press, Princeton, NJ).

Banerjee, Biswajit, 1981, Some aspects of rural-urban migration in India: A case study of Delhi, unpublished Ph. D. thesis (University of Oxford, Oxford).

Banerjee, Biswajit, 1983, Social networks in the migration process: Empirical evidence on chain migration in India, Journal of Developing Areas, Jan., 185–196.

Becker, Gary S., 1971, The economics of discrimination, 2nd ed. (University of Chicago Press, Chicago, IL).

Berreman, Gerald, D., 1979, Caste and other inequities (Folklore Institute, Delhi).

Béteille, A., 1969, Castes old and new. Essays in social structure and social stratification (Asia Publishing House, Bombay).

Béteille, André, 1974, Studies in agrarian social structure (Oxford University Press, Delhi).

Birdsall, Nancy and M. Louise Fox, 1981, Why males earn more: Location, job preferences and job discrimination among Brazilian schoolteachers, Mimeo. (World Bank, Washington DC).

Blinder, Alan S., 1973, Wage discrimination: Reduced form and structural estimates, Journal of Human Resources, Fall, 436–455.

Bonacich, Edna, 1979, The past, present and future of split labor market theory, in: C.B. Marrett and C. Leggon, eds., Research in race and ethnic relations. A research annual, Vol. 1 (Jai Press, Greenwich, CT).

Bose, Pradip Kumar, 1981, Social mobility and caste violence. A study of the Gujarat riots, Economic and Political Weekly, April 18, 713–716.

Brown, Randall S., Marilyn Moon and Barbara S. Zoloth, 1980, Incorporating occupational attainment in studies of male–female earnings differentials, Journal of Human Resources, Winter, 1–28.

Cain, Glen G., 1976, The challenge of segmented labor market theories to orthodox theory: A survey, Journal of Economic Literature, Dec., 1215–1257.

Commissioner for Scheduled Castes and Scheduled Tribes, various years, Annual report (Government of India Press, Delhi).

Cox, Oliver Cromwell, 1959, Caste, race and class. A study in social dynamics (Monthly Review Press, New York).

Darity, William A., Jr., 1982, The human capital approach to black–white earnings inequality: Some unsettled questions, Journal of Human Resources 17, no. 1, 72–93.

Department of Social Welfare, 1969, Report of the Committee on Untouchability, Economic and educational development of the scheduled castes and connected documents (Delhi).

Dumont, Louis, 1966, A fundamental problem in the sociology of caste, Contributions to Indian Sociology 9, Dec., 17–32.

Dushkin, Lelah, 1979, Backward class benefits and social class in India, 1920–1970, Economic and Political Weekly, April 7, 661–667.

Fukutake, Tadashi, 1967, Asian rural society: China, India, Japan (University of Tokyo Press, Tokyo).

Joshi, Heather and Vijay Joshi, 1976, Surplus labour and the city. A study of Bombay (Oxford University Press, Delhi).

Knight, J.B. and M.D. McGrath, 1977, An analysis of racial wage discrimination in South Africa, Oxford Bulletin of Economics and Statistics 39, no. 4, 245–271.

Knight, J.B. and R.H. Sabot, 1982, Labour market discrimination in a poor urban economy, Journal of Development Studies 19, no. 1, 67–87.

Lambert, Richard D., 1963, Workers, factories and social change in India (Princeton University Press, Princeton, NJ).

Lubell, H., 1973, Urban development and employment in Calcutta, International Labour Review 108, July, 25–41.

Lynch, Owen M., 1969, The politics of untouchability. Social mobility and social change in a city of India (Columbia University Press, New York).

Marshall, Ray, 1974, The economics of racial discrimination: A survey, Journal of Economic Literature, Sept., 849–871.

Moffatt, Michael, 1975, Untouchables and the caste system: A Tamil case study, Contributions to Indian Sociology (N.S.) 9, no. 1, 111–122.

Morris, Morris David, 1965, The emergence of an industrial labor force in India. A study of the Bombay cotton mills, 1854–1947 (University of California Press, Berkeley/Los Angeles, CA).

Oaxaca, Ronald, 1973a, Sex discrimination in wages, in: Orley Ashenfelter and Albert Rees, eds., Discrimination in labor markets (Princeton University Press, Princeton, NJ) 124–151.

Oaxaca, Ronald, 1973b, Male–female differentials in urban labor markets, International Economic Review 3, Oct., 603–709.

Papola, T.S., 1977, Mobility and wage structure in an urban labour market: A study in Ahmedabad, in: Subbiah Kannappan, ed., Studies of urban labour market behaviour in developing countries (International Institute for Labour Studies, Geneva).
Srinivas, M.N., 1962, Caste in modern India and other essays (Asia Publishing House, Bombay).
Srinivas, M.N., 1969, Social change in modern India (University of California Press, Berkeley, CA).
Stiglitz, Joseph, 1973, Approaches to the economics of discrimination, American Economic Review, Papers and Proceedings, 63, no. 2, 287–295.
Swinton, David H., 1977, A labour force competition theory of discrimination in the labor market, American Economic Review, Papers and Proceedings, 67, no. 1, 400–404.
Wadhawa, Kamlesh Kumar, 1975, Minority safeguards in India (Thomson, Delhi).

[11]

Blacks, Hispanics, and White Ethnic Groups: Are Blacks Uniquely Disadvantaged?

By REYNOLDS FARLEY*

The National Academy's *A Common Destiny* described black Americans, and observed that while substantial progress was made, blacks remained far behind whites on social, health, and economic indicators.

Are blacks unique? If we consider Hispanics, other racial minorities, and white ethnic groups, will we find that some groups are even less prosperous than African-Americans? Is the black-white comparison too simple? This paper, part of my larger investigation of racial-ethnic differences (1989), addresses these issues.

I. Defining Racial and Ethnic Groups

The 1980 Census asked persons to identify their race by checking one of 15 circles. All respondents also answered a question about their Hispanic origin. A 19.3 percent sample answered a question about their ancestry. This query, used for the first time in 1980, replaced questions about birthplace of parents. Respondents could write any terms they wished, and typically the first two were coded. There was no allocation for nonresponse to the ancestry question, and about 11 percent left the question unanswered. Another 6 percent wrote the single term, American.

An exhaustive and mutually exclusive array of racial/ethnic groups was created using these questions (see also Stanley Lieberson and Mary Waters, 1988, ch. 2). First, 4 Hispanic groups were defined from the Spanish-origin question. Next, non-Hispanics were classified by their race. Aleuts and Eskimos were grouped with American Indians (by race) to form an American Natives category, and then 7 nonwhite racial groups were identified. A residual category of "other races" included Hawaiians, Guamanians, and other infrequently reported races.

Those who identified themselves as white by race and were not Hispanics were classified by their first reported ancestry. I identified 37 white ethnic groups, each having 60,000 persons between the ages 25–54; a number that allowed the fitting of models of earnings using the one-percent sample. The list of white ethnic groups includes American Indians. There were numerous individuals (approximately 2 million) who selected white as their race and then wrote American Indian for their ancestry. This group should be distinguished from the smaller Native American group (C. Matthew Snipp, 1980, ch. 2). The list includes a category of whites who wrote American for their ancestry, those who left the ancestry question blank, and whites not elsewhere classified (NEC): people whose first ancestry was not among the 36 used in this analysis. English and German each made up about 15 percent of the population. The third largest group, blacks, was the only other one comprising 10 percent or more. The 4 smallest groups (Croatian, Rumanian, Lebanese, and Armenian) each comprised less than .1 percent.

II. Economic Characteristics

Table 1 shows the percent in households whose pre-tax cash incomes either fell below the poverty line or exceeded six times the poverty line (a group I label affluent). To be impoverished, a household of four had to have an income of less than $11,600 in 1987 dollars; to be affluent, in excess of $69,600.

The white ethnic groups (except Americans and American Indians) had poverty rates between 4 and 8 percent, or well below the national average of 11 percent. Among Filipinos, Japanese, Koreans, and Asian Indians, poverty rates were equivalent to those of white ethnic groups, but 6 groups were distinguished by elevated poverty. The most

*Population Studies Center, University of Michigan, Ann Arbor, MI 48104.

TABLE 1—SIZE AND CHARACTERISTICS OF 50 MUTUALLY EXCLUSIVE RACIAL/ETHNIC GROUPS IN 1980

	Percent			Men 25–54	
	Below Poverty Line	Affluent[a]	Per Capita Income[b]	Mean Yrs. College	Percent Prof./ Mgr.[c]
U.S. Total	11	12	$11.2	1.7	28
Hispanic Groups					
Cuban	12	9	10.6	1.7	25
Mexican	22	3	6.8	.7	11
Puerto Rican	34	2	6.1	.6	13
Other Spanish	16	7	8.9	1.5	21
Racial Minorities					
Amer. Natives	25	5	6.9	1.0	19
Asian Indians	8	12	13.2	5.3	60
Black	27	4	7.1	1.0	14
Chinese	13	16	11.9	3.6	42
Filipino	6	9	10.9	2.8	27
Japanese	5	23	14.6	2.9	42
Korean	8	11	10.2	3.4	36
Vietnamese	34	3	5.8	1.4	17
Other Races	21	7	8.8	2.2	26
White Ethnic Groups					
American	10	9	10.0	1.0	18
Amer. Indian	13	6	9.0	.8	15
Armenian	9	19	13.6	2.6	38
Austrian	5	25	15.5	3.3	49
Belgian	7	14	12.3	2.0	36
Canadian	6	7	13.4	2.2	40
Croatian	4	16	13.2	2.1	38
Czech	6	16	13.3	2.2	35
Danish	5	16	13.2	2.3	34
Dutch	8	12	11.7	1.7	29
English	8	15	12.5	2.0	32
Finnish	7	13	11.5	2.1	31
French	8	10	11.6	1.5	27
French-Canadian	6	11	11.7	1.5	25
German	6	14	12.3	1.8	30
Greek	7	16	12.2	2.0	35
Hungarian	6	18	13.5	2.3	36
Irish	8	13	11.8	1.8	29
Italian	6	14	12.1	1.8	31
Lebanese	7	17	13.1	2.8	40
Lithuanian	5	20	14.6	2.6	42
Norwegian	6	15	12.7	2.2	33
Polish	5	11	12.8	2.0	32
Portuguese	7	10	10.9	1.1	19
Rumanian	6	27	15.3	3.3	49
Russian	6	32	17.9	4.0	59
Scandinavian	5	16	12.3	2.7	41
Scots-Irish	5	18	14.1	2.4	37
Scottish	5	20	14.4	2.7	40
Slovak	4	13	13.4	1.8	27
Swedish	5	17	13.7	2.4	37
Swiss	6	18	13.6	2.5	36
Ukrainian	5	17	13.6	2.5	36
Welsh	5	18	13.0	2.6	39
Yugoslavian	7	18	13.7	2.1	33
NEC	6	14	12.4	2.4	36
Not Rpt.	5	11	11.7	2.3	23

Source: U.S. Bureau of the Census, *Census of Population: 1980*, Public Use Microdata Sample.

[a]This reports the percent of individuals in households whose pre-tax cash income equalled at least six times the poverty line.

[b]Shown in thousands: 1987$.

[c]This shows the percent of employed men holding professional or managerial jobs in April 1980.

impoverished, Puerto Ricans and Vietnamese, had rates triple the national average, while among blacks, American Natives, Mexicans, and Other Races, poverty was double the national rate. Only two groups, Vietnamese and Puerto Ricans, were more frequently impoverished than blacks.

Several white groups and one Asian race were overrepresented among the affluent. Nationally, about one person in eight lived in such a household, but one-third of Russians did so. More than one-fifth of Rumanians, Austrians, Lithuanians, and Japanese were in prosperous circumstances.

Per capita incomes are shown in Table 1 in 1987 dollars. Two groups stood out for their meager incomes: Vietnamese (92 percent born outside the United States) had a per capita income just one-half the national average, while Puerto Ricans (about one-half island born) had incomes only $300 above that of the Vietnamese. American Natives, Mexicans, and blacks had small incomes, about 60 percent of the national average. The least prosperous European group (the Portuguese) had incomes exceeding those of blacks by 54 percent.

Russians, whose incomes were $2,500 greater than those of their closest rivals, Austrians and Rumanians, were exceptionally prosperous. Three others (Japanese, Lithuanians, and the Scottish) had incomes $3,000 or more in excess of the overall average.

Information about the educational attainment and occupational achievements of men aged 25–54 is also presented in Table 1. The summary assessment of attainment is per capita years of college education. The national average was 1.7 years, but Asian Indians were exceptional in that they averaged in excess of 5 years of college, or 1.3 years more than the second ranking group, the Russians. Austrians, Chinese, Koreans, and Rumanians had averages exceeding 3 years. At the other extreme were Americans, American Natives, and blacks who averaged just 1 year of college, and 2 groups, Mexicans and Puerto Ricans, whose average was below 1 year.

The final column reports the percent of employed men holding professional or managerial jobs. Overall, 28 percent worked at these positions, but 2 groups stood out for their unusually high proportions: Asian Indians and Russians. In 8 groups, fewer than 20 percent were so employed. Mexicans were least likely to be working as professionals or managers followed by Puerto Ricans, blacks, American Indians, Vietnamese, Americans, American Natives, and one European-origin group, the Portuguese.

III. The Earnings of Men

Does race or ethnicity make a difference? Why are there such substantial discrepancies in economic status? Do some groups invest in education and live in high wage areas, while others quite school and remain in the rural South? Or, are there systematic differences in the rates of financial return groups receive for their human capital investments? A complete disaggregation of differences is beyond the scope of this paper, but groups differ greatly in the characteristics associated with earnings and racial minorities, and Hispanics receive smaller returns for human capital investments than white ethnic groups.

Table 2 describes men aged 25–54 who reported any positive earnings in 1979. To facilitate a comparison, I eliminated men who were foreign born and considered only those 40 groups in which there were 300 or more in the 1980 one-percent sample. In the table, Puerto Rican refers to men born in the United States.

The first column shows mean earnings in 1987 dollars, while the second reports earnings as a percent of the national average of $23,400. There is additional evidence of the prosperity of Eastern European ancestries since Russian, Austrian, and Yugoslavian men had earnings 20 percent or more above average. Other white ethnic groups (with the exception of Americans and American Indians) had earnings 95 to 119 percent of the mean. At the low end were Puerto Ricans, Mexicans, and American Natives, but blacks were at the bottom with earnings 80 percent of the national average. The procedure used here underestimates actual racial-ethnic differences by assuming full employment. In fact, only 83 percent of black men ages 25–54 reported any earnings in 1979, compared to 96 percent of the Russians.

TABLE 2—ANNUAL EARNINGS OF MEN 25–54 AND DIFFERENCES FROM THE NATIONAL AVERAGE FOR 40 MUTUALLY EXCLUSIVE RACIAL/ETHNIC GROUPS IN 1980

			Differences Attributable to	
	1979 Annual Earnings[a]	As Percent of Total	Own Characteristics[b]	Own Rates of Return[c]
U.S. Total	$23.4	100		
Hispanic Groups				
Mexican	19.3	83	−11	−6
Puerto Rican	19.6	84	−8	−3
Other Spanish	21.3	91	−2	−7
Racial Minorities				
Amer. Natives	19.1	82	−12	−12
Black	18.6	80	−12	−8
Chinese	26.8	115	+18	−13
Japanese	26.4	113	+14	−6
Other Races	20.3	87	−1	−16
White Ethnic Groups				
American	21.3	91	−9	0
Amer. Indian	20.8	89	−10	−4
Austrian	29.4	126	+17	+6
Belgian	27.2	116	+7	+8
Canadian	23.7	101	+7	0
Czech	25.5	109	+7	+3
Danish	25.4	109	+9	+2
Dutch	23.5	101	+2	−1
English	24.1	103	+1	+1
Finnish	27.3	117	+5	+5
French	23.2	99	−1	+1
French-Canadian	23.8	102	+2	+2
German	24.4	104	+3	+1
Greek	25.7	110	+10	+1
Hungarian	27.8	119	+10	+8
Irish	24.5	105	+2	+3
Italian	25.5	109	+5	+6
Lithuanian	27.3	117	+11	+3
Norwegian	24.7	106	+6	+3
Polish	25.6	110	+6	+3
Portuguese	25.4	109	+3	−3
Russian	32.4	139	+22	+8
Scandinavian	25.7	110	+8	+2
Scots-Irish	25.4	109	+7	+1
Scottish	25.7	110	+9	+1
Slovak	26.5	114	+9	+3
Swedish	25.6	110	+9	+2
Swiss	24.2	104	+8	−4
Ukrainian	25.5	109	+8	+3
Welsh	25.7	110	+10	+2
Yugoslavian	28.0	120	+9	+15
NEC	24.6	105	+4	+1
Not Rpt.	22.1	95	−7	0

Source: See Table 1.

[a]Shown in thousands: 1987$. Estimates of earnings assume a person worked 2000 hours. Analysis is restricted to all persons reporting positive earnings in 1979.

[b]This is the percent difference between the overall average earnings and the hypothetical earnings of a group assuming their own characteristics and the rates of return of the entire sample.

[c]This is the percent difference between the overall average earnings and the hypothetical earnings of a group assuming their own rates of return but the characteristics of the entire sample.

To investigate causes of these differences, I used an earnings model and a regression standardization procedure. The log of hourly earnings was regressed upon years of precollege education, years of college, marital status (to distinguish married men who earn more), age, and a series of variables that identified the regions and men who lived outside metropolises. Equations were fit for the entire sample and for every group.

For each race-ethnicity, I took the earnings equation for the entire sample and inserted the characteristics of the group to estimate what their earnings would have been if they had the rates of return of the entire sample but their own characteristics. These hypothetical earnings were compared to the national average to assess the net effects of a group's characteristics. They are shown in Table 2 as a percent of the overall mean. Mexicans, for example, had characteristics that cost them an amount equal to 11 percent of the national average.

Next, I used the earnings equations for each group and inserted the characteristics of the total sample. This produced a second hypothetical earnings estimate for every group which was compared to the national average to assess the effects of a group's rates of return. This disaggregation does not unambiguously account for a group's overall difference from the national average.

We expect that groups differ in their earnings because of differences in their geographic locations, education, age, and marital status. Figures in the column Own Characteristics confirm this. The earnings of Russian, Chinese, Austrian, Japanese, and Lithuanian men were raised by 10 percent or more above the average because of their favorable characteristics, while those of Mexicans, American Natives, and blacks were limited because of their characteristics.

Title VII of the 1964 Civil Rights Act outlawed discrimination in the labor market. If this earnings model is appropriate, and if employers comply with the law, we would expect that the numbers showing differences attributable to a group's rates of return would be close to zero. This is the situation for most white ethnic groups. Four white ethnic groups (Belgians, Hungarians, Russians, and Yugoslavians) had earnings that were augmented, but the racial minorities and Hispanics had their earnings limited by lower than average rates of return. The net cost of being an American Native, black, Chinese, or Other Races exceeded 8 percent of the overall mean earnings. It is impossible to demonstrate discrimination using census samples, but these numbers imply that if a specific set of characteristics were possessed by Hispanics or racial minorities, they were less rewarded than if they were possessed by white ethnic groups.

Several additional conclusions may be drawn. First, the high earnings of Eastern European men came about primarily because of their characteristics. Second, Chinese and Japanese reported large earnings but the net effect of membership in these groups was a reduction in earnings. To earn a great deal, Chinese and Japanese must have greater educational attainments than whites (see Ronald Takaki, 1989). Third, the least prosperous of the white groups were those who wrote American or American Indian for their ancestry or left the question blank. Their low earnings were due to their characteristics: their meager educations and concentrations in rural areas. Finally, Mexicans, American Natives, and blacks were at a double disadvantage. Their characteristics limited their earnings, and their rates of return were also below average.

IV. Conclusion

Would the National Academy's Committee have drawn different conclusions if they had considered an array of racial, Hispanic, and ethnic minorities? Is the black-white comparison too simple? The answer to both questions is no. After examining the characteristics of 50 racial-ethnic groups, I found that the Vietnamese and Puerto Ricans were more impoverished than blacks and, in terms of per capita income, Mexicans and American Natives were similar to blacks. There was considerable variation in the status of the 37 white ethnic groups and Eastern European groups had exceptionally high incomes. However, all of the white ethnic groups were more prosperous than blacks. The only white group whose educational attainment or occupational status approximated that of blacks were people who identified themselves as white by race but American Indian by ancestry.

When the analysis focused on earnings of native born men, blacks were the most disadvantaged with earnings below those of Native Americans, Mexicans, and Puerto Ricans. Blacks and men from these three groups had characteristics associated with low earnings. In addition, blacks, other racial minorities (including Asians), and Hispanic groups had rates of return that were lower than those of white ethnic groups.

REFERENCES

Farley, Reynolds, "Race and Ethnicity in the U.S. Census: An Evaluation of the 1980 Ancestry Question," unpublished manuscript, Population Studies Center, University of Michigan, 1989.

Jaynes, Gerald and Williams, Robin, *A Common Destiny: Blacks and American Society*, Washington: National Academy Press, 1989.

Lieberson, Stanley and Waters, Mary C., *From Many Strands*, New York: Russell Sage, 1988.

Snipp, C. Matthew, *American Indians: The First of This Land*, New York: Russell Sage, 1988.

Takaki, Ronald, *Strangers from a Different Shore*, Boston: Little Brown, 1989.

U.S. Bureau of the Census, *U.S. Census of Population: 1980*, PC80-S1-10, Special Report, *Ancestry of the Population by State: 1980*, Washington, 1983.

[12]

Race and Human Capital

By JAMES P. SMITH*

While human capital has been used with some success to analyze recent changes in racial income differences, scholars have repeatedly pointed to a major empirical problem that appears to severely limit the historical relevance and scope of skill-based theories as applied to racial questions. The challenge they raise is legitimate. Put simply, if measured skill disparities between the races narrowed throughout the twentieth century, why did income ratios first begin to converge in the 1960's?

In this paper, I address this question relying on some unexploited census data by race on education, literacy, occupations, and income. Using these data that begin with the 1890 Census, I present new estimates of age-specific relative income positions of black men for all postslavery birth cohorts. In addition to reconciling the apparently inconsistent skill and income series, these income ratios offer a very different historical record than many economists believe to have been the case. To cite a prominent example, Gunnar Myrdal's classic work (1944) saw the economic position of his contemporary black America not only as dismal, but made even more so by its sense of hopelessness, given the absence of any hint of progress or change. While Myrdal's pessimism is understandable, it appears that even in his day seeds had long been sown that were already permanently altering and improving the relative economic status of black men.

I. Background

The success of human capital explanations for racial income differences has historically been uneven at best. Morton Zeman's 1955 dissertation, a detailed and careful analysis of the 1940 Census, served as the standard empirical reference until the micro-level 1960 Census tapes became available. Zeman evaluated the importance of human capital's two main faces: years of schooling and on-the-job training. While incomes of men of both races increased with schooling and age, Zeman discovered that the rate of increase across either dimension was considerably higher for white men. Whether the added skill involved an extra year in school or another on the job, black-white income ratios declined by one-third of 1 percent for every 1 percent rise in white income. Racial income differences within schooling or age groups dominated racial differences in the amount of human capital possessed. The elimination of racial differences in schooling or age would have reduced the southern racial income gap by less than one-quarter and that in the North by about 5 percent. Essentially, Zeman's work implied that giving blacks the same amount of schooling as whites would do little to alter racial income disparities. The problem, rather, was different pay for the same skill and differential racial payoffs to acquiring more skill.

Throughout the 1950's, events appeared to confirm Zeman's research. Studies based on the 1950 and 1960 Censuses indicated that, if anything, there may have been a deterioration in the relative economic position of blacks (Alan Batchelder, 1964). The initial micro-level studies based on the 1960 Census by Giora Hanoch (1965), Lester Thurow (1969), and others did little to amend this view. Their work painted a consistent picture of low returns to schooling for blacks as well as a sharp deterioration in relative black economic potential over job careers. In light of these findings, the emphasis in the economic literature concentrated on reasons for racial differences in the value of skill.[1]

*Senior Economist, The Rand Corporation, 1700 Main Street, Santa Monica, CA 90406. Comments by Gary Becker, Robert Hauser, Jacob Mincer, and Ted Schultz are gratefully acknowledged. I am indebted to the oftentimes heroic assistance of Chris Witsberger. The research received support from the Ford Foundation and the National Science Foundation.

[1]On the schooling dimension, market discrimination against black skilled labor and government discrimination resulting in lower quality of black schools were the principal competing factors advanced to explain de-

TABLE 1—YEARS OF SCHOOLING OF U.S. MALES BY YEARS OF BIRTH

Birth Years	Age in 1973	Black	White	Difference
1907–16	57–66	7.1	10.6	3.5
1917–26	47–56	8.6	11.6	3.0
1927–36	37–46	10.1	12.2	2.1
1937–46	27–36	11.4	12.9	1.5
1947–51	22–26	11.9	13.0	1.1

Source: Robert Hauser and David Featherman (1978).

Two developments led to more emphasis being assigned to human capital factors during the late 1960's and early 1970's. First, there was a sustained and impressive rise in black-white income ratios. Second, micro analysis based on the 1967 Survey of Economic Opportunity and 1970 Census indicated that rates of return to education, especially at upper schooling levels, appeared as high for blacks as for whites (Finis Welch, 1974). In addition, reanalysis of the 1960 Census revealed that first-generation studies had significantly understated rates of return to education for blacks.[2] On the issue of job-related investments, Welch pointed out that cross-sectional data showing declining black-white income ratios with age may not reflect life cycle factors at all if changes across birth cohorts are larger for blacks than whites. In joint work, Welch and I (1977) provided evidence that over recent years, black male incomes did not fall behind those of comparable whites as their careers evolved, lending some support to a cohort interpretation for at least recent cross sections.

The historical validity of an emphasis on human capital factors has rightly been questioned (see Orley Ashenfelter, 1977; Henry Levin, 1978; and William Darity, 1982).[3]

TABLE 2—RATIOS OF MEAN PERSONAL INCOME OF BLACK AND WHITE MALES, 1948–78

Year	Ratios	Year	Ratios
1948	.530	1968	.612
1953	.533	1973	.643
1958	.538	1978	.669
1963	.566		

Source: U.S. Bureau of the Census, *Consumer Income*, Series, P-60.

The basic issue raised is illustrated in Table 1 which summarizes trends in educational attainment by race and post-World War II changes in racial income differences. The twentieth-century schooling story is clear. With each successive birth cohort, racial differences in education levels narrowed, until a 3.5-year gap for the oldest cohort was reduced to only a 1.1-year advantage for whites in the youngest cohort. As new cohorts entered the labor force over the last forty years, the competitive human capital disadvantage

clining black-white income ratios with schooling. On the job investment side, discrimination-based theories dominated, either using the language of denying blacks access to jobs with human capital growth or simply confining blacks to secondary labor markets.

[2]Apparently, due to the use of group data and an age control rather than experience. (See my article with Welch, 1977.)

[3]While the basic point remained the same, the language used became progressively stronger and the problem was viewed as increasingly lethal. "Where does this leave us? In my view, it leaves us with a very considerable puzzle. Attributing the steady increase in relative earnings to the gradual increase in their skills (as measured, say, by schooling) requires an explanation of why the gradual increase in skills of black men had so little effect on their relative earnings before the mid 1960's" (Ashenfelter, p. 297). "Thus, the human capital interpretation seems to be applied in an *ad hoc* fashion to 1964 and beyond while ignoring the lack of earnings equalization during the first half of this century when the trend towards educational equalization was much more dramatic" (Levin, p. 28). "Human capital differences, therefore, are offered only as the dominant explanation for racial income differences for a limited episode—the 1960s and later. Usually, the theory is not claimed by its proponents to be historically general in applicability. ...The human capital approach may well be a dead letter" (Darity, p. 80).

TABLE 3—MEAN SCHOOLING LEVELS BY BIRTH COHORT (YEARS OF SCHOOLING)

Birth Cohort	White Males	Black Males	White Females	Black Females
1951–54	12.64	11.82	12.70	12.24
1946–50	12.68	11.93	12.45	11.86
1941–45	12.32	11.25	12.14	11.33
1936–40	12.00	10.46	11.81	10.89
1931–35	11.69	9.78	11.52	10.37
1926–30	11.38	9.11	11.33	9.87
1921–25	11.14	8.44	11.12	9.03
1916–20	10.74	7.65	10.79	8.36
1911–15	10.15	6.75	10.36	7.70
1906–10	9.72	6.26	10.02	7.16
1901–05	9.19	5.72	9.45	6.46
1896–1900	8.74	5.42	8.96	6.03
1891–95	8.18	4.96	8.42	5.52
1886–90	7.74	4.72	8.11	5.13
1881–85	7.56	4.38	7.95	4.67
1876–80	7.44	4.11	7.88	4.27
1871–65	7.22	3.56	7.58	3.59
1866–70	7.07	3.06	7.45	2.89
pre–1865	6.76	2.37	7.13	1.99

of blacks appears to have continuously diminished.

This was not so for income. Before 1960, there was little change in relative income by race. Black-white male income ratios did rise sharply after the mid-1960's and have continued to do so for the last fifteen years.[4] See Table 2.

The appreciable rise in relative black income that appears to begin suddenly during the mid-1960's is roughly coincident with the passage of the 1965 Civil Rights Act. This correspondence in timing is the key piece of evidence for those who assign an almost exclusive role to antidiscrimination legislation (Richard Freeman, 1973). Add to this the basically negative results for human capital factors in studies based on the 1940 and 1950 Censuses and the issue is joined: side by side with steady long-term convergence of human capital characteristics, why is there silence on the income front?

II. Schools

To address this question, I begin with a summary of my historical education data.[5] Table 3 presents new estimates of average schooling completed by five-year birth cohorts,[6] starting with persons born in the first

[4]Indeed, a common initial reaction to the 1960's acceleration was to view it as an historical aberration, a short-run by-product of the boom conditions of that decade. As the improvement continued unabated into the late 1970's, when business cycle conditions were less than robust, the idea that this was only a transitory improvement was put aside.

[5]Between 1870 and 1930, the census included questions on illiteracy, defined as the ability to read and write English or another language. Beginning with the 1940 Census, the literacy questions were replaced with questions on educational attainment.

[6]My estimates are based on published census data from the 1940 and 1970 Censuses and the 1979 *Current Population Survey* (*CPS*). Published data include single year of schooling distributions by five-year age groups separately by race and sex. Each cross-sectional census provides an estimate of schooling distributions for a set of birth cohorts. By linking and blending these five cross sections, one can span the birth cohorts listed in Table 3. Figures on education by birth cohort are averages of distributions across census years, so that data for a single birth cohort could potentially come from five cross sections. This averaging did not significantly alter the time-series description that one would obtain within any census year. As is well known, birth cohort tracking across census years shows unbelievably large increases (beyond any reasonable age of school attendance) in average schooling levels. This problem is particularly acute for blacks. This education inflation is often attributed to exaggeration of schooling accomplishments as education norms in society rise.

TABLE 4—RACIAL DIFFERENCES IN MEAN SCHOOLING LEVELS (ADDITIONAL YEARS OF SCHOOLING OF WHITES)

Birth Cohort	Men	Women
1951–54	.83	.46
1946–50	.75	.60
1941–45	1.07	.81
1936–40	1.54	.92
1931–35	1.91	1.15
1926–30	2.27	1.47
1921–25	2.71	2.09
1916–20	3.09	2.44
1911–15	3.41	2.69
1906–10	3.46	2.86
1901–05	3.46	3.00
1896–1900	3.32	2.93
1891–95	3.23	2.90
1886–90	3.02	2.98
1881–85	3.18	3.28
1876–80	3.33	3.62
1871–75	3.67	4.00
1865–70	4.01	4.55
pre-1865	4.39	5.13

five years after the Civil War. To isolate differential secular trends, Table 4 lists racial differences in school completion for each birth cohort. Finally, a more complete characterization of schooling distributions is given in Table 5, evaluated for selected birth cohorts that represent key historical turning points.

The 120-year post-Civil War period turns out not to be a simple story of steady and constant narrowing of human capital differences between the races, as backward extrapolation of twentieth-century data would have led one to expect. For those born in this century, as we have seen earlier, the underlying trend was indeed one of convergence. Similarly, racial differences in mean schooling levels diminished sharply for both sexes during the first quarter-century after the Civil War. Matters took a different course, however, for the generations born between 1886 and 1905. During this period, racial disparities in school completion expanded for males and stabilized for women. This 20-year reversal has had important implications for the economic history of blacks right to the present. And as these generations slowly pass through the 10-year records of the census, they affect our interpretation of income trends.

A convenient way of summarizing the historical data is to separate this 120-year span into three distinct segments: the initial post-Civil War phase of convergence (1865–86), the period of divergence (1886–1905), and finally, the more familiar narrowing of schooling differences during the twentieth century.

A. *1865–1886*

The story of black education in the South before the Civil War is simple indeed. Slave insurrections in the early part of the nineteenth century led to the legal proscription of formal instruction. By 1835, every southern state had a law prohibiting the schooling of slaves, and some even forbade instruction of freedmen. At the start of the Civil War, consequently, 95 percent of black southerners were completely illiterate. At its end, the differences between the races in school completion that I describe in Table 3 were enormous, with whites of either sex finishing 4 to 5 more years of school than blacks.

Although schooling levels would remain low for blacks throughout the nineteenth century, the first 20 years after the Civil War saw the effective origin of mass Negro education in the South. Between 1870 and 1880, the number of black southern children enrolled in school rose by almost 500 percent as the proportion of young blacks in school increased from 9 percent to almost one-third (Welch). In contrast, during this 20-year subperiod, changes in schooling distributions across white male birth cohorts listed in Table 5 were relatively modest, especially compared with what was to come. The modal level of school completion was *exactly* 8 years of grade school. Fully one-third of all white men born in this period received their grade school diploma but never advanced beyond that point. Even by the 1886–90 birth cohorts, only 30 percent of white males went beyond elementary school, and less than one-fifth earned a high school diploma.

Throughout these first two decades after the Civil War, the effective margin for black children was whether to attend school at all, and if so, whether to proceed as far as the fourth or fifth grade. However, we shall see

TABLE 5—SCHOOLING DISTRIBUTIONS OF SELECTED MALE BIRTH COHORTS

	Years of Schooling						
Birth Cohorts	0	< 5	< 9	8	< 12	12	12+
A. Black							
Pre-1865	45.9	81.6	96.5	4.2	98.6	0.9	1.4
1866-70	33.8	73.5	94.9	6.1	97.1	1.3	1.6
1886-90	15.7	54.1	88.0	10.1	93.2	3.5	3.3
1906-10	7.1	35.1	75.9	12.6	88.1	7.3	4.6
1926-30	2.3	11.7	43.7	12.4	67.6	20.2	12.1
1946-50	1.0	1.7	8.4	3.9	26.3	46.2	27.5
B. White							
Pre-1865	7.7	25.3	83.9	34.8	88.9	5.3	5.8
1866-70	6.6	22.4	81.2	35.6	87.4	6.1	6.5
1886-90	5.6	18.9	70.6	29.7	81.5	9.0	9.8
1906-10	1.3	6.1	44.7	23.2	64.1	19.0	16.1
1926-30	0.8	3.0	20.7	10.3	41.0	32.3	26.7
1946-50	0.5	1.9	7.7	2.9	18.8	36.8	44.4

TABLE 6

	White Men		Black Men	
Birth Cohort	Go On	Complete High School	Go On	Complete High School
A. School Continuation Probabilities for Elementary School Graduates				
1916-20	83.1	59.7	75.6	41.2
1906-10	70.4	44.7	65.7	32.4
1896-1900	58.6	36.2	57.0	29.2
1886-90	49.8	31.3	54.3	30.8
1876-80	44.0	29.0	51.4	29.1
B. Increase in Average Schooling by Year of Birth[a]				
	North	South	North	South
1888-1908	2.30	1.75	2.09	2.01
1908-28	1.64	1.58	1.78	1.94

[a]*Source:* Public Use Tapes of 1960 U.S. Census.

that these first 4 years of school were critical in shaping the economic history of blacks, for they would eventually eradicate black illiteracy.

B. *1886–1906*

The next 20 years, 1886–1906, represent a temporary stall during which human capital of blacks, as measured by years in school and quality of schooling, fell behind that of whites. This subperiod roughly coincides with the erosion of black political power in the South as the forces of disfranchisement worked their way through the system. But events in the North were of equal import in causing this reversal.

In the North, the principal development was the spread of public high school education on a wide scale. No longer did the eighth grade constitute the normal end of a school career for a white child. The speed at which white high school attendance and completion became common during this subperiod is illustrated in Table 6, which lists school continuation propensities, conditioned on elementary school graduation.[7]

[7]I have calculated elementary graduate progression rates using 8 years of school. However, the appropriate year to use is ambiguous because historically, elementary schools did not have uniform lengths. Many elementary schools, particularly in the South, contained only 7 grades.

Across the span of years that covers those born in 1886 to those born in 1916, the fraction of white males who continued their education beyond elementary school rose dramatically. By the birth cohort of 1916, more than 8 in 10 white male elementary graduates continued in school, and 60 percent would earn their high school diplomas—almost double the rates that existed 30 years earlier. In contrast, these high school completion rates were stable (at around 30 percent) among blacks between 1886 and 1910.[8] Table 6, panel B, attests to the lead taken by the North in the development of the public high school. Between birth years 1888 and 1908, the largest increases in mean education were achieved by northern-born whites. In contrast, for those born between 1908 and 1928, the largest schooling gains would be registered among southern-born blacks.

Political developments in the South also played a role in causing this period of reversal. With the return to office of conservative Democrats in the elections of 1876–77 and the end of Reconstruction, whatever equivalence had previously existed between the quality of black and white southern schools began eroding, a process that accelerated with disfranchisement.

Starting with Horace Bond (1934), a number of scholars have documented the impact of the loss of black political power on black southern schools. The ultimate legacy was a sharp decline in the relative quality of black southern schools during the late nineteenth century and early part of the twentieth century.[9] There is not space to repeat their documentation here, but I will illustrate with one famous example. In 1886, Mississippi passed a law that allowed counties to divert state funds allocated to black schools. Since state allocations were made to the county independently of pupils' race, the effect of diverting funds to white children on a per capita basis was greatest whenever the ratio of black to white pupils was highest. By 1910, counties with a black majority spent 7 to 30 times as much on white as on black students, while "white" counties spent only 2 to 3 times as much on white pupils. This same Mississippi law also provided for teacher salaries to be related to teacher scores on examinations. From that point (1886), Table 7 demonstrates that black and white teacher salaries drifted apart.

TABLE 7—AVERAGE MONTHLY SALARY OF MISSISSIPPI TEACHERS, 1875–95

Year	White	Black
1875	57.5	53.3
1885	28.7	28.6
1890	33.4	23.2
1895	33.0	21.5

Source: Bond.

C. *1906–50*

Because trends in the twentieth century are so widely known, my summary of this subperiod is brief. In terms of schooling quantity, we know that as each new generation of blacks and whites born in this century arrived in the labor force, the difference in schooling achieved by race continuously narrowed. As Tables 3 and 5 show, these changes were never dramatic or sharp. Only for black cohorts born after the depression of the 1930's did high school diplomas become a realistic goal. And, of course, the black college graduate is mostly a product of our own day. The message conveyed by nominal years of schooling is reinforced by data on schooling quality, which tell a clear twentieth-century story of improving relative quality of black schools.[10]

[8]Note that black progression rates were initially higher than those of whites. Those blacks who reached the eighth grade were clearly a very select group. Later in this century, progression rates for high school graduates to college were also higher for black men, a reflection of a similar phenomenon.

[9]Because the date of disfranchisement and the ensuing deterioration in black schools varied across southern states, the southern component of my argument cannot be neatly placed into any single 20-year time frame. However, they roughly coincide with the period in which racial disparities in school quantity expanded.

[10]To cite but two examples, in 1920, black youths attended school only two-thirds as many days per year as white students, but by 1954, there were no real

III. The Effects of Schools

In the remainder of this paper, I will try to document how this history of black schools shaped postslavery swings in the relative economic status of blacks. The first link in the chain of my argument concerns the influence of schools on black literacy.

A. *Literacy*

Table 8 presents illiteracy rates by race for the 100-year period from 1870 through 1969. In each decade, the percentage of blacks recorded by the census as unable to read and write declined significantly, but high rates of illiteracy persisted well into the twentieth century. At the turn of the century, 35 years after the Civil War, almost one-half the black population remained illiterate. Forty years later, at the outbreak of World War II, the fraction was one-tenth. In short, it took 75 years for blacks to equal the basic literacy rate that whites enjoyed at the end of the Civil War.

Table 8—Percentage Illiterate by Race Population 10 Years and Older

Year	All	Whites	Blacks
1870	20.3	11.5	81.4
1880	17.3	9.4	70.0
1890	13.3	7.7	57.1
1900	10.7	6.2	44.5
1910	7.7	5.0	30.4
1920	6.0	4.0	22.9
1930	4.3	2.7	16.3
1940	2.9	2.0	11.5
1952	2.5	1.8	10.2
1959	2.2	1.6	7.5
1969	1.0	0.7	3.6

Source: 1870–1930 from *Fifteenth Census of the United States*: *1930 Population*, Vol. 11, *General Report Statistics by Subjects*, ch. 13–"Illiteracy." 1940–69: "Illiteracy in the United States," *Current Population Reports*, Series P-20, Nos. 45 and 217, November 1969.

Table 9 illustrates the effect of schools on literacy and the reason why black illiteracy remained so high well into the twentieth century. In each census year, this table lists by age group the proportion of black men who were illiterate. There is now abundant evidence that literacy is a skill that is almost exclusively acquired in schools. For example, we find that over 80 percent of men with a year of schooling or less were unable to read or write. In contrast, among men who completed the fourth grade, only 7 percent were illiterate.[11] Not surprisingly, then, the patterns in Table 9 indicate a sharply rising proportion of black illiterates as we move from younger to older age groups in any census year. The effects of schools are seen most dramatically in the youngest age groups. Illiteracy rates of these blacks aged 10 to 14 fell rapidly as public schooling spread. The fraction of illiterates was half as high in 1900 as it was in 1880, and it would be cut in half again by 1920.

However, if we follow a birth cohort over their lifetime, Table 9 also demonstrates that the adult black population remained largely untouched by the increased ability of their children to read and write. If a black man reached adulthood without this ability, the chances were over 90 percent that he would never be able to write his name or read a newspaper. The idea that after slavery was abolished large numbers of adult blacks successfully acquired, on their own, elementary reading or writing skills is a myth. Average illiteracy in the black population remained

black-white differences in days attended. Similarly, in 1920, teachers of black students had 1.75 times as many pupils as the average teacher in the country. By 1954, this difference had been reduced to 1.18. See my article with Welch for a more complete summary.

[11] Proportion of males, 35 to 44 years old, illiterate by schooling (1947):

Years of Schooling	Percent
0	87.9
1	82.5
2	52.8
3	27.6
4	7.1

Source: Special Reports of U.S. Census (1948). Because the census asked either years of schooling or literacy, cross classifications for earlier periods are not possible.

TABLE 9—PROPORTION OF BLACK MALES ILLITERATE, BY AGE

Age	1969	1952	1930	1920	1910	1900	1890	1880
10–14			5.3	11.4	18.9	30.1	39.8	66.2
15–19			8.1	14.1	20.3	31.8	42.6	62.7
20–24			12.2	17.0	23.9	35.1	49.3	
25–34	1.3	6.4	13.0	17.9	24.6	39.3	56.8	
35–44		6.6	16.8	23.3	32.3	52.0	70.5	
45–54	5.5	11.5	24.2	34.1	47.0	68.1	80.8	73.1
55–64		18.1	34.4	49.4	63.0	78.4	86.3	
65+	16.7	33.3	55.7	68.3	74.5	85.4	90.2	
15–24	0.6	3.9	10.5	15.5	22.1	33.4	45.6	

Source: See Table 8.

TABLE 10—MALE ILLITERACY RATE BY COHORT

Birth Year	Cohort Age 10[a]	Age 40[b]	Proportion Illiterate Blacks	Fathers	Whites	Fathers
1840	1850	1880	74.8	> 85.0	8.0	–
1850	1860	1890	60.6	> 85.0	7.7	–
1860	1870	1900	43.0	83.2	6.3	–
1870	1880	1910	27.7	74.8	5.5	8.0
1880	1890	1920	22.0	60.6	5.3	7.7
1890	1900	1930	17.3	43.0	3.4	6.3
1900	1910	1940	14.1	27.7	2.0	5.5
1910	1920	1950	7.5	22.0	1.2	5.3
1920	1930	1960	6.1	17.3	0.7	3.4
1930	1940	1970	3.4	14.1	0.5	2.0
1940	1950	1980	1.7	7.5	0.4	1.2
1950	1960	1990	0.8	6.1	0.3	0.7
1960	1970	2000	0.4	3.4	0.3	0.5

Source: See Table 7.
[a]Year of schooling.
[b]Midway through work career.

high and changed slowly because improvements in the aggregate occurred only as new generations were born, schooled, and eventually replaced the much older, mostly illiterate black population.

The stability of illiteracy rates among the adult population allows us to measure long-term movements across different generations of blacks and whites. This is illustrated in Table 10, in which the year index in the first three columns measures year of birth, year of schooling, and year in which each birth cohort is midway through their labor market career. Assuming a 30-year generational lag, we also match illiteracy rates of fathers with each birth cohort. The first clear signs of the benefits of the black southern schools created during the Reconstruction period appear with the birth cohorts of 1860 and 1870. The fraction illiterate of the 1870 cohort was 27.7 percent, almost 50 percentage points below that of the cohort born 30 years earlier.

For simplicity, if we take a 40-year-old as the average worker in a year, the 1870 cohort would eventually represent the average black male worker in 1910. Fathers' illiteracy, which serves as a crude proxy for family background, may indicate why advances in relative market earnings of blacks were initially so slow. The fathers of our average black workers in 1910 were slaves born in 1840, and three-quarters were illiterate. Thus, the improvements in schools that start with the 1860 birth cohort first appear as im-

TABLE 11—"PSEUDO" LOG EARNINGS FUNCTION OF BLACK MALES AGED 14–64: 1900 CENSUS[a]

Variables	
South Atlantic Resident	−.3729
	(11.2)
South Central Resident	−.4671
	(14.3)
Age Spline:	
14–24	.1437
	(32.9)
25–34	.0156
	(3.79)
35–44	−.0105
	(2.21)
45+	−.0157
	(4.61)
Illiterate	−.1523
	(7.44)
Constant	6.310
	(148.8)
R^2	.465
Sample size	2962

[a] *t*-statistics are shown in parentheses.

provements in family background with the birth cohort of 1890, a group that represents our average black worker in 1930. Fortunately, this long and dark shadow of the past has an optimistic side. Eventually, the narrowing of racial income differences accelerated. Not only did each new generation of blacks have more schooling relative to contemporary whites than their parents did, but also they had parents with more education relative to whites than their parents did.

If schools were able to at least impart basic literacy skills, the next step is to relate literacy to income, a connection that also serves as our transition into the next section. Fortunately, the 1900 micro data file of the U.S. Census enables us to establish the connection.[12] Table 11 contains a pseudo earnings function for black men based on the 1900 Census. The pseudo label is used because earnings were not directly available from the 1900 file. Rather, an earnings amount was assigned to each worker based on his sex, race, age, and occupation. (These earnings weights are described in the next section.) Therefore, by construction, regressors must operate exclusively through occupational assignment. In essence, this income weight gives a metric that summarizes some very complex movements across occupations. In our 1900 sample, 45 percent of all black working men were illiterate. My estimate is that illiteracy depressed their income by 15 percent, a result that is strongly statistically significant. Because it ignores within-occupation income differences associated with literacy, this estimate is certainly an understatement.

B. *Income*

Few would question the central role of black schools in the eventual elimination of black illiteracy. The link between schools and income, however, is far more uncertain and the role of schools in the economic resurgence of black America is more controversial. One difficulty in establishing any historical connection is that reliable income data by race are a relatively recent phenomenon. The first decennial census to include income questions was the 1940 Census. Before that survey, only scattered bits of racial income data are available, based typically on small and nonrepresentative samples. To trace out a truly long-term history, one must of necessity resort to indirect methods of estimating income by race. Fortunately, the census has published occupation distributions of the work force, separately by race and sex beginning in 1890. Most important, these occupation distributions were typically stratified by age.[13]

This age stratification is an unexploited dimension of census occupational data that

[12] The 1900 Census is a nationally representative sample of the population of the United States. The sample consists of 100,438 individuals, representing a sampling rate of 1/760 of the population. This micro sample was assembled by scholars at the Center for Studies in Demography and Ecology, University of Washington, from manuscripts of the 12th Census of the United States.

[13] Since 1890, the only census with no age stratification by race occurred in 1910. In addition, in 1920, only broad age intervals (i.e., 25–44, 45–64) are available. In all other censuses, five- or ten-year age brackets are used. Clearly, the micro files available beginning with the 1960 Census allow maximum flexibility.

permits us to follow different birth cohorts over their labor market careers. Since these data begin in 1890, the first black birth cohort that we can follow from virtually the start to the end of this labor market life was the first generation not born in slavery (1865–70); but even for blacks born in the last 30 years of slavery, we can observe partial slices of their labor force histories.

The task of assembling and linking these occupation data was formidable. The most vexing issue involved the construction of a meaningful and consistent set of occupational groupings across such a long time span. With each successive census, the number of occupational categories varied and the meaning of some occupations, even with the same title, often changed. In particular, three fundamental revisions were made by the census in their occupational coding system —in 1910, 1940, and 1970. Although the census has published historical series by sex, there exist no historical data stratified by race, sex, and age. Therefore, a major component of this research was the construction of an occupational taxonomy that covered the time span 1890 to 1980.

The system I have constructed places black and white men in 133 occupation categories for the entire period from 1890 to 1979.[14] Using this occupational coding system, black-white male income ratios were calculated for each birth cohort at different points in their life cycles. Each occupation was assigned a race, sex, and age-specific average income. Although I have experimented with income weights from different years, Table 12 is based on 1970 Census incomes and the 35–49 age group.[15] Our measure of relative income can change only when the distribution of blacks and whites across occupations changes over time. Within-occupation changes in relative incomes of blacks during the twentieth century will not affect this index, a point to which I return below.

Before discussing the cohort and age-specific detail available in Table 12, time-series swings in the average racial income ratio (over all age groups) in each census year merit a brief discussion. These are described in the final two rows of Table 12. According to my index, the relative income status of black men rose from 1890 to 1920, remained relatively constant between 1920 and 1940, increased sharply during the 1940's, and ended with the steady and significant post-1960 rise in relative black incomes.[16] Table 12 indicates not only that black-white income ratios rose after 1960, but also that the 1960 income ratio is clearly larger than that which prevailed throughout the 1920–40 period, and that the 1920–40 ratios exceeded the ratio of 1890. Affirmative action pressures of the 1960's cannot have been the exclusive driving force of black progress; the historical antecedents for some of the trends must have occurred earlier.

More germane to the issue addressed in this paper are the cohort-specific income ratios and the differential experiences of cohorts over their respective lifetimes. To highlight the central point, the generations

[14]At each stage in this process when additional aggregation over occupation groups was required, checks were made to test the sensitivity of the conclusions to the level of aggregation. I found no evidence that the level of aggregation into these 133 groups distorts the trends described in the text. For example, Table 12 was also computed for the post-1940 period using the more plentiful occupational groups available over this subperiod. The results were essentially identical to those using my 133 codes. The details of this process of making this series comparable are laborious, but are available from the author on request.

[15]Experiments indicate that it did not matter whether these income weights were based on the 1960 or 1970 Census. I also experimented with age groups 20–64, 14–75, and 5-year age groups. The results were insensitive to these experiments. In addition, comparisons with actual observed changes after 1940, when income data became available, indicate that at least over this period my index does not distort the actual changes that occurred. Clearly, my index understates the rate of post-1960 improvement by ignoring within-occupation narrowing of racial wage differentials.

[16]These decade-by-decade comparisons are necessarily made against the backdrop of major historical upheavals that can easily dwarf the type of slowly evolving forces that we argue were reshaping black America. For example, the Great Depression could easily have overwhelmed the factors at issue in this paper, for blacks surely bore more than their proportional share of its burdens. Thus, the 1940–30 comparison in Table 12 could easily suppress the slow economic evolution emphasized here.

TABLE 12—ESTIMATED BLACK-WHITE MALE INCOME RATIOS BY BIRTH COHORTS

Birth Cohort	Census Year 1890	1900	1910	1920	1930	1940	1950	1960	1970	1980
1956–60										.653
1951–55										.625
1946–50									.646	.624
1941–45									.608	.610
1936–40								.571	.583	.573
1931–35								.561	.582	.593
1926–30							.555	.555	.577	.583
1921–25							.542	.546	.571	.554
1916–20						.501	.532	.537	.562	.583
1911–15						.488	.516	.536	.562	
1906–10					.509	.480		.526	.548	
1901–05					.500	.482	.508	.524		
1896–1900				.515	.498	.483		.519		
1891–95					.494	.478	.503			
1886–90					.492	.469	.501			
				.494						
1881–85		.488			.481	.465				
1876–80					.458	.445				
1871–75	.472	.463			.452					
1866–70				.387	.438					
1856–65	.454	.451								
1846–55	.435	.428								
1836–45	.417	.398								
1826–35	.397									
All Ages 10–75	.433	.442	.455	.476	.479	.474	.516	.542	.590	.611
Ages 20–64	.439	.449		.484	.486	.479	.522	.543	.585	.605

born within the 20-year period of education retrogression are separated from the others in Table 12. To facilitate comparisons, Table 13 lists 20-year growth in average schooling by race. The cohort-specific patterns in these tables are remarkable. Both of the two historical periods of clear racial convergence in education—the first 25 years after slavery and the twentieth century—show steady across-cohort improvement in the relative income of black men. In contrast, the subperiod in which no strong across-cohort trends exist in relative income of blacks were those born within the era of education retrogressions. Using the 1930, 1940, and 1950 Censuses, the changes within the period of education retrogression average less than 1 percentage point. Table 12 also demonstrates that the rate of improvement for blacks accelerated as we move towards younger cohorts. This acceleration makes sense in light of the speedup in racial convergence in education levels during this century (see Table 13), and of the point emphasized above that a substantial lag occurs before family background effects become operative.

TABLE 13—CHANGES IN AVERAGE EDUCATION LEVELS

Birth Cohorts	Black Males	White Males	Difference
1866–85	1.66	0.69	0.97
1886–1905	1.54	1.99	−0.45
1906–25	2.55	1.65	0.89
1926–45	2.81	1.31	1.50

The generations born between 1886 and 1905 have an effect on our interpretation of time-series changes in the relative income of blacks that lasts for half a century. These generations were the male labor force aged 20–34 in 1920, 25–44 in 1930, 35–54 in 1940, and 45–64 in 1950. Thus, they would dominate census surveys for close to 40 years. As long as they remained a large part of the total labor force, there was no reason to expect, on the basis of human capital factors alone, much convergence in income ratios. Indeed, it is not until the 1960–70 census comparisons that these generations leave the labor market. And this is the census comparison for which the economics profession first took notice of improvement in economic conditions for black men.

C. *Labor Market Careers*

To this point, I have emphasized across-cohort trends and ignored within-cohort evolution over life cycle careers. The empirical origin of theories that blacks do not progress as rapidly as whites over their careers probably dates back to the 1940 Census, which first showed that black-white male income disparities increase systematically with age. This pattern has become a feature common to all cross-sectional studies of black-white earnings differences. It has been replicated in all the succeeding decennial censuses, and each of the 30-odd yearly *Current Population Surveys* beginning in the late 1940's.

The observation is well known that, by themselves, individual cross sections cannot test theories of life cycle discrimination. However, if we link these cross sections—for example, by reading across rows in Table 12—we can follow the actual experience of birth cohorts over their labor market careers. If we consider men who entered the labor force during the twentieth century (for example, those born after 1886), black-white income ratios did not decline over life cycles. The cross-sectional decline apparently results from more rapid cohort effects for blacks, and not from differential life cycle career paths. Among men born before 1886, Table 12 does provide evidence of a less rapid career income growth for black men, although obviously not as pronounced as the cross section would predict.

By construction, the ratios presented in Table 12 can only detect life cycle decay in the relative economic status of blacks that have their origin in movement across occupations. This table does demonstrate the important point that any cross-sectional decline in relative incomes of blacks due to different occupational distributions for men of different ages is a cohort and not a life cycle phenomenon. However, within occupations, incomes of blacks may be falling relative to whites, or more white-intensive occupations may exhibit faster career wage growth, even if race income neutrality prevails within occupations. If either of these two events occurred, relative income ratios of blacks would decline with age, but we would not capture it in Table 12.

Because of the absence of income data by race, it is not possible to observe actual income ratios over the long historical time span covered in Table 12. However, for more recent periods we can calculate series that are based on actual incomes. Tables 14 and 15 present my estimates of mean income ratios over the 1940–80 census years.[17] As one would expect, these actual income ratios are more erratic than those imputed using the more stable occupational distributions. While not without exception, the patterns depicted using ratios of actual incomes are consistent with the principal conclusions I have advanced using Table 12. Although each cross-sectional series in Tables 14 and 15 indicates a sharp decline with age, in the vast majority of cases black-white male income ratios either remained stable or actually rose over careers.[18] It is also worth noting that over the subperiod in which these two tables overlap, actual income series confirm trends in the imputed income series. Most important, the time period of retrogression in

[17]For the 1960–80 period, the actual income ratios are derived from the census and *CPS* micro data files. I calculated the 1940 series from tables of Zeman, which listed mean earnings by schooling and region. The 1950 series was derived from published tables listing income distributions by race, age, and schooling. Over the 1960–80 period, I have also calculated weekly wage ratios. The results with weekly wages were essentially identical to those with income. To preserve comparability with the 1940 and 1950 Censuses, only the income series is presented in the text. Because of small sample sizes, Table 15 stratifies schooling by 10-year cohort groups.

[18]The two main exceptions are 1921–25 and 1911–15 cohorts, principally during the first 10 years. There is a recovery during the remainder of the life cycle, but it takes most of it to achieve it. It is impossible to know for certain whether these are important exceptions or whether the income ratios are suspect.

TABLE 14—BLACK-WHITE INCOME RATIOS, 1940–80

Birth Cohort	Census Year				
	1940[a]	1950[b]	1960[c]	1970[c]	1980[d]
1950–60					74.9
1951–55					76.0
1946–50				82.6	76.1
1941–45				71.8	70.0
1936–40			69.1	64.7	69.0
1931–35			60.7	60.5	62.6
1926–30			54.9	57.2	62.7
1921–25		60.5	53.6	55.3	62.3
1916–20		55.0	50.4	54.1	67.4
1911–15	57.4	49.8 (1906–15)	48.9	54.3	
1906–10	45.4		47.2	55.5	
1901–05	41.7 (1896–1905)	47.3 (1896–1905)	48.0		
1896–1900			45.9		
1891–95	42.5 (1886–95)	46.6 (1886–95)			
1886–90					
1881–85	42.9 (1876–85)				
1876–80					

[a]Derived from tables in Zeman, using 1940 Census.
[b]1950 U.S. Census Special Reports, "Education," Table 12.
[c]1 in 100 decennial U.S. Census (computer tape).
[d]1980 *Current Population Survey* (computer tape).

TABLE 15—BLACK-WHITE MALE INCOME RATIOS 1940–80, BY YEAR OF SCHOOLING

Birth Cohort	Census Year				
	1940	1950	1960	1970	1980
Years of Schooling = 8–11					
1946–55					73.2
1936–45				72.8	76.4
1926–35			65.9	69.7	75.1
1916–25		68.4	68.6	69.9	82.6
1906–15	57.8	64.0	63.8	72.0	
1896–1905	51.8	62.5	61.0		
1886–95	51.6	63.0			
1876–85	51.7				
Years of Schooling = 12					
1946–55					75.1
1936–45				74.6	79.0
1926–35			65.1	70.3	72.0
1916–25		68.7	63.8	64.9	78.6
1906–15	55.3	61.6	57.8	65.0	
1896–1905	49.0	54.0	49.0		
1886–95	47.1	52.2			
1876–85	44.0				
Years of Schooling = 16+					
1946–55					88.5
1936–45				76.7	82.9
1926–35			62.5	78.0	79.1
1916–25		63.4	52.9	59.5	70.9
1906–15	49.6	53.4	45.7	54.9	
1896–1905	42.6	50.9	43.7		
1886–95	40.2	48.4			
1876–85	40.6				

education is a time of little increase in relative black male income in Table 14. Table 15, which presents these relative income series stratified by education level, indicates that school-quality trends are consistent with secular changes in levels. Within each schooling class, general trends do not support career retrogression for black men.

Given the initial stocks of human capital with which blacks and whites start their careers, black men of recent birth cohorts apparently do not face very different career prospects from those of white men. The fundamental problem is the wide disparities that exist when market competition begins, not what evolves over the labor market career. This conclusion is not a denial of the importance of labor market discrimination, but only about the form that it takes. The still large initial income differences between the races at the beginning of the career may well owe much to racial discrimination.

IV. Conclusion

During this century, America has undergone an evolutionary process, spawned in large part in its schools, that permanently altered and improved the relative economic position of black Americans. Because this process evolved slowly and because its implications for economic welfare were often not realized until decades after the seeds were planted, the importance and even existence of this evolution have been largely ignored or dismissed. But the historical evidence suggests that we have witnessed in this century a gradual but significant improvement in the quality and quantity of skills that blacks are able to carry with them into the labor market to compete with white workers. And as the human capital of blacks increased relative to whites, so also did their earnings.

REFERENCES

Ashenfelter, Orley, "Comment on Smith-Welch, 'Black/White Male Earnings and Employment: 1960–1970,'" in Thomas Juster, ed., *The Distribution of Economic Well-Being*, National Bureau of Economic Research, Studies in Income and Wealth, No. 41, Cambridge: Ballinger 1977.

Batchelder, Alan, "Decline in the Relative Income of Negro Men," *Quarterly Journal of Economics*, November 1964, *78*, 525–48.

Becker, Gary, *The Economics of Discrimination*, Chicago: University of Chicago Press, 1957.

Bond, Horace Mann, *The Education of the Negro in the American Social Order*, New York: Prentice Hall, 1934.

Darity, William A., "The Human Capital Approach to Black-White Earnings Inequality: Some Unsettled Questions," *Journal of Human Resources*, Winter 1982, *18*, 72–93.

Freeman, Richard B., "Changes in the Labor Market for Black Americans 1948–1972," *Brookings Papers on Economic Activity*, 1: 1973, 67–120.

Hanoch, Giora, "Personal Earnings and Investments in Schooling," unpublished doctoral dissertation, University of Chicago, 1965.

Hauser, Robert and Featherman, David, *Opportunity and Change*, New York: Academic Press, 1978.

Levin, Henry M., "Education and Earnings of Blacks and the *Brown* Decision," unpublished manuscript, September 1978.

Miller, Herman P., *Income of the American People*, New York: Wiley & Sons, 1955.

Myrdal, Gunnar, *An American Dilemma*, New York: Harper and Brothers, 1944.

Smith, James P. and Welch, Finis, "Black-White Male Wage Ratios: 1960-1970," *American Economic Review*, June 1977, *67*, 323–38.

Thurow, Lester, *Poverty and Discrimination*, Washington: The Brookings Institution, 1969.

Welch, Finis, "Education and Racial Discrimination," in Orley Ashenfelter and Albert Rees, eds., *Discrimination in Labor Markets*, Princeton: Princeton University Press, 1974.

Zeman, Morton, "A Comparative Analysis of White-Non White Income Differentials," unpublished dissertation, University of Chicago, September 1955.

U.S. Bureau of the Census, Special Reports of U.S. Census, *Current Population Reports*, 1947, P-20, No. 20, September 1948; 1950, P-E, No. 5B.

______, *Consumer Income*, Series P-60, various issues.

[13]

THE EFFECT OF DISCRIMINATION ON EARNINGS: EVIDENCE FROM MILITARY TEST SCORE RESULTS*

DAVE M. O'NEILL

ABSTRACT

The test score performance of a large sample of youth on the Armed Forces Qualification Test, cross-classified by schooling and race, was used to estimate the relative importance of current and past discrimination in explaining 1960 racial differentials in earnings. Our results indicate that, for schooling levels below college graduate, between 50 and 55 percent of the differentials were attributable to (then) current labor market discrimination and the remaining 50 to 45 percent to the lagged effect of past discrimination, both market and nonmarket. Since these results must be viewed in the context of the imperfect statistical procedure that produced them, a detailed discussion of biases is presented.

I. STATEMENT OF THE PROBLEM

Census data for 1940, 1950, and 1960 as well as various annual survey data show that Negro males of the same age and (nominal) schooling attainment as whites have lower annual earnings. More detailed statistical analysis of the decennial Census data show that most of these differentials remain even after controlling for such earnings-associated factors as type of residence, marital status, geographic location, and migrant-nonmigrant

---

The author is Research Director, Manpower Studies Group, Institute for Naval Studies, Center for Naval Analyses, an affiliate of the University of Rochester.

* The author wishes to thank Gary Becker, Jacob Mincer, Zvi Griliches, and Finis Welch for helpful comments. Also, my colleagues at the Center for Naval Analyses, Burton Gray and Michael Canes, suggested useful changes and modifications. The research was partially supported by the National Bureau of Economic Research and the Center for Naval Analyses.

TABLE 1
MEAN EARNINGS OF MALES 25–34 YEARS OLD, BY YEARS OF SCHOOL COMPLETED AND COLOR, FOR THE U.S.[a]

Years of School Completed	Nonwhite	White
Elementary		
0–7	$2,332	$3,537
8	2,994	4,357
High school		
1–3	3,240	4,998
4	3,717	5,480
College		
1–3	4,072	5,964
4+	4,760	7,146

Source: 1960 Census of Population, Special Report, Earnings by Education and Occupation, Table 1.

[a] Mean earnings of males in the experienced civilian labor force with earnings in 1959.

status.[1] These persistent earnings differentials can be viewed as the result of both present and past discrimination on the part of whites, with this discriminatory behavior taking place in both market and nonmarket activities.[2]

Past discrimination in the provision of school facilities and school resources, a type of nonmarket discrimination, causes Negro high school graduates to enter the labor market with a lower potential marginal productivity, even to nondiscriminating firms, than white high school graduates of the same age. Moreover, past discrimination in the labor market, a type of market discrimination, has probably led many Negro youths to try less hard

1 See the statistical results in Giora Hanoch, "An Economic Analysis of Earnings and Schooling," *Journal of Human Resources,* 2 (Summer 1967), pp. 310–29; Finis Welch, "Labor Market Discrimination: An Interpretation of Income Differences in the Rural South," *Journal of Political Economy,* 75 (June 1967), p. 234, Table 1; and George Stigler, *The Theory of Price* (3rd ed.; New York: Macmillan Co., 1966), ch. 18, p. 295, n. 14.

2 This framework was suggested by the work of Welch, "Labor Market Discrimination . . . ," who emphasized the distinction between pre-labor market discrimination and labor market discrimination per se. The classic analysis of labor market discrimination is Gary Becker, *The Economics of Discrimination* (Chicago: University of Chicago Press, 1957).

when attending school, again causing them to enter the labor market subsequently with a potential productivity below that of whites.

Thus the effects of past discrimination, both market and nonmarket, live on in the present and lead to a situation in which current observed racial earnings differentials are a compound, of unknown proportions, of the effects of past and present behavior.

My purpose in this article is to utilize data on the test scores of young men on the Armed Forces Qualification Test (AFQT) in order to make estimates of the relative importance of current and past discrimination in explaining 1960 racial differentials in earnings. More specifically, the question I attempt to answer is this: If current labor market discrimination against Negroes had vanished completely in 1961, by how much would we have expected racial earnings differentials, within age-education cells, to have narrowed in the short run? I think I have devised a quantitative method which, although crude, leads to results that are interesting.

A recent study by Finis Welch attempted a quantitative analysis of racial earnings differentials within schooling classes in terms of present and past discrimination.[3] His approach to the problem focused on quantifying some dimensions of the quality of formal schooling, estimating income value weights for these dimensions, and applying the estimated weights to racial differentials in the dimensions of schooling quality.

Welch concluded that, for his data framework, quality of schooling differentials could account for about 27 percent of racial earnings differentials within schooling classes, implying that the short-run effect of completely eliminating labor market discrimination could be quite significant; that is, a narrowing of about 70 percent might take place.

My approach to the problem in this article has both advantages and disadvantages relative to Welch's approach. The advantages stem from its potential comprehensiveness in being able to quantify the market productivity effects of a host of factors, including not only the quality of schooling and motivation-to-learn effects of past discrimination, but also factors such as family environment which can operate to influence market productivity, given the level of schooling quality. The disadvantages of my approach lie in its dependence on using one type of individual performance (test scores) to explain another type of individual performance (productivity in the market place). With this approach one cannot distinguish how much each of the various component causal factors (e.g., Welch's two quantifiable dimensions of school quality) is contributing to the total effect of past discrimination on current earnings differentials.

3 Welch, "Labor Market Discrimination . . . ."

TABLE 2

PERCENT DISTRIBUTION OF MALE YOUTHS, AGE 19–21, BY SCORE ON THE ARMED FORCES QUALIFICATION TEST, BY YEARS OF SCHOOL COMPLETED AND RACE: FOR THE U.S.[a]

Test Score[b]	None	Elementary School 1–4	Elementary School 5–6	Elementary School 7–8	High School 1–2	High School 3–4	College 1–2	College 3–4	College 5+
					White[c]				
0–9	84.7	73.6	47.0	16.7	5.3	.6	.1	.1	—
10–30	9.8	22.4	44.3	50.5	35.3	13.2	3.5	1.6	—
31–64	4.4	3.4	7.8	27.5	44.4	46.6	30.3	21.1	15.8
65–92	1.1	.5	.9	4.9	13.3	32.1	44.7	44.3	42.1
93–100	—	.1	.1	.4	1.6	7.5	21.4	32.9	42.1
					Negro				
0–9	92.6	90.9	81.4	58.6	34.1	7.7	.1	—	—
10–30	7.4	8.1	17.3	36.0	51.3	50.0	27.6	18.2	—
31–64	—	1.0	1.3	5.1	13.5	36.8	53.1	57.7	50.0
65–92	—	—	—	.2	1.0	5.1	16.3	20.4	50.0
93–100	—	—	—	—	—	.4	2.8	3.6	—

Source: B. D. Karpinos, "The Mental Test Qualification of American Youths for Military Service and Its Relationship to Educational Attainment," *Proceedings of the American Statistical Association,* Social Statistics Section, 1966.

[a] The distributions are based on the performance of youths during the period January 1953 to July 1958. A 50 percent sample (750,000 youths) of all youths examined during this period was used to tabulate test score performance by years of schooling.

[b] The test scores of individuals were derived by converting their raw scores (number of correct answers adjusted for guessing) into percentile values based on the distribution of raw scores achieved by a representative sample of youths in 1949. Thus the entry in the tables for whites with no years of schooling of 84.7 percent means that this fraction of youths did only as well as the lowest 10 percent of the 1949 group.

[c] Non-Negro nonwhites are included in the white distribution.

However, I would submit that in this particular problem area factors such as family environment during childhood, which are so difficult to quantify and measure, may turn out to play such a significant causal role in influencing market productivity that the approach used in this paper is justified in spite of its methodological disadvantages.[4]

4 Surely this is the thrust of the message from people such as Daniel P. Moynihan who stress the prime importance of the absence of the father in the Negro household in shaping the future opportunities of the Negro child.

TABLE 3

ARITHMETIC MEAN TEST SCORE, BY RACE AND YEARS OF SCHOOL COMPLETED

Years of School Completed	Arithmetic Mean[a]	
	Negro	White
None	5.6	8.7
Elementary		
1–4	6.2	9.9
5–6	7.7	15.4
7–8	12.4	28.1
High school		
1–2	19.1	40.4
3–4	32.2	57.2
College		
1–2	46.3	70.9
3–4	50.6	76.9
5+	63.0	81.2

Source: See Table 2.

[a] Estimated using the midpoints of test score class intervals as estimates of the mean scores for each interval.

II. EMPIRICAL ANALYSIS

Racial Differentials in Test Score Performance on the AFQT

Tables 2 and 3 and Figure 1 present and summarize the information contained in one available body of data on Armed Forces Qualification Test (AFQT) score performance cross-classified by the schooling completed and race of the young men taking the test. These data were obtained from a 50 percent sample of the records of all individuals who were called up for the draft or attempted to enlist during the period January 1953 to July 1958. The sample was composed of three-quarters of a million young men.

The AFQT, which is given to every youth when he is initially examined for military service, contains 100 questions equally distributed among the following four areas: vocabulary or verbal concepts; arithmetic; spatial relations; and mechanical ability, that is, ability to interrelate tools and equipment.

The AFQT is *not* designed to measure only innate ability characteristics; it is an achievement-type test rather than an IQ-type. As our data show, performance on the AFQT is highly correlated with schooling level. Benjamin Karpinos, a medical statistician in the Office of the Surgeon

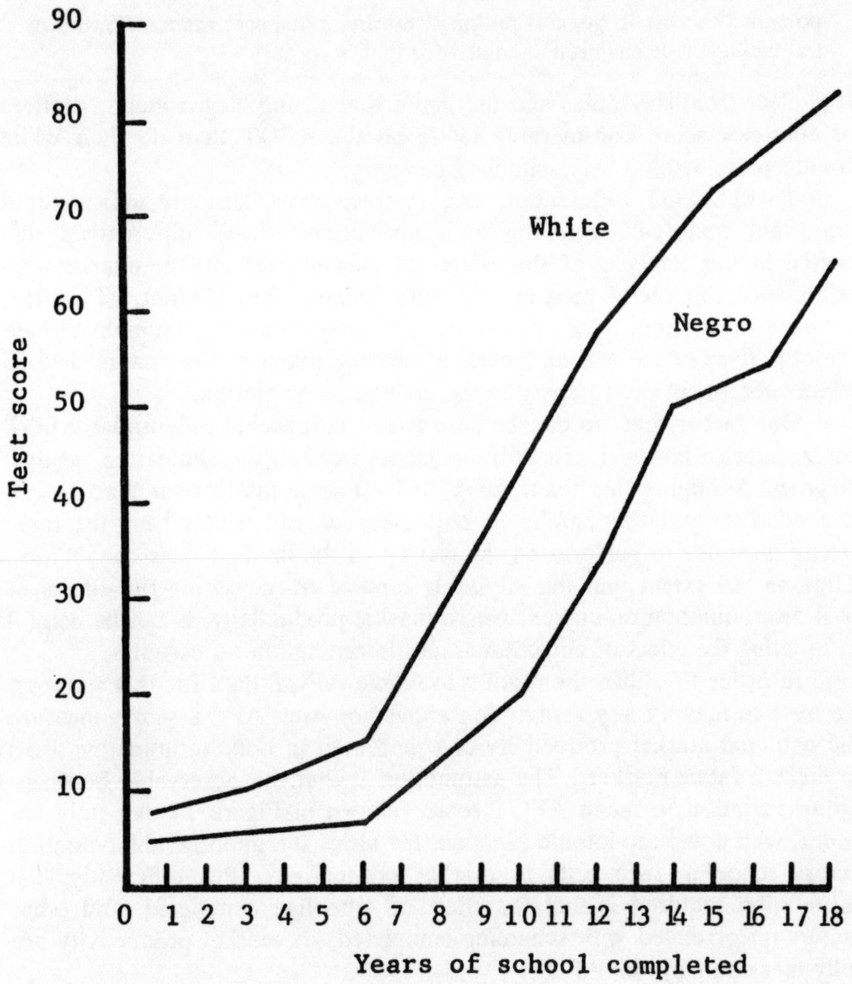

FIGURE 1

MEAN TEST SCORE ON AFQT BY YEARS OF SCHOOL COMPLETED

Source: See Table 3.

General has succinctly stated the goals of the AFQT:

> . . . [T]he AFQT was delegated a dual objective: *a.* To measure the examinee's general mental ability to absorb military training within a reasonable length of time, so as to eliminate those who do not possess such ability—a qualification device; and *b.* to provide a uniform measure of the examinee's potential general usefulness in the service, if qualified on the tests—a classification device. It was hence specifically intended to predict

potential success in general military training and performance ("military trainability"). It has been validated for that purpose.[5]

It is clear from the tables and the figure that young Negro males, draftees or enlistees, score considerably lower on the AFQT than do their white counterparts within every schooling category.

These AFQT differentials are, in themselves, strongly indicative of important quality-of-schooling and motivation-to-learn differentials discussed in our analysis of the effects of past market and nonmarket discrimination on racial productivity differentials. They do not, of course, measure these productivity differentials directly, but are presumably, given the objectives of the test designers, measuring many of the factors that do affect subsequent productivity in the civilian labor market.

One factor that we can be sure is not influencing differential AFQT performance, however, is current labor market discrimination against Negroes. Assuming that the military, at least since the Korean War period, is a nondiscriminating employer, both Negroes and whites have the same strong incentive to perform on the test up to the limit of their capabilities. Thus, to the extent that the AFQT is capable of measuring the effects of past discrimination on current Negro market productivity, it can be helpful in isolating the effect of current market discrimination on earnings.

In order to utilize the readily available AFQT data for this purpose, we have to make a key assumption about how well AFQT scores measure the potential market productivity of young men in nondiscriminating firms in civilian labor markets. The assumption is that the observable between-group variation in mean AFQT score (shown in Figure 1) can fully account, with some monotonic function, for all of the unobservable variation across schooling-race cells in market productivity. Put differently, the assumption required is that the effect of schooling completed, and other factors uncorrelated with schooling completed, on market productivity are fully measured by the AFQT.

With this assumption, the data in Table 3 and Figure 1 can be used to convert Negro years of schooling into "equiproductive" years of white schooling. Then the observed white earnings–schooling completed profile (Table 1) can be utilized to deduce predictions of Negro earnings–schooling completed profiles that would exist with zero level current market discrimination.[6]

---

5 B. D. Karpinos, "The Mental Qualification of American Youths for Military Service and Its Relationship to Educational Attainment," *Proceedings of the American Statistical Association*, Social Statistics Section, 1966.

6 This assumes that Negroes with the same productivity would have the same tastes for market and nonmarket sources of income.

Is this a reasonable assumption with regard to the AFQT? It is hard to say a priori.[7] For measuring variation in potential market productivity across individuals (within group variation), clearly it would be a gross overestimate of the power of the AFQT.

This, however, is not our situation. For purposes of measuring variation in mean productivity across large groups of individuals, the predictive power of the AFQT should be much greater. Many of the intangible personality factors which influence individual productivity and elude AFQT measure will tend to have approximately the same values across large groups of individuals. The most likely source of error is that the productivity effects of schooling will not be completely measured by the AFQT. Another source of error stems from the fact that factors unrelated to subsequent market productivity (for example, pure desire to excel on tests) surely cause some variation in the AFQT, and this can possibly create group differentials that do not correspond to productivity differentials. The possible biases in our estimates of discrimination effects resulting from these sources will be discussed after our results are presented.

Earnings Differentials and Current Market Discrimination

Table 4 presents estimates of the proportion of the observed 1960 racial earnings differentials that could have been attributed to current (as of 1960) market discrimination against Negroes. These estimates were derived by using the data in Tables 1 and 3 in combination with our above-discussed assumption about the AFQT as a measure of market productivity.[8]

First, the AFQT-schooling curves in Figure 1 were used to convert Negro schooling levels into "equiproductive" years of white schooling. Thus, for example, to convert the Negro schooling completed level H.S. 4, we find the point on the Negro curve giving the mean AFQT score for the H.S. 4 group; then a horizontal line at that AFQT score level is drawn over to the white curve and the associated white schooling level for that AFQT level is read off.

Estimates of Negro earnings to be expected in the complete absence of current market discrimination were obtained by assigning the observed white earnings associated with the calculated "equiproductive" years of white schooling. The various columns in Table 4 contain the results of these calculations.

7 If one were willing to assume that group pay differentials in the military were equal to productivity differentials in the civilian sector, then military personnel data banks could be utilized to make a more direct test of this assumption.

8 Another assumption relating to the target population coverage as between AFQT-schooling data and the 1960 Census earnings-school data is also required. We will discuss this in detail below.

TABLE 4

ESTIMATED CONTRIBUTIONS OF CURRENT MARKET DISCRIMINATION TO 1960 RACIAL EARNINGS DIFFERENTIALS BY SCHOOLING-COMPLETED LEVEL, FOR MALES 25–34 YEARS OLD

Years of School Completed	Observed Earnings			Effect of Current Market Discrimination			
	White ($)	Nonwhite ($)	Differential (1) — (2) ($)	Equiproductive Years of White Schooling	White Earnings for Equiproductive Schooling Levels ($)	Absolute Effect of Current Market Discrimination (5) — (2) ($)	% Effect of Current Discrimination (5) — (2) / (3)
	(1)	(2)	(3)	(4)	(5)	(6)	(7)
Elementary							
0–7	3.537	2,332	1,205	n.a.	n.a.	n.a.	n.a.
8	4.357	2,994	1,363	4.6	3,680	686	50.3
High school							
9–11	4,998	3,240	1,758	7.2	4,140	900	51.1
12	5,480	3,717	1,763	9.5	4,680	963	54.6
College							
13–15	5,964	4,072	1,892	11.2	5,160	988	52.2
16+	7,146	4,760	2,386	11.8	5,320	560	23.5

Source: Tables 1 and 3.

n.a. Our procedure could not be applied here because the shapes of the AFQT-schooling curves in Figure 1 implied that Negroes with four years of school completed score lower than whites with zero years of school completed.

Our results indicate that, for schooling levels below college graduate, between 50 and 55 percent of the 1960 earnings differentials were attributable to current labor market discrimination, and the remaining 50 to 45 percent to the lagged effects of past discrimination, both market and nonmarket.

Another important aspect of our results is the dip in the current discrimination effect for the College 4+ group. This suggests that, contrary to most a priori conjectures, quality of schooling rather than current market discrimination is probably the main cause of the observed low economic return to Negro college education.

When our results are compared with those of Welch, we find a significantly smaller impact of current market discrimination on racial earnings differentials. This is what one would expect, given the more comprehensive nature of our measure of the effects of past discrimination. Also, Welch's approach to distinguishing the effects of present and past discrimination lumped the effect of past market discrimination on Negro motivation-to-learn while in school together with the effect of current market discrimination. However, our results still indicate that, as of 1960, substantial gains in Negro earnings could have been made via the elimination of then current labor market discrimination.

III. SOURCES OF BIAS AND CONCLUDING COMMENTS

We turn now to a discussion of the possible directions of bias in our results.

If schooling's effect on earnings is not fully captured by the AFQT, then our procedure will tend to underestimate the effect of current market discrimination. This is because Negroes with the same AFQT as whites have completed more years of schooling and are therefore more productive by some unknown amount. This bias might account for the sharp dip in our estimate of the current discrimination effect at the college graduate level.

The possible effect of the nonproductivity component of variation in the AFQT across individuals is difficult to specify. If this component causes systematic positive differentials in AFQT by race (white greater than Negro), then it would create another source of underestimation of the current market discrimination effect. Thus it is sometimes argued that the aptitude and achievement tests used by private corporations to distinguish among job applicants tend to be biased against Negroes, the contention being that the tests measure the effects of personal characteristics that ultimately prove to be irrelevant for productivity on the job and that whites tend to acquire more of these characteristics than do Negroes of the same schooling attainment.

Finally, the difference between the population coverage in our two basic bodies of data also creates some difficulties in interpreting the results. The cohort of individuals covered by the AFQT data would have been only about 24 to 26 years old when the 1960 Census was taken. The group covered by our earnings data, however, was 25 to 34 years old in 1960. I would conjecture that this "misphasing of cohorts" situation leads to an overestimate of the current market discrimination effect because it is likely that there has been a steady secular trend toward narrowing of factors such as quality-of-schooling differentials so that our aged 25–34 earnings cohort would have exhibited larger racial differentials in AFQT performance.

Even if we had our cohorts phased precisely in terms of age, however, we would still have a problem of differential coverage because the military testing network probably does not select randomly from the various cohorts of young men who come of military age. The average AFQT score of men in the civilian labor force may differ from the average AFQT score of men who are tested by the military, and this effect may vary significantly with both schooling level and race. The possibility of variation by race would obviously create another source of bias in our results. However, it does not appear possible to speculate on the direction of bias from this source.

In sum, it would appear that we are in the unhappy position of not being able to assert with any great certainty the *direction* of bias in our estimating procedure. We have isolated two sources that almost certainly go in the direction of underestimating our effect, one source that probably leads to overestimation, and one source that cannot be specified a priori.

About all one can say here is that future studies in this area should concentrate research efforts on bringing together bodies of data on AFQT results and on earnings, by schooling and race, that will at least avoid the bias problems created by lack of identical population coverage.

If we blink the bias problem and assume that our results are not far from reality, what is their message, if any, for attitudes toward public policy in this area?

The major finding is that, as of 1960, there was plenty of room for improving the earnings prospects of Negroes by eliminating discriminatory behavior in the labor market during the decade of the 1960s. However, another message from our results is that perhaps as much as half of the 1960 differentials were the lagged effect of discrimination that took place prior to 1960. This component of the differentials could be expected to persist for a long time even if market discrimination against Negroes had fallen to zero in 1961.

Thus the persistence of *some* racial differential in earnings during the 1960s does not in itself indicate a "white backlash" or even the absence of a *decline* in market discrimination against Negroes. Only careful analysis of the earnings differential data in the forthcoming 1970 Census of Population, along with related bodies of AFQT data, will be able to detect evidence of movements in market discrimination during the turbulent 1960s.

[14]

Journal of Economic Perspectives—Volume 4, Number 4—Fall 1990—Pages 25–45

The Role of Human Capital in Earnings Differences Between Black and White Men

June O'Neill

During the past 50 years, the earnings of black men have increased substantially both in absolute terms and relative to those of white men, as shown in Figure 1. In 1940 the black-white weekly earnings ratio among men ages 25–34 was 49 percent; by 1980 it had increased to 79 percent. During the 1980s, however, the overall black-white earnings gap did not narrow, and at younger ages the gap actually widened. Although the 1980s is not the first decade since 1940 in which black men made little or no gains in relative earnings—the 1950s was another—the lack of progress in the 1980s is nevertheless puzzling and a source of concern.

This article examines the factors underlying the differential in earnings between black men and white men, with a focus on the role of human capital. Since 1940, successive generations of black men entering the labor force have been increasingly more educated relative to white men, both in terms of years of school completed and in the quality of schooling obtained. As the education and income levels of black parents increased, racial differences in the transmission of human capital in the home were also likely to have narrowed. This convergence in educational differences combined with the migration of blacks out of the South contributed to the narrowing in the racial gap in earnings over the 1940–80 period, particularly in the first half of the period.

But human capital factors—education and migration—were not the only source of convergence in black-white differences in earnings. The patterns of change in the earnings gap support the contention that declining labor market discrimination against blacks has also contributed to the rise in the black-white earnings ratio. Moreover, the acquisition of human capital itself has been strongly affected by societal and governmental discrimination, since blacks were long provided with greatly inferior schooling resources.

■ *June O'Neill is Professor of Economics and Finance and Director of the Center for the Study of Business and Government, Baruch College, City University of New York, New York, New York.*

Figure 1
Black–White Weekly Wage and Salary Ratios for Men

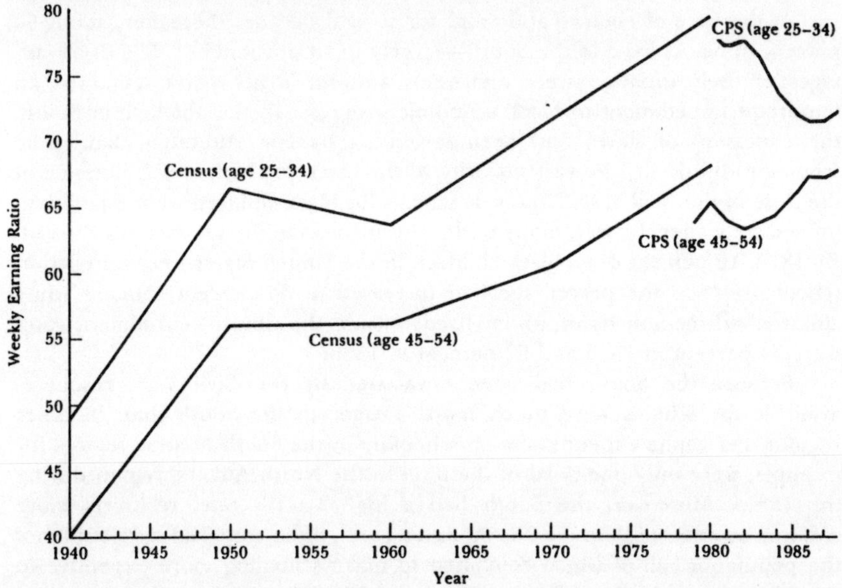

Although black-white differences in schooling have declined substantially over time, large differences in educational achievement (as measured by achievement test scores) persist. These differences are likely to be related to factors such as remaining differences in the quality of schools attended and in family background. Indeed, current differentials in educational achievement and in work experience are found to account for most of the current black-white gap in earnings among younger men. Moreover, the importance of these skill differentials has been heightened in the 1980s by changing patterns of demand for workers which have shifted in a direction favoring those with the most skill. This development helps explain the lack of relative gains in the wages of black men during the 1980s.

The discussion focusses on men, rather than on all blacks. Because of the dramatic changes in women's labor market activity in the past 50 years and the differences in these patterns between black women and white women, meaningful analysis of racial differences in economic status requires separate treatment by gender. The black-white wage gap has remained considerably larger among men than among women, making racial differences among men an issue of particular concern.[1]

[1]Over the past decade the black-white wage gap among women has been 10 percent or less, depending on the data source. For a comprehensive treatment of black-white differences in women's economic status see Zalokar (1990).

Historical Background

At the time of emancipation and for several decades thereafter, about 90 percent of blacks lived in the South—largely in rural counties.[2] The disadvantages of their situation were enormous and for many years remained an important impediment to black economic progress. In the antebellum South, the education of slaves had been forbidden by law. Although clandestine schooling did occur, the vast majority of the black population was illiterate at the close of the Civil War. However, schools for black children were established immediately after the war, many under the auspices of the Freedmen's Bureau. By 1870, 10 percent of all black children in the United States were enrolled in school; by 1880 the percentage had increased to 34 percent. Among white children—three-fourths of whom lived outside the South—enrollment rates were 54 percent in 1870 and 62 percent in 1880.

Because the South had been devastated by the Civil War, resources available for schools were much more meager in the South than in other regions. Per capita expenditures on schooling in the South Atlantic region, for example, were only one-third of the level in the North Atlantic region during the 1880s. Moreover, the South had a higher birth rate, relatively more children to educate than the North, and a rural, often scattered distribution of the population, all of which combined to make schooling more expensive to provide. Within this poorest of regions, racial hostility and the disenfranchisement of blacks resulted in an even smaller share of resources going to black children in the segregated southern schools. As recently as 1920, the length of the school year for southern whites was three-quarters of that for northern whites; but the school year for southern black children was only three-quarters as long as it was for white southern children. Similar large disparities existed in other indicators of school resources, like pupil-teacher ratios and teacher salaries.

As the southern economy grew, the differences in school resources between the South and the rest of the country narrowed. School resources provided to black children in the South also increased markedly, particularly after 1920. For example, the length of the school term for southern blacks rose from 0.76 of that of southern whites in 1920 to 0.89 in 1940, and to 0.96 in 1953. Over the same period the student-teacher ratio, which was 46 percent larger in black schools in 1920, fell to near equality with white schools; and teacher salaries rose from 55 percent to 90 percent of the white level. Thus, by 1953, on the eve of the Supreme Court ruling that segregated schools are inherently unequal and therefore unconstitutional, black-white differences in tangible school resources had narrowed considerably in the South (Brown v. Board of Education of Topeka, Kansas; 347 U.S. 483). Differentials in school resources continued to

[2]This section draws on a study I wrote with James Cunningham, Andy Sparks, and others, published by the U.S. Commission on Civil Rights (1986).

narrow after 1953, and according to the Coleman Report (1966) were negligible by the mid-1960s.

The markedly lower level of school resources publicly provided to black children earlier in the century was likely to have reduced both the amount of schooling they obtained and the quality of that schooling. Schooling attainment of black children was also influenced by the poverty of their parents. In an analysis of the determinants of racial differences in enrollment in four southern states in 1900, Margo (1987) finds that school characteristics, such as the number of months the schools were kept open, could account for only a portion of the differential in attendance. The literacy, occupational status and wealth of parents accounted for more than half of the gap. In cotton-farming areas, the opportunity costs stemming from the possibility of a child being employed rather than attending school also played a role in reducing school attendance. The rise in parental incomes and literacy in the South and migration to urban areas were factors contributing to the increase in school enrollments among black children, which by 1940 were 90 percent of white enrollment rates nationwide.

It should come as no surprise that racial differences in years of school completed were extremely large in the early part of the century. Data collected on World War I recruits show that black southern draftees had completed on average only 3.3 years of school compared to 7.2 years by the native white draftee (National Academy of Sciences, 1921). The black northern draftee, however, had completed 5.6 years of school, slightly more than the white foreign-born draftee. Blacks from the north were more likely to be urban and to have attended better schools; but only about 10 percent of blacks at that time would have been northern-born and educated.

Today, blacks still complete fewer years of school than whites, but Table 1 shows how the differential has narrowed sharply over time. In 1940, the gap in years of school completed was close to four years among men aged 25–34; in 1988, the gap was only .66 years in that age group. Black men are currently about 90 percent as likely to complete high school as white men. But college completion rates are farther apart. Among men ages 25–34 in 1988, 15.4 percent of black men had completed college compared to 27.9 percent of white men.

Earnings Differentials from 1940 to 1980

The differences observed in school completion levels would be expected to generate racial differences in earnings. Therefore, black-white earnings ratios for men with the same level of schooling should be higher than the earnings ratio for all levels of schooling combined. Table 2 uses data from the decennial census to illustrate this pattern for the 1940–1980 period (the 1980s are examined below), detailing the basic relationships between race, earnings,

Table 1
Changes in the Education Level of Black Men and White Men, 1940–1988

	Mean Years of School Completed (Men with Earnings)			*Percent with 4 years High School or More*[a]		*Percent with 4 years College or More*[a]	
	White	Black	Difference	White	Black	White	Black
U.S. Census		Ages 25–34			Ages 25–29		
1940	10.04	6.38	3.66	41.4	13.5	9.1	2.4
1950	10.89	7.77	3.12	57.7	25.6	14.2	3.8
1960	11.60	9.22	2.37	67.8	40.8	19.4	6.1
1970	12.54	10.86	1.68	77.7	60.5	24.5	8.9
1980	13.47	12.41	1.05	86.3	75.4	25.3	11.2
CPS		Ages 20–34			Ages 25–34		
1980	13.24	12.22	1.02	90.3	79.0	30.1	12.6
1988	13.25	12.59	0.66	91.1	83.2	27.9	15.4

[a]The Census data on high school and college completion refer to all civilian men, not just earners. The CPS data on school completion refer to men with earnings.
Source: U.S. Commission on Civil Rights, October 1986, and Microdata files Current Population Survey, March supplements for 1980 and 1988, microdata files.

schooling and region. For instance, the black-white earnings ratio for men ages 25–34 in 1940 at all levels of schooling combined was 48.9 percent in 1940. Within the same age group, the ratios within specific education levels were 61 to 62 percent. As differences in education diminished over time, the differences between the aggregate ratio and the ratios within schooling levels also narrowed. In 1980, the earnings ratio at ages 25–34 was 79.4 percent for all schooling levels combined, while the ratios within schooling levels ranged from 80.5 percent to 87 percent.

Regional differences also narrowed after 1940. In 1940, the black-white earnings gap was considerably larger in the South than outside the South even within schooling levels. The relative earnings of blacks rose in part because of migration out of the South to other regions. In addition, earnings levels rose generally in the South relative to the North and within the South the earnings gap between blacks and whites also declined.

Clearly, the narrowing in years of school completed and regional differences between blacks and whites contributed to the convergence in earnings. However, these factors cannot explain a large portion of the change. Within each specific age, region and education group, the black-white earnings ratio rises between 1940 and 1980 and these within group increases are substantial. For example, at the high school graduate level within the South, the earnings

Table 2
Black-White Weekly Earnings Ratios, for Male Wage and Salary Workers, by Region, Age, and Education: 1940, 1960, 1980

	Ages 25–34			Ages 45–54		
	1940	1960	1980	1940	1960	1980
All Regions:						
8–11 Years	62.3	71.6	81.6	56.4	69.1	79.1
High School	61.9	69.8	80.5	42.4	65.7	78.5
College	61.2	69.9	87.0	26.4[b]	52.8	78.5
All Levels[a]	48.9	63.7	79.4	40.3	56.2	68.2
South:						
8–11 Years	59.8	64.4	80.4	48.0	61.0	72.3
High School	53.1	63.2	79.5	--[c]	55.1	72.1
College	55.7	68.4	83.5	--[c]	58.6	66.8
All Levels[a]	42.4	57.6	77.1	36.5	50.2	63.4
Non-South:						
8–11 Years	70.1	80.8	87.3	62.2	76.8	87.4
High School	70.6	75.6	85.5	51.3[b]	69.4	84.2
College	--[c]	73.3	91.4	--[c]	50.4[b]	73.9
All Levels[a]	66.9	74.0	84.9	51.9	68.1	75.1

[a]Includes 0–7 and 13–15 years, not shown separately.
[b]Based on less than 100 observations, but more than 50 observations.
[c]Based on fewer than 50 observations.
Note: Earnings are for wage and salary workers only. Data on 0–7 and 13–15 years of school is included in the totals, but not shown separately.
Source: Census of Population, 1940–1980; Public Use Sample. Reported in U.S. Commission on Civil Rights, October, 1986.

ratio for 25–34 year-olds rose from 53 percent in 1940 to 79.5 percent in 1980 —an increase of 26.5 percentage points.

What other factors can account for the rise in the relative earnings of black men during these decades? I discuss two key factors: a rise in the skills of blacks relative to whites within education categories because of higher quality schooling or parental inputs, and a decline in labor market discrimination against blacks.[3]

[3]A third explanation originating with Richard Butler and James Heckman (1977) is that rising black male earnings partly reflect a selection factor since the labor force participation of black men has declined relative to that of white men. If lower-wage black men withdrew disproportionately from the labor force, the earnings of remaining black wage earners would show an apparent wage gain, but the increase would be illusory. These selection factors would only be relevant for the period since the mid-1960s when black male market activity began to decline relative to that of whites. The analysis in this article includes detailed adjustments for schooling, age and other factors on which selection would be based. It is possible that selection factors explain some of the unexplained rise in black male earnings, particularly in the period after 1960. However, even under extreme assumptions about the earnings of labor force dropouts, they cannot explain a major portion of the earnings rise (U.S. Commission on Civil Rights, 1986).

Quality of Schooling

The argument that the education of blacks became relatively more productive over time because of improvements in school quality has been elaborated in several important papers (Welch, 1966, 1973a, b; Smith and Welch, 1977; Smith, 1984). These authors have associated school quality with tangible school resources such as expenditures per pupil, student/teacher ratios, length of the school term and teacher salaries. The reduction and virtual elimination of racial disparities in these measures of school resources has been cited as evidence that relative school quality for blacks increased.

There is certainly a correspondence in timing between the narrowing of the differential in school resources and the subsequent reduction in the earnings differential. Successive cohorts of black men have had very different exposure to school resources. The cohort of workers who were 25–34 years of age in 1940 would have received their schooling between 1912 and 1929 if they attended for eight years; the cohort ages 25–34 in 1980 would have been in school between 1952 and 1969 for the first eight years. As noted, school resources provided to black children in the South increased dramatically between 1920 and 1953.

But do increased school resources actually lead to more of the kind of learning that increases market productivity and earnings? In answering this question it is important to distinguish between time periods, because the black-white gap in basic school resources was extremely large around World War I, and then fell to relatively small magnitudes by the mid-1950s. For example, in 1920 in Louisiana the number of pupils per teacher was close to 50 in the segregated black schools compared to 30 in the white schools, and the school term was only 126 days in black schools—50 days shorter than in white schools (Card and Krueger, 1990). Such large differentials seem likely to generate real differences in educational outcomes and the elimination of these differentials might be expected to improve the school learned skills and the productivity and earnings of blacks relative to those of whites.

A recent paper (Card and Krueger, 1990) does find a link between increases in measured school resources in a person's state of birth and in the monetary return to schooling as an adult. (The monetary return is the increase in earnings associated with an additional year of schooling.) Card and Krueger relate school inputs to earnings for cohorts born in 1920–29, 1930–39, and 1940–49. They find that the black-white convergence in the pupil-teacher ratio can account for most of the convergence in the rate of return to schooling when men born in the 1920s are compared with those born in the 1930s, but a smaller share (one-half) of the convergence in returns when the 1930s and 1940s birth cohorts are compared. These findings support the view that relative gains in school resources account for much of the otherwise unexplained narrowing in the black-white earnings gap between cohorts who would have been in their twenties in 1950, 1960, and 1970. However, the effect is likely to be negligible for cohorts reaching their twenties in 1980 and beyond because racial differences in school resources had been substantially eliminated by the time they were in school.

Another line of research relates differences in school resources to educational outcomes as measured by achievement test scores. These scores are correlated with earnings and presumably the skills that they try to measure are the route by which school resources affect earnings. The large volume of research in this area (reviewed by Hanushek, 1986) has found little relation between school resource measures and student performance on tests of academic achievement and, therefore, would appear to contradict the findings of Card and Krueger. However, almost all of the studies reviewed by Hanushek relate to the effects of differences in class size, teacher salaries and other school characteristics during the years since 1970. The range of differences in these characteristics is likely to be much smaller than that which existed between blacks and whites in the South and the North in the earlier periods analyzed by Card and Krueger.[4]

Historical evidence on the change over time in black-white differentials in academic achievement can be obtained from results of achievement tests administered by the military since World War I. These results can be roughly compared with the historical changes in school resources. The Armed Forces Qualifications Test (AFQT) has been used by the armed services for many years to test individuals for fitness for military service. It is an achievement test of verbal and mathematical skills and reflects the quality of schooling received as well as the effects of parental background. As I show below, AFQT scores are highly correlated with earnings for both blacks and whites.

Most of the cohorts whose earnings are measured in the 1940–80 censuses received their schooling well in the past, when data on military test scores are more fragmentary than for later cohorts. Evidence from the testing of recruits for the World War I draft suggests that test score differentials between blacks and whites, even at the same education level, were much larger around 1918 than they became several decades later when schools attended by black children had greatly improved. Memoir XV of the National Academy of Sciences (1921) which analyzes the results of the army "alpha" test (a predecessor of the AFQT) shows that among fourth-grade graduates the median score of southern black draftees was only 36 percent of the median score of white native-born draftees.[5] But the median score of northern blacks at the fourth grade level

[4]It should also be recognized that the absence of an effect of school resources does not mean that schools do not matter. The characteristics of schools that do matter, however, do not seem to be related to the inputs that public schools typically spend their money on.

[5]The black-white differentials in army alpha scores are likely to underestimate what the actual differential would be for a more representative group. Those who were administered the test were prescreened for literacy and those who could not read and write were given the army "beta" test which is not primarily a test of school learned skills. The "Memoirs" report that only 35 percent of the Southern black draft took the alpha test compared to 86 percent of the native white draft and 67 percent of the northern black draft.

Table 3
Mean AFQT Percentile Test Scores of Men Ages 19–21 by Race and Education

Years of school completed	1953–58		1980		Difference	
	Black	White	Black	White	1953–58	1980
Elementary						
5–6	7.7	15.4	4.5	7.3	7.7	2.8
7–8	12.4	28.1	9.4	14.9	15.7	5.5
High school						
1–2	19.1	40.4	14.0	30.4	21.3	16.4
3–4	32.2	57.2	19.4	46.5	25.0	27.1
College						
1–2	46.3	70.9	39.2	65.8	24.6	26.6
3–4	50.6	76.9	49.7	80.2	26.3	30.5

Note: Mean percentile scores on the Armed Forces Qualification Test (AFQT) for 1953–58 are based on data obtained from a 50 percent sample (0.75 million men) of the records of all individuals called up for the draft or attempting to enlist between 1953 and 1958. Scores are reported for all tested, including those rejected. Scores for 1980 are based on the results of the AFQT administered by the Defense Department to a national sample of youth.
Sources: 1953–58, D. O'Neill (1970). 1980 National Longitudinal Survey of Youth, microdata files (U.S. Commission on Civil Rights).

(who presumably had attended superior northern schools) was 85 percent of the native white score.

To be sure, problems of sample and test comparability arise between the World War I results and those of later periods. In recent times, however, national samples of black men of draft age appear to have scored closer to whites of the same age and schooling level. For example, among high school graduates ages 18 to 22 in 1980 the black median AFQT score was 65 percent of the white median.[6]

The relative rise in achievement test scores of black men seems to have occurred largely in the period between 1918 and the mid-1950s since differentials in AFQT scores are surprisingly similar in the 1950s and in 1980.[7] Table 3 provides mean AFQT scores for two cohorts of men who took the AFQT in these two time periods. The first group consists of a 50 percent sample of all men tested for the draft or enlistment during the 1953–58 period. The second group consists of a large, nationally representative sample of men participating

[6]These comparisons of median scores are calculated from the National Longitudinal Survey of Youth (NLSY) results discussed below.

[7]Both data sources are based on results of the AFQT administered to large nationally representative samples of young men and both provide information on age and education level of those tested. I do not know of any other test score results that have been released by the armed forces that contain the required detail by race and schooling.

in the National Longitudinal Survey of Youth (NLSY) who were administered the AFQT in 1980. The NLSY data have been tabulated for the same age group (19–21 years) as the 1950s data and for the same educational levels. At levels of education below the third year of high school the differential in scores narrowed between the 1950s and 1980. But at all other levels of education the differentials widened slightly.

The admittedly sparse historical data point to a narrowing of black-white differences in academic achievement when the World War I draft is compared with men tested in the 1950s. The World War I draft would have received their schooling around 1905–1915 while the men tested in the 1950s would have been in school during the 1940s and early 1950s. Between the two points in time the initially large black-white differential in school resources was greatly diminished. Although differences in school resources continued to narrow after the forties and early fifties and were eventually eliminated, black-white differences in AFQT scores do not show any further decline. These test score comparisons suggest that relative improvements in academic skills are not likely to account for the continuing rise in black-white earnings ratios for cohorts reaching their twenties between 1960 and 1980 (although they are consistent with such an explanation for earlier cohorts).

Additional evidence for this point can be found in Table 2, which reveals that earnings ratios not only increased between cohorts, but also rose for the cohort as it aged. For instance, the black-white earnings ratio for 25–34 year old high school graduates was 69.8 percent in 1960; in 1980 when this cohort reached ages 45–54, the ratio was 8.7 percentage points higher.[8] Since school quality is essentially fixed for a cohort as it ages, forces other than school quality must have produced the rise.

The Role of Declining Discrimination

Declining labor market discrimination is a likely candidate for explaining some of the rise within cohorts in black-white earnings ratios. By this I do not mean that specific affirmative action policies were necessarily responsible for the change, although they may have contributed. Market discrimination appears to have declined even before 1960, since black-white earnings ratios rose for cohorts as they aged over the 1940-1960 period. These increases, however, were smaller in the South before 1960 than they were after 1960. Undoubtedly

[8]At a moment in time (that is, in the cross-section) black-white earnings ratios tend to decline with age. This reflects the fact that older groups are from earlier cohorts who went to school and received their training during a time when opportunities for blacks were more limited. Cohort profiles might also show a decline in the ratio if blacks gained less from work experience than whites.

the Civil Rights Act, by repealing legally enforced segregation, had particularly profound effects in the South.

Of course, the effects of declining market discrimination need not be confined to changes within age cohorts. It is also plausible that reduced discrimination contributed to the relative rise in black men's earnings between successive cohorts entering the labor force. As barriers to entering occupations, industries, and specific firms are removed, blacks entering the labor force are likely to have a wider choice of jobs and training opportunities that provide cumulative career benefits.

There is also likely to be considerable interaction between discrimination and the acquisition of human capital. If a group perceives that the return to additional training will not be rewarded, they are less likely to invest in the training. It will always be difficult, therefore, to distinguish the effects of human capital from the effects of declining discrimination on the earnings gap.

The Wage Gap in the 1980s

In a break with the pattern of rising relative wages of the preceding two decades, the average weekly earnings of black men declined slightly relative to those of white men during the years 1977 to 1988. The decline, illustrated in Table 4, is largest among younger black men (ages 25–34) with twelve years or more of education—particularly college graduates—and among men ages 35–44 who had completed high school or one to three years of college. The black-white earnings ratio was stable, or rose, however, among men with less than twelve years of schooling at all ages and among men ages 45–54 at all education levels.

The small decline in the relative earnings of black men at all education levels combined is perhaps not surprising in view of the kinds of changes that have occurred in the structure of earnings in the 1980s. As several authors have documented, the earnings of less skilled workers—whether defined in terms of education or occupation—declined in the 1980s both absolutely (in real terms) and relative to those of skilled workers. (See, for example, Blackburn, Bloom and Freeman, 1990; Kosters, 1989; Murphy and Welch, 1989.) Moreover, the relative decline in earnings of less skilled workers has been most pronounced at younger ages. Because black workers have less schooling and are in less skilled occupations than white workers, the economy-wide decline in demand for less skilled workers and the rising premiums to highly skilled workers would be expected to increase the black-white wage gap.

A more puzzling question, however, is why the black-white wage gap increased sharply within certain age and schooling levels as it did among high school and college graduates under the age of 35. One hypothesis is that structural changes in employment by industry had a disproportionately large

Table 4
Black-White Weekly Earnings Ratios among Men, by Age and Schooling, Three Year Averages 1977–79 through 1986–88.

Age and years of school completed	1977–1979	1980–1981	1983–1985	1986–1988
Ages 25–54				
0–11	74.0	72.8	75.4	78.2
12	76.7	77.6	73.0	73.6
13–15	82.2	79.0	78.3	79.6
16 +	82.5	75.2	78.7	77.8
Total	71.2	70.2	69.0	69.6
Ages 25–34				
0–11	74.5	75.9	70.6	81.6
12	79.6	80.9	73.6	75.5
13–15	85.4	83.7	80.1	82.1
16 +	96.4	84.8	85.1	74.4
Total	78.1	77.7	72.4	72.4
Ages 35–44				
0–11	76.0	72.1	73.6	80.4
12	79.5	78.0	76.7	74.4
13–15	84.3	81.4	77.2	81.3
16 +	77.1	73.6	83.5	81.0
Total	70.5	68.2	69.4	70.3
Ages 45–54				
0–11	72.8	71.8	78.8	72.5
12	72.0	74.3	73.0	74.0
13–15	74.0	73.6	78.3	82.0
16 +	73.6	71.9	73.6	81.7
Total	63.9	63.5	65.8	67.9

Note: Earnings are for wage and salary workers who worked at least twelve weeks during the calendar year and were full-time for at least half of the time they worked. Earnings ratios are based on averages over the three years indicated. Age and schooling are as of the survey week which is in the following year.
Source: U.S. Bureau of the Census, *Current Population Survey*, March Supplements, 1978–1989, Microdata files.

effect on black men. For example, there has been a decline in the employment of men in durable goods manufacturing and those who were displaced may have had to settle for employment in less well paid industries. Possibly blacks were in this situation more often than whites.

To investigate the effects of changes in workers' industrial attachments and other characteristics on the change in the wage gap, I used regression analysis to estimate the change in the black-white differential in earnings from 1977 through 1987 controlling for industry, geographic location, marital status, individual year of age and education, and the skill level and blue collar identity of the person's occupation.[9] This regression analysis shows that among younger workers (ages 20–34) who have completed one year of college or more, the black-white weekly earnings gap increased sharply—by about 1.4 percent a year over the decade. Among younger workers with 0–12 years of schooling the earnings gap widened at a rate of only 0.4 percent a year. At older ages (35–54 years), the earnings differential decreased in both of the broad education categories but the change is not significant.

The analysis also reveals that compositional shifts have had little effect on these rates of change. That is, the black-white earnings differential widens almost as much within industry, occupation and detailed education and age groups, as it does when these additional factors are not taken into account. Shifts in industrial composition over the decade did tend to have a more negative impact on blacks than on whites, particularly at the high school level and below, but the effects were small and were offset by other compositional changes.[10]

What does have a significant impact on the change in the earnings gap are changes in the wage structure associated with the monetary return to skill. Most important are the increases in the premiums associated with additional years of schooling at the college level and with higher occupational skill levels. For example, among whites and blacks ages 20–34, with one or more years of college, the return to an additional year of college increased by 0.3 percent a year, and the earnings increment associated with an occupation requiring an additional year of training increased by 0.2 percent a year.[11] However, the earnings of blue collar workers declined sharply, by 0.6 percent a year. Since blacks in this group (ages 20–34, with one year or more of college) have fewer

[9]In these regressions, data from the Current Population Survey (March supplements) on earnings and the different explanatory variables were pooled over the years from 1977 through 1987 for blacks and whites combined. A variable interacting the year and race estimates the annual rate of change in the black-white differential over the period. Separate regressions were run for the two education and age categories. Separate models were also estimated, each of which contains different specifications of the independent variables. In this way the effect of adding variables—such as a set of industry dummies—is obtained by observing the change in the race/year interaction term when the additional variables are included.

[10]When individual years of schooling within the broader educational categories are held constant, the wage gap increases somewhat more rapidly since the continuing rise in the relative education of blacks was a force reducing the wage gap. When controls are added for industry and occupation the rate of increase in the gap is again narrowed somewhat. At most, shifts in industry and occupation can account for 14 percent of the widening in the wage gap among younger college educated men. Among younger men who completed only high school or less, industry and occupational shifts can account for about one-third of the widening in the gap. But the magnitude of the change in the gap is relatively small for the latter group.

[11]The skill level of an occupation was estimated by using the Dictionary of Occupational Titles (DOT) rankings of the years of Specific Vocational Preparation (SVP) required to perform the occupation (3-digit level).

years of schooling and are in less skilled occupations, they benefitted less than whites from the increases in the skill premium. Blacks are also more likely to hold blue collar jobs than whites in this age-schooling group and therefore were also more negatively affected by the relative decline in blue collar wages. The effects of these changes in the wage structure on the change in the black-white wage gap were more substantial among younger men at the college level than among other groups largely because the relative wage changes associated with skill were larger for this group. In addition black-white differences in years of schooling, occupational skill level and blue collar attachment were larger for this group than for the other age and education categories.

My analysis indicates that overall changes in the premia for skills can account for more than one-third of the decline in the black-white wage gap among younger men with college training. The remainder is linked to the finding that the wage premium for an additional year of college training increased significantly faster for white men than for black men over the decade. Of course, this explanation is not satisfactory in itself, since it immediately raises the question why the schooling and occupational skill premiums did not increase as fast for blacks as for whites at the college level.

Part of the explanation may be related to affirmative action considerations. In a study of the effects of affirmative action, Smith and Welch (1984) conclude that young college-educated blacks were the major beneficiaries of affirmative action as firms under scrutiny by the federal government bid up their wages as they sought to comply with federal regulations. Smith and Welch attribute the high relative wage of young black college graduates in the early 1970s to an "affirmative action bubble" and a decline in the mid-1970s to the difficulty of sustaining the bubble. The black/white wage ratio among young college graduates was close to parity in the late 1970s according to the data shown in Table 4, which may reflect a rekindling of affirmative action pressures which could not be sustained.

Another hypothesis is that the return to unmeasured components of skill—such as educational achievement—increased just as the premium associated with completing an additional year of college increased. A recent paper by Juhn, Murphy, and Pierce (1990) reaches this conclusion. Black-white differences in educational achievement are wider at the college level than at lower levels of schooling. An increase in the return to achievement would therefore have a larger impact at the college level.

The Effect of Achievement on Earnings in the 1980s

As shown in Table 3, blacks score lower than whites within given educational levels on the AFQT test. A natural question is whether these substantial differences in scores explain any of the differential in earnings between blacks and whites at the same level of schooling. Earnings are bound to be influenced by a wide range of skills that are not measured by achievement tests, like managerial skills, artistic talent, and physical dexterity. However, in an era where higher levels of schooling are commanding a premium, it might be expected that those who score high on achievement tests, which reflect cognitive skills of the kind developed in school, might also command a premium. Test scores, of course, reflect more than the value added in schools, since they reflect human capital acquired in the home as well.

The National Longitudinal Survey of Youth (NLSY) contains observations on earnings and AFQT scores as well as a considerable amount of detail on actual work experience, schooling and other characteristics. Black-white differences in AFQT are larger at the college level than at the high school level. Among men with 0–12 years of schooling the difference in scores is 0.96 of the white standard deviation. Among those with one or more years of college the black-white difference in AFQT scores is 1.35 times the white standard deviation. The actual years of work experience of blacks is lower than that of whites, particularly at the high school level, and it is lower while attending school as well as after leaving school. However, blacks have more experience in the armed forces. Blacks also work in occupations with a lower skill level (measured as the years of specific vocational preparation required, or SVP).

Using regression analysis to explain wages I find that a person's score on the AFQT in fact shows a strong positive correlation with the wage, holding schooling constant.[12] The effect of an increase in the AFQT scores on the hourly wage is larger at the college level than at the high school level, which is consistent with the findings of Hause (1972). Moreover, the effect of AFQT scores is larger for blacks than for whites. When schooling, age and region are held constant, an increase of one standard deviation in the AFQT score of black men increases their wages by 10.6 percent, while the comparable increase in scores among whites increases their wages by 7.0 percent.[13]

Consistent with the studies reviewed by Hanushek, standard measures of school quality have no effect on the wages of young men in the NLSY sample. Information from school records was available on the student/teacher ratio, the percentage of teachers with advanced degrees and other measures of the resources of the youth's high school. When substituted for AFQT or entered

[12]The AFQT test was administered to the NLSY sample in 1980 when the group was 15–22 years of age. Therefore, many had not yet completed their schooling. In an effort to control for potential bias in the AFQT coefficient, following Griliches and Mason (1972) who faced the same problem, I distinguished between years of schooling completed at the time of the AFQT test (1980) and years completed after taking the test.

[13]Regression results for blacks and whites separately (all levels of schooling combined) are given in the Appendix. The model specification shown includes a large number of explanatory variables including industry, occupational skill and years of work experience. The AFQT coefficients, while still large and significant, are smaller than in a regression holding constant only schooling, region, and age. The addition of the explanatory variables indicated somewhat dilutes the effect of AFQT because the additional variables are themselves influenced by changes in AFQT scores, or the educational achievement they reflect.

into the regression as additional variables (alone or in combination) these school resource measures were never significant and often as not had the wrong sign.[14]

To estimate the effect of differences in AFQT scores on the black-white earnings gap I utilized the regression coefficients, estimated separately for blacks and whites, to construct two kinds of predicted wages. In one, the mean characteristics of whites were substituted into the black regressions. (See the Appendix for examples of the black and white regressions and for more detailed findings.) The result should predict what black wages would be, on average, were blacks to be given the mean characteristics of whites while continuing to be remunerated according to the parameters of the black labor market. There is, however, an index problem since the remuneration of job-related characteristics in fact differs for blacks and whites; for example, the effect of AFQT scores on wages differs by race, as noted. Therefore, in a second exercise the mean characteristics of blacks were substituted into the white regressions, thus predicting what pay whites would receive if they were given the job related characteristics of blacks but continued to be remunerated for these characteristics according to the white pay structure.

Table 5 presents two sets of predicted wage ratios, given this tool. Part A of the table shows the predicted black wage (given average white characteristics) as a percentage of the white wage. Part B of the table shows the actual wage of black men as a percentage of the predicted white wage (given average black characteristics). Five different model specifications were used because of differences in the interpretation that might be placed on the results. The different model specifications are numbered by columns across the top of the page, and then identified by what combination of factors are being held constant by the "yes" indicated under the five columns. Schooling, AFQT scores, region, and potential experience are not likely to be the consequences of direct discrimination in the labor market. However, actual work experience, industry and the occupation's skill level may reflect both choice and elements of discriminatory treatment.

The black-white hourly earnings ratio is 82.9 percent before adjusting for any characteristics. In Panel A, after adjusting for region, schooling and potential work experience—which are the standard variables used in analysis of Current Population Survey data—the ratio rises to 87.7 percent. The addition of AFQT raises the ratio to 95.5 percent, at which point close to three-quarters of the gap is explained. Adding actual work experience virtually closes the gap. Industry and occupational skill level do not add very much to the explanation of the gap.

The unadjusted black-white earnings ratio is similar at the high school and college levels. However, separate analyses conducted for the group with one

[14] I also find that these school resource measures have no effect on AFQT scores for either blacks or whites, which is entirely consistent with the studies reviewed by Hanushek. Black and white youth in the NLSY sample are, however, shown to attend schools with nearly identical school resource measures.

Table 5

Effect of Adjusting for Differences in AFQT Scores and Other Characteristics on the Black-White Hourly Wage Ratio, Men Ages 22–29, 1987, National Longitudinal Survey of Youth.

	Actual black / white ratio	*Predicted black / white wage ratios*				
		(1)	*(2)*	*(3)*	*(4)*	*(5)*
A. Predicted black wage (given white characteristics) as percent of actual white wage:						
All Schooling Levels	82.9	87.7	95.5	99.1	101.2	91.2
0–12 years	84.5	85.0	90.4	93.8	96.7	87.7
13 years and over	85.9	95.6	108.0	110.4	107.5	97.9
B. Actual black wage as percent of predicted white wage (given black characteristics)						
All Schooling Levels	82.9	85.2	90.4	94.7	97.3	88.7
0–12 years	84.5	84.2	88.8	93.6	96.3	88.2
13 years and over	85.9	89.0	103.9	100.5	100.6	90.9
Factors held constant:						
Region		yes	yes	yes	yes	yes
Schooling		yes	yes	yes	yes	yes
Potential work experience		yes	yes	yes	yes	yes
AFQT Score			yes	yes	yes	
Actual work experience				yes	yes	
Industry					yes	yes
Skill of 3-digit occup. (SVP) and whether blue collar					yes	yes

Note: Predicted wages were estimated as follows: Separate hourly wage regressions were estimated for black and white men. A predicted wage for blacks (whites) was estimated by substituting white (black) mean characteristics into the regression results for black (white) men. The predicted wage varies depending on the explanatory variables in the model. Five model specifications are shown. The analysis is restricted to full-time workers who are not self-employed. See Appendix for samples of the regressions.
Source: National Longitudinal Survey of Youth

year of college or more and the group with less than 12 years of school does produce different results. As one would expect based on the sizable black-white difference in scores and the large size of the AFQT coefficient, the adjustment for AFQT differences for the college group raises the black-white ratio to over 100 percent. At the high school level, adjusting for AFQT differences raises the black-white earnings ratio to 90 percent. Work experience, industrial attachment and occupational skill level raise the ratio to 96.7 percent. Thus, racial differences in labor market experience at the high school level tend to have a larger influence on the outcome than at the college level.

The results in Panel B differ from those in Panel A largely at the college level. The reason is that at the college level, the white coefficients on schooling and AFQT scores are generally lower than the black coefficients. Since white coefficients weight the results in Panel B while black coefficients weight the results in Panel A, variables with large black-white differences in characteristics —in particular, the AFQT coefficient—make a bigger difference in Panel A.

To address the question whether the skills measured by AFQT are commanding a higher premium in 1987 than they did earlier in the decade, I compared the results of wage equations for men ages 22–25 in 1983 with those for men reaching the same age in 1987. I found that the AFQT coefficient (showing the effect on the log of the hourly wage of a one point increase in the AFQT score) did rise for the combined group of men of all races and for whites and blacks separately. The coefficient for all men ages 22–25 was .0023 in 1983 and .0032 in 1987. For black men, the increase was somewhat larger: from .0026 to .0039. There are problems associated with this comparison due to the fact that we are not comparing individuals who took the test at the same age and education level. The results, however, can be taken as a bit of evidence that the returns to the qualitative dimension of education rose during the 1980s, just as the return to an additional number of years of schooling increased.

Concluding Comments

Several years ago, Richard Freeman (1981) commented that "background differences appear to have become a more important impediment than market discrimination to attainment of black-white economic parity among the young." Freeman was referring to an analysis of racial differences in earnings and other economic indicators among young men in 1969. This same conclusion can be applied to the black-white earnings gap among young men today. In 1987, differences in background factors, as summarized by differences in years of school completed and in AFQT scores, explained three-quarters of the hourly earnings difference between black men and white men under age 30. Differences in work experience accounted for most of the remaining gap.[15]

Black-white earnings ratios have fallen slightly during the 1980s. The erosion is not attributable to widening differences in levels of schooling; in fact, differences in years of school completed have actually narrowed somewhat. The problem seems more to do with the increasing premium in the market to high levels of skill of the sort learned in school. As a result, differences in school quality or family and socioeconomic background that lead to differences in the acquisition of human capital are highlighted and now have an even greater impact on economic outcomes than they did in the past.

[15]Differences in the work experience of young men are also related to differences in family background and neighborhood factors (Hill and O'Neill, 1990).

Appendix
Wage Regressions

Underlying the "adjusted" black-white wage ratios shown in Table 5 are a series of wage regressions estimated separately for blacks and whites at all schooling levels combined and again separately by education level (0–12 years and 13 years and more of schooling). Regression coefficients and sample means are shown in the accompanying table for blacks and whites, all schooling levels combined. The specification shown contains the maximum number of independent variables utilized which is regression model #4 in Table 5.

The analysis is restricted to those who worked 35 hours or more in a week. The variables are defined in the Appendix Table on the following page. The basic data source is the National Survey of Youth (NLSY) 1987 microdata file. The "SVP" of an occupation refers to the years of specific vocational preparation required for average performance on the occupation, as measured by the Dictionary of Occupational Titles (DOT). The DOT measure for occupations at the 3 digit level was added to the data set.

Appendix Table

Regressions of the Log of Hourly Wages of Black Men and White Non-Hispanic Men, Ages 22–29 in 1987, National Longitudinal Survey of Youth *(t-stats in parentheses)*

			Variable Means			
	Black Men Coefficient	*White Men Coefficient*	*Black Men Mean*	*St. Dev.*	*White Men Mean*	*St. Dev.*
Dependent variable:						
Log hourly wage			1.91	0.46	2.13	0.48
Independent variables:						
Years of schooling, 1980	0.0465	0.0511	10.82	1.80	11.35	1.87
	(4.65)	(7.39)				
Years of schooling since 1980	0.0425	0.0403	1.56	1.79	1.83	2.05
	(3.14)	(4.18)				
AFQT score in 1980	0.0039	0.0019	47.99	20.65	73.09	23.20
	(5.31)	(4.14)				
Currently enrolled (0, 1)	−0.1245	−0.1227	0.05		0.07	
	(−2.07)	(−3.16)				
Potential wk exp. (Years since age 18 not enrolled in school or in armed forces)	−0.0206	−0.0228	6.61	2.61	6.16	2.84
	(−2.00)	(−2.74)				
Years worked 26 weeks or more since age 18	0.0392	0.0482	4.15	2.66	4.73	2.80
	(4.85)	(6.92)				

Appendix Table (continued)

	Black Men Coefficient	White Men Coefficient	Variable Means: Black Men Mean	St. Dev.	White Men Mean	St. Dev.
Years in armed forces	0.0434 (3.75)	0.0274 (2.13)	0.36	1.13	0.15	0.68
Years worked while enrolled	0.0280 (2.09)	0.0255 (2.96)	0.87	1.09	1.44	1.43
Tenure on current job (yrs)	0.0304 (5.12)	0.0310 (8.07)	2.17	2.41	2.78	2.73
Blue collar occupation (0, 1)	0.0429 (1.39)	0.0010 (0.04)	0.55		0.50	
SVP of occupation	0.0394 (5.12)	0.0342 (6.99)	1.56	1.72	2.42	1.97
SMSA (0, 1)	0.1108 (3.33)	0.1196 (5.84)	0.84		0.75	
Northeast (0, 1)	0.1479 (4.33)	0.0863 (3.39)	0.20		0.22	
West (0, 1)	0.1750 (3.42)	0.0825 (3.02)	0.06		0.16	
Midwest (0, 1)	0.0158 (0.45)	−0.0100 (−0.44)	0.16		0.32	
Industry dummies						
Agriculture	0.0189 (0.21)	−0.1104 (−1.74)	0.02		0.03	
Mining, construction	0.3194 (5.42)	0.2434 (5.69)	0.13		0.13	
Manufacturing	0.2302 (4.39)	0.1902 (4.95)	0.21		0.25	
Trans., Util.	0.3000 (4.96)	0.2605 (5.58)	0.10		0.08	
Fin, ins, rl. est, bus. serv.	0.1497 (2.61)	0.1994 (4.53)	0.11		0.12	
Professional services	0.0568 (0.93)	−0.0468 (−0.96)	0.09		0.08	
Public administration	0.2900 (4.17)	0.2515 (4.52)	0.06		0.04	
Retail trade	0.0065 (0.12)	−0.0293 (−0.71)	0.15		0.15	
Wholesale trade	0.0907 (1.25)	0.0981 (1.86)	0.04		0.04	
Intercept	0.6423 (4.71)	0.7894 (8.73)				
R-Sq. adj.	0.3631	0.328				
Sample size	902	2055				

■ *The author is grateful to Terry Koh and Hengzhong Liu for their programming assistance and to a grant from the Baruch College Fund for financial support. I am also indebted to Carl Shapiro, Joseph Stiglitz and Timothy Taylor for their unusually detailed and helpful comments.*

References

Blackburn, McKinley L., David E. Bloom, and Richard B. Freeman. "The Declining Economic Position of Less Skilled American Men." In Burtless, Gary, ed., *A Future of Lousy Jobs? The Changing Structure of U.S. Wages.* Washington, D.C.: The Brookings Institution, 1990.

Butler, Richard, and James J. Heckman, "The Government's Impact on the Labor Market Status of Black Americans: A Critical Review." In Hausman, Leonard J., et al., eds., *Equal Rights and Industrial Relations.* Madison: Industrial Relations Research Association, 1977, pp. 235–81.

Card, David, and Alan Krueger, *Does School Quality Matter? Returns to Education and the Characteristics of Public Schools in the United States*, mimeo, February 1990.

Coleman, James, et al., *Equality of Educational Opportunity.* Washington, D.C.: Government Printing Office, 1966.

Freeman, Richard B., "Black Economic Progress after 1964: Who Has Gained and Why?" In Rosen, Sherwin, ed., *Studies in Labor Markets.* Chicago, University of Chicago Press, 1981, 247–94.

Griliches, Zvi, and William M. Mason, "Education, Income and Ability," *Journal of Political Economy*, May/June 1972, *80*, S75–S103.

Hanushek, Eric A., "The Economics of Schooling: Production and Efficiency in Public Schools," *Journal of Economic Literature*, September 1986, *24*, 1141–77.

Hause, John C., "Earnings Profile: Ability and Schooling," *Journal of Political Economy*, May/June 1972, *80*, S108–S138.

Hill, M. Anne, and June O'Neill, *Underclass Behaviors in the United States: Measurement and Analysis of Determinants*, mimeo, March 1990.

Juhn, Chinhui, Kevin M. Murphy, and Brooks Pierce, "Accounting for the Slowdown in Black-White Wage Convergence," Conference Paper, Wages in the 1980s, American Enterprise Institute for Public Policy Research, 1990.

Kosters, Marvin H., *Wages and Demographics*, American Enterprise Institute, November 1989.

Margo, Robert A., "Accounting for Racial Differences in School Attendance in the American South, 1900: The Role of Separate But Equal," *Review of Economics and Statistics*, November 1987, *69*, 661–666.

Murphy, Kevin, and Finis Welch, "Wage Premiums for College Graduates: Recent Growth and Possible Explanations," *Educational Researcher*, May 1989, *18*, 17–26.

National Academy of Sciences, Memoir XV, *Psychological Examining in the United States Army.* Yerkes, Robert M., ed., Washington, Government Printing Office, 1921.

O'Neill, Dave M., "The Effect of Discrimination on Earnings: Evidence from Military Test Score Results," *Journal of Human Resources*, 1970, *4*, 477–86.

Smith, James P., "Race and Human Capital," *American Economic Review*, September 1984, *4*, 685–98.

Smith, James P., and Finis Welch, "Black-White Male Wage Ratios: 1960–1970," *American Economic Review*, June 1977, *67*, 323–38.

Smith, James P., and Finis Welch, "Affirmative Action and Labor Markets," *Journal of Labor Economics*, April 1984, *2*, 269–302.

U.S. Commission on Civil Rights, *The Economic Progress of Black Men in America*, Clearinghouse Publication 91, October 1986.

Welch, Finis, "Measurement of the Quality of Education," *American Economic Review*, May 1966, *56*, 379–392.

Welch, Finis, "Black-White Differences in Returns to Schooling," *American Economic Review*, December 1973a, *63*, 893–907.

Welch, Finis, "Education and Racial Discrimination." In Ashenfelter, Orley, and Albert Rees, eds., *Discrimination in Labor Markets.* Princeton: Princeton University Press, 1973b, pp. 43–81.

Zalokar, Nadja, *The Economic Status of Black Women: An Exploratory Investigation*, Staff paper, U.S. Commission on Civil Rights, January 1990.

[15]

ON THE DECOMPOSITION OF WAGE DIFFERENTIALS

Jeremiah Cotton*

Abstract—The often used method for decomposing wage differentials into human capital and discrimination components is reformulated so that both the disadvantage, or "cost," discrimination imposes on a black or minority wage earner and the advantage, or "benefit," it bestows on a white or majority wage earner can be estimated.

Introduction

THE theories of human capital investment and economic discrimination taken together suggest that differences in the average wages of racial groups occur both because of differences in their average skills or productivity characteristics and differences in the way the market treats or evaluates membership in a particular group, the level of skills notwithstanding. Moreover, according to the dual labor market hypothesis the chief way the market is able to maintain and perpetuate such treatment differences is by routing minorities in disproportionate numbers into the secondary sector of the labor market and mainly white males into the primary sector.

There have been a number of empirical studies in which attempts have been made to decompose observed racial wage and earnings differentials into these hypothesized "skill" and "treatment" components. One of the most often used decomposition methods was first employed in demography by Kitagawa (1955) and later popularized in the sociology literature by Duncan (1968) and Althauser and Wigler (1972), and in the economics literature by Oaxaca (1973) and Blinder (1973).

In his seminal work on labor market discrimination, Becker (1971) defined a competitive market discrimination coefficient for labor of different productivity as the difference between their observed wage ratio and the wage ratio that would prevail in the absence of discrimination. Oaxaca (1973) expressed this difference in percentage terms as:[1]

$$D = \frac{\overline{W}^w/\overline{W}^b - MP^w/MP^b}{MP^w/MP^b} \qquad (1)$$

where $\overline{W}^w/\overline{W}^b$ is the observed white–black average wage ratio, and MP^w/MP^b is the ratio of the white–black average marginal products, which by assumption is the average wage ratio in the absence of discrimination. Expressed in logarithmic form, (1) becomes the white–black average wage differential:

$$\ln \overline{W}^w - \ln \overline{W}^b = \ln MP^w - \ln MP^b + \ln(D+1). \qquad (2)$$

The difference between the marginal products, $\ln MP^w - \ln MP^b$, is that part of the wage differential that is due to differences in white and black productivity, and $\ln(D+1)$ is the treatment, or discrimination component.

Now, in general, $\ln \overline{W}$ can be estimated by $\sum_{j=0}^{K} B_j \overline{X}_j$, where the $\overline{X}_j$'s are average productivity-determining characteristics, and the B_j's are least-square regression coefficients. Thus, (2) can be written as

$$\ln \overline{W}^w - \ln \overline{W}^b = \sum B_j^w \overline{X}_j^w - \sum B_j^b \overline{X}_j^b \quad (j = 0, \ldots, K \text{ implied}). \qquad (3)$$

With some elementary manipulations the terms on the right-hand side of (3) can be decomposed into either

$$\ln \overline{W}^w - \ln \overline{W}^b = \sum B_j^b(\overline{X}_j^w - \overline{X}_j^b) + \sum \overline{X}_j^w(B_j^w - B_j^b) \qquad (4)$$

or

$$\ln \overline{W}^w - \ln \overline{W}^b = \sum B_j^w(\overline{X}_j^w - \overline{X}_j^b) + \sum \overline{X}_j^b(B_j^w - B_j^b). \qquad (5)$$

The first terms on the right-hand sides of (4) and (5) are estimates of $\ln MP^w - \ln MP^b$, and the second terms are estimates of $\ln(D+1)$. Oaxaca explained these alternative forms of the decomposition in the following manner:

> On the basis of either of two assumptions, we can estimate the white–black wage ratio that would exist in the absence of discrimination: If there were no discrimination, 1) the wage structure currently faced by blacks would also apply to whites; 2) the wage structure currently faced by whites would also apply to blacks. Assumption one (two) says that blacks (whites)

Received for publication August 28, 1986. Revision accepted for publication October 14, 1987.

* University of Massachusetts, Boston.

[1] Oaxaca investigated sexual rather than racial wage differences. However, inasmuch as the subsequent analysis focuses on racial wage differences I have taken the liberty of substituting "white" for "male" and "black" for "female" in the reproductions of his formulas and the quote from his text.

would on average receive in the absence of discrimination the same wages as they presently receive, but that discrimination takes the form of whites (blacks) receiving more (less) than a nondiscriminating labor market would award them. (Oaxaca, 1973, p. 695)

The formulations in (4) and (5) correspond to Oaxaca's first and second assumptions, respectively. In his empirical work he treated the issue as essentially an index number problem and obtained estimates from both formulations, using them to establish the range within which the true values of the components presumably would fall. Some subsequent decompositioners followed Oaxaca's example of estimating both forms, while others opted for one form or the other, or some variant of both.[2] Several analysts who used (5) did so because they believed the wage structure that would prevail in the absence of discrimination was more likely to be close to the white wage function than to the wage function of blacks.[3]

So far the principal concern of those who have considered this procedure has been largely statistical in nature. Among some of the adherents the problem of omitted variables has been the main worry. Since the second component is a residual, for it to be an exact measure of labor market discrimination all of the factors that determine the wage must be present and properly accounted for. If they are not, if perhaps because of data limitations some have been excluded and others poorly measured, then the residual will reflect these omitted influences as well, and will therefore either over- or underestimate the extent of discrimination.[4] This is a long-standing problem and at present nothing very much can be done except to recognize the check it places on the interpretation of results.

The criticism, however, that comes closest to revealing the main flaw in the construction of the Oaxaca decomposition is that made by Butler (1982). His most telling argument is that the attempt to measure labor market discrimination by differences in white–black regression coefficients confounds market, or demand-side sources of discrimination with those that originate on the nonmarket, or supply-side. Such coefficients are taken

[2] See, e.g., Bloch and Smith (1977) and Kiefer and Smith (1977). The form used by Masters (1974) and Diaz-Etchevehere (1977) in respective black–white and Mexican-American–white earnings comparisons combined the first term of (4) with the second term of (5):

$$\ln \overline{W}^w - \ln \overline{W}^b = \sum B_j^b\left(\overline{X}_j^w - \overline{X}_j^b\right) + \sum \overline{X}_j^b\left(B_j^w - B_j^b\right) + \sum\left(\overline{X}_j^w - \overline{X}_j^b\right)\left(B_j^w - B_j^b\right). \tag{2.1}$$

This, however, necessitated the addition of a third term, called the "interaction" term. Masters interpreted this term as a measure of the relative magnitude of discrimination against blacks who have above-average educational and other productivity skills. See also Althauser and Wigler (1972) and Iams and Thornton (1975).

[3] See, e.g., Gwartney and Long (1978) and Cotton (1985). Curiously, Masters took the same approach in defense of the second component of his decomposition (see footnote 2 above), arguing that the alternative form, $\Sigma \overline{X}^w(B^w - B^b)$ assumed that "we could give whites the black earnings function without changing that function. This assumption is less realistic than assuming no change in the white earnings function when it is given to blacks because they are only a small percentage of the population." (Masters, 1974, p. 343, footnote 3). Yet in his choice of his second term he apparently neglected his own good advice.

[4] Suppose data are available on only G of the K productivity characteristics that are assumed to fully determine the wage. Then the racial wage equation for the ith individual is

$$\ln W_i^r = \sum_{j=0}^{G} B_j^r X_{ij}^r + e_i^r \tag{4.1}$$

where

$$e_i^r = \sum_{j=G+1}^{K} B_j^r X_{ij}^r.$$

The racial wage differential formed from (4.1) would be operationally equivalent to the fully specified differential only if $E(e_i^r) = 0$. Since there is no reason to assume that this would be the case we have

$$\begin{aligned} E(\ln W_i^r) &= \sum_{j=0}^{G} B_j^r E(X_{ij}^r) + E(e_i^r) \\ &= \sum_{j=0}^{G} B_j \overline{X}_j + \overline{m}^r \\ &= (B_0^r + \overline{m}^r) + \sum_{j=1}^{G} B_j^r \overline{X}_j^r. \end{aligned} \tag{4.2}$$

The effect of the omitted characteristics are captured in the intercept. The decomposition of the wage differential now takes the form:

$$\ln \overline{W}^w - \ln \overline{W}^b = \sum_{j=1}^{G} B_j^w\left(\overline{X}_j^w - \overline{X}_j^b\right) + \sum_{j=1}^{G} \overline{X}_j^b\left(B_j^w - B_j^b\right) + \left(B_0^{\#w} - B_0^{\#b}\right) \tag{4.3}$$

where $B_0^{\#r} = B_0^r + \overline{m}^r$. The last two terms of the sum comprise the residual component and Jones (1983) has shown that it is impossible to assign a unique value to either element of this component. Thus, the residual is a mixture of discrimination and other omitted influences. However, it must be noted that many of these omitted factors, e.g., school quality or family background, may be themselves the result of past discrimination and to control for them may be tantamount to controlling for significant sources of discrimination.

from reduced-form equations and are therefore an amalgam of both demand and supply structural coefficients. And because of past supply-side discrimination in the provision of education and other skill-acquiring opportunities, the demand for black labor might be more elastic than the demand for the more capital-compatible white labor even in the absence of discrimination. In which case even though blacks and whites are identical in all other respects the white B_j's will be larger than the black B_j's and any measure of discrimination based on their differences will be overstated.

Butler is correct in questioning the comparisons of black and white regression coefficients. He is not correct, however, to assume that these are the coefficients that would prevail in the absence of discrimination. For without discrimination we would not expect differences in the black and white B_j's to persist. Perhaps in the short run just after discrimination has been eliminated one might observe blacks and whites with different average skills because of different opportunities in the past, but in the long run as blacks are assured of competing on equal terms in the same markets as whites the differences in supply characteristics can be expected to diminish along with differences in the demand for black and white labor. Indeed it is this very expectation of continuing convergence of black and white skills that is heralded by the proponents of the vintage hypothesis.[5]

In this paper it is contended that the Oaxaca decomposition procedure is flawed because of its failure to portray adequately the most critical of Becker's original conditions, viz., the wage structure that would prevail in the absence of discrimination. If Oaxaca's first assumption were used, i.e., if we assumed that blacks would receive the same wage in the absence as in the presence of discrimination, then barring envy or malice towards white wage earners (and unrequited benevolence toward employers), blacks would have no particular economic reason for desiring an end to such discrimination since their wages would be unaffected by the change and the only other effect would be to lower white wages. On the other hand, if we use the second assumption and once again bar extra-market malevolence or benevolence, whites would have no objection to ending discrimination since their own wages would not be affected thereby.

[5] See Smith and Welch (1977), (1978).

Separately considered, each assumption abstracts from the central reality of wage and other forms of economic discrimination: not only is the group discriminated against undervalued, but the preferred group is overvalued, and the undervaluation of the one subsidizes the overvaluation of the other.[6] Thus, the white and black wage structures are both functions of discrimination and we would not expect either to prevail in the absence of discrimination.

The Nondiscriminatory Decomposition

The derivation of a more suitable decomposition formula starts with Becker's assumption that in the absence of discrimination in perfectly competitive markets whites and blacks would be perfect substitutes in production. Or put another way, in the absence of discrimination the only reason wage differences would arise would be because of differences in productivity characteristics. Therefore, in the absence of discrimination the wage structures are assumed to be equal: $B^{*w} = B^{*b} = B^*$, where B^* is the nondiscriminatory wage structure.

Now consider the hypothetical term, $\Sigma B_j^*(\bar{X}_j^w - \bar{X}_j^b)$. This is the difference in the current white and black average productivity characteristics evaluated as the market would in the absence of discrimination. It is therefore the "true" value of the skill component of the wage differential.

Consider also the hypothetical term, $\Sigma B_j^* \bar{X}_j^w$. These are the current white average productivity characteristics valued as they would be in the absence of discrimination. The difference between this term and the first term on the right-hand side of (3) is solely due to differences in the way whites are currently treated and the way they would be treated in the absence of discrimination,

$$\sum B_j^w \bar{X}_j^w - \sum B_j^* \bar{X}_j^w = \sum \bar{X}_j^w (B_j^w - B_j^*).$$

[6] Some Marxists claim that the only beneficiaries of discrimination are capitalist employers and that both white and black workers lose or are "undervalued." (See Reich, 1968.) And while in general agreement, Harris (1978) suggests that perhaps the rate of exploitation of black labor exceeds that of white labor. Others such as Baron (1975) and Baran and Sweezy (1966) appear to believe that once capitalism passed from its competitive to its monopoly stage the profitable use of discrimination diminished for the capitalist class. Now ideological and psychological factors rather than pecuniary ones account for the persistence of racism.

This is therefore that part of the treatment component of the wage differential which, if positive, is due to whites' "pure" treatment advantage. A similar situation exists with respect to blacks, and we have

$$\sum B_j^* \overline{X}_j^b - \sum B_j^b \overline{X}_j^b = \sum \overline{X}_j^b \left(B_j^* - B_j^b \right).$$

This is that part of the treatment component which, if positive, measures blacks' "pure" treatment disadvantage. The average wage differential is therefore decomposed as

$$\begin{aligned} \ln \overline{W}^w - \ln \overline{W}^b = & \sum B_j^* \left(\overline{X}_j^w - \overline{X}_j^b \right) \\ & + \sum \overline{X}_j^w \left(B_j^w - B_j^* \right) \\ & + \sum \overline{X}_j^b \left(B_j^* - B_j^b \right). \quad (6) \end{aligned}$$

In this decomposition the treatment or discrimination component is made up of two elements, one representing the amount by which white productivity characteristics are overvalued (the "benefit" of being a white worker), and the other the amount by which black productivity characteristics are undervalued (the "cost" of being a black worker).[7]

A graphic distinction between the Oaxaca decomposition and the formulation in (6) is shown in figure 1. As drawn, the three simplified wage functions are assumed to depend solely on productivity characteristic $\overline{X}$. The Oaxaca decomposition of the wage differential is $(B^w\overline{X}^w - B^w\overline{X}^b) + (B^w\overline{X}^b) - B^b\overline{X}^b)$. This is the equation (5) version of the decomposition and it overestimates the "true" productivity difference and underestimates the "true" treatment difference. The decomposition given in (6) is $(B^w\overline{X}^w - B^*\overline{X}^w) + (B^*\overline{X}^w - B^*\overline{X}^b) + (B^*\overline{X}^b - B^b\overline{X}^b)$.

The major operational weakness of (6), however, is the fact that the B^* vector is unobserved and therefore must be estimated if the formulation is to be useful for empirical work. Such an estimator of course is subject to criticism inasmuch as its construction must be based on a number of rather strong assumptions about the nature of B^*. The first of these assumptions is a restatement of the conclusions previously drawn about the expected outcomes of wage and other forms of economic discrimination, viz., in the absence of discrimination whites would receive a lower average wage than they currently receive and blacks would receive a higher average wage. Thus,

$$\sum B_j^w \overline{X}_j > \sum B_j^* \overline{X}_j > \sum B_j^b \overline{X}_j.$$

Second, it is assumed that in the absence of discrimination the prevailing market structure will be some function of the forces that currently determine the white and black wage structures. This assumption is simplified by specifying B^* as a linear function of B^w and B^b, the respective white and black wage structures. Third, it is assumed that the nondiscriminatory wage structure will be closer to the current white wage structure than to the current black wage structure.[8] This third assumption is operationalized by weighting the white and black wage structures by the respective proportions of white and black males in the employed civilian male labor force.[9] Thus, the estimator of

FIGURE 1.—DECOMPOSITION OF THE WHITE–BLACK WAGE DIFFERENTIAL

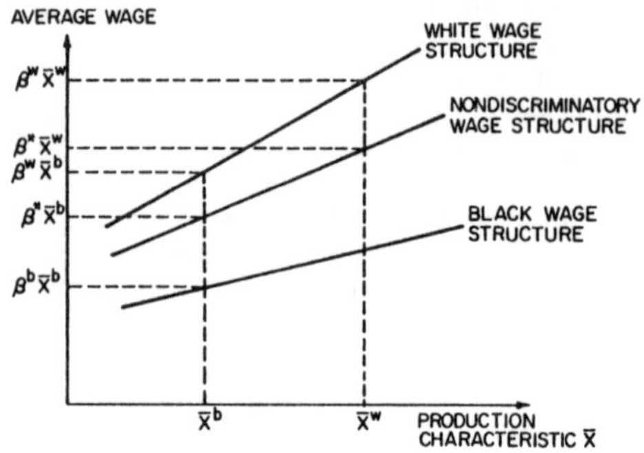

[7] The interpretation of, say, $\Sigma B^* \overline{X}^b$ is no more difficult than the interpretation of the Oaxaca term, $\Sigma B^w \overline{X}^b$. The former values the black characteristics "as if there were no discrimination" and the latter values the black characteristics "as if blacks had the white wage structure." Nor for that matter is it any more difficult than the interpretation of B, the regression coefficient, as the change in the dependent variable "if a unit change occurred in the independent variable"—a most hypothetical event indeed.

[8] Bergmann (1971, p. 310) concluded that "for the great majority of whites the end of discrimination would have only a minor effect on rates of pay. Those whites in the lowest bracket would bear the brunt of the change."

[9] Some decompositioners who recognized that the nondiscriminatory wage structure should lie between the wage structure of the majority group and that of the minority group arbitrarily assigned equal weight to both groups (See Coleman et al., 1971; Lopreato and Poston, 1977; and Reimers, 1983). Reimers wrote a general expression for the skill component of the wage differential in matrix form as

$$(X^w - X^b)(DB^w + (I - D)B^b) \quad (9.1)$$

where I is the identity matrix and D a diagonal matrix of

B^* used in this note is defined as

$$B^* = f_w B^w + f_b B^b \quad (7)$$

where f_w and f_b are the proportions. In 1979, the year covered by this study, approximately 90% of the males in the employed civilian male labor force were white, while about 9% of such workers were black.[10]

Finally, implicit in this formulation is the assumption that neither total *actual* output nor the total wage bill would change in the absence of discrimination. The only effect would be a redistribution of income and jobs. Thus, there is no expectation that the elimination of discrimination would also eliminate the tendency toward an underutilization of the labor force. As Thurow (1969, pp. 134–135) has observed, although total *potential* output would be greater in the absence than in the presence of discrimination, "to the extent that there is a surplus of labor of all types and skills, eliminating discrimination and reshuffling the labor force would result in a redistribution of income but no real gain in actual output."

In order to compare the results from the nondiscriminatory formula in (6) with the alternative formulations of the Oaxaca decomposition given in (4) and (5), each will be used to estimate the components of the wage differential of white and black males.

Empirical Wage Model and Decomposition Results

The data used in this analysis were taken from the 1% sample of the Public Use Samples of the 1980 Census. Coverage was restricted to white and black males 16 years and over who had positive earnings and hours worked and who resided in the Northeastern states of New York and Pennsylvania; the Midwestern states of Illinois, Indiana, Michigan, Ohio and Wisconsin; the Southwestern states of California and Texas; and the Southern states of Georgia and North Carolina. There were 21,341 white males and 2,785 black males in the samples.

The mean values of the explanatory variables of the wage model along with their respective regression coefficients are given in table 1. The comparative performance of the two most important variables in the model, education and work experience, was generally as expected. White males had about a year and a half more schooling than blacks and the average rate of return to an additional year of schooling for whites was considerably greater than that for blacks. In addition, the wage–experience profile of white males was well above the black male profile.

The log hourly wage for white males was 2.0125, and the corresponding geometric mean wage was \$7.48. For blacks the log wage was 1.7987, and the geometric mean wage was \$6.04. Thus, the resulting log wage differential was 0.2138, and the mean wage difference was \$1.44.

The decomposition of these differentials using equation (6), the hypothetical formulation that incorporates an estimate of the nondiscriminatory wage structure, is given in the first row of table 2. There it is estimated that approximately 49% of the log wage difference was due to white males' skill or productivity advantage evaluated as it would have been in the absence of discrimination. Translated into dollars and cents it means that about 71¢ of the \$1.44 wage gap was due to skill differences between whites and blacks. The white male treatment advantage accounted for some $22\frac{1}{2}$% of the log wage differential, or about 32¢ of the mean wage gap. This is the difference in the wage white males currently receive and what they would receive in the absence of discrimination.

The treatment disadvantage component for black males was over 28% of the log wage difference and represented about 41¢ of the \$1.44 wage gap. This is the difference in the current black male wage and the wage they would receive if there were no discrimination.

In the last two rows of table 2 estimates of the skill and treatment components obtained by using the Oaxaca decomposition formulas of equations (4) and (5) are presented. As expected, equation (4) underestimates the "true" value of the skill differential and overestimates the treatment component, whereas equation (5) does the reverse.

weights. When $D = 0$, the expression is equal to the skill component of (4), and when $D = I$, it is equivalent to that of (5). Reimers chose $D = (0.5)I$ as the weights for the nondiscriminatory wage structure. The formulation derived in (6), however, would suggest an approximate value of $D = (0.9)I$. For all the reasons adduced in the text the latter value would appear to be closer to the true value of the weights for the nondiscriminatory wage structure.

[10] See *Employment and Earnings* 27 (4) (Apr. 1980), table A-59. The relative proportion of white to black males in the civilian male labor force has been fairly constant at 10 to 1 since 1973.

TABLE 1.—MEAN VALUES AND REGRESSION COEFFICIENTS OF MODEL VARIABLES (ESTIMATED STANDARD ERRORS IN PARENTHESES)

	White		Black	
Variables	Mean Values	Regression Coefficients	Mean Values	Regression Coefficients
Education	12.13	0.0756[a] (0.0112)	10.65	0.0427[a] (0.0145)
Work Experience	16.44	0.0377[a] (0.0086)	16.27	0.0212[b] (0.0111)
Work Experience^2	468.86	−0.0006[a] (0.00002)	464.32	−0.0004[a] (0.0001)
Married, Wife Present	0.768	0.2909[a] (0.0255)	0.604	0.1801[a] (0.0486)
Once Married	0.086	0.1147[a] (0.031)	0.173	0.1466[a] (0.0333)
Urban Residence	0.411	0.1219[a] (0.0099)	0.792	0.1733[b] (0.0826)
Veteran	0.538	0.0239 (0.0211)	0.411	0.1325[b] (0.0772)
Government Worker	0.196	−0.0276[b] (0.0131)	0.289	−0.0199 (0.0207)
Region:				
Northeast	0.324	0.0638[b] (0.0392)	0.439	0.1114 (0.0917)
Southwest	0.244	0.0955 (0.0665)	0.23	−0.0678[a] (0.0214)
South	0.098	−0.1052[a] (0.0412)	0.097	−0.1931[a] (0.0537)
Industry:				
Construction	0.102	0.2891[a] (0.0488)	0.066	0.4148[a] (0.1809)
Mfg. Durables/ Nondurables	0.341	0.1966[a] (0.0475)	0.352	0.3979[b] (0.2088)
Trans. & Pub. Util.	0.123	0.2311[a] (0.049)	0.144	0.6812[a] (0.2773)
Wholesale/Retail Trade	0.141	−0.0267 (0.0444)	0.105	0.1717 (0.1502)
Insurance/Real Estate	0.057	0.1582[a] (0.0617)	0.041	0.3794 (0.2496)
Household Service	0.0007	0.0953 (0.1595)	0.0069	0.2512 (0.2779)
Miscellaneous Service	0.117	−0.1249[a] (0.0423)	0.163	0.3002[b] (0.1681)
Public Administration	0.083	0.1169[a] (0.0378)	0.085	0.4671[a] (0.2128)
Constant	1.0	0.3133[a] (0.0527)	1.0	0.4606[a] (0.2128)
R^2	0.281		0.196	
SSE	0.4057		0.4171	
N	21,341		2,785	
ln Hourly Wage	2.0125		1.7987	
Mean Hourly Wage (Geometric Mean)	$7.48		$6.04	

[a]Significant at the 0.01 level or less.
[b]Significant at the 0.10 level or less.

TABLE 2.—DECOMPOSITION OF WHITE–BLACK MALE WAGE DIFFERENTIAL USING DECOMPOSITION EQUATIONS (4), (5) AND (6)
(PERCENTAGE OF WAGE DIFFERENTIAL IN PARENTHESES)
WHITE–BLACK LOG WAGE DIFFERENTIAL = 0.2138

Nondiscriminatory Decomposition Equation	Skill Differential	White Treatment Advantage	Black Treatment Disadvantage
(6)	0.1050 (49.1%)	0.0481 (22.5%)	0.0607 (28.4%)
Oaxaca Decomposition Equations	Skill Differential	Treatment Differential	
(4)	0.0099 (4.6%)	0.2039 (95.4%)	
(5)	0.1102 (51.5%)	0.1036 (48.5%)	

Indeed, had we only these two equations with which to capture the values of the white–black skill and treatment components we would have a very wide range to deal with. According to equation (4), only about 5% of the wage differential was due to skill differences and the other 95% to treatment differences. On the other hand, equation (5) estimated that nearly 52% of the differential was due to a skill gap and about 48% to differential treatment.

Conclusion

The main defect in previous attempts to decompose wage differentials has been shown to be due to a failure of past decompositioners to appreciate fully the underlying theory of discrimination that should have guided both the construction of their decomposition formulas and the interpretation of the resulting components. As a consequence they ended up either underestimating or overestimating the hypothesized skill and treatment differences.

The form of the decomposition procedure derived in this paper not only yields more nearly accurate estimates of the components of the wage differential but also models the true state of differential treatment by estimating the "cost" to the group discriminated against as well as the "benefits" accruing to the favored group.

REFERENCES

Althauser, Robert P., and Michael Wigler, "Standardization and Component Analysis," *Sociological Methods and Research* 1 (Aug. 1972), 97–135.

Baran, Paul, and Paul Sweezy, *Monopoly Capitalism* (New York: Monthly Review Press, 1966).

Baron, Harold, "Racial Domination in Advanced Capitalism: A Theory of Nationalism and Division in the Labor Market," in R. C. Edwards et al. (eds), *Labor Market Segmentation* (Lexington, Mass.: D. C. Heath, 1975).

Becker, Gary S., *The Economics of Discrimination*, second edition (Chicago: University of Chicago Press, 1971).

Bergmann, Barbara, "The Effect on White Incomes of Discrimination in Employment," *Journal of Political Economy* 79 (Mar./Apr. 1971), 294–313.

Blinder, Alan S., "Wage Discrimination: Reduced Form and Structural Estimates," *Journal of Human Resources* 8 (Fall 1973), 436–455.

Bloch, Farrell, and Sharon P. Smith, "Human Capital and Labor Market Employment," *Journal of Human Resources* 12 (Fall 1977), 550–559.

Butler, Richard J., "Estimating Wage Discrimination in the Labor Market," *Journal of Human Resources* 17 (Fall 1982), 606–621.

Coleman, James, C. C. Berry, and Z. D. Blum, "White and Black Careers During the First Ten Years of Work Experience," Johns Hopkins University Center for Social Organization, Report No. 123, 1971.

Cotton, Jeremiah, "A Comparative Analysis of Black–White and Mexican-American–White Male Wage Differentials," *Review of Black Political Economy* 13 (Spring 1985), 51–69.

Diaz-Etchevehere, Hugo, "An Analysis of Earnings Differentials between Anglos, Mexican-Americans and Blacks in Five Southwestern States," Ph.D. dissertation, University of Wisconsin-Milwaukee, 1977.

Duncan, Otis D., "Inheritance of Poverty or Inheritance of Race?" In D. P. Moynihan (ed.), *On Understanding Poverty* (New York: Basic Books, 1968), 85–105.

Gwartney, James, and James Long, "The Relative Earnings of Blacks and Other Minorities," *Industrial and Labor Relations Review* 31 (April 1979), 336–346.

Harris, Donald J., "Capitalist Exploitation and Black Labor: Some Conceptual Issues," *Review of Black Political Economy* 8 (Winter 1978), 133–151.

Iams, Howard M., and Arland Thornton, "Decomposition of Differences: A Cautionary Note," *Sociological Methods and Research* 3 (Feb. 1975), 341–352.

Jones, F. L., "On Decomposing the Wage Gaps; A Critical Comment on Blinder's Method," *Journal of Human*

Resources 18 (Winter 1983), 126–130.

Kiefer, Nicholas M., and Sharon P. Smith, "Union Impact and Wage Discrimination by Region," *Journal of Human Resources* 12 (Fall 1977), 521–534.

Kitagawa, Evelyn M., "Components of a Difference between Two Rates," *Journal of American Statistical Association* 50 (Dec. 1955), 1168–1194.

Lopreato, Sally C., and Dudley L. Poston, "Differences in Earnings and Earnings Ability between Black Veterans and Nonveterans in the United States," *Social Science Quarterly* 57 (Mar. 1977), 751–766.

Masters, Stanley H., "The Effect of Educational Differences and Labor Market Discrimination on the Relative Earnings of Black Men," *Journal of Human Resources* 9 (Summer 1974), 342–360.

Oaxaca, Ronald L., "Male-Female Wage Differentials in Urban Labor Markets," *International Economic Review* 14 (Oct. 1973), 693–709.

Reich, Michael, "Racial Discrimination and the White Distribution of Income," Ph.D. dissertation, Harvard University, 1968.

Reimers, Cordelia, "Labor Market Discrimination Against Hispanic and Black Men," this REVIEW 65 (Nov. 1983), 570–579.

Smith, James P., and Finis Welch, "Black–White Male Wage Ratios: 1960–1970," *American Economic Review* 67 (June 1977), 323–338.

______, "Race Differences in Earnings: A Survey and New Evidence," The Rand Corporation R-2295-NSF (Mar. 1978).

Thurow, Lester C., *Poverty and Discrimination* (Washington, D.C.: The Brookings Institution, 1969).

U.S. Department of Labor, "Employment Status of the Civilian Noninstitutional Population by Sex, Age, Race and Hispanic Origin," *Employment and Earnings* 27 (4) (Apr. 1980), table A-59.

Part II
Direct Tests of the Presence of Economic Discrimination

[16]

ROGER JOWELL AND PATRICIA PRESCOTT–CLARKE

Racial Discrimination and White-collar Workers in Britain

INTRODUCTION

The United Nations Institute for Training and Research (UNITAR) have conceived, as one of their projects, a series of national studies concerned with estimating the effectiveness of measures against racial discrimination. The first such study has been carried out in Britain[1] by the Institute of Race Relations working in co-operation with UNITAR. The ultimate intention of the national studies is that there should be a comparison of anti-discriminatory measures and resulting recommendations on improving the effectiveness of such measures.

For the British project, a number of papers re-assessing the existing data were prepared.[2] These covered the absorption of immigrants and minority groups into British society, demographic and statistical background, employment, housing, education, anti-discriminatory legislation, other government measures, and the police. Papers were also prepared on the Race Relations Board, and on the Community Relations Commission and the local committees, and here work included some interviewing.[3] A further range of interviews was carried out with immigrant leaders.[4] Finally, Social and Community Planning Research were commissioned to carry out a survey of white-collar job applicants and discrimination: the subsequent paper is their research report and is printed here in its original form.

Why was it decided to collect data on job applications and discrimination within the present study? The answer to this lies in the way in which the concept of discrimination was treated, and in the relative paucity of evidence on this particular area of discrimination. It was recognized[5] that discrimination was not simply an act, or series of acts, but rather a process involving such factors as in-group,

ROGER JOWELL is Co-director of Social and Community Planning Research (S.C.P.R.) and PATRICIA PRESCOTT-CLARKE is a research officer at S.C.P.R.

out-group, act of discrimination, and relationship to society as a whole. It followed that anti-discriminatory measures might be directed primarily at one or more of these parts of a discriminatory process. In order to look at the working of such anti-discriminatory measures it seemed valuable to look more closely at discrimination —in this case, to examine the prospective engagement of white-collar workers set against the introduction of the Race Relations Act of 1968.

SIMON ABBOTT

THE DISCRIMINATION STUDY

This report outlines the aims, methods, and results of a study carried out during the spring and summer of 1969 to test the degree of job discrimination in white-collar employment within four areas of high immigrant concentration:

The areas studied were:

Nottingham/Derby/Leicester;
Reading/Windsor/Slough;
Birmingham/Wolverhampton;
Greater London

The piloting for the study was carried out during January and February 1969; and the main research spanned the period from April to August.

The study was carried out on a fairly small scale and was also regarded as a methodological pilot of a hitherto untested research technique in this area. As will be seen from the body of this report, the technique proved to be extremely successful and promises to provide a valid and economical method of discrimination testing, not only in employment, but in a variety of possible contexts.

The study was prepared and carried out by S.C.P.R. in consultation with the Institute of Race Relations.

Appendices to this report contain detailed documentation of the main research instruments employed.

Basic Approach

The aim of the study was to investigate any differences in treatment accorded to limited samples of immigrant and white British applicants for jobs.

Our first approach to the brief was to use the established and tested method of measuring discrimination, i.e. sending a series of matched coloured and white 'actors' to job interviews. The P.E.P. study employed this method successfully and, despite certain inherent drawbacks of the technique, it is still widely used in the United States. It is, of course, almost the only feasible method of testing discrimination in manual employment. We were, however, concerned with white-collar jobs—for which postal applications were possible and, in many cases, necessary—so that we were in a position to evaluate and decide on three possible approaches:

(i) A sample survey to find out the actual employment situation of a group of white and coloured employees (or aspiring employees). This was ruled out on several grounds, the most important being that it would contribute little in the way of concrete evidence. It is, of course, true that this technique would have revealed the extent to which comparable groups of British whites and immigrants were managing to find employment; the relative status structures of their employment situations; the extent to which they were holding 'preferred' jobs or 'forced choice' positions; and so on. But all this information—however relevant it may have been to the many human problems involved—would have avoided the basic question contained in our research objective: to what extent are white and coloured applicants treated differently when applying for the same jobs and with the same appropriate qualifications? No amount of scrutiny of the present employment or unemployment situation (or of attitudes towards it) could answer this question. Nor could any answer have been *inferred* if the results had shown both groups to be equally economically active and equally satisfied with their present respective positions. As has been pointed out, the same finding could well emerge from a similar survey in South Africa.

(ii) The P.E.P. approach of sending 'actor applicants' to prospective employers. This was ruled out, after serious consideration, for various technical reasons. Firstly, it is an extremely expensive technique and—because of budgetary limitations—would have meant a large reduction in the coverage of our survey. Secondly, the inherent drawbacks of the technique are simply not capable of validation and therefore impossible to allow for in the analysis of the results.

An important problem relates to the question of motivation. It has been suggested that there could well be a conscious or unconscious motivation on the part of coloured actors to *prove* discrimination, and that this would bias the results. This is, of course, an extremely tenuous argument. It is equally likely (and equally unprovable) that there would be a conscious or unconscious motivation on the part of white actors to *disprove* discrimination. Nevertheless, the strength of the criticism lies precisely in the fact that both arguments *are* unprovable, because it is virtually impossible to measure, or control for, differing levels of motivation. The problem was simply that a fairly important and relevant consideration could not adequately be allowed for in the research design and analysis, unless the scale of the operation had been large enough for these factors to have cancelled themselves out.

Precisely the same argument applied to personality differences between the actors. This encompasses a whole range of relevant variables: e.g., how plausible or credible they are; how (appropriately) modest they are; how fluent they prove to be in answering questions; how well they sell themselves; and so on. There is no reason to expect that these positive characteristics would not be randomly distributed between white and coloured actors, *provided* that the sample of actors and jobs was large enough to counteract biases in either direction. But our sample—within the budget—could not have been large enough. This meant again that discrimination could have been either exaggerated or underrated in our findings, simply because of uncontrollable and unquantifiable personality biases.

Arising from these drawbacks, the most important reason for rejecting the job interview approach was the need for reliable baseline information which could be used for purposes of *monitoring* levels of discrimination over time. This is, of course, much more important now, in view of the extension of the Race Relations Act to cover employment. We felt that, for monitoring purposes, it was essential to control all possible variables which could conceivably affect the results differently between one study and the next. If levels of discrimination were to be measured at regular intervals, the changes (if any) had to be accountable for by real shifts in practice, and not be blurred by possible alterations in the research input. In other words, we were concerned that budgets for monitoring would—in practice—rarely be large enough to allow motivational and personality variations to be randomised out. So we needed a technique which could successfully neutralise them as relevant variables.

It was these objections—in addition to the desirability of exploring new techniques—which finally persuaded us to adopt the third approach, described below.

(iii) A postal approach of sending matched written applications in reply to advertised vacancies. By opting for written applications, we were able effectively to eradicate the two major 'unknowns' of the job interview approach. On the other hand, we were also opting for a very different measurement from that tested in the P.E.P. study. The test variable with which we were concerned was more fundamental and more decisive: it was the extent to which differences in treatment occurred in the granting of job *interviews*. In other words, we were assessing the propensity of different types of employer to *consider* different types of applicant for different types of job. The study was insufficient in scale to draw any generalised national conclusions from the results. Its chief aims were to test the levels of discrimination found within the areas we surveyed; to test the feasibility of the postal technique; and to develop the technique as an economical and accurate tool of measurement.

In comparing our findings with previous studies, it is important to remember several major differences both in the content and context of the research. Firstly, we were measuring a different stage of possible discrimination, i.e. it can reasonably be assumed that discrimination in the granting of interviews would be lower than (and probably different from) any discrimination found in the allocation of jobs. The decision to interview an applicant is clearly much less conclusive than the decision to employ one.

Secondly, we were concerned only with white-collar jobs. In order for us to 'invent' suitable applicants with equal qualifications for the advertised vacancies, we were, in effect, creating a group of immigrant applicants who—in terms of both qualifications and job experience—were probably far in advance of the great majority of their 'real' counterparts in Britain today. There must, for example, be very few Pakistani area sales managers with ten years' experience in leading manufacturing firms all over Britain; and very few Indian advertising executives with the pedigree of having managed several large British offices, dealing with a variety of clients and products.

If these types of applicant were not invited for interview (while their white counterparts were) this would indeed be discrimination at a debilitating level. We do not take the view that we should have restricted ourselves to a more 'realistic' range of job types, i.e. those for which the bulk of immigrants are currently applying. What we were trying to assess was the extent to which immigrants with equal qualifications would (or do) suffer in relation to their British-born, white counterparts. While it is doubtless true that the immigrants' qualifications may have been regarded as suspect by potential employers, this would, of course, still apply to 'real' immigrants in 'real' situations. The result, in both cases, would be discrimination against the immigrant, regardless of the reason or even the justification. What we were measuring was the degree of discrimination, not the extent of prejudice or the rationale behind it: how much do immigrants with equal qualifications get accorded equal treatment? No more and no less.

Thirdly, the passage of the Race Relations Act will probably have made inroads into the levels of discrimination since the period of the last major study conducted by P.E.P. We cannot, of course, know the extent or types of changes that the Act has promoted. What we do know is that the context in which this research was conducted is different from that in which previous work has been undertaken.

Research Method

We decided early on to restrict the letters of application to actual vacancies, rather than trying to apply 'blind' to a series of unsuspecting firms. In this way, we were able substantially to reduce wastage: the firms were intending to make an appointment and, provided that our two matched applicants were at least as good as any others who applied, they were *both* likely to be invited for an interview or sent an application form. Had we applied 'blind', we would probably have encountered a large (and wasted) number of negative responses to both our applicants.

We restricted the scope of the study to four job categories in four different areas of the country:

Job Types	*Areas*
sales and marketing vacancies	Greater London;
accountancy and office management	Birmingham/Wolverhampton;
electrical engineering	Nottingham/Derby/Leicester;
secretarial	and Reading/Windsor/Slough

In all, 128 jobs were applied for by 256 applicants (i.e. two matched applicants per job—one British-born white and one immigrant). The 128 jobs were spread evenly between the four job types *and* the four areas; thus, within each area and each job type, thirty-two job applications were made:

8 from West Indians matched against British-born whites
8 from Asians matched against British-born whites (i.e. 4 Sikh Indians and 4 Pakistanis)
8 from Australians matched against British-born whites
8 from Cypriots matched against British-born whites

The notion of choosing four different types of immigrant was to ensure that variables both of country of origin and mother tongue were included. Our four groups could, therefore, be described respectively as:

Coloured English-speaking
Coloured non-English-speaking
White English-speaking
White non-English-speaking

Nevertheless, these descriptions related only to the applicants' *likely* mother tongue, not to their relative fluency in English. All letters of application—from British-born whites and immigrants alike—were of a comparable standard of literacy; and all immigrant applicants had received their higher or further education in Britain. (In fact one–half of the sample had also received their secondary schooling in Britain.)

The typical sequence of events, from the appearance of the advertisement to the result of the application, was as follows:

Advertisement appears in, say, Wolverhampton paper	(Day 1)
Paper arrives at S.C.P.R. offices; advertisement extracted; and letters of application formulated	(Day 2)
Letters of application hand-written by two 'hand-writers' (the same two for the whole study); and letters posted to the two Wolverhampton posters (the same two for the whole study)	(Day 3)
Letters posted from the two Wolverhampton addresses	(Day 4)
Letters arrive at firm	(Day 5)
Replies arrive at the two Wolverhampton addresses	(up to 3 weeks later)
Replies posted to S.C.P.R. offices	(same day)
Replies arrive at offices; booked-in; and 'scored'; successful applicants' letters sent off declining offer of interview	(1 day later)

The 'scoring' was naturally very straightforward. We were not looking for possible reasons or justifications for differences in treatment, but merely recording the results of each application:

A score of 0 signified that both applicants were treated equally, i.e. both asked for interview, both sent application forms, or both refused.

A score of -1 signified that the immigrant applicant received an unfavourable response in relation to his white counterpart.

A score of $+1$ signified that the immigrant applicant received a more favourable response than his white counterpart.

In order to allocate scores of this kind, we had to be sure that all exogenous variables (which could have influenced the responses received) were accounted for in the research design. Our applicants had to be identically matched in terms of all possible relevant variables so that the crucial factors of colour and country of origin could be isolated and tested.

This is, of course, an impossible task to achieve on two individual applicants. Handwritings would necessarily be different; the two postal addresses might be perceived in different terms; letter styles had to be different enough for them not to be spotted as 'fakes'; and so on. What we were concerned with, however, was that these exogenous factors were neutralised *over the sample as a whole*, and that only certain selected and controlled factors were *identical* for any two matched applicants. Ideally, of course, all pairs of applicants would have been identically matched; but from the point of view of authenticity, there had to be minor variations. Five 'profile variables' were therefore neutralised between matched applicants in the following way:

(i) *Age:* the two applicants for each job were always given ages which were within one year of each other.

(ii) *Marital status:* the two matched applicants were always given the same marital status; and they did not differ—in terms of number of children—by more than one child.

(iii) *Present and previous employers:* no applicant's *present* employer was ever named, but was described broadly as a 'large' or 'leading' firm in the relevant field; *previous* employers—which were named—were always a group of companies, so that references could not be taken up without further information from the applicant.

(iv) *Salary:* no details of present salary were ever provided by any of the applicants; where 'present salary' was demanded in the job advertisement, the job was excluded from the universe. (This was done on the basis of our pilot results, which showed that marginal salary differences often seemed to have a very major influence on whether or not a candidate was invited for interview. Since it did not warrant inclusion in the research design, we felt it better to exclude it completely from the range of relevant influences.)

(v) *Date of sending applications:* all matched applications were always made to arrive on the same day; and this was never in excess of one week after the advertisement had appeared. On several occasions, the time span from appearance of the advertisements to despatch of letters was less than three days.

Two other variables could equally have been neutralised, but we preferred to include them as 'test variables' so that we could isolate and test their relevance. These were:

(i) *Country of schooling:* all of our immigrant applicants received their *primary* schooling in their country of origin; however, one-half of them (spread equally between all types) received their secondary schooling in Britain and the other half reported having arrived in Britain immediately after secondary school.

(ii) *Level of qualification and experience:* each pair of matched applicants was allocated a minimum of six 'O' levels; beyond that the qualifications were matched to specific job requirements so that—for one-half of all immigrants (spread equally between all types)—the immigrant was given a *higher* qualification or greater length of appropriate experience than his British-born counterpart; and for the other half, their qualifications were identically matched. (A higher qualification always meant either one [more] 'A' level, in the case of junior posts, or two [extra] years of experience, in the case of senior posts.)

Finally, there were three further variables which—in the very nature of the study—had to be 'test variables':

(iii) *Country of origin:* the 128 British-born white applicants were matched (with equal frequency) against four different groups of immigrant applicants—West Indians, Asians, Australians, and Cypriots. These groups were identified by their names (in the case of Asians and Cypriots) *and* by a mention in their letter of application about when they had arrived in Britain. All immigrants stated in their letters that they were now permanently resident here.
The names allocated to all applicants were standardised, so that one male name and one female name were used throughout the study for each national group, e.g. the British-born applicant was always John Robinson or Mary Robinson; the Cypriot was always George Demetriades or Helen Demetriades.

(iv) *Job type:* similarly, the 128 jobs were divided equally between four job categories—sales and marketing, accountancy and office management, electrical engineering, and secretarial. Each job type was applied for with equal frequency in each of the four areas and was included on the basis of an advertisement appearing in either local or national press, or, in a few cases, specialist professional journals. Once a vacancy had been found (in one of the four job categories), it was always included in our sample, unless it specified that salary must be mentioned in the application or unless the firm had already been selected for another vacancy.

(v) *Letter of application:* as we have mentioned, each pair of letters had, of course, to differ in style, so that the authenticity of the two applications was retained. This stylistic difference could have been a biasing factor (equivalent to 'personality' in a personal interview context) unless it was capable of randomising out. Similarly, handwriting and home address (which had to differ between two matched applicants) had to be neutralised over the sample as a whole. Two *standard* letters were therefore devised and used throughout the study. Style A was always written in handwriting X and posted from address number 1 in each area; Style B was always written in handwriting Y and posted from address 2 in each area. This was, therefore, a composite variable, incorporating and neutralising three possible biasing factors. The two letters were naturally identical in content, in degree of motivation, in literacy, etc. But they varied in style and ordering sufficiently to appear to have been authored by two different applicants. Space was left appropriately in each letter for the insertion of relevant qualifications, experience, background, etc., all of which were obtained from 'experts' in the four relevant job categories. The two basic letter-types were, of course, allocated with equal frequency to each different type of applicant.

Thus the research method was an experimental design, comprising five interlaced variables: country of origin, job type, country of schooling, level of qualification, and letter of application. This enabled an analysis of variance to be carried out on the scores, so that mean differences between each of the five variables could be identified and their significance tested. For *each* of the four *job types*, for example, the following design balance was achieved:

Table 1

		Country of Origin	*Qualifications**	*Schooling†*	*Letter Style‡*
Immigrant	1	West Indian	Higher	Abroad	A
	2	"	"	"	B
	3	"	"	U.K.	A
	4	"	"	"	B
	5	"	Equal	Abroad	A
	6	"	"	"	B
	7	"	"	U.K.	A
	8	"	"	"	B
	9	Asian	Higher	Abroad	A
	10	"	"	"	B
	11	"	"	U.K.	A
	12	"	"	"	B
	13	"	Equal	Abroad	A
	14	"	"	"	B
	15	"	"	U.K.	A
	16	"	"	"	B
	17	Australian	Higher	Abroad	A
	18	"	"	"	B
	19	"	"	U.K.	A
	20	"	"	"	B
	21	"	Equal	Abroad	A
	22	"	"	"	B
	23	"	"	U.K.	A
	24	"	"	"	B
	25	Cypriot	Higher	Abroad	A
	26	"	"	"	B
	27	"	"	U.K.	A
	28	"	"	"	B

Table 1 (continued)

		Country of Origin	Qualifications*	Schooling†	Letter Style‡
Immigrant	29	Cypriot	Equal	Abroad	A
	30	,,	,,	,,	B
	31	,,	,,	U.K.	A
	32	,,	,,	,,	B

* A higher qualification relative to the British counterpart.

† Schooling abroad relates to secondary schooling. All British counterparts were schooled in the U.K.

‡ In each case, the British applicant was allocated the alternative style of letter.

Results

1. As we have mentioned, all *pairs* of applications were allocated one of three possible scores: 0 = no discrimination, − 1 = discrimination against immigrant (whatever his country of origin), and + 1 = discrimination in favour of immigrant. Table 2 shows the distribution of the actual scores.

Table 2

		Total	%
Score 0	Both applicants invited for interview	51	40
	Both received application forms	26	20
	Both received acknowledgments only	3	2
	Both received no reply	5	4
	Both refused interviews	16	13
	One refused, one no reply	1	1
	No discrimination	102	80
Score −1	Briton interview, immigrant refused	12	9
	Briton interview, immigrant no reply	5	4
	Briton interview, immigrant app. form	1	1
	Briton app. form, immigrant refused	3	2
	Briton app. form, immigrant no reply	2	2
	Discrimination against immigrant	23	18
Score +1	Immigrant interview, Briton refused	1	1
	Immigrant app. form, Briton no reply	2	1
	Discrimination in favour of immigrant	3	2
	TOTAL	128	100

2. The null hypothesis was that the aggregate score would not differ significantly from zero. It could, of course, be argued that our null hypothesis should have been a *positive score*, since one–half of the immigrants were given higher qualifications for the jobs than their British-born counterparts. Nevertheless, the basis of the design was such as to neutralise the differences between candidates to an extent that any variations in the

granting of an interview should have been ruled out. Stated unscientifically, it might have been fairer to say that the aggregate score over the sample as a whole should have been *at least* zero.

3. In the event, the aggregate score was *− 20*, a statistically significant difference from zero (at the 99 per cent level). This aggregate score predictably concealed the fact that different immigrant groups received very different treatments, i.e. the figures in Table 2 only show the total refusals for all immigrants and therefore do not yet reveal the effect of the race factor for coloured, as opposed to white, immigrants.

4. Firstly, taking a broad view of the results, it can be seen that the success rate of the British-born whites (i.e. being invited for interview or sent an application form) was very high. Of the 128 applicants, 100 were successful, i.e. *78 per cent.*

   Australians were just as successful, *78 per cent* of them being granted an interview or sent an application form.

   West Indians and Cypriots were less successful, with identical results: *69 per cent* of both groups received a positive response to their applications.

   Asians were, by far, the least successful: just under *35 per cent* of them were invited for interview or sent an application form.

5. Immigrants with higher qualifications than their white counterparts and immigrants who had received their secondary schooling in the U.K. received only *slightly* more favourable treatment than other immigrants, but the differences were not significant.[a]

		Success Rate
Immigrants with:	higher qualifications	69%
	equal qualifications	56%
Immigrants with:	secondary schooling in U.K.	70%
	secondary schooling abroad	58%

6. Since we had taken four immigrant groups to examine variations between colour and language, we can now assess these as independent variables. Taking language as a variable first, we tested two 'English-speaking' immigrant groups and two 'non-English-speaking' groups. (The language variable was, of course, in terms of imputed mother-tongue differences only, since *all* letters indicated clearly a complete fluency in English.) The results were as follows:

[a] Where references are made (here and later) to differences being 'not significant', they imply that the result could have occurred by chance in more than 5 cases out of 100.

		Success Rate
English-speaking:	Australians	78%
	West Indians	69%
Non-English-speaking:	Cypriots	69%
	Asians	35%

In each case, the white group was more successful than the coloured group; and in the case of the non-English-speaking groups, the difference was statistically significant (at the 99 per cent level).

7. It is interesting to note that there was no discrimination against Australians in relation to their British-born counterparts. (Both groups achieved a success rate of 78 per cent.) This would imply that 'foreignness', in itself, may be insufficient grounds for discrimination by British employers, i.e. the 'xenophobia argument' as a cause of discrimination is not borne out by these results. Additional 'disabilities' of either colour or mother-tongue differences (and preferably both) are apparently necessary to induce the onset of active discrimination at this level.
8. Using colour as an independent variable, we found substantial differences between the success rates of white and coloured immigrants (accounted for by the high Australian and low Asian success rates):

	Success Rate
White immigrants (Australians/Cypriots)	74%
Coloured immigrants (West Indians/Asians)	52%

9. There were virtually no differences in the degree of discrimination between either the four areas or the four job types covered in the study. Nor were there any differences between the two groups of Asians which we covered, i.e. half were Indian Sikhs (identified by country of schooling and surnames) and half were Pakistanis.
10. An analysis of variance, carried out on the full sample of jobs, is shown below. As will be seen, only 'country of origin' emerged as a significant variable (out of the five variables tested).

Table 3
Analysis of Variance

Variation Between	*Degrees of Freedom*	*Sum of Squares*	*Mean Square*	*F Ratio*
Letter type	1	·026	·026	·15
Job type	3	·188	·063	·37
Country of origin	3	2·750	·917	*5·36
Qualifications	1	·125	·125	·73
Schooling	1	·278	·278	1·63
	9	3·367		

* Significant at the 99 per cent level.

(Continued overleaf)

Table 3 (continued)

Variation Between	*Degrees of Freedom*	*Sum of Squares*	*Mean Square*	*F Ratio*
Letter/job interaction	3	·536	·179	1·05
Letter/country interaction	3	·099	·033	·19
Letter/qualification interaction	1	·287	·287	1·68
Letter/schooling interaction	1	·009	·009	·05
Job/country interaction	9	1·437	·160	·94
Job/qualification interaction	3	·062	·021	·12
Job/schooling interaction	3	·159	·053	·31
Country/qualification interaction	3	1·000	·333	1·95
Country/schooling interaction	3	·847	·282	1·65
Qualification/schooling interaction	1	·035	·035	·20
	30	4·471		
Residual	88	15·037	·171	
TOTAL VARIATION	127	22·875		

11. In examining 'country of origin' further, we found that the difference between British-born and West Indian *or* Cypriot success rates was *not* significant at the 10 per cent level. However, the difference between British-born and Asian success rates was *significant* at the 1 per cent level, i.e. this result would have occurred by *chance* in only one out of one hundred similar tests.

12. None of the cases of discrimination found would have been even remotely apparent to the disadvantaged applicant. We list below some of the typical replies for each of the four job types:

(a) *Reply to British applicant:*

Dear Miss Robinson,

Thank you for your letter of the 9th inst., in answer to our advertisement for a secretary. I should be glad to see you, if you would kindly telephone me to arrange an interview. I enclose a copy of our catalogue and also a form for you to complete and bring with you to the interview.

Yours sincerely,

Reply to Indian applicant:

Dear Miss Kaur,

Thank you very much for your answer to my advertisement for a secretary. The standard of all applications was excellent, but I have chosen someone with more experience in publishing.

Yours sincerely,

N.B. *Miss Robinson's* secretarial experience had been in chemical manufacturing and metal manufacturing.
Miss Kaur's secretarial experience had been with a transport firm and a *publishing* firm.
In all other respects the two applicants were identical.

(b) *Reply to British applicant:*

Dear Mr. Robinson,

Thank you for your application dated 4th July for the post of Cost Accountant.

Would you please telephone the writer to arrange a convenient time for you to come to this office for interview.

Yours sincerely,

Reply to Indian applicant:

Dear Mr. Singh,

Thank you very much for your letter of 4th July. I am very sorry to have to advise you that other applicants appear to fit the job description better and I am therefore unable to take your application any further.

Yours sincerely,

N.B. *Mr. Singh* had both longer and more relevant experience than *Mr. Robinson*. The two letters above were written on the same day.

(c) *Reply to British applicant:*

Dear Mr. Robinson,

Thank you for your letter dated 1st August 1969 regarding our vacancy for a Sales Representative.

We have pleasure in enclosing an application form . . . and will be in further contact with you as soon as possible after receipt, when an interview will be arranged.

Yours sincerely,

Reply to West Indian applicant:

Dear Mr. Gardiner,

We thank you for your application for the position of representative with this company, but regret to advise you that we will not be proceeding further with this appointment due to internal re-organisation.

Thanking you for your interest, we remain,

Yours sincerely,

N.B. The two letters arrived within a week of each other.

(d) *Reply to British applicant:*

Dear Mr. Robinson,

Thank you for your letter of 31st July in response to our advertisement for an electronics engineer.

We should like you to attend for interview so that we can discuss the position further, and would ask you to telephone . . . as soon as possible so that we can arrange this . . . .

Yours sincerely,

Reply to Indian applicant:

Dear Mr. Singh,

Thank you very much for your letter of 31st July in connection with an advertisement for an electronics engineer.

There was a big response to this advertisement and we have studied all letters carefully before making our final short list of candidates. It seemed to us that you were really a little too well-qualified for the type of job we were offering and therefore regret to inform you that we decided against including your name on the short list.

We would like to wish you every success in obtaining the type of position for which your qualifications fit you.

Once again, our thanks for your interest.

Yours sincerely,

N.B. Mr. Robinson and Mr. Singh had identical qualifications.

Conclusions

1. To our knowledge, this was the first study to be carried out in Britain on the propensity of employers to discriminate at this level of staff selection. It is a peculiarly decisive and absolute form of discrimination: the employer is (deliberately) denying himself the opportunity of even considering an applicant whose qualifications appear to be suitable; and the disadvantaged applicant is denied the chance even of competing with other applicants, whether or not his qualifications are better than theirs.
2. The results of the study show Asian immigrants to be the chief sufferers from this form of discrimination; West Indians and Cypriots in our sample were also disadvantaged, but not at a

statistically significant level; Australians suffered no discrimination in relation to their British counterparts. These findings differ from those of the P.E.P. report in that—in the present study—Asians, rather than West Indians, appear to be the main target for discrimination. But we were measuring a different kind of disadvantage and were looking at white-collar jobs only. It is probably true that Asian immigrants are more frequent applicants for the type of job covered in our study. It seems certain that they are more frequently rejected from being granted an interview.

3. The scale of the study was necessarily small and it was inevitably in some senses a pilot project. As such, it has proved extremely successful. It has shown, firstly, the relative economy, flexibility, and precision of a postal approach to discrimination-testing; and, secondly, the way in which measurements arising from such studies can be used for monitoring changes in the level of discrimination. The methods outlined in this report could be applied to a wide range of testing situations, e.g. holiday camps, hotels or boarding houses, new housing estates, and many others. Although the scale needs to be larger if generalised national conclusions are to be drawn, the basic methodology can be applied with good effect, even in very limited and specific situations.
4. The findings of the study give little cause for encouragement: immigrants who completed all their secondary schooling (and further or higher education) in Britain did not encounter significantly less discrimination than more recent arrivals; those immigrants who had higher qualifications than their white counterparts were not treated (significantly) differently from those with equal qualifications; and, most important, in none of the cases of discrimination found, could a complaint feasibly have been made under the Race Relations Act by the disadvantaged applicant: he or she would simply never have known that discrimination was taking place. All refusals were (predictably) polite, benevolent, and often charming: e.g. 'We would like to wish you every success in obtaining the type of position for which your qualifications fit you.' No doubt Asian immigrants, in particular, will have to face the fact that their country of origin is frequently the only significant qualification taken into account.

APPENDIX

(*i*) *Standard Letters of Application**

Dear Sir,

With reference to your advertisement in *The Daily Telegraph* of nth July, for the post of *Electrical Engineer*, I wish to apply for the vacancy.

* The italicized sections in all letters are exclusive to the particular applicant.

I am *29* years old and received my secondary schooling in *Karachi*, where I obtained six 'O' levels *and three 'A' levels.*

I arrived in England from *Pakistan* in *1958*. After leaving school I attended *Bristol University* and obtained a *B.Sc.(Hons.) degree in electrical engineering*. I am now permanently resident in Britain *and am married with three children.*

On leaving *University* I joined '*Y*' *Industries* and was employed there for *five* years. My responsibilities concerned *the application of solid state control schemes to the company's range of synchros and fractional horse power machinery.* I left in *1966* to take up my present job in a leading *paper machinery* company where I am now *engaged on design problems related to manufacturing machinery for various grades of paper and corrugated board.*

From the description of the advertised vacancy, I feel that I would be interested in the kind of work involved. I would certainly be pleased to attend an interview, if you think my qualifications and experience are suitable.

Yours faithfully,

(signed) Ahmed Khan

Dear Sir,

I was interested to read of the vacancy in your organisation for the post of Electrical Engineer.

I think my experience is suited to this position and I would be glad of the opportunity to visit you and discuss it in more detail.

I am *28* years of age and have been working as *Design and Contract Engineer* with a major company in *the paper industry* for the last *three years*. The work includes *consideration of all aspects of design techniques in the electrical components of heavy machinery. I am married and have two children.*

My educational qualifications are as follows:

Six 'O' levels } obtained at a *grammar*
Three 'A' levels } school in *Basingstoke*
B.Sc. (*Hons.*) *degree in Electrical Engineering from London University*

My first job on leaving *University* was with '*X*' *Industries as a machine designer working on small motors.* I stayed there for *five* years before moving to my present post.

I hope that the description above will enable me to obtain an interview.

Yours faithfully,

(signed) John Robinson

(*ii*) *Standard Letters of Refusal*

Dear Sir,

Thank you for your letter *of nth July* inviting me to attend an interview *at 9.30 a.m.* on *nth August*.

Since writing to you in answer to your advertisement, I have been offered and accepted a post elsewhere. I would like, however, to thank you for asking me to attend this interview.

Yours faithfully,

(signed) Ahmed Khan

Dear Sir,

Since my recent application to you for the post of *Electrical Engineer*, I have had a discussion with my employers and, as a result, have decided to remain with my present organisation.

I thank you for considering my application and apologise for any inconvenience.

Yours faithfully,
(signed) John Robinson

(*iii*) *Standard Names Used by Job Applicants*

Nationality	*Male*	*Female*
British	John Robinson	Mary Robinson
Asian: Indian (Sikh)	Santokh Singh	Ranwi Kaur
Pakistani	Ahmed Khan	Sushma Khan
Australian	Paul Harris	Avril Harris
Cypriot	George Demetriades	Helen Demetriades
West Indian	Errol Gardiner	Eva Gardiner

(*iv*) '*Addresses*' *of Applicants*

In selecting the two addresses for each area, an attempt was made to locate them in a fairly 'mixed' neighbourhood. All our possible contacts for addresses in and around the Reading area happened to be in 'white', middle-class areas, and to avoid the possibility (however slight) of an applicant claiming to live in the same or nearby street as a prospective employer, it was decided that all candidates for jobs in Reading/Windsor/Slough should be currently resident in London. The following list indicates the general locality of each address.

Base Area	*Address*	
	Letter A	*Letter B*
Greater London	London, S.E.1.	London, N.1.
West Midland Conurbation	Great Wyrley, Nr. Walsall	Great Barr, Birmingham 22A
Reading/Windsor/Slough	London, S.W.15.	London, N.W.3.
East Midlands	Nottingham NG7 1BB	Nottingham NG7 1DW

(*v*) *Newspapers Used as Advertised Job Sources*

NATIONALS

The *Daily Telegraph*
The *Sunday Times*

LOCALS

Derby Evening Telegraph
Leicester Mercury
Evening Post and News (Nottingham)
Evening Post (Reading)
Birmingham Evening Mail
Slough Observer
Windsor, Slough and Eton Express

Suitable trade journals were initially also scanned as sources of suitable job advertisements, but proved unproductive and were discontinued. A large majority of these advertised vacancies were duplicated in the daily press.

(vi) Detailed Table of Results

					0						-1			
		Total	Both Interview	Both Application Forms	Both Refused	Both No Reply	1 Refused 1 No Reply	Acknowledgement Only	1 Interview 1 Refused	1 Application Form 1 Refused	1 Interview 1 No Reply	1 Application Form 1 No Reply	1 Interview 1 Application Form	+1
	ALL	128	51	26	16	5	1	3	12	3	5	2	1	3
Area	Nottingham	32	13	5	6	3		1	3			1		
	Reading	32	13	6	3		1	1	3	1	2		1	1
	Birmingham	32	11	8	5	2			3	1	1			1
	London	32	14	7	2			1	3	1	2	1		1
Nationality	Australian	32	17	8	4	1		1			1			
	Cypriot	32	13	8	5	1			3	1				1
	West Indian	32	15	6	4	1		1		1	2	1		1
	Indian	16	4	1	2		1	1	4		2		1	
	Pakistani	16	2	3	1	2			5	1		1		1
Job Type	Sales Marketing	32	4	14	3	1			1	3	3	1		2
	Electrical Engineering	32	12	5	4	2		3	4			1	1	
	Accountancy	32	17	4	4	1	1		4		1			
	Secretarial	32	18	3	5	1			3		1			1
Immigrant's Qualifications	Equal	64	23	11	10	3		1	7	2	5			2
	Higher	64	28	15	6	2	1	2	5	1		2	1	1
Immigrant's Schooling	U.K.	64	31	12	9	1	1	1	3	3	2	1		2
	Abroad	64	22	14	7	4		2	9		3	1	1	1
Immigrant's Colour	Coloured	64	21	10	7	3	1	2	9	2	4	2	1	2
	White	64	30	16	9	2		1	3	1	1			1
Native Language	English	64	32	14	8	2		2		1	3	1		1
	Not English	64	19	12	8	3	1	1	12	2	2	1	1	2

RACIAL DISCRIMINATION AND WHITE-COLLAR WORKERS IN BRITAIN 417

References

[1] Simon Abbott (ed.), *The Prevention of Racial Discrimination in Britain* (Oxford University Press for Institute of Race Relations and UNITAR, forthcoming).

[2] By Sheila Patterson, Brian Cohen, Bob Hepple, Elizabeth Parker, Julia McNeal, Louis Kushnick, and Nicholas Deakin.

[3] These papers were prepared by Hannan Rose, Brian Cohen, and others.

[4] By R. Manderson-Jones and Jyothi Kamath.

[5] See the related paper 'Defining Racial Discrimination', in 'Quarterly Forum' in this issue of *Race*.

[17]

Excerpt from *The Extent of Racial Discrimination,* 1–55.

I Introduction

This report presents the findings of a study designed to assess the extent of the discrimination faced by Asians and West Indians when seeking jobs and housing in England. It is the second of a series of reports from the PEP Study of Racial Disadvantage. The first report[1] (which has already been published) was concerned with the extent to which employers and trade unions have taken steps to prevent racial discrimination and to secure equality of opportunity for all groups. Later reports will be concerned with the housing policies and practices of local authorities and with the general situation of Asians and West Indians, as shown by a survey among a large and representative national sample.

The general aim of the research programme is to measure the size and nature of the disadvantages suffered by members of the racial minorities compared with the white population, and to assess, as far as possible, how far these disadvantages are associated with discrimination on grounds of race, and how far they spring from other causes. From the other parts of the project we shall be able to measure the total gap between the minority and the white populations, and to understand the attitudes and behaviour of those who are in a position to discriminate. In order to extract the full meaning from this information we also need to have an objective assessment of the extent of discrimination. We hope that this will show whether discrimination is still a major aspect of the general disadvantage suffered by Asian and West Indian people in this country.

It is important to be clear about what we mean by an objective assessment of the extent of racial discrimination. It is possible to obtain *indirect* evidence that discrimination is occurring in a number of ways. For example, in our survey of employers we have shown that even in areas where at least 4 per cent of the population are new Commonwealth immigrants nearly one-fifth of plants employ no workers from the minority groups, that the great majority of minority workers are concentrated within a small minority of plants, that plants have a far greater proportion of applicants than of employees from the minority groups, and that after a careful analysis of all the evidence, the variations between plants in the concentrations of minority workers can hardly be accounted for except on the assumption that some of

[1] David J. Smith, *Racial Disadvantage in Employment,* PEP Broadsheet No. 544.

the plants discriminate against the minorities in recruitment. Again case studies of particular plants have provided a number of examples of discriminatory practices, though these findings do not provide a firm statistical base for wider generalisations.

This kind of evidence is useful and pertinent, but it needs to be supplemented by a more direct and more precise measure of the extent of discrimination. We have concluded that this can only be done by carrying out experiments; that is, by arranging for white and Asian and West Indian testers to apply for jobs and homes in person, by telephone and by letter in a set of carefully controlled situations, so that the success rate can be compared for the different racial groups. Personal and telephone testing was successfully used in the earlier PEP project carried out in 1966–67; the correspondence method has been tried and tested by Jowell and Prescott-Clarke.[3] These earlier projects have established the viability of the methods; they also provide a point of comparison with certain of our results, so that some conclusions can be drawn about changes in the level of discrimination since 1967 and since 1969. Our own work was carried out in late 1973 and early 1974.

Objectivity and the legal definition

The 1968 Race Relations Act introduced a legal definition of racial discrimination, which forms the basis of the work of the Race Relations Board. This work, and this definition, are shaped by the need to establish whether there is clear-cut evidence that discrimination has occurred in a particular case. By contrast it is not our objective to draw indubitable conclusions about particular cases: where we state that there is evidence that discrimination has occurred we are not claiming that this could necessarily be established for each individual case in a court of law (though it might well be proved for some). What we do claim is that over the whole range of tests which we have carried out the relevant factors have been carefully controlled; and therefore, that the percentage of cases in which the immigrant applicant was differently treated represents an unbiassed estimate of the overall extent of discrimination in the situations included in the tests.

The nature of the measure

To say that we aimed to 'measure' the extent of discrimination is not to imply that a single, comprehensive or conclusive measure can be provided. Discrimination occurs in different fields (employment, housing), in different contexts (recruitment, promotion) and at different stages (screening applications, final interview). There can be no single, comprehensive measure; there can only be a series of separate, but related, attempts to establish what is happening at a number of critical points.

Any testing method is bound to have inherent limitations which mean that the results can provide only *minimum* estimates of the amount of discrimination that actually occurs. In correspondence testing, for example, a pair of

[3] Jowell and Prescott-Clarke, ***Racial discrimination and white-collar workers in Britain***, RACE, Vol. XI, April 1970.

written applications are sent in for the same advertised job, one from a 'white applicant' and the other from, say, a 'West Indian applicant'. Where one applicant is invited to an interview while the other is not, this is treated as a case of discrimination (given that the qualifications and experience of the two applicants, as stated in the letters, are similar). Where both applicants are invited to an interview, this is treated as a case of no discrimination. But of course, if the applicants had been real, and had been able to attend the interviews, the employer would still have had the opportunity to discriminate at the interview stage: the testing method tells us nothing about the level of discrimination that would have occurred then. If discrimination is often encountered at the screening stage it is most unlikely that it would be reversed at later stages—that is, that the immigrant would be unduly favoured. For this reason we can be confident that actual levels of discrimination are at least as high as those shown by the tests. In fact the results of our work suggest that discrimination tends to be higher where it is possible to carry out the test at a later stage in the application procedure. Therefore it is likely that correspondence testing, which is restricted to the earliest stage, produces an under-estimate of the actual level of discrimination. The same type of limitation applies to telephone testing and to personal testing for house purchase, which can take into account only the number of houses initially offered by an estate agent; there are many further arduous stages to be gone through before the purchase of a house is actually finalised. Even in the case of personal applications by testers for unskilled jobs, the testing ends at the stage where the applicant is made a casual offer. For these reasons actual levels of discrimination are *at least* as high as shown by tests, and probably a good deal higher.

It is important, too, to make a distinction between three 'measures' of discrimination:

(1) The number of cases in which members of minority groups have had experiences where they personally believed that they had been the victims of discrimination;

(2) The number of cases in which members of minority groups have actually been the victims of discrimination, whether or not they were aware of it;

(3) For a given situation, the proportion of cases in which a member of a minority group will be discriminated against, if he puts himself in that situation.

It is necessary to make these distinctions because, first, discrimination can often take place without the victim being aware of it; and secondly, West Indians and Asians may tend to avoid situations in which they have come to expect discrimination. The first of these points is obvious and straightforward. In many of the cases described in these tests the Asian or West Indian applicant would not have been aware that there had been any discrimination, because apparently valid reasons were given for the refusal. Therefore the actual number of cases of discrimination must exceed the number known to the individuals concerned. The second point requires some further explanation.

The research which PEP carried out in 1966–67 showed that the minority groups tend to avoid situations in which they might be subjected to discrimination; for example, many of them had never applied to rent accommodation from a white landlord who was a complete stranger, although they often had great difficulty in finding rented accommodation. In fact, in most cases where Asians and West Indians had not experienced discrimination it was possible to explain this by showing that they had avoided situations where discrimination might occur.

It was argued after the publication of our earlier report that the 'situation tests' exaggerated the extent of discrimination, because the testers put themselves in situations which the majority of Asians and West Indians would tend to avoid. Even on its own ground this argument was weak, because the study showed that many Asians and West Indians had actually experienced discrimination (which they knew about) in just those situations which were recreated in the tests, though they might tend to avoid these situations to some extent. More important, it illustrated a fundamental misconception of the objective of the testing itself. It is precisely because potential victims may tend to avoid the possibility of discrimination that the experimental method is necessary. It is for this reason (together with the difficulty of verifying them) that claims of discrimination are not a reliable measure of the extent of the problem.

The minority groups will make choices, when looking for jobs or housing, within a framework of expectations which includes the likelihood of discrimination in some circumstances, but not in others. Such expectations may be based on personal experiences or on a general 'folklore'; they may or may not be sound. They *are* sound *if* the person is right in thinking that he would be discriminated against in the situations that he avoids. In that case, he is behaving rationally in avoiding such situations, since he could not gain from them. A person who avoids certain situations on the sound expectation that they could give rise to discrimination against him is hampered and restricted without being the victim of any concrete discriminatory act. Such a person may be harmed by discrimination just as much as one who actually exposes himself to it (except that he avoids the personal sense of shock caused by a manifest injustice).

In fact, in societies where the inferior status of certain groups is officially sanctioned, there is little need for the superior groups to reject members of the inferior ones by acts of discrimination, since the required patterns of behaviour are built into the law and into the mentality of all groups.

For these reasons, neither of the first two measures that we have mentioned —claims of discrimination by members of minority groups and the actual cases of discrimination against them in the course of their normal lives—is the best indication of the importance of discrimination in a society. The best measure is how often the minorities are discriminated against in certain key situations, even though many of them may tend to avoid such situations in real life. This is what our research is designed to establish.

Outline of the method

The correspondence testing covered applications for the following kinds of white collar jobs:

Salesman (male)

Accountant (male)
Management trainee (male)
Clerical (male)
Clerical (female)
Secretary (female)

It was carried out in six different towns. A total of 305 tests were completed, each test involving a pair of matched applications. In every case one of the two applicants was a native white English person, while the other was either an Italian, a West Indian, an Indian, or a Pakistani. The two applicants always had similar (British) qualifications and experience.

A team of actors was used to carry out tests in four situations:

(1) Personal application for unskilled or semi-skilled manual jobs;
(2) Telephone enquiries about skilled manual jobs advertised in newspapers;
(3) Enquiries about house purchase, mainly by personal visits to estate agents, but occasionally by telephone in response to advertisements;
(4) Enquiries about rented accommodation, mainly by telephone in response to advertisements, but also by personal visits to leading London accommodation agencies.

These tests were carried out in London and Birmingham. Two sets of actors were used, each set consisting of a native British white actor, a West Indian, an Indian, a Pakistani, and a Greek. Two actors from the set were involved in each individual test; one of the pair was always the white actor while the other was one of the other four. A total of 516 tests were carried out.

The methods used will be described and discussed in detail in the main sections of this report.

II The actor testing

1 METHOD

Conditions to be satisfied

If tests carried out by actors are to be valid and reliable, a number of conditions must be satisfied; these can be considered under the following heads:

- motivation of the actors
- consistency of recording
- checkability
- credibility
- match between the actor's 'story' and the situation
- the separation of the racial from the foreign element
- level of actor variability.

Motivation of the actors

If in the testing the white British actors were trying hard to obtain offers of jobs and housing while the immigrant actors were (consciously or unconsciously) hoping to be turned down, then the balance of the experiment would be upset; the white actors might be given preference because they seemed more eager or gave a better impression, and not because of racial discrimination. To ensure that this did not occur, great care was given to the selection and briefing of the actors, and they were continually observed during the course of the testing and asked about their personal opinions and feelings about what happened. Before the testing began it was established that none of the actors had ever been active in immigrant or other political organisations, and that none had knowingly been the victim of racial discrimination. All were professional actors and it became clear before the testing began that their main concern was to do a good job, that is, to play their roles convincingly. One of the main purposes of our briefings was to emphasise the importance of sustaining the roles and to discuss and work through any problems that might arise in doing this.

It became clear from observation of the actors and discussion with them during the testing that motivation presented no problem. All of them were pleased when they were made an offer, and annoyed when they were turned down. When the immigrant actors first met with discrimination they were genuinely surprised and hurt. Even though they knew or suspected that discrimination occurred, it came as a shock to be brought up against it face to face.

Consistency of recording

A set of standard forms was evolved for recording the details of each test; this was the raw data used for analysis in the office. Therefore the actors did not themselves decide whether the result of a test was to be classified as a case of discrimination.

The actors always worked in pairs, and one member of each pair was always one of the three white British testers, while the other was varied. The three white British testers therefore represented a stable element in the situation. Each one carried out a large number of tests, and was in a position to help his partner with any doubts he might have about the procedure.

Checkability

In the case of the personal tests it is not possible for the experimenter to observe the actor's performance directly. However, he can ask questions about it afterwards, and such questioning will reveal any serious departures from the correct procedure. This kind of checking was done throughout.

In the case of the telephone tests the experimenter can sit with the tester while he makes the call. This provides an excellent check on the telephone tests themselves; it also provides an indirect check on the personal tests, because the general manner and approach used by an actor on the telephone will tend to carry over to the personal testing situation. In about half of the cases the telephone tests were observed.

Credibility

If the person approached by the actor did not believe that the application was genuine then the whole experiment would be undermined. There is no evidence at all to suggest that this ever happened. First, no respondent ever said anything that showed any doubt about the authenticity of the applicant. Secondly, respondents always behaved in a perfectly natural way. Thirdly, both white British and immigrant actors were frequently offered jobs and accommodation.

In addition, we took pains to ensure, in a general way, that the actors were capable of sustaining the roles that were given to them. Thus, all of them had at some time done unskilled or semi-skilled jobs, and all but one of them owned their own homes, so that the situations which they confronted in the personal testing were not at all strange to them.

We were particularly concerned to ensure that the actors' approach was natural, and that they avoided imitating any crude stereotype. The applications for skilled jobs presented special problems, which we shall discuss later; in the event they proved to be far less serious than we thought they might be.

Match between 'story' and situation

It is important that the qualifications of an applicant for a job should be the appropriate ones, that a house buyer should name a suitable price range, and so on.

To ensure credibility it was found that a rather flexible approach had to be used, particularly in the case of house purchase and skilled jobs. While the house price or the qualifications had to be the same for the two actors involved in a particular test, they also had to be varied according to the level of prices in the area or the requirements of a particular skilled job. This represents a slight departure from the methods used in the earlier PEP study. At that time house prices may have been more uniform, and relatively few tests were carried out involving skilled jobs.

The separation of the racial from the foreign element

It is relevant to know how many times in total a white applicant is given preference over a West Indian applicant with similar qualifications and experience, but it is also important to establish how far this is specifically because of race rather than because of the West Indian's foreign origin. To meet this point, Greek testers were included in the experiment. This gives us a measure of the extent of discrimination against an immigrant who is not of a different race: to the extent that discrimination in this case is lower than it is against West Indians and Asians, this shows that discrimination against West Indians and Asians contains an element of what can strictly be termed colour prejudice.

Actor variability

It might be suggested that the results of tests such as these are governed by the personal qualities of particular actors, rather than by the racial differences between them. It should be pointed out, of course, that if variations between particular actors were an important factor, this would not necessarily lead to an over-estimate of the extent of discrimination: it could equally work in the other direction.

Nevertheless we have taken account of this factor by using two different teams of actors for the two situations where personal testing was used. This allows us to make a statistical estimate of the effect of varying the identity of the actors, compared with the effect of varying their racial origin, in producing the overall result.

The situations and roles

Unskilled and semi-skilled jobs

The testers were sent to areas where there were a large number of establishments fairly close together which offered unskilled and semi-skilled work. Most of the tests were carried out at manufacturing plants. The testers were not necessarily responding to advertisements, though in many cases vacancies were advertised at the factory gate. For these reasons there were a substantial number of cases in which neither applicant was offered work. The testers presented themselves to the gatekeeper or receptionist and said they were looking for work. In some cases they were turned away immediately; in others they were sent to see the appropriate person.

Examples of the roles adopted by two of the testers are given below.

West Indian: Age 29. Educated in primary and secondary school in Jamaica. Came to Britain with his parents at the age of 16. Took a job as a bus conductor in 1963 and remained in that job for five years. He then moved to a canning factory working on the production line. He is now wanting to leave

8

his present job because he no longer wants to work on permanent night shifts. Present wage about £30 net, including bonuses and overtime. Married with two children.

White British: Age 31. Born and bred in Glasgow. He has held three jobs in Glasgow in the past 14 years: warehouseman in a distillery (1960–64), packer in a dairy produce firm (1964–69), production line in a cereals factory (1969–73). He is married to a girl from London, with two children. He is now moving to the London area. Present wage about £27 net, including bonuses and overtime.

These two backgrounds are sufficiently different to avoid arousing suspicion among respondents; at the same time the differences are not significant from the point of view of a potential employer. Backgrounds for the other testers were worked out on a similar pattern.

The details of job experience were changed in some cases to ensure that the experience was relevant to the type of work at a particular plant. Such changes were controlled by the experimenter.

The second white British tester came from Grimsby, and the details were changed accordingly. The details for the other immigrant testers were similar, apart from the country of origin. The Asian testers spoke English very fluently, and without a very marked accent. The West Indians also spoke with only a slight accent.

Skilled jobs

The actors responded by telephone to advertisements in newspapers. The difficulty was to ensure that the actors had the technical knowledge required to sustain a telephone conversation about the job. This was overcome in two ways. First, jobs involving highly specialised skills were avoided; examples of the type of job selected are fitter, bricklayer, carpenter. Secondly, actors and experimenter studied a range of advertisements in different newspapers for the same types of commonly advertised skilled jobs, and it was found that a good picture of the qualifications and experience required for these jobs emerged.

The basic background of each tester remained the same as for the non-skilled tests, including the length of time spent in each job. However the actual jobs done had to be varied to suit each particular application.

In practice it was found that the testers were seldom required to give detailed information over the telephone. Generally the respondent would either describe the job and ask a few simple and basic questions before inviting the tester to an interview, or he would say that the job had been taken before any discussion had taken place.

The job experience and qualifications of each minority tester made it clear that while he had been educated in the country of origin he had learnt the appropriate skill in this country.

The testers always gave their names at the beginning of the conversation; in the case of the Asians this was enough to make it clear that they were of Asian origin though it was not possible in all cases to ensure that the respondent knew whether the Asian was from India or Pakistan. In the case of the West Indian the Christian name used was Leroy, which contains some suggestion of the country of origin, but to ensure that the employer was left in no doubt it was also necessary for the tester to speak with a definite West Indian accent. In the case of the Greek the name was enough to show foreign-ness; a slight accent was also used.

House purchase
The bulk of the house purchase tests involved personal visits to estate agents, but a few were telephone enquiries about houses which had been advertised.

In all cases the immigrant was an accountant, while the white British actor was a salesman. The immigrant was earning about £4,000 per annum, the white tester about £3,800. As usual, both were married with two children, but neither had working wives. In the earlier PEP house purchase tests, the testers in one of their roles were working class and were looking for something within a low price range. Because of the radical change in the market for houses since that time it is no longer possible to sustain this role in most areas, since very little cheap accommodation is available for purchase. For this reason the testers were confined to a middle-class role on this occasion.

It was not possible to keep constant the price range within which the testers were looking, because of the wide variations in what was available in different areas. Instead the testers assessed price levels in each area in which they worked, and then sought houses within the middle range, but said that they might be ready to pay a little more. An analysis of the prices mentioned to estate agents by testers is shown in Appendix 1 (a).

Testers were ready to mention the amount which they had available to put down as a deposit on a mortgage. This amount depended on the purchase price that the tester expected to pay; it was calculated as 30 per cent of the expected price for the immigrant and 25 per cent for the white tester. In fact, although the information was available, estate agents very seldom asked about deposits.

Rented accommodation
The testers replied by telephone to advertisements in the newspapers for rented accommodation. In the past PEP research, testers visited accommodation which was advertised on notice boards, but because of the general shortage of privately rented accommodation this is no longer a viable method, since little accommodation is now advertised in this way.

There was considerable variation in the rents of the advertised accommodation both between areas and within areas. Further information on the rents is given in Appendix 1 (b). The role of the tester was adapted to suit the rent and other details given in the advertisement. For example, if the advertisement stated: 'would suit single, professional man', the testers telephoned as single accountants and salesmen. It was originally thought that salary would have to be adapted to suit the circumstances but in fact salaries were never asked for. The testers gave a fairly lengthy introduction in which they gave their names, stated their interest in the accommodation and asked if they could come to see it. The race of the tester was communicated in the same way as before.

A small number of personal tests were also carried out among London accommodation agencies.

Matching

In a number of these situations, as we have explained, it was necessary to adapt the role of the tester and the information given to some extent from one test to the next. It should be stressed that since the testers worked in pairs it was always possible for them to ensure that for any given test they gave closely comparable details. In addition the details given were recorded so that the experimenter could later check that they had been adequately matched.

The design

The testing was carried out in London and Birmingham. In Birmingham a single white British tester was used throughout, while two sets of immigrant testers were used, one set for two of the situations and the other set for the other two. In London two white British testers were used (neither of them was the one used in Birmingham) together with the same two sets of immigrant testers. In the case of unskilled jobs and house purchase all possible pairs of white British tester plus immigrant tester were used to provide for an assessment of actor variability. Code letters have been assigned to the testers as follows:

White British testers	*Immigrant testers*		
X	West Indian	A	F
Y	Indian	B	G
Z (Birmingham only)	Pakistani	C	H
	Greek	D	I

With the help of these code letters, the pairings used are shown below.

	London				*Birmingham*
Unskilled jobs	XA	XF	YA	YF	ZA
	XB	XG	YB	YG	ZB
	XC	XH	YC	YH	ZC
	XD	XI	YD	YI	ZD
Skilled jobs	XA				ZF
	XB				ZG
	XC				ZH
	XD				ZI

	London				Birmingham
House Purchase	XA	XF	YA	YF	ZF
	XB	XG	YB	YG	ZG
	XC	XH	YC	YH	ZH
	XD	XI	YD	YI	ZI
Rented Accommodation	YF				ZA
	YG				ZB
	YH				ZC
	YI				ZD

	Total tests	*Effective tests**
Unskilled jobs		
London	145	91
Birmingham	33	11
Total	178	102
Skilled jobs		
London	45	39
Birmingham	39	37
Total	84	76
House purchase		
London	159	152
Birmingham	31	27
Total	190	179
Rented accommodation		
London	46	34
Birmingham	18	17
Total	64	51
Total London	395	316
Total Birmingham	121	92
Grand total	516	408

* Excluding 'double refusals'

12

The number of tests carried out are shown in the table above. Where an, offer was made to neither tester there is no evidence for or against discrimination, and such cases have therefore been excluded from the analysis for most purposes. The first column of the table shows the total number of tests (including double refusals) while the second column shows the number of effective tests (excluding these).

Since each test involved a pair of contacts, this means that 1,032 contacts were made altogether.

Order

One element of the design was common to all situations: the immigrant actor always made the first approach (before the white British actor). There was a period of half an hour to an hour between the two contacts, and it was always possible that the job or home might be taken during this period. By always putting the immigrant tester first we have ensured that to the extent that this has happened it has favoured the immigrant.

2 THE FINDINGS

Discrimination in the four situations

The results of each individual test have been classified according to whether discrimination was shown or not. Discrimination is defined as a case where one tester was made an offer, while the other was made none, or one where a better offer was made to one tester than to the other. There were some cases in which there was, apparently, discrimination against the white British tester and in favour of the immigrant. To take account of this we have expressed the results in terms of *net* discrimination against the immigrant. Net discrimination is the gross number of cases in which there was discrimination against the immigrant *less* the number of cases in which there was discrimination against the white British tester. If it is assumed that the cases of 'discrimination' against the white tester are the result of a random effect, then this procedure ensures that this effect is removed from our final estimate.

There are two difficulties of classification which require some discussion. In the case of unskilled jobs, there were seven tests in which an offer of a low paid job was made to the immigrant, while no offer was made to the white British tester. It seems likely that these plants were looking for cheap labour; they may have assumed that the immigrant would be ready to accept such jobs and that the white British tester would not. If this interpretation is valid these should not be treated as cases of genuine reverse discrimination when calculating the level of net discrimination. A more cautious treatment is to regard them as genuine cases of reverse discrimination even though there may be some doubt about them: this will of course result in a lower estimate of the level of net discrimination. Two different estimates of net discrimination for unskilled jobs will be given, corresponding to these two methods of classification.

The jobs offered in these seven doubtful cases of reverse discrimination were as follows:

General handyman in machine shop at £25 per week
Unskilled machine work (engineering) at £25 per week
General labourer at £22 per week
Cleaning and sweeping in a rolling mill at £20 per week
General labourer at £20 per week
Machine operator in electrical engineering at £20 per week (plus bonus of £3 to £5)
Labourer at £19 per week.

Classification of the house purchase tests also poses some difficulties. Here there were comparatively few cases in which the estate agent did not offer any houses, and discrimination was expressed by the offer of a different range of houses to the two testers. It was clear in some cases that the range offered to the white British tester was superior (normally because more houses were offered). In other cases about the same number of houses were offered to both testers, but they were different houses in different areas. In these latter cases the estate agent appears to be directing the immigrant to particular areas, but making a genuine attempt to find him a suitable house. They are in a sense cases of discrimination, but it is discrimination of rather a special kind. We shall therefore provide two sets of summary figures for house purchase; the first set counts all cases of different treatment as discrimination, while the second set excludes cases where a different but not obviously inferior range of houses was offered.

The levels of gross and net discrimination are given in the table overleaf for tests involving Asians and West Indians. (The tests involving Greeks will be shown in a separate table.)

A substantial level of discrimination is shown in all of the situations, but the level is definitely highest in the case of unskilled jobs. We cannot be sure whether this reflects a real difference or whether it relates to the methodology. As was pointed out in the discussion of the method, in the case of unskilled job applications it was possible to carry out the tests at a later stage in the process than for any of the other situations. Here the applications could be made in person, the qualifications and experience required are simple and straightforward, and the potential employers are in the habit of making a decision on the spot. It is possible that comparable levels of discrimination would be found in the other situations if the testing could be carried forward to a later stage.

It is worth considering what these substantial levels of discrimination imply in relation to the present application of the law. The tests indicate that an Asian or West Indian when applying for an unskilled job will face discrimination in at least one-third and perhaps as much as a half of all cases. The report of the Race Relations Board for 1973 states that during that year a total of 150 complaints were received relating to recruitment to employment; opinions of discrimination were formed in 16 per cent of all employment cases (including cases other than recruitment to employment). Thus opinions of discrimination were formed in perhaps 20 or 30 cases relating to recruitment to employment. By contrast, at a rough approximation, the levels of

Discrimination against Asians and West Indians in each of the four situations

	Unskilled jobs		Skilled jobs		House purchase Different treatment		House purchase Inferior treatment		Rented accommodation	
No. of tests*	81		65		137		137		41	
	No.	%	No.	%	No.	%	No.	%	No.	%
Gross discrimination	39	48	14	22	24	18	18	13	12	29
Net discrimination	37	46	13	20	23	17	17	12	11	27
or	30	37**								

* Here, and in succeeding tables, cases where an offer was made to neither tester are *not* included.
** To arrive at the lower figure (30 cases, or 37 per cent), 'doubtful cases' are treated as genuine cases of reverse discrimination.

discrimination in recruitment shown by our tests imply that the actual number of such cases over a year is of the order of tens of thousands.

We must be cautious in making comparisons between the levels of discrimination shown in the different situations, since the differences may reflect the fact that the testing can be taken to a later stage in some situations than in others. For example, we would not conclude from these results that there is less discrimination against applicants for skilled than against those for unskilled jobs. However, the level of discrimination by estate agents against house purchasers does appear to be low compared with the other situations, particularly if the cases of different, but not necessarily inferior, treatment are regarded as being less serious: if, that is, directing immigrants to particular areas is regarded as less serious than refusing a job or a service, or offering something inferior.

Greek testers were also included in the design so that we could assess how far the discrimination stems from the race of the applicant and how far from the fact that he originates from another country. The table opposite shows the levels of discrimination against the Greek testers in the four situations.

The levels of discrimination against Greeks are much lower than against Asians and West Indians. The numbers are rather small for us to make a separate comparison for each situation. Adding the results for the four situations together we find that net discrimination against Greek testers is 11 per cent, compared with 24 per cent for Asian and West Indian testers. Therefore the specifically racial as opposed to the foreign element accounts for rather more than half of the total effect.

Actor variability

In the case of unskilled jobs and house purchase, for which both sets of actors were used, it is possible to compare the amount of variation in the results between individual actors with the variation between actors of different races. The statistical technique used is the analysis of variance, and the method of computation is given in Appendix 1(c). In the case of unskilled jobs the race of the actor accounts for six times as much of the variance as the identity of the actor; in the case of house purchase the ratio is four and a half. In the case of unskilled jobs, once the influence of the identity of the actor has been extracted, the difference in the success rates between actors of different races is significant at the 95 per cent level of confidence—that is, the result would occur by chance in less than 1 in 20 cases. In the case of house purchase the result reaches significance at a marginally lower level of confidence.

This analysis demonstrates that, compared with his racial origin, the personal characteristics of a particular actor have only a slight influence on the result.

The minority groups compared

The numbers of observations are not large enough to allow us to compare the level of discrimination against the different minority groups for each situation separately, but a reasonable comparison can be made across all situations. The table below shows the levels of gross and net discrimination against each

Discrimination against Greeks in each of the four situations

	Unskilled jobs		Skilled jobs		House purchase: Different treatment		House purchase: Inferior treatment		Rented accommodation	
No. of cases	21		11		42		42		9	
	No.	%	No.	%	No.	%	No.	%	No.	%
Cases of discrimination	2	10	1	9	5	12	1	2	1	11

Note: There were no cases of 'reverse discrimination' involving Greek testers; therefore there can be no distinction between gross and net discrimination, and a single figure only is given.

minority group for all situations together.

Differences in the levels of discrimination against West Indians, Indians and Pakistanis are very slight, and are not statistically significant. West Indians, Indians and Pakistanis are likely to meet with about the same amount of discrimination in these situations.

If the doubtful cases of reverse discrimination for unskilled jobs are not treated as genuine (as in the calculation of 'net discrimination (1)' in the table) then the gross and net figures are much the same for each of the minority groups. This is because, apart from the doubtful cases, reverse discrimination occurred in only five of the tests. If, however, the doubtful

Discrimination against each minority group for the four situations combined

	West Indians		Indians		Pakistanis		Greeks	
No. of cases	104		111		109		84	
	No.	%	No.	%	No.	%	No.	%
Gross discrimination	30	29	32	29	27	25	9	11
Net discrimination (1)	28	27	31	28	25	23	9	11
Net discrimination (2)	27	26	26	23	24	22	9	11

Note: For 'net discrimination (1)' the doubtful cases have *not* been treated as true cases of reverse discrimination, while for 'net discrimination (2)' they *have* been so counted and have therefore been included in the figure to be subtracted from the gross figure.

cases are treated as genuine (as in the calculation of 'net discrimination (2)'), we find that the greatest difference between gross and net discrimination occurs among Indian testers: this is because in five out of the seven doubtful cases, an Indian tester was involved.

Comparison with 1967

Extensive actor testing was carried out by PEP in 1967 as part of the enquiry 'Racial discrimination in England'. A team of three actors was used, a West Indian, a Hungarian and a white tester; the three testers worked together, rather than in pairs, as in the present project. In the case of house purchase, personal applications were made to 42 estate agents evenly spread across the six towns included in the study. In the case of rented accommodation, 60 personal applications were made to landlords and a further 120 applications were made to landlords by telephone. Testing was also carried out in connection with recruitment to employment, but here the firms approached were ones which the informants in a survey claimed had discriminated against them. The results of these latter tests showed that informants' claims of discrimination were mostly justified, but they do not provide a basis of comparison with the present research, because the firms tested were not a random sample, but a set of firms against which claims of discrimination had been made.

However the earlier accommodation tests were carried out on a roughly similar basis to the present ones, and they do form the basis for a comparison over time. The fact that three testers were previously used for each test does not invalidate the comparison, since the results for the West Indian tester can easily be extracted. Since in the present tests we have found no significant difference between the results for West Indians, Indians and Pakistanis, we propose to compare the present combined results for Asian and West Indian testers with the earlier results for the West Indian tester. The areas in which the tests were carried out were not the same in the two projects, but this would be unlikely to explain any substantial differences.

The results for 1967 and 1973 are compared in the table below.

	1967 % discrimination against West Indian tester	*1973* % discrimination (net) against West Indian and Asian testers
Rented accommodation (telephone)	62	27
Rented accommodation (personal)	75	NA
House purchase (personal)	64	17 (different treatment)
		12 (inferior treatment)

The comparison shows that there has been a sharp decrease in the level of discrimination in these situations since 1967, before the enactment of the 1968 Race Relations Act. This decrease has been sharper for house purchase through estate agents than for rented accommodation. While in 1967 discrimination was about as high for house purchase as for the other situations, in 1973 there seems to be less discrimination for house purchase than for rented accommodation, or for recruitment to manual employment.

There has also been a qualitative change in the behaviour of estate agents. In nine out of the 27 occasions on which estate agents discriminated in 1967 they did this by telling the West Indian that a mortgage would be impossible, or by giving him different information about mortgage terms. In 1973, however, there were no cases of discrimination involving mortgage terms. It may be, of course, that this reflects a change in the behaviour of building societies.

In 1967 a large number of the advertisements for rented accommodation stated that 'coloureds' would not be accepted. Such advertisements were excluded from the tests, so that the results show the level of discrimination for advertisements which did not openly exclude West Indians and Asians. Advertisements of this kind disappeared following the 1968 Race Relations Act, and only covert discrimination remained feasible. This change is an important result of the Act in itself. It also means that the decrease in discrimination in rented accommodation is under-stated in our table.

The results clearly show that since 1967 discrimination in the field of accommodation has decreased to a considerable extent. At the same time discrimination against applicants for rented accommodation is still substantial.

As we have explained, a direct comparison cannot be made for recruitment to manual employment. Nevertheless the general drift of the 1967 results suggests that here, too, discrimination was taking place on a massive scale. In 1973 discrimination against applicants for unskilled jobs in particular is still substantial (46 per cent of cases): yet it has probably decreased considerably since 1967. **[20]**

III Correspondence testing

1 METHOD

Correspondence testing is a tightly controlled method of assessing the level of discrimination against applicants for white collar jobs. This method was first used by Jowell and Prescott-Clarke in 1969. We have used essentially the same method as they, but with a few modifications.

Written or typed letters of application are sent for a sample of advertised jobs. Two applications are made for each job, one in the name of a white British applicant, and the other in the name of an immigrant. Where both applicants are invited to an interview this is treated as a case of 'no discrimination', but where one applicant is invited to an interview and the other is not, this is treated as a case of discrimination.

The advantage of the method is that all features of the application can be carefully controlled. The disadvantage is that it only tests for discrimination at the first 'screening' stage of the recruitment process. However we have not been able to devise a testing method for white collar jobs that overcomes this difficulty.

The variables

Country of origin of the immigrant

One of the two applicants was always white British. The other was either:

Italian
West Indian
Indian, or
Pakistani.

The inclusion of the Italian allows us to assess the effect of race as opposed to foreign origin.

The immigrant applicants always stated in their letters: 'I came to England in 1956 from Jamaica/India/Pakistan/Italy after completing my primary schooling. I have been permanently resident in the UK since that time.' The white British applicants always mentioned the town where they went to school, but did not, of course, explicitly state that they were white or that they were born in England: this would be the natural assumption for the recipient to make. The names of the applicants were a further aid to the establishment of the country of origin.

Type of job
Our aim was to cover a broad range of white collar jobs in terms of pay and prospects, and also to include at least one job which is commonly done by immigrants. The following six types of job were included:

Salesman (male)
Accountant (male)
Management trainee (male)
Junior clerical (male)
Junior clerical (female)
Secretary (female)

The variable of sex is built into this design in a limited way, since it is possible to make a direct comparison between the results for male and female applicants for junior clerical jobs. In some cases the advertisements for these jobs specified the sex required, but where this was left open in the advertisement we allocated it to either the male or female category at random. In general, what the list above indicates is the sex of our *applicants*; this does not necessarily imply that sex was specified in the advertisement.

Region
The testing was carried out in one town within each of the six regions of England which contain substantial numbers of immigrants:

London
Remainder of the South East (Slough/Windsor)
East Midlands (Nottingham)
West Midlands (Birmingham)
Yorkshire (Leeds)
North West (Manchester)

Letter type
Clearly identical letters cannot be sent for the same job; therefore two different letters have to be devised. There may be some danger that the exact form of the letter influences the response (even though the substance of the two letters is the same) but the design controls for this by allocating each letter to the immigrant in exactly half of all cases.

Strictly speaking, letter type cannot be regarded as a variable in the same sense as region, type of job and country of origin. This is because the content of the letter must vary considerably between the different jobs, so that it is not possible to say which of the two letters used for 'salesman' corresponds with the first of the two used for 'secretary'. In other words it does not make sense to add up the results for letter type A across all jobs and to ask whether it produced a better response than letter type B.[1] Nevertheless it is possible to say whether the type of letter used has a significant effect on the result for any individual type of job.

[1] This is a logical point on which we differ from Jowell and Prescott-Clarke. In their study letters for different types of job were considered to be adaptations of the same basic letter.

Associated with the differences in letter type there were also marginal differences in qualifications and experience, since the two applicants could not have gone to the same schools and had exactly the same jobs without arousing suspicion. However, these differences did not amount to a qualitative difference in level of qualifications and experience. If job experience in one of the letters happened to have a special relevance to a particular advertised job, then this job was excluded.

The invariable factors

The level of qualifications and experience of the two applicants was always the same. Applications for secretarial jobs were typed while the other applications were handwritten.

The letters from immigrant applicants always stated that they had had their primary schooling in the country of origin and their secondary schooling in England. Therefore both applicants had similar standard British qualifications. It was also established by implication that the immigrant applicants were fluent in spoken and written English; the standard of the letter itself also made this clear. The applicants' names confirmed the information about country of origin which was explicitly stated in the letter. Altogether ten names were used, one for each sex within each country of origin.

The ages of the two applicants were always within one year of each other, their marital status was always the same, and they did not differ in terms of children by more than one child. Present and previous employers were never named; instead they were described in a general way, for example 'a leading paint manufacturer'. Details of present salary were never given. In most cases matched applications were posted on the same day, though in some cases there was a difference of one or two days. On rare occasions this appeared to have had an influence, because a reply refusing an interview to one applicant was sent after an acceptance had been sent to the other applicant; in such cases the test was discarded and replaced.

The overall design

The method is an experimental design comprising four interlaced variables.

The number of cells is:

4 (country of origin)
X 6 (job type)
X 6 (region)
X 2 (letter type)
=288

It was decided to carry out one test in each cell, except that the salesman category would be duplicated to increase the number of observations: that is, there were two observations in each cell involving a job as salesman. Thus the number of observations required was 336, or in other words 672 letters of application.

Non-response and replacement

Where both applicants are invited to interview (or in some cases sent an application form to fill in) this is evidence that there has been no discrimination at the screening stage. But the interpretation is less straightforward where both applicants are refused, or where both receive no reply, or indeed where one is refused and the other receives no reply. Jowell and Prescott-Clarke treated these cases, too, as evidence of no discrimination. But clearly, where an employer refuses both applicants, or replies to neither of them, this may be because the job has already been filled, or because neither of the applicants has the necessary qualifications, or because other, better applications have been received. There is really no evidence about discrimination at all; only if the applications had been received sooner, or if the qualifications and experience had been different, would the employer have had the opportunity to discriminate. We decided from the start that we would treat such cases as 'test not valid' and replace them.

In Jowell and Prescott-Clarke's study, which was carried out in 1969, the tests that we have treated as invalid amounted to only 22 out of a total of 128 (17 per cent). In our study, carried out in 1973 and early 1974, we found that employers were far more likely than this to refuse or fail to reply to both applicants; in fact, this happened in about one-third of cases. This difference may be due to a change in the job market between 1969 and 1973–74 for the types of job tested. In particular, the later part of our testing unfortunately coincided with the three-day week; during this period there were certainly fewer jobs advertised than usual, and there were probably more applicants for each advertised job. In the circumstances, therefore, it is hardly surprising that our applicants had a lower success rate overall than those in the earlier study.

We have no doubt that, logically, replacement is the correct solution to this problem. On the other hand it does lead to severe practical difficulties; it means, in effect, that it is never possible to finish the work completely, because each set of replacements leads to a fresh set of invalid tests that have to be replaced. In the event we succeeded in completing 305 out of the 336 that were scheduled. In practice this slight incompleteness imposes few limitations on the interpretation of the results.

Selection of advertisements and administration

The jobs were selected from ones advertised in the local newspapers of the towns where the testing was carried out, or from national newspapers in the case of some of the London jobs. The letters were written or typed in London then forwarded to an address in the relevant town, from where they were posted. This same address would be the one given in the letter, so that the replies would eventually be received there. As soon as they were received they were forwarded back to London. Invitations to interviews were declined either by letter or by telephone.

Numbers of observations

We have explained that 31 of the 336 tests in the design have not been completed. It is important to ensure that the gaps are not distributed in such a way as to lead to any systematic bias.

The table below shows the number of tests completed by the country of origin of the immigrant applicant within region.

	Italian	West Indian	Indian	Pakistani
Region:				
Yorkshire	13	13	14	14
West Midlands	13	14	12	14
North West	9	14	13	12
East Midlands	10	14	9	9
South East	13	14	14	13
London	13	14	13	14
Total	71	83	75	76

It can be seen that the cells are well balanced.

Adding together the figures for the six regions, the table below shows the number of tests completed by country of origin by type of job by letter type.

	Italian	West Indian	Indian	Pakistani
Sales A	11	12	10	11
Sales B	11	12	11	10
Accountant A	5	6	5	6
Accountant B	5	6	6	5
Management trainee A	3	6	5	4
Management trainee B	4	6	4	6
Clerical A male	6	6	6	6
Clerical B male	4	5	4	4
Clerical A female	6	6	6	6
Clerical B female	6	6	6	6
Secretary A	5	6	6	6
Secretary B	5	6	6	6
Total	71	83	75	76

Again the table shows that the balance is good. The objectives of the original design have been substantially achieved even though 31 of the 336 tests have not been completed.

2 THE FINDINGS

The level of discrimination

As in the actor testing there were some cases in which there was apparent discrimination against the white British applicant. This is allowed for when calculating the 'net' discrimination by taking the number of cases in which there was discrimination against the immigrant and subtracting from it the number of cases in which there was discrimination in the opposite direction. The gross and net levels of discrimination are shown in the table below for Asian and West Indian applicants and for Italian applicants separately.

Level of discrimination against Asians and West Indians and against Italians

	Asians and West Indians		Italians	
Number of tests	234		71	
	No.	%	No.	%
Gross discrimination	84	36	13	18
Net discrimination	70	30	7	10

Taking the net figures, an Asian or West Indian applicant was discriminated against in 30 per cent of cases, while an Italian applicant faced discrimination in only 10 per cent of cases.

In the light of the fact that the method only identifies discrimination at the screening stage a level of 30 per cent is very substantial. The very much lower figure for the Italian applicant shows that the discrimination is associated largely with racial rather than simply with foreign origin.

The differences in the success rates between white British applicants, Italians, and Asians and West Indians are large, but it is worth examining the possibility that these results could have been obtained by chance, even though no real differences existed. For this purpose a statistical test can be used—the chi-squared test—to assess how confident we can be, from these results, that the three groups of applicants do obtain different success rates. If such a test shows that a difference is significant at the 99 per cent level of confidence, this means that there is only one chance in a hundred that a real difference does not exist.

The results of these tests are as follows:

Comparison between the success rate of white British applicants and that of Asians and West Indians—significant at *well over* the 99.9 per cent level of confidence.

White British applicants versus Italians—significant at the 99 per cent level of confidence, and nearly significant at the 99.9 per cent level.

Italians versus Asians and West Indians—significant at the 98 per cent level of confidence.

The results of these tests demonstrate beyond doubt that these results cannot be the product of chance variations, and therefore that there is discrimination against Asians and West Indians, and that Italians also face discrimination, but to a lesser extent.

In some cases discrimination involved an actual refusal, while in others one of the applicants received no reply. The results of the tests in these terms are shown in the table below.

	Tests involving Asians or West Indians		Tests involving Italians	
Number of tests	234		71	
	No.	%	No.	%
Discrimination against immigrant:				
Immigrant refused, white British accepted	51	22	7	10
No reply to immigrant, white British accepted	33	14	6	8
Discrimination against white British:				
Immigrant accepted, white British refused	2	1	—	—
Immigrant accepted, no reply to white British	12	5	6	8
No discrimination:				
Both accepted	136	57	52	75

While there were 20 cases of reverse discrimination, only two of these involved an actual refusal of the white British applicant; in the remaining 18 cases, the white British applicant received no reply. It is probable that these cases arise because of the methods adopted by employers to deal with large numbers of job applicants, rather than because of a deliberate and positive preference for the immigrant applicant. For example, an employer who has received a large number of replies may choose to consider only the first 20 that come to his notice. Of course this implies that a similar number of the apparent cases of discrimination against the immigrant arise for the same reasons, and this is allowed for in calculating net discrimination. It does suggest, however, that the case in which an employer positively prefers an Asian or West Indian applicant to a white British applicant with similar qualifications occurs very seldom.

Comparison between regions

The level of discrimination against Asians and West Indians is much the same in each of the six towns where the testing was carried out. A chi-squared test shows that the differences between towns fail to reach significance even at the 90 per cent level of confidence.

Discrimination against Asian and West Indian applicants by type of job

	Salesman		Accountant		Management trainee		Junior clerical (male)		Junior clerical (female)		Secretary	
Number of tests	66		34		31		31		36		35	
	No.	%	No.	%	No.	%	No.	%	No.	%	No.	%
Gross discrimination	21	32	13	38	14	45	17	55	12	33	7	19
Net discrimination	16	24	12	35	13	42	15	48	8	22	6	17

The effect of letter type

As we have explained when discussing the method, it is not possible for the two applicants for the same job to write exactly the same letter. For each type of job, therefore, two slightly different letters had to be used, but the balanced design ensures that the two letters are allocated an equal number of times to the white British and to the immigrant applicant. It follows that, even if one of the letters were more successful than the other, no bias would be introduced into the results.

An analysis of the results according to the type of letter which was allocated to the immigrant applicant shows some apparent differences, but there is more than a one in ten chance that these could be random effects. This analysis (which is shown in Appendix 2(c)) demonstrates that the country of origin of the applicant has a far more powerful effect on the result than the stylistic differences which it was necessary to introduce into the letters.

Comparison between types of jobs

Taking the tests involving Asian or West Indian applicants, the table opposite shows the levels of gross and net discrimination for each type of job separately.

At first sight there do appear to be considerable differences in the levels of discrimination for different types of job, but because the sample sizes are rather low these differences are statistically significant at only the 87 per cent level of confidence. This means that there is a rather less than one in seven chance that they could be the result of random variations.

A striking feature of these results is that the two job categories for which discrimination is lowest are the two female ones. There is a strong suggestion here that within those white collar jobs that women have traditionally done (clerical and secretary) there is less racial discrimination against women than against men. If we compare the male and female junior clerical categories we find that the difference, though large, is not statistically significant at the 90 per cent level. However, a different sort of comparison can be made if we are prepared to regard junior clerical and secretarial jobs as coming into a qualitatively different and more junior category than the three other types of job, which are mainly done by men. If this distinction is thought to be a sound one, then it is legitimate to compare the level of discrimination against men with that against women, for the junior clerical and secretarial categories alone. In effect this means making a comparison between secretary plus clerical (female), and clerical (male). In fact this difference is significant at the 98 per cent level of confidence.

This result implies that women may face less discrimination than men in the more junior jobs in which they have traditionally worked, but this conclusion requires further confirmation. The results also suggest that the level of discrimination may vary between the different white collar jobs done by men, but on this point more clear-cut data will be required to form the basis for a definite interpretation.

Comparison between minority groups

We have established:

that Asians and West Indians face substantial discrimination;
that they face far more discrimination than Italians;
and that Italians do face discrimination to a significant extent.

We now consider whether there are differences between the levels of discrimination against West Indians, Indians and Pakistanis. The gross and net levels of discrimination are shown for applicants from the four different countries in the table below.

Level of discrimination by country of origin

	West Indies		India		Pakistan		Italy	
Number of tests	83		75		76		71	
	No.	%	No.	%	No.	%	No.	%
Gross discrimination	31	37	23	31	30	39	13	18
Net discrimination	27	33	20	27	23	30	8	11

The table shows that the levels of gross and net discrimination are about the same for West Indian, Indian and Pakistani applicants. (As we have already seen they are very different for Italian applicants.) In fact the differences between West Indians, Indians and Pakistanis fail to reach significance even at the 70 per cent level of confidence.

This strengthens the conclusion that it is colour prejudice which underlies most of the discrimination shown in these tests. The particular country of origin of the applicant seems to have very little influence.

Comparison with 1969

It is useful to compare the results of our study with those of the study carried out in 1969 by Jowell and Prescott-Clarke, to see whether there is any evidence of a change in the level of discrimination since that time. Whereas in the case of the actor testing our point of comparison was 1967, before the Second Race Relations Act, in this case the comparison is with a time shortly after the Act was passed.

We have said that our method is largely borrowed from the earlier study, but there are a number of important differences. We have already discussed the question of 'invalid tests' in which there is a refusal or no reply to both applicants; the earlier results can be re-worked to bring them into line with the present ones in this respect. The earlier study included Australian and Cypriot applicants in place of our Italians; comparisons can be restricted to the Asians and West Indians who were common to both studies. Three other differences are more difficult to take into account:

(1) Our applicants all had their secondary schooling in Britain, while half of the applicants in the earlier study had their secondary schooling in the country of origin.
(2) All of our matched pairs of applicants had equivalent qualifications and experience, while in half of the tests in the earlier study the immigrant had superior qualifications.

(3) In our study there were equal numbers of West Indians, Indians and Pakistanis, while in the earlier one there were twice as many West Indians as either Indians or Pakistanis.

Because there were only 64 tests which involved Asian or West Indian applicants in the earlier study, it is not possible to re-work the results so as to bring them into line with the present ones in these three respects. The differences will have to be borne in mind when looking at the comparative results, which are shown in the table below.

Levels of discrimination against Asians and West Indians—1969 and 1973–74

	All Asians and West Indians		Asians		West Indians	
	1969	1973–74	1969	1973–74	1969	1973–74
Number of tests	53	234	26	151	27	83
	%	%	%	%	%	%
Gross discrimination	34	36	54	35	15	37
Net discrimination	30	30	50	28	11	33

Note: The figures for 1969 have been re-worked as described on page 30 from Jowell and Prescott-Clarke's published data.

The overall levels of discrimination shown in the two studies are very similar. Thus net discrimination was 30 per cent in both 1969 and 1973–74, while the figures for gross discrimination were 34 per cent in 1969 compared with 36 per cent in 1973–74. However this conceals an important difference in the results for Asians and West Indians separately. In 1969 far more discrimination was recorded against Asians than against West Indians; thus the net discrimination for Asians was 50 per cent compared with only 11 per cent for West Indians. In spite of the small sample size this difference is significant at the 99.9 per cent level of confidence. On the other hand, as we have seen, in 1973–74 about the same level of discrimination was recorded against both Asians and West Indians.

The apparent implication is that discrimination against West Indians has increased, while discrimination against Asians has gone down. However, the differences in procedure between the two studies are enough to make us doubt whether changes of this kind have really occurred. In the earlier study half of the Asian and West Indian applicants were given superior qualifications to the matched white applicant, so that, all things being equal, a lower level of discrimination would be expected than in the present study. This could explain the apparent increase in the level of discrimination against West Indians. The question then arises why the same effect has not been registered in the case of the Asian applicants. The explanation may lie in the particulars of schooling given in the two studies. In the earlier study half of the Asian and West Indian applicants had gone to secondary school in the country of origin. In the case of the Asians this may have counted very heavily against them, because employers may have concluded that their standard of English would be very low. In the present study all applicants had had their secondary schooling in England, so that this worry about the Asians could not arise.

Other differences between the studies could be cited; for example the areas in which the tests were carried out and the range of jobs covered. We have said enough to show that it would be unwise to make too detailed a comparison. What the comparison does make clear is that for Asians and West Indians combined the levels of discrimination recorded in 1969 and 1973–74 were roughly of the same order. Overall there is no evidence of a substantial increase or decrease over the past five years.

Examples of discrimination

In cases where there was discrimination this would never have been apparent to the applicants concerned. Employers showed some imagination in inventing reasons for turning down an application. A selection of letters is reproduced below (in the original spelling).

To the white applicant:
Date: 10th December, 1973

Dear Mr X,

Many thanks for your reply to our advert, in the Y. E. Post. Basically the work would entail calling on working Mens Clubs and pubs in Yorks. selling Electric Lamps and tubes.

If you think this is the type of work you are looking for, please would you be good enough to phone me at my home any evening after 6.0 pm. Leeds (telephone number given). I can then arrange a suitable time for an interview.

Yours faithfully,

To the West Indian applicant:
Date: 10th December, 1973

Dear Sir,

Many thanks for your advert in the Y. E. Post. Unfortunately, since placing the advert the fuel situation has worsened and the management have decided against incresing the sales force at this present time. We will of course keep your name and address for future reference when the fuel crisis eases.

Yours faithfully,

In some cases the employer was more blunt.

To the white applicant:
Date: 17th September, 1973

Dear Mr X,
We thank you for your interest in employment with this Company and would now ask you to complete and return the enclosed application form.
We will make further contact with yourself when we have assessed all the applications for this position.

Yours faithfully,

To the Pakistani applicant:
Date: 17th September, 1973

Dear Mr X,
We have received your letter with interest but regret to inform you that we have no suitable vacancy at the present moment.
However, should a suitable vacancy arise in the near future we will make further contact.

Yours sincerely,

Ingenuity in inventing reasons for the refusal is further illustrated by the following pair of letters.

To the white applicant:
Date: 12th February, 1974

Dear Mrs X,

Position of Secretary

Thank you very much for your letter of the 9th February applying for the position of Secretary.
Perhaps you would be kind enough to telephone the office as soon as ever possible to arrange a mutually convenient time for you to come in to see us.
I look forward to hearing from you.

Yours sincerely,

To the Pakistani applicant:
Date: 12th February, 1974

Dear Mrs X,
Thank you very much for your letter of the 9th February replying to our advertisement in The Manchester Evening News for a Secretary.
Unfortunately, we have a policy in the office not to employ married women as we unfortunately, had a bad experience recently.

Yours sincerely,

Finally, the following example vividly illustrates how wide the gap between the treatment of the two applicants can be.

To the white applicant:
Date: 17th January, 1974

Dear Mr X,

I was very pleased and interested to receive your reply to our recent advertisement for Salesmen.

I am sure we would both agree that it is extremely important for you to be given every opportunity of finding out as much as possible about our activities as a Company, exactly what is involved in selling for us, and naturally, what rewards success as a Salesman would bring.

The vital question is, of course—how to achieve these objectives. We believe we have the best answer through a very informal meeting of no more than ten or twelve people, all interested in discovering as much as possible about a Sales career with us. The meeting lasts for about two-and-a-half hours and at least half of that time is given over to an open discussion on the Company and the job.

I would emphasize that nothing is raised or discussed which might be considered personal or private to anyone present. The complete informality for which we aim relieves the tensions so often associated with interviews, and, almost without exception, everyone feels the results achieved have been well worth the time spent.

It is with pleasure that I invite you to attend such a meeting at the Midland Hotel, Peter Street, Manchester, on (date mentioned) commencing at 10.30 a.m., and I certainly hope that you will want to accept this invitation.

I am enclosing an Application Form which I would like you to complete and bring with you. If, for any reason, you are unable to come but would like to arrange an alternative appointment for you, please send the completed form to me through the post.

Yours sincerely,

To the Indian applicant:
(A badly reproduced, duplicated letter)
Date: 17th January, 1974

Dear Sir,

I thank you for your reply to our recent advertisement for Salesmen.

I very much appreciate your interest, and it is with regret, therefore, that I have to tell you that we shall not be asking you to attend for interview.

I would also like to apologise for the lack of the "personal touch" in this letter. You will understand, of course, that in trying to reply promtly to everyone who has written to us, it is impossible to answer each applicant individually.

Yours sincerely,

IV Summary and conclusions

The results of our tests demonstrate that there is still substantial discrimination against members of the minority groups when seeking jobs and housing. They also show that this discrimination is more related to race than to foreign origin, since the level of discrimination against Italians or Greeks is comparatively low. In all of our tests we have found that West Indians, Indians and Pakistanis face about the same amount of discrimination. It is fair to conclude that this is the result of colour prejudice.

Our tests probably under-estimate the true extent of discrimination, because they cannot follow through the application to the later stages. The testing method is most satisfactory in the case of unskilled jobs, since the tests can be carried out personally, and employers are in the habit of deciding on the spot whether or not to take a man on. It is significant, therefore, that in this situation we found the highest level of discrimination. Asian and West Indians applying for unskilled jobs faced discrimination in 46 per cent of cases. This finding implies that there are tens of thousands of acts of discrimination of this kind in a year. By contrast the Race Relations Board dealt with only 150 complaints of discrimination relating to recruitment to employment in 1973.

Discrimination by estate agents against house purchasers (at least at the initial stage) is lower than for any of the other situations. Within white collar jobs there is some evidence that women face less discrimination than men when applying for that limited range of jobs which women have traditionally done.

There is no evidence that discrimination is more prevalent in some parts of the country than in others. It seems to be about equally common in all those areas which have substantial immigrant populations.

Since 1967, before the Second Race Relations Act, there has been a sharp decrease in the level of discrimination against West Indians and Asians when seeking accommodation. In the case of employment an exact comparison cannot be made, but the general drift of the 1967 findings showed that at that time discrimination in recruitment to employment was taking place on a massive scale. From our present findings it seems likely that discrimination in this field, too, has decreased since 1967.

Although the level of discrimination seems, therefore, to be lower now than it was before the Act, the general conclusion from these findings must be that the number of cases of discrimination that are dealt with by the law (either by means of conciliation or by means of legal sanctions) forms a very small proportion of the number of acts of discrimination that actually occur. [36]

Appendix 1

Technical details of the actor testing

(a) House purchase

Of the 190 house purchase tests carried out, 27 were enquiries about specific houses that had been advertised, while the remaining 163 were general enquiries made to estate agents in person. The 27 enquiries about specific houses were all carried out in the London area, while the 163 general enquiries to estate agents were divided between London and Birmingham (132 in the London area, 31 in the Birmingham area).

An analysis of the prices of the specific houses advertised is shown below.

£8,000–£9,999	2
£10,000–£11,999	5
£12,000–£14,999	12
£15,000–£19,999	8
	27

When approaching estate agents in the remaining tests, as explained in the report, the testers always mentioned a price range, and this range was adjusted to suit the price levels in the area. The areas and price ranges mentioned are listed below.

London and suburban areas

London SW17	£8,000–£12,000	Bromley	Up to £13,000
London SE13	£15,000–£20,000	Croydon	£13,000–£15,000,
London SE4	£15,000–£20,000		£12,000–£14,000,
London SE3	£15,000–£20,000		£10,000–£12,000
London SE12	Up to £10,000	Hounslow	About £12,000
London SW11	About £12,000	Pinner	About £15,000
London SW4	Up to £15,000	Sudbury	About £12,000
London SW2	£12,000–£13,000	Wembley	About £12,000
London NW11	About £15,000	Richmond	About £15,000
London SW16	£12,000–£13,000	Surbiton	About £12,000
London SE9	About £10,000	Northwood	About £15,000
London N3	£12,500–£14,500		

Birmingham Area	
Central Birmingham	£8,000–£10,000, £8,000–£12,000
Birmingham 23	Up to £9,000
Birmingham 30	Up to £9,000
Birmingham 26	About £10,000
Solihull	About £10,000, £8,000–£12,000

(b) Rented accommodation

Of the 64 tests carried out, 17 were personal visits to accommodation agencies in London, while the remaining 47 were telephone enquiries in response to advertisements for rented accommodation in the newspapers; of these telephone enquiries, 18 were carried out in the Birmingham area, while the remaining 29 were carried out in the London area.

The telephone enquiries were always in response to an advertisement for a specific flat (or occasionally house), but in many cases it turned out that an agency had placed the advertisement. In such cases the agency would often offer an alternative flat if the one advertised had already been let. Our assessment of whether or not discrimination occurred would then relate to the whole treatment of the tester, including whether alternative accommodation was offered.

When carrying out the personal tests among accommodation agencies, the testers always said they were looking for something at about £20 a week; this high level of rent was appropriate to the London area, and even then, there were some cases where nothing was available for this amount.

The rents of the advertised accommodation for which tests were carried out are listed below, for London and Birmingham separately.

Weekly rents

London area	*Birmingham area*
Eight at £20.00	
£19.00	£30.00
£18.90	£25.00
£18.80	£16.00
Seven at £18.00	£13.00
£16.80	£12.50
Two at £16.00	Five at £12.00
£15.75	£10.50
Three at £15.00	Two at £10.00
£13.00	Two at £8.00
£12.00	£4.00
£9.50	In two cases the rent was not stated
In one case the rent was not stated	

(c) Actor variability

The effect of actor variability was assessed by means of a one-way analysis of variance. This analysis was carried out separately for the data on house purchase and for the data on unskilled jobs. (The design did not allow for this type of analysis in the case of the other two situations.)

The raw material for the analysis was the success rate for each individual actor (that is, the percentage of cases in which he was offered a job or house). In calculating these success rates, cases in which neither actor was made any offer were excluded, as they have been throughout the analysis. The preparation of the data as success rates means that for the purpose of the analysis, each *actor* was treated as a single observation. The results of the analysis would probably be more decisive if each *test* were treated as an observation, but in that case a two-way analysis of variance would be required, and this would lead to technical difficulties, since the numbers of observations in each cell would not be equal, as required for the normal form of the two-way analysis of variance.

The data are shown below in the form required for the analysis, together with the statistics that have been derived from them.

Unskilled jobs

	West Indian	Indian	Pakistani	Greek	White	Total
Tester A	25	62	53	90	90	
Tester B	64	57	43	89	95	
Sum	89	119	96	179	185	668
Mean	44.5	59.5	48	89.5	92.5	66.8
No. of cases	2	2	2	2	2	10

	Sum of squares	Degrees of freedom	Estimate of variance	F
Total	4,995.6	9		
Between columns	4,159.6	4	1,039.9	6.219
Within columns	836.0	5	167.2	
Critical value of $F_{4.5}$ (.05 level) = 5.19				

Therefore the between column differences are significant at the 95 per cent level of confidence after the within column differences have been extracted.

House purchase

	West Indian	Indian	Pakistani	Greek	White	Total
Tester A	79	76	94	100	100	
Tester B	94	79	95	90	99	
Sum	173	155	189	190	199	906
Mean	86.5	77.5	94.5	95.0	99.5	90.6
No. of cases	2	2	2	2	2	10

	Sum of squares	Degrees of freedom	Estimate of variance	F
Total	772.4	9		
Between columns	604.4	4	151.1	4.497
Within column	168.0	5	33.6	
Critical value of $F_{4,5}$ (.05 level) = 5.19				

Therefore the between column differences just fail to reach significance at the 95 per cent level of confidence after the within column differences have been extracted.

(d) The raw results

Unskilled jobs

	Total	Offer to white British none to immigrant	Better offer to white British	Same offer to both	Offer to immigrant none to white British		No offer to either
London					(1)*	(2)**	
West Indian	40	11	1	11	1	—	16
Indian	38	3	8	12	4	1	11
Pakistani	28	6	3	9	1	—	9
Greek	36	2	—	19	—	—	15
Birmingham							
West Indian	8	1	3	—	—	—	4
Indian	9	—	1	1	2	—	5
Pakistani	10	2	—	—	1	1	7
Greek	6	—	—	—	—	—	6
Total	175	25	16	52	9	2	73

* Including 'doubtful' cases of reverse discrimination.

** Excluding 'doubtful' cases.

41

Skilled jobs

	Total	Job or interview offered to white British but not to immigrant	Offers to both	Offer to immigrant but not to white British	No offer to either
London					
West Indian	19	3	14	1	1
Indian	10	2	7	—	1
Pakistani	10	3	7	—	—
Greek	6	—	2	—	4
Birmingham					
West Indian	10	3	7	—	—
Indian	10	2	6	—	2
Pakistani	10	1	9	—	—
Greek	9	1	8	—	—
Total	84	15	60	1	8

House purchase

(i) Estate agents and advertised houses combined

	Total	Offer to white British tester only	*Different treatment* (a) Less good offer to immigrant (e.g. less choice)	*Different treatment* (b) Different houses offered	Same offer to both	Better offer to immigrant tester	No offer to either tester
London							
West Indian	29	1	2	1	22	—	3
Indian	40	1	5	2	28	—	4
Pakistani	53	1	4	2	45	1	—
Greek	37	—	—	4	33	—	—
Birmingham							
West Indian	10	—	—	1	9	—	—
Indian	10	1	2	—	6	—	1
Pakistani	5	—	1	—	2	—	2
Greek	6	—	1	—	4	—	1
Total	190	4	15	10	149	1	11

(ii) *Telephone enquiries about advertised houses*

Number of tests	27
Viewing offered to white British tester only	1
Immediate viewing offered to white British tester, no definite offer of viewing to immigrant tester, but viewing not actually refused	2
Viewing offered to both testers	24

(iii) *Personal enquiries among estate agents*

	Total	Houses to white British tester only	*Different treatment* (a) Less good offer to immigrant (e.g. less choice)	*Different treatment* (b) Different houses offered	Same offer to both	Better offer to immigrant tester	No offer to either tester
West Indian	39	1	2	2	31	—	3
Indian	49	2	7	2	33	—	5
Pakistani	32	—	3	2	24	1	2
Greek	43	—	1	4	37	—	1
Total	163	3	13	10	125	1	11

Rented accommodation

(i) *Personal tests among accommodation agencies (in London only)*

	Total	Better offer to white British tester	Same offer to both testers	Better offer to immigrant tester	Offer to neither tester
Origin of immigrant tester:					
West Indian	8	1	3	1	3
Indian	—	—	—	—	—
Pakistani	9	3	4	—	2
Greek	—	—	—	—	—
Total	17	4	7	1	5

(ii) *Telephone tests in response to advertised accommodation*

	Total	Better offer to white British tester	Same offer to both testers	Better offer to immigrant tester	Offer to neither tester
Origin of immigrant tester:					
West Indian	8	2	5	—	1
Indian	20	5	13	—	2
Pakistani	9	1	3	—	5
Greek	10	1	9	—	—
Total	47	9	30	—	8

Appendix 2

Technical details of the correspondence testing

(a) The letters

The standard wording of the letters is given below. The blanks were, of course, filled in as appropriate in each actual letter.

(i) *Salesmen*

Introduction—immigrant applicants

Dear Sir,

With reference to your advertisement in the .... of .... for the post of .... I should like to apply for the vacancy. I came to England in 1957 from .... after completing my primary schooling. I have been permanently resident in the UK since that time.

Introduction—white British applicants

Dear Sir,

I am writing in reply to your advertisement of .... in the .... for ...., for which I feel I am suitably qualified.

Continuation—Letter Type A

I received my secondary education in .... where I passed four 'O' levels in English, Maths, Geography and History.

My first job on leaving school was with a bakery where I worked firstly in dispatch and then as a van salesman. I later joined the sales force of a company which manufactured paper cups. In 1971 I took up my present position selling to retailers for a firm of dairy produce packers.

I am now 27 years of age and am married with one child. I hope my qualifications will enable me to obtain an interview.

Yours faithfully,

Continuation—Letter Type B

I am at present employed as a member of the sales team of a national confectionary manufacturer selling to retail outlets in the .... area.

I am 28 years old and am married with two children. I was educated at a grammar school in ...., which I left having got three 'O' levels.

I then went on to work in an insurance company in a clerical capacity. I took my present job in 1970 after having spent a number of years as a salesman first with a television rental company and then selling to interior decorators and do-it-yourself shops for a paint firm.

I should naturally be happy to attend an interview at any time that is convenient to you.

Yours faithfully,

(ii) *Accountants*

Introduction—immigrant applicants

Dear Sir,

With reference to your advertisement in the .... of .... for the position of .... I should like to be considered for the vacancy. I came to England in 1956 from .... after completing by primary schooling. I have been permanently resident in the UK since that time.

Introduction—white applicants

Dear Sir,

I am writing in reply to your advertisement of .... in the .... for the post of .... for which I feel I am suitably qualified.

Continuation—Letter Type A

I received my secondary education in .... where I passed seven 'O' levels and three 'A' levels. After leaving school I was articled to accountants and obtained my ACA and ACWA qualifications in 1968.

My first job on completing my exams was with the same firm where I remained for two further years. In 1970 I took up my present position as Assistant to the Chief Accountant in a Mail Order company where I have responsibility for costing, budgeting, forecasting and producing monthly statements and working with computerised records.

I am now 29 years of age and am recently married. I hope that my qualifications will enable me to obtain an interview.

Yours faithfully,

Continuation—Letter Type B

I am at present employed as an accountant with a large supermarket and grocery chain, where I have gained experience in mechanised accounting and systems work.

I am 28 years old and am married with one child. I was educated at a grammar shool in .... which I left having obtained eight 'O' levels and two 'A' levels. I then went on to be articled to a firm of accountants in .... where I studied for my ACA and ACWA exams. I took my present job in 1969 shortly after becoming fully qualified.

I should be happy to attend an interview at any time convenient to you.

Yours faithfully,

(iii) *Management Trainees*

Letter Type A

Dear Sir,

I left school this summer and have recently heard that I have passed two 'A' levels in .... and .... with grades of 'C' and 'E' respectively.

I have seen in the Cornmarket *Careers for School Leavers* information concerning openings in your organisation as ....

Apart from the 'A' levels I also have five 'O' levels in Maths, English, Physics, Chemistry and Geography.

(I came to England in 1965 from .... where I had attended primary school. My family is now permanently resident in the UK.)[1]

I should be very pleased to come for an interview at any time suitable to you.

Yours faithfully,

Letter Type B

Dear Sir,

I am starting to look for a career, after finishing school in .... this year and I am very interested in the .... which I believe you offer school leavers. I shall be very much obliged if you could consider me for one of these posts, if there are any vacancies. (I am particularly interested in posts in the .... area.)

I have two 'C' Grade 'A' level passes in .... and .... and five 'O' levels in English Language, History, Elementary Maths, Physics and Biology.

(I came to England in 1965 from .... where I had attended primary school. My family is now permanently resident in the UK.)[1]

Yours faithfully,

---

[1] Included for immigrant applicants only.

(iv) *Clerical (male) and clerical (female)*

Introduction—Immigrant applicants

Dear Sir,
With reference to your advertisement in the ....
of .... for .... I should like to apply for the vacancy. I came to England in 1965 from .... after completing my primary schooling. I have been permanently resident in the UK since that time.

Introduction—white British applicants

Dear Sir,
I am writing in reply to your advertisement of ....
in the ...., for which I feel I have suitable qualifications.

Continuation—Letter Type A

I received my secondary education in ....
After leaving school I attended evening classes at a college of further education where I obtained 'O' level passes in English Language and Literature, Maths and Geography.

My first job on leaving college was with the Gas Board where I was an accounts clerk. In 1971 I took up my present position as a clerk with responsibility for the computerised sales and purchase ledger in a shoe wholesaling concern.

I am now 19 years of age and am unmarried. I hope the qualifications I have described will allow me to get an interview.

Yours faithfully,

Continuation—Letter Type B

I am at present employed as a wages clerk with a mail order company in
....

I am almost 20 years old and am single. I was educated at a secondary school in .... which I left when I was 15. I then went to evening classes at the local college where I sat my 'O' levels and passed History, English, Maths and Economics. I took my present job two years ago after having spent two years working as a clerk for the local authority.

I should be happy to attend an interview at any time convenient to you.

Yours faithfully,

(v) *Secretary*

Introduction—immigrant applicants

Dear Sir,
With reference to your advertisement in the......................................
of .... for the post of .... I should like to be considered for the vacancy. I came to the UK in 1958 after completing by primary schooling in .... I have been permanently resident in England since that time.

Introduction—white British applicants

Dear Sir,

I am writing in reply to your advertisement of .... in the .... for the post of .... for which I feel I am suitably qualified.

Continuation—Letter Type A

I received my secondary education in .... where I passed five 'O' levels. After leaving school I attended a secretarial college where I did a year's full-time course. My typing speed is now 60 wpm and my shorthand is 110 wpm.

My first job on leaving college was with an architectural partnership where I worked for two of the junior partners. I later worked for the director of a dye company and in 1970 I took up my present position as personal secretary to the Marketing Director of a frozen food firm.

I am now 25 years of age and am recently married. I hope my qualifications will enable me to obtain an interview.

Yours faithfully,

Continuation—Letter Type B

I am at present employed as the Secretary of the Chief Buyer of a large department store.

I am 26 years old and have been married for two years. I was educated at a grammar school in .... which I left when I was sixteen with five 'O' levels. I spend the next year at a secretarial college where I attained speeds of 120 in shorthand and 60 in typing.

I took my present job in 1969 after having spent a number of years working firstly with a textile company and then as secretary to a solicitor.

Yours faithfully,

(b) Significance testing

Our original intention was to analyse the results by means of a four-way analysis of variance, but in the event we decided against this for two reasons. First, some of the cells in the design had not been completed, and secondly, we realised that letter type was not a true variable (for the reasons explained in the text). Instead the analysis was carried out by means of a series of chi-squared tests, which proved to be a perfectly satisfactory method.

In each chi-squared test the columns were the different categories of the variable (for example, regions). Three figures appeared in each column:

the number of cases of discrimination against the immigrant;
the number of cases of discrimination against the white British applicant;
the number of cases of no discrimination.

Invalid tests (those in which both applicants were refused or received no reply) were, of course excluded.

As an example of layout, the test for differences between regions is given below.

	Yorkshire	West Midlands	North West	East Midlands	South East	London	Total
Discrimination against immigrant	15	13	17	13	9	18	85
Discrimination against white British	—	—	3	2	5	4	14
No discrimination	26	27	19	17	27	19	135
Total	41	40	39	32	41	41	234

$\chi^2 = 15.014$ df$=10$
Critical value of χ^2 at the .10 level$=15.987$

Null hypothesis accepted.

Where a test is carried out between the white applicants and others the format has to be changed, for otherwise the cells in the matrix would not be independent of each other, which is a condition required for this type of test. Therefore the data are presented in this case as the number of applicants who were accepted and the number who were not accepted (that is, who were refused, or who received no reply). This format meets the requirement that the cells should be independent.

A list of the tests carried out, together with their results, is given below.

1. Whites versus Asians and West Indians
   $\chi^2 = 63.244$ df=1
   Critical value of χ^2 (.001 level) = 10.827

2. Whites versus Italians
   $\chi^2 = 10.063$ df=1
   Critical value of χ^2 (.001 level) = 10.827
   (.01 level) = 6.635

3. Italians versus Asians and West Indians
   $\chi^2 = 7.823$ df=2
   Critical value of χ^2 (.05 level) = 5.991
   (.02 level) = 7.824

4. Between regions for Asians and West Indians only
   $\chi^2 = 15.015$ df=10
   Critical value of χ^2 (.10 level) = 15.987

5. Between West Indians, Indians and Pakistanis
   $\chi^2 = 4.251$ df=4
   Critical value of χ^2 (.10 level) = 7.779
   (.30 level) = 4.878

6. Between job types, among Asians and West Indians only
   $\chi^2 = 15.195$ df=10
   Critical value of χ^2 (.10 level) = 15.987
   (.20 level) = 13.442

7. Between letter types for *secretary* only
   $\chi^2 = 2.5$ df=2
   Critical value of χ^2 (.10 level) = 4.605
   (.20 level) = 3.219

8. Between letter types for *accountant* only
   $\chi^2 = 3.238$ df=2
   Critical value of χ^2 (.10 level) = 4.605
   (.20 level) = 3.219

9. Junior clerical (male) versus junior clerical (female) among Asians and West Indians only
   $\chi^2 = 3.212$ df=2
   Critical value of χ^2 (.10 level) = 4.605
   (.20 level) = 3.219

10. Secretary and junior clerical (female) versus junior clerical (male)
   $\chi^2 = 8.035$ df=2
   Critical value of χ^2 (.01 level) = 9.210
   (.02 level) = 7.824

(c) The effect of letter type

The tests for each job type can be sorted into those in which the immigrant applicant was allocated letter type A, and those in which he or she was allocated letter type B. In each case the white British applicant was allocated the other letter type. The table below shows the net level of discrimination for each of these conditions.

Letter type allocated to the immigrant applicant

	A		B	
	No. of tests	Net discrimination (no.)	No. of tests	Net discrimination (no.)
Job type:				
Salesman	44	11	44	9
Accountant	22	10	22	4
Management trainee	18	7	20	7
Junior clerical (male)	24	7	17	7
Junior clerical (female)	24	5	24	4
Secretary	23	5	23	1

It would not be logical to add together all of the situations in which the immigrant was allocated one or other letter type, because the letters vary too much depending on the job being applied for. This means that six individual comparisons have to be made, one for each type of job.

The table shows that the results are much the same whichever way the letters are allocated; the differences, such as they are, are at their largest for tests involving accountants and secretaries. However, since the numbers of observations in each case are small (under 25) a considerable amount of chance variation is to be expected. A chi-squared test for each of these two job types (where the variations are at their highest) shows that there is no significant difference at the 90 per cent level of confidence between the cases where the immigrant had the one letter and those where he had the other.

We conclude that the differences between the letters had no significant influence on the result. Of course, even if it did have an influence, this would not invalidate the main finding, since the two letters were allocated to the white and immigrant applicants an equal number of times.

(d) The raw results

(I) Results of the tests by region

	Discrimination against immigrant	Discrimination against white British	No discrimination
Region:			
Yorks and Humberside	17	—	37
West Midlands	15	2	36
North West	18	4	26
East Midlands	17	3	22
South East	11	6	37
London	20	4	30

(ii) Result of the tests by country of origin of immigrant by type of job by letter type

Job type and letter type allocated to immigrant:	West Indian: Discrimination against immigrant	West Indian: Discrimination against white British	West Indian: No discrimination	Indian: Discrimination against immigrant	Indian: Discrimination against white British	Indian: No discrimination	Pakistani: Discrimination against immigrant	Pakistani: Discrimination against white British	Pakistani: No discrimination	Italian: Discrimination against immigrant	Italian: Discrimination against white British	Italian: No discrimination
Salesman A	4	—	8	2	—	8	5	2	4	2	—	9
Salesman B	4	1	7	2	1	8	4	1	5	3	1	7
Accountant A	3	—	3	2	—	3	3	—	3	2	—	3
Accountant B	1	—	5	2	—	4	2	—	2	—	—	5
Management trainee A	3	—	3	2	—	3	1	—	3	1	—	2
Management trainee B	6	—	—	—	1	3	2	—	4	1	—	3
Clerical (male) A	4	—	2	3	—	3	4	2	—	—	2	4
Clerical (male) B	2	—	3	2	—	2	2	—	2	1	—	3
Clerical (female) A	2	1	3	3	—	3	1	1	4	2	1	3
Clerical (female) B	1	1	4	3	1	2	2	—	4	—	—	6
Secretary A	1	—	5	1	—	5	2	—	4	1	—	4
Secretary B	—	1	5	1	—	5	2	—	4	—	1	4

[18]

Measuring Racial Discrimination with Fair Housing Audits: Caught in the Act

By JOHN YINGER*

A survey technique called a fair housing audit provides a direct measure of racial discrimination in housing and an opportunity to test hypotheses about its causes. Audits conducted in Boston in 1981 uncovered extensive discrimination; black housing seekers were told about 30 percent fewer available housing units than were whites. This paper finds that the primary cause of this discrimination is economic: Housing agents cater to the racial prejudice of current or potential white customers.

With the help of a survey technique called a fair housing audit, several recent studies have demonstrated that, despite the Civil Rights Act of 1968, racial and ethnic discrimination in housing continues to be widespread. This paper examines the discrimination uncovered by a large audit study conducted in Boston in 1981 and analyzes the econometric issues that arise in evaluating fair housing audit data. The audit technique also makes it possible to test hypotheses about the causes of discriminatory behavior by housing agents. This paper states and carries out such tests.

In a fair housing audit, an individual from the white majority and an individual from a minority group, who have been matched according to their family and economic characteristics, successively visit a landlord or real estate broker in search of housing. By comparing the treatment minority and majority auditors receive, a researcher can isolate discrimination, which is defined as systematically less favorable treatment for the minority auditors.

Fair housing audits were developed by fair housing organizations as an investigative tool. They were first used for research in the pioneering study by Ronald Wienk et al. (1979) and have since been used in four other large studies, all of which pay careful attention to sampling, survey writing, auditor training, and survey management.[1] This paper examines data from the audit study conducted by Judith Feins, Rachael Bratt, and Robert Hollister.

Fair housing audits are an important methodological advance. Previous research examined discrimination indirectly by looking for its impacts on urban residential structure, such as higher prices in largely black areas and more centralized patterns of black residence (see my paper, 1979). Fair housing audits, on the other hand, literally catch discriminators in the act of discriminating. As a result, audits provide direct measures of discrimination and an unprecedented opportunity to study the circumstances under which discrimination occurs.

I. Measuring the Level of Discrimination

Fair housing audits yield information on the treatment black (or any other minority) and white housing seekers receive from hous-

*Professor of Economics and Public Administration, The Maxwell School, Syracuse University, Syracuse, NY 13244. I thank Judith Feins, who provided the data; Wilhelmina Leigh, Gary Solon, two anonymous referees, and participants in a seminar at the Institute of Public Policy Studies, University of Michigan, for helpful comments; and Howard Bloom and Michael Stoto for valuable advice on an early version of the material on audit methodology.

[1] The studies, all reviewed in my paper (1984), are Jon Hakken (1979); Judith Feins, Rachael Bratt, and Robert Hollister (1981) (summarized in Feins and Bratt, 1983); Franklin James, Betty McCummings, and Eileen Tynan (1983); and William Holshouser (1984). For a detailed review of study design and management issues, see Wienk et al., Feins et al., or myself (1984).

ing agents. In the broadest sense, racial discrimination exists whenever black auditors receive less favorable treatment than their white teammates. Treatment has many dimensions, however; each auditor is told about a certain number of units, quoted a certain rent or asking price, given certain signals about credit checks and financing, and so on. Although discrimination can occur in all types of treatment, this paper follows the existing studies in focusing on discrimination in the provision of information about available housing. After all, blacks cannot gain access to housing unless they know it exists.[2]

I employ three measures of housing availability: the number of housing units offered to the auditor as serious possibilities; the number of units the auditor was invited to inspect; and the number of units the auditor actually inspected.[3] For each measure, I estimate the level of discrimination and test the associated hypothesis that discrimination exists.

A. *A Simple Model of Discriminatory Treatment*

A fair housing "audit" consists of two or more "visits" to a housing "agent," some visits by black auditors and some visits by their white teammates. An audit study consists of audits carried out for a random sample of the advertised housing units in a given housing market using a set of trained auditors. Let us describe audit data with two subscripts: a identifies the audit and i identifies the individual auditor. The number of visits or observations equals the number of audits, say N, multiplied by the average number of auditors per audit. In most studies, including the 1981 Boston study, each audit consists of two visits, one by a minority auditor and one by a majority auditor, so the number of visits is $2N$.

Now let A measure an action taken by a housing agent toward an auditor, such as the number of apartments the auditor is invited to inspect; let R be a binary variable for minority status, where R equals one for a black and zero for a white auditor; and let e stand for a random error. Then the relationship between A and R is

$$(1) \qquad A_{ai} = \alpha + \beta R_i + e_{ai}.$$

The ordinary least squares (OLS) estimate of β, say b, is a measure of the level of discrimination. If a higher value of A implies more favorable treatment, then a negative value for b implies that agents discriminate against minority auditors in action A. The t-test for β is a test of the hypothesis that discrimination exists. Note that b is the difference in the mean treatment of blacks and whites and the OLS t-test is equivalent to a standard difference-of-means test.

B. *Eliminating Bias Through the Audit Study Design*

The first statistical question to ask about equation (1) is whether b is biased. Many variables other than R influence the treatment an auditor receives, so the question is whether b is biased because these variables are left out of the equation. According to the well-known theorem, left-out-variable bias in b equals the sum, across all left-out variables, of the true coefficient of the left-out variable multiplied by the partial correlation between that variable and R (see J. Johnston, 1972, p. 169). The audit design eliminates bias by identifying variables that are likely to have large true coefficients—that is, large effects on A—and insuring that the correlation between these variables and R equals zero.

[2] For evidence about discrimination in other types of treatment, see my paper (1984). Discrimination in credit checks or the provision of mortgages is difficult to study with audits, but other methods can be used. See Robert Schafer and Helen Ladd (1981).

[3] Auditors try to visit all units to which they are invited, but not all invitations are genuine and they do not always succeed. One kind of discrimination, racial steering, may exist even if blacks and whites are told about the same number of available units; blacks may learn about units in black areas and whites about units in white areas. The Boston data provide some evidence of steering: after controlling for differences in the total number of units seen, on average black auditors saw .31 apartments and .21 houses that were not shown to their white teammates. See my paper (1984).

Three categories of left-out variables might influence treatment: whether the auditor precedes or follows his or her teammate(s); characteristics of the audit, including conditions in the housing market at the time of the audit and characteristics of the housing agent; and characteristics of the auditor. The audit design eliminates bias from all three categories.

Teammates cannot visit an agent at the same time, and their order of visit might influence their relative treatment. For example, a rental agent might discourage the second auditor if her teammate looked like a good prospect. To insure that order of visit would not be correlated with R, and therefore would not be a source of bias in b, Feins et al. assigned order randomly.

Sending auditors to the same agency during a short time span insures that agency characteristics and housing market conditions are the same for teammates and therefore are not correlated with R. Teammates visit the same agency but may encounter different agents. This possibility is not a source of bias. If the assignment of an agent to a customer is a random process, or if it depends on customer characteristics other than minority status, then variation in treatment across agents is not correlated with R. If, on the other hand, agent assignment depends on the customer's minority status, then differences in teammates' treatment due to the assignment process constitute discrimination and appropriately influence b.

The treatment an auditor receives is also influenced by his or her age, income, and family characteristics. In an audit study, teammates are matched on these characteristics, so that they are not correlated with R and therefore are not a source of bias. All the auditors in a team are assigned income and family characteristics. A study manager controls matching by teaming auditors with the same indelible characteristics, such as sex and age, and by assigning similar income and family characteristics to teammates.

All auditor characteristics that might influence treatment cannot be identified and incorporated into the matching process. Teammates may receive different treatment, for example, because of different personal styles. Audit studies minimize the potential bias from hard-to-measure auditor characteristics by giving all auditors the same thorough training and by avoiding auditors whose personalities might induce unusual treatment by agents.[4]

C. *An Error-Components Model of Discriminatory Treatment*

The audit study design implies that the random error in equation (1) has three components. The first, λ_a, is associated with audit a; that is, it measures variation in treatment due to factors shared by the teammates who participate in a given audit, including shared individual characteristics, agency characteristics, and market conditions. By definition, factors that are shared by teammates are not correlated with R. The second component, μ_i, refers to auditor i; that is, it measures variation in treatment due to auditor characteristics other than race that are not shared by teammates. Auditor assignment, matching, training, and selection are designed to insure that auditor characteristics with large impacts on treatment are reflected in λ_a, not μ_i. What remains in μ_i is small, random variation in the treatment of individuals that is not correlated with R. The third component, ε_{ai}, measures the component of treatment that is unique to auditor i's participation in audit a. Sending auditors to the same agency at about the same time insures that agency characteristics and market conditions, are reflected in λ_a, ε_{ai}. Randomizing order insures that order, the effect of which is in ε_{ai}, is not correlated with R. In symbols,

$$A_{ai} = \alpha + \beta R_i + \lambda_a + \mu_i + \varepsilon_{ai}. \quad (2)$$

Because the error components are not corre-

[4]Auditor training and selection and the assignment of roles eliminate auditor characteristics as a source of bias but also limit the generality of the results; an audit study does not reveal the level of discrimination against minorities with characteristics outside the range observed in auditors.

TABLE 1—THE LEVEL OF DISCRIMINATION IN HOUSING AVAILABILITY

	Measure of Availability					
	Rental Audits			Sales Audits		
	Possi-bilities	Invited To See	Inspected	Possi-bilities	Invited To See	Inspected
Measures of Treatment (Number of Housing Units)						
White Average = Constant Term	2.077	1.959	1.308	2.195	2.119	1.322
Level of Discrimination Against Blacks = $-b$	0.594	0.712	0.433	0.576	0.542	0.314
Test Statistics for the Level of Discrimination						
Bivariate Regression[a]						
Standard Error	0.153	0.150	0.101	0.172	0.178	0.097
t-Statistic[b]	3.877	4.734	4.302	3.343	3.055	3.247
R-Squared	0.046	0.067	0.056	0.046	0.038	0.043
Paired Difference-of-Means Test[c]						
Standard Error	0.119	0.123	0.089	0.125	0.139	0.077
t-Statistic[b]	5.007	5.779	4.883	4.623	3.902	4.074
R-Squared[d]	0.715	0.688	0.634	0.753	0.708	0.699
Number of Audits	156	156	156	118	118	118

Source: Author's calculations based on the Feins et al. 1981 Boston data.
Notes: Possibilities = number of housing units discussed as serious possibilities; Invited to see = number of housing units invited to inspect; Inspected = number of housing units actually inspected.
[a]And standard difference-of-means test.
[b]A t-statistic above 3.291 occurs by chance only once in 2000 trials.
[c]And bivariate regression plus audit dummies or *GLS* regression.
[d]Only applies to regression with audit dummies.

lated with R, the *OLS* estimate of β, namely b, is unbiased.

Although *OLS* yields an unbiased b, the *OLS* standard error for b is biased upward and could lead researchers or enforcement officials to conclude that discrimination does not exist when in fact it does. This bias arises because of the error component λ_a, which implies that the error terms for black and white auditors are correlated.[5] Consider the case of two auditors per audit. Let e_{aB} and e_{aW} be the error terms in equation (1) for the black and white auditors, respectively. Now define $\rho = \text{Cov}(e_{aB}, e_{aW})/\text{Var}(e_{ai})$. Then *OLS* overstates the standard error of b by a factor of $1/(1-\rho)^{1/2}$.[6] If $\rho = 0.5$, for example, the *OLS* formula overstates s_b by 41 percent.

With two auditors per audit, this error in s_b can be eliminated with a paired difference-of-means test, which uses the same b

[5]In principle, μ_i and the error component for order of visit, which is in ε_{ia}, could also lead to biased standard errors. A *GLS* procedure to account for μ_i would be complex but would add little; because the study design keeps μ_i small, its effect on the standard errors is small (for evidence, see fn. 11). Auditor dummies cannot be used to correct for μ_i because they are perfectly collinear with R. And as shown in Section II, a dummy variable for order, which corrects for the order error component, is never significant.

[6]In a bivariate regression of Y on X, the variance of b is

$$Var(b) = E\left[\sum_j w_j^2 e_j^2 + 2\sum_{j \neq k} w_j e_j e_k\right],$$

where j and k stand for observation, $w_j = x_j/\Sigma x_k^2$, and $x_j = (X_j - \bar{X})$. See Johnston (p. 20). In my case, $X_j = R_j$, $E(e_j^2) = \sigma^2$, and if teammates' observations appear together, $E(e_j e_k) = \text{Cov}(e_B, e_W)$ for teammates (j = odd, $k = j+1$) and $E(e_j e_k) = 0$ otherwise. Furthermore, $\rho = \text{Cov}(e_W, e_B)/\sigma^2$ (see text), $\Sigma w_k^2 = 1/\Sigma x_k^2$ (see Johnston, p. 19), and $x_j = (R_j - \bar{R})$ equals 0.5 for blacks and -0.5 for whites. Thus, $\text{Var}(b) = \sigma^2\{[1/[(.25)(2N)] + \rho(2N)(.5)(-.5)/[(.25)(2N)]^2\} = 2\sigma^2(1-\rho)/N$. It follows that the usual *OLS* formula, which assumes $\rho = 0$, overstates s_b, which is the square root of $\text{Var}(b)$, by a factor of $1/(1-\rho)^{1/2}$.

as the standard difference-of-means test, but incorporates the covariance between e_{aB} and e_{aW} into the calculation of s_b.[7] Identical results can be obtained from two regression models. A "fixed effects" model includes a dummy variable for each audit; the coefficient of the dummy variable for audit a is an estimate of λ_a. A "random effects" model treats the correlation between teammates' errors as part of the error structure and derives a generalized least squares (*GLS*) procedure to account for it. This *GLS* procedure is employed in Section II and is described in the Appendix.[8]

D. *Results from the 1981 Boston Audits*

Table 1 presents my analysis of the audit data collected by Feins et al. in Boston in 1981.[9] The second row contains the estimated level of discrimination in three measures of housing availability in both the rental and sales markets. The level of discrimination is high in all six cases.[10] For example, discrimination in "invitations" in the rental audits is 0.712 apartments; on average, blacks were invited to inspect 1.247 apartments, whereas white were invited to inspect 0.712 apartments more (or 57 percent more) than blacks. Overall, blacks must search much harder than whites to find equivalent housing; a black renter would have to visit 8 housing agents to receive as many invitations to inspect as a white receives from 5 agents.[11]

The correct t-test, in the seventh row of Table 1, indicates that these estimates of discrimination are highly significant. A comparison of third and sixth rows reveals that the incorrect bivariate regression yields standard errors that are biased upward by as much as 38 percent—but that still indicate significance. In a different audit study, a failure to correct a bias of this magnitude might lead one to conclude that discrimination does not exist when in fact it does.

II. Testing Hypotheses About Discriminatory Behavior

Table 1 documents that discrimination exists, but provides no insight into its causes. Discrimination is, of course, illegal regardless of its causes, but an analysis of causes helps to determine why discrimination persists and to design more effective policies to eliminate it. Consequently, this section explains and tests hypotheses about the

[7] In the paired test, the t-statistic is the difference in average treatment of blacks and whites divided by an estimate of s_b equal to the square root of $[\mathrm{Var}(A_{aW})+\mathrm{Var}(A_{aB})-2\,\mathrm{Cov}(A_{aB}, A_{aW})]/N$.

[8] With two visits per audit and no control variables, these three methods are algebraically equivalent. This equivalence can be demonstrated with the results in Yair Mundlak (1978). A fixed effects model estimates β on the basis of variation in the data within groups (in my case within audits), but ignores variation between groups. A random effects model estimates β on the basis of a weighted average of within- and between-group variation. Because of the audit design, however, there is no between-group variation in R (every audit involves a zero and a one) and the *GLS* estimate collapses to the *OLS* estimate with audit dummies. Estimating each audit error is the same as analyzing differences between teammates, so all three methods are the same. Because a *GLS* procedure is consistent and asymptotically efficient, the other procedures share these desirable properties, and one might as well use the simplest procedure, namely the paired difference-of-means test. A more formal proof of these results is available from the author. I am grateful to Gary Solon for suggesting this line of argument.

[9] Feins et al. also present bivariate regression results for these three treatment variables. My results differ slightly from theirs because they weighted the data to count each neighborhood equally and they did not eliminate the bias in s_b.

[10] Audits avoid bias in b by insuring that teammates share factors that might influence treatment. Thus, a simple measure of the success of the design is the proportion of the variance in treatment explained by audit dummies. In Table 1, adding audit dummies boosts the R-squared from about 0.05 to about 0.7; most of the factors that influence treatment are indeed shared by teammates.

[11] Paul Courant (1978) shows that discrimination of this form can lead to a high degree of racial residential segregation and to a higher price for equivalent housing in black than in white areas. Schafer (1979) found large price differentials (up to 34 percent for some housing types) between largely black and largely white areas of Boston in 1970. The audit results and Courant's analysis suggest that these price differentials may have continued into the 1980's.

causes of discriminatory behavior by housing agents.

A. *The Hypotheses*

The literature on discrimination indicates that a housing agent might deny blacks access to housing because of his (or her) own prejudice or because of the prejudice of his white customers (see my paper, 1979). A third possibility is that housing agents treat blacks and whites differently because they expect blacks and whites to prefer different neighborhoods.[12] In this section, I apply these hypotheses to discrimination in the provision of information about available housing and test them using audit evidence. A similar set of hypotheses and tests (derived independently) for a different set of treatment variables is presented by John Simonson and Wienk (1984), using the audits carried out by Wienk et al.

The first hypothesis is that an agent's own prejudice leads him to discriminate in order to avoid dealing with blacks. According to this agent-prejudice hypothesis, variation in the strength of racial prejudice among housing agents leads to variation in the level of discrimination. Prejudice tends to increase with age, for example, and men tend to be more prejudiced than women (see George Simpson and Milton Yinger, 1985). More discrimination by older or by male brokers would therefore provide support for this hypothesis. The strength of an agent's prejudice, and hence the level of discrimination, also may vary with characteristics of the black auditor that matter to the agent but not to his potential white customers. The sex of a married black customer, for example, cannot matter to white residents (who would have both husband and wife as neighbors), but it might matter to the agent (who only deals with one spouse).

The second hypothesis is that an agent who depends on the business of a prejudiced white community discriminates in order to avoid alienating his current or potential white customers. Rental agents for all-white apartment buildings discriminate against blacks because the entry of a few blacks could lead to the exit of many or all white tenants and hence to extensive turnover costs. Real estate brokers cultivate contacts in their community to attract potential buyers and sellers. In a prejudiced white community, therefore, brokers discriminate against blacks to avoid alienating most of their potential clients, namely white residents.

These incentives to discriminate break down once a neighborhood starts to undergo racial transition. If blacks are willing to outbid whites for apartments, complete racial turnover may yield an increase in rental income that compensates a landlord for his turnover costs. And once racial transition begins, a real estate broker cannot be blamed for introducing blacks and he may be able to generate extra commission income by encouraging rapid turnover.

In sum, the white-customer-prejudice hypothesis predicts extensive racial discrimination in established white areas, but no discrimination in areas experiencing rapid racial transition.

The Boston audits took place in six neighborhoods, which are described in Table 2. Back Bay/Beacon Hill and Central are mostly white with significant increases in population but very small increases in black population between 1970 and 1980. The other four neighborhoods are more integrated, with racial compositions between 8 and 41 percent black, but they had widely varying patterns of racial change between 1970 and 1980. Dorchester and Hyde Park/Roslindale experienced large inflows of blacks and large outflows of whites—that is, they experienced rapid racial transition. Jamaica Plain lost white population, but gained few blacks. And the South End, which became a desirable location both for young, white professionals and for black families, saw rapid growth in both its black and white populations.

The customer-prejudice hypothesis predicts that discrimination will be high in Back Bay/Beacon Hill and Central and nonexistent in Dorchester and Hyde Park/Roslindale. It also predicts continuing discrimination in Jamaica Plain, where blacks' demand

[12] This hypothesis was proposed by an anonymous referee.

TABLE 2—CHARACTERISTICS OF STUDY NEIGHBORHOODS

	1980 Characteristics			1970–80 Change as Percentage of 1980 Population		No. of	Percentage of Owner Units in Subareas		Percentage of Renter Units in Subareas	
Neighborhood	Population	Percent Renter	Percent Black	Black	Other	Subareas	< 20% Black	> 5% Black	< 20% Black	> 5% Black
BackBay/ Beacon Hill	30,212	82.1	4.2	2.2	6.7	1	100.0	0.0	100.0	0.0
Central	21,797	90.0	3.0	1.8	9.8	3	100.0	0.0	100.0	0.0
South End	27,125	86.9	40.8	7.7	8.7	1	0.0	100.0	0.0	100.0
Dorchester	82,912	65.2	24.7	11.3	−40.5	11	62.4	73.5	54.4	82.2
Hyde Park/ Roslindale	62,849	48.0	8.1	6.7	−25.3	9	75.3	38.4	82.6	36.0
Jamaica Plain	39,331	74.9	19.1	1.6	−23.1	5	72.5	59.5	44.4	85.4

Source: Boston Redevelopment Authority.

for housing does not appear to be growing, and in the South End, where many locations are currently attractive to whites.

White residents' prejudice, and hence agent discrimination, may also vary with the black auditor's characteristics. Survey evidence suggests that whites are more receptive to black neighbors with higher incomes and that whites may be more opposed to school integration than to residential integration, per se (see Simpson and Yinger). We can test the hypotheses that housing agents respond to these feelings by determining whether discrimination is stronger against either low-income blacks or blacks with school-age children.

The third hypothesis is that agents' actions reflect their perceptions about black and white preferences. According to surveys, most whites prefer not to move into an integrated neighborhood, and most blacks prefer an integrated neighborhood to an all-black one, although they also prefer not to be the first black in a previously all-white neighborhood (see Howard Schuman, Charlotte Steed, and Lawrence Bobo, 1985). Agents do not know the racial preferences of individual auditors; indeed, teammates are instructed to ask for the same housing and to express interest in all available units. On the other hand, agents may be aware of average preferences; this hypothesis assumes that agents attribute to each auditor the average preferences for his or her race. Agents' perceptions and actions are linked because showing apartments or houses is costly; an agent may not show a housing unit to a customer unless he believes there is a reasonable probability that the customer will rent or buy that unit.[13] According to the above assumption, therefore, an agent will not show housing in integrated neighborhoods to whites or housing in all-white neighborhoods to blacks.

To test this perceived-preference hypothesis, we must decide which neighborhoods are attractive to each race. One survey found that 50 percent of whites would "consider" moving into a neighborhood that was 21 percent black and that 95 percent of blacks would move into a neighborhood that was 14 percent black (Reynolds Farley, Suzanne Bianchi, and Diane Colasanto, 1979). If agents try to please the majority of their customers, it therefore seems reasonable to assume that any area less than 20 percent black is acceptable to whites, and any area greater than 5 percent black is acceptable to blacks. Several of the neighborhoods in the Boston study are large and heterogeneous, so the overall racial composition may not be an accurate guide to their attractiveness. For-

[13] Simonson and Wienk identify several characteristics of black customers that might signal a low probability of completing a transaction—and therefore might lead to discriminatory treatment.

tunately, a special census tabulation breaks the largest neighborhoods into relatively homogeneous subareas. Table 2 presents the percentage of owner and renter units in subareas that, according to the above assumptions, are acceptable to whites and to blacks.

Based on the data in Table 2, the perceived-preference hypothesis predicts that discrimination will be relatively high in Back Bay/Beacon Hill and Central, where all the units are acceptable to whites and none are acceptable to blacks. In the South End, however, this hypothesis predicts no discrimination against blacks. (Indeed, the data in Table 2 indicate that no units are in areas acceptable to whites and therefore suggest that there might even be discrimination against whites. Subarea data are not available for the South End, however, so the heterogeneity mentioned earlier is not captured by these data.) In Dorchester and Jamaica Plain, the number of units acceptable to blacks and whites is about the same, so this hypothesis predicts no discrimination. In Hyde Park/Roslindale, many more units are acceptable to whites than to blacks, so this hypothesis predicts discrimination against blacks.

The perceived-preference hypothesis and the white-customer-prejudice hypothesis yield the same predictions in Back Bay/Beacon Hill, Central, and Dorchester. In the South End and Jamaica Plain, however, the customer-prejudice hypothesis predicts discrimination against blacks, whereas the perceived-preference hypothesis does not. The reverse is true for Hyde Park/Roslindale, where the perceived-preference hypothesis predicts discrimination, but the customer-prejudice hypothesis does not. We can decide which hypothesis to embrace by examining the levels of discrimination in these last three neighborhoods.

B. *Estimation Strategy*

Hypotheses about nondiscriminatory behavior are built into the audit study design. Teammates are matched on income, for example, because income is expected to influence their treatment. I now add direct controls for nondiscriminatory behavior by introducing into equation (2) the variables defined in Table 3. A variable to indicate the sex of the auditor, for example, controls for the possibility that female auditors are treated more favorably than males.[14]

To test the hypotheses about discriminatory behavior, let us introduce into equation (2) a series of interaction terms between race and the control variables in Table 3. Consider, for example, race interacted with whether the housing agent was female. A positive coefficient for this variable would indicate that female agents discriminate less than male agents. The interaction terms are expressed as deviations from a mean. For a particular auditor, the variable just mentioned, for example, equals the minority status of that auditor multiplied by the difference between the female-agent variable for that auditor and the average value of the female-agent variable for black auditors. This formulation allows us to continue to interpret the coefficient of the race variable as the average level of discrimination, as in equation (2). The coefficients of the interaction terms measure variation around this average.

Now let X^j_{ai} be control variable j for audit a and auditor i, and let γ_j be its coefficient. Furthermore, let $\bar{X}^j_{aB}$ be the average value of X^j_{ai} for all visits by black auditors. Then adding control variables and interaction terms to equation (2) yields

$$(3)\quad A_{ai} = \alpha' + \beta' R_i + \sum_j \gamma_j X^j_{ai} + \sum_j \delta_j R_i \left(X^j_{ai} - \bar{X}^j_{aB} \right) + \lambda'_a + \mu'_i + \varepsilon'_{ai}.$$

Applying *OLS* to equation (3) yields unbiased estimates of the parameters, but the controls do not fully eliminate the audit error component, λ'_a, and the standard errors of *OLS* coefficients are biased upward.[15]

[14] If matching eliminates correlation between the controls and R, then adding controls will not affect b. Table 4 shows that, by this test, matching was successful in the 1981 Boston audits.

[15] In the Boston audits, the R-squared with controls tends to be about half the R-squared with audit dummies, which fully capture λ_a; i.e., controls account for about half the variation in λ_a.

TABLE 3—DEFINITIONS AND AVERAGE VALUES FOR CONTROL VARIABLES

	Rental Audits		Sales Audits	
Variable	Black Auditor	White Auditor	Black Auditor	White Auditor
Auditor's Assigned Characteristics Income[a]	2.18	2.03	3.73	3.69
Role = single parent[b]			0.01	0.01
= childless couple	0.48	0.48	0.56	0.56
= couple with young children	0.04	0.04	0.25	0.27
= couple with older children			0.07	0.04
= previous owner			0.07	0.07
Auditor's Indelible Characteristics				
Age[c]	3.01	2.73	2.97	2.69
Sex (1 = Female)	0.54	0.54	0.47	0.47
Agent's Characteristics				
Race (1 = Nonwhite)	0.03	0.01	0.02	0.02
Young (1 = < 35-years-old)	0.57	0.57	0.36	0.36
Old (1 = > 50-years-old)	0.09	0.10	0.19	0.16
Sex (1 = Female)	0.49	0.46	0.46	0.48
Other Audit Information				
Auditor's order of visit (1 = 1st)	0.50	0.50	0.53	0.47
Audit was in June (not May)	0.46	0.46	0.33	0.35
Audit was in afternoon	0.57	0.61	0.58	0.64
Unit was a condominium[d]			0.37	0.37

[a]Income defined as follows: $10,000 = 1; increments of $10,000 to $50,000 = 5; increments of $15,000 to > $80,000 = 7.

[b]Only one audit team was assigned the single-parent role, so the coefficient of this variable measures the relative treatment of this audit—not the relative treatment of single parents.

[c]Age defined as follows: < 25 = 1; 25–29 = 2; ...; 60–64 = 9; > 65 = 10.

[d]This variable counts audits in which either auditor was quoted a condominium fee, but misses condominiums if neither auditor was told that the advertised unit was available.

The *GLS* procedure in the Appendix can be used to eliminate this bias.[16]

C. *Results from the 1981 Boston Audits*

Tables 4 and 5 present the *GLS* results for variation in discriminatory behavior.[17] In Table 4, the coefficients of R, which still measure the average level of discrimination, are close in magnitude and significance to the estimates in Table 1. The other entries in Table 4 are coefficients of nonneighborhood interaction terms: the neighborhood results are in Table 5.

Few of the nonneighborhood variables have a statistically significant impact on dis-

[16]In equation (3), as in (2), X_a can be eliminated by differencing; i.e., by expressing the model as a difference between each black auditor and her white teammate. However, this formulation forces one to estimate the γ_js based solely on the within-audit variation in the X_js, despite the fact that most of the variation in these variables occurs between audits. This problem can be solved in two ways. First, unbiased estimates of the γ_js can be obtained using equation (3) and these estimates can then be used as a restriction in the differenced version of equation (3). This procedure has intuitive appeal, but unlike the *GLS* procedure in the text, its statistical properties are not known. (It turns out, however, that this paired approach and *GLS* yield similar results, at least for the 1981 Boston sample. Results for the paired approach are available from the author.) Second, one can ignore teammate differences in the X_js; after all, the audit design insures that these differences are small. This alternative is employed by Simonson and Wienk, but it is inappropriate for the Boston audits, because blacks are assigned slightly more favorable values than are their teammates for a few characteristics, such as income, and the left-out differences may be correlated with R. See Table 3.

[17]The *GLS* results for nondiscriminatory behavior are available from the author. Few controls are significant.

TABLE 4—ESTIMATED VARIATION IN DISCRIMINATORY BEHAVIOR

Variable	Measure of Rental Availability			Measure of Sales Availability		
	Possi-bilities	Invited To See	Inspected	Possi-bilities	Invited To See	Inspected
Average Level of Discrimination						
Auditor's Race	0.5757	0.6596	0.4502	0.4815	0.4972	0.3419
(= R)	(4.5510)	(5.0640)	(4.8490)	(3.1060)	(2.9470)	(3.8480)
Impact of Control Variables on the Level of Discrimination						
Auditor's Assigned Characteristics						
Income	0.1385	0.0849	0.0233	0.0657	0.0153	0.2068
	(0.7410)	(0.4390)	(0.1690)	(0.4960)	(0.1060)	(2.7380)
Childless Couple	−0.1305	−0.1710	−0.3554	0.7215	0.9129	−0.1863
	(0.4020)	(0.5080)	(1.4780)	(1.3600)	(1.5720)	(0.6150)
Couple, Child ≤ 6	−0.8675	−0.5022	−0.6397	0.1557	0.4617	−0.6757
	(1.1600)	(0.6490)	(1.1590)	(0.2630)	(0.7130)	(2.0030)
Couple, Child > 6				0.3417	−0.2387	−0.9226
				(0.3190)	(0.2040)	(1.5030)
Previous Owner				0.3648	0.8880	0.4768
				(0.4640)	(1.0350)	(1.0620)
Auditor's Indelible Characteristics						
Age	−0.109	0.0210	−0.0458	0.0621	0.0464	−0.1769
	(0.0400)	(0.0760)	(0.2330)	(0.1760)	(0.1220)	(0.8690)
Sex	0.2942	0.2818	0.2671	0.0976	0.2708	0.5896
	(0.6920)	(0.6530)	(0.8740)	(0.1880)	(0.4820)	(1.9710)
Agent's Characteristics						
Race	−1.0398	−1.1316	−1.2366	0.3100	0.1514	0.2948
	(0.8360)	(0.8640)	(1.3160)	(0.2850)	(0.1270)	(0.4760)
Young	0.3488	0.1641	0.0564	−0.2601	−0.1351	−0.0645
	(1.1390)	(0.5300)	(0.2580)	(0.7340)	(0.3540)	(0.3160)
Old	0.0953	−0.3136	−0.4013	0.0286	0.2139	0.2443
	(0.1890)	(0.6140)	(1.1090)	(0.0620)	(0.4340)	(0.9240)
Sex	−0.3339	−0.3684	0.2636	0.1701	−0.0855	0.1647
	(1.2410)	(1.3380)	(1.3460)	(0.5500)	(0.2550)	(0.9280)
Other Audit Information						
Order	0.1977	0.1884	−0.1139	0.1401	0.0876	−0.2430
	(0.5790)	(0.5760)	(0.5000)	(0.3640)	(0.2200)	(1.0650)
June	−0.2618	−0.2524	−0.1536	0.1961	0.2682	0.1175
	(1.0470)	(0.9740)	(0.8300)	(0.5660)	(0.7070)	(0.5940)
Afternoon	−0.5967	−0.6361	0.0612	−0.1503	0.2219	0.1052
	(2.0460)	(2.1570)	(0.2930)	(0.4430)	(0.6100)	(0.5360)
Condo				0.1396	0.3487	0.0357
				(0.3300)	(0.7540)	(0.1480)
R-Squared	0.2995	0.3172	0.2479	0.3647	0.3360	0.3317

Source: Author's calculations based on the Feins et al. 1981 Boston data.

Notes: Row 1 is $-b$ (-1 times the coefficient of R); the other rows are coefficients of variables in Table 3 interacted with R (a negative sign implies that discrimination increases with that variable). The sample is visits; dependent variables are defined in Table 1; *GLS* regressions also include control variables in Table 3, a dummy variable for each neighborhood in Table 2 (less 1), and neighborhood dummies interacted with R; interactions between R and the controls are expressed as deviations from the mean for blacks. Absolute values of t-statistics are shown in parentheses. The two-tailed 10 [5] (1) percent level of significance is 1.645 [1.960] (2.576).

criminatory behavior; in most cases, discrimination takes place regardless of the characteristics of the auditor or of the agent. In the rental market, discrimination in offering serious possibilities or in invitations to inspect is higher in the afternoon, after controlling for order—a result not predicted by any of the hypotheses. In the sales market, discrimination in actual inspections is stronger against low-income blacks and black families with children. (Estimated discrimination is even higher against black families with older children, although the coefficient is not quite significant at the 10 percent

TABLE 5—ESTIMATED LEVEL OF DISCRIMINATION BY NEIGHBORHOOD

	Rental Discrimination				Sales Discrimination			
Neighborhood	No. of Audits	Possi-bilities	Invited To See	Inspected	No. of Audits	Possi-bilities	Invited To See	Inspected
Sample Average	156	0.58^c	0.66^c	0.45^c	118	0.48^c	0.50^c	0.34^c
		(4.55)	(5.06)	(4.85)		(3.11)	(2.95)	(3.85)
BackBay/ Beacon Hill	46	0.68^c	0.65^c	0.07	16	0.03	0.04	0.75^c
		(2.97)	(2.74)	(0.43)		(0.59)	(0.07)	(2.57)
Central	31	0.97^c	1.04^c	0.98^{c,d}	16	1.09^c	0.99^b	0.90^{c,d}
		(3.40)	(3.49)	(4.61)		(2.44)	(2.04)	(3.54)
South End	36	0.05^d	0.34^a	0.42^b	14	0.89^b	0.61	0.63^c
		(0.21)	(1.28)	(2.19)		(1.92)	(1.21)	(2.37)
Dorchester	11	0.17	0.55	0.61^b	24	0.46	0.76^b	−0.14^d
		(0.34)	(1.06)	(1.65)		(1.18)	(1.79)	0.61
Hyde Park/ Roslindale	13	0.46	0.46	0.27	28	−0.06	0.11	−0.17^d
		(1.02	(1.00)	(0.80)		(0.16)	(0.29)	0.80
Jamaica Plain	19	0.99^c	0.87^b	0.60^b	20	0.64^b	0.61^a	0.65^c
		(2.80)	(2.37)	(2.30)		(1.70)	(1.48)	(3.02)

Notes: Sample average is from Table 4. Other entries equal (−1) times the coefficients of neighborhood dummies interacted with R from regressions like those described in Table 4, except that all six neighborhood interactions are included and R is excluded. Absolute values of t-statistics are shown in parentheses.

^{a} = Significantly different from zero, 90 percent level.
^{b} = Significantly different from zero, 95 percent level.
^{c} = Significantly different from zero, 99 percent level.
^{d} = Significantly different from average, 95 percent level.

level.) These results support the hypothesis that when it comes to actually showing houses to customers, real estate brokers are trying to keep out the black households that would most upset their potential white customers. In addition, black females encounter less discrimination in actual inspections than do black males; this result supports the hypothesis that some agents have particularly strong prejudice against black males and therefore avoid showing them houses.

Table 5 reveals substantial variation in discrimination across neighborhoods.[18] In Central and Jamaica Plain, the estimated level of discrimination in both the sales and rental markets is high and statistically significant for all three treatment variables. In Hyde Park/Roslindale, on the other hand, discrimination is low and insignificant and in one case is significantly below average. In Back Bay/Beacon Hill, the South End, and Dorchester, significant discrimination exists for one or two treatment variables, usually including actual inspections. For a black customer, housing agents may be willing to provide information, but they avoid taking the next step in a housing transaction, namely showing available units. The results for the sales market in Dorchester are somewhat contradictory; estimated discrimination in inspections is negative and significantly below the average level, despite significant discrimination in invitations to inspect.

These results provide strong support for the white-customer-preference hypothesis and a strong rejection of the perceived-preference hypothesis. As predicted by both hypotheses, there is discrimination in Back Bay/Beacon Hill and in Central. As predicted by neither, there is some discrimination in Dorchester, although in the sales market the

[18]In Table 5, the average level of discrimination is the coefficient of R in a regression with a set of neighborhood dummy variables (defined as deviations from the mean with one left out) interacted with R. The levels of discrimination by neighborhood are the coefficients of neighborhood dummy variables (defined as zero or one with none left out) interacted with R in a regression without R. These results measure discrimination by neighborhood because all auditors first asked about an advertised unit in a given neighborhood, and then asked about similar units in the same neighborhood.

discrimination in invitations appears to be canceled by equal treatment in actual inspections. In the other three neighborhoods, where the two hypotheses yield different predictions, the results all support the customer-preference hypothesis. To be specific, there is discrimination in the South End and in Jamaica Plain, but none in Hyde Park/Roslindale.

Thus, housing agents discriminate primarily to retain the business of their actual or potential white customers. This incentive to discriminate breaks down when a neighborhood undergoes rapid racial transition; under these circumstances, discrimination may disappear (as in Hyde Park/Roslindale) or linger (as in Dorchester). Agent prejudice may be another source of discrimination in some cases, such as the nonshowing of houses to black males.

III. Conclusion

Well-managed fair housing audit studies provide direct, compelling tests of the existence of discrimination in housing. Unbiased measures of the level of discrimination (and its standard error) can be obtained with a very simple technique, namely the paired difference-of-means test. The application of this technique to the 1981 Boston audits reveals extremely high levels of discrimination. On average, for example, black auditors are invited to inspect 36.3 percent fewer apartments than their white teammates. Discrimination of this magnitude constitutes a serious social problem and cries out for stronger government action.

Fair housing audits also provide an unprecedented opportunity to study discriminatory behavior. In the Boston audits, racial discrimination in housing generally does not vary with the characteristics of the black auditor or the characteristics of the housing agent, although in actually showing houses for sale, it is stronger against lower-income blacks and black families with children. On the other hand, discrimination does vary by location, with high discrimination in white areas and no discrimination in some areas undergoing racial transition. These results indicate that the primary cause of racial discrimination in housing is that housing agents illegally promote their economic interests by catering to the racial prejudice of their current or potential white customers.

Appendix

To derive the *GLS* procedure, rewrite equation (1) in matrix form:

$$\text{(A1)} \qquad \mathbf{A} = \mathbf{R}\boldsymbol{\beta} + \mathbf{e},$$

where $E(\mathbf{e}) = 0$, $E(\mathbf{ee}') = \sigma^2\Omega$, and Ω is a symmetric, positive definite matrix. Now place visits for teammates next to each other. Then Ω has the following 2×2 blocks on the diagonal, zeroes elsewhere;

$$\text{(A2)} \qquad Z = \begin{bmatrix} 1 & 0 \\ 0 & 1 \end{bmatrix}.$$

The *GLS* estimator is based on a matrix Q such that $Q'Q = \Omega^{-1}$. With audits, Q is a block diagonal matrix with Z replaced by

$$\text{(A3)} \qquad Z^* = \begin{bmatrix} w_1 & w_2 \\ w_2 & w_1 \end{bmatrix}$$

where
$$w_1 = \frac{1}{2}\left[\frac{1}{\sqrt{1+\rho}} + \frac{1}{\sqrt{1-\rho}}\right]$$

$$w_2 = \frac{1}{2}\left[\frac{1}{\sqrt{1+\rho}} - \frac{1}{\sqrt{1-\rho}}\right]$$

Equation (A3) defines a special case of Marc Nerlove's (1971) estimator.

To employ (A3), one must estimate ρ from the residuals of an *OLS* regression. With an estimated ρ, *GLS* is consistent and asymptotically efficient (see Thomas Fomby, R. Carter Hill, and Stanley Johnson, 1984, ch. 8), but second-stage observations for teammates are not independent and half the degrees of freedom are consumed. Second, one must premultiply **A** and **R** by Q. This matrix multiplication replaces an auditor's value for each variable, V, with a weighted average of that auditor's value and her teammate's value:

$$\text{(A4)} \qquad V^*_{ai} = w_1 V_{ai} + w_2 V_{ai'},$$

where i' denotes the teammates' visit. Applying *OLS* to the transformed variables yields the *GLS* estimator (Johnston, ch. 7).

REFERENCES

Courant, Paul N., "Racial Prejudice in a Search Model of the Urban Housing Market," *Journal of Urban Economics*, July 1978, *5*, 329–45.

Farley, Reynolds, Bianchi, Suzanne and Colasantro, Diane, "Barriers to the Racial Integration of Neighborhoods: The Detroit Case," *Annals of the American Academy of Political and Social Science*, January 1979, *441*, 97–113.

Feins, Judith D. and Bratt, Rachael G., "Barred in Boston: Racial Discrimination in Housing," *APA Journal*, Summer 1983, 344–55.

______, ______, **and Hollister, Robert,** "Final Report of a Study of Racial Discrimination in the Boston Housing Market," Abt Associates, November 1981.

Fomby, Thomas B., Hill, R. Carter and Johnson, Stanley R., *Advanced Econometric Methods*. New York: Springer-Verlag, 1984.

Hakken, Jon, *Discrimination Against Chicanos in the Dallas Rental Housing Market: An Experimental Extension of the Housing Market Practices Survey*, Washington: U.S. Department of Housing and Urban Development, 1979.

Holshouser, William, "Final Report of a Study of Racial Discrimination in Two Boston Housing Markets," Abt Associates, 1984.

James, Franklin J., McCummings, Betty L. and Tynan, Eileen A., "Discrimination, Segregation, and Minority Housing Conditions in Sunbelt Cities: A Study of Denver, Houston, and Phoenix," Center for Public-Private Sector Cooperation, Graduate School of Public Affairs, University of Colorado-Denver, 1983.

Johnston, J. *Econometric Methods*, 2nd ed., New York: McGraw-Hill, 1972.

Mundlak, Yair, "On the Pooling of Time Series and Cross Section Data," *Econometrica*, January 1978, *46*, 69–85.

Nerlove, Marc, "A Note on Error Components Models," *Econometrica*, March 1971, *39*, 383–96.

Schafer, Robert, "Racial Discrimination in the Boston Housing Market," *Journal of Urban Economics*, April 1979, *6*, 176–96.

______ **and Ladd, Helen F.,** *Discrimination in Mortgage Lending*, Cambridge: MIT Press, 1981.

Schuman, Howard, Steeh, Charlotte and Bobo, Lawrence, *Racial Attitudes in America*, Cambridge: Harvard University Press, 1985.

Simonson, John C. and Wienk, Ronald E., "Racial Discrimination in Housing Sales: An Empirical Test of Alternative Models of Broker Behavior," unpublished manuscript, 1984.

Simpson, George E. and Yinger, J. Milton, *Racial and Cultural Minorities: An Analysis of Prejudice and Discrimination*, 5th ed., New York: Plenum Press, 1985.

Wienk, Ronald E. et al., *Measuring Discrimination in American Housing Markets: The Housing Market Practices Survey*, Washington: U.S. Department of Housing and Urban Development, 1979.

Yinger, John, "Prejudice and Discrimination in the Urban Housing Market," in P. Mieszkowski and M. Straszheim, eds., *Current Issues in Urban Economics*, Baltimore: Johns Hopkins University Press, 1979.

______, "Measuring Racial and Ethnic Discrimination with Fair Housing Audits: A Review of Existing Evidence and Research Methodology," paper submitted to the HUD Conference on Fair Housing Testing, Washington, D.C., December 6–7, 1984.

Boston Redevelopment Authority, *Boston Population and Housing by Neighborhood Area, 1980* (Demographic Information from the U.S. Bureau of the Census) September 1983.

[19]

PETER A. RIACH AND JUDITH RICH

Measuring discrimination by direct experimental methods: seeking gunsmoke

Throughout the 1970s and 1980s, the fashionable technique for establishing whether or not discrimination exists in the labor market was regression analysis. Oaxaca (1973) was foremost in the application of regression analysis as a technique to estimate the proportion of the black–white, or male–female, wage differential that was attributable to differences in productivity, and, on the other hand, the proportion not attributable to productivity-related characteristics, such as education, training, and labor force experience. The profession's enthusiasm for these statistical studies is vividly captured by Ashenfelter and Oaxaca (1987, p. 322):

> To most economists the insistence on finding "smoking gun" evidence of discriminatory actions, intent, or motivation seems quite irrelevant to determining whether market discrimination exists. In crude terms, for economists evidence of discrimination merely requires the presence of "unexplained" differences in compensation or employment.

While "most economists" might think this way, an increasingly vocal minority have been expressing concern about the specification problems associated with the regression procedure, and have evinced interest in locating the "smoking gun." For instance:

> In light of such sensitivity of the magnitude of discrimination to plausible alternative specifications of the underlying regression equations, and the fact that neither productivity nor discrimination itself is directly observable, some skepticism has arisen about the adequacy of this technique for measuring discrimination. [Blau and Ferber, 1987, p. 318]

> [I]t may be instructive to consider the direct evidence of discriminatory attitudes that has been accumulated by other social scientists. [Blau and Ferber, 1987, p. 319]

Peter A. Riach is Head of the Department of Economics at Leicester Polytechnic, England. Judith Rich lives in Melbourne, Australia.

> Discrimination can, after all, take many forms besides sex-based wage differentials, and seems unlikely to be completely captured by so crude a measure as a log-earnings regression. Perhaps the present analysis will stimulate further research on these other relatively neglected aspects of sex discrimination. [Kuhn, 1990, p. 297]

> Much of the economic literature on discrimination refers implicitly to the use of sex as a screen in hiring but it is in the field of psychology that controlled experiments to demonstrate its existence have been carried out. Fidell conducted an experiment involving sending brief curricula vitae of ten imaginary psychologists to U.S. university and college psychology departments. [Chiplin and Sloane, 1976, p. 79].

Direct tests of discrimination

As Blau and Ferber and Chiplin and Sloane acknowledge, the quest for "smoking guns" has predominantly been the province of noneconomist social scientists, although one notable exception is Yinger's (1986) measurement of racial discrimination in the housing market, aptly subtitled "Caught in the Act." In this article, Yinger reports on the technique of fair housing audits, whereby carefully matched members of different racial groups successively approach a landlord or a real estate broker to determine if there is any systematic, differential treatment on the basis of race. He explains that, in contrast to research that had tested for discrimination indirectly "by looking for its impacts on urban residential structure, such as higher prices in largely black areas and more centralized patterns of black residence," fair housing audits provide a direct measure of discrimination and "literally catch discriminators in the act of discriminating" (1986, p. 881). Yinger also claims that the technique is an important methodological advance and that it was first used in a pioneering study published in 1979 (i.e., Wienk, et al., 1979).

This claim was, in fact, incorrect: in 1966, a London-based research unit, Political and Economic Planning, conducted what they termed "situation tests," to assess the extent of racial discrimination in England. The method involved sending teams of three carefully matched actors to landlords and real estate agents to test for discrimination in the housing market; to employment agencies and employers to test for discrimination in the labor market; and to car insurance providers, car rental firms, and hotels to test for discrimination in services. The three-person team was comprised of a white Englishman, a white (Hungarian) immigrant, and an immigrant of color. This study was published in report form over the organization's name (Political and Economic Planning, 1967), and subsequently was published in an amended book version (Daniel, 1968). The same organization conducted a followup study in 1973, using actors again for direct approaches in the labor and housing markets (McIntosh and Smith, 1974).

While "situation tests" or "audits" involve the use of white applicants as a control group, it is impossible to ensure that all aspects of the applicants' performance are identical during their interaction with housing market sellers or labor market buyers. It is only if the applicants are distinguished by race, and *by race alone*, that we can safely conclude that racial discrimination has occurred when they encounter differential treatment. The problem with personal, and necessarily private, approaches is that there is no way to know or to demonstrate that *only* race distinguished the other party's perception of the applicants. Yinger argues that this difficulty is minimized by thorough training and by selecting participants carefully on personality grounds (Yinger, 1986, p. 883). Nevertheless, there is always the issue of motivation—particularly that, consciously or unconscioulsy, black applicants may seek to prove the existence of discrimination, and thereby bias the results. This was a criticism raised about the original Political and Economic Planning study by Ward (1969). Likewise, there could, on occasions, be doubts about the motivations of white applicants, and consequently the overriding difficulty is that the researcher using this method has no way of demonstrating to the reader that, in their interactions with other market transactors, applicants came across as identical in all essential respects other than race. The reader, therefore, must either rely on the assurance of the researcher and, in turn, his participants that motivation and all other nonrace factors were carefully controlled for, or dismiss the findings.

Written confirmation of gunsmoke

It was in order to meet the above criticism that an alternative technique for measuring labor market discrimination directly was devised by Jowell and Prescott-Clarke (1970). This technique has become known as "correspondence testing," and involves sending carefully matched pairs of written job applications in response to advertised vacancies, to test for discrimination in labor hiring at the initial stage of selection for interview. In order to avoid detection, the letters obviously cannot be identical, but in all essential characteristics, such as age, qualification, and experience, candidates are closely matched so that the only effective distinguishing characteristic is race. Moreover, to control for the possibility that the style of a particular letter might influence employer response, letter type is alternated and allocated equally between the racial groups. The advantage of this correspondence technique is that the researcher is able to exercise precise control over the content of applications, to control for any unintended bias in letter type by equal allocation among the racial groups, and to *demonstrate* the controlled and objective nature of the procedure to the reader. This includes the publication of the standard letters of application. Moreover, the researcher is able to retain documentation of all her or his activities—i.e., letters of application—and replies in the form of letters and telegrams. Thereby, conforming with the position adopted by Dewald, Thursby, and Anderson in their study of replication in empirical economics, "authors of empirical articles should feel a professional responsibility to maintain program and data files for a reasonable amount of time after publication and to provide these to other researchers" (1986, p. 601).

The disadvantage of "correspondence testing" is that it only tests for discrimination in labor hiring at the initial stage of selection for interview. Some employers may delay their discriminatory activity until the interview, and until making the final choice from among the interviewed short-list. Thus, correspondence testing does not measure the full extent of discrimination in the hiring decision, but, on the other hand, it does highlight one quite decisive form of discrimination—that of denying the applicant the chance even to compete for a job.

Correspondence testing has been used to measure racial discrimination in the British labor market on several occasions: by Jowell and Prescott-Clarke (1970), McIntosh and Smith (1974), Hubbock and Carter (1980), and Brown and Gay (1985). It has also been used to test for racial discrimination in the Australian labor market by Riach and Rich (1991). The British studies matched Afro-Carribeans, Indians, and Pakistanis against the indigenous Anglo-Saxon community; the Australian study matched recent Greek and Vietnamese immigrants against the long-established Anglo-Celtic community. In all cases, substantial and statistically significant discrimination against nonwhite job applicants was documented, despite the existence in both countries of legislation proscribing such activity. In view of U.S. preeminence in antidiscrimination policy and legislation, a replication of this work in the U.S. labor market would be particularly interesting. Unlike econometric work, where published data are universally available, the logistics of correspondence testing, and the need for speedy responses to advertisements and interview invitations, requires researchers on the spot.

Correspondence testing has also been used to measure sexual discrimination in the Australian labor market (Riach and Rich, 1987). Statistically significant discrimination against women was found in the most senior job tested—computer analyst programmer—and in the one manual occupation tested—gardener. Discrimination was encountered in both the private and public sectors of the economy. As U.S. equal employment opportunity policy for females is more vigorous and and of longer standing than Australian policy, a comparative study in the U.S. labor market would be most valuable in assessing policy performance.

Correspondence testing would obviously be applicable as a method for obtaining a direct measure of discrimination in any market where written contact was customary. This would include insurance, hotel accommodation, and new housing development. It could even be used to provide "smoking gun" evidence for enforcement agencies. *The Guardian* reported on November 9, 1989 that, in response to a complaint of discriminatory activity by a property developing company, the Commission for Racial Equality had conducted telephone tests. White and Asian applicants had telephoned for details about houses in a new development: only the white applicants received the details requested. Therefore, it is possible to foresee that correspondence testing will one day take its place alongside regression analysis as evidence acceptable in courts of law (Ashenfelter and Oaxaca, 1987).

Policy implications

Recent U.S. literature has related the incidence of discrimination to its likelihood of detection:

> Employers are more likely to indulge in discrimination when there is a low probability that such action will be detected . . . .Women lacking accurate statistical information are not sufficiently confident to conclude that they are being discriminated against. These women will tend not to report discrimination. [Barbezat and Hughes, 1990, pp. 284–285]

A point repeatedly noted in the correspondence studies cited above is that, given existing labor market practice, in all cases where discrimination was detected there would have been no way in which the rejected applicant could have been aware, let alone able to prove, that race or sex was the criterion for being refused an interview. Rejected applicants normally received a letter simply stating that their application was not being proceeded with, but on those occasions where an explanation was offered, employers demonstrated quite a capacity for imaginative untruths. For instance, in one British study, a white, married, secretarial applicant was invited to interview, while a Pakistani applicant received the following letter:-

> Thank you very much for your letter of the 9th February replying to our advertisement in the Manchester Evening News for a Secretary. Unfortunately, we have a policy in the office not to employ married women as we unfortunately, had a bad experience recently. [McIntosh and Smith, 1974, p. 33]

In our Australian study of sexual discrimination, on an occasion when both applicants had claimed to be graduates of four years standing, one applicant was invited to interview, while the other was declined because "due to an enforced salary ceiling we are looking for a recent graduate."

Therefore, to improve the capacity of labor market participants to detect discrimination, and to provide them with prima facie evidence for presentation to enforcement authorities, we have recommended that, in the letter of rejection, employers be required to specify the name of the person appointed and to provide a brief resumé of her or his qualifications and experience (Riach and Rich, 1987). Such information is generally available informally in the academic labor market: we are simply recommending that the practice be formalized and made universal. We believe that such a policy is the logical concomitant of equal opportunity legislation which puts the onus of initiating complaints on aggrieved labor market suppliers. Besides providing victims with prima facie evidence of their treatment, this disclosure requirement, by heightening the probability of detection, would be very likely to diminish discriminatory activity by employers. A complementary policy we have recommended is for equal opportunity agencies to have greater authority to initiate inquiries and, in particular, to conduct random audits of short-listing and appointment procedures (Riach and Rich, 1987).

On the basis of direct tests in the U.S. housing market, Yinger concluded that, despite the 1968 Civil Rights Act, racial discrimination in housing was still widespread. Consequently he called for stronger government action (Yinger, 1986, p. 892). One Australian and several British direct tests in the labor market have disclosed substantial and persistent racial discrimination, despite legislation proscribing it. Quite clearly, current policies and institutions in the three countries are not achieving their stated purpose. Therefore, if legislators are genuine in their concern for equality of opportunity, new initiatives must be explored. Our two policy proposals were intended as a contribution to the overdue debate about the strengthening of equal opportunity legislation. Regular monitoring of antidiscrimination measures is necessary, and we believe that correspondence testing could make an efficient and economical contribution here, despite the Ashenfelter/Oaxaca aversion to smoking guns.

REFERENCES

Ashenfelter, Orly, and Oaxaca, Ronald. "The Economics of Discrimination: Economists Enter the Courtroom." *American Economic Review*, May 1987, *77*, 321–325.

Barbezat, Debra A., and Hughes, James W. "Sex Discrimination in Labor Market: The Role of Statistical Evidence: Comment." *American Economic Review*, March 1990, *80*, 277–285.

Blau, Francine D., and Ferber, Marianne A. "Discrimination: Empirical Evidence from the United States." *American Economic Review*, May 87, *77*, 316–320.

Brown, Colin, and Gay, Pat. *Racial Discrimination: 17 Years after the Act*. London: Policy Studies Institute, 1985.

Chiplin, Brian, and Sloane, Peter J. *Sex Discrimination in the Labour Market*. London: MacMillan, 1976.

Daniel, W.W. *Racial Discrimination in England*. Harmondsworth: Penguin, 1968.

Dewald, William, G.; Thursby, Jerry G.; and Anderson, Richard, G. "Replication in Empirical Economics: *The Journal of Money, Credit and Banking* Project." *American Economic Review*, September 1986, *76*, 587–603.

Hubbock, Jim, and Carter, Simon. *Half a Chance?* London: Commission for Racial Equality, 1980.

Jowell, Roger, and Prescott-Clarke, Patricia. "Racial Discrimination and White-Collar Workers in Britain." *Race*, April 1970, *11*, 397–417.

Kuhn, Peter J. "Sex Discrimination in Labor Markets: The Role of Statistical Evidence: Reply." *American Economic Review*, March 1990, *80* 290–297.

McIntosh, Neil, and Smith, David J. *The Extent of Racial Discrimination*. London: Political and Economic Planning Broadsheet No. 547, 1974.

Oaxaca, Ronald. "Male-Female Wage Differentials in Urban Labor Markets." *International Economic Review*; October 1973, 14, 693–709.

Political and Economic Planning. *Report on Racial Discrimination*. London: Political and Economic Planning, 1967.

Riach, P.A., and Rich, J. "Testing for Sexual Discrimination in the Labour Market." *Australian Economic Papers*, December 1987, *26*, 165–178.

———. "Testing for Racial Discrimination in the Labour Market." *Cambridge Journal of Economics*, September 1991, *15*, 239–256.

Ward, Robin. "A Note on the Testing of Discrimination." *Race*, October 1969, *11*, 218–233.

Wienk, Ronald E., et al. *Measuring Discrimination in American Housing Markets: The Housing Market Practices Survey*. Washington, D.C.: Department of Housing and Urban Development, 1979.

Yinger, John. "Measuring Racial Discrimination with Fair Housing Audits: Caught in the Act." *American Economic Review*, December 1986, *76*, 881–893.

[20]

THE URBAN INSTITUTE AUDIT STUDIES: THEIR RESEARCH AND POLICY CONTEXT

Ronald B. Mincy

INTRODUCTION

In recent years concern about the poor labor market performance of young males has dominated public, academic, and policy-making discussions of social distress among inner-city blacks and Hispanics. When compared with young white males of the same age, young black and Hispanic males have higher unemployment rates, lower labor force participation rates, and lower mean wages. The decreasing labor market participation among black males is a new phenomenon. Without a firm foothold in the labor market, young black and Hispanic males are unable to form and support families. Many observers believe that this has contributed to rising rates of female-headed and welfare-dependent families in black and Hispanic communities.

Sociologists and other social scientists have revisited a few arguments to explain these labor market outcomes. The most frequently cited explanations emphasize changes in the structure of urban labor demand that have produced skills or spatial mismatches to the detriment of young black and Hispanic workers. Competition from women and recent immigrants is another argument advanced to explain poor labor market outcomes. Only rarely do theorists raise the possibility that labor market discrimination explains the poor labor market performance of black and Hispanic males.

Because discrimination has been such a neglected subject, the Urban Institute (UI) audit studies of hiring are potentially very important. The results of these studies—if they hold up to scrutiny—will remind observers that labor market discrimination still limits the employment opportunities of young males in some metropolitan areas where poverty and social distress remain high. The purpose of this chapter is to review these findings in light of (1) the literature on the role of labor markets in high rates of social distress among blacks and

Hispanics, (2) theoretical and empirical research on labor market discrimination, (3) findings from hiring audits in the United States and Great Britain, and (4) developments in public policies toward labor market discrimination.

LABOR MARKETS AND THE URBAN UNDERCLASS

Explanations of the social distress of inner-city minorities usually ignore the role that employment discrimination can play in reducing the employment opportunities of blacks and Hispanics. Instead, most observers emphasize changes in urban economics or changes in attitudes as factors. Beginning with *The Declining Significance of Race*, Wilson (1980) has drawn attention away from racially and ethnically centered explanations for inner-city dislocations, instead emphasizing the adverse effects of changes in the structure of urban economies (Wilson 1987). The most important structural change has been the decline in manufacturing establishments in urban areas and the replacement of manufacturing jobs by jobs in the high-skilled or low-skilled service sectors.

Other observers have also de-emphasized issues of race and ethnicity. Kasarda (1988) argues that the decline in employment opportunities for young black males in Chicago and, by extension, in other major metropolitan areas is the result of spatial mismatch. According to Kasarda, during the 1970s and 1980s opportunities for low-skilled employment moved from central-city areas with large concentrations of black and Hispanic residents to the suburbs, where few blacks and Hispanics live. Low-skilled employment thus became inaccessible to inner-city residents. Ellwood (1986) argues that "race not space" explains the reduction in employment opportunities, although he does not discuss the implications of continued discrimination for public policy. More conservative writers, such as Meade (1986), have explicitly pronounced that discrimination is no longer a barrier to employment opportunities for blacks and Hispanics because of successful civil rights enforcement.

By turning attention away from issues of race and ethnicity these authors hope to encourage policymakers to shift their focus. Old policies tried to correct the human capital deficiencies of individual workers or the misdeeds of individual employers. New policies, according to these authors, should try to adjust for macro-structural changes in the economy or for changes in attitudes about the social obligations of citizens. Even if these larger forces could account for some growth in poverty and dislocations among inner-city blacks and Hispanics, the effect of the change in focus has been that discrimination has disappeared from view.

PREVIOUS STUDIES

Because of the predictions of economic theory, empirical work by economists has emphasized wage discrimination and neglected hiring discrimination. Economists have focused on wage discrimination because the earliest theories of discrimination rested on assumptions about employer preferences for minority and majority workers. In these theories, only wage discrimination could account for hiring discrimination (Cain 1986).

Hiring discrimination can result because employers, workers, or customers prefer majority workers. If some employers in a labor market practice hiring discrimination to indulge their own preferences for majority workers, wage and hiring discrimination results. Employers with such preferences hire only majority workers and, because they are in greater demand, pay them higher wages than nondiscriminating employers pay minority workers. If some employers practice hiring discrimination to indulge worker or customer preferences, however, there should be no wage discrimination. In other words, data on hiring discrimination are consistent with employer, worker, or customer discrimination, but data on wage discrimination reveal that employer preferences dominate.

Another branch of the economic theory of discrimination also focuses on wages. In these statistical theories, employers pay different wages to minority workers because race and ethnicity are inexpensive ways to predict the productivity of workers. If employers have reason to believe that majority workers are more productive than minority workers, then color or accent provides an inexpensive signal of a worker's productivity. To offset the expected lower productivity of minority workers, employers offer all minority job applicants lower wages, even if particular minority applicants may be as productive as the average majority applicant. In low-wage labor markets, such wage discrimination can result in hiring discrimination when the wage offer to minority workers falls below the legal minimum, so that employers cannot legally hire them.

Besides economists' studies of wage discrimination, a few new studies by other social scientists simply document the extent of hiring discrimination. The most important studies for comparision are previous audit studies that focus on discrimination in entry-level employment, relying for data on personal contacts between auditors and employers. (The studies of discrimination in higher-level positions get much of their data from employer responses to cover letters and resumes, while the hiring process for entry-level jobs rarely uses cover letters and resumes.)

McIntosh and Smith (1974) tested for discrimination against Greek, Indian, Pakistani, and West Indian immigrants applying for unskilled and semiskilled jobs in Britain. The authors found substantial discrimination against nonwhite immigrants and much less discrimination against white (Greek) immigrants. This finding suggested that British employers discriminated on the basis of both color and immigrant status. The UI studies examined both kinds of discrimination by U.S. employers.

Two features of the McIntosh and Smith study make it difficult to generalize from their results. First, they did not rely on a random sample of employers. Instead, they sent auditors to make "cold contacts" with any employer in two areas of British cities with high concentrations of low-skilled manufacturing employment. An unknown number of these employers lacked an opportunity to discriminate because they lacked vacancies. Further, the results could not be generalized beyond the two areas studied or beyond manufacturing employers.

A second troubling feature of the McIntosh and Smith audits was their reliance on professional actors who were not necessarily matched to form visually comparable teams. Instead, in one city the researchers matched one white actor with eight immigrant actors (two West Indians, two Pakistanis, two Indians, and two Greeks) to form eight audit teams. In another city, the authors matched two white actors with the same group of immigrants. The researchers gave both immigrant and nonimmigrant auditors biographies mentioning previous experience in unskilled jobs. Still, there were many idiosyncratic differences between the members of the audit teams that could have accounted for differential treatment.

Culp and Dunson (1986) conducted the only previous and closely related study of entry-level employment discrimination by U.S. employers. They relied on a nonrandom sample of 21 graduating, but non-college-bound, male high school seniors. Many blacks wanted to participate in the study, partly because they had not found full-time jobs by the summer after they graduated. By contrast, few whites wanted to participate, and some who began the study failed to complete the audit phase because they later found full-time employment.

At best, the Culp and Dunson study hints at what an actual audit might find. The researchers did not pair the students or give them falsified biographies to convince prospective employers that the students were comparable on productivity characteristics. And because of attrition in the sample, the researchers were unable to have the students apply for vacancies with the same employers. Instead, Culp and Dunson first examined the employment-relevant characteristics of their entire sample of seniors. Then they looked at how large employers in the same county treated the subsample of students who completed the study. But because these students made cold contacts rather than responding to known vacancies, once again, an unknown number of contacted employers lacked an opportunity to discriminate.

Culp and Dunson presumed that employers would find that their sample of black and white seniors had similar employment-relevant characteristics. Specifically, all the students had limited previous employment experience and few references. Four black students and one white student completed a survey questionnaire about their treatment by 45 contacted employers.

The four blacks reported less favorable treatment by employers, who were less likely to treat them courteously (i.e., to call them "Mr.," offer them a seat, shake their hand, engage them in a conversation, and so on). Besides these aspects of employer behavior—which are important because they can discourage applicants—there were at least two clear signs of discrimination: Employers were less likely to tell the black applicants about employment prospects, and they quoted black applicants lower wages. While there was evidence that differential treatment varied by industry, none of the results were statistically significant.

URBAN INSTITUTE AUDIT STUDIES

The UI audits (Cross et al. 1990; Turner et al. 1991) were executed with great care and were improvements over previous studies in three important respects. The earlier studies were hampered by incomplete matching of white and nonwhite auditors, nonrandom samples of employers, and uncertainties about the availability of vacancies.

While there had been a previous study of employment discrimination against blacks in the United States, until the UI audits there had been no study of employment discrimination against Hispanics.

The UI research teams chose, matched, and trained auditors carefully. All the auditors were college students who had applied for jobs as study participants. First, the research staff evaluated each applicant and eliminated applicants they felt were too zealous, had inadequate motivation, or were difficult to match. Second, the staff matched the successful black or Hispanic applicants with successful white or Anglo applicants of similar height, weight, and general appearance. Third, outside project consultants reevaluated audit teams, making a few necessary changes. Once the research staff had finalized the audit teams, who consisted of one Anglo and one Hispanic (or one white and one black) auditor, auditors worked with the same team member in the field.

These and other procedures contributed to high-quality audits. The auditors applied for jobs requiring no more than a high school education, so they were all overqualified. Auditors had falsified, but believable, biographies to support the illusion of comparability on productivity characteristics. Employers thus saw credible applicants, and, as far as possible, the only basis for choosing one team member over another was race and ethnicity.

Employer selection and auditor training emphasized standardization. The researchers selected employers from a random sample of advertisements for entry-level jobs in the Sunday editions of major metropolitan newspapers, which resulted in some variance in employer characteristics, such as size and industry. Auditor teams contacted employers within three days. By relying on advertised vacancies instead of cold contacts, the studies had fewer trials in which there was no opportunity to discriminate, though employers had sometimes filled vacancies before the initial auditor call.

Each audit followed a standard procedure, beginning with a phone call to find out if the advertised vacancy was still available. White (or Anglo) and black (or Hispanic) auditors alternated making the first call. If permitted, the auditor made a personal visit to the employer to obtain and complete an application and request a personal interview. If the employer granted the interview, the auditor presented his qualifications using the interview skills he learned during training sessions. After the interview, the auditor called the employer to learn of the employer's decision. If offered a job, the auditor declined within a few hours. At every stage of this process, the auditor completed standardized forms detailing the employer's response in various requests and some indications of the way the employer had treated the auditor. Finally, auditors received a flat salary, which removed any incentive for them to discover discrimination where there was none.

Brief Review of Findings

The UI audit studies examined the outcomes of young black, Hispanic ("foreign looking and foreign sounding"), and Anglo (or white) men seeking entry-level employment. Audits involving Hispanic and Anglo applicants took place in Chicago and San Diego. Audits involving black and white applicants took place in Chicago and Washington, D.C.

The two sets of audits used a common three-stage model of the effect of hiring discrimination on employment of young black and Hispanic men (figure 4.1). In this model, young men seek entry-level employment by reviewing advertisements in major metropolitan area newspapers. After identifying vacancies for which they qualify, potential applicants call to find out whether vacancies are still available and whether they can fill out an application.[1] Opportunities for unfavorable treatment begin at this point and proceed through two further stages. First, if the employer permits only one applicant to fill out an application, that applicant is counted as having received favorable treatment at the application stage. Second, if the employer permits both auditors to complete applications but grants an interview to only one applicant, that applicant is counted as having received favorable treatment at the interview stage. Third, the employer interviews both applicants but makes only one applicant an offer, that applicant is counted as having received favorable treatment at the offer stage.

The Hispanic/Anglo and black/white audits used somewhat different questions about job-seeking outcomes. The Hispanic/Anglo audits were aimed at finding out (1) whether Anglo applicants progressed further through the hiring process than did Hispanic applicants and (2) whether Anglo and Hispanic applicants had different numbers of completed applications, interviews, and job offers. Thus the study included the possibility of reverse discrimination.

Besides these two outcomes, the black/white audits also were aimed at finding out whether black and white auditors experienced differential treatment at various stages in the hiring process. For example, black applicants may have been required to wait longer for interviews, or may have met with clerical staff instead of with managers who would be making hiring decisions. Even if employers accepted appli-

Figure 4.1 DIFFERENTIAL OUTCOMES AND DIFFERENTIAL TREATMENT IN THE HIRING PROCESS

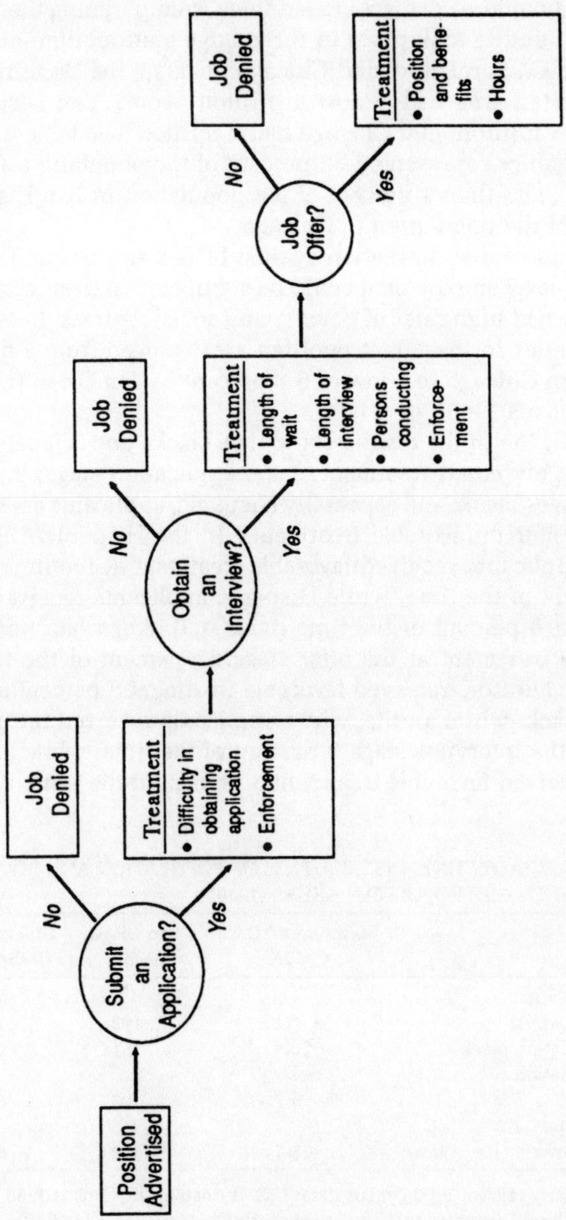

Source: Turner et al. 1991.

cations from black applicants and interviewed them, such differential treatment could have discouraged them from pursuing the job further.

The UI audits took place in three large metropolitan areas: Washington, D.C., San Diego, and Chicago. In 1990, the Washington, D.C., metropolitan area had almost 4 million people, San Diego had just under 2½ million, and Chicago had 7 million (see table 4.1).[2] Blacks and Hispanics represented 32 percent of the population in Washington, D.C., less than 1 percent of the population in San Diego, and 31 percent of the population in Chicago.

Findings of discrimination against blacks and Hispanics applying for entry-level employment could be significant in these cities because each city had high rates of poverty and social distress. In 1980, family poverty rates in these metropolitan areas ranged from a high of 16.8 percent in Chicago to a low of 9.2 percent in San Diego (U.S. Bureau of the Census 1988).

Overall, the audit results show that blacks and Hispanics experience roughly equal treatment at the application stage; but at subsequent stages black, and especially Hispanic, applicants are more likely to encounter unfavorable treatment.[3] In the Hispanic/Anglo audits, Anglo applicants received favorable treatment at the interview stage 22 percent of the time, while Hispanic applicants received favorable treatment 6 percent of the time (table 4.3). Anglo auditors received favorable treatment at the offer stage 22 percent of the time, while Hispanic auditors received favorable treatment 8 percent of the time. In the black–white audits, white applicants received favorable treatment at the interview stage 9 percent of the time, while black applicants received favorable treatment 3 percent of the time. White audi-

Table 4.1 RACIAL/ETHNIC DISTRIBUTION OF POPULATION AND POVERTY FOR FOUR METROPOLITAN AREAS (1980)

Measure	Washington, D.C., CMSA	San Diego SMSA	Chicago CMSA[a]	Denver CMSA
Total population (in thousands)	3,924	2,498	7,261	1,848
% of population black	26.6	0.1	19.6	0.1
% of population Hispanic[b]	5.7	0.2	11.5	0.1
% of families below poverty line, 1979	15.1	9.2	16.8	10.3

Sources: Early release 1990 census data; U.S. Bureau of the Census 1988.
[a]Includes the six counties that were part of the Chicago SMSA in 1980.
[b]Persons of Hispanic origin can be of any race.

Table 4.2 STAGE AT WHICH UNFAVORABLE TREATMENT OCCURRED

Stage	Black/white audit (%)	Hispanic/Anglo audit (%)
Application		
Anglo or white favored	2	6
Black favored	0	—
Hispanic favored	—	2
Interview		
Anglo or white favored	9	22
Black favored	3	—
Hispanic favored	—	6
Job offer		
Anglo or white favored	8	22
Black favored	4	—
Hispanic favored	—	8

Sources: Cross et al. 1990; Turner et al. 1991.

tors received favorable treatment at the offer stage 8 percent of the time, while black auditors received favorable treatment 4 percent of the time.

These results are revealing beyond what they tell us about discrimination. Consider what the results meant to the sample of young men who were seeking employment. For the UI researchers, the only valid audits were those in which employers allowed at least one auditor to complete an application. In some cases employers allowed neither auditor to complete one, but both kinds of audits convey information about the difficulty these young men experienced finding jobs.

Counting both kinds of audits, only about half of the employers who advertised vacancies allowed both auditors to complete an application. Thus even without any discrimination on the part of employers, jobs are scarce. Further, black and Hispanic applicants could expect to be offered a job at most 5 percent of the time they filled out applications. In the face of these results, the low and falling parts of labor force participation of black and Hispanic men should not surprise observers.

Unfavorable treatment experienced by blacks and Hispanics varied across metropolitan areas. Black auditors in Washington, D.C., experienced more unfavorable treatment than did black auditors in Chicago, and Hispanic auditors in Chicago experienced more unfavorable treatment than did Hispanic auditors in San Diego.

Within metropolitan areas, there also were variations by occupation and industry. For example, Hispanic auditors in Chicago experienced more unfavorable treatment in applying for jobs in management and service occupations and in the manufacturing and construction industries. Black auditors in Washington, D.C., experienced more unfavorable treatment in applying for jobs in service industries and in white-collar or sales occupations. These findings are consistent with hypotheses that discrimination is more likely to occur in higher-paying or higher-status jobs and in jobs with substantial amounts of customer contact. Finally, the black–white audits showed that unfavorable treatment of black applicants occurred in subtle ways. For example, employers steered black applicants to less favorable jobs (with lower wages, less desirable hours, or lower status), made negative comments to them about the job, made them wait longer for interviews, or interviewed them for shorter periods of time.[4]

DENVER AUDIT STUDY

James and DelCastillo (1991) recently completed an audit study of hiring discrimination in the Denver metropolitan area. Like the UI studies, this study focused on young black and Hispanic men who applied for entry-level employment, using high-quality audits. The researchers carefully selected, trained, and matched auditors and used a random sample of employers who had advertised vacancies in a major metropolitan newspaper. Unlike the UI studies, the Denver study found almost no evidence of discrimination. The only evidence of discrimination was that large employers (with 15 or more employees) never favored the black applicant. Several methodological and substantive issues could account for differences in the results of these studies.

First, auditor selection, training, matching, and compensation differed in ways that make comparisons of the two groups of audits difficult. The most important difference was the characteristics of the Hispanic auditors. The UI Hispanic/Anglo audits used "foreign-looking and foreign-sounding" Hispanics. The Denver audits had no such requirements.[5] Recent amendments to the Immigration Reform and Control Act provide for stiffer sanctions against employers who hire undocumented aliens. A possible and perverse side effect of these sanctions is discrimination against persons who appear to be illegal immigrants because of their Hispanic appearance or accent. The U.S. General Accounting Office commissioned the UI studies to determine the extent of such discrimination, but because effects of changes in immigration law were not under examination in the Denver audits, those audits used native-born Hispanics who did not necessarily have Hispanic accents or appear Hispanic.

Other methodological differences could also account for the different results. For example, the Denver study recruited Anglo and white auditors from college campuses but contacted local civil rights agencies to recruit black and Hispanic auditors, who may therefore have been more aggressive than the white and Anglo auditors in the job search process. In particular, black and Hispanic auditors made more post-interview follow-up calls than did white or Anglo auditors, though orientation and training should have eliminated any such differences.

Finally, the Denver and UI studies paid auditors differently. Denver auditors received a bonus when at least one member of the team completed an application. They received another bonus when at least one member completed an interview and a third bonus when at least one member got a job offer. James and DelCastillo provided these bonuses so that the auditors would have monetary incentives similar to the incentives real job searchers have. Whether these incentives differentially affected team members is unclear because black and Hispanic auditors made more follow-up calls. By contrast, UI auditors received a flat salary, which removed any incentive to find discrimination but also removed the monetary incentive real job seekers have.

These and other aspects of the Denver and UI studies create arguable biases that hamper comparisons between the Denver and UI results.[6] The more important point, however, is that the Denver and UI studies used higher-quality audits than did previous audit studies. Therefore, while comparisons across these studies are risky, each presents reliable evidence of discrimination in the respective labor markets.

Assuming the Denver results are reliable, what could account for the absence of any findings of discrimination in Denver? The authors emphasize two factors. First, blacks in Denver made up a smaller fraction of the metropolitan area population than did blacks in the UI audit cities (Chicago and Washington, D.C.). Perhaps low-skilled white and Anglo workers in Denver felt less threatened by blacks and, therefore, put less pressure on Denver employers to discriminate against them.

Second, blacks and Hispanics in Denver have higher levels of educational attainment on average than do minorities in Chicago and Washington, D.C. Denver employers would thus have historically observed less disparity in the educational attainment of entry-level minority and nonminority workers, which could have contributed to their lower levels of statistical discrimination against minority workers. Unfortunately, the authors provide no evidence for this theory, and data for 1980—on the proportions of blacks and Hispanics who completed high school and college in the respective cities—provide very weak support (table 4.3)

IMPLICATIONS FOR POLICY AND RESEARCH

The UI studies documented significant hiring discrimination against young black and Hispanic men in three metropolitan areas where indicators of poverty and social distress are high. A high-quality audit of employers in Denver revealed almost no discrimination. Since these audits represented improvements over the previous research, their results are the most reliable evidence available of the extent of discrimination. This evidence has important implications for future research and policy, especially antidiscrimination policy.

Labor Market Performance

The most obvious implication is as a reminder to the public, policymakers, and researchers that discrimination constrains the already limited employment opportunities of black and Hispanic males in some metropolitan areas. To improve the poor labor market performance of these men, policies must pay more attention to the demand for their labor. Policymakers can improve the labor market performance of young black and Hispanic men by using three strategies: (1) reducing discrimination against them, (2) increasing their human capital, and (3) increasing the demand for their labor, for example,

Table 4.3 PERCENTAGE OF BLACKS AND HISPANICS IN FOUR SMSAs COMPLETING HIGH SCHOOL AND COLLEGE (1980)

	Blacks		Hispanics	
SMSA	4 years of high school	4 years of college	4 years of high school	4 years of college
Chicago	29.6	8.4	20.1	6.2
Washington, D.C.	32.8	14.7	27.2	27.4
Denver	34.5	14.2	29.4	8.4
San Diego	35.3	11.1	25.6	7.8

Source: Census tracts, 1980 Census of Population and Housing, U.S. Bureau of the Census, PHC80-2 series.

through public service employment. The hiring audit data suggest that the third strategy should receive top priority.

Many observers blame supply-side factors for the low labor force participation rates of young Hispanic and, especially, black males. For example, Meade (1986) argues that these young males have high reservation wages and poor human capital. The employment audit results provide significant evidence against this interperetation because the supply-side characteristics of minority and nonminority workers are identical.

The demand side is responsible for the differential results. That is, the audits took place in labor markets with few opportunities, even for young men willing to work at prevailing wages. Only half the employers who advertised vacancies allowed both auditors to complete an application. Despite nearly 30 years of forceful antidiscrimination policies, since the Civil Rights Act of 1964, white and Anglo men were two to three times more likely to get a job offer in the UI audits than were equally overqualified black or Hispanic men. This meant that blacks and Hispanics could expect to get a job offer for at most 5 percent of the unfilled vacancies they found. Given these odds, observers should not be surprised that labor force participation rates of these men are low and falling.

Antidiscrimination Policies

State and federal budget crises may not permit new expenditures to increase the demand for young black and Hispanic men. Still, policymakers should guarantee that the opportunities created by the market are equally available to all workers. Policymakers now use widely or selectively targeted sanctions to achieve this goal. Widely targeted sanctions affect the decisions of all employers in a labor or product market simultaneously; selectively targeted sanctions affect the decisions of those employers who have direct contact with enforcement agencies.

Current Policies for Targeting Sanctions

The most important vehicle for widely targeted sanctions is Executive Order No. 11246, as amended by Executive Order No. 11375 and administered by the Office of Federal Contract Compliance Programs (OFCCP). These orders impose a basic obligation on federal contractors not to discriminate, require them to take affirmative action to employ minorities and women, and require them to get similar commitments from their subcontractors (Amaker 1988). Because the orders affect all employers who bid on federal construction contracts, the sanctions for violations are widely targeted. These sanctions include back-pay orders, retroactive seniority requirements, cancellation or suspension of existing contracts, and debarment from bids on future government contracts.

The major vehicle for selectively targeted sanctions is Title VII of the Civil Rights Act, which allows individuals to sue employers for employment discrimination. The act also gives the Equal Employment Opportunity Commission (EEOC) authority to impose sanctions for discrimination by private employers and federal agencies in administrative or judicial proceedings. Historically, the EEOC has used this authority to establish an arsenal of broad legal principles which private citizens have used to win multimillion-dollar judgments against discriminating employers (Leonard 1990). Title VII also gives the Justice Department responsibility to bring suits against state and local government units charged with employment discrimination.

Affirmative action involves weak and unstable sanctions. Its weakness derives from its being targeted only against government contractors; its instability derives from its reliance on enforcement by federal agencies whose commitment is subject to swings in political will.

The employment audit data suggest that affirmative action requirements imposed on government contractors have little potential to reduce employment discrimination against young black and Hispanic males. Indeed, 85 percent or more of the audited employers were in retail trades and service industries, which have few federal government contractors (Smith and Welch 1984). So there is no reason to expect that policymakers can increase their impact on the hiring practices of employers who fill entry-level positions by continuing to widely target government contractors. Further, in a series of studies reviewed by Leonard (1990), economists have shown that this type of antidiscrimination program has had only modest effects on black employment.

From 1964 until 1981, enforcement of antidiscrimination policies by the EEOC, the OFCCP, and the Justice Department established new legal precedents for the fight against discrimination. But subsequent actions by the same federal agencies have weakened antidiscrimination policies considerably. Many observers who bemoan this reversal fail to realize that it was inevitable. The most effective way to promote or change policy is through leadership and control of federal agency purse strings. Thus, in the 1980s, the heads of these federal agencies challenged the principles established by their predecessors, including (1) the use of timetables and numerical goals in the affirmative action plans of federal contractors and (2) race-conscious hiring plans in judgments and conciliation agreements involving state and local government bodies found guilty of past discrimination. Further, the EEOC and the Justice Department reduced the number of complaints of discrimination by private employers settled by administrative and judicial law.

Before 1989, selectively targeted sanctions, brought through private litigation under Title VII, were the most effective antidiscrimination strategy (Leonard 1990). But recent Supreme Court decisions, especially *Wards Cove Packing Co. v. Atonio*, 490 U.S. 642 (1989), weakened selective sanctions. Because of this decision, plantiffs must go beyond showing that employment practices result in numerical imbalances. They must identify the practices specifically and show that they are not a business necessity. Obviously, hiring audits can provide powerful documentation for such efforts.

Using Hiring Audits to Target Sanctions

As discussed earlier, widely targeted sanctions have limitations, and selective sanctions impose high costs on plantiffs, who must pay for legal representation and wait months for a complaint to be adjudicated in the courts. While many have complained about selective targeting, it may be the most effective strategy for enforcement when there is no systematic pattern to the employment discrimination (Wallace 1973). When there are patterns, however, policymakers can target sanctions to affect a wide range of employers.

The earlier discussion of the economic theory of discrimination suggests that patterns of discrimination vary by industry. Responding to competitive market pressures, employers discriminate to indulge worker or customer preferences. If they don't discriminate against minorities, they must pay their workers higher wages or lose customers to other firms that employ only majority workers. Thus, markets in which worker and customer preferences dominate decisions about hiring are appropriate markets for widely targeted sanctions.

One such appropriate market is the construction industry, where employers sometimes discriminate against minorities to indulge their workers. Construction worker preferences for nonminority co-workers are a simple extension of nepotism, which has operated in unionized construction for decades. By requiring all construction contractors with federal contracts (and their subcontractors) not to discriminate, policymakers make it easier for employers to resist the discriminatory demands of their workers. This antidiscrimination policy also extends to unions, which have been subjected to scrutiny by the EEOC (Wallace 1973).

Construction is not the only product market where policymakers should try to reduce competitive pressures on employers to discriminate in hiring. Two other obvious candidates for widely targeted sanctions are the retail trade and service industries in highly segregated areas. These industries have many positions with high customer contact and employ large numbers of entry-level workers. If the economic theory is correct and customers in highly segregated areas are more likely to prefer service by majority workers, hiring discrimination in these industries will be widespread.

Widely targeted sanctions in these industries could work in two ways. Policymakers could audit every retail or service employer in a highly segregated area (or every employer with an advertised vacancy) and sanction discriminating employers. Alternatively, policymakers could audit a random sample of retail and service employers. If the audits uncovered employers who discriminate, policymakers could affect the hiring decisions of nonsampled employers through publicity—for example, by letting the public know, through journalists, that an "ongoing program" of random audits in the area was the source of the evidence used to bring suit against the discriminating employers. Such publicity would raise the expected cost of discrimination to all retail and service employers in the area.

The evidence from the audit studies also suggests that discrimination in entry-level employment varies from one metropolitan area to another. This kind of evidence could help policymakers allocate scarce enforcement resources more effectively. For example, the audits suggest that because blacks in Chicago and Washington, D.C., suffer more from discrimination than do blacks in Denver, the scope of any equal opportunity enforcement effort should be smaller in Denver.

Evidence gathered by hiring audits also could strengthen selective sanctions. Courts have already ruled that audit testers in the housing discrimination area have standing to bring suits against housing owners who discriminate. Similar standing could be granted in the hiring discrimination area. Thus, audits could be used to show whether specific hiring practices systematically favor majority applicants. These practices include, for example, (1) differential screening of minority and nonminority applicants by accepting fewer applications from minorities, denying them personal interviews, or conducting shorter interviews with them; and (2) supplying less favorable information to black or Hispanic applicants about wages or promotion opportunities.

Suggestions for Future Research

While the UI audits provide valuable information for researchers and policymakers, two features need adjustment in future work. First, the audits gathered and reported very little information on wages and other terms or conditions of employment. This information is valuable for research and for use as evidence in selective sanctions. Economists need information about wage offers (and other terms and conditions of employment) to help determine whether employer, worker, or customer preference drives hiring discrimination. This information also can help determine whether antidiscrimination policies should be targeted widely or selectively.

Litigants need such information to provide unambiguous evidence of discrimination. Subjective evaluation of candidates is an arguably valid reason for not accepting an application from a non-Anglo male, not granting an interview, or cutting an interview short. But there is no valid reason for quoting Anglo and non-Anglo applicants different wages, hours, or working conditions for the same job. Audits seeking to gather such information would require larger samples because many employers exclude black and Hispanic applicants before they have a chance to ask about wages and other conditions of employment.

Second, future research should try to reconcile the results of the hiring audits in Denver and in the UI cities. There were methodological differences between these studies, but there also was a major substantive difference. Blacks and Hispanics represent small fractions of the population in Denver, but they represent large fractions of the population in the UI cities. Theory predicts that there should be less discrimination in cities like Denver. A more reliable test of this hypothesis could be undertaken using another city where minorities represent a small fraction of the population, using the UI methodology. Unfortunately, a test of discrimination against "foreign-looking and foreign-sounding" Hispanics in a city with few Hispanics is not feasible because immigrants locate in areas where there is an established immigrant community.

Finally, the UI audits focused on male applicants—for good reasons—but many observers would like to see the results of employment audits involving women. The number of critical variations multiplies quickly. Some observers are most concerned about the economic status of women; they want to know whether employers favor men over women for entry-level jobs in traditionally male occupations. Other observers want to know whether employers pay men and women differently for comparable jobs. Answering that question would shift the focus away from hiring decisions and require more data on wages for comparable jobs.

Observers concerned about the economic status of blacks and Hispanics are also interested in questions that audits involving women could answer. For example, do employers favor women over men, especially minority men, for jobs in industries with high customer contact? The shift in urban employment from manufacturing to service and low-wage retail industries gives this question more importance. Still other observers want to know whether employers favor white or Anglo women over black or Hispanic women in certain occupations. The steadily increasing number of female-headed families in the black and Hispanic communities adds importance to this question. Setting priorities among these variations will be a difficult task.

The Role of Audits

Poverty and social distress among blacks and Hispanics have increased dramatically in the past two decades. Explanations for these changes emphasize the poor labor market performance of young men and rarely consider the role of employment discrimination. The Urban Institute hiring audits show that young black and Hispanic males experience substantial discrimination when they apply for entry-level employment. But discrimination does not exist everywhere. The recent audit of employers in the Denver metropolitan area found almost no evidence of discrimination.

These studies are important because they remind observers that employment opportunities are scarce for young male workers. Overqualified young men, willing to work for prevailing wages, found few vacancies in the four major metropolitan areas studied. Thus, increasing the demand for the skills of young male workers is the best way to improve the labor market performance of young black and Hispanic men. Besides poor demand for their labor, young black and Hispanic men face substantial discrimination in metropolitan areas where they are no longer racial and ethnic minorities. After 30 years of hotly debated antidiscrimination policy, this is an intolerable situation.

Antidiscrimination policies have been ineffective for these young men, either because they rely on costly, selective sanctions that few of them can afford or because they rely on sanctions widely targeted at employers who hire few young men.

The audit results suggest ways of making selectively and widely targeted sanctions more effective. Under rules forthcoming from recent Supreme Court decisions, hiring audits can provide the evidence plaintiffs need to show how specific hiring practices systematically favor majority applicants. But the direction of antidiscrimination policy may make it harder for policymakers to use this evidence. Since 1981, federal agencies charged with enforcing antidiscrimination laws have tried to restrict remedies for discrimination to actual victims. If their effort continues, only audits involving real job applicants will be able to be used to sanction discriminating employers. Nevertheless, policymakers can use publicized hiring audits and the threat of sanctions to increase the costs of discrimination for all employers serving customers in one product market, thus enabling these employers to resist customer demands for hiring discrimination.

Notes

This chapter is a product of the Underclass Research Project. I thank Susan Wiener for her research assistance.

1. The UI research teams treated the initial telephone calls differently. The Hispanic auditors had accents so that employers could determine ethnicity from the initial telephone contact. Therefore, the Hispanic–Anglo research team counted an audit valid if, on the basis of the initial telephone call, employers refused to allow the Hispanic auditor to obtain and complete an application but allowed the Anglo auditor to do so. The black–white research team did not assume that employers could identify a black accent over the telephone. Therefore, this research team invalidated audits in which the employer screened out one auditor on the basis of the initial telephone call. Instead, the first opportunity for discrimination (i.e., for a valid audit) occurred when employers allowed both auditors to obtain applications.

2. The data in table 4.1 reflect the six Chicago counties that were in the Chicago SMSA in 1980. The other consolidated metropolitan areas in the table had the same (or virtually the same) counties in 1980 SMSAs and 1990 consolidated CMSAs.

3. Discrimination is only one of the reasons that employers deny job offers to black and Hispanic job seekers. Therefore, at best, the UI studies document whether whites and Anglos were systematically favored over black and Hispanic applicants. For this reason, the studies report findings in terms of the number or percentage of audits in which employers treated particular types of auditors unfavorably. I follow this language. The findings suggest discrimination if differences in unfavorable treatment between two members of a team of auditors are statistically significant.

4. Additional findings from the employment audits is presented in the appendix.

5. The Hispanic auditors had dark hair and dark complexions, but did not necessarily have accents.

6. A lengthy correspondence between the authors of the UI and Denver studies is available for the interested reader.

References

Amaker, Norman C. 1988. *Civil Rights and the Reagan Administration*. Washington, D.C.: Urban Institute Press.

Cain, Glen G. 1986. "The Economic Analysis of Labor Market Discrimination: A Survey." In *The Handbook of Labor Economics, Volume I*, edited by O. Ashenfelter and R. Layards. Netherlands: Elsevier Science Publishers B.V.

Culp, Jerome, and Bruce H. Dunson. 1986. "Brothers of a Different Color: A Preliminary Look at Employer Treatment of White and Black Youth." In *The Black Youth Employment Crisis*, edited by R. Freeman and H. Holzer. Chicago: University of Chicago Press.

Cross, Harry, Genevieve Kenney, Jane Mell, and Wendy Zimmerman. 1990. *Employer Hiring Practices: Differential Treatment Of Hispanic and Anglo Job Seekers*. Washington, D.C.: Urban Institute Press.

Ellwood, David. 1986. "The Spatial Mismatch Hypothesis: Are There Teenage Jobs Missing in the Ghetto?" In *The Black Youth Employment Crisis*, edited by R. Freeman and H. Holzer. Chicago: University of Chicago Press.

James, Franklin J., and Steve W. DelCastillo. 1991. "Measuring Job Discrimination by Private Employers Against Young Black and Hispanic Males Seeking Entry Level Work in the Denver Metropolitan Area." Unpublished Report. Denver: University of Colorado.

Kasarda, John D. 1988. "Jobs, Migration, and Emerging Urban Mismatches." In *Urban Change and Poverty*, edited by Michael G. H. McGeary and Laurence E. Lynn, Jr. Washington, D.C.: National Academy Press.

Leonard, Jonathan S. 1990. "The Impact of Affirmative Action Regulation and Equal Employment Law on Black Employment." *Journal of Economic Perspectives*, 4 (fall): 47–63.

McIntosh, Neil, and David J. Smith. 1974. *The Extent of Racial Discrimination*, XL, Broadsheet No. 547. London: PEP, The Social Science Institute.

Meade, Lawrence M. 1986. *Beyond Entitlement: The Social Obligations of Citizenship*. New York: Free Press.

Ricketts, Erol, and Isabel Sawhill. 1988. "Defining and Measuring the Underclass." *Journal of Policy Analysis and Management*, 7 (2): 316–25.

Smith, James P., and Finish Welch. 1984. "Affirmative Action and Labor Markets." *Journal of Labor Economics*, 2 (2): 269–301.

Turner, Margery A., Michael Fix, and Raymond Struyk. 1991. *Opportunities Denied, Opportunities Diminished: Racial Discrimination in Hiring*. UI Report 81–9. Washington, D.C.: Urban Institute Press.

U.S. Bureau of the Census. 1988. *County and City Data Book, 1988*. Washington, D.C.: U.S. Government Printing Office.

Wallace, Phyllis A. 1973. "Employment Discrimination: Some Policy Considerations." In *Discrimination in Labor Markets*, edited by Orley

Ashenfelter and Albert Rees. Princeton, N.J.: Princeton University Press.

Wilson, William Julius. 1987. *The Truly Disadvantaged*. Chicago: University of Chicago Press.

———. 1980. *The Declining Significance of Race: Blacks and Changing American Institutions*. Chicago: University of Chicago Press.

[21]

AN OVERVIEW OF AUDITING FOR DISCRIMINATION

Michael Fix, George C. Galster, and Raymond J. Struyk

The concept of auditing for discrimination is straightforward. Two individuals (auditors or testers) are matched for all relevant personal characteristics other than the one that is presumed to lead to discrimination, e.g., race, ethnicity, gender. They then apply for a job, a housing unit, or a mortgage, or begin to negotiate for a good or service. The results they achieve and the treatment they receive in the transaction are closely observed, documented, and analyzed to determine if the outcomes reveal patterns of differential treatment on the basis of the trait studied and/or protected by antidiscrimination laws. The technique of auditing for discrimination was first broadly used in the area of housing (Wienk et al. 1979) and has subsequently been adapted at least experimentally to activities such as seeking employment (Cross 1990; Turner, Fix, and Struyk 1991), applying for a mortgage (Center for Community Change 1989), seeking home owner's insurance (Squires and Velez 1988), negotiating the price of a car (Ayres 1991), seeking taxi services (Ridley 1989) and applying for membership in a health club. Auditing is used for both research and enforcement. When used in the enforcement context it is typically referred to as testing rather than auditing. Research auditing is designed to measure the extent of discrimination in a market, requiring a large number of tests in order to obtain statistical reliability for the findings. Studies of employment discrimination, for example, typically require two hundred or more tests within a metropolitan area to achieve acceptable statistical reliability for differences in treatment of minority and majority auditors. Moreover, the sample of "opportunities" to be audited must be carefully drawn. This involves both defining the sampling frame with precision, i.e., what subset of all opportunities can be or will be included, and randomly selecting the opportunities for testing to insure a representative sample.

Enforcement auditing (testing) in contrast, is designed to develop evidence of discrimination against an individual or firm for use in legal proceedings. In this instance the firm is selected on the basis of a formal complaint or other reason to suspect discriminatory behavior. A single carefully executed test may be sufficient, although the results of several tests are typically presented as evidence. The results of an audit study for a metropolitan area can help establish the context in which the results of individual tests are presented, and can help target individual audits (by neighborhood or industry, for example).

The utility and value of auditing have grown in the current legal and political environment. It is a particularly effective instrument for detecting the more subtle forms of discrimination that have evolved since the civil rights revolution of the 1960s. Auditing can make plain the need for sustained, expanded, or redirected civil rights enforcement activity. Auditing also provides direct evidence of discrimination that may, in some cases, offer an evidentiary alternative or supplement to plaintiffs whose cases would otherwise rest on statistical evidence alone. This chapter provides an overview of past use of auditing, or testing, for discrimination and discusses how it might be applied in the future. We believe that auditing to establish the general incidence of discrimination and testing to support litigation against discriminatory practices have the potential to improve the effectiveness of civil rights law and enforcement.

The chapter is divided into seven sections. The first section sets the context by describing recent trends in public attitudes and expert understanding of the scope and character of discrimination. These trends have been influenced by auditing and, in turn, will shape its future. The second section sketches the strengths and limits of auditing for both research and enforcement purposes, emphasizing ethical issues that have been raised. In the third section we review the major results of the employment, housing, and credit audits conducted to date. The fourth section explores a series of methodological issues raised in this volume and elsewhere relating to the design of audits and interpretation of their results. The fifth section looks at the impact that audit results may have had on the shape of recent civil rights legislation, focusing on the Fair Housing Amendments Act of 1988, a law that expanded existing civil rights protections. We contend that the extensive documentation of housing discrimination, to which audits contributed, was instrumental in this expansion. The sixth section examines the potential role of auditing and testing in a comprehensive enforcement strategy, focusing on the case of housing. We conclude with a discussion of the implications of auditing for civil rights policy.

THE CONTEXT FOR EXPANDING THE USE OF AUDITING

We summarize two strands of related developments in housing, housing credit, and employment rights in recent years to set the stage for the ideas considered later in this chapter and the rest of the volume. First, public attitudes about equal rights and affirmative action have diverged in housing and employment; such divergent attitudes can be expected to affect the extent of discrimination in each area and to influence decisions made by Congress and the courts. Second, important differences among housing, housing credit, and employment exist in the corpus of evidence on discrimination and its reflection in conventional wisdom and expert opinion. A key issue is the extent to which audit findings are consistent with attitudinal differences and variation in expert opinion on different areas.

Trends in the Attitudes of Whites

Congressional legislation and, to a lesser extent, the decisions of the courts are influenced (as they should be) by the attitudes of the nation's citizens. This has indeed been the case for civil rights in recent years.

Table 1.1 presents the responses to questions about the attitudes of whites to equal opportunities in housing and employment for blacks over the 1963–1990 period.[1] Each question included in the table has been asked in the same form over a long period by a prominent national survey organization. Following the lead of Schuman et al. (1985), we assemble the questions in the table into three groups:

> *Principles.* Questions that ask respondents whether they endorse broad principles of nondiscrimination and desegregation in important areas of social life.
>
> *Government Role/Implementation.* Questions that deal with steps that the government (usually but not always the federal government) might take either to reduce discrimination or segregation or to improve the economic status of blacks.
>
> *Social distance.* Questions that ask how respondents would react in situations that involve some degree of integration at a personal level. Thus the questions deal with the principle of integration, not in an abstract way or in terms of government enforcement, but rather at the level of the individual's behavior or feelings. (Pp. 72–3)

Table 1.1 TRENDS IN WHITE ATTITUDES TOWARDS BLACKS IN HOUSING AND EMPLOYMENT, 1963–1990

	Year of survey																												Last minus first
	63	64	65	66	67	68	69	70	71	72	73	74	75	76	77	78	79	80	81	82	83	84	85	86	87	88	89	90	
A. Housing																													
1. Questions concerning principles																													
Residential choice, 1 alt. (NORC)[a]																													
% Agree slightly	21	—	—	—	—	25	—	18	—	15	—	—	—	18	21	—	—	17	—	15	—	14	15	—	12	15	14	14	−7
% Disagree slightly	20	—	—	—	—	25	—	19	—	23	—	—	—	26	29	—	—	29	—	32	—	25	28	—	22	24	23	25	+5
% Disagree strongly	19	—	—	—	—	19	—	34	—	40	—	—	—	34	28	—	—	38	—	39	—	48	44	—	56	54	55	53	+34
Residential choice, 2 alt. (ISR)																													
% Blacks have rights	—	—	—	—	—	73	—	—	—	88	—	—	—	—	—	—	—	—	—	—	—	—	—	—	—	—	—	—	+15
2. Implementation questions																													
Open housing (NORC)																													
% No discrimination	—	—	—	—	—	—	—	—	—	—	34	—	34	35	—	37	—	40	—	—	46	51	—	51	52	56	59	55	+21
3. Social distance questions																													
Next door (Gallup)																													
% Might	24	—	23	21	24	—	—	—	—	—	—	—	—	—	—	10	—	—	—	—	—	—	—	—	—	—	—	4	−20
% No	55	—	63	66	63	—	—	—	—	—	—	—	—	—	—	86	—	—	—	—	—	—	—	—	—	—	—	93	+38
Great numbers (Gallup)																													
% Might	28	—	30	31	32	—	—	—	—	—	—	—	—	—	—	33	—	—	—	—	—	—	—	—	—	—	—	18	−10
% No	23	—	28	30	28	—	—	—	—	—	—	—	—	—	—	46	—	—	—	—	—	—	—	—	—	—	—	68	+45
Same block (NORC)																													
% No	63	64	69	71	—	77	—	—	—	85	—	—	—	—	—	—	—	—	—	—	—	—	—	—	—	—	—	—	+22
B. Employment																													
1. Questions concerning principles																													
Equal jobs (NORC)																													
% As good a chance	85	—	—	89	—	—	—	—	—	97	—	—	—	—	—	—	—	—	—	—	—	—	—	—	—	—	—	—	+12

2. Implementation questions											
Federal job intervention											
1. Gov't see to job and living standard	— — — — — — — — — — — — —	13 —	12 —	11 —	7 —	10 —	10 —	10 —	10 —	9	−4
2.		6 —	5 —	5 —	3 —	7 —	6 —	7 —	6 —	6	0
3.		9 —	8 —	8 —	7 —	9 —	9 —	11 —	8 —	9	0
4.		20 —	20 —	17 —	19 —	18 —	20 —	20 —	21 —	18	−2
5.		13 —	12 —	10 —	15 —	13 —	16 —	16 —	16 —	16	+3
6.		8 —	8 —	11 —	12 —	16 —	13 —	13 —	14 —	14	+6
7. Gov't let each person		19 —	17 —	18 —	17 —	12 —	12 —	9 —	17 —	13	−6
get ahead on his own		13 —	16 —	20 —	21 —	16 —	14 —	14 —	7 —	15	+2

Sources: Data for 1963–83, Schuman et al. (1985), tables 3.1, 3.2, 3.3; 1984–90, NORC General Social Surveys, Gallup and Hujick (1990), and ISR unpublished tabulation.

[a]NORC is the National Opinion Research Center; ISR is the Institute for Social Research at the University of Michigan.

Question wordings and variants:

Residential choice, 1 alternative (NORC): "Here are some opinions other people have expressed in connection with black–white relations. Which statement on the card comes closest to how you yourself feel? White people have a right to keep blacks out of their neighborhoods if they want to, and blacks should respect that right."

1. Agree strongly
2. Agree slightly
3. Disagree slightly
4. Disagree strongly

Residential choice, 2 alternatives (ISR): "Which of these statements would you agree with: White people have a right to keep black people out of their neighborhoods if they want to, or, black people have a right to live wherever they can afford to, just like anybody else?"

1. Keep blacks out
2. Blacks have rights

(Variant: In 1964 replace "anybody else" with "white people.")

continued

Table 1.1 TRENDS IN WHITE ATTITUDES TOWARDS BLACKS IN HOUSING AND EMPLOYMENT, 1963–1990 *(continued)*

Open housing (NORC): "Suppose there is a community-wide vote on the general issue. There are two possible laws to vote on. One law says that a homeowner can decide for himself who to sell his house to, even if he prefers not to sell to blacks. The second law says that a homeowner cannot refuse to sell to someone because of their race or color. Which law would you vote for?"

1. Homeowner can decide
2. No discrimination

Next door (Gallup): "If black people came to live next door, would you move?"

1. Yes, definitely
2. Might
3. No

Great numbers (Gallup): "Would you move if black people came to live in great numbers in your neighborhood?"

1. Yes, definitely
2. Might
3. No

Same block (NORC): "If a Negro with the same income and education as you have moved into your block, would it make any difference to you?"

1. Yes
2. No

Equal jobs (NORC): "Do you think Negroes should have as good a chance as white people to get any kind of job, or do you think white people should have the first chance at any kind of job?"

1. As good a chance
2. White people first

Federal job intervention (ISR): "Some people feel that the government in Washington should see to it that every person has a job and a good standard of living. Others think the government should just let each person get ahead on his own. And, of course, other people have opinions somewhere in between. Where would you place yourself on this scale, or haven't you thought much about this?" (7-point scale shown to respondents).

1. Government see to job and good standard of living
2.

. . . .

7. Government let each person get ahead on his own.

Turning to the responses to the housing questions first, one sees truly remarkable changes in attitudes of whites in support of the rights of black people over the past quarter century in all three areas—principles, government role/implementation, and social distance. The figures indicate a major increase in racial tolerance. Importantly, these changes continued to evolve during the 1980s. Particularly telling is the response to the government role question, which asks if a home owner should be able to decide whom he is willing to sell his home to: Over the 1980s the percentage of respondents saying he should not be able to discriminate rose by 15 percentage points.

Questions dealing with employment rights indicate a more mixed picture. On the one hand, as early as 1972 nearly all respondents agreed in principle that blacks should have as good a chance at obtaining any kind of job as whites. On the other hand, for the one question on the government's role for which longitudinal data exist throughout the 1980s, the pattern of responses shows little change over the 1972–88 period in the percentage of respondents who believed the government "should see to it that every person has a job and a good standard of living." In the area of employment, then, there is an abiding reluctance to allow government to determine outcomes. This suggests that there are differences in attitudes of whites on issues involving housing versus employment—differences that may inform the formulation of antidiscrimination policy in the two areas.

Current Knowledge about Discrimination

What is the conventional wisdom in the public policy and research communities about the extent of discrimination against blacks in housing availability, employment, and mortgage credit, and upon what is it based?[2]

Before the advent of audits, research findings typically come from studies employing multivariate analyses. In these studies the analyst controls for factors, such as age and education, that could reasonably be expected to account for the outcomes observed for majorities and minorities separately—such as being employed or having a mortgage loan approved. The analyst then identifies a residual difference between the two groups, that is, a difference putatively not associated with attributes included in the analysis. Some unknown share, possibly all, of the residual is suspected of being due to discrimination; but often the share cannot be identified. Moreover, many problems emerge in attempting to fully specify the multivariate models, which introduces uncertainty about whether the magnitude of the residual itself is correct.[3] Further, such studies cannot report the incidence of discrimination, only the magnitude of the resulting impact. In short, a good deal of uncertainty about the level of discrimination is the rule in such studies (Price and Mills 1985).[4]

Employment. In the broadest terms, economists have found that blacks operate at a disadvantage in the labor market relative to comparable whites in terms of earnings, occupations, and employment levels (Jaynes and Williams 1989, 146–7).[5] Most economists would attribute at least some of this difference to discrimination in the market; part of the difference is also due to residential segregation that puts lower-skilled blacks a greater distance from suburban blue-collar jobs than their white counterparts. Residential segregation, in turn, may result at least partially from housing discrimination. Young black men, who appear especially disadvantaged, have received the most intense study (e.g., Freeman and Holzer 1986; Rees 1986; Freeman 1990). Most recently, analysts have been struck by the decline in the employment rates of all black men compared with white men during the 1980s when their relative wages appear to have risen; a similar pattern has not been observed for black women (Jaynes 1990).

Beneath the surface of this general agreement on the existence of employment discrimination, however, there is much controversy. On the basis of standard statistical methods, some analysts have suggested sharp declines in the extent of discrimination; others[6] contend that differences in blacks' outcomes relative to whites' are culture-based and not reasonably attributed to discrimination.[7] Ballen and Freeman (1986), after controlling for differences in factors affecting the probability of employment, such as education and age,[8] identified a large difference in the rates at which white versus inner-city black youth make the transition between unemployment and employment. They suggested that this residual difference may have been due in part to employers' adverse reaction to employment histories involving numerous short-duration positions—a pattern more common among inner-city black youth. But the authors were unable to provide a quantified explanation of the residual, that is, the share attributable to discrimination.

There has been and is a large and continuing controversy about the role suburbanization of blue-collar jobs has played in reducing black employment opportunities.[9] Ihlanfeldt and Sjoquist (1990) have provided convincing econometric evidence that location does matter; after controlling for other factors such as individual characteristics and family background, they found the range of the racial gap in employment rates attributable to job access to be 30 to 50 percent. Note that, again, 50 to 70 percent of the racial gap remains to be explained—some of which is presumably attributable to discrimination. And numerous complaints about discrimination on the basis of race in hiring, but especially wages and promotions, continue to be filed with state and federal administrative agencies and courts (Donohue and Siegelman 1991).

In sum, analyses of discrimination in employment have generated substantial consensus that blatant discrimination in hiring and wages has been largely eliminated (Donohue and Heckman 1990). Moreover, the statistical estimates indicate that there is little, if any, discrimination against black women in comparison with white women (Jaynes and Williams 1989, 146).[10] Yet there remains sharp disagreement about the extent of continuing, more subtle forms of discrimination against minorities; indeed, there is substantial uncertainty about the ability to identify more subtle discriminatory acts (e.g., Strauss 1990). Such controversy is to be expected, given the problems noted earlier in accurately identifying discrimination in hiring and wages from statistical data.

Indeed, congressional hearings on the Civil Rights Acts of 1990 and 1991 focused almost exclusively on the impact of recent Supreme Court decisions on future patterns of litigation. Questions about, or data on, the extent of discrimination were rarely raised.[11] Our understanding of the extent and character of discrimination in mortgage credit markets is even less developed.

Credit. The popular discussion of possible discrimination in lending has been dominated by two simple empirical observations:

- ☐ The rate at which loans are originated per 1,000 owner-occupied dwellings in predominantly white neighborhoods is two to three times greater than the rate in predominantly black neighborhoods.
- ☐ The rejection rate for black mortgage loan applicants is more than twice as high as the rate for white applicants. Moreover, there is a strong suspicion that would-be minority applicants are often discouraged from making an application.[12]

While these findings could result from factors other than discrimination, many in the policy community find this hard to accept. There is a presumption that where there is so much smoke there must be fire (U.S. Senate 1990, 119).

In stark contrast, the responsible supervisory agencies (Federal Reserve Board, Office of the Comptroller of the Currency, etc.) have testified repeatedly that simple tabulations of differences in white-black loan rates and volumes are not meaningful because they fail to control for a host of germane factors influencing the demand for and supply of mortgage loans. Moreover, their examiners have uncovered few, if any, discriminatory actions in mortgage lending by thrifts and banks.[13] Nevertheless the differences in lending rates, buttressed by a number of cases of discrimination documented by private fair-housing groups, have produced an apparently strong disposition in Congress to believe discrimination is occurring in mortgage lending.

Most rigorous statistical analyses of mortgage discrimination have not produced definitive results. Analysts employ the standard methodology described at the beginning of this section. Data on the aggregate number or volume of loans made to neighborhoods or census tracts have been analyzed, as have individual loan applications. Even analyses employing microdata on applicants, however, suffer from having to use indicators of the characteristics of the area in which the property to be purchased is located, rather than information on the specific property. Until recently, the most careful studies employing microdata on mortgage applications yielded mixed results as to the presence of discrimination (Schafer and Ladd 1981; King 1980).[14] However, a recent study (Munnell et al. 1992) conducted by the Federal Reserve Bank in Boston, which examined data from mortgage applications, found that Boston blacks and Hispanics were more frequently denied loans than whites who represented similar credit risks. Given the evidence that there is discrimination at the application stage of mortgage lending, it is reasonable to presume there is also discrimination at the pre-application stage. But little analysis has been done of the extent to which black applicants are discouraged at this preapplication stage—except for the pioneering audit projects reviewed by George Galster (see chapter 7 of this volume).

Housing Availability. Today's conventional wisdom—of widespread discrimination in housing transactions—has been profoundly shaped by the release in 1979 of the results of the Housing Market Practices Survey—the first national audit study of housing availability (Wienk et al. 1979).[15] This study documented that a black home seeker experienced unfavorable treatment in 28 percent of inquiries about the availability of rental units and in 15 percent of those about home owner units advertised in a major metropolitan newspaper. Over a typical housing search in which the minority home seeker contacts several rental or sales agents, the probability of encountering unfavorable treatment at least once thus becomes very large. These national findings have been bolstered by literally dozens of audit studies conducted at the local level and a large number of media stories on their results and the sometimes spectacular awards received by plaintiffs who bring housing discrimination suits (Galster 1990b; 1991a). Scattered audits in several cities conducted between 1978 and 1983 suggest more variable, but similar outcomes for Hispanics.[16] Against this background it is hardly surprising that the presence of discrimination in the housing market is not seriously contested. Indeed, the marshaling of evidence on this score in the congressional report for the Title VIII amendments is striking (U.S. House of Representatives 1988).

ADVANTAGES AND ETHICS OF AUDITING

As we have seen, our knowledge of discrimination is uneven and the tools available to social scientists for measuring it are limited. What, then, are some of the defining strengths and liabilities of auditing in this context?

Among the chief advantages of auditing are the comparative level of confidence its results inspire, the political persuasiveness of those results, its ability to detect subtle forms of discrimination, and its efficiency as an enforcement tool. Critics of auditing point to ethical problems raised by the deception it involves, its invasion of privacy, its use of human subjects without their knowledge or consent, the problem of tester motives and their implications for reliability, difficulties in interpreting the results of audits, and the feasibility of using testing for comparatively complex transactions such as hiring. (In this section we do not go into the statistical issues involved in measuring discrimination on the basis of audit data. These are discussed in the section beginning on p. 25, after we have summarized the audit results.)

Ultimately, the principle guiding judgments on the merits of conducting audits must be whether the benefits that will accrue to society substantially exceed the costs that will be borne by the firms being audited and the costs of actually conducting the audit.

In discussing the comparative advantages and disadvantages of auditing we need to distinguish between the use of audits for research and the use of audits for enforcement. The purpose of research audits is to measure and understand discrimination in order to guide policy—that is, to identify types of transactions that need to be covered by antidiscrimination protections; to identify industries, practices, or regions as targets for enforcement; or to specify effective remedies for discrimination. The deterrent impact of such activities is indirect and differs from that associated with litigation against alleged violators, where the goal is to detect, punish, and deter discrimination. In research studies discriminators do not learn that their practices have been discovered, and there is no direct imperative for them to change their ways. The same, obviously, is not true in the enforcement context.

The Arguments for Auditing

One major advantage of auditing is the comparatively high level of confidence attached to the results, owing to the fact that auditing is usually based on close observation of individuals (e.g., employers, real estate agents) reacting spontaneously to a controlled choice between two or more candidates who are alike except for the presence of a protected trait.[17] With characteristics other than the protected trait controlled for, systematic patterns of differential treatment can be identified.[18] Another value of audits is their ability to present evidence on unequal treatment, while at the same time informing the character of that treatment. That is, audits can detect and distinguish opportunity-denying behavior (e.g., rejection of one job candidate in favor of another) and opportunity-diminishing behaviors such as steering minorities to lower paying jobs. In so doing, well-designed audits can present strong evidence on the incidence, character, and impacts of unequal treatment.

At the same time, it is important to appreciate the limited capacity of other methods of detecting and measuring discrimination. There are basically three alternative research strategies: (1) analysis of statistical imbalances in the distribution of goods, workers, etc; (2) self-reports of possible discriminators (e.g., employers); and (3) victimization studies.

As we have noted, analysts using only statistical data to detect and measure discrimination must control for a host of possibly germane factors before ascribing such unfavorable outcomes as high unemployment rates or higher car payments to the practices of employers, car dealers, and the like. Obviously, the complexity of the analysis and the number of judgments that must be made reduce confidence in the results, as does the heavy reliance on statistical evidence demonstrating "undue coincidence" between race or ethnicity and, say, employment or wage outcomes.

Self-reported results of the incidence and character of discrimination are obtained either through telephone or mail surveys or through face-to-face interviewing. Mail or telephone survey methods can be comparatively effective only when the type of discrimination in question would not constitute an obvious violation of law and when candid responses can be expected. These factors were present in the General Accounting Office's mail survey of employer responses to the employer sanctions provisions of the 1986 Immigration Reform and Control Act (U.S. General Accounting Office 1990). Even here, though, the survey was criticized because some believed its results—which reported widespread discrimination—were due to a mix of misunderstanding and self-interest among the respondents (Bowsher 1990).

Another strategy for exploring discriminatory practices is simply to interview persons in a position to discriminate face to face. This strategy was adopted by two researchers at the University of Chicago, Joleen Kirschenman and Kathryn Neckerman (1991). They found employers in Chicago surprisingly willing to reveal their prejudices vis-à-vis young minority workers. But despite the insights into discrimination this kind of work provides, it has not been used to provide statistical estimates of discrimination.

Finally, victimization surveys draw only on those who believe that they have been discriminated against and who have chosen to come forward. Although such studies are informative, they make no pretense at providing statistically meaningful evidence on the incidence or impact of discrimination.

The limitations that characterize one of more of these approaches—susceptibility to self-interested responses or the inability to generate statistically meaningful results—do not apply to auditing.

The results of auditing are also distinguished by their political legitimacy. This stems not only from confidence in their accuracy, but also from the kind of "story" that auditing tells.[19] The departing premise of audits is a team of candidates who are equivalently qualified (in some cases the minority candidate is slightly better qualified). As a result, any systematic pattern of unfavorable treatment that emerges reveals decisions that are based on factors other than merit. This type of selection violates the most basic notions of fairness and justice. It thus differs from other illegal discriminatory activities that present somewhat more ambiguous moral questions. (An example would be the adoption of neutral practices that are found to have an unfavorable, if unintended, impact on minorities.) The political influence of audits owes in part, then, to the fact they forcefully demonstrate what appears to be patently unfair treatment.

The legitimacy of these controlled tests has a corollary in the enforcement context. Firms whose day-to-day practices are evenhanded will escape detection in audits even when the composition of their work forces or their lending patterns might "look bad on paper." In the case of employment, this might be a desirable policy outcome where a firm's work force is racially imbalanced as a result of historical processes over which the firm had no control. However, it would constitute a less just result where a firm has historically discriminated but has recently changed its policies.

Auditing is useful not only for its scientific and political credibility but also for its sensitivity to otherwise concealed practices. Thus it is especially valuable in an era in which discrimination has grown more subtle and less detectable than was once the case.[20] Discrimination in hiring—an issue that has drawn little analytic attention[21] and represents a constantly declining share of the rising volume of employment discrimination cases[22]—provides a good example of the important policy implications of this ability to detect concealed practices. Contact between the applicant and the employer during the hiring process is typically fleeting, the eventual outcome is unknown to the candidate, and the process itself rarely signals exclusionary intent. As a result few complaints are filed, leading to a general perception that discrimination in hiring is not as important a social problem as discrimination in promotions or terminations, which generate a far larger number of complaints. Public and private enforcement resources are then allocated (and potentially misallocated) on the basis of a possible misperception.

As we have noted, close observation of the comparative outcomes of matched testers as they advance through the hiring process allows one to detect and measure unequal treatment and outcomes, even when they are masked by apparently courteous treatment. But auditing has a further value. And that is its ability to detect and measure opportunity-*diminishing* as well as opportunity-*denying* behaviors. Opportunity denial means that the home or job seeker was refused the possibility of pursuing the home or job advertised or a similar opportunity: The door was closed. For example, a rental agent would tell the minority auditor that no units were available but would tell his white teammate that one or more units were available; or the majority job candidate would be granted an interview or job while his minority counterpart was refused one. Opportunity-diminishing behaviors include those subtle signals of encouragement and discouragement that are hard to detect and that may "save" the discriminator from taking actions that more clearly are violations of the law. The

Urban Institute Employment Discrimination Study, for example, measured differential treatment of black and white job applicants not only in terms of advancement in the process but also in terms of:

—Difficulty in obtaining an application for a job;
—Negative comments;
—Positive comments;
—Interview waiting time;
—Length of the interview;
—Number of interviewers; and
—Quality of job offered (hours, fringe benefits, etc.).

Not only are these behaviors detectable through auditing; in most instances they lend themselves to quantification and even to the development of cumulative measures.

Among such opportunity-diminishing behaviors, audits offer perhaps the best window on the nature and extent of steering. Steering is a process that makes available different, and typically inferior, opportunities to minorities and that sustains existing patterns of segregation and discrimination. Like other opportunity-diminishing behaviors, steering is especially resistant to other forms of detection. In the employment context, take, for example, the case of an audit team responding to an advertisement placed by a car dealer. Both team members apply for and are offered jobs. However, the minority is assigned to the used-car lot, where the commissions are lower and the clientele poorer; the other member of the team is assigned to the new-car lot, where the reverse is the case. In this and similar cases the discrimination involved would escape many statistical assessments.

Another argument that is made for testing is that it can make the enforcement process more efficient. Carefully administered audits are likely to lead to fewer "false positives" or false legal claims than evidence of mere statistical imbalances in neighborhoods or workplaces. In addition, early studies suggest that housing discrimination cases that are based on audits are far more likely to settle before trial and in favor of the plaintiff than are cases brought using other forms of evidence. A more recent study of testing's impact is less conclusive (Turner et al. 1992).[23] By stimulating early settlement, tests reduce costs for the parties, for state and federal court systems, and for administrative agencies and tribunals. Thus adoption of testing by law enforcement agencies could make more efficient use of public enforcement resources.

Beyond these economies, testing provides public and private enforcement agencies with a tool that can help them root out discriminatory practices in a systematic manner rather than simply responding to complaints that might be filed.

The Ethics of Auditing

The use of auditing for both enforcement and research purposes has been criticized on ethical grounds.

One critique, forcefully advanced by Sissela Bok in her book *Lying* (1979, 198–203), condemns the use of deception in social science. A central premise of the book is that the use of deception in all its forms is a "slippery slope" and that its institutionalization will do more harm than good. Deceit for purportedly noble goals will breed deceit for less admirable purposes. Thus Bok would claim that the use of deception in tests for discrimination in housing and employment will only legitimize questionable practices like the use of pseudostudents to monitor the ideological content of college professors' lectures.

Another ethical critique of auditing focuses on the fact that the agent whose behavior is being monitored is effectively used in an experiment without his knowledge or consent, breaching legitimate expectations of privacy. Critics also claim that despite the fact that the researchers may make every effort to limit the intrusiveness of the experiment, some harm is done to the agent in the cost of time lost from other pursuits.

An ethical issue that applies only to testing for enforcement is the issue of entrapment. Critics of auditing who make this argument charge that the purportedly illegal behavior detected was induced by the audit process itself.

Responding to these ethical criticisms requires a balancing of interests and an acknowledgment of the goals and advantages of auditing.[24]

With regard to the critique that testing invades a legitimate privacy interest, the behaviors that have been monitored in the studies documented in this volume all involve public, commercial, or professional acts. In most instances there has been a special invitation issued to the public—via a published ad for a job, apartment, or loan—regarding the transaction that is later monitored. Moreover, the behaviors that have been monitored are all publicly regulated at some level, either by laws barring discrimination or by professional codes of conduct. It could be argued that such activities are similar to the operation of a motor vehicle and, thus, subject to the unannounced monitoring that is accepted practice there. As Christopher Edley argues (chapter 9), such public behavior creates, in effect, an implied consent to this kind of policing that makes it possible.

With regard to enforcement and claims that auditing constitutes entrapment, it is important to distinguish between auditing and other contexts in which this defense is raised. In the audit context no attractive lures (drugs, money) are presented to the discriminator that might tempt or induce him to act in an illegal manner. (Indeed, the reverse could be said to be the case when minority candidates present more favorable credentials than white candidates.) In fact, the purpose of audits is to observe the conventional practices of the monitored firm or individual and not to stimulate exceptional and illegal behaviors.

In the case of auditing for research purposes, it is clear that no real harm, discomfort, or liability attaches to the firm or employee audited. In all cases audits have been structured in a manner to make them as unintrusive as possible, occupying a few moments to an hour of the real estate agent's, employer's, or car salesman's time.[25] Because auditors of hiring practices or housing rentals or sales are instructed to turn down offers soon after they are made, there is no harm to members of the pool of legitimate applicants.

The legitimacy of testing in these separate contexts is reinforced by the fact that there is no good analytic alternative for determining the prevalence and character of discrimination. The courts have led the way in recognizing that testing may provide the only credible way of developing information about discrimination:

> [Because] it is frequently difficult to develop proof in discrimination cases . . . the evidence provided by testers is frequently valuable, if not indispensable.[26]

> [M]any times the evidence gathered by a tester may . . . be the only competent evidence available to prove that the defendant has engaged in unlawful conduct.[27]

Further, there is no alternative to the clandestine character of the test. To request consent would lead to staged (vs. spontaneous) behavior and would defeat the essential purpose of the study.[28]

Audits for both research and enforcement serve an important public purpose: to locate the manifest injustice of discrimination on the basis of race, ethnicity, and gender when it exists, and in doing so, to begin to counteract it. Moreover, as we have noted, the linkage of research to public policy has been unusually close. This has been clearest in the use of audits to support and guide the Fair Housing Act Amendments. Plainly these studies do not constitute exclusively academic inquiries.

On balance, it is our judgment that the costs imposed on the kind of businesses that have been audited to date do not outweigh the benefits that accrue to society from the comparatively precise information these audits provide.

AUDIT FINDINGS IN BRIEF

The results of the most recent and reliable audit studies indicate that substantial levels of unfavorable treatment of blacks and Hispanics remain in America's housing market and in hiring for entry-level jobs.[29] Additionally, it appears that there is some variation in the extent of unfavorable treatment among metropolitan areas, although not between central cities and their suburbs.

Because other chapters in this volume present detailed results of the housing and hiring audits discussed here, this section presents only selected highlights. The results for the housing market are from the recently completed Housing Discrimination Study, in which about 3,800 audits were conducted in the summer of 1989 in 25 metropolitan areas where blacks or Hispanics represented at least 12 percent or 7 percent of the population, respectively (i.e., the same as their shares in the national population). The results are representative for all metropolitan areas with 1980 central-city populations of at least 100,000.[30]

The study's sampling plan was structured so that a few hundred audits were conducted in each of five "in-depth" sites, which yielded statistically reliable results for those individual sites. The study conducted black-white and Hispanic-Anglo audits for both rental and sales units.

The results for hiring are from two pilot studies. The first, carried out in the summer of 1989, tested for unfavorable treatment of accented Hispanics compared with Anglos in San Diego and Chicago (Cross et al. 1990). The second study involved black-white audits in Chicago and Washington, D.C., in the summer of 1990 (Turner, Fix, and Struyk 1991). Both of these studies were deliberately limited in the range of unfavorable treatment covered. First, both tested only for discrimination against young men seeking entry-level jobs—a critical part of the market from the perspective of the career opportunities of minority males.[31] In addition, the audit for Hispanics was conducted as part of a larger study of the potential adverse impact of the employer sanctions provisions of the Immigration Reform and Control Act of 1986 on job attainment by Hispanics (General Accounting Office 1990). The law's framers were concerned that its ban on hiring undocumented aliens would lead to discrimination against foreign-sounding and -looking persons who were legally authorized to work. Consequently, the Hispanic auditors were persons who looked Hispanic and had definite accents.

All three of these audit studies were conducted by the Urban Institute and followed the same sampling methodology and field procedures. In each study the available apartment, home, or job was identified through a random sample of advertisements appearing in the major local newspaper the weekend preceding the audit. The sample was selected exclusively from newspapers and not other, more informal listings (such as jobs posted at plant bulletin boards or apartment rentals on church bulletin boards) or personal recommendations of units for sale or rent or jobs available, because no practical sampling frame for these informal sources could be developed. Without such a frame the representativeness of the opportunities sampled would be unknown. However, this sampling strategy did mean that only limited segments of the labor and housing markets were audited.

Audit teams were assigned qualifications suitable for acquiring each housing unit or filling the job vacancy. They then conducted the audit following carefully defined procedures. The sampling procedure adopted meant that any findings of unfavorable treatment should be interpreted as the unfavorable treatment encountered by a qualified person who identified and pursued a housing or employment opportunity announced in the area's major weekend newspaper.

The procedure followed in these studies is similar in some ways to experimental designs using random assignment. In the experiments with random assignment persons eligible for some type of assistance or other "treatment" (an experimental employment and training program, for example) are randomly assigned to groups receiving different types of assistance or treatment, including, possibly, a "no treatment" control group. The effect of the treatment is inferred from differences in outcomes (changes in housing consumption, work effort, service utilization) among the different groups (Campbell and Stanley 1963).

In audits there are two levels of random assignment: the employment or housing opportunity to be audited can be randomly assigned to an audit team as is the order in which the auditors visit the housing or employment agent. Like analyses done under experimental designs, the outcomes for majority auditors serve as "controls" for the outcomes of the minority auditors. The major difference is that the "treatment" itself (i.e., race) cannot be randomly assigned, although audit studies strive to control for other germane factors affecting the hiring decision through the matching of the audit team members.

The validity of the audit findings hinges on the closeness of the match between the members of each audit pair and the veracity of their reporting. Special care was taken in the hiring audits to ensure similarity. Audit pairs had similar education attainment in real life and were of the same physical appearance and personality type. Careful training included mock interviews in which the pair learned to respond similarly to typical questions asked in real interviews. Biographies presented to would-be employers were synchronized. In brief, extensive effort was devoted to minimizing any systematic differences between the members of each audit team in their qualifications for and approach to obtaining a job.

The figures in tables 1.2 and 1.3 show the percentage of times in which either the minority or the majority auditor received unfavorable treatment. Two types of unfavorable treatment are distinguished: opportunity denying and opportunity diminishing. A discussion of the alternative ways these numbers can be used to measure "discrimination" appears in the following section of this chapter.

The figures show that opportunity denial occurred 20 percent of the time in the black-white hiring audits and 31 percent in the Hispanic-Anglo hiring audits. Stated alternatively, about one time in three a young accented Hispanic applying for a job advertised in the newspaper was denied an application, refused an interview, or not offered a job when his Anglo partner experienced the opposite outcome. In the housing sector, in contrast, this type of treatment occurred about 8 percent of the time when either blacks or Hispanics sought to purchase a home. Black renters were essentially refused any sort of information ("door slamming") 15 percent of the time, while Hispanic renters were treated this way 12 percent of the time. In short, opportunity-denying treatment is more common in hiring transactions involving entry-level positions than in the housing acquisition process.

Opportunity-diminishing behavior includes treatment that lowers the chance of the candidate's obtaining the housing unit or job sought but stops short of eliminating the person from the home or job acquisition process. In renting, for example, opportunity was considered diminished for one auditor if the other was told of more units being available, shown more units, or quoted more favorable rental terms.

Table 1.2 AUDIT ESTIMATES OF UNFAVORABLE TREATMENT IN HOUSING

Characteristic	Coverage	Opp'y deny minority(%)[a]	Opp'y deny White/Anglo(%)[b]	Opp'y deny/ diminish minority(%)[c]	Opp'y deny/diminish White/Anglo(%)[c]
1. Black/White Rental	National	15	5	46	18
2. Black/White Sales	National	8	1	50	20
3. Hispanic/Anglo Rental	National	12	6	43	20
4. Hispanic/Anglo Sales	National	8	3	45	21

[a]The minority rental or home seeker was essentially denied any information while the information was given to the majority.

[b]The majority rental or home seeker was essentially denied any information while the information was given to the minority.

[c]Opportunity diminishing acts are defined as follows: while either the minority or majority auditor was able to learn about the unit requested he was treated less well than his counterpart. In housing, for example, one tester is offered fewer units, or the minority tester is "steered" to neighborhoods with more minorities.

Table 1.3 AUDIT ESTIMATES OF UNFAVORABLE TREATMENT IN EMPLOYMENT

Characteristic	Coverage	Opp'y deny[a] minority(%)	Opp'y deny[b] White/Anglo(%)
Black/White	Chi; D.C.	20	7
Hispanic/Anglo	Chi; S.D.	31	11

Sources: Cross et. al. (1990), figure 5.1: Turner, Fix and Struyk (1991), Table 5, and unpublished tabulations.

[a]The minority auditor was denied the opportunity of advancing as far in the hiring process as his majority counterpart or the majority auditor received a job when his minority partner did not.

[b]The majority auditor was denied the opportunity of advancing as far in the hiring process as his minority counterpart or the minority auditor received a job when his majority partner did not.

For those seeking to purchase a home, such behavior included steering purchasers to different, less desirable neighborhoods and providing less information on potential financing sources. In hiring, opportunity was considered diminished when, for example, one auditor had difficulty in obtaining the employment application, had to wait substantially longer before being interviewed, or was offered a position inferior to that offered to his audit partner.[32] The *combined* incidence of opportunity-denying and opportunity-diminishing treatment for housing is high. On average, blacks encountered unfavorable treatment 46 percent of the time when renting a home and 50 percent of the time when trying to purchase one. For Hispanics the respective rates of unfavorable treatment were almost as high: they encountered unfavorable treatment 43 percent of the time in rentals and 45 percent in sales (see table 1.2). The pervasiveness of opportunity-diminishing treatment is evident by contrasting these figures with those for opportunity denial.

Only one of the pilot hiring audit studies—black-white audits in Chicago and Washington—was structured to capture opportunity-diminishing treatment. The results for these two sites viewed together suggest that such adverse treatment occurs in 36 percent of hiring transactions involving a young black man.

How does one explain the greater overall incidence of unfavorable treatment of minorities in housing in light of the greater incidence of opportunity-denying behavior in hiring? The answer, in part at least, stems from the greater opportunity that housing agents—who often control multiple housing opportunities—have to discourage applicants without denying them some putative assistance. To clarify this point, we discuss the two types of unfavorable treatment further.

Opportunity Denial. The denial of an opportunity to pursue the advertised unit or job or any alternative can occur at any of three distinct stages of the hiring process: obtaining the application, having the interview, or receiving the offer. But in the case of housing the denial occurs typically at the outset, with a refusal to provide information on any unit. The result is the same in both instances: The applicant has no further chance to pursue the job or housing opportunity. However, the opportunities for denial are greater in hiring because the denial can occur at any of a number of stages in the process.

Opportunity Diminishing. In the hiring process, candidates for entry-level positions typically proceed through a fairly well-defined process. There is usually only one available position, and it is controlled by the offeror. The housing transaction is different because the agent controls multiple units, and the process of negotiation between the agent and the home seeker can take many directions. Since many of the units that an agent offers may be inferior to the one advertised (which is the one sought and presumably preferred), the home seeker's opportunity to find *some* acceptable unit is diminished but not completely denied. For example, units other than the one advertised might be offered to the minority home seeker while the advertised unit is shown to his majority partner. The substitute units might be smaller or larger than the one requested or, in the case of sales units, in a different neighborhood. In contrast, in the hiring process, the firm has few if any substitute jobs to offer an applicant. So the opportunity to appear responsive by offering a substitute, even an inferior substitute, is more limited and occurs less frequently in hiring than in housing.

This line of reasoning suggests that comparisons of the incidence of unequal treatment in different types of transactions are complex and should be made with caution. Nevertheless, the basic finding of the audit studies seems valid: Opportunity-denying behavior is more common in hiring, while the combined incidence of opportunity-denying and opportunity-diminishing behavior is higher in housing.

A final question concerns the extent of variation in unfavorable treatment among metropolitan areas.[33] (For simplicity's sake, the table below reports majority-favored outcomes alone as a way of portraying varying patterns of differential treatment across metropolitan areas.) Two rather different patterns appear in the housing audits (table 1.4). There is little variation in the incidence of unfavorable treatment of blacks but a greater dispersion in unfavorable treatment of Hispanics. For example, the lowest incidence in Anglo-Hispanic sales audits is

Table 1.4 VARIATION IN THE LEVEL OF UNFAVORABLE TREATMENT OF MINORITIES ACROSS METRO AREAS

	Black-White (%)		Hispanic-Anglo (%)	
Site	Rental	Sales	Rental	Sales
Housing[a]				
Chicago	45	39	46	39
New York	40	44	53	61
Los Angeles	44	36	41	38
Atlanta	41	49	NA	NA
San Antonio	NA	NA	31	46
Hiring[b]				
Chicago	17		33	
Washington, D.C.	23		NA	
San Diego	NA		29	

Sources: Housing—unpublished results; Hiring—Cross et al. (1990), tables A.1, A.2; Turner, Fix, and Struyk (1991), table 9.

Note: Each entry is the percentage of audits in which minorities were treated less favorably than their majority group counterparts.

a. Includes both opportunity-diminishing and opportunity-denying behavior. See notes to table 1.2.

b. Opportunity denying only.

39 percent (Los Angeles) and the highest is 61 percent (New York). The results for the hiring audits, limited as they are, suggest a smaller range of unfavorable treatment across metro areas for Hispanics.[34]

No significant differences in the incidence of unfavorable treatment in housing sales and rentals were found between central cities and suburbs within the same metropolitan area.[35] Similarly, no significant differences were detected in the hiring patterns of firms located in central cities versus suburbs. But note that only firms advertising positions were audited (Turner, Fix, and Struyk 1991; Kenney and Wissoker, forthcoming). There may be a difference here in that suburban firms that advertise positions may be less inclined to discriminate compared with all suburban firms than are central-city firms that advertise compared with all central-city firms.

The burden of the evidence, then, is that significant levels of unequal treatment exist in housing markets and in hiring of young workers for entry-level positions; some forms of unequal treatment are worse in some places than in others, but the variation is surprisingly low overall.

Can we claim that the unfavorable treatment just summarized represents discrimination? The straightforward character of auditing and the strength and persuasiveness of its results mask a number of controversial and complex underlying methodological and definitional issues in the translation of unfavorable treatment to discrimination. Some of these are unique to audits, others are shared by studies using experimental designs. These issues are addressed in the next section and appendices 1.A and 1.B, as well as elsewhere in this volume, most notably in chapters 2 and 5.

METHODOLOGICAL ISSUES RELATED TO DESIGNING, INTERPRETING, AND STATISTICALLY EVALUATING AUDITS[36]

How can we be sure that differential treatment is due to race or ethnicity (hereafter referred to simply as race) rather than other factors? What statistical tests are appropriate for interpreting audit findings? Are there flaws in the design of audits themselves that leave the results open to doubt?

This section grapples with these difficult questions. We begin by stressing that different definitions of discrimination imply different interpretations of the differential treatment data provided by audits. We present four alternative definitions of discrimination and demonstrate how the definition chosen governs the statistics analyzed to interpret audit results. The role of random factors related to the behavior of auditors, agents, and the audit process is crucial to this discussion, because how they are treated determines how we assess audit results. (A more detailed discussion is provided in appendix 1.A.) Next, we discuss a number of other methodological concerns raised in this volume and elsewhere about auditing for discrimination. Finally, we show that in the Urban Institute's national housing discrimination study and in three of four employment discrimination sites there is clear and convincing evidence of discrimination, regardless of which definition or statistical test is chosen.

What Do We Mean by Racial Discrimination?

"The unequal treatment of equals on the basis of race" is a straightforward and generally accepted definition of discrimination. This definition is not precise enough, however, to allow us to interpret the results of audits in a world where random factors are mixed up with systematic factors in determining how two persons of different races (but otherwise equal) are treated when they apply for a job, a mortgage, or an apartment for rent. By random events we mean idiosyncratic variations in the behaviors of auditors and agents, and variations in the circumstances facing teammates associated with the audit method itself, that may or may not produce observed differences in treatment between auditor teammates. By systematic differences in treatment we mean differences observed consistently over a large number of audits or in circumstances where random variations are minimal.

"Unequal treatment" in the context of auditing typically refers to an action that is not evenhanded. This is different from evenhanded application of standards or rules that happen to result in more majority than minority applicants being successful. In legal terms, auditing is designed to uncover "differential treatment," not "disparate impact."

Disentangling random from systematic factors produces at least four alternative operational definitions of disparate treatment:

(1) Discriminatory Inclination: When evaluating equally qualified applicants, agents systematically assign penalties on the basis of race, whether those so penalized ultimately are given equal access to the particular market (or opportunity) or not.

(2) Gross Unfavorable Treatment: When confronting equally qualified applicants, agents give greater access to the particular market to majority auditors, whether for random or systematic reasons.

(3) Systematic Unfavorable Treatment: When confronting equally qualified applicants, agents give greater access to the particular market to majority auditors because of a systematically applied penalty based on race.[37] Under this definition, neither penalties that do not result in unequal access nor instances of unequal access that are due to random factors are counted as discriminatory.

(4) Net Market Effects: In a set of comparisons of equally qualified applicants, the number of majority-favored actions (for whatever reason) exceeds the number of minority-favored actions (for whatever reason), thereby creating, on net, reduced access for minorities to the particular market.

Each definition has its strengths and weaknesses. Since subsequent chapters use different definitions, at least implicitly, we discuss differences here to set the stage for interpreting the rest of the volume.

Yinger's "true behavior" (chapter 2) is an application of definition (1). The "discriminatory inclination" notion is based on how economists conventionally model a discrete choice (to favor one auditor or not): by positing that the observed dichotomous choice was produced by some continuous "latent variable" measuring the agent's evaluation of the auditor. The "act" of unequal treatment in this case is imposing a race penalty or bonus. This racial penalty or bonus may, however, be small compared to the effects of randomness, so that minorities are not necessarily provided less access to a particular market even though the agent holds a discriminatory inclination directed against them. This fact suggests a weakness of definition (1): audit data do not distinguish between systematic penalties and random factors, requiring complex statistical techniques to try to distinguish between the two. In addition, some would argue that society's primary concern is with inclinations that result in unequal treatment.

Turner (chapter 3) implicitly employs definition (2), gross unfavorable treatment. Unequal treatment of equals is discrimination, regardless of reason.[38] Being explicitly disfavored is harmful in and of itself. A strength of this definition is that it avoids the need to distinguish systematic from random events. A weakness is its implication that a purely random process that produces differential treatment (like the flipping of a fair coin) discriminates. To avoid this implication, it is typically assumed that differences in treatment observed in audits are infrequently caused by randomness.

Proponents of definition (3), "systematic unfavorable treatment," argue that one must both have an inclination and act systematically in disfavoring minorities before one can be found to have discriminated. It is important to recognize that random factors play an asymmetric role in this definition. Random factors that overcome agents' minority-disfavoring inclinations, thereby resulting in minorities having equal or even greater access, are ignored. But random factors that overcome agents' majority-disfavoring or equal-treatment inclinations, thereby resulting in minorities having less access, must be subtracted from the gross measure of unfavorable minority access. A weakness of this definition, like definition (1), is that it requires one to differentiate the systematic from the random. Furthermore, the appeal of this definition wanes if the size of the racial penalty grows small compared to the influence of randomness on the outcomes. That is, if an agent always assesses a small racial penalty but random influences on treatment overwhelm the effects of the penalties, the agent could end up favoring the minority almost as often as the majority. In this case a court might have difficulty finding discrimination because the evidence would be virtually indistinguishable from that produced by someone who assessed no racial penalty and favored some people over others for purely random reasons.[39]

Heckman and Siegelman (chapter 5) argue for definition (4), the "net market-effects" definition. They argue that the net result of acts that both favor and disfavor minorities is the most relevant concept for policymakers and minorities alike. Take, for instance, a case where minorities are treated less favorably in 30 percent of audits and are treated more favorably in 5 percent of audits (whereupon the net would be 25 percent). The results are dramatically different from the case where both the majority and minority auditors are favored (and disfavored) in 30 percent of the tests (where the net would be 0 percent). This intuitive appeal of the "net" measure is also its weakness, however, because it allows nonrandom acts that may have been systematically favoring majorities to be offset by nonrandom acts that may have been systematically favoring minorities—running the risk of concluding that no discrimination exists, when in fact there may be discrimination against both groups. Put differently, should discrimination against minorities by some be negated by favoritism toward minorities by others?

There is no "best" definition of racial discrimination. But it is important to be clear about one's definitional standpoint, because it can crucially shape one's conclusion about whether discrimination exists in the firm(s) or market(s) being audited.[40]

Each of the four definitions of discrimination employs a different statistical measure.

For ease of notation, let: f represent the proportion of those agents audited who systematically assess a penalty on minorities (i.e., have discriminatory inclinations); P_{maj} the proportion of cases favoring the majority auditor in market access (called "gross majority-favored" in this volume); P_{min} the proportion of cases favoring the minority auditor in market access ("gross minority-favored"); P_{rmaj} the proportion of cases favoring the majority auditor in market access due only to random factors; P_r the proportion of cases where agents have a minority-disfavoring proclivity but minorities do not get less market access because of randomness. The difference $P_{maj} - P_{min}$ is called "net majority-favored." The statistical measures indicating the existence of discrimination corresponding to each definition are as follows:

Definition of Discrimination	Existence Measure
(1) Discriminatory Inclination	$f > 0$
(2) Gross Unfavorable Treatment	$P_{maj} > 0$
(3) Systematic Unfavorable Treatment	$P_{maj} - P_{rmaj} > 0$
(4) Net Market Effects	$P_{maj} - P_{min} > 0$

For assessing whether discrimination exists, each definition looks to see if the particular statistical measure it deems relevant is greater than zero. Note that $f = P_{maj} - P_{rmaj} + P_r$.

Do Audits Provide Data on the Appropriate Statistical Measure?

Audits provide unambiguous measures of gross majority- and minority-favored frequencies; thus, the net majority-favored measure can be easily computed as well. But which of these measures is correct differs according to the definition chosen.

Perhaps the most serious disagreement arises over the test of the existence of discrimination: the so-called "gross versus net debate." All would agree that discrimination exists if the test listed for definition (4) is satisfied, but those employing definition (1) or (2) would argue that the net $P_{maj} - P_{min}$ (and $P_{maj} - P_{rmaj}$ if one were able to obtain it) provides an overly conservative test of the existence of discrimination. Those employing either definition (3) or (4) would reply that the gross P_{maj} (and f, if one were able to obtain it) is not, in itself, convincing. Of course, all would agree that demonstrating discrimination under the $P_{maj} - P_{min} > 0$ test (espoused by definition (4)) would be sufficient to demonstrate it under all definitions.[41]

Debate over the correct measure also has centered on whether and how audit studies account for randomness in their results. The 1977 Housing Market Practices Survey audit study (Wienk et al., 1979), for example, held that the gross minority-favored figure was a good proxy for differential treatment due purely to random factors, i.e., that $P_{min} = P_{rmaj}$. Under this interpretation the net measure becomes an accurate indicator of discrimination from perspectives (3) and (4).[42] Those holding to definition (1) or (2) argue that the $P_{min} = P_{rmaj}$ assumption discounts the possibility of systematic favoritism expressed toward minorities, and overstates P_{rmaj}. On this view, the net measure understates incidence.

New theoretical and empirical work is underway to determine the effects of randomness on audit results. One noteworthy theoretical effort is described by Yinger in chapter 2. Ongoing empirical work centers on audits involving pairs of same-race auditors; "sandwich" audits that involve three auditors, two auditors of one race and a third of another; and repeat audits of the same agents.

Other Methodological Issues

Matching of Auditors. It has been claimed that it is virtually impossible to match auditors on all characteristics that are perceived by the agent as relevant. This criticism is frequently voiced in the field of employment, where a wide variety of personal characteristics are indicative of prospective productivity and auditors may be interviewed more intensively than in the case of a housing audit. Heckman and Siegelman (chapter 5) contend that there may be crucial "unobservable" characteristics of potential workers that hypothetically cannot be matched. They also put forward a theoretical argument that matching auditors on observable characteristics might actually accentuate the differences in unobservables and, under certain conditions, overstate the measured extent of discrimination.

Heckman and Siegelman emphasize a crucial issue, especially for employment audits. More work needs to be done on matching auditor teammates to each other and matching both to prospective jobs being audited. In particular, future audits should seek to quantify (and thereby potentially standardize) dimensions of auditor personality and behaviors. Batteries of psychological and behavioral tests might prove useful in this regard. Matching auditors on bona fide financial and credit history characteristics is especially difficult in the context of mortgage audits (see Galster, chapter 7). Explorations that include teams matched at different skill levels relative to the job requirements might also provide illuminating results, because "overqualified" pairs may face different levels of discrimination from "underqualified" pairs.

Audit Management Approaches. How one recruits, trains, and reimburses auditors raises important questions. James and DelCastillo (1992), for example, have criticized the Urban Institute employment audits for using college-educated youths as auditors, instead of representatives of the minority population that are more representative in demeanor, behavior, speech, and other characteristics. One suggestion is to conduct employment audits involving "clusters" of auditor teams. The auditors in each cluster would be similar in both their actual and fictitious backgrounds, but actual and fictitious backgrounds would differ across clusters. The practical difficulties of recruiting such a diverse stable of auditors may be substantial, however. And using poorly educated auditors may risk compromising the quality of the audit information obtained and recorded.

With regard to auditor training, it has been argued that auditors are likely to be predisposed to find discrimination. In the research context this is referred to as experimenter effects, when the auditors produce the results they intuitively feel are "right." In the enforcement context this predisposition is amplified by the possible recovery of punitive and compensatory damages. As one commentator has written:

> Although substantial efforts have been made in the design of the test and the techniques it employs in an attempt to enhance its validity, a

> fundamental flaw may remain. This shortcoming relates to the test's dependence on objective sensory impressions in an environment where objectivity is particularly apt to be elusive. . . . [T]he testing process itself demands a formidable psychological and emotional commitment from its participants. At best, this commitment can complicate the testers' ability to distinguish between what he is trained to detect and what is perceived. Arguably, this interest also could create a predisposition that also would attack the objectivity necessary for valid results. Factors such as these taint the process and fuel the contention that the fair housing test is susceptible to fabricating its own evidence and thereby making up its own case. (Millspaugh 1984, 240)

We acknowledge the importance of rigorous auditor training and monitoring, so that the objectivity of the evidence is preserved. Exacting auditor selection and training techniques have been and will continue to be developed as the auditing procedure evolves. In the future these might draw on lessons learned in jury selection to ensure impartial conduct and reporting of results.

A final management issue concerns compensation for auditors. James and DelCastillo claim that the Urban Institute's strategy of paying auditors whether or not they obtained a job application, interview, or offer, encouraged "passive behavior" that was unrepresentative of actual job-seeking behavior. Those authors' Denver employment audits gave bonuses to auditors depending upon the stage in the hiring process they attained, on the assumption that such incentives would stimulate more representative (i.e., "real") job-seeking behavior. We believe such incentives are more likely to distort the audit results. Great care is taken during auditor training to instill behavior that improves comparability between the two members of a team. Differential bonuses hinging on "success" may encourage auditors when confronting agents to draw upon their personal, idiosyncratic resources and thereby disrupt the routinized behaviors learned during training.

Sampling Strategies. How one selects agents to be audited may strongly affect the results. For example, if one samples only agents or firms that have amassed a long record of consumer complaints, the result is likely to be higher measured discrimination than if one took a random sample of all agents or firms. A closely related question is the mechanism through which auditors gain access to an agent.

The audit studies reported in this volume all relied upon metropolitan newspapers as the basis for selecting a random sample of advertisements. This sampling strategy has the shortcoming of covering only a portion of available jobs or dwellings. Most openings are found by bona fide customers through other channels, such as signs, word of mouth, or the community newspaper. We believe, however, that auditing metropolitan newspaper ads is a conservative strategy—probably producing an underestimate of discrimination occurring in an area. This is because those who wish to discriminate are likely to prefer an advertising medium that is more selective in the audience it reaches than the metropolitan newspaper. As Heckman and Siegelman point out in chapter 5, this belief is supported indirectly by survey evidence showing that minorities searching through general newspapers for jobs have a higher rate of success than those using other means. Pilot audits conducted by the Fair Employment Council in Washington, D.C., also indicate lower rates of discrimination against both Hispanics and blacks in jobs advertised in metropolitan newspapers than those advertised in suburban newspapers or in employment agencies (Bendick et al., 1991, 1993). In any event, further research is needed to determine whether other sampling frames are feasible and affordable, and the extent to which audit results using those sampling frames might differ.

A second sampling issue relates not to which agents or firms are audited, but what sorts of jobs or dwellings are focused upon. Does one concentrate on a particular range of housing rents or values, or a particular skill level or industrial category of jobs? In the housing market it is not difficult to audit homes or apartments of any price range; one merely needs to provide the appropriate purchasing power in the auditors' scenario. But in the employment market in-person auditing of any but entry-level jobs may be difficult. Many available higher level positions are listed and, ultimately, filled within the firm. Other professional positions may be advertised externally, but may have such a small pool of potential applicants that in-person auditors might be obvious. Note, however, that McIntyre et al. (1980) and Bendick et al. (1991) have conducted pilot audits using resumes, instead of in-person auditors, to investigate a variety of professional positions. Yet other professional or craft occupations have licensing and technical requirements that would be virtually impossible (and probably illegal) to falsify. It remains an open question, therefore, how wide a spectrum of skills and occupations is amenable to investigations by the in-person auditing technique, and what the potential of audits based on matched resumes is.

Measurement of Unfavorable Treatment. Up to this point we have assumed that we could observe unambiguously whether an auditor was receiving unfavorable treatment in comparison to the teammate. Such might not always be the case in the instance of neighborhood or occupational steering. Minority auditors may, for example, be shown more dwellings than their majority teammates, but these dwellings might all be in neighborhoods occupied predominantly by minorities or with concentrations of low-quality dwellings and inferior public services. Such steering is clearly illegal under fair housing statutes, yet our audits might register instances of "minority-favored" treatment on the criterion of "numbers of dwellings shown." As Yinger points out (chapter 2), such misclassifications of results can have important impacts that would lead us to understate discrimination. If we were to include the cases of inferior housing units to which minorities have been steered, the net white-black difference in homes made available per audit would rise from .48 to .57, and the net Anglo-Hispanic difference from .52 to .66. The analogous case in employment testing is when minority auditors are given more job offers when the jobs in question are menial (as observed by James and DelCastillo, 1992) or do not involve contact with the public.

One might be tempted to score audits on the basis of the "quality" of the dwellings shown or jobs offered, not simply on their number. Operationally, however, quality scoring quickly becomes arbitrary. How should an audit be scored in the hypothetical case where the minority teammate is shown two homes in neighborhoods that are 10 percent minority-occupied and the majority teammate is shown one in a neighborhood that is 7 percent minority-occupied? How does one grade the quality of a job, or devise an index of degree of contact with the public? If one had such grades and indices, how large would the differences between teammates need to be before one judged a result "unfavorable?" Since consensus on such issues is unlikely, researchers using quality scoring should report findings for several alternative scoring schemes, to demonstrate the sensitivity of results to the scoring method used.

Applicability of Auditing Beyond the Housing Market. Audits have been criticized on feasibility grounds. For example, Sen. Alan Simpson (R-Wyo.) has asserted that testing is inappropriate for transactions that are putatively more complex than is the sale or rental of a housing unit, as they introduce a level of subjectivity that complicates judgments about the discriminatory intent and outcomes. Simpson stated on the floor of the Senate on February 22, 1991:

> While the Department of Housing and Urban Development has conducted similar tests of discrimination in public housing [sic], the employer-employee relationship is far more complex than that of landlord-tenant.

> There are so many more variables present in deciding whether to hire someone, that I believe that it is necessary for Congress to establish some reasonable ground rules with respect to this sort of "testing."

In response, Senator Simpson introduced legislation that would effectively undermine the use of testing under Title VII of the Civil Rights Act of 1964.[43]

Critics' concerns about the complexity of the hiring process and other similar transactions may be overstated. In the first place, where hiring involves entry-level jobs, the process is usually a summary one, very similar to the rental of a housing unit. Further, audits in the areas of lending, employment, and auto sales all focus on the "front end" of the transaction in question, where records are rarely kept, and practices are often uniform. It is possible to monitor the early phases of these transactions without becoming involved in the kind of complex interpersonal exchanges that would entail outcomes based largely on subjective criteria.

Where discriminatory activities involve more complex transactions—in hiring for a midlevel white-collar position, perhaps—testing may be less useful a tool unless the testers assume their own identities, which raises complicated recruitment and statistical issues. Moreover, in such cases the benefits of the auditing process may not outweigh the cost imposed on the employer, since several interviews involving a significant amount of senior management time could be involved.

Clear and Convincing Evidence?

Taken as a whole, the audit-based data in this volume provide strong evidence that racial-ethnic discrimination, however defined, continues in many American metropolitan housing markets and at least some labor markets, and seriously limits minorities' access to these markets. Even conservative standards of interpretation confirm this conclusion.

Consider first the question of the existence of discrimination. The Housing Discrimination Study (as well as its predecessors, the 1977 Housing Market Practices Survey and dozens of local audits conducted by fair housing organizations) reveals that discrimination against blacks and Hispanics exists in the vast majority of the metropolitan areas audited. This is true regardless of discrimination definition or statistical test employed.

The main challenge has come in the field of employment audits. But recall that a conservative test of the existence of discrimination, regardless of one's definition, is whether the difference between majority-favored and minority-favored audits is significantly greater than zero (i.e., $P_{maj} > P_{min}$). Heckman and Siegelman employ three alternative statistical tests—sign test, large sample chi-squared test, exact small-sample (binomial) test—and find evidence of discrimination in the Urban Institute studies when considering all black-white audits combined, all Hispanic-Anglo audits combined, and all individual employment audits sites except Chicago's black-white audits. These statistical results combining all auditor pairs are permissible, given Heckman and Siegelman's tests for homogeneity.

The evidence from the pilot employment audits to date, therefore, shows that discrimination exists against foreign sounding/looking Hispanic males in San Diego and Chicago and against black males in Washington, D.C.[44] It is not clear in the case of blacks in Chicago (or Denver blacks and Hispanics, based on the James and DelCastillo results, 1992). More employment audits are needed to clarify the geographic extent of racial employment discrimination and test whether racial differentials are similar for men and women.[45]

The differential effect of race on *overall* access to housing and labor markets is not in doubt, however. Regardless of definitional perspective, all analysts would agree that the magnitude of the limitation faced by minorities in a market is given by the net majority-favored measure. The Housing Discrimination Study showed that blacks in the sales market have, on average, 21 percent fewer homes recommended or shown to them than their teammates; in the rental market the comparable figure is 25 percent fewer apartments. Hispanics in the sales market have, on average, 22 percent fewer homes made available to them than their teammates; in the rental market the figure is 11 percent fewer apartments. In the Chicago and Washington black-white employment audits, blacks were offered 23 percent fewer jobs than their teammates. In the Chicago and San Diego Hispanic-Anglo employment audits, Hispanics were offered 34 percent fewer jobs than their teammates.

These racial impacts offer clear and convincing evidence that we have yet to achieve equal opportunity in America.

CONSEQUENCES OF STRONG DOCUMENTATION

Strong documentation of discrimination has two direct results: The frame of reference for debating the strengthening of equal opportunity legislation is altered, and the analysis of differential outcomes by scholars is transformed.

The clearest illustration of the first point comes from comparing passage of congressional amendments to Title VIII of the Fair Housing Act of 1968 with the 1990 defeat of proposed amendments to Title VII of the Civil Rights Act of 1964. The unequivocal documentation of the widespread existence of discriminatory treatment against minority home seekers with audit data from the Housing Market Practices Survey helped change the terms of debate from *whether* to strengthen Title VIII to *how* to strengthen it in a way that would both create an efficient enforcement mechanism and maintain constitutional guarantees of due process. The contrast with the deliberations in 1990 on amending Title VII, where evidence on discrimination was both less central and less definitive, is strong. Mashaw (1990), among others, argued that clear proof of discrimination would be essential for any strengthening of Title VII. However, a law doing so was proposed and enacted in 1991: The Civil Rights Act of 1991.

We recognize, of course, that many other factors were at work in the two cases. Opposition to strengthening housing legislation may be weaker because in a housing sale the buyer and seller do not have a continuing relationship, as do an employer and employee. Additionally, as was pointed out earlier, public opinion gives little support for the idea that the government should intervene in the labor market. Finally, a powerful if unexpected impetus for enacting The Civil Rights Act of 1991 was rising concern with sexual harassment in the workplace—a concern that was dramatized on the eve of the law's passage by sexual harassment allegations against now-Justice Clarence Thomas (Simiscalco and Giansello 1992).

Equally important, the documentation of discrimination in the housing sector has fundamentally changed the way researchers are structuring their analyses of discrimination—a shift that has altered the conventional wisdom. In the 1970s, housing researchers conducted analyses of differences in the prices blacks and whites paid for housing, homeownership rates, the rates at which the two groups consumed various types of housing, and the type of areas in which they lived. In each of these cases the analytic method attempted to control for all factors besides race that might account for the differences, with the residual attributed at least partially to discrimination.[46] In short, the primary effort was given to measuring the presence and extent of discrimination by trying to discern its effects.

Once the presence of discrimination was definitively documented and quantified for 40 metropolitan areas, research gradually shifted to explaining the role of discrimination in observed outcomes. For example, Galster and Keeney (1988) and Galster (1991) analyzed the interrelationships among housing discrimination, interracial occupational disparities, incomes of blacks relative to incomes of whites, and residential segregation across cities. A greater incidence of housing discrimination was found to increase segregation, which in turn produced greater occupational disparities, relatively lower black incomes, and higher poverty rates.

Strikingly, much of the recent research involving discrimination in employment is of the type done in the housing field in the years preceding the documentation of housing discrimination. The following list of "dependent variables" in housing and employment studies illustrates this point:

Housing	*Employment*
house prices and rents	wages
housing choices and consumption levels	occupation type
residential segregation	workplace segregation

Thus, a similar shift in analysis would be useful in documenting hiring discrimination (particularly for entry-level positions) and in making such measures of discrimination available for a substantial number of metropolitan areas. For example, analysis could be undertaken of the causes of variation in minority relative to white wage rates or minority employment rates across markets using discrimination measures as one explanatory variable. These advances would, in turn, have clear implications both for defining social problems and for the policy interventions that address them.

TESTING AS AN ENFORCEMENT STRATEGY: THE CASE OF HOUSING

This section looks first to the experience in the housing sector to assess the effectiveness of testing in combating discrimination by providing relief for individual complainants; it then examines whether testing can be carried out at high volume. Finally, the section outlines a strategy for the use of testing and auditing in a comprehensive enforcement program.

Effectiveness in Combating Discrimination

The record on the effectiveness of testing programs in combating housing discrimination is based almost exclusively on experience before implementation of the amendments to Title VIII in March 1989. Two gauges of success are relevant: first, the effectiveness of testing in resolving individual cases, and second, the effectiveness of testing in reducing the incidence of discrimination in a local housing market.

Numerous leaders of state and local and public and private fair-housing groups have testified to the effectiveness of careful housing tests in obtaining favorable out-of-court settlements or court decisions involving individual acts of discrimination.[47] The only systematic, statistical evidence on the effectiveness of having testing evidence available comes from the evaluation of the Fair Housing Assistance Program (FHAP) sponsored by the Department of Housing and Urban Development (HUD) in the mid 1980s. Part of this study analyzed case closures in the early 1980s by agencies receiving funding under FHAP. Regression models were estimated of the likelihood of a complainant's obtaining relief with the assistance of the agency. According to that analysis, the likelihood of some form of relief increased by 54 percent when testing evidence was available, after controlling for the agency involved, type of respondent, type of issue, case duration, and other factors (Wallace et al. 1985, table 5.4).

A more recent Urban Institute study of the disposition of fair housing complaints filed by private fair housing groups has generated weaker results. Multivariate and logit analyses revealed that testing played a limited role in determining complaint outcomes after other factors were taken into account. However, the number of cases observed was limited and the controls exerted on the types of cases examined were fewer than was the case in the Wallace study.[48]

Evidence is sparse on the more general question of whether aggressive campaigns of testing can indeed reduce the level of discrimination. Galster (1990) reviewed the experiences of agencies that have mounted ongoing, comprehensive programs of random testing. He concluded:

> Although the evidence is limited, it appears that such collective enforcement techniques can create a potent deterrent. Cleveland Heights, OH, has undertaken a series of random tests in its community since the late 1970s. This program, coupled with efforts to educate the real estate industry about fair housing and well-publicized suits against major real estate brokerage firms, has produced a dramatic decline in the observed incidence of discriminatory acts, as revealed by the tests

themselves. Similar efforts by the Kentucky Commission on Civil Rights have returned comparable dividends. (P. 145)

An important question is whether testing—either in support of developing evidence in response to complaints or on a random basis—can be conducted at a high volume and thus create a "critical mass" of settlements that would collectively change the behavior of rental and real estate agents in larger communities. The answer is clearly affirmative, based on the numbers achieved in the recent housing and hiring audits. About 30 valid audits were completed weekly in each of the five in-depth sites in the Housing Discrimination Study. Similarly, an average of at least 40 valid audit completions were obtained in Washington, D.C., and Chicago in the Employment Discrimination Study.[49] The strains on management of mounting such high numbers of audits were significant in both studies but would likely decline if testing programs of this volume were sustained indefinitely and adjustments were made to manage the work flow. Note that these volumes are probably the upper limits for a program of random audits, since the two studies used most or all of the housing and employment ads for units and positions meeting the audit programs' criteria.

Testing in support of litigation has already reached high aggregate levels in the housing area. One estimate is that in 1990 about 4,500 such tests were conducted by private fair-housing groups—roughly evenly divided between those done in the course of pursuing complaints and those done as part of systematic testing programs.[50]

Finally, what does testing cost? Conducting a test to develop evidence costs from $300 to $600, depending broadly on local wage rates. This is the cost, including overhead and management, of identifying the firm to be audited, briefing the auditors, organizing and conducting the audit, debriefing the auditors, and analyzing the results. It does not include attorney's costs for using this information in legal proceedings.

Testing/Auditing as Part of a Comprehensive Enforcement Effort

Being able to develop strong evidence of discrimination—in this case, through testing—is a crucial element in an enforcement strategy. However, testing must be part of a larger process. Convenient opportunities to file complaints must be available for those who suspect they have been discriminated against, and adequate resources must be devoted to pursuing types of discrimination not amenable to identification or verification through testing.

Development of strong evidence must be coupled with a speedy and effective legal process. One of the most notable features of the 1988 amendments to Title VIII was a strengthened and speedier legal process.[51] Speed was achieved by authorizing hearings before administrative law judges (ALJs) under tight time schedules, while due process was guaranteed by the right of the complainant or respondent to request to have the case heard in a federal district court.[52]

The ALJ process is widely perceived to be notably faster than taking the case to a district court, although precise figures are hard to assemble. In addition, the process benefits the complainant because HUD or the responsible agency in jurisdictions with equivalent laws bears the cost of preparing the case and prosecuting it before the ALJ. Obviously, this arrangement can be more advantageous to aggrieved parties than bringing a private civil suit for alleged discriminatory acts—the common approach in employment discrimination cases. But if the complainant engages a private attorney and prevails, he can then apply to the ALJ for attorney's fees and costs. If HUD files the case and the respondent prevails, HUD may be liable for reasonable attorney's fees.

Importantly, the potentially large costs associated with providing these legal services to an unknown number of complainants appear to be a key factor in making jurisdictions hesitant about revising their laws to conform to the new federal statute and to committing themselves to prosecuting valid complaints.

In summary, the effectiveness of testing in the area of housing has increased because it has been joined with efficient complaint processing and judicial procedures. We now turn to three distinct roles that testing and auditing have to play in a comprehensive enforcement program.

Complaint Processing. Private fair-housing groups, and state and local fair-housing agencies to a lesser extent, have conducted tests in investigating complaints. Conducting the tests immediately after the complaint is filed has been instrumental in obtaining temporary restraining orders in numerous cases and in obtaining more out-of-court settlements favorable to the complainant. Clearly this type of testing is an essential element of a contemporary enforcement strategy. Because HUD has begun to contract for testing as part of its investigations, the use of testing in this context will certainly rise in the years ahead.

Random Testing. A central finding of all the housing audit studies is that discrimination is typically subtle, with the victims seldom realizing that it has occurred. Indeed, one recent HUD estimate is that less than 1 percent of illegal acts of housing discrimination become the subject of a complaint.[53] Consequently, enforcement needs to go beyond responding to complaints. Identifying those who discriminate will require a substantial program of random tests, conducted explicitly to develop evidence of such behavior. Earlier, we noted that a few jurisdictions have conducted these testing programs with considerable effect.

Some assistance with such testing is available to private fair-housing groups under HUD's Fair Housing Initiative Program.[54] A major expansion in the resources available to support programs of random testing is needed for an ongoing, comprehensive program in every metropolitan area. Achieving this objective will require not only additional funding but also support for expanding the coverage of testing organizations to communities lacking active fair-housing programs. Such support could involve assistance in establishing fair-housing groups where they do not now exist, inducing state agencies to fill the void, or, failing these options, having HUD undertake this testing by either contracting with outside groups or managing the process itself.

A Systematic Auditing Program. The results on the extent of housing discrimination for the five in-depth sites in the Housing Discrimination Study underscore the variance in discrimination among areas, although housing discrimination remains a serious problem in all metropolitan areas for which reliable data are available. A program of audits—at both the national and the metropolitan level—is clearly essential for ascertaining the extent to which public policy and changing attitudes are reducing discriminatory behavior. While HUD has been a leader in conducting periodic national audit studies, similar studies should be undertaken at the metropolitan level as well. The metro-specific results could be used in targeting scarce federal enforcement resources.

To date housing audit studies have focused on race and ethnicity. In the future they should be expanded to encompass discrimination based on sex, family status, and age.[55] Having a full inventory of the incidence of discrimination against various groups could be the basis for an efficiently targeted program of random testing.

FUTURE DIRECTIONS FOR AUDITING

Lessons from Housing

The experience with auditing in the housing context makes clear its capacity and its value. First, national, federally funded audits have firmly established the incidence of high levels of both opportunity-denying and opportunity-diminishing behavior disadvantageous to both blacks and Hispanics. The evidence from audits has changed perceptions of opportunity in housing, enabling and guiding policy change. And national studies have demonstrated conclusively that audits can be conducted economically and at high volume.

Second, there is evidence that the use of auditing for enforcement has expedited settlements of legal challenges in favor of plaintiffs, at manageable costs. In addition to the power of audits to help remedy individual cases of discrimination, there is evidence that testing can lead to a decrease in discrimination at the city or county level.

Third, auditing has been an important element in an innovative and generally fruitful collaboration between the federal government (i.e., HUD) and private, nonprofit, and state and local organizations dedicated to fair housing. The government provides limited support for testing, sets basic rules governing its implementation, and now provides a forum for hearing disputes stemming from challenges to which tests have given rise. In return, these nonfederal agencies assume responsibility for field activity and enforcement. In the final analysis, the courts, to which all defendants have recourse, serve to set minimum standards for the fairness and quality of the testing that takes place.

In sum, the coherent approach adopted in the area of housing may represent something of a model for other areas of policy—most notably credit and employment, to which we now turn.

Credit Studies

If housing represents the most fully developed area of activity in terms of scientific methods, institutional commitments, and institutional history, credit is the least developed area covered in this volume.

George Galster's review of early credit-related audits makes clear both the feasibility and the advisability of testing in this area (see chapter 7 of this volume). The studies reviewed indicate that discrimination at the pre-application stage occurred in a small fraction of transactions. Where tests have been concentrated on institutions suspected of discriminating, however, higher levels of discrimination have been found. As Galster points out, these early studies made valiant efforts to pioneer the use of testing within a comparatively complex framework. Galster cautions, though, that the studies tend to "fall short of social-scientific standards of clarity, replicability, and statistical validity."

On the strength of this review it seems clear that a next step will be to develop and implement a pilot study that examines a range of lending and related practices (including home appraisal and mortgage insurance) across several metropolitan areas. The study would draw not only on prior experiments in the credit area but also on advances in housing and employment audits. As Galster notes, such a test, for feasibility purposes, would need to focus on the preapplication stage as the first phase of a broader testing program. But that should not be a problem. Many analysts believe that it is in the preapplication phase that most of the discrimination takes place. Indeed, it is during this phase, prior to development of a traceable paper trail, that individuals and institutions have the greatest incentive to discriminate. Further, the difficulties associated with going beyond the preapplication phase (including operational problems associated with avoiding discovery and issues relating to fraudulent misrepresentation) raise feasibility issues.

Employment Studies

We believe that the employment audits conducted by the Urban Institute not only have established the feasibility of testing in the employment context but have gone some distance toward establishing a workable methodology for fieldwork and analysis.

The results of these early metro-area studies indicate that the incidence of opportunity-denying behavior in hiring is higher than in housing. At the same time, the incidence of opportunity-diminishing behavior is relatively lower in hiring, and overall discrimination in hiring may be more variable across cities than is the case for housing. These initial findings also suggest that discrimination in hiring is worse for accented, foreign-appearing Hispanics than for blacks and is no worse in suburban than in central-city settings.

As in the area of credit, testing in employment may have its greatest power in illuminating that phase of the employment transaction—hiring—about which the least is known, in which employers have the greatest incentive to discriminate, and that may hold the most significant policy implications.

The feasibility of conducting hiring audits may well be limited to entry-level jobs and to the early screening phases (the review of resumes, for example) of more sophisticated jobs. If this is the case, it certainly does not invalidate the conclusions being drawn here. Still, one must be careful not to project these findings to the labor market as a whole.

We mentioned earlier the fact that employment discrimination cases brought under Title VII have grown many times faster than the overall federal civil caseload (Donohue and Siegelman 1991). We also noted that firings account for an increasingly large share of this growing caseload, while hiring cases account for a steadily declining percentage.

These developments have several implications for antidiscrimination efforts and for testing. First, if policymakers look to complaints, they may tend to overlook the abiding problem of discrimination in hiring, focusing attention on other stages of the employment process and thereby misallocating resources. As a result, policies may reflect the interests of minorities who are better off and work in integrated settings. (Both are frequently characteristics of complainants in discharge cases, Donohue and Siegelman point out.)

Second, Donohue and Siegelman contend that the patterns of litigation emerging from Title VII give employers a growing incentive to discriminate against minorities at the hiring stage, where the applicant will be less aware of discrimination, less able to prove it, and less inclined to try. As in the case of credit, it is at the initial hiring stage where the paper record is least complete, enabling and, in some cases, effectively encouraging discriminatory behaviors.

Auditing for research and enforcement can address both of these effects. If further pilot tests continue to affirm the validity of auditing for employment discrimination and its capacity to do so at high volume, it may make sense for the federal government to conduct a national audit of hiring discrimination modeled on HUD's approximately decennial Housing Discrimination Study. Support for the design of early studies has been provided by private foundations, but given that civil rights enforcement is a public responsibility, it makes sense for this larger, more expensive effort to be funded by the federal government.[56] Use of audits in the enforcement context to test for discrimination in hiring makes substantial sense given that hiring discrimination may be underrepresented in Title VII litigation. It also makes sense given the incentives that may be established by Title VII to exclude minorities at the hiring stage.

As chapter 8 in this volume indicates, the legal issues surrounding the use of testing in employment were being litigated in the fall of 1991 in a case brought by the Fair Employment Council of Washington. The case invokes the validity of auditing under both Section 1981 and Title VII. Thus, it is likely to inform the validity of the U.S. Equal Employment Opportunity Commission's (1990) policy guidance announcing that the agency would accept charges based on evidence provided by testers. Expanding the use of testing in employment to the enforcement context raises a number of policy issues. First, to what extent would it be advisable for the federal government to help build an infrastructure of private organizations resembling the fair-housing councils that exist in many metro areas? Second, should the federal government provide direct financial support of testing in employment, as it has in housing? And, if so, should that support be conditioned on conducting tests that conform to certain federally designated procedural standards, as is the case in housing?

Random or targeted testing in the employment area may lend itself to other uses. For example, the Office of Special Counsel of the Department of Justice or the EEOC might consider using random or targeted testing to determine which employers are inadvertently discriminating on the basis of national origin or alienage in response to the 1986 Immigration Reform and Control Act. Findings of discrimination could initially result in guidance on compliance rather than punishment, at the same time providing valuable feedback to the agency on the nature and incidence of discrimination.

In sum, the audit studies discussed in this volume have established the feasibility and advisability of testing in a variety of contexts. It seems to us that audits hold the power to clarify the extent of discrimination, which helps government perform its continuing obligation to counteract it. It makes sense to continue to expand their use for both research and enforcement purposes in the areas of credit and employment.

Notes

Funding to support this work has been provided by The Rockefeller Foundation. The authors thank Larry Pearl, Ron Wienk, Genevieve Kenney, Douglas Wissoker, and Cliff Schrupp for advice and information during the preparation of this chapter.

1. Attention is restricted to white attitudes because comparatively few questions have been asked of blacks consistently over the same period. Schuman et al. (1985, table 4.1) report two questions for this period dealing with housing and employment. As early as 1964—and consistently thereafter—blacks reported essentially unanimous support for the statement of principle that "black people have a right to live wherever they can afford to, just like anybody else." Similarly, in 1964 blacks gave an overwhelmingly positive response (92 percent) to the following question on implementation of the rights of blacks in obtaining jobs: "Should the government in Washington see to it that black people get fair treatment in jobs or leave these matters to the states and local communities?" However, there was some diminution in support for this position by 1974, when 82 percent of blacks still agreed with it.

2. We restrict the discussion to blacks to keep the discussion brief. Analyses similar to those described have been conducted for Hispanics versus Anglos and white women versus white men.

3. Sometimes these studies have employed aggregate data. For example, Bradbury et al. (1989) analyzed the ratio of mortgage loans to structures in Boston neighborhoods as a function of variables measuring the demand for and supply of units and mortgages and the percentage of households in the neighborhood that were black. They interpreted the coefficient of the race variable as suggesting discrimination in lending against blacks.

4. It should be noted that notwithstanding such uncertainty, the courts have been willing to accept evidence of discrimination produced using these methods. See Ashenfelter and Oaxaca (1987) for details.

5. There is substantial inequality in earnings among blacks (even compared with white men), with those with limited education falling further behind (Jaynes and Williams 1989, 275–6).

6. See Shulman (1989) for a summary of the studies and a rebuttal. Heckman (1989) gives greater detail on some of the methodological problems of identifying declines in wage differentials between blacks and whites.

7. Darity (1989) summarizes these studies and argues that other evidence refutes this interpretation.

8. Many more studies have been done attempting to explain differences in wages received by blacks and whites. See, for example, O'Neill (1990) and Haworth et al. (1975).

9. Most recently, for a review of this literature, see Holzer (1991) and Holzer and Vroman (1991). Holzer and Vroman conclude that "the review of the literature indicated widespread support for the idea that labor demand has shifted away from less-educated workers in the past two decades, thus leading to some degree of skill mismatch . . . there is growing evidence that intra-metropolitan movements of firms and population have reduced the demand for black, inner-city residents. But the extent to which these sources of mismatch explain the employment problems of less-educated black males has remained open to question" (p. 36).

10. There is also agreement on the effectiveness of affirmative action programs combined with improved education and other federal action in increasing black employment shares in certain industries during the 1960s and 1970s, although there is far less agreement on the impact on overall employment levels. See, for example, Leonard (1990) and Heckman (1989).

11. U.S. House of Representatives (1990); U.S. Senate (1989).

12. For a summary of these findings, see Fishbein (1989) and Galster (1992).

13. See the testimony of these agencies in U.S. Senate (1990).

14. Beginning in 1990 higher-quality data on mortgage loan applications started being collected from most financial institutions doing such lending under the Home Mortgage Disclosure Act. However, these data do not include detailed information about the specific properties for which mortgage financing is sought. See Wienk (1992).

15. More recent, technically stronger results from another national audit study covering both blacks and Hispanics are discussed later in this chapter, and are presented in greater detail in chapter 2.

16. See Hakken (1979); James et al. (1984); and Galster (1991a).

17. In tests that are carefully administered, comparability is sought by, for example, (a) creating fictional biographies; (b) carefully screening and matching testers so that they

are similar in tangible features such as size, age, and speech, as well as in such intangible features as demeanor and temperament; (c) providing intensive training; and (d) maintaining close oversight of tester performance. See, generally, Turner, Fix, and Struyk (1991).

18. Individual cases of unfavorable treatment may result, however, not from discrimination but from random factors. See the section on methodological issues **(p. 00)** for a detailed discussion.

19. On the need for the social sciences to tell a coherent and compelling story in order to stimulate public action, see Peter Marris (1982).

20. As one scholar has written, "modern forms of both racial prejudice and discrimination have become more subtle, indirect, procedural, and ostensibly non-racial" (Pettigrew 1985, 674).

21. Most studies of discrimination in labor markets focus exclusively on wage versus hiring discrimination. See Donohue and Siegelman (1991).

22. While hiring charges outnumbered termination charges by 50 percent in 1966, the ratio was reversed by more than 6 to 1 by 1985 (Donohue and Siegelman 1991, 8).

23. This result, discussed later in this chapter, was found in a multivariate analysis of outcomes in complaints filed under the Department of Housing and Urban Development's Fair Housing Assistance Program (Wallace et al. 1985). However, later findings from a large-scale Urban Institute research project that systematically compared outcomes in housing discrimination cases brought using audits with those brought without them, produced less conclusive results (Wienk and Simonson 1992).

24. There is substantial precedent for such a balancing of interests. For example, federal policy for the protection of human subjects holds that the following conditions can justify the omission of informed consent:

> An IRB [institutional review board] may . . . waive . . . informed consent provided. . .
> (1) The research involves no more than minimal risk to human subjects:
> (2) The waiver or alteration will not adversely affect the rights and welfare of the subjects;
> (3) The research could not practicably be carried out without the waiver or alteration: and
> (4) Whenever appropriate, the subjects will be provided with additional information after participation.

56 Federal Register 117, p. 28017, June 18, 1991.

25. For example, Ian Ayres (1991) has written regarding the fair-driving testers' efforts to mitigate the process of wasting the salespersons' time: "The study has several features designed to mitigate the problem of wasting the salespersons' time during the negotiation process. Most important, the testers visited the dealerships during the least busy times of the week (from the hours of 9–12 and 1–5 Monday to Friday). During these times few people shop for cars, and there are often several salespeople without customers to serve. In addition, testers were instructed that if all salespeople of a dealership were busy, they should return to the dealership at another time. . . . Steps were also taken to minimize the time that testers spent with the salespeople. The test itself was designed to be completed in 10 to 15 minutes and the testers were instructed to spend no more than an hour at the dealership" (p. 822).

26. *Richardson v. Howard*, 712 F.2d 319, 321 (7th Cir. 1983).

27. *Zuck v. Hussey*, 394 F. Supp. 1028, 1051 (E.D. Mich. 1975), aff'd mem., 547 F.2d 1168 (6th Cir. 1977).

28. Nevertheless, broad knowledge of the existence of such tests might reduce the level of discriminatory behavior that takes place. As a result, broad notice—like that used to make the public aware of tax audits—has some merits.

29. Statistically reliable audit findings are not available for mortgage transactions. See chapter 7 in this volume for details.

30. The results are summarized in Turner, Struyk, and Yinger (1991); also see chapters 2 and 3 of this volume.

31. These studies are summarized in appendix A of this volume. An additional hiring audit study involving both Hispanic-Anglo and black-white tests was conducted in Denver in 1990. The results are not included in the main discussion because the audit procedures followed there were somewhat different from those involved in the other two pilot tests. Details are in James and DelCastillo (1991), and are also discussed in chapters 4 and 5 of this volume.

32. These are only illustrations from much larger lists of the items included in opportunity-diminishing acts. The following rules were applied in the hiring audits to determine which auditor was treated more favorably: (1) If one auditor advanced to a further stage in the hiring process (i.e., obtaining an application, being given an interview, being offered a job) than his partner, he was defined as being treated more favorably; (2) when both auditors advanced to the same stage in the hiring process, if one experienced fewer opportunity-diminishing acts than his partner, then he was defined as being treated more favorably.

33. These data refer to simple differences in unfavorable treatment and make no attempt at disentangling random from systematic behaviors. The estimates in table 1.2 for housing, in contrast, are based on multivariate procedures that purge the random component. Nevertheless, analysis in the Housing Discrimination Study shows that estimates of discrimination and unfavorable treatment are generally quite close. For details, see Yinger (1991b).

34. James and DelCastillo (1991) found no statistically significant levels of hiring discrimination against either blacks or Hispanics in Denver (using somewhat different procedures). Taken at face value, these results indicate a much larger spread for hiring audits than indicated by the other two pilot studies.

35. Yinger (1991a), chap. 6.

36. Craig Coelen, Genevieve Kenney, and Douglas Wissoker made invaluable suggestions that are reflected in this section and in appendix 1.A. Yinger defines systematic as "what would occur if one teammate were able to experience the same circumstances as the other;" see chapter 2.

37. Note that we do not equate systematic with intentional. Differential treatment may be systematic even when it is so habitual, and unconsciously applied, that it may not be conscious.

38. Just as majority-favored audits indicate discrimination against minorities, so do minority-favored audits indicate discrimination against the majority.

39. This case is described in more detail in appendix 1.A.

40. Note that two other questions could be asked here: 1. How much less likely are minorities to receive favorable treatment? 2. How many fewer options (numbers of jobs, dwellings, etc.) are made available to minorities? Regardless of definitional perspective, there is a consensus that the former question is answered by the statistic: proportion majority-favored minus proportion minority-favored, and the latter by a simple difference in the number of total options afforded the group of majority auditors and those afforded the group of minority auditors. These amount to the same thing when the outcomes are simple measures of proportions. Such estimates for housing audits are presented by Yinger (chapter 2), and estimates for hiring audits are presented by Heckman and Siegelman (chapter 5).

41. A related area of disagreement is as follows. Although from the perspective of one holding definition (3) it is clear that P_{maj} will overstate the incidence of discrimination

whenever P_{rmaj} is positive, whether f will be larger or smaller than $P_{maj} - P_{rmaj}$ cannot be determined a priori. (See appendix 1.A for an illustration.)

42. An important qualification is demonstrated in appendix 1.A. The cases of P_{min} are likely to be a poor proxy for P_{rmaj} because P_{rmaj} represents cases of P_{maj} where randomness has overcome minority-favored and equal-favored treatment proclivities. See also chapter 2.

43. Senator Simpson's proposal, which is set out in his own proposed version of the Civil Rights Amendments of 1991, would prohibit employment testers from misrepresenting their education, experience, or other qualifications for the job being offered. This requirement was offered because Senator Simpson viewed it as being "only fair for employers who might be subject to liability under Title VII because of testing programs." *Congressional Record* S 2259-63, Feb. 22, 1991.

44. When they apply for entry-level jobs advertised in the major metropolitan newspaper. Recently the Washington results were replicated by Bendick et al. (1993).

45. Bendick et al.'s Latino (1991) and black (1993) audits suggested they are not.

46. For a systematic review of these studies, see Yinger et al. (1979), Yinger (1979), and Galster (1992).

47. Such commentary was common, for example, at the 1984 HUD Conference on Fair Housing Testing; for a summary of the proceedings, see Heintz (1985). See also chapter 8 of this volume.

48. The authors themselves conclude:

This does not necessarily imply that testing does not represent important evidence in individual complaints, or that it is an ineffective mechanism for investigating fair housing complaints. Instead, it seems likely that the most important determinants of both investigative procedures and complaint outcomes are unobserved factors, such as the underlying merits of individual complaints, the quality of testing evidence, and the specific nature of the testing evidence. (Wienk and Simonson, 1992)

49. Data from the Urban Institute work flow logs.

50. See, generally, Wienk and Simonson (1992).

51. In this instance, the case is referred to the Department of Justice for prosecution.

52. Figure in Galster (1990a).

53. Funding for the program in fiscal year 1991 is $5.8 million. HUD's legislative proposals for fiscal year 1992 request expansion of eligibility to state and local agencies whose equivalency status is withdrawn in 1992 because their government does not modify its fair-housing laws to be consistent with the revised federal fair-housing statute.

54. For a further discussion of avenues for expanding the coverage of these studies, see Struyk (1985).

55. There may also be room here for state action. States played a critical role in monitoring discrimination triggered by the Immigration Reform and Control Act's employment discrimination provisions. See California Fair Employment and Housing Commission (1990); New York state Inter-Agency Task Force on Immigration Affairs (1988).

APPENDIX 1.A

INTERPRETING AUDITS USING DIFFERENT DEFINITIONS OF DISCRIMINATION

This appendix provides illustrations of how the implicit definition of discrimination one employs crucially shapes how one statistically evaluates and interprets the results of audits. A closely related issue is how one believes random events affect the audit results.

Because the issues quickly grow complex, we start by considering audits repeatedly conducted on a single agent in an idealized, nonrandom world. We then allow randomness to enter and assess its impact on our audit results. Finally, we expand our hypothetical audits to cover many agents. We employ the same four codes denoting definitions of discrimination and the same symbols as provided in the text. Throughout we consider the questions of the existence and the incidence of discrimination, that is: Does discrimination occur? How often does it occur?

Auditing a Single Agent in a Nonrandom World

Distinctions among the four definitions of discrimination become moot in a world without randomness, i.e., where the single agent being audited behaves consistently, all auditor matches are perfect, and no stochastic events impinge on the audit activities that affect either the agent's or auditors' actions. In such a world, there will be a one-for-one correspondence between the racial penalties agents assess when evaluating applicants and the failure of those so penalized to gain equal access compared to their teammates. The distinction between random and systematic differences in treatment is rendered moot. Finally, the agent will evince favoritism (if any) toward either majority or minority auditors, not both.

As illustration, what if the agent being audited had a discriminating inclination towards minorities, and therefore consistently assessed a race penalty on minority applicants for vacant apartments? We would expect to see that 100 percent of the audits favored the majority (i.e., "gross majority-favored" = 100 percent). This figure would simultaneously provide an indicator of the existence and an accurate estimate of incidence of this agent's discrimination, whether one considers penalty being assessed or explicit acts of differential access, because $f = P_{maj} = 100$ percent.

Thus, in repeated audits of a single agent in a nonrandom world, gross and net measures of favoritism would be identical and equal to both inclinations proclivities and explicit acts of discrimination. Any of the four definitions of discrimination yield the same result regarding the existence and incidence of discrimination.

Auditing a Single Agent When Randomness Occurs

Unfortunately, the above unanimous conclusion evaporates when any one of several potential forms of randomness enter the audit results. First, auditors are unlikely to be matched perfectly on all relevant characteristics, and even if they were in some abstract sense, an agent's evaluations of these matches may not always correspond. Auditors may not behave uniformly in each encounter with an agent, depending on their health, mood, or reaction to the agent. Second, agents are likely to have a random component to their behavior; they may be unable to treat auditors of the same race identically in repeat trials. Finally, external events can intervene to affect agents' behaviors because the auditors do not confront the agent simultaneously. Idiosyncratic events may have immediately preceded the visit by one teammate that were not present during the other's visit: a bona fide applicant appears to take the job or dwelling, the agent receives some upsetting news, etc.

Consider the consequences of any of these sorts of random influences on results of repeated audits of a single agent. We analyze four alternative cases, and show how the veracity of the gross (P_{maj}) and net ($P_{maj} - P_{min}$) measures as tests for the existence and incidence of discrimination varies according to the definition chosen.

Case I. First, suppose we audit an agent who, we assume, never assesses a racial penalty ($f = 0$). Even though this person tries to be evenhanded, randomness is likely to lead to some audits in which the minority is favored but, on average, just as many in which the majority is favored; let us assume 10 percent each as illustration, i.e., $P_{maj} = P_{min} = 10$ percent. (Eighty percent of the audits would reveal equal treatment.) Thus, the net majority-favored figure would be zero. Now only the gross unfavorable treatment definition (2) of discrimination would claim that the gross majority-favored 10 percent is a correct measure of the incidence of discrimination against minorities; all other definitions would argue that the true incidence was zero, and thus the net measure would be the correct indicator.

Case II. Consider next the results of auditing an agent who tries to assess a penalty against minorities (f = 100 percent), but the penalty is small relative to the effect of inconsistencies in the agent's behavior and/or other randomness generated by the auditors or by external effects. In this case what we would have seen as 100 percent majority-favored in a nonrandom world is obscured: randomness so overwhelms the slight penalty being applied to minorities that we are likely to see many instances of equal treatment and roughly equivalent numbers of minority- and majority-favored outcomes ($P_r >> P_{min} = P_{maj}$). Indeed, the outcome may be quite indistinguishable from the case described in the previous paragraph. Yet, which definition of discrimination one chooses becomes more important.

In this case, if one adopts the discriminatory inclination definition (1) of discrimination, one would wish for a 100 percent incidence of penalties being assessed against either the black or white auditor; unfortunately, neither the gross (P_{maj}) or net ($P_{maj} - P_{min}$) figure comes close. The gross unfavorable treatment definition (2) would indicate that the gross majority-favored figure accurately gives the incidence of discrimination. The systematic unfavorable treatment definition (3) would agree, because here randomness only serves to push instances of proclivity penalties out of P_{maj}. That is, P_{rmaj} represents those who did not assess a penalty but were erroneously categorized in P_{maj} by the audits; and here $P_{rmaj} = 0$. Definitions (1), (2), and (3) would agree that discrimination exists, however. But definition (4) would, as above, claim that discrimination overall did not exist because the market effect (i.e., net measure) was not significantly different from zero.

Case III. If the agent has an inclination to assess a sizable race penalty that is unlikely to be overwhelmed by random effects, we would expect an audit to reveal more majority-favored than minority-favored cases. For illustration, assume the results were: $P_{maj} = 65$ percent majority-favored, 20 percent equal treatment, $P_{min} = 15$ percent minority-favored. The latter two results must have been produced by random effects that favored minorities ($= P_r$) and thus offset (and, in the case of minority-favored, overwhelmed) the race penalty being exacted 100 percent of the time by the agent.

Definition (1) would say that the gross 65 percent measure badly understates the "true" 100 percent incidence of discriminatory inclination. Definitions (2) and (3) would agree that 65 percent was a correct measure of incidence, as in Case I. Definition (4) would agree with the other three definitions that discrimination exists here because the net figure ($P_{maj} - P_{min} = 50$ percent) is greater than zero.

Case IV. Reverse Case III: the agent has an inclination to assess a sizable race bonus in favor of minorities. The audits reveal: $P_{min} = 65$ percent minority-favored, 20 percent equal treatment, $P_{maj} = 15$ percent majority-favored. Definition (1) would produce a finding of zero discrimination against minorities because $f = 0$; definition (4) would reject the hypothesis that $P_{maj} - P_{min}$ was greater than zero and so would support this conclusion. Definition (2), as usual, would insist that gross majority-favored $P_{maj} = 15$ percent is an accurate incidence and, presuming it is significantly greater than zero, would conclude that discrimination against minorities exists. (Of course, this definition would also claim that the majority was discriminated against 65 percent of the time.) But (3) would argue for zero incidence of discrimination against minorities, because these 15% were due purely to random reasons: $P_{maj} - P_{rmaj} = 0$. As usual, definition (4) would argue that P_{maj} overstates existence; a net less than zero ($P_{maj} - P_{min} = -50$) obviously would not support the finding of discrimination against minorities.

Summary. Let us summarize the conclusions of the prior cases of single-agent audits. The appropriateness of gross (P_{maj}) and net ($P_{maj} - P_{min}$) majority-favored figures as estimates of the existence and incidence of discrimination against minorities, as seen from the perspective of the various definitions of discrimination, is:

Definition	Case I	Case II	Case III	Case IV
(1) Discriminatory Inclination	gross overst.	gross underst.	gross underst.	gross overst.
(2) Gross Unfavorable Treatment	net correct gross correct	net underst. gross correct	net underst. gross correct	net correct gross correct
(3) Systematic Unfavorable Treatment	net underst. gross overst.	net underst. gross correct	net underst. gross correct	net underst. gross overst.
(4) Net Market Effects	net correct gross overst. net correct	net underst. gross overst. net correct	net underst. gross overst. net correct	net correct gross overst. net correct

The above makes plain that definitional perspective and interpretation of audit results are inextricably linked. In addition, it shows that even if one assumes one definition of discrimination, the accuracy of the simple gross or net measures for investigating existence or incidence of discrimination may be questioned when randomness affects audit results. Only definitions (2) and (4) tautologically finesse this issue: the former by equating discrimination with gross majority-favored incidence and the latter equating discrimination with sizable market effect on net. By contrast, both (1) and (3) must distill the effects of randomness from the observed gross and net audit results in order to estimate the existence and incidence of discrimination within their conceptual framework. This problem is made even more difficult when we consider the scenario typically confronted in audits: a single audit on a large number of agents from many different institutions.

Auditing Many Agents when Randomness Occurs

The difficulty in the straightforward interpretation of audit results is heightened when they represent the composite profile of many agents, their inclinations to assess racial penalties or bonuses, and the degree to which randomness can outweigh such inclinations in shaping the ultimate behavior observed. An additional source of randomness enters the picture here as well: auditor teammates may not always see the same agent. The main point of this subsection is to demonstrate how variations in the distributions of the sizes of race penalties/bonuses assessed, relative to the size of the random effects, crucially influence how those holding to discrimination definitions (1) or (3) evaluate the simple gross and net results from an audit.

We will proceed, as before, by comparing three alternative hypothetical examples involving different assumptions about the relative impacts of race penalties/bonuses vs. randomness. As the basis for each, assume that the sample of 100 agents audited consists of 40 who have proclivities to penalize minorities ($f = 40$ percent), 40 who have proclivities to assess no penalties or bonuses, and 20 who have proclivities to give bonuses to minorities. It is clear, therefore, that the discriminatory inclination definition (1) would like to uncover the "true" incidence of 40 percent with the audits. The "true" incidence as seen from the perspective of the systematic unfavorable treatment definition (3) will vary from case to case, depending on the assumptions made about the impacts of randomness on those holding discriminatory inclinations toward minorities (P_{rmaj}).

Case A. Assume that the distributions of race penalties/bonuses across agents relative to the size of random effects is such that 10 percent of agents starting in any given inclination category end up having behaviors in the audit that place them in the "adjacent" category. That is, 10 percent (i.e., 4) of the majority-favoritists and 10 percent (i.e., 2) of the minority favoritists end up treating both teammates the same; of those with no proclivity for assessing race penalties/bonuses, 10 percent (i.e., 4) end up favoring the majority auditor and 10 percent the minority auditor. This would yield:

Proclivity	Majority-Favored 40	No Difference 40	Minority-Favored 20
Observed Original	36	32	18
Due to Random	4	6	4
Total	40	38	22 (net = 18)

Here, the Majority-Favored lost four to the No Difference group due to random factors (P_r = 4), but gained an equal number from the No Difference group for the same reason (P_{rmaj} = 4). But fewer Minority Favored were observed in the No Difference group than vice versa, because there were half as many agents in it.

Thus, in this case those using the discriminatory inclination definition (1) would be pleased with the gross majority-favored figure (P_{maj} = 40), because it precisely measures the percentage of agents who have a proclivity to assess race penalties. However, those using systematic unfavorable treatment definition (3) would not count the four in the majority-favoritist group who did not end up treating auditors differently, nor those originally in the No Difference group who only favored majority auditors for random reasons (P_{rmaj} = 4). Their precise estimate of discrimination incidence would, therefore, only be 36 percent (= $P_{maj} - P_{rmaj}$), which is overstated by the gross measure.

Case B. Assume that those who favor the majority all have an inclination to assess large penalties on minority applicants, such that no random event will lead to anything but majority-favored outcomes being observed in an audit (P_r = 0). Now, if all else stayed the same as above, we would observe:

Proclivity	Majority-Favored 40	No Difference 40	Minority-Favored 20
Observed Original	40	32	18
Due to Random	4	2	4
Total	44	34	22 (net = 20)

From the perspective of either definition (1) or (3), the gross majority-favored figure (P_{maj} = 44 percent) now overstates the "true" incidence, which in this case equals 40 percent from both perspectives.

Case C. Assume that those with inclinations to favor the majority only penalize minorities a small amount, such that random events end up pushing 50 percent (i.e., 20 agents) into the No Difference audit result category, all else equal ($P_r = 20$). This would yield:

Proclivity	Majority-Favored 40	No Difference 40	Minority-Favored 20
Observed Original	20	32	18
Due to Random	4	22	4
Total	24	54	22 (net = 2)

From the perspective of definition (1), the gross measure ($P_{maj} = 24$ percent) badly understates the "true" value (40 percent), but from the perspective of definition (3) the gross measure continues to overstate the "true" value ($P_{maj} - P_{rand} = 20$ percent).[1]

The above cases should demonstrate sufficiently that the gross incidence of majority-favored audits may (but not necessarily does) badly over- or understate the "true" incidence of those with an inclination to discriminate (definition (1)), depending on the relationship between the sizes of the race penalties these agents assess and the random effects that impinge on the audit process which lead to those with certain inclinations being observed acting differently from their inclinations. Systematic unfavorable acts of discrimination (definition 3) will always be upwardly bounded by the gross measure because P_{rmaj} is non-negative; the gross measure's degree of overstatement will be directly related to P_{maj}: the extent to which random factors result in those who do not have a proclivity to assess penalties against minorities being observed in the majority-favored category nevertheless. Finally, note how those using the market effects perspective of definition (4) would assess the above cases. In the first two, they would agree that discrimination exists because the net figure is significantly greater than zero; in the last case they would not.

Note to Appendix 1.A.

1. Indeed, it should be obvious from these examples that the gross measure will always provide an upper-bound estimate to the incidence of discrimination against minorities from the perspective of definition (3), since randomness can never produce discrimination.

APPENDIX 1.B

LINKING AUDIT METHODOLOGY TO CONVENTIONAL ESTIMATION APPROACHES

This appendix explores how the gross and net measures of discrimination used in audit studies relate to those more familiar to most economists. We first present a simple model that puts the measures from the audit literature in the context of the broader labor economics literature. We then discuss what happens to the interpretation of audit findings when the extent of discrimination varies by employer/auditor characteristics. Finally, we discuss whether it is possible to derive separate estimates of the incidence and severity of discrimination.

Consider first the case of individual, non-paired observations, which is the standard in economics. Here is a conventional formulation: Faced with an individual applying for a job, an employer determines whether to hire ($y=1$) or not to hire ($y=0$) by the rule

$$y = \begin{matrix} 1 \text{ if } y^* > 0 \\ 0 \text{ if } y^* < 0, \end{matrix} \qquad (1.B.1)$$

where

$$y^* = \beta' x + \alpha z + \epsilon, \qquad (1.B.2)$$

with x = covariate vector, z = race ($z = 1$ for the majority, $z = 0$ for the minority), and the disturbance ϵ is distributed standard normal independent of x and z. The bonus granted to the majority applicant is given by α. The covariate vector includes employer characteristics (e.g., industry), job characteristics (e.g., skill requirements), and applicant characteristics (e.g., productivity or human capital). With y^* unobserved, this is a probit model. It implies that

$$\Pr(y = 1|\, x, z) = E(\, y|\, x, z) = F(\beta' x + \alpha\, z), \qquad (1.B.3)$$

where $F(\cdot)$ is the standard normal cumulative distribution function. So for a given x, the difference between the hiring probabilities for a majority and a minority applicant is

$$n(x) = E(y|\, x, z = 1) - E(y|\, x, z = 0) \quad (1.B.4)$$
$$= F(\mu + \alpha) - F(\mu),$$

where $\mu = \beta' x$. On the presumption that α is positive, indicating a preference for the majority, $n(x)$ is positive. If we had repeated observations at a single value of x, and if all employers were following the same rule (1), then we would expect the difference between the proportions of majority and minority applicants hired to be $n(x)$. This is what the net measure based on data from paired audits would pick up in the simplest case.

In practice, of course, there would be variability in x across observations. If we suppose that at each value of x we observed one majority and one minority applicant, the net measure would correspond to the difference in hiring rates:

$$E[n(x)] = E(y|\, z = 1) - E(y|\, z = 0)$$
$$= \sum_x [E(y|\, z = 1, x) - E(y|\, z = 0, x)] \cdot Pr(x) \quad (1.B.5)$$
$$= \text{average of } n(x) \text{ across the distribution of } x.$$

While α, the bonus given to the majority applicant in the employer's latent evaluation y^*, is measured directly in the probit model, the implied difference in hiring rates, $E[n(x)]$, provides a more intuitive measure of discrimination. Tests for the existence of discrimination take the form $H_0{:}\alpha = 0$, $H_1{:}\alpha > 0$ or, equivalently, $H_0{:}E[n(x)] = 0$, $H_1{:}E[n(x)] > 0$.

How would the conventional, individual-level formulation carry over to the audit-pair situation, where each employer sees a matched pair of applicants? For the simplest case, we may suppose that the employer makes two independent decisions. In that case, the table of joint probabilities would be

		White	
		$y = 1$	$y = 0$
Black	$y = 1$	$F(\mu+\alpha)\, F(\mu)$	$[1-F(\mu+\alpha)]\, F(\mu)$
	$y = 0$	$F(\mu+\alpha)\, [1-F(\mu)]$	$[1-F(\mu+\alpha)][1-F(\mu)]$

In this table, the gross majority-favored measure corresponds to the probability that the majority applicant is hired and the minority applicant is not, that is, to

$$g(x) = F(\mu+\alpha)[1\text{-}F(\mu)].$$

The gross minority-favored measure, which corresponds to the probability that the majority applicant is not hired and the minority is, corresponds to

$$[1\text{-}F(\mu+\alpha)]\ F(\mu).$$

These gross measures have no analogue in the economics literature. The net measure corresponds to the difference between the two gross measures, namely

$$F(\mu+\alpha) - F(\mu),$$

which is just the $n(x)$ defined above for individual-level data.

Currently, researchers using the gross measure of discrimination test whether the proportion of times the majority applicant is hired and the minority applicant is not is significantly different from zero (with attendant statistical problems noted in Heckman and Siegelman's chapter 5 of this volume). This assumes that every incident of differential treatment is due to discrimination. However, random factors are very likely to play some role in hiring decisions (as indicated by the specification of a random disturbance term in the hiring model). To obtain an estimate of differential treatment that would occur in the absence of discrimination, same race audit pairs could be used. An appropriate test of discrimination, then, would test whether the proportion of times the majority gets a job and the minority does not is equal to (vs. greater than) the proportion of times one same-race auditor gets a job and the other same-race auditor does not.

When data from audit pairs are used to estimate equation (2), the estimate of the bonus, α, will not depend on x. Since both auditors are matched on observable characteristics and visit the same employers, the measure of the effect of race (α) will be independent of x. The estimate of $E[n(x)]$ can be obtained most simply by subtracting the proportion of audits in which the minority is hired and the majority is not from the proportion of audits in which the majority is hired and the minority is not. This is quite different from the individual-level formulation under which the estimate of α depends on the x's included in the model because the x's differ by race. So, as before, tests for the existence of discrimination take the form $H_0{:}\alpha=0$, $H_1{:}\alpha>0$ or, equivalently, $H_0{:}E[n(x)]=0$, $H_1{:}E[n(x)]>0$.

One might also want to allow for dependence of the two decisions made by an employer. Since the auditors went into the hiring process with similar resumes, they could be expected to be comparably suited for the job: in other words they will tend to be over- or underqualified for the same jobs. One way to allow dependence is to introduce an employer-specific effect that correlates the disturbances of the two y^* equations in the context of a bivariate probit model. One recent attempt to estimate such a model produced a very large and statistically significant firm-specific correlation coefficient (Kenney and Wissoker, forthcoming) suggesting that the job hiring probabilities are indeed dependent on one another in audit studies.

Interdependence of Race and Employer/Applicant Characteristics

Until this point, we have assumed that the extent of discrimination is independent of employer and applicant characteristics. However, this assumption may be invalid. First, economic theory suggests that the extent of discrimination differs across employers by the profitability of discrimination and whether an employer is subject to affirmative action regulations. Second, discrimination may vary with the characteristics of applicants, such as skill level, which by construction vary over a very narrow range in audit studies.

These considerations suggest a model in which employer, job, and auditor characteristics (x) are fully interacted with race (z). Such models may yield estimates of how discrimination interacts with employer and job characteristics, but will not provide evidence on how skill level and discrimination relate unless auditors are drawn from many different skill levels. Furthermore, if the extent of discrimination does depend on the skill level of applicants, the audits will yield an estimate of discrimination only for the skill level at which the auditors are matched. In addition, it should be noted that in a model where race and employer/auditor characteristics interact, the correct estimate of the net measure of discrimination is based on an average over the empirical distribution of x.

The dependence of the net measure of discrimination on x makes clear the need to carefully interpret the estimates obtained from the audit studies. Audit studies are based on a set of auditors with a narrow range of applicant characteristics, both real and constructed. The measures of discrimination that result from audit studies are clearly only appropriate for the range of characteristics observed.

Finally, Heckman and Siegelman in chapter 5 of this volume argue that the skill level at which auditors are matched relative to the requirements of the job being sought can systematically affect the rate at which the black and white auditors are hired. In their model, the productivity level of the auditors depends on an observable/matched component and an "unobservable" unmatched component that is observable only to prospective employers. Heckman and Siegelman show that even if the means of the unobservable characteristics are the same for the white and black auditors, the relative hiring rates for the black and white auditors will vary with the skill level of the auditors if the variance of the unobservable characteristic depends on race. Their analysis underscores the need to minimize the extent to which "unobservables" differentiate black and white applicants and to expand audit studies to encompass broader skill levels.

Untangling Incidence and Severity in Audit Studies

This model also provides a context for examining the incidence and severity of discrimination. Incidence refers to the share of employers who discriminate. Severity refers to the intensity of discriminatory preferences and is revealed through consistency of unfavorable differential treatment toward minorities. The formulation above assumes that all employers follow rule (1), that is, have the same α and hire if $y^*>0$; do not hire if $y^*<0$. With α positive, one might say that the incidence of discrimination is 100 percent. Given a majority and minority who are identical on x and ϵ, the majority always receives a higher value of y^*, and thus a higher hiring probability. Therefore, one could have a trivially small value of α, manifested in a trivial difference in hiring rates, and nevertheless insist that the incidence of discrimination is 100 percent.

Of course, it is possible to allow for a distribution of rules—in particular of values of α—across employers. In such a case, equation (2) could be modified as

$$y^* = \beta' x + \alpha_i z + \epsilon, \qquad (1.B.2b)$$

where α_i is the bonus applied by firm *i*. If some α values were positive, others zero, and still others negative, the incidence of discrimination would be less than 100 percent. However, current audit studies (with one audit per employer) lack information on the distribution of α_i across firms. To get a handle on incidence from current audit studies, therefore, one is forced to make strong assumptions about the distribution of α_i and how it relates to observed characteristics (for example, see Yinger's chapter 2 of this volume).

With repeated observations at each firm, α could be estimated for each firm and the proportion of employers with $\alpha_i>0$ and the average value of α_i could be estimated separately. Clearly, a large number of audits would be required per firm to obtain a precise estimate of the incidence of discrimination. This may not be feasible, because of dangers of detection and because one is constrained by the number of audit pairs. In addition, limited resources force a tradeoff between how many firms can be audited and how many audits can be done per firm. This tradeoff may not favor increasing the number of audits per firm versus the number of firms audited.

Note to appendix 1.B.

This appendix owes its existence to the insights of Arthur S. Goldberger, Douglas Wissoker, and Genevieve Kenney.

References

Amaker, Norman. 1988. *Civil Rights and the Reagan Administration*. Washington, D.C.: The Urban Institute Press.

Ashenfelter, O., and R. Oaxaca. 1987. "The Economics of Discrimination Thirty Years Later: Economists Enter the Courtroom." *American Economic Review* 77(2): 321–5.

Ayres, Ian. 1991. "Fair Driving: Gender and Race Discrimination in Rental Car Negotiations." *Harvard Law Review* 104(4): 817–72.

Ballen, J., and R. B. Freeman. 1986. "Transition between Employment and Nonemployment." In *The Black Youth Employment Crisis*, edited by R. Freeman and H. Holzer, 75–112. Chicago: University of Chicago Press.

Bendick, Marc, Charles Jackson, and Victor Reinoso. 1993. *Measuring Employment Discrimination Through Controlled Experiments*. Washington, DC: Fair Employment Council of Greater Washington.

Bendick, Marc, Charles Jackson, Victor Reinoso, and Laura Hodges. 1991. "Discrimination Against Latino Job Applicants." *Human Resource Management* 30 (4): 469–484.

Bok, Sissela. 1979. *Lying: Moral Choice in Public and Private Life*. New York: Vintage.

Bowsher, C. A. Letter and attached memorandum from Asst. Comptroller Gen. for Program Evaluation and Methodology E. Chelimsky to Sen. Alan K. Simpson (R-Wyo.), June 26, 1990.

Bradbury, K., K. E. Case, and C. R. Dunham. (1989). "Geographic Patterns of Mortgage Lending in Boston, 1982–87." *New England Economic Review* (Sept./Oct.): 3–29.

California Fair Employment and Housing Commission. 1990. "Public Hearings on the Impact and Effectiveness in California of the Employer Sanctions and Anti-Discrimination Provisions of the Immigration Reform and Control Act of 1986," January 11.

Center for Community Change. 1989. "Mortgage Lending Discrimination Testing Project." Unpublished report. Washington, D.C.: U.S. Department of Housing and Urban Development.

Cross, Harry, Genevieve Kenney, Jane Mell, and Wendy Zimmermann. 1990. *Employer Hiring Practices: Differential Treatment of Hispanic and Anglo Job Seekers*. Washington, D.C.: The Urban Institute Press.

Darity, William, Jr. 1989. "What's Left of the Economic Theory of Discrimination?" In *The Question of Discrimination: Racial Inequality in the U.S. Labor Market*, edited by S. Shulman and W. Darity, Jr., 335–76. Middletown, Conn: Wesleyan University Press.

Donohue, J. J., and James J. Heckman. 1990. "Re-evaluating Federal Civil Rights Policy." Paper presented at the Georgetown University Law Center Conference on "The Law & Economics of Racial Discrimination in Employment," November 30.

Donohue, John J., and Peter Siegelman. 1991. "The Changing Nature of Employment Discrimination Litigation." *Stanford Law Review* 43(3): 983–1033.

Duleep, Harriet O., and N. Zalokar. 1991. "The Measurement of Labor Market Discrimination When Minorities Respond to Discrimination." In *New Approaches to Economic and Social Analyses of Discrimination*, edited by R. Cornwall and P. Wannava. New York: Praeger.

Fishbein, A. 1990. "Discrimination in Home Mortgage Lending." Testimony at hearings before the Subcommittee on Consumer and Regulatory Affairs of the Senate, Committee on Banking Housing and Urban Affairs. October 24.

Freeman, R. 1990. "Employment and Earnings of Disadvantaged Young Men in a Labor Short Economy." Working Paper No. 3444. Cambridge, Mass.: National Bureau of Economic Research.

Freeman, R., and H. Holzer. 1986. *The Black Youth Employment Crisis*. Chicago: University of Chicago Press.

Gallup, G. H., Jr., and L. Hujick. 1990. "Racial Tolerance Grows, Progress on Racial Equality Less Evident." *The Gallup Poll News Service* 55(6).

Galster, George. 1990a. "Federal Fair Housing Policy: The Great Misapprehension." In *Building Foundations: Housing and Federal Policy*, edited by D. Dipasquale and L. C. Keyes, 137–56. Philadelphia: University of Pennsylvania Press.

———. 1990b. "Racial Steering by Real Estate Agents: A Review of the Audit Evidence." *Review of Black Political Economy* 18: 105–129.

———. 1991a. "Racial Discrimination in Metropolitan Housing Markets During the 1980s: A Review of the Audit Evidence." *Journal of Planning Education and Research* 9: 165–75.

———. 1991b. "Housing Discrimination and Poverty of Urban African-Americans." *Journal of Housing Research* 2: 87–122.

———. 1992. "Research on Discrimination in Housing and Mortgage Markets: Assessment and Future Directions." *Housing Policy Debate* 3: 639–684.

Galster, G., and W. M. Keeney. 1988. "Race, Discrimination, and Economic Opportunity: Modeling the Nexus of Urban Racial Phenomena." *Urban Affairs Quarterly* 24: 87–117.

Goering, J. 1986. *Housing Desegregation and Federal Policy.* Chapel Hill: University of North Carolina Press.

Hakken, Jon. 1979. "Discrimination Against Chicanos in the Dallas Rental Housing Market: An Experimental Extension of the Housing Market Practices Survey." Washington, D.C.: U.S. Department of Housing and Urban Development.

Haworth, J. G., J. Gwartney, and C. Haworth. 1975. "Earnings, Productivity, and Changes in Employment Discrimination." *American Economic Review* 65(1): 158–68.

Heckman, J. J. 1989. "The Impact of Government on the Economic Status of Black Americans." In *The Question of Discrimination: Racial Inequality in the U.S. Labor Market*, edited by S. Shulman and W. Darity, Jr., 50–80. Conn.: Wesleyan University Press.

Heintz, K. 1985. "HUD Conference on Fair Housing Testing: Final Summary Report." Washington, D.C.: U.S. Department of Housing and Urban Development.

Holzer, H. 1991. "The Spatial Mismatch Hypothesis: What Has the Evidence Shown?" *Urban Studies* 28(1), 105–22.

Holzer, H., and W. Vroman. 1992. "Mismatches and the Urban Labor Market." In *Urban Labor Markets and Job Opportunity*, eds. George E. Peterson and Wayne Vroman. Washington, D.C.: Urban Institute Press.

Ihlanfeldt, K. R., and D. L. Sjoquist. 1990. "Job Accessibility and Racial Differences in Youth Employment Rates." *American Economic Review* 80(1): 268–76.

James, F. J., B. I. Cummings, and E. A. Tynan. 1984. "Minorities in the Sunbelt." New Brunswick, N.J.: Center for Urban Policy Research, Rutgers University.

James, Franklin J., and Steve W. DelCastillo. 1991. "Measuring Job Discrimination by Private Employers Against Young Black and Hispanic Males Seeking Entry Level Work in the Denver Metropolitan Area." Unpublished Report. Denver: University of Colorado.

Jaynes, G. D. 1990. "The Labor Market Status of Black Americans: 1939–1985." *Journal of Economic Perspectives* 4(fall): 9–24.

Jaynes, G. D., and R. M. Williams, Jr. (1989). *A Common Destiny: Blacks and American Society.* Washington, D.C.: National Academy Press.

Kenney, Genevieve M., and Douglas A. Wissoker. Forthcoming. "An Analysis of the Correlaters of Discrimination Facing Young, Hispanic Jobseekers." *American Economic Review.*

King, Thomas. 1980. "Mortgage Lending, Social Responsibility and Public Policy: Some Perspectives on HMDA and DRA." *American Real Estate and Urban Economics Association Journal* 8: 77–90.

Kirschenman, Joleen, and Kathryn Neckerman. 1991. "We'd Love to Hire Them, But . . . , The Meaning of Race to Employers." In *The Urban Underclass*, edited by C. Jencks, and P. E. Peterson, 203–32. Washington, D.C.: Brookings Institution.

Leonard, Jonathan S. 1990. "The Impact of Affirmative Action Regulation and Equal Employment Law on Black Employment." *Journal of Economic Perspectives* 4(fall): 47–63.

Marris, Peter. 1982. *Meaning and Action*. London: Routledge Kegan and Paul.

Mashaw, J. 1990. "Implementing Quotas." Paper presented at the Georgetown University Law Center Conference on "The Law and Economics of Racial Discrimination in Employment."

McIntyre, S., et al. 1980. "Preferential Treatment in Preselection Decisions According to Race and Sex." *Academy of Management Journal* 23: 738–749.

Millspaugh. 1984. "Fair Housing Testing: Its Legal Status and Policy Implications." *University of Baltimore Law Review* 13: 240.

Munnell, A., L. Browne, J. McEneaney, and G. Tootell. 1992. *Mortgage Lending in Boston: Interpreting the HMDA Data*. Federal Reserve Bank of Boston, paper 92–7.

New York State Inter-Agency Task Force on Immigration Affairs. 1988. "Workplace Discrimination Under the Immigration Reform and Control Act of 1986." November 4.

O'Neill, J. 1990. "The Role of Human Capital in Earnings Differences Between Black and White Men." *Journal of Economic Perspectives* 4(fall): 25–45.

Pettigrew, Thomas F. 1985. "New Patterns of Racism: The Different World of 1984 and 1964." *Rutgers Law Review* 37: 674.

Price, R. and Edwin Mills. 1985. "Race and Residence in Earnings Determination." *Journal of Urban Economics* 17: 1–18.

Rees, A. 1986. "An Essay on Youth Joblessness." *Journal of Economic Literature* 24: 613–28.

Ridley, Stanley E., James A. Bayton, and Janice H. Outtz. 1989. "Taxi Service in the District of Columbia: Is it Influenced by Patron's Race and Destination?" Paper prepared for the Washington, D.C. Lawyer's Committee for Civil Rights.

Schafer, Robert, and Helen Ladd. 1981. *Discrimination in Mortgage Lending*. Cambridge, Mass.: MIT Press.

Schuman, H., C. Steeh, and L. Bobo. 1985. *Racial Attitudes in America*. Cambridge, Mass.: Harvard University Press.

Shulman, S. 1989. "A Critique of the Declining Discrimination Hypothesis." In *The Question of Discrimination: Racial Inequality in the U.S. Labor Market*, edited by S. Shulman and W. Darity, Jr., 126–52. Middletown, Conn.: Wesleyan University Press.

Siniscalco, Gary, and John Giansello. 1992. "An Analysis of the Civil Rights Act of 1991." Papers presented at the American Bar Association 1992 Mid-winter Meeting of the Labor and Employment Law Section, March 4–7. La Quinta, California.

Squires, Gregory, and W. Velez. 1988. "Insurance Redlining and the Process of Discrimination." *Review of Black Political Economy* 16: 63–75.

Strauss, David A. 1990. "The Law and Economics of Race Discrimination in Employment." Paper presented at a conference held at Georgetown University Law Center, on "The Law and Economics of Race Discrimination in Employment: An Agenda for the Next Generation," November 30.

Turner, Margery, Michael Fix, and Raymond Struyk. 1991. *Opportunities Denied, Opportunities Diminished: Discrimination in Hiring*. Washington, D.C.: The Urban Institute Press.

Turner, Margery A., Raymond Struyk, and John Yinger. 1991. "Housing Discrimination in America: Summary of Findings from the Housing Discrimination Study." Washington, D.C.: The Urban Institute.

U.S. Equal Employment Opportunity Commission. 1990. "Policy Guidance on the Use of EEO Testers." *EEOC Compliance Manual* (BNA), Section 405 (November 20): 6899.

U.S. General Accounting Office. 1990. "Immigration Reform: Employer Sanctions and the Question of Discrimination." GAO/GGD 90-62. Washington, D.C.: March.

U.S. House of Representatives, Committee on Education and Labor and Committee on the Judiciary. 1990. Joint Hearing on H.R. 4000, Civil Rights Act of 1990. February 20 and 27, March 13 and 20.

U.S. Senate, Subcommittee on Consumer and Regulatory Affairs of the Committee on Banking, Housing and Urban Affairs. 1990. Hearing on Mortgage Discrimination. May 16.

———. Committee on Labor and Human Resources. 1989. Hearing on S. 2104, Civil Rights Act of 1990. Serial No. 101-649, February 23 and 27, March 1 and 7.

Wallace, J., W. L. Holshouser, T. S. Lane, and J. Williams. 1985. "The Fair Housing Assistance Program Evaluation." Washington, D.C.: U.S. Department of Housing and Urban Development.

Wienk, Ronald, Clifford E. Reid, John C. Simonson, and Frederick J. Eggers. 1979. "Measuring Racial Discrimination in American Housing Markets: The Housing Practices Survey." Washington, D.C.: U.S. Department of Housing and Urban Development.

Wienk, Ron, and John Simonson. 1992. "FHIP: An Evaluation of the Testing Demonstration." The Urban Institute, June.

Yinger, J. 1991a. "Lessons About Discrimination Against Blacks and Hispanics from the Housing Discrimination Study." Washington, D.C.: The Urban Institute.

———. 1991b. "Housing Discrimination Study: Incidence of Discrimination and Variation in Discriminatory Behavior." Washington, D.C.: U.S. Department of Housing and Urban Development.

———. 1979. "Prejudice and Discrimination in the Urban Housing Market." In *Current Issues in Urban Economics*, edited by P. Mieszkowski and M. Straszheim, Baltimore, Md.: Johns Hopkins University Press.

Yinger, J., G. Galster, B. Smith, and F. Eggers. 1979. "The Status of Research into Racial Discrimination and Segregation in American Housing Markets: A Research Agenda for the Department of Housing and Urban Development." *Occasional Papers in Housing and Community Affairs* 6: 55–175.

Part III
Identifying Winners and Losers from Discrimination

[22]

Divide and conquer: microfoundations of a Marxian theory of wage discrimination

John E. Roemer*

Microfoundations for a divide-and-conquer model of wage discrimination are provided by positing that workers' psychologies permit racial integration of firms to weaken workers' unity and hence reduce their bargaining power against employers. In this bargaining—as opposed to competitive—model of wage determination, there are discriminatory equilibria at which both white and black workers are worse off and employers are better off than would be the case without worker dissension. Furthermore, owing to the bargaining structure, market forces cannot unravel the discriminatory wage bargain.

1. Introduction

■ The Marxian theory of wage discrimination between workers of different races is that capitalists use a divide-and-conquer strategy to force wages of both black and white workers down. The persistence of discrimination is explained by the persistence of racism in society, which allows capitalists to make use of such a strategy. According to this theory, capitalists gain and all workers lose from discrimination, which is a conclusion much at variance with Becker's neoclassical theory of discrimination (Becker, 1957). The Marxian position has been elaborated and empirically investigated in recent years by Reich (1976, 1977). The models presented here will also draw from recent theories of labor market segmentation (Doeringer and Piore, 1971; Edwards, Reich, and Gordon, 1975).

It has been somewhat of a task for economic theory to produce microeconomic models of the labor market in which discrimination persists at equilibrium. To put the problem in a nutshell, one would expect that any wage differentials which do not reflect productivity differentials would be competed away in equilibrium. Various explanations of discriminatory equilibria have been put forth by neoclassical writers (Arrow, 1972; Becker, 1957; Miyazaki, 1977; Spence, 1974; Thurow, 1969; Welch 1967). These writers achieve the result by positing actual or perceived differences in productivity of the two types of worker or by positing "tastes" for discrimination among employers or workers. The Marxist theory, however, has not been explicitly formulated as a competitive microeconomic model, so the theory remains in a state of rela-

* Associate Professor of Economics, University of California, Davis.

This work was partially supported by a fellowship from the Social Science Research Council. I would like to acknowledge useful comments, made on an earlier version of this paper, by Victor Goldberg, Hajime Miyazaki, and Sam Rosenberg.

tive vagueness. The task of this article is to construct such a model, to show that a divide-and-conquer strategy is a competitive, profit-maximizing strategy for firms, which will result in discriminatory equilibria, even in the presence of a competitive labor market. (There will, however, be some constraints on competition, internal to the firm.) It is hoped that this demonstration will put the Marxian model on the same logical footing as the models I have called neoclassical, as a candidate for explaining racial wage discrimination.

There is anecdotal evidence in the labor history literature which implies that employers have deliberately integrated their work forces to prevent unity of the workers and consequent strikes.[1] Various models of individual worker psychology could be constructed. Some of these would embody the docile behavior which apparently comes with integration and produces the divide-and-conquer effect; others would not. Here we shall examine only one wage psychology, that pictured in Figure 1, which produces the divide-and-conquer effect.

Consider Figure 1a. If the firm hires a workforce which has a fraction η of white workers, we shall posit that intrafirm bargaining for wages will produce an outcome at which white workers must be paid at least $h_1(\eta)$, and black workers at least $h_2(\eta)$. If the firm hires an all black ($\eta = 0$) or all white ($\eta = 1$) workforce, the bargaining strength of the workers is such that they can force a high wage to be paid. (We shall assume $h_i(0) = h_i(1)$, which is of no great consequence to the argument.) The effect of divisiveness among workers, due to racism, is maximized at proportion η^*, where the wages are lowest and the wage differential is greatest. The u-shaped character of the h curves embodies the psychology of racial discord between the two groups

[1] It is useful to introduce this essay with several quotations from studies of labor history to suggest the existence of the phenomenon which is posited:

> When the labor shortage ended, those Negroes who had proved their use were retained in service in substantial numbers. In the summer of 1928 several officials of the Carnegie Steel Company declared that they could well get along without the Negro, but that they did not choose to do so. Instead, they kept him in their plants in a ratio of about 10 percent of the total number of employees. The Negro is now recognized as a permanent factor in industry and large employers use him as one of the racial and national elements which help to break the homogeneity of their labor force. This, incidentally, fits into the program of big concerns for maintaining what they call "a cosmopolitan force," which frees the employer from dependence upon any group for his labor supply and also thwarts unity of purpose and labor organization. Or, as the personnel manager of a very large company near Chicago put it: "It makes fraternizing among the employees difficult." (Spero and Harris, p. 163)

And from a description of farm practices:

> A notable fact about farm labor in California is the practice of employers to pay wage scales on the basis of races, i.e., to establish different wage rates for each racial group, thus fostering racial antagonism and, incidentally, keeping wages at the lowest possible point. As a part of this general strategy, "it is a common custom of the ranchers to entrust a particular work to a group of laborers of the same nationality." In this manner, of course, the races are kept segregated and pitted one against the other. Because of their differences in custom, language, and appearance, the Hindus were a particularly valuable intermediary group. They were used, and still are to some extent, as a wedge to separate the Mexican and Oriental groups. How general the custom is of pitting one race against the other is indicated by the fact that, in 1937, the bookkeeper of Hotchkiss Ranch (one of the large farm-factories in the San Joaquin Valley) had to be a trained linguist, as he was dealing with four or five racial groups. The foreman of the Griffen Ranch, in the same area, stated to a reporter that: "Last year our Hindu workers struck. So this year we mixed half Mexicans in with them, and we aren't having any labor trouble." (McWilliams, p. 118)

FIGURE 1

WORKERS' MINIMAL WAGE FUNCTIONS $h_i(\eta)$

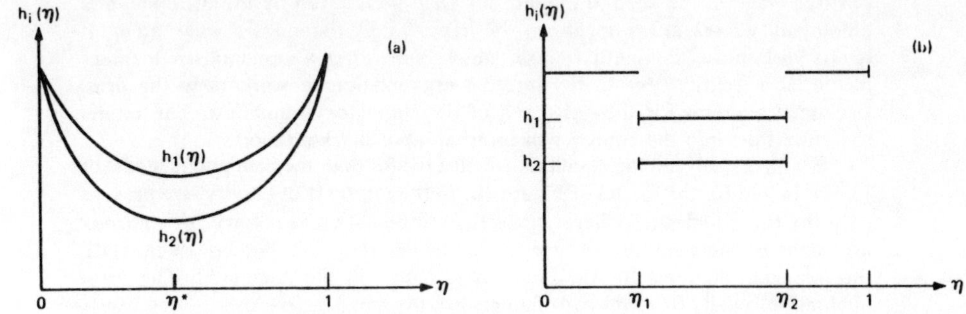

of workers which weakens the bargaining power of the workforce. That the wage differential approaches zero as the workforce becomes homogeneous is a consequence of the lack of racial divisiveness among the homogeneous workforce.

Another variant of the model assumes that the divisiveness effect is characterized as in Figure 1b. In this case there are thresholds at η_1 and η_2. If $\eta_1 \leq \eta \leq \eta_2$ then divisiveness operates, and firms must offer wages above the minimal values h_1 and h_2 to white and black workers, respectively. For η small or large, divisiveness is inoperative, and all workers must be paid the high wage.

This article will study two models. In both, we assume the following:

(1) There is a finite supply of black and white workers, with a proportion of white workers in the population of η_{pop}.

(2) Workers are perfect substitutes in production, and the production function for all firms is $f(L) = L$, where L is the amount of labor employed.

(3) All firms face a fixed (world) price p for the output.

Assumptions 2 and 3 are adopted to make the model as simple and translucent as possible. The two models differ in their assumption concerning the reservation wages of workers. In Model 1, the reservation wage of a worker of a given type (black or white) is the *highest* wage his type is currently receiving in the economy. This model contains a serious limitation to competition in the labor market, for clearly with this assumption about the reservation wage, an unemployed worker will not compete for the job of an employed worker. It is not surprising, then, that discriminatory equilibria will exist in this model. In the second model, the reservation wage of a worker-type is assumed to be the *lowest* wage currently being paid to that type of worker (employed or unemployed). This introduces a much sharper form of labor market competition, and the main result is that, nevertheless, discriminatory equilibria persist. (In particular, in the second model, as long as the unemployment of black (white) workers exists, black (white) workers will be willing to work for any positive wage.)

A final introductory comment on the noncompetitive structure of these models, which allows discrimination to persist, should be made. The bargaining process *within* the firm is not competitive in the neoclassical sense. An unemployed white worker, for instance, may be willing to work for a miniscule positive wage in the second model: but once he is hired by the firm which is employing whites in proportion η, he immediately demands a wage $h_1(\eta)$. It is this violation of competitiveness, which constitutes a monopolistic element in the labor market due to the internal organization of workers in the firm, that must account for the existence of discriminatory equilibria. The model therefore falls into the category of internal labor market theories.

We have analyzed the equilibria which exist for both the continuous model of Figure 1a and for the model of Figure 1b. In the interests of brevity, we present only the threshold model here, since the mathematics necessary for rigorous argument in the continuous case are more detailed. We do, however, state the relevant theorems for the continuous model in the Appendix. The main qualitative results from the two models are the same.

2. Model 1: divide and conquer with a high reservation wage

■ To define the concept of equilibrium, we describe how a firm operates. It offers a pair of wages $(w_1,w_2) \equiv w$, which it promises to pay white and black workers, respectively. If these wages attract both white and black workers, then it can hire a workforce in whatever proportions it chooses. If the firm hires whites and blacks in proportions η and $1 - \eta$, then the wages w must be *feasible* at η (see below), and the firm must make a nonnegative profit. Notice that the *average wage per worker* and *per unit output* will be $\eta w_1 + (1 - \eta)w_2$. We denote this convex combination of wages:

$$\eta w_1 + (1 - \eta)w_2 \equiv \vec{\eta}\cdot w.$$

Since the production function is $f(L) = L$, the unit profits will be

$$\pi \equiv p - \vec{\eta}\cdot w.$$

Definition 1:[2] A *T1 equilibrium* is a triplet $Q = \langle \eta,w_1,w_2 \rangle$ such that:

(1) $p \geq \vec{\eta}\cdot w$ (profits are *nonnegative* at Q);
(2) $h(\eta) \equiv (h_1(\eta),h_2(\eta)) \leqq w$ and $w_1 \geq w_2$ (Q is *feasible*); and
(3) there does not exist a triplet $\langle \eta',w_1',w_2' \rangle$ such that:

(a) $w' > w$
(b) $\vec{\eta}'\cdot w' < p$ (Q is *undominated*).
(c) $\langle \eta',w' \rangle$ is feasible

The rationale for this definition is as follows. The market is in equilibrium when, if firms are operating at Q, no other firm can enter the market and start operation. (A "new" firm can, of course, be an old firm offering a new contract.) For the new firm to attract workers of both types, it must offer a wage pair w' strictly greater than the wages currently paid by the firms in operation, since we assume *the reservation wage for each worker is the highest wage paid to his type*.[3] The challenging firm, then, must offer wages to attract *both* types of

[2] Convention on vector ordering: $v > w$ means $v_i > w_i \forall i$; $v \geqq w$ means $v_i \geqq w_i \forall i$; $v \geq w$ means $v \geqq w$ and $v \neq w$.

[3] The requirement 3(a) makes sense if all workers are already employed before the challenging firm enters. If there are some unemployed workers, we might wish to weaken 3(a) to a weak inequality. This, however, will be dealt with in Model 2.

FIGURE 2

LOWEST FEASIBLE AVERAGE WAGE FUNCTION $\omega(\eta)$

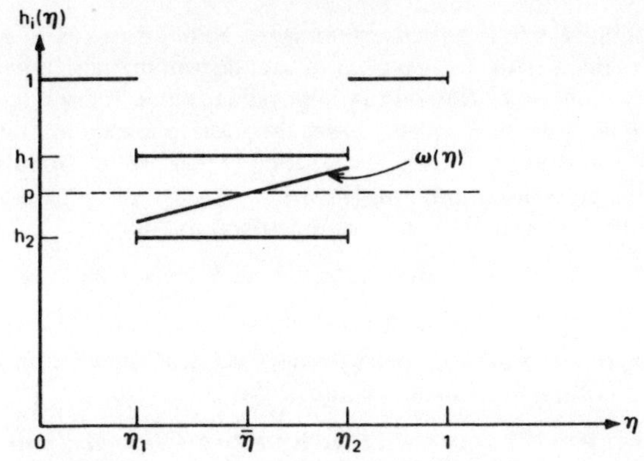

workers, and then choose a proportion η' which is feasible and profitable. Hence, the definition of equilibrium states that no new entrant can challenge the existing firms which operate at Q. (There is a minor technical point here: we assume that $p < 1$. Otherwise, a firm could offer a wage pair sufficiently high to attract just one kind of worker and could operate at positive profits. In this case, the model becomes moot.)

Notice that as part of the definition of feasibility, it is assumed that black workers can never be paid more than whites. The rationale is this: white workers will not object if black workers are paid the same wage as they are, but will not allow a greater wage to be paid to blacks. This is part of the divide-and-conquer assumption.

We proceed to characterize the set of T1 equilibria under the assumption that the price level p is as illustrated in Figure 2. (We consider the case $1 > p \geq h_1$ below.) Clearly, an equilibrium can only exist for values of η such that $\eta_1 \leq \eta \leq \eta_2$, for outside that interval, the average wage paid must render profits negative. Define the *lowest feasible average wage* function as

$$\omega(\eta) \equiv \eta h_1 + (1 - \eta)h_2;$$

$\omega(\eta)$ is illustrated in Figure 2. Obviously, any T1 equilibrium must be in the interval $[\eta_1,\bar{\eta}]$ or else profits would be negative.

Consider the triplet, $Q = \langle \eta,w_1,w_2 \rangle$, an equilibrium candidate. Notice that if Q is an equilibrium, profits must be zero there (that is, $\vec{\eta}\cdot w = p$). Otherwise, a challenging firm can offer wages slightly higher than $\langle w_1,w_2 \rangle$, attract all the workers of both types at these wages, and, therefore, hire in proportions η and still make positive profits. So we assume $\vec{\eta}\cdot w = p$ at Q.

Notice, furthermore, that if $\eta > \eta_1$, then there is a wage offer at η_1 which will dominate Q. This follows because when $\eta > \eta_1$, we have $\vec{\eta}_1\cdot w < \vec{\eta}\cdot w$ as long as $w_2 < w_1$. Consequently, a firm can offer wages $\langle w_1 + \delta, w_2 + \delta \rangle$ for small δ, attract workers of both types, hire them in proportions η_1, and operate at positive profits.

Hence the only *discriminatory* T1 equilibria (*i.e.*, $w_1 \neq w_2$) are at η_1. Conversely, all triplets $\langle \eta_1,w_1,w_2 \rangle$ which are feasible and zero-profit are T1 equilibria, since any challenger (according to part (3) of the definition of T1 equilibrium) must offer wages strictly greater than $\langle w_1,w_2\rangle$. But at any value $\eta \geq \eta_1$, this will produce negative profits.

Let us inquire where *nondiscriminatory* equilibria exist (*i.e.*, $w_1 = w_2$). Since profits must still be zero at a nondiscriminatory equilibrium, we must have $w_1 = w_2 = p$. But this is impossible, since the white wage is not feasible when $w_1 \geq h_1 > p$. In this case, then, there are no nondiscriminatory equilibria. If, however, $1 > p \geq h_1$, then there is a nondiscriminatory equilibrium for all η in the interval $[\eta_1,\eta_2]$.

The results for Model 1 can be summarized as follows:

Theorem 1. Let the price be given at p, where $h_1 > p > h_2$. Then:

(a) There exist discriminatory T1 equilibria at η_1 and only at η_1. These equilibria consist of all wage pairs $\langle w_1,w_2\rangle$ which are feasible and zero-profit.

(b) There are no nondiscriminatory equilibria.

If, on the other hand, $1 > p \geq h_1$, then (a) above still holds, but:

(b′) There is a nondiscriminatory equilibrium $\langle \eta,p,p\rangle$ at every $\eta\epsilon[\eta_1,\eta_2]$.

In either case:

(c) At anytime, an economy can sustain only one discriminatory T1 equilibrium.

Only statement (c) still requires proof. If $\langle \eta_1,w_1^\alpha,w_2^\alpha\rangle$ and $\langle \eta_1,w_1^\beta,w_2^\beta\rangle$ are two discriminatory equilibria, then with proper choice of the labels α and β, $w_2^\alpha > w_2^\beta$ and $w_1^\alpha < w_1^\beta$. Consequently, all white workers in firm α cease working, since their reservation wage is w_1^β, and all black workers in firm β cease working since their reservation wage is w_2^α. Hence only one discriminatory equilibrium can be sustained. *Q.E.D.*

Therefore, in the case of a high reservation wage, discriminatory equilibria exist. One can note the simple economic idea behind Theorem 1. White workers are a costly but necessary input into production, since without them production at nonnegative profit levels is impossible. We expect, then, that optimization on the firm's part will lead to minimizing the costly input, which is precisely what happens at η_1.

The main deficiency of the T1 concept of equilibrium is that unemployed workers exert no pressure on wages. It is not startling that without this competitive pressure on price from excess supply, discriminatory equilibria exist. In the next section, we therefore consider an alternative assumption about the reservation wage.

3. Model 2: divide and conquer with a low reservation wage

■ In the last model, the reservation wage of the type i worker was the highest wage currently being paid to his type. In this model, the reservation wage is the lowest wage currently being paid to his type. In particular, if there are unemployed black workers, then the black reservation wage is zero. Even if a black worker is working, his reservation wage is zero because if he refused to take a wage cut, his alternative would be to join the existing ranks of the unemployed. On the other hand, if all black workers are employed and the lowest wage being paid them is w^2_{min}, then no black worker will work for less than w^2_{min}, since when all blacks are employed, a particular worker assumes a job is available for him which pays at least that minimum wage. Consequently:

Definition 2: The *reservation wage* for type *i* worker is:

$$\underline{w}_i = \min_j w^i_j,$$

where $\{w^i_j\}$ are the wages being paid to type *i* workers; this set includes the wage zero if there are unemployed workers of type *i*.

Definition 3: A *T2 equilibrium* is a set of triplets $Q = \langle \eta, w_1, w_2 \rangle$ such that:

(1) each Q is a T1 equilibrium; and
(2) if $(w_1,w_2) > (\underline{w}_1,\underline{w}_2)$ and w is feasible at η, then $\vec{\eta} \cdot w \geq p$.

Thus, a T2 equilibrium is one in which no challenger can make positive profits by offering wages which will attract both types of workers.

We analyze the existence of discriminatory T2 equilibria. Since all T2 equilibria must be, more weakly, T1 equilibria, we may limit the search for T2 equilibria to points of the form $\langle \eta_1, w_1, w_2 \rangle$, where $\vec{\eta}_1 \cdot w = p$ and $\langle w_1, w_2 \rangle \geqq \langle h_1, h_2 \rangle$. Suppose $\eta_{pop} > \eta_1$. Then, if all firms are hiring at η_1 (as they must be in a discriminatory equilibrium), there must at least be some unemployed white workers. In that case, the unemployed white workers, whose reservation wage is therefore zero, can be attracted to and held in the firm at a wage h_1. Hence, with $\eta_{pop} > \eta_1$, the only possible white wage at T2 equilibrium is h_1. Therefore, since profits are zero at the T2 equilibrium, the black wage must be that unique value $\bar{w}_2$ such that:

$$\eta_1 h_1 + (1 - \eta_1)\bar{w}_2 = p.$$

This shows that the only possible T2 equilibrium is at $Q = \langle \eta_1, h_1, \bar{w}_2 \rangle$. It is left to show that Q is in fact a T2 equilibrium when $\eta_{pop} > \eta_1$: that is, that no entrant can make a feasible wage offer which dominates $(h_1, \bar{w}_2)$ and still earn positive profit. Notice that there is only one type of unemployed worker at Q. If both types were unemployed, the wage offer (h_1, h_2) would be acceptable, and positive profits would be possible. Since $\eta_{pop} > \eta_1$, it is the white workers who are unemployed; all black workers are employed at the wate $\bar{w}_2$. Hence, the reservation wage for black workers is $\bar{w}_2 > 0$. Although the white workers' reservation wage is zero, they must be paid a wage at least h_1 to hold them in the firm. It follows immediately that nonnegative profits cannot be made at any wage offer which dominates $(h_1, \bar{w}_2)$ for any feasible fraction $\eta \geq \eta_1$. Thus $Q = \langle \eta_1, h_1, \bar{w}_2 \rangle$ is a T2 equilibrium.

We summarize the situation for T2 equilibria:

Theorem 2:

(a) If $\eta_{pop} > \eta_1$, there is a unique discriminatory T2 equilibrium, $Q = \langle \eta_1, h_1, \bar{w}_2 \rangle$, where $\bar{w}_2 = p - \eta_1 h_1 / 1 - \eta_1$. In this case there are white unemployment and black full employment.
(b) If $\eta_{pop} < \eta_1$, there is a unique discriminatory T2 equilibrium, $Q = \langle \eta_1, \bar{w}_1, h_2 \rangle$, where $\bar{w}_1 = p - (1 - \eta_1)h_2/\eta_1$. In this case there are black unemployment and white full employment.
(c) If $\eta_{pop} = \eta_1$, any T1 equilibrium is a T2 equilibrium.

(d) *Nondiscriminatory* T2 equilibria only exist if $p \geq h_1$. If $1 > p \geq h_1$, then $\langle \eta_{pop}, p, p \rangle$ is the unique nondiscriminatory equilibrium, and it exists only if $\eta_{pop} \in [\eta_1, \eta_2]$.

Part (a) has been demonstrated. Parts (b), (c), and (d) follow easily with similar argumentation.

Hence, even in the T2 case, where unemployment exerts competitive pressure on the wage, discriminatory equilibria exist. Furthermore, an interesting observation follows from the existence of nondiscriminatory equilibria. At such equilibria, divisiveness lowers the wages of workers (below what they would be in the segregated firm), even though discrimination is not evident. Hence, *the absence of discriminatory wages cannot be taken as evidence of the absence of the divide-and-conquer effect.* Since in modern society wage discrimination has become somewhat difficult and even illegal for the firm, one might expect the entire divide-and-conquer effect to be embodied in a low general wage rate rather than in a wage differential.

4. Some possible objections

■ Several comments should be offered on possible anomalies of this model. For the United States, the value of η_{pop} is about .8. Certainly $\eta_1 < .8$. It, therefore, follows from Theorem 2 that there will be white unemployment and black full employment at a discriminatory equilibrium, which is not in accordance with what appear to be the facts. How can this be explained as consistent with the divide-and-conquer formulation?

First, note that the existence of discriminatory equilibria only at the *low* value of $\eta = \eta_1$ is not a *curiosum* of the two models examined here. On the contrary, this result is robust under any reasonable formulation of the divide-and-conquer mechanism. This follows since the logic of cost minimization is to economize on the use in production of the costly input—white workers.

However, one cannot immediately compare the actual unemployment situation we observe with the unemployment in the models. For the model, the relevant populations are white and black workers of equal skill. The model's jurisdiction must also be limited to an area within which there is labor mobility. We are then led to ask: among workers of a particular level of skill in a particular area, what is the fraction of white workers? This fraction η_{pop} may be substantially below .8 for unskilled groups. It may easily be below the value η_1, which in a particular area might be in the range $.3 \leq \eta_1 \leq .5$. Hence, Theorem 2 is not inconsistent with black unemployment in a particular area at a discriminatory equilibrium.

We might also ask: What determines the value η_1, which is a psychological parameter? η_1 is the proportion of white workers necessary to trigger the divide-and-conquer effect. If we accept the conventional wisdom that racial antagonisms in a city are greater when η_{pop} is smaller, then we might conclude that as η_{pop} rises, a larger proportion of white workers in the plant is necessary to trigger the divide-and-conquer mechanism: that is, η_1 rises as η_{pop} rises. If so, then even relatively large values of η_{pop} (measured on the population of unskilled workers) might still preserve the ordering $\eta_{pop} < \eta_1$.

These tentative remarks are meant simply to defend the models against what appears at first sight to be an anomalous result. In principle, empirical tests can be designed to test whether racial unemployment data are consistent with the model's predictions.

Another objection might be raised. Suppose the economy is at a discriminatory equilibrium $(\eta_1, h_1, \bar{w}_2)$. Why cannot an entrepreneur form a coalition with black workers and offer to hire them at $\bar{w}_2 + \delta$? In that case, the entrepreneur and the black workers will all be better off; in return, the black workers must forego their ability to exercise their strength in unity, which could extract for them a wage of 1, but which would drive the firm out of business. Or, in another variant, why do they not accept the entrepreneur's offer, and then bargain up to a wage of p, not forcing the firm out of business? An answer to this is that perhaps on the margin it does occur. It can be argued, nevertheless, that big firms will not make such offers to workers. Notice that in the case postulated here of the firm with the segregated workforce, the wage $\bar{w}_2 + \delta$ is below the value which workers are able to achieve with their degree of unity (that is, 1), whereas in the case of discriminatory equilibrium, the workers' unity cannot win them higher wages. Hence, the employers in these segregated firms are always at the mercy of a militant workforce, whereas employers in integrated firms have insurance against being "held up" by the workers. Big firms, it can be argued, might opt for the strategy with insurance.[4]

5. Conclusion

■ The mechanism which triggers the divide-and-conquer effect is this: if black and white workers are mixed in certain proportions, racial discord is introduced in their ranks because of their particular psychologies, and their bargaining ability is consequently reduced. The firm can then lower the wages it is required to pay either group. Since whites are the more costly workers to hire, equilibrium occurs at a point where white workers are hired in that minimal proportion necessary to trigger the dissension effect. Although the equilibrium is discriminatory, it cannot be unravelled.

A comparison should be made with Becker's 1957 neoclassical model of wage discrimination. In Becker's model, and in similar neoclassical models, workers face wage discrimination because of tastes by firms or by workers themselves for homogeneity in the workforce. First, we should not posit firms as being invested with these irrational tastes. That is antithetical to both the Marxian and neoclassical notions of the firm as a profit-maximizing, capital-accumulating entity. In fact, this is Becker's conclusion, for in long-run equilibrium, firms with these inefficient tastes will not survive, and, therefore, discrimination will not survive. Concerning the tastes of workers for discrimination, the argument is different. It cannot be argued that these tastes do not exist: however, I will maintain that such tastes are not sufficiently strong to become translated into higher reservation wages which workers demand if they are to work with others of another race. But, more to the point, the mechanism generating discrimination in the Becker model is qualitatively different from the one posited here. In the former, the mechanism is competitive; in the latter it is a bargaining mechanism with shelters against competition and with monopoly rents. In the present model, higher wages are foregone, at integrated values of η, not because workers prefer integration, but, on the contrary, because integration creates dissension which weakens their bargaining position.

---

[4] It is beyond our scope here to examine further whether firms would choose the insurance strategy or the strategy of coalition with black workers. We remark that, according to Marxian theory, no coalition of workers and capitalists can be secure; hence, the choice of the insurance strategy by firms, posited here, is consistent with a more complete Marxian theory of the firm.

There is a weakness in this formulation which necessitates a closing *caveat*. The model, like all models which take the psychological structure of agents—in this case, the h curves—as exogenously given, tends to blame the victim. Who, after all, is responsible for wage discrimination here? The workers who are so irrational as to permit the divisiveness embedded in the h curves to rule. It must, therefore, be added that in a full Marxian or radical treatment, the present model would be a partial equilibrium analysis in this important sense: a complete analysis would inquire into what institutions and practices in capitalist society are responsible for endowing workers with the h-curve psychology. This, perhaps, indicates the sharpest difference between the neoclassical and radical approaches to the problem of discrimination: while the former tends to accept individual psychologies (*i.e.*, preferences) as a datum, the latter claims that psychologies are endogenous, and in fact are manipulated in such a way as to produce an equilibrium outcome beneficial to capitalists. Certainly, this paper makes no pretense of analyzing this important issue; and it is for this reason that the model presented provides only a foundation for a Marxian/radical treatment, and does not itself represent a complete theory.

Appendix

■ The existence theorems concerning equilibria for the continuous model of Figure 1a are sketched here.

Theorem A1 (T1 equilibrium): Let $\hat{\eta}$ be minimum of the least average wage function, $\omega(\eta) = \bar{\eta} \cdot h(\eta)$. If $h(0) > p > \omega(\hat{\eta})$, then:

(a) there exists a nondiscriminatory T1 equilibrium at which all workers are paid wage p;
(b) there exists a discriminatory T1 equilibrium $\langle \hat{\eta}, h(\hat{\eta}) \rangle$ at which each worker is paid a wage precisely on the appropriate h curve;
(c) if there exists more than one discriminatory equilibrium, which in general is the case, then there exists precisely an interval of η's for which such equilibria exist;
(d) all discriminatory equilibria except the one referred to in part (b), have precisely one of their wages lying on the appropriate h curve, while the other wage lies above its h curve;
(e) two equilibria cannot exist simultaneously in the economy; i.e., all firms hire at the same pair of wages and the same proportions η, with the exception of the nondiscriminatory case, where the proportions may vary between firms.

Theorem A2 (T2 equilibrium):

(a) If and only if $\eta_{pop} < \bar{\eta}_2$, there is at most one T2 equilibrium at which there is black unemployment, and that occurs at a certain proportion $\bar{\eta}_2$. $\bar{\eta}_2$ is in fact a T2 equilibrium. At that equilibrium, blacks are paid $h_2(\bar{\eta}_2)$, and whites are paid, in general, a wage greater than $h_1(\bar{\eta}_2)$.
(b) There is at most one T2 equilibrium at which there is white unemployment, and that occurs at a certain value $\bar{\eta}_1$. At that equilibrium, whites are paid a wage $h_1(\bar{\eta}_1)$, and blacks are paid, in general, a wage greater than $h_2(\bar{\eta}_2)$. This point is in fact a T2 equilibrium if and only if $\eta_{pop} > \bar{\eta}_1$.

Theorem A3: Consider the three equilibrium states of the economy:

(i) black unemployment only
(ii) white unemployment only
(iii) full employment.

Then, an economy can be specified (that is, there exists a specification for the *h* curves, and a value η_{pop}) such that a discriminatory T2 equilibrium exists exhibiting (i), (ii), or (iii) above, or in which any combination of (i), (ii), and (iii) can occur at different equilibria for the economy. Also, at most one T2 discriminatory equilibrium can be sustained in an economy at a time.

References

ARROW, K. "Some Mathematical Models of Race Discrimination in the Labor Market" in Anthony Pascal, ed., *Racial Discrimination in Economic Life*, Lexington, Mass.: D.C. Heath, 1972.

BECKER, G. *The Economics of Discrimination*. Chicago: University of Chicago Press, 1957.

DOERINGER, P. AND PIORE, M. *Internal Labor Markets and Manpower Analysis*. Lexington, Mass.: D.C. Heath, 1971.

EDWARDS, R., REICH, M., AND GORDON, D. *Labor Market Segmentation*. Lexington, Mass.: D.C. Heath, 1975.

MCWILLIAMS, C. *Factories in the Field*. Boston: Little, Brown and Co., 1939.

MIYAZAKI, H. "The Rat Race and Internal Labor Markets." *The Bell Journal of Economics*, Vol. 8, No. 2 (Autumn 1977).

REICH, M. "Who Benefits from Racism? The Distribution among Whites of Gains and Losses from Racial Inequality." Department of Economics, University of California, Berkeley, Mimeo, 1976.

———. "The Neoclassical Approach to Racial Discrimination: A Survey and Critique." Department of Economics, University of California, Berkeley, Mimeo, 1977.

SPENCE, A.M. *Market Signalling*. Cambridge: Harvard University Press, 1974.

SPERO, S. AND HARRIS, A. *The Black Worker*. Port Washington, N.Y.: Kiddikat Press, 1966 (reprinted from 1930 first edition).

STONE, K. "The Origins of Job Structures in the Steel Industry." *Review of Radical Political Economy*, Vol. 6, No. 2 (Summer 1974).

THUROW, I. *Poverty and Discrimination*. Washington, D.C.: Brookings Institution, 1969.

WELCH, F. "Labor Market Discrimination: An Interpretation of Income Differences in the Rural South." *Journal of Political Economy* (June 1967).

[23]

White Workers are Hurt by Racism: Econometric Evidence

THE ECONOMETRIC FINDINGS, theoretical analysis, and historical evidence presented in the previous three chapters each support a bargaining power theory of income distribution in which racial inequality hurts most white workers. Racial divisions weaken worker solidarity and bargaining power; capitalists gain and most white workers lose.

Racial discrimination may nonetheless benefit skilled workers and professionals in occupations with entry barriers that keep blacks and others out. Most workers in the United States do not belong to such privileged occupations, but it is important to incorporate this qualification into the analysis. Since these beneficiaries have relatively high incomes to begin with, I account for this qualification by restating the main hypothesis as: racial inequality increases inequality among whites by benefiting capitalists and high-income whites and by hurting most white workers.

This hypothesis concerning the effect of racial inequality on the white income distribution does not by itself exclude other effects with possibly quite different distributional implications. For example, racial discrimination in housing may increase the income of ghetto property owners, and racial discrimination in schooling through underfunding of ghetto schools may keep taxes down for all property owners (assuming they bear the burden of school financing). But the econometric results in Chapter 4 indicate the dominance of the bargaining power effects over these others.

Notice that the validity of the bargaining power theory does not depend on the particular mechanisms by which racial inequality is produced. No matter how racial inequality is created, it will have the effect of weakening working-class solidarity. Even if racial inequality resulted entirely from schooling and housing market discrimination, with employers playing no active role, the principal effect would be to produce racial divisions among workers from which employers benefit. This analysis implies that capitalists benefit from racial divisions whether or not they individually or collectively practice racial discrimination.

For these reasons, I have not investigated here the specific mechanisms of discrimination. These reasons also support the use of a racial inequality measure that deliberately does not control for racial differences in individual characteristics nor otherwise attempt to separate the various forms of discrimination from one another.

Nevertheless, it is possible and important to explore further the mechanisms that link racial inequality's effects to diminished worker solidarity and bargaining power. An elaboration of these mechanisms enriches our understanding and further supports the class conflict theory of the effects of racial inequality. In this chapter I explore two mechanisms that connect racial inequality to inequality among whites:

1. The effect of racial inequality on worker solidarity in wage bargaining. Racial inequality exacerbates inequality among whites because racial antagonisms inhibit union bargaining strength and militancy, thereby reducing the total income share of labor.
2. The effect of racial inequality on the solidarity of coalitions of black and low- and middle-income whites in the political arena. Racial inequality exacerbates white inequality because racial antagonisms reduce the redistributive nature of expenditures on local public services. That is, racial antagonisms result in a reduced effective supply of public services, such as public schooling and welfare, that are available to low- and middle-income whites.

WHITE WORKERS ARE HURT

These mechanisms are testable empirically using the cross-metropolitan area model of income distribution developed in Chapter 4. In this chapter I discuss the unionism and public services mechanisms in relation to these econometric tests. I also discuss in detail the expected relation between unionism and the earnings distribution in a metropolitan area, and present the results of the econometric tests. The findings show that both of these mechanisms do work to hurt most whites. Finally, drawing on detailed industry data on wages, unions, and profit rates, I report the results of a more direct test of the bargaining-power model. These findings also show that greater racial inequality in earnings is associated with lower wages, less unionism, and higher profit rates.

MECHANISMS: UNIONISM AND PUBLIC SERVICES

The first mechanism suggests that the bargaining strength of labor unions is lessened by racial inequality. The fear of a cheaper and underemployed black labor supply in the area affects labor when it presents and negotiates its wage demands. Racial antagonisms on the shop floor deflect attention from labor grievances relating to working conditions, permitting employers to cut costs without a substantial decline in net worker productivity. Racial divisions among labor inhibit the development of united worker organizations both within the workplace and in the labor movement as a whole. As a result, unionization and union militancy will be less, the greater are the extent of racial divisions.

Some economists have pointed to greater racial inequality to explain why the extent of unionization is much lower in the South than elsewhere in the United States. Differences in industrial structure between the regions do not account for this lower extent of unionism.[1] Southern unionization is significantly lower within nearly every industry that has an

[1] F. Ray Marshall, *Labor in the South* (Cambridge: Harvard University Press, 1965), chapter 18.

appreciable number of employees in both the South and the rest of the nation. The greater virulence of racism in the South seems to be one of the principal factors responsible for the inability of unions to develop a larger base there.[2]

The hypothesis that unions are hurt by racism may seem surprising to some, given the egregious racism of much of organized labor. Indeed, many students of the labor movement have demonstrated that discriminatory policies have been practiced by organized labor from its earliest history.[3] In their early years, for example, the constitutions of many craft unions expressly prohibited blacks from joining. It is often argued that union pressure comprises one of the primary forces compelling otherwise profit-seeking employers to conform to prevailing white social customs and attitudes against blacks.[4] An exclusionary racial policy, goes the argument, benefits white union members because it increases their bargaining power and income.

In evaluating this argument, however, it is important to distinguish between actual practice and the objective economic self-interest of union members. Racial exclusion increases bargaining power only when entry into an occupation or industry can be limited effectively. Industrial unions are much less able to restrict entry than are craft unions or organizations such as the American Medical Association. Historically, racial exclusion has been most practiced by skilled craft unions, and has probably benefited them, while it has

[2] Marshall, p. viii and chapters 1–2.

[3] Philip Taft, *Organized Labor in American History* (New York, 1964), pp. 665–670; Sterling Spero and Abram Harris, *The Black Worker* (New York: Atheneum, 1968), pass.; F. Ray Marshall, *The Negro Worker* (New York: Random House, 1967); Herbert Hill, "The Racial Practices of Organized Labor: The Age of Gompers and After," in Arthur Ross and Herbert Hill, eds., *Employment, Race and Poverty* (New York: Harcourt, Brace and World, 1967).

[4] For example, see Leonard Rapping, "Union-Induced Racial Entry Barriers," *Journal of Human Resources* (Fall 1970).

WHITE WORKERS ARE HURT

often weakened or destroyed industrial unions.[5] For example, many CIO unions would not have developed so rapidly in the late 1930s had they not stressed racial equality in their internal organization.

Moreover, census data indicate that the incomes of blacks and whites in labor unions are less unequal than incomes of those not in labor unions. These findings, presented in Table 7.1, are sustained even with more detailed occupational breakdowns. They are consistent with the hypothesis developed here that unions have, on the whole, a narrowing effect on racial inequality and that racial inequality inhibits unionism.

The second mechanism suggests that racial inequality creates divisions in working-class solidarity in the political arena where the level and distribution of public expenditures are determined. Racism thereby affects the distribution among whites of publicly provided services. These racial divisions reduce the ability of blacks and low- and middle-income whites to join in a united political movement that would press for the public services that benefit these groups. Two of the most important of these publicly provided services are schooling and welfare.

A certain amount of inequality in public services would exist even without racial divisions. Consider, for example, the distribution of schooling resources among social classes. The geographic segmentation of whites by social class and the tradition of local financing of school expenditures result in a high correlation between local expenditures on schooling and the per capita income of the locality. The desire of many

[5] Robert Analavage gives an account of a present-day example of this phenomenon: "Laurel Strike is Broken," in David Mermelstein, ed., *Economics: Mainstream Readings and Radical Critiques* (New York: Random House, 1970), pp. 131–135. In another recent case, an employer had to be enjoined by the National Labor Relations Board to cease the use of inflammatory racial arguments during union representation elections. See Sewell Manufacturing Co. 138 NLRB 66 (1963), cited in Marshall, *Labor in the South* p. 326.

TABLE 7.1 Effect of Union Membership on Relative Incomes of Nonwhites, 1970

	Male		*Female*	
*Year-Round, Full-Time Workers**	*In Labor Unions*	*Not in Labor Unions*	*In Labor Unions*	*Not in Labor Unions*
All Occupations	83	62	91	82
Blue Collar	90	72	95	104
White Collar	85	70	86	95
Service	73	77	101	89

* Entries refer to ratio of nonwhite to white median income.

SOURCE: U.S. Bureau of the Census, *Social and Economic Status of Blacks in the United States, 1972*, P-23 Series, no. 46, Table 43, p. 55.

teachers to work in the same neighborhoods in which they live, and their preference for students of upper social classes, biases the quality of teacher inputs within a school district in favor of the children of the rich.[6]

Racial discrimination and racial antagonisms exacerbate inequality in schooling among whites in several ways. First, black ghettos tend to be located near poor white neighborhoods more often than near rich white neighborhoods.[7] Since the inferiority of black schools often results from the fiscal deprivation of an entire school district or central city, poor whites living in the central city are simultaneously affected.

[6] Henry Levin has shown that teachers in effect charge more for their services when they teach in ghetto schools.

[7] The geographical contiguity of black and poor white neighborhoods can be deduced both from theoretical considerations and available empirical evidence. In the pure model of urban residential location, the household's decision on how far from the city center to locate depends basically on its income level and its subjective tradeoff between desire for housing space and the transportation costs of commuting to work. Given a high income elasticity of demand for housing space and the fact that transportation costs rise

WHITE WORKERS ARE HURT

Second, racial antagonisms dilute both the desire and the ability of poor white parents to improve educational opportunities for their children. Antagonisms between blacks and poor whites drive wedges between the two groups and reduce their ability to join in a united political movement pressing for improved and more equal education.[8] Moreover, many poor whites recognize that however inferior their own schools, black schools are even worse. This provides some degree of satisfaction and identification with the status quo, reducing

linearly with distance from the city center, whereas the cost of a unit of housing falls more than linearly with distance from the center, it follows that, differences in taste aside, lower-income families will reside in central cities. The poor will be concentrated in the center of cities, and the rich will live in the environs.

This pure model is not sufficient, however, to explain the concentrations of blacks in central cities. Blacks are concentrated in central cities not only because they are poor, but also because of intense racial discrimination in the residential housing market. Economic and racist forces have thus thrown lower-income blacks and whites together in the central cities. Moreover, the rapid growth of the black population in central cities and the resultant expansion of pressures on the geographical limits of the ghetto have accentuated this pattern. It has been empirically established that when ghettos expand, they tend to do so in the direction of poor white neighborhoods. The so-called deterioration of urban neighborhoods occurs first as the local housing stock ages and the average income level of its residents (mostly white) declines.

This stage always precedes the stage in which a neighborhood begins to "tip," or turn black. In other words, the geographical contiguity of blacks and poor whites is observable at the neighborhood, and even block, level, and is particularly evident at the edges of the ghetto. See Luigi Laurenti, *Property Values and Race: Studies in Seven Cities* (Berkeley: University of California Press, 1960); Karl Taeuber and Alma Taeuber, *Negroes in Cities* (Chicago: Aldine Press, 1965), and Beverly Duncan and Otis D. Duncan, *The Negro Population of Chicago: A Study in Residential Succession* (Chicago: University of Chicago Press, 1956). In a recent study, Karl Taeuber examined the extent of racial segregation in white city neighborhoods according to the social class of the neighborhood, and found that the upper-income districts showed significantly greater degrees of racial segregation. See Karl Taeuber, *Patterns of Negro-White Residential Segregation* (Santa Monica: Rand Corporation, 1970).

[8] For examples of labor union involvement in political campaigns that are intended to influence publically provided services, see David Greenstone, *Labor in American Politics* (New York: Random House, 1968).

the desire of poor whites to press politically for better schools in their neighborhoods. Finally, pressure by teachers' groups to improve all poor schools has been reduced by racial antagonisms between predominantly white teaching staffs and black children and parents.

In a similar fashion racial antagonisms reduce the political pressure on governmental agencies to provide other public services that are "pro-poor" in their distributional impact. In the case of welfare, racial inequality reduces the ability of poor blacks and whites to press for higher welfare stipends. Piven and Cloward have argued that political demands by the poor are a major determinant of legislator-determined welfare stipends as in the Aid to Families with Dependent Children program (AFDC).[9] Racial inequality, therefore, can significantly determine the average level of AFDC payments in an SMSA.

The mechanisms stated above can be expressed in the following set of equations, where the control variables are those discussed in Chapter 4.

(1) Unionism = g (racial inequality, market control variables)
(2) White schooling inequality = h (racial inequality, market control variables)
(3) Welfare payment levels = j (racial inequality, market control variables)

The greater the extent of racial inequality, the weaker will be the unions, the more unequal will be the white schooling distribution, and the lower will be the level of public welfare payments.

Bargaining Power and Unions

The economic literature examining the influence of unions and collective bargaining on wages, productivity, and income

[9] Frances Piven and Richard Cloward, *Regulating the Poor* (New York: Random House, 1971).

WHITE WORKERS ARE HURT

distribution has become both voluminous and controversial.[10] Not surprisingly, economists disagree on how much, or even whether, bargaining power affects workers' wages. At one extreme, some economists view union strength as the sole determinant of wage rates and labor's share of income. At the other extreme, there is the view epitomized by Milton Friedman: "In a dynamic world, economic forces are always arising that tend to change relative wage rates. . . . In the absence of unions, these forces will operate more or less directly on wage rates. Given unions, the same forces will be present but they will operate indirectly on wage rates through the mediation of the union. . . . In many cases, so to speak, unions are simply thermometers registering the heat rather than furnaces producing the heat."[11]

[10] Much of the early literature is summarized and reviewed in H. Gregg Lewis, *Unionism and Relative Wages in the United States* (Chicago: University of Chicago Press, 1963). Two reviews of the controversy that also contain good bibliographies are Richard Perlman, *Labor Theory* (New York: Wiley, 1969), and Richard Perlman, ed., *Wage Determination: Market or Power Forces?* (Boston: D.C. Heath, 1964). There was little empirical research on the impact of unionism in the 1960s as research interests in microincome determination shifted from the "structural" variables of the 1940s and 1950s to individual differences in human capital endowments. However, as noted below, unionism returned to the attention of researchers in the 1970s.

For studies suggesting that unionism and oligopolistic product market structure interdependently result in higher wage increases than in non-unionized and competitive industries, see William Bowen, *Wage Behavior in the Postwar Period: An Empirical Analysis* (Princeton: Princeton University Press, 1960), and Martin Segal, "The Relation Between Union Wage Impact and Market Structure," *Quarterly Journal of Economics* (February 1964); Harold Levinson, "Unionism, Concentration and Wage Changes: Towards a Unified Theory," *Industrial and Labor Relations Review* (January 1967).

An early example of the shift to analyzing the "quality of the labor supply" is Leonard Weiss, "Concentration and Labor Earnings," *American Economic Review* (March 1966). For one explanation of the reasons for this shift, see Barry Bluestone, "The Tripartite Economy: Labor Markets and the Working Poor," *Poverty and Human Resources* (July–August 1970), and Howard Wachtel and Charles Betsey, "Employment at Low Wages," *Review of Economics and Statistics* (May 1972).

[11] Milton Friedman, "Some Comments on the Significance of Labor Unions for Economic Policy," in David M. Wright, ed., *The Impact of the Union* (New York: McGraw-Hill, 1951).

WHITE WORKERS ARE HURT

Nonetheless, it is important to examine the many empirical studies of union impact and to assess whether unions do increase workers' wages. Here I discuss some of the issues involved in this literature and indicate the implications of previous research for the structure of my cross-sectional model of income distribution.

Economists generally do agree that workers in highly unionized sectors receive higher average wages than those in nonunionized sectors. Estimates based on industry or establishment data for the 1950s indicate that wages of union workers averaged about 10 to 15 percent higher than those of comparable nonunion workers in otherwise similar environments. More recent investigations, also using industry and establishments as the unit of observation, find a greater differential; one study (by Throop) indicates a differential of 26.0 percent in 1960, and another (by Ryscavage) finds differentials ranging from 20 to 40 percent in 1973.[12] The studies

[12] Weiss, "Concentration and Labor Earnings"; Adrian Throop, "The Union, Non-Union Wage Differential and Cost-Push Inflation," *American Economic Review* (March 1968); Paul Ryscavage, "Measuring Union-Non-Union Earnings Differences, *Monthly Labor Review* (December 1974). See also Vernon Clover, "Compensation in Union and Non-Union Plants, 1960–65," *Industrial and Labor Relations Review* (January 1968).

In the 1970s large microdata sets became available that permitted using the individual worker, rather than the industry or establishment, as the unit of observation. Studies using these data sources found consistently higher union wage effects than did Lewis. Many labor economists have attributed these higher estimates not to greater union bargaining power, but to the improved quality of the new data or to upward biases created by treating an individual's union membership status as exogenous to the wage relationship.

For example, Ashenfelter and Johnson found that union effects on wages were reduced by half or more if union status is itself treated as an endogenous variable in wage determination. However, an interesting paper by Leigh critically reviews the Ashenfelter-Johnson model and a half-dozen subsequent attempts to obtain simultaneous equation estimates of union wage effects. Leigh's own estimates indicate that adjustments for simultaneity *increase* the estimated impact of unions on earnings. See Orley Ashenfelter and George Johnson, "Unionism, Relative Wages, and Labor Quality in U.S. Manufacturing Industries." *International Economic Review* (October 1972); Duane Leigh, "Racial Differentials in Union Relative Wage Effects: A Simultaneous Equations Approach," *Journal of Labor Research* (Winter 1980).

find that the size of individual union, nonunion differentials varies, depending on the type of union and industry, the age of the union, and the stage of the business cycle.

But because unionism is intertwined with other aspects of labor and product-market structures, it is not easy empirically to isolate unionism itself as the *cause* of the union, nonunion wage differentials. The presence of unions tends to be highly and positively correlated with city size, plant size, capital-intensive techniques, high levels of product market concentration, and a labor force that has a high proportion of adult white males and an above-average level of years of schooling. Since each of these variables is itself correlated positively with wage rates independently of unionism, the gross union, nonunion wage differential does not provide unequivocal evidence that unionism is the causal factor producing higher wages. This difficulty permits a wide range of interpretations on the impact of unions.

Moreover, some economists have suggested that the causality between wages and unionism may work in both directions. The labor market forces that create higher wages may also facilitate union organizing efforts. Employers may adjust to unionism by increasing the skill and educational levels of the workers they hire, by installing machinery, or by making other changes in the conditions of employment in order to augment worker productivity.

Conversely, the absence of a union, nonunion wage differential does not prove conclusively that unions have no impact on wages. Unions may exert important "spillover" effects on nonunion employers, forcing them to increase wages to the union level in order to remain competitive. Alternatively, the nonunion employers may raise wages to union levels in order to forestall incipient unionism in their own firms; to counter, in other words, the "threat effects" of unionism.[13] Unions

[13] Sherwin Rosen, "Trade Union Power, Threat Effects and Extent of Organization," *Review of Economic Studies* (April 1969). However, studies examining the impact of unionism on management find greater productivity in unionized plants. See Sumner Slichter, James Healy, and Robert Livernash,

may also be effective in extending union rates to an entire labor market by influencing legislative bodies.

Finally, the independent effects of unionism on wages may be difficult to identify because unionism may be necessary but not sufficient for wage increases. Some of the empirical studies suggest that unions have their greatest independent effects on wages when they are newly organized.[14] During recessions the union, nonunion differential generally increases, because unions have negotiated multiyear contracts, with wage increases scheduled in advance, while nonunion wage increases are retarded by the slowdown in the demand for labor. When recession and inflation occur simultaneously, however, as during the 1970s, multiyear contracts can retard union wages if sufficient allowances for cost-of-living increases are not included in the contract. Many unions found themselves in this predicament when inflation accelerated in the mid-1970s.

Many of the earlier analyses of union impact, beginning with Paul Douglas in 1930, compared changes in union and nonunion wages over time.[15] After 1950 most studies attempted cross-sectional comparisons of wage differences at a particular moment in time. Two early cross-sectional studies of union impact illustrate some of the difficulties mentioned in the previous paragraphs.[16] In one of the earliest empirical

---

The Impact of Collective Bargaining on Management (Washington, D.C.: Brookings Institution, 1960) and Charles Brown and James Medoff, "Trade Unions and the Production Process," *Journal of Political Economy* (May–June 1978).

[14] See, for example, Arthur Ross and William Goldner, "Forces Affecting the Inter-Industry Wage Structure," *Quarterly Journal of Economics* (May 1950); Orley Ashenfelter and George Johnson, "Unionism, Relative Wages, and Labor Quality."

[15] Paul Douglas, *Real Wages in the United States*, 1890–1926 (Boston: Houghton Mifflin, 1930).

[16] Harry Douty, "Union and Nonunion Wages," in W.S. Woytinsky, ed., *Employment and Wages in the United States* (New York, 1951); John E. Maher, "Union, Nonunion Wage Differentials," *American Economic Review* (June 1956). Both of these studies and others are discussed in Robert Ozanne, "Impact of Unions on Wage Levels and Income Distribution," *Quarterly Journal of Economics* (May 1959).

WHITE WORKERS ARE HURT

attempts to measure union impact, Harry Douty examined union and nonunion wage rates within detailed occupations across different industries. Douty found that wages of workers in unionized plants exceeded wages of workers in nonunionized plants in 87 percent of the occupations studied. This seemed to Douty to be significant proof of union impact. However, in comparing union and nonunion workers, Douty did not control for sex of the work force, region, city size, or other variables that were correlated with both wage rates and probability of unionism. In a subsequent study by John Maher, an attempt was made to control for such variables. Instead of looking at national data, Maher limited himself in his study to selected male occupations in paint and varnish plants in Cleveland and in footwear plants in one part of New England. His findings indicated a zero union, nonunion wage differential. But Maher's conclusions that unions have no impact on wages are just as open to criticism, omitting as they do the possible "spillover" effects of unionism, as mentioned above.

The Maher study also illustrates problems that arise in the measurement of the variables. How should we relate the extent of union power to the percentage of workers that are organized by the union? Maher's data required him to assume that plants where less than half of the workers are covered by wage agreements are "nonunion," while those over half organized are "union." Many other statistical studies assume that union power is simply proportional to the percentage of the workers who are organized. But what if union power faces certain threshold levels? It seems plausible that unions command relatively little influence until they have organized 60 percent of a work force, that they cross a power threshold between 60 and 80 percent, and attain little increased power beyond that level.

The more sophisticated econometricians that have followed Douty and Maher have tried to confront these problems. They employ more detailed data and more complicated models and estimation techniques. But collinearity among the independent variables continues to plague these studies.[17] In sum, attempts to isolate the independent effects of unions on wages and employment seem to have come up against many conceptual and empirical difficulties that permit continuing differences of interpretation.

Nonetheless, one can distinguish four different types of income differentials on which unions may have an impact, beginning with more micro differentials and ending with more macro effects. First, unions may have an impact on wage differentials among individuals in the same occupation. There is wide agreement that the union ethic of "equal pay for equal work," union hostility to piece rates, and the more formal structuring of labor markets that accompanies unionism have produced considerable narrowing of interpersonal wage differentials within detailed occupational categories.[18] Wages for similar work have been somewhat equalized among workers in the same plant, and among workers in different firms and industries.

Second, unions may have an impact on interoccupational and interindustry earnings differentials. Craft-type unions have generally attempted to increase interoccupational differentials between skilled and unskilled workers, whereas industrial-type unions have generally sought to narrow these

[17] For examples, see Weiss, "Concentration and Labor Earnings," Frank Stafford, "Concentration and Labor Earnings: A Comment," *American Economic Review* (March 1968); Michael Boskin, "Unions and Relative Real Wages," *American Economic Review* (June 1972); Ryscavage, "Measuring Union-Nonunion Earnings Differences"; Ronald Oaxaca, "Estimation of Union/Nonunion Wage Differentials Within Occupational/Regional Subgroups," *Journal of Human Resources* (Fall 1975); Ashenfelter and Johnson, "Unionism, Relative Wages, and Labor Quality."

[18] See Clark Kerr, "Wage Relationships—The Comparative Impact of Market and Power Forces," in John T. Dunlop, ed., *The Theory of Wage Determination* (New York: St. Martin's Press, 1957).

differentials.[19] Early empirical studies suggested that inter-occupational wage differentials have narrowed considerably among blue collar occupations, among white collar occupations, and between blue and white collar occupations, over the first half of this century. But little of this narrowing was considered to be a direct result of union policies.[20] However,

[19] In many basic industrial sectors, the policy of industrial unions has often been to attain equal absolute wage gains for all of its members, skilled and unskilled, thus tending to reduce relative differences in wages.

[20] The role of unions in these narrowing trends is evaluated negatively in Lloyd G. Reynolds and Cynthia Taft, *The Evolution of the Wage Structure* (New Haven: Yale University Press, 1956), p. 186, and in Kerr, "Wage Relationships," pp. 188–189.

The narrowing trends are much attenuated after 1950. The long-run decline in wage differentials among manufacturing occupations has been documented in studies by Keat and by Ober. See Paul G. Keat, "Long-run Changes in Occupational Wage Structure, 1900–1956," *Journal of Political Economy* (December 1960); Harry Ober, "Occupational Wage Differentials, 1907–1947," *Monthly Labor Review* (November 1953). Long-term trends in white collar differentials have not been systematically studied, in part because of the fragmentary data that are available. The available data suggest that at the turn of the century, clerical and other low-level white collar workers received, on the average, about double the average wage of blue collar manufacturing workers; today the average white collar clerical and sales workers earn *less* than the average blue collar worker. For example, in 1890 the average annual earnings was $848 for clerical workers in manufacturing and steam railroads and $439 for blue collar workers in manufacturing. By contrast, in 1964 the median annual earnings was $5,300 among *male* clerical and sales workers and $5,855 among skilled craftsmen. See *Historical Statistics of the United States, Colonial Times to the Present* (Washington, D.C.: U.S. Government Printing Office, 1959), p. 92, and U.S. Bureau of the Census, "Trends in the Income of Families and Persons, 1947–74," *Technical Paper No. 17* (Washington, D.C.: U.S. Government Printing Office, 1968), p. 140.

The earnings gap between professional and low-level white collar work has also fallen, though again systematic data are not available. We do know that high school teachers in major cities earned nearly three times the wage of an average manufacturing production worker in 1904, but earn only 50 percent more today. See Keat, "Long-Run Changes in Occupational Wage Structure," and U.S. Bureau of the Census, *Technical Paper No. 17*. Incidentally, this narrowing is not inconsistent with the observed constancy of the rate of return to schooling, since occupational entry was much less dependent on schooling credentials in the past than it is today.

recent multivariate analysis by Sherwin Rosen and by Orley Ashenfelter suggests that unions have had a significant narrowing impact on interoccupational differentials.[21]

Interindustry differentials have also narrowed somewhat, but the conventional wisdom suggests that on the whole unionism had very little to do with this trend.[22] Again, the evidence is mixed. Reynolds, for example, has argued that greater union effectiveness in high-wage industries has tended to *widen* interindustry wage differentials.[23]

The effects of unionism on income differentials in a particular SMSA may differ from the effects of unionism in the nation as a whole. These differences are relevant to an examination of income distributions within SMSAs. They arise because the relative importance of craft unions and industrial unions varies across SMSAs, and because some unions in an SMSA may have strong ties to national labor unions. Interindustry differentials within the SMSA may be increased because such unions are keyed to *national* wage agreements and national labor markets, irrespective of local labor market wage levels.[24] Steel, auto, and meat-packing are examples of industries in which national labor union activity has been particularly evident.[25] On the other hand, a number of

[21] Sherwin Rosen "Unions and the Occupational Wage Structure in the United States," *International Economic Review* (June 1970); Orley Ashenfelter, "Racial Discrimination and Trade Unionism," *Journal of Political Economy* (May–June 1972).

[22] Kerr, "Wage Relationships"; Goldner, "Forces Affecting the Inter-Industry Wage Structure"; Lewis, *Unions and Relative Wages*.

[23] See Lloyd Reynolds, "The Influence of Collective Bargaining on the Wage Structure in the United States," in Dunlop, *Theory of Wage Determination*. Gail Pierson has fitted Phillips-curve-type wage equations to ten strongly unionized and several less strongly unionized manufacturing industries for the period 1953–1963. She found significantly greater wage increases in the unionized group. See Gail Pierson, "Union Strength and the Phillips Curve," *American Economic Review* (June 1968).

[24] Such unionism, it should be noted, tends to reduce inter-area differentials.

[25] See Lloyd Ulman, *The Rise of the National Trade Union* (Cambridge: Harvard University Press, 1960).

unions may form a coalition across industries within an SMSA. In most major cities the city-wide AFL-CIO Central Labor Councils provide at least the institutional shell of such a coalition.[26] Such a coalition might conceivably reduce inter-industry differentials within the SMSA. The net effect of unionism on interoccupational and interindustry differentials will depend, then, on the relative sizes and strength of craft unions and industrial unions, the extent to which unions are tied to national labor markets, and the extent of overall solidarity of unions in the SMSA.

A third impact of unions may impinge on the earnings differential between unionized and nonunionized workers. Differentials may arise within an industry between organized and unorganized plants as well as between industries that are organized and those that are not. As we have seen, much empirical research has examined the nature and causes of these differentials.[27]

Finally, unionism may affect the size distribution of income by changing the relative shares of labor and capital in favor of labor. Many economists express skepticism that labor can raise its share of total income, since unions represent no more than one-fourth of the total labor force, and any gains unions make for organized sections of the labor force may occur at the expense of unorganized sections. Unions are stronger in oligopolistic industries, and unorganized workers might be hurt by the capacity of such industries to pass wage increases on to consumers in the form of higher prices.

Moreover, if unions raise wages of their own members relative to nonunionized workers, capital will be substituted for labor in the unionized sector, and the resulting flow of labor into the nonunionized sector may depress the level of wages in that sector. The magnitude of this effect depends on the relative capital intensities in the two sectors as well as the elasticities of substitution between labor and capital.

[26] Greenstone, *Labor in American Politics.*

[27] See note 12 above.

WHITE WORKERS ARE HURT

A theoretical and empirical analysis along these lines has been carried out by Johnson and Mieszkowski. They estimate that in a competitive economy, a 1 percent increase in the union wage markup produces a gain in union wages that exceeds the loss in nonunion wages, so that the aggregate wage bill would be increased by up to 0.25 percent.[28] Insofar as the economy is not competitive and unions can extract a share of monopoly profits, the gains in labor's share will be greater and will come more at the cost of capital and less at the cost of the unorganized sector.[29]

This review of the literature suggests that although different types of unions can exert effects in opposing directions, unions on the whole probably narrow the income distribution. The magnitude of this expected impact across metropolitan areas depends on the size and strength of unions and the relative importance of craft and industrial unions. The size and strength of the unions depends in turn on their internal

[28] A statistically sophisticated attempt to examine the relationship between unionism and labor's share would employ a modern macroeconomic model so as to separate fluctuations in labor's share due to the rhythm of the business cycle from those due to the independent effect of unionism. Such an analysis should, however, account for the labor movement's political clout as one of the factors that increases the political costs of high unemployment and so shifts the nature of fiscal policy and the business cycle. I do not know of any such study, although there have been Phillips-curve-type attempts to measure the impact of the Kennedy-Johnson wage-price guideposts. See George Perry, "Wages and the Guideposts," *American Economic Review* (September 1967). There is also an emerging literature on political business cycles. See for example, Edward Tufte, *Political Control of the Economy* (Princeton: Princeton University Press, 1978).

[29] See Harry G. Johnson and Peter Mieszkowski, "The Effects of Unionization on the Distribution of Income: A General Equilibrium Approach," *Quarterly Journal of Economics* (November 1970).

In an article that is somewhat more pertinent to the present study, Clark Kerr reported that "[the] degree of unionization by SMSA is not significantly related to labor's share of manufacturing income in the SMSA's according to our calculations"; unfortunately, Kerr does not offer any clues as to his data, sample, statistical method, or quantitative results. See Clark Kerr, "Trade Unionism and Distributive Shares," *American Economic Review* (1954), pp. 279–292.

WHITE WORKERS ARE HURT

cohesiveness and solidarity (here racial divisions become important) and on the industrial structure of the metropolitan area. Areas with a high concentration of oligopolistic, capital-intensive industries are more likely to have larger union movements, and these unions will be able to win greater wage increases for their members.

Mechanisms: Econometric Evidence

I present here results of tests of the hypotheses concerning the unionism and public services mechanisms through which racial inequality operates to increase income inequality among whites. I discuss first the empirical counterparts of the variables and then turn to the findings themselves.

Variable Specification

An ideal unionization variable would account for each aspect of the phenomenon of unionism that has an impact on the distribution of income. These aspects include union structure and membership, degree of union militancy, and ties to national unions, as discussed in the previous section. Unfortunately, reliable data on unions and on union membership are very difficult to obtain. It is even more difficult to classify unions by craft versus industrial, degree of militancy, propensity to strike, and so forth. The variable used here, and the only one available for my sample, is based on union membership statistics collected by the U.S. Bureau of Labor Statistics. It is defined as the percentage of plant workers in all industries in an SMSA who are employed in establishments where a majority of workers are covered by a labor-management contract.[30] In the equations in which unionism appears

[30] These data are reported in U.S. Department of Labor, Bureau of Labor Statistics, *Wages and Related Benefits: 82 Labor Markets, 1960–61*, Bulletin No. 1285-83, Table 8-33b, p. 121; U.S. Department of Labor, Bureau of Labor Statistics, "Area Wage Surveys, Selected Metropolitan Areas, 1968–69," Bulletin No. 1625-90, Table 3. Only establishments employing fifty persons or more are included in this survey data. No data were available for seven of the SMSAs in the sample: Sacramento, San Diego, San José, Rochester, Fort Worth, Tampa, and Gary. The exclusion of these SMSAs may impart some

as a dependent variable, I expect that the coefficient of both the racial inequality and the percentage of employment in manufacturing variables will be positive. Unions will be stronger when racial inequality is low, and when manufacturing employment is high.

Turning next to schooling, an appropriate measure of schooling inequality would isolate and measure the effect of the local schooling systems on the distribution of earnings capacities among whites in the SMSA. An ideal variable would measure the degree of inequality in the distribution of postschooling individual earnings capacities *net* of the "pre-school" distribution, net, that is, of the capacities relevant for later labor market years that parents transmit to their children beginning in the preschool years and continuing outside of school in later years. In this way, the effects of the schooling system alone would be isolated from those of family background.

Two sets of empirical problems are immediately present. First, how does one isolate empirically the effects of parental social-class inequality from those of schooling? Second, how does one measure the effects of schooling on individual earnings capacities? These two problems of theory and measurement have perennially bedeviled attempts to estimate educational production functions and the economic effects of schooling.[31] There is both a paucity of adequate intergenera-

bias into my results, but I have no strong a priori notions of the direction of the bias. Two of the seven are Southern, a proportion comparable to that for the entire sample; on the other hand, none of the seven are among the larger SMSAs in my sample. A comparison of the means, standard derivations, and correlation matrices of all the variables for this subsample of forty-one SMSAs with those of the entire sample did not reveal any significant biases in the subsample.

[31] Some of the most important studies are in W. Lee Hansen, ed., *Education, Income and Human Capital* (New York: National Bureau of Economic Research, 1972); see, in particular, Samuel Bowles, "Towards an Educational Production Function." On the issues raised in this paragraph and the following one, see also Herbert Gintis, "Education, Technology and Worker Productivity," *American Economic Review* (May 1971); Samuel Bowles, "Schooling and Inequality from Generation to Generation," *Journal of Political Economy*

WHITE WORKERS ARE HURT

tional and longitudinal data on schooling and theoretical disagreement as to the nature of the inputs and outputs of schools that are pertinent in determining earnings.[32]

It is not my purpose to examine these problems in a systematic fashion here. The only available input measures of schooling inequality in an SMSA—per pupil expenditures—are collected on a school district basis. Since much of schooling inequality occurs *within* school districts and since a school district often comprises an entire central city, the school district unit is much too aggregated for the present purposes. Moreover, a number of recent studies have cast considerable doubt on the appropriateness of per pupil expenditures as a measure of schooling inputs.

For these reasons, I use an output rather than an input measure of schooling inequality. A convenient, and for my sample, the only available, measure of schooling output is years of schooling completed. I measure schooling inequality by a Gini coefficient of years of schooling completed for a cohort of white males aged twenty-five to twenty-nine. The purpose of using a young five-year age cohort is to control for the upward secular trend in years of schooling completed and to approximate most closely inequalities among recent students.

I obtained a white frequency distribution of years of schooling by subtracting nonwhites from total frequencies for fifteen schooling classes.[33] I used midpoints of intervals as class means, and computed a Gini coefficient of years of

---

(May–June 1972); Samuel Bowles and Herbert Gintis, "IQ in the U.S. Class Structure," *Social Policy* (January 1973); Christopher Jencks et al., *Inequality: A Reassessment of the Impact of Family and Schooling* (New York: Basic Books, 1972); Martin Carnoy, ed., *Schooling in a Corporate Society* (New York: David McKay, 1972).

[32] A recent study by Peter Meyer, "The Reproduction of the Distribution of Income" (Ph.D. diss., University of California, Berkeley, 1979), advances beyond the previous literature.

[33] The data sources are *U.S. Census of the Population*, parts 2-51, Table 103 (1960), and Table 148 (1970).

schooling with the same formula used in computing Gini coefficients of income. In the equations in which schooling inequality is the dependent variable, I expect that the coefficient of the racial inequality variable will be negative; the less the racial inequality, the less will be the white schooling inequality.

Finally, I also include an equation to test the hypothesis that levels of welfare stipends are related to the extent of racial inequality. I use the average 1960 SMSA level of monthly stipends to recipient families in the Aid to Families with Dependent Children (AFDC) as the dependent variable in this equation.[34] I expect to find positive signs for both the racial inequality and the median family income coefficients in this equation.

Unions

Table 7.2 presents results for a series of tests of the unionization hypotheses, using the subsample of forty-one SMSAs for which unionization data are available. The first two equations indicate the influence of racial inequality and the control variables on the extent of unionization. PCTMFG is positive and significant in these equations, as one would expect. The racial inequality variable is also positive, as expected, and significant at the 5 percent level in equation 1 and at the 1 percent level in equation 2. According to equation 2, at the sample means, a 1 percent increase in the ratio of median black to white incomes (reduction in racial inequality) is associated with a 0.6 percent increase in the degree of unionization.

[34] The data came from a survey of state welfare agencies by Marjorie Honig, to whom I am grateful for making this data available. Data were not available for the following fourteen SMSAs: Sacramento, San Bernardino, San José, Albany, Buffalo, Rochester, Akron, Columbus, Dayton, Toledo, Gary, Minneapolis, Paterson, and Portland. A comparison of the means, standard derivations, and correlation matrix of all the variables for this subsample of thirty-four SMSAs with those for the entire sample indicated that no significant biases were introduced by the exclusion of the above SMSAs.

TABLE 7.2 Unionism Equations, 1960 (n = 41)

Equation Number	*Dependent Variable*	*Constant*	*B/W*	*PCTMFG*	*WHICOL*	*PCTGOVT*	*MDWINC*	UNIONISM	R^2
1	UNIONISM	−.637	.646	.863	.291		.086		.544
			(2.20)	(3.58)	(0.90)		(2.55)		
	elasticity		.52	.31	.16		.75		
	beta		.29	.17	.06		.36		
2	UNIONISM	−.491	.787	.601		−0.838	.090		.558
			(2.68)	(1.95)		(−1.40)	(2.71)		
3	G_w	.423	−.092	−.125	.098			−.038	.679
			(−2.78)	(−4.31)	(2.82)			(−2.49)	
	beta		−.30	−.47	.26			−.25	
	Non-Southern SMSAs (n = 31)								
4	UNIONISM		−.028	.450	.527				.214
			(−0.04)	(1.69)	(1.69)				
5	G_w	.406	−.093	−.086	.094			−.0312	.399
			(−2.18)	(−2.76)	(2.56)			(−1.35)	

Simple Correlations (n = 41)

	G_w	*S1*	*B/W*	*PCTMFG*	*WHICOL*	*MDWINC*
UNIONISM	−.60	−.50	.49	.61	.12	.40

WHITE WORKERS ARE HURT

These results both bear out my hypotheses and contradict much conventional wisdom on the relation between unions and racism. The positive sign of B/W in equation 1 indicates that, at least as far as degree of organization is concerned, unions on the whole are better off when there is less racial inequality. Although some unions—particularly craft unions—may benefit from discriminatory practices and racial exclusion, such policies do not appear to produce gains for unions in the aggregate.

Evidence on the relation between unionism and racial inequality is also provided by Ashenfelter and by Leigh.[35] Their findings are worthy of summary here.

Ashenfelter first presents evidence that unions have a narrowing effect on the interoccupational wage structure. Since blacks are concentrated in the low-skill, low-wage occupations, unions tend to reduce the average income differential between blacks and whites, holding other variables constant. According to Ashenfelter's calculations, the average black/white wage ratio of all workers is about 1 to 2 percent higher than the average black/white wage ratio of nonunion workers.[36] Ashenfelter then looks separately at the effects of craft and industrial unions, using a large microeconomic data set from the 1967 *Survey of Economic Opportunity*. His results suggest that craft unions depress the black/white wage ratio, while industrial unions increase it. The disequalizing effect of craft unions occurs for two reasons. First, craft unions are less likely to have black members than industrial unions; second, craft unions tend to increase the interoccupational wage differential, whereas industrial unions tend to narrow it. Ashenfelter estimates that craft unions in the construction industry reduce the black/white male wage ratio by 5 percent, while industrial unions tend to increase this ratio by about

[35] Orley Ashenfelter, "Racial Discrimination and Trade Unionism"; and Duane Leigh, "Racial Discrimination and Labor Unions: Evidence from the NLS Sample of Middle-Aged Men," *Journal of Human Resources* (Fall 1978).

[36] Ashenfelter, "Racial Discrimination and Trade Unionism," pp. 16 and 24.

4 percent.[37] He finds that unions, on net, increase the average black/white wage ratio by about 3 percent.

Leigh has reexamined Ashenfelter's analysis by using data for 1969 from the National Longitudinal Surveys of middle-aged men. This data set contains explicit information on the type of union—industrial or craft—representing workers. Leigh could therefore identify craft unionists directly, whereas Ashenfelter could only identify craft unionists in construction. Nonetheless, Leigh's findings are substantially the same as Ashenfelter's.[38]

Ashenfelter, Leigh, and I find similar correlations between unionism and racial inequality, but we draw opposite causal inferences. Both inferences probably have validity, although I have not tried to assess their relative importance. Both inferences are consistent with the class-bargaining-power model I have proposed. Neither inference is consistent with the Becker hypothesis that capitalists lose and white workers gain from discrimination.

Table 7.2 also provides some evidence on the direct effect of unionism on the white income distribution. The simple correlation between G_w and unionism is $-.60$, indicating that unions are strongly associated with greater income equality, but a causal interpretation requires multivariate analysis. Equation 3 in Table 7.2 shows that, controlling for the effects of industrial structure and racial inequality on the income inequality variable, an increase in unionism is still associated significantly with a reduction in income inequality. The UNIONISM variable has the expected sign, is significant at the 1 percent level, and has a beta of .25, the same order of magnitude as the betas for the other explanatory variables.

This equation significantly understates the impact of unions.

[37] Ibid., p. 23.

[38] Leigh, "Racial Discrimination and Labor Unions," pp. 572–576. These results are sustained in Leigh's simultaneous equations estimate in which union status is exogenous (not in the sense of my model, but rather of that discussed in note 12). See Leigh, "Racial Differentials in Union Relative Wage Effects."

WHITE WORKERS ARE HURT

The UNIONISM variable is highly correlated with PCTMFG, and the latter may be picking up some of the union effects. Moreover, the data underlying the UNIONISM variable contain considerable measurement error, the variable itself is an imperfect measure of labor's bargaining strength, and the overall variation in this variable is restricted by the general weakness of unions in the United States. In view of all these handicaps, I interpret these results as providing striking support (the pun is intended) of the hypothesis that unions exert a significant egalitarian effect on income distribution.

Equation 3 in Table 7.2 also shows that racial inequality affects white inequality, both directly and indirectly, through its effect on unionism. The direct and indirect effects of racial inequality on white inequality can be decomposed quantitatively by use of the following relation:

$$r_{G_w,B/W} = b_{G_w,B/W} + b_{G_w,u} \cdot r_{u,B/W} + \sum_i b_{G_w,i} \cdot r_{i\,B/W},$$

where: r_{kj} = simple correlation coefficients

b_{kj} = standardized regression coefficients (beta weights)

u = subscript for unionism

i = runs over control variables.

The direct effect of racism is then the first term on the right-hand side of the above equation, while the indirect effect through unionism is represented by the second term. The relations can be illustrated by a path diagram:

WHITE WORKERS ARE HURT

The computed results are:

Direct effects of racial inequality:	−.30
Indirect effects via unionism:	−.13

Finally, Table 7.2 presents estimates of the same equations for the non-South subsample. The industrial-structure variables continue to be significant in equation 4, but the B/W variable is not. The hypothesized relation between unionization and racial inequality apparently holds only on an interregional level. As the institutional literature suggests, the regional differences in unionization may be related to the greater degree of racial inequality in the South. The B/W variable is still significant in equation 5.

Schooling Inequality and Public Welfare

The effect of racial inequality on white schooling inequality is reported in Table 7.3. In equation 1, the coefficient of B/W is negative, as predicted, and is significant at the 1 percent level. PCTMFG has a negative sign, and is the only other variable that enters significantly into this equation. More than half of the variance is explained by the equation. Similar results obtain for the non-South subsample (see equation 3). B/W again appears with a negative coefficient, significant at the 1 percent level. The significance of the control variables in this equation again is much lower than in the G_w or S1 equations.

The high association between schooling inequality among young white males and racial income inequality in these equations supports the specific hypotheses of this chapter concerning the effects of racism on schooling inequality. The results also further support the validity of B/W as a measure of racism. A spurious correlation between B/W and EDGINW is much less likely than a spurious correlation between B/W and G_w. The much higher statistical association between B/W and EDGINW therefore diminishes the likelihood of spuriousness in the observed statistical association between G_w and B/W.

As equations 2 and 4 indicate, both B/W and EDGINW are insignificant when EDGINW is added to the G_w equation. This

TABLE 7.3 White Schooling Inequality Equations, 1960

Equation Number	*Dependent Variable*	*Constant*	*B/W*	*PCTMFG*	*WHICOL*	*MDWINC*	*EDGINW*	R^2	*n*
1	EDGINW	.563	−.563	−.185	.117	.014		.566	48
			(−6.22)	(−1.86)	(−1.25)	(−1.30)			
2	G_w	0.43	−.056	−.123	.080	−.012	.087	.661	48
			(−1.44)	(−4.93)	(2.26)	(−3.63)	(1.60)		
	beta		−.18	.46	.20	.27	.18		
Non-Southern SMSAs									
3	EDGINW		−.321	−.0475	−.173			.396	36
			(−2.99)	(−0.72)	(−2.08)				
4	G_w	0.36	−.065	−.086	.094	−.0046	.110	.358	36
			(−1.24)	(−2.96)	(2.49)	(−0.91)	(1.36)		

Simple Correlations (n = 48)

	G_w	*S1*	*B/W*	*PCTMFG*	*WHICOL*
EDGINW	.55	.55	−.77	−.44	−.25

WHITE WORKERS ARE HURT

increase in the standard error occurs because the simple correlation coefficient between the two variables is −.77. Moreover, EDGINW is not a truly exogenous variable in this equation, since we would expect the degree of white income inequality itself to influence the degree of schooling inequality.

The results in equations 2 and 4, together with the high correlation between B/W and EDGINW, suggest that much of the effect of racial inequality on income inequality occurs indirectly through the effect on schooling inequality. A decomposition of the direct and indirect effects, using the same technique as with unionism, produced the following results:

Direct effect of racial inequality:	−.18
Indirect effect via schooling:	−.13

The equation estimate relating racial inequality to the average SMSA level of monthly stipends in the Aid to Families with Dependent Children (AFDC) program is indicated in Table 7.4. The important control variable here is MDWINC, for it measures the general wage level of the SMSA and the capacity of the state and city to fund welfare programs. MDWINC has the expected sign and is significant at the 1 percent level in all the equations. PCTMFG, WHICOL, and PCTNW are not significant in these equations.

The racial inequality variable has the expected positive sign and is significant at the 1 percent level in all the equations in Table 7.4. The results indicate that SMSAs with less racial inequality have more generous transfer programs, presumably in response to greater pressure from the poor.

It is possible that the causation here works in the reverse direction: the higher AFDC benefits cause a higher B/W. This would happen if (1) AFDC stipends are high relative to median black incomes, and (2) a high proportion of black families, higher than among white families, receive AFDC payments. But underlying data clearly indicate that, in 1960, neither the average AFDC stipend nor the mean percentage of black families receiving AFDC payments was sufficiently high to produce a spurious correlation between median black income (the numerator of B/W) and the AFDC variable.

TABLE 7.4 AFDC Equations, 1960 (n = 34)

Equation Number	Dependent Variable	Constant	*B/W*	*PCTMFG*	*WHICOL*	*MDWINC*	*PCTNW*	R^2
1	AFDC	−173.	243.1	.071	−.779	25.0		.685
			(4.28)	(0.09)	(−0.38)	(2.69)		
2	AFDC	−197.	280.4			19.0	31.42	.497
			(3.03)			(2.80)	(0.32)	
			Non-Southern SMSAs (n = 22)					
3	AFDC	−207.	300.0	.272	−.655	23.0		.521
			(3.47)	(0.24)	(−0.25)	(3.47)		
4	AFDC	−272.	460.4			11.0	190.0	.375
			(3.24)			(6.84)	(1.17)	

Simple Correlations (n = 34)

	B/W	*MDWINC*	*PCTNW*
AFDC	.61	.49	−.36

WHITE WORKERS ARE HURT

Once again, the results support the hypotheses of this study: higher levels of AFDC stipends are associated with lower levels of racial inequality.

Evidence from 1970 Data

As in the investigation for 1960, I have examined two mechanisms for 1970 that link racial inequality with inequality among whites: the impact of racial inequality on inhibiting (1) the extent and strength of unionism in an SMSA, and (2) the capacity of poor and middle-income whites to unite in the political arena to obtain greater resources, such as for public schooling. I examine the first mechanism by estimating an equation with the extent of union membership in an SMSA in 1970 as the dependent variable (UNIONISM); I examine the second with an equation explaining the 1970 degree of schooling inequality among young white males, as measured by a Gini coefficient of years of schooling completed in 1970 among white males aged twenty-five to twenty-nine (EDGINW). These results are presented in Table 7.5.

In equation 1 of Table 7.5, the B/W variable appears with a positive coefficient, as expected, and is significant at the 15 percent level. At the sample means, a 1 percent increase in B/W (decline in racial inequality) is associated with a 0.33 percent increase in the extent of unionism. The coefficient, t-statistic, and elasticity at the means are each about two-thirds of that found with 1960 data. In 1970, unions were still stronger where there was less racial inequality, but the extent of the association was less than in 1960.

In equation 2 of Table 7.5, reporting the estimates of the same unionism equation for the non-Southern SMSAs only, the B/W variable does not appear significantly. This variable also did not appear significantly with 1960 data. In 1970 it still seemed to be the case that the relation between unionism and racial inequality occurred as in interregional phenomenon.

The estimates of the schooling-inequality hypotheses are reported in equations 3 and 4 of Table 7.5. The B/W coefficient in equation 1 is negative as expected, and significant at the

TABLE 7.5 Unionism and White Schooling Inequality, 1970

Equation Number	*Dependent Variable*	*Constant*	*B/W*	*PCTMFG*	*WHICOL*	*MDWINC*	R^2	*n*
1	UNIONISM	−.224	.225	.827	.009	.0099	.624	44
			(1.48)	(6.61)	(.048)	(1.22)		
2[a]	UNIONISM	.159	−.115	.688	−.028	.0015	.433	31
			(−0.47)	(4.27)	(−0.11)	(0.12)		
3	EDGINW	.218	−.048	−.003	−.049	−.0032	.199	44
			(−1.53)	(−0.01)	(−1.27)	(−2.07)		
4[a]	EDGINW	.193	−.045	.103	−.518	−.0014	.085	32
			(−0.82)	(0.36)	(−1.04)	(−0.60)		

[a] Indicates non-Southern subsample.

15 percent level. However, the magnitude and significance of this and all the other coefficients, as well as the R^2, are much lower than for 1960. I suspect that the general increase in schooling levels between 1960 and 1970 render the Gini coefficient of schooling years completed less valid as a measure of inequality in schooling resources in 1970. This may explain the changed results for the two years. Similar remarks apply to the non-South equation, where the B/W variable is not significant.[39]

Wages, Unions, Profits, and Racial Inequality

The theoretical model concerns the effects of racial inequality on workers' wages and employers' profits. Yet the empirical investigations have made use of and examined the relation between racial inequality and the size distribution of income in an SMSA. A more direct test of the model would be desirable. While the most direct test would employ the relevant data on individual firms, such data unfortunately are not available for a statistically adequate sample. Relevant data from the Census Bureau and the Internal Revenue Service are available, however, for three-digit detailed industries in 1970. A brief discussion will indicate how I use industry data on wages, unions, and profits to make more direct tests of the model.

My argument states that greater racial inequality between black and white workers makes alliances between them more difficult, hindering the development of joint bargaining power against employers. At the microeconomic level of the firm or, better yet, at the establishment or shop-floor level, racial inequality in annual earnings is due more to occupational and seniority differences then to the pure wage discrimination of unequal pay for equal work. Nonetheless, the differences that exist can and often do affect the solidarity of the workers in negotiating wages and working conditions.

[39] The 1960 results I obtained concerning the relation between racial inequality in an SMSA and average AFDC stipend levels drew on data gathered by Marjorie Honig. I have not been able to obtain comparable data for 1970 and therefore could not repeat this analysis.

WHITE WORKERS ARE HURT

I therefore expect that *lesser* racial inequality should be associated with (1) *higher* earnings for white workers and (2) stronger unions. These implications are the opposite of what one would expect to find if white workers and their unions were thought to benefit from racial inequality.

A bargaining-power model of wage determination suggests, at the same time, a bargaining-power model of profit determination. Holding productivity and output prices constant, an increase in wages will come out of profits. I therefore also expect to find that lesser racial inequality is associated with lower profit rates.

Table 7.6 reports results for three equation, relating racial inequality to wages, unionism, and profit rates, respectively.[40] These equations are estimated across those industries for which data are available, including data for control variables. Note that since my hypotheses concern the establishment or firm, while the data are at the industry level, the estimates are

[40] Some of the variables, such as union membership, are not available with as much disaggregated detail as others. To make efficient use of the available data and permit inclusion of independent control variables, I constructed a conformable set of observations for each equation by employing weighting procedures to reaggregate some observations. This explains the different sample sizes for each of the equations in Table 7.6.

White and nonwhite workers' earnings refer to median annual wage and salary income in the industry for males who are in the experienced civilian labor force. The B/W variable is the ratio of nonwhite-to-white earnings. The unionism variable refers to proportion of employees in labor unions and is based on household-survey data. The profit rate is measured as the ratio of after-tax profits to stockholders' equity in the industry. AGE is median age of male workers, PCTNW refers to the percentage of nonwhites in the industry labor force, and PCTYR refers to the proportion of the industry labor force that worked fifty or more weeks in 1969.

Data sources for these variables are: U.S. Bureau of the Census, *Census of the Population, 1970*, "Subject Reports: Industrial Characteristics," Tables 5, 6, and 7 (earnings, percent year-round workers); 32 (age); 33 (percent nonwhite); U.S. Internal Revenue Service, *Corporation Returns, 1970*, Table 1 (profit rate); U.S. Department of Labor, Bureau of Labor Statistics, *Selected Earnings and Demographic Characteristics of Union Members, 1970*, Bulletin No. 417 (union membership).

Table 7.6 1970 Industry Equations

Equation Number	*Dependent Variable*	*Constant*	*B/W*	*Age*	*PCTNW*	*PCTYR*	R^2	*n*
1	Median White Earnings	5197	3178 (2.16)	−138.3 (−1.90)	−63.6 (−2.13)	83.4 (4.36)	.542	47
2	Unionism	−1.03	1.15 (3.15)	.014 (1.27)	−.252 (−0.36)	.019 (0.04)	.336	27
3	Profit Rate	.205	−.140 (−2.61)		−.217 (−2.15)		.145	83

likely to understate the true relationships among the variables I am studying.

As equations 1 and 2 in Table 7.6 indicate, racial inequality in an industry appears to be a significant determinant of white male workers' annual earnings in the industry and of the proportion of union members among workers in the industry.[41] A reduction in racial inequality (higher B/W) is associated with higher earnings for white workers and with more unionism, controlling for other variables in both cases. At the sample means, the elasticity of the B/W variable is .29 in the earnings equation, and 2.30 in the unionism equation. Each of these results is consistent with the conflictual bargaining-power model.

Equation 3 indicates that a reduction in racial inequality is associated with a fall in the industry profit rate. A 1 percent decline in racial inequality produces a 0.44 percent decline in the profit rate. This result is again consistent with my model.

These results, taken together with the 1970 SMSA equations in Tables 7.4 and 7.5, provide further confirmation of my hypotheses. Capitalists benefit and most white workers lose from racial inequality. Whether or not these effects are apparent to the respective agents is not clear, but they seem to be still present in the United States in 1970.

Conclusion

The class conflict analysis of racial inequality identifies specific and testable mechanisms through which racial inequality works to hurt most white workers and benefit capitalists. Unions are weaker and the supply of public services to low- and middle-income whites are lessened by racial divisions.

[41] A years-of-schooling variable could not be included in the earnings equation because these data are only available at a very high level of aggregation. The same is true for weekly hours and weeks worked, though these influences are picked up to some extent by the PCTYR variable. Data limitations thus precluded the inclusion of a number of control variables in these equations.

WHITE WORKERS ARE HURT

These mechanisms are tested here econometrically using the cross-SMSA model developed in Chapter 4, and applying a cross-industry model as well. The empirical findings generally support the class conflict theory. These results thus complement the econometric evidence presented in Chapter 4, the theoretical analysis presented in Chapter 5, and the historical evidence presented in Chapter 6. Racial inequality benefits capitalists and hurts most whites.

[24]

RACIAL INEQUALITY AND WHITE EMPLOYMENT: AN INTERPRETATION AND TEST OF THE BARGAINING POWER HYPOTHESIS

Steven Shulman

This article disputes the argument and the evidence used to conclude that white workers are hurt by discrimination against blacks. Racism may increase the bargaining power of white workers if it unifies white ethnics, and may benefit them if it reduces job competition. The distributional consequences of discrimination will vary with the intensity of aggregate unemployment and the degree of racial segmentation in the labor market. The impact of racial inequality on the probability of employment is evaluated with a cross-sectional model using census summary data on SMSAs. Results show that racial inequality improves white male and female employment prospects in 1980, and suggest the same for 1970.

The bargaining power hypothesis explains the persistence of labor market discrimination in capitalism. Labor and management are presumed to have opposing interests which are resolved through formal and informal conflict and negotiation. Wage and other outcomes are determined by the balance of power which, in the context of a given set of economic and political conditions, depends upon the processes of group formation and resource utilization. Discrimination is held to separate and differentiate black and white workers, thereby reducing the solidarity of labor and increasing the bargaining power of capital. Competitive market mechanisms would then tend to reproduce discrimination just as they reward and reproduce any profit maximizing strategy.[1]

A number of authors working within the tradition of radical political economy have concluded from the bargaining power hypothesis that racial discrimination hurts white as well as black workers by weakening their bargaining position.[2] Some have characterized this interpretation of the bargaining power hypothesis as "the" radical or Marxist model of discrimination.[3] Erik Olin Wright, for example, comments that "[t]he analysis of racism as a divide and conquer strategy has perhaps been the central theme in Marxist treatments of the subject."[4] However, it does not necessarily follow from the bargaining power hypothesis that discrimination is inimical to the economic interests of white workers. Other authors, equally firmly situated within the radical paradigm and equally committed to the bargaining power hypothesis, conclude that white workers as well as capitalists benefit from discrimination.

Herbert Hill, for example, argues that racial identification unified white ethnics and that both craft and industrial unions have consistently discriminated to preserve employment advantages for white workers. Daniel Fusfeld and Timothy Bates develop a crowding model in which blacks supply a form of coerced labor into the secondary sector while whites enjoy improved economic opportunities from the reduction of competition in the primary sector. Edna Bonacich argues that the threat of substitution of cheaper black labor encouraged white workers to erect "racist structures" of exclusion and caste to insulate themselves from competition. William Darity, Jr. describes the labor market as a terrain for ethnic-racial competition and conflict along group lines in which whites strive to protect their preferred positions in an occupationally stratified system.[5]

These authors agree that capital and labor engage in class conflict over the distribution of income and control of the labor process. However, they interpret the bargaining power hypothesis in a broader sense than "divide-and-conquer." Racial identification not only divides black workers from white workers, but also unifies and assimilates white ethnic groups. Depending upon the relative strengths of these opposing tendencies, racism may result in either a net increase or decrease in the bargaining power of white workers. The distributional outcomes of discrimination are thus seen to be contingent upon historical circumstances rather than preordained by the logic of divide-and-conquer. Furthermore, employment and occupational discrimination reduce job competition for the favored group. Racism can thus insulate whites from downturns, enhance their occupational mobility and make their wages more downwardly rigid even if it also inhibits wage growth, unionization and progressive public policies. The distributional impact of discrimination is complex and variable, which is why, as Bonacich puts it, "the question of whether white workers gain or lose from racism [is] a false, or at least oversimplified issue."[6]

This article provides evidence in support of the broader, historically contingent interpretation of the bargaining power hypothesis. It supports the view that the impact of discrimination on white workers depends upon labor market conditions, in particular its degrees of racial segmentation and aggregate tightness. These forces may work in opposing directions. The article also describes a simple econometric test of the impact of racial inequality on white and black unemployment in 1970 and 1980.

DISCRIMINATION, SEGMENTATION, AND UNEMPLOYMENT

The broad interpretation of the bargaining power hypothesis suggests that racial inequality may increase white workers' bargaining power if it unifies white ethnics and insulates them from labor market competition, but may also decrease white workers' bargaining power if it enables capital to divide-and-conquer labor as a whole. The former may be considered the "insulation effect" and the latter the "solidarity effect." The insulation effect implies that white workers benefit from racial inequality while the solidarity effect means that they suffer distributional losses.

Distributional consequences can be interpreted in either absolute or relative terms. Because the issue at stake is the incentive of white workers to discriminate, absolute measurements are more appropriate here. White workers could make gains relative to capital even if discrimination lowered the incomes of both, or conversely white workers could suffer losses relative to capital even if discrimination raised their standard of living. In the first case relative gains would not indicate that white workers have an incentive to discriminate, while in the second case relative losses could not be used to justify the conclusion that white workers have a material stake in promoting racial equality. Michael Reich, for example, disputes white workers' "perception that fighting racism means sacrifice" on the basis of a demonstration that more equality between blacks and whites results in more equality between wealthier and poorer whites.[7] The conclusion does not necessarily follow from the premises. The perception of white workers may be correct if discrimination shifts income from all blacks to all whites with white capital gaining proportionately more than white labor. In this case, racism would raise the standard of living of white workers even though it lowers their income relative to capital. Consequently, the distributional question in this article is understood in terms of the impact of racial inequality on the absolute incomes of white workers.

Income changes can be due to fluctuations in employment as well as wages, and can be difficult to assess since the two may move in opposite directions. The impact of discrimination on white wages is particularly difficult to predict since the benefit from reduced job competition (insulation effect) may be offset by the loss of working-class unity (solidarity effect). The employment impact is less ambiguous since it is only the insulation effect that directly affects the probability of a hire. Solidarity between black and white workers influences the wage bargain, but the quantity of employment is rarely determined by negotiation, and in any event will be buffeted by the wage bargain both in terms of costs and demand. I will therefore concentrate on the issue of employment in evaluating the distributional impact of racial inequality on white workers.

White workers can improve their employment prospects if they are able to insulate themselves from job competition by black workers. Competition in the labor market means that comparable workers are potential substitutes. If the substitutability of black and white workers is inhibited, then white workers will glean benefits in the same manner that a supplier of any commodity gleans benefits from a reduction in competition. Restrictions on substitutability result from the institutional forces that segment job markets and the discriminatory forces that attach racial categories to job segments. To the degree that labor markets are segmented along racial lines, white workers will then enjoy greater job security and lower unemployment.

The racial identification of job segments does not require that white workers act as a cartel, although the history of the labor movement strongly suggests a systematic attempt to institutionalize white privilege.[8] Capitalists, almost all of whom are white, are able and willing to give preferential treatment to white workers as long as the benefits exceed the costs. The benefits to the capitalist are reduced labor solidarity, which may mean that white workers "purchase" their improved job security at the expense of lower wages. Capitalists are further able to offset class conflicts with their white workers by establishing an identity of interests along racial lines. This hegemonic relation can reduce unit labor costs to the degree that team efficiency rises with social homogeneity.[9] From this perspective, the failure of the labor movement to consistently fight racism and the triumph of business unionism over social unionism no longer appear as anomalies, but rather as the expected outcomes of a racial hierarchy that rewards class compromise by both capitalists and white workers. Segmentation is conjoined with discrimination as a result of profit maximization, not conspiracies or cartels.

Capitalists also face costs from giving preferential treatment to white workers. Neoclassical economists emphasize the increase in search costs if qualified black applicants are passed over, or in lowered productivity if less qualified white applicants are hired.[10] What neoclassicists fail to recognize is that such costs will vary with the tightness of the labor market. If aggregate unemployment is high, search time will not have to be extended nor wages raised to find qualified white applicants. Furthermore, the opportunity cost for foregone output is lower in a recession than in an expansion. Capitalists are thereby able to reap the benefits of discrimination while facing minimal costs from doing so during a downturn. Preferential treatment would thus be more likely to be observed in periods of high unemployment.[11]

The insulation effect is therefore more likely to predominate when labor markets are segmented and slack. However, these determinants of labor market behavior are not necessarily simultaneous. Segmentation is a product of institutional forces such as custom, technology and the capital-labor "accord"[12] while aggregate unemployment is a consequence of macroeconomic conditions. In the immediate post-war period, for example, segmentation was strong while labor markets were relatively tight. White workers benefited from barriers to black mobility[13] while capitalists used the productivity gains from labor-management cooperation (in part a product of racial privilege) to offset the costs created by racial exclusion during a period of low unemployment.[14] This arrangement broke down in the mid-1970s as slow economic growth, intensified international competition and other developments eroded the distributional basis of the labor accord.[15] This event occurred in the context of—and perhaps was partly caused by—the demise of some of the traditional mechanisms of racial subordination, and in particular a decline in occupational segregation. Black occupational mobility improved over the slow growth years of the 1970s as well as over the rapid growth years of the 1960s. Educational differences also fell rapidly over this period.[16] Labor markets thereby became less segmented along the lines of race (at least in terms of employed persons). At the same time, aggregate unemployment over this period rose considerably so that the costs of racial exclusion fell. Racial privilege in this period benefited capitalists as it reduced labor solidarity, kept wages low and further weakened the labor movement, while white workers were buffered to some degree from the destructive impact of prolonged, high unemployment. Consequently, preferential treatment for white workers continued, though after the mid-1970s it was motivated more by macroeconomic conditions than by labor market structure.

Discrimination has therefore been sustained as segmentation offset tight labor markets in the immediate post-war period, and as slack labor markets offset the decline in segmentation since the mid-1970s. These trends in segmentation and unemployment suggest that labor market restructuring over the 1970s has not altered the distributional consequences of racial discrimination. White workers are expected to have made employment gains both before and after the mid-1970s as a result of preferential treatment. While the mechanisms generating preferential treatment were different in the two periods, the results were the same.

The distributional impact of discrimination in both periods depends on the relative strengths of segmentation and unemployment. It cannot be logically predetermined as the divide-and-conquer interpretation would have it. Instead, the net benefit or loss that discrimination confers upon white workers must be empirically displayed.

EMPIRICAL METHOD

The most well known empirical support for the solidarity effect comes from Reich.[17] Reich uses cross-sectional census summary data on SMSAs to show that income inequality among whites is positively correlated with income inequality between blacks and whites. On the basis of this demonstration he concludes that racial equality increases the solidarity of labor and thereby its bargaining power. As the bargaining power of labor rises, the functional distribution of income will shift in favor of wages, so that the gap between wealthier and poorer whites will fall. Closure of the income gap between blacks and whites thus corresponds to closure of the income gap among whites.

Unfortunately, Reich's results are rendered unreliable by several econometric and interpretive problems. First, his equations are misspecified since he does not include the human capital and labor market control variables that influence the functional distribution of income.[18] Second, income inequality among whites, as a proxy for the state of class conflict, may also influence the family income ratio between blacks and whites insofar as Reich's theory posits income to be a function of class conflict.[19] The estimated coefficients of Reich's equations may thus suffer from simultaneity bias. Third, Reich's results are not robust. Other studies using cross-sectional and time-series data have failed to replicate his results.[20] Fourth, he fails to separate out the issues of wages and employment despite the fact that losses in terms of one may be offset by gains in terms of the other. Fifth, his dependent variable is drawn on 1969 data (census income data is one year prior to the decennial year) while his independent variables are drawn on 1970 data, thus chronologically confounding the direction of causality. Finally, as noted above, his conclusion that white workers are hurt by racism does not follow from his results since income inequality among whites may be offset by income inequality between blacks and whites.

The cross-sectional model developed here is similar to Reich's in that the data are taken from the 1970 and 1980 census summary statistics on the fifty most populous SMSAs.[21] The purpose is to demonstrate that evidence for the insulation effect can be gleaned from the same data base used by Reich to illustrate the solidarity effect. The hypotheses tested are that the insulation effect reduced white unemployment in both 1970 and 1980. If whites made employment gains from racial inequality in 1970, then support is provided for the argument in the previous section that labor market segmentation allowed whites to benefit from reduced competition for jobs prior to the mid-1970s. If whites continued to make employment gains from racial inequality in 1980, then support is provided for the contention that the decline in racial segmentation resulting from the erosion of the labor accord was offset by the rise in aggregate unemployment. In this case, the insulation effect would continue to dominate the solidarity effect in 1980 as well as 1970.

I follow Reich in using the ratio of black-to-white median family (B/W) as the measure of overall racial inequality. This is an imperfect measure of labor solidarity since it can be influenced by factors such as household headship, number of earners, number of children, governmental policies, etc. However, many of these factors can ultimately be related to the discriminatory inequities which also take their toll upon labor solidarity. Furthermore, solidarity occurs in the community as well as on the shop floor, and in this sense a broad measure such as the family income ratio may be more appropriate than a ratio of individual wages. For these reasons, as well as to sustain comparability with Reich's study, the family income ratio is used as the measure of overall racial inequality. If the insulation effect is operative, then racial inequality will reduce job competition for whites, so that a drop in B/W will be positively correlated with a drop in white unemployment (and vice versa).

The dependent variable used to measure the probability of employment is the ratio of the unemployment rate of each race-sex group to the total unemployment rate, i.e. UR_i/UR_t where UR is the unemployment rate, i is black or white men or women, and t is total. This ratio expresses the intensity of population-specific unemployment for a given set of labor market conditions. Use of this dependent variable is conceptually equivalent to placing UR_i on the left-side and UR_t on the right-side of the equation, but it avoids the simultaneity bias inherent in this apparently simpler formulation. A decline in UR_i/UR_t reflects an improvement in the employment position of group i relative to the overall availability of employment. Since the variation in overall labor market conditions between SMSAs is standardized within the dependent variable, the probability of employment for group i can then be expressed simply as a function of its supply-side characteristics (plus B/W as the focus variable). Regional and industrial control variables are also included to further standardize the equation for labor demand variations due to the structure of urban labor markets. The equation to be tested can thus be written as

$$UR_i / UR_t = \alpha_1 + \alpha_2 (B/W) + \alpha_3 (LS_i) + \alpha_4 (LD)$$

where LS_i is a vector of labor supply characteristics for group i, and LD is a vector of labor demand characteristics for the SMSA as a whole.[22]

Phrased more precisely, then, the hypothesis to be tested is that α_2 is significantly positive for whites in 1970. Equations on black males and females are included for the purpose of comparison. The expectation is that α_2 in the black equations will be negative since the insulation effect will correlate a lower family income ratio with higher black unemployment as a result of crowding. The equations are then rerun with 1980 data to see if labor market restructuring over the mid-1970s undermined the insulation effect. If it did not, then α_2 will also be positive for whites and negative for blacks in the 1980 equations.

Supply-side control variables include the fraction of persons twenty-five years old and over who have graduated from high school but not college (HS_i), the fraction of such persons with a college degree (COL_i), median age (MA_i) and the fraction of all households that are female-headed (FHH_j where j is total black or total white). These variables explain the deviation of UR_i from UR_t in terms of the characteristics of group i. More schooling is expected to reduce unemployment by improving the prospect of a job offer. Because I use two variables reflecting degree attainment (as opposed to one variable on years of schooling completed), their impact can capture the screening hypothesis (i.e., credentialism) as well as traditional human capital theory (which explains the negative correlation between education and unemployment in terms of the impact of general training on the costs of specific training). The coefficients on HS_i and COL_i are thus expected to be negative. The coefficient on MA_i is also expected to be negative since young persons are more likely to experience frictional unemployment. Finally, FHH_j is expected to have a positive coefficient on males since men without families are less threatened by job loss. Its coefficient for females is uncertain since women with dependent children may have more need for wages than other women, but also may face more constraints in the job market.[23]

Labor demand control variables include a regional dummy (1 = south) and two industrial structure variables, the percent of total employment in manufacturing (MFG) and the percent of total employment in the government sector (GOVT). SOUTH reflects regional differences in history, culture and development, MFG reflects differences in unionization and industrialization, and GOVT reflects the organization and impact of the public sector. The inclusion of these variables represents a conservative statement of the hypothesis since the impact of discrimination will be partially captured in the industrial and regional controls, thereby lowering the significance of the B/W coefficient.[24] The signs on the estimated coefficients of the LD variables are expected to vary by race-sex group.

Results from the OLS procedure are listed in Tables 1 and 2.

DISCUSSION OF RESULTS

Results on the focus variable provide weak support for the hypothesis that whites made employment gains from racial discrimination in 1970, and stronger support for the hypothesis in 1980. The positive signs on the B/W coefficients in the white equations show that less racial equality is associated with less unemployment (for a given degree of labor market tightness) for both white males and females in 1970. However, the confidence levels fall below the conventional 90 percent cutoff, so that the econometric support for the hypothesis in 1970 must be taken as tentative. Nonetheless, given that any influence on UR_i will also affect UR_t so that the impact on the ratio can wash out, and given that the impact of inequality will to some extent be picked up by the industrial and regional controls, the t-statistics on the B/W coefficients in the 1970 white equations remain suggestive. The implication that racial exclusion yields employment gains for white workers is strengthened by the significantly negative B/W coefficient in the black female equation. Black women suffer employment losses by virtue of the same process that allows whites to enjoy employment gains. The coefficient is insignificant in the black male equation, a finding that may indicate the family income ratio is a

TABLE 1
OLS Results: 1970

Dependent Variable: UR_i/UR_t

Variable	White Men	Black Men	White Women	Black Women
Constant	0.65	1.84	1.03	2.17
	(1.82)	(2.26)	(2.60)	(2.44)
HS_i	0.18	-1.04	-0.20	-0.76
	(0.47)	(-1.34)	(-0.54)	(-0.78)
COL_i	-0.33	-0.66	-0.81	2.11
	(-1.07)	(-0.32)	(-0.99)	(0.59)
MA_i	0.002	-0.03	-0.004	0.04
	(0.52)	(-0.95)	(-1.00)	(1.58)
FHH_j	1.88	2.45	-0.73	-3.26
	(1.72)	(1.84)	(-0.52)	(-1.89)
SOUTH	-0.13	-0.53	0.03	0.02
	(-3.45)	(-4.49)	(0.59)	(0.15)
MFG	-0.01	0.003	0.003	0.03
	(-2.52)	(0.40)	(0.73)	(3.96)
GOVT	-0.01	0.003	0.003	0.02
	(-2.23)	(0.37)	(0.63)	(1.72)
B/W	0.37	0.11	0.44	-1.99
	(1.55)	(0.12)	(1.55)	(-2.07)
R^2	.52	.51	.21	.42
Mean UR_i/UR_t	0.79	1.64	1.04	1.78

Notes: 1) Symbols defined in text
2) T-statistics in parentheses

poor indicator of the racial barriers facing black men (since a disproportionate number live outside of families), or that discrimination is a less important determinant of employment for black men than black women.[25]

These results did not disappear by 1980; indeed, the positive B/W coefficient increased in significance to above the 90 percent level in both white equations while its magnitude nearly tripled for white women. As employment shifted toward the service sector over the 1970s, white women made especially strong gains from the insulation effect.[26] The results for blacks were largely unchanged. This evidence suggests that labor market restructuring over the mid-1970s did not undermine the impact of the

TABLE 2
OLS Results: 1980

Dependent Variable: UR_i/UR_t

Variable	White Men	Black Men	White Women	Black Women
Constant	0.48	1.85	-0.07	5.22
	(1.02)	(1.51)	(-0.22)	(6.55)
HS_i	0.01	0.001	-0.002	-0.002
	(1.16)	(0.15)	(-0.56)	(-0.32)
COL_i	-0.01	-0.01	0.005	-0.01
	(-1.96)	(-0.73)	(1.44)	(-0.50)
MA_i	-0.002	-0.02	0.01	-0.05
	(-0.31)	(-0.50)	(2.37)	(-3.31)
FHH_j	1.51	2.65	0.48	-2.48
	(1.41)	(2.26)	(0.54)	(-2.93)
SOUTH	-0.14	-0.32	0.06	0.01
	(-3.57)	(-2.79)	(1.66)	(0.08)
MFG	-0.002	0.01	-0.003	0.02
	(-0.55)	(0.97)	(-1.11)	(3.38)
GOVT	-0.002	0.01	-0.01	0.01
	(-0.33)	(0.41)	(-2.22)	(1.20)
B/W	0.38	-0.86	1.16	-2.34
	(1.79)	(-0.88)	(6.71)	(-3.51)
R^2	.57	.58	.58	.48
Mean UR_i/UR_t	.86	2.00	.86	1.77

Notes: 1) Symbols defined in text
2) T-statistics in parentheses

insulation effect on the probability of white employment. High unemployment increased the propensity to discriminate despite the fact that racial segmentation among employed persons declined. The offsetting tendencies created by changes in segmentation and in unemployment are apparently dominated by the latter.

Results on the control variables are generally as expected. Many of them have low significance levels due to their simultaneous impact of UR_i and UR_t. The labor supply variables (education, age and household composition) are either insignificant or tell self-evident stories. The labor demand variables are somewhat more complicated. SOUTH lowers black and white male unemployment in both 1970 and 1980, but is positive (with generally low significance levels) in the female equations. Men benefited from the movement of professional, construction and manufacturing jobs from the frost belt to the sun belt. MFG lowers white male unemployment and raises black female unemployment in 1970, displaying the race/sex division of labor characteristic of manufacturing jobs at that time. The loss of significance in the white male 1980 equation shows that deindustrialization eliminated the employment benefits white males made from manufacturing. GOVT had the same impact as MFG in 1970, again indicating the prevalence of a race/sex division of labor, but by 1980 was significant only in the white female equation. Its negative sign suggests that white women may have been the major beneficiaries of affirmative action in the public sector.

Given that any influence on UR_i will also be reflected in UR_t and therefore will tend to be washed out in UR_i/UR_t, given the standardization for basic supply-side and demand-side characteristics of urban labor markets, and given that some of the impact of discrimination will be siphoned off in the control variables, the signs and significance levels on the B/W coefficients in the white equations provide reasonably strong support for the thesis that white workers can make employment gains from racial inequality. These results show that the insulation effect continued to improve the probability of white employment in 1980 despite the labor market restructuring of the mid-1970s. Racial inequality continues to be symptomatic of a systematic skew in the distribution of job opportunities toward whites.

SUMMARY AND CONCLUSIONS

This study demonstrates that the distributional impact of racial inequality on white workers is more complex than the "divide-and-conquer" interpretation of the bargaining power hypothesis would suggest. The author argues that the question of white gain from discrimination is conditional upon circumstances. Racial identification may increase or decrease the bargaining power of white workers depending upon the degree of substitutability between black and white workers and the intensity of aggregate unemployment. Labor market segmentation institutionalized the insulation effect by identifying job categories with racial categories in the immediate post-war period. In the mid-1970s, however, racial segmentation of the labor market declined, implying that the insulation effect fell in importance. This tendency, however, was offset by the increase in unemployment over the same period, a change that would be expected to intensify the gains white workers and capitalists can make from preferential treatment. Labor market restructuring over the 1970s thus had a contradictory impact on the distributional outcomes of racial inequality. Empirical results on the relative probability of employment tentatively support the contention that the insulation effect was operative in 1970, and strongly support the contention that whites made employment gains from racial inequality in 1980.

The distributional conclusions that can be drawn from this study are not as simple as that suggested by Reich and others who analyze discrimination solely as a divide-and-conquer strategy of the capitalist class. Discrimination indeed divides the working class, and it is plausible that white workers suffer wage losses as a result. However, racism also unifies whites by giving disparate ethnics a common identification. It is conceivable that racial discrimination can benefit whites in some ways (e.g., employment) but hurt them in others (e.g., wages), benefit them in the short-term but hurt them in the long-term, benefit their bargaining position in one set of historical circumstances but hurt it in another, etc. The divide-and-conquer interpretation of the bargaining power hypothesis is too narrow to capture the potentially complex distributional effects of racial discrimination on white workers.

The political conclusions that follow from this perspective are concordantly more complicated than those proposed by the divide-and-conquer model. That analysis suggests that white and black workers have common interests in the capital-labor conflict at the point of production. The political strategy of "unite and fight" is simple and appealing. Unfortunately, it is then difficult to understand why the white working-class has adopted this strategy so infrequently and with such little commitment.[27] The history of white workers' efforts to exclude and subordinate blacks is far more extensive and consistent than their sporadic attempts to unite with them. The divide-and-conquer model can only explain this phenomenon in terms of false consciousness, i.e., that the perceptions of white workers conflict with their actual interests. But this inference sits uncomfortably within the materialist tradition which informs the radical paradigm.[28]

This study suggests that race consciousness bears a systematic relation to economic circumstances. White workers have a stake in the distribution of income between blacks and whites as well as between capital and labor. Furthermore, the distributional question is not the dividing line between the radical and orthodox analyses of discrimination. In fact, the view that white workers can make certain gains from racism can be seen as more consistent with the methodological underpinnings of the radical framework, and has been propounded by a variety of scholars working within this tradition. The radical and orthodox analyses of discrimination are instead divided over the question of the culpability of the wage-labor system in perpetuating discrimination. Radicals may argue about how capitalism reproduces racism, but all agree that it does.

NOTES

Kim Christensen, William Darity, Jr. and Elaine McCrate made helpful comments on an earlier draft of this paper.

1. Samuel Bowles, "The Production Process in a Competitive Economy: Walrasian, Neo-Hobbesian, and Marxian Models," *American Economic Review*, Volume 75 (September 1985).

2. For example, see Michael Reich, *Racial Inequality: A Political-Economic Analysis* (Princeton NJ: Princeton University Press, 1981); John E. Roemer, "Divide and Conquer: Microfoundations of a Marxian Theory of Wage Discrimination," *Bell Journal of Economics*, Volume 10 (Autumn 1979); and Albert Syzmanski, "Racial Discrimination and White Gain," *American Sociological Review*, Volume 41, (June 1976).

3. For example, see E. M. Beck, "Discrimination and White Economic Loss: A Time Series Examination of the Radical Model," *Social Forces*, Volume 59 (September 1980); and Norman R. Cloutier, "Who Gains From Racism? The Impact of Racial Inequality on White Income Distribution," *Review of Social Economy*, Volume XLV (October 1987).

4. Erik Olin Wright, *Class Structure and Income Determination*, (NY: Academic Press, 1979), p. 202.

5. Herbert Hill, "Black Labor and Affirmative Action: An Historical Perspective," in *The Question of Discrimination: Racial Inequality in the U.S. Labor Market* (Steven Shulman and William Darity, Jr., eds., Wesleyan University Press, 1989); Daniel R. Fusfeld and Timothy Bates, *The Political Economy of the Urban Ghetto* (Carbondale IL: Southern Illinois University Press, 1984), pp. 179-190; Edna Bonacich, "Advanced Capitalism and Black/White Race Relations in the United States: A Split Labor Market Interpretation," *American Sociological Review*, Volume 41 (February 1976); William Darity, "What's Left of the Economic Theory of Discrimination?" In *The Question of Discrimination*, op. cit.

6. Edna Bonacich, "Class Approaches to Ethnicity and Race," *Insurgent Sociologist* 10 (Fall 1980), p. 14.

7. Reich, op. cit., p. 311. The only effort by Reich to use an absolute measure of distributional impact (which he agrees is a more "direct test") is in his Table 7.6 (p. 302). He uses median white earnings across industries as the dependent variable, and attempts to show that they are positively correlated with the ratio of nonwhite-to-white earnings. The equation, however, is unconvincing. First, he includes an age variable whose coefficient is significantly *negatively* correlated with earnings. Second, he includes (without justification) a percent nonwhite variable whose coefficient is also significantly negative. If white earnings go up when nonwhite employment goes down, then it could be concluded that whites make wage gains from employment discrimination against blacks.

8. Hill, op. cit.

9. See Elizabeth Moss Kanter, *Men and Women of the Corporation* (NY: Basic Books, 1977), for a discussion of this process with respect to the sex typing of occupational roles.

10. For example, see Thomas Sowell, *Markets and Minorities* (NY: Basic Books, 1981).

11. Steven Shulman, "Competition and Racial Discrimination: The Employment Effects of Reagan's Labor Market Policies," *Review of Radical Political Economics*, Volume 16 (Winter 1984).

12. Richard Edwards and Michael Podgursky, "The Unraveling Accord: American Unions in Crisis," in *Unions in Crisis and Beyond*, ed., R. Edwards, et. al. (Dover MA: Auburn House, 1982).

13. Herbert Hill, "The AFL-CIO and the Black Worker: Twenty-five Years After the Merger," *The Journal of Intergroup Relations*, Volume 10 (Spring 1982).

14. Edwards and Podgursky, op. cit., for example, comment that the accord—which they partially credit for the productivity increases of the period—"primarily organized white male workers" (p. 21).

15. Edwards and Podgursky, op. cit., pp. 28–34.

16. Reynolds Farley, *Blacks and Whites: Narrowing the Gap?* (Cambridge MA: Harvard University Press, 1984), pp. 16–22, 46–50.

17. Reich, op. cit., ch. 4.

18. Cloutier, op. cit.; Beck, op. cit.

19. Rhonda M. Williams, "Capital, Competition, and Discrimination: A Reconsideration of Racial Earnings Inequality," *Review of Radical Political Economics*, Volume 19 (Summer 1987), p. 6.

20. Cloutier, op. cit., fails to replicate Reich's results with the use of 1980 census summary data on an expanded set of SMSAs. Beck, op. cit., finds no support for the solidarity effect using time-series data. He describes Reich's findings as "spurious" because "the positive relationship . . . between the income ratio and white economic status may be the result of both terms covarying with changes in the demand for labor" (p. 162). Sysmanski, op. cit., does replicate Reich's results, but only by committing the same econometric errors.

21. Nassau is not listed separately in the 1970 census. The sample size for the 1970 equations is therefore 49. There is no reason to believe that this difference between the 1970 and 1980 sample biases the results. White variables for 1970 are computed as total minus black minus Spanish speaking.

22. One obvious objection that might arise at this point is the possibility of simultaneity since causality could clearly run from unemployment to family incomes, i.e., from the left side of the equation to the right side. However, the census income data is from the year prior to the decennial year, while the unemployment data is on the decennial year itself. Since unemployment in the decennial year cannot be held to influence family incomes in the year prior, simultaneity is not a problem here. As noted in the text, the same is not true of Reich's specification: his dependent variables are drawn on 1969 data while his control variables are drawn on 1970 data.

23. Family structure may also influence unemployment if socialization patterns and learned work behaviors vary systematically between two-parent and one-parent families. However, there is little evidence in support of this proposition.

24. The significance levels on the focus variable in all equations are considerably higher if the industrial and regional controls are excluded. Results are robust with respect to alternative specifications, including alternative forms of the dependent variable (e.g., employment-to-population rates, with the total unemployment rate included on the right side).

25. Elsewhere I show that EEOC complaints of discrimination (as a proxy for actual discrimination) are positively correlated with the probability of white employment and negatively correlated with the probability of black employment. The impact is approximately twice as strong in the black female equation as in the black male equation. Why

this would be the case is uncertain, although it may have to do with the interaction of race discrimination and sex discrimination. See Steven Shulman, "Discrimination, Human Capital and Black-White Unemployment: Evidence from Cities," *The Journal of Human Resources*, Volume 22 (Summer 1987).

26. It is interesting to note the comparison in the mean values of UR_i/UR_t in 1970 versus 1980. Almost no change is recorded for black women and little change for white men. In contrast, the ratio fell sharply for white women and rose sharply for black men. These changes reflect the employment advantages white women experienced in the expanding clerical and service sectors, and suggest that black men lost employment advantages as wage differentials declined. See Andrea Beller, "The Economics of Enforcement of an Antidiscrimination Law: Title VII of the Civil Rights Act of 1964," *Journal of Law and Economics*, Volume 21 (1978); and Shulman (1987), op. cit.

27. Wright, op. cit., p. 205, for example, states that "[b]lack and white workers may well have conflicting immediate interests under certain circumstances (as do many other categories of labor within the working class), and still share fundamental class interests." In comparison to "fundamental" class interests, immediate interests are concrete and perceivable, and thereby may account for the failure of white workers to consistently fight racism. The distinction may sustain the classical Marxist analysis of racism, but it unfortunately does not simplify the problem of formulating political strategy.

28. Michael Omi and Howard Winant, *Racial Formation in the United States: From the 1960s to the 1980s* (London: Routledge & Kegan Paul, 1986), p. 33.

Part IV
Assessing Antidiscrimination Measures

[25]

DETECTING AND REMOVING DISCRIMINATION UNDER EQUAL OPPORTUNITIES POLICIES

S. Dex
University of Keele

P. J. Sloane
University of Aberdeen

Abstract. This paper surveys part of the recent voluminous literature on the economics of discrimination, focusing on two key questions. First, how should discrimination be measured and can in fact unambiguous estimates be derived, as the basis for detecting where discrimination is present and setting in train measures to eliminate it? Second, to what extent has the implementation of equal opportunities legislation improved the relative standing of women and minority workers in the labour force? This section includes a discussion of the likely effects of recent changes in the law such as the equal value amendment in the UK or the introduction of comparable worth in the USA. The survey concludes that our ability to detect discrimination at all precisely is still rudimentary and consequently policy measures are likely to be inefficient for this reason.

Keywords. Discrimination; estimation; policy implementation.

1. Introduction

Computer searches on the topic of the economics of discrimination can produce more than one thousand references dating from the early 1970s from North American and British sources alone, though the North American literature still dominates. Becker's (1957) seminal work stimulated and moulded much of the subsequent discussion which took up both the theoretical and empirical issues which he raised. The popularity of this subject matter is, however, far more related to specific policy issues, interest in which greatly increased in the 1960s, especially in the USA, as discrimination became a major legislative issue. An important branch of the discussion followed the issue into the US courts, where economists' multivariate regression techniques have now become standard tools in discrimination cases. Interest in the provision of accurate measures of discrimination has obviously grown alongside these policy concerns.

0950-0804/88/01 0001-27 $02.50/0

JOURNAL OF ECONOMIC SURVEYS Vol. 2, No. 1

In this paper we intend to review the past decade of work on the measurement and policy aspects of discrimination. We are ignoring more theoretical debates through limitations on space. There have been earlier reviews but these have either concentrated on other issues, for example, methodological (Cain, 1976; Dex, 1979), costs of discriminating (Dex, 1986), offer radical (Darity and Williams, 1985) or general surveys (Sloane, 1985). This review concentrates on whether we have a widely accepted method of measuring discrimination that can be adopted in empirical work, in court cases and in measuring whether the extent of discrimination has changed over time, and on whether policy measures have had any impact.

It is only by answering these questions that we can help to provide a clearer framework for the controversies which are now taking place. There are those who debate whether discrimination now exists at all in the USA. Some libertarian economists espouse the virtues of competition, over government programmes, in eliminating discrimination. Others argue on empirical grounds that government policies have had little effect. Assessing the validity and accuracy of these arguments requires a recognized measure of discrimination and a theoretical understanding of the processes which both created and maintain it. Our review suggests that we are not yet in such a privileged position that we can give clear answers to these questions.

First some definitions might be helpful. The focus of this paper is on labour market discrimination as conventionally understood by economists. Most commonly, discrimination is said to occur when individuals of the same level of productivity are paid different amounts; this would be wage discrimination. Wage discrimination also occurs if individuals who are paid the same amount do not have the same levels of productivity; this has become known as reverse discrimination in the literature which attempts to measure discrimination. A type of discrimination which is far less often considered by economists is the case where individuals of similar levels of productivity are employed disproportionately to their numbers in the relevant population; this is employment discrimination, and it may or may not accompany wage or earnings discrimination.

It is also relevant to distinguish discrimination which takes place after, or on the point of, entry into, the labour market, post-entry discrimination, or labour market discrimination, from that which might have already taken place, pre-entry discrimination (Chiplin and Sloane, 1976). The distinction is important since groups who have experienced pre-entry discrimination are likely to have lower levels of productivity when they enter the labour market. They will find themselves badly off in the job market, but not necessarily because they are experiencing post-entry discrimination. This review is concerned only with post-entry labour market discrimination. Section 2 reviews the state of the art in measuring discrimination and Section 3 assesses the impact of equal employment policies. Finally, in Section 4, we come to some conclusions about the state of knowledge on the policy and measurement aspects of the economics of discrimination.

2. Human capital and the measurement of discrimination productivity measures

The empirical work which has grown out of Becker's (1964) and Mincer's (1974) work on human capital theory is nothing if not highly elaborate and sophisticated. The early formulations posited that the earnings of individual workers would be a function of their past investment in themselves, that is their education and work experience. The productivity of an individual's human capital would, therefore, be dependent upon these characteristics and experiences. Since the traditional definition of discrimination used by economists has been that discrimination occurs when individuals of similar productivities are paid differing amounts for the same work, it is easy to see how the human capital framework has become the main vehicle for measuring discrimination. It is also understandable that measurement of productivity would grow more and more sophisticated. Reviews exist of some of the general developments in the human capital framework (Siebert, 1985) and of how it has been applied to women workers (Blau, 1984).

The productivity of an individual's human capital is now thought to be potentially related to the quality, as well as the amount, of education (Link *et al.*, 1976, 1980; Hoffman, 1979; Akin and Garfinkel, 1980), the type as well as the amount of work experience and training (Duncan and Hoffman, 1979; Blakemore and Low, 1983; Olson and Becker, 1983), job turnover (Borjas, 1980, 1984; Flanagan, 1974; Bartel, 1981; Shorey, 1983), absenteeism (Leigh, 1983), personality (Filer, 1983), expectations about future labour market participation (Polachek, 1981; Blackmore and Low, 1984; Abowd and Killingsworth, 1983), and even culture (Chiswick, 1983a, 1983b; Sowell, 1981, 1983, 1984). Dissent has been expressed, however, about the measures used to capture many of these variables (Medoff and Abraham, 1980, 1981; Darity and Williams, 1985).

2.1. *Estimating discrimination*

The standard procedure for deriving a measure of discrimination is to estimate for a sample of individuals a Mincer human capital equation of the form

$$\log E_t = a + b_1 S + b_2 X_t + b_3 X_t^2 + \varepsilon_1 \qquad (1)$$

where E = earnings at time t
S = years of schooling
X = years of experience
a = intercept term
b_1, b_2, b_3 are coefficients of the variables
ε_1 = stochastic error.

In some cases qualifications are substituted for years of schooling or some qualitative measure of education is included in the equation. Using this basic framework a large number of attempts have been made to measure discrimination, usually by the residual method, whereby separate equations are run for the different groups (such as men and women or blacks and whites) and earnings are decomposed into differences resulting from varying endowments and coefficients, and the unexplained differential arising in the constant term. Estimates can vary considerably for particular groups and depend on decisions made in the process of investigation.

First additional 'productivity' variables are incorporated as available according to the data set used. This means that one should be very cautious in comparing estimates of discrimination derived from different studies. For one thing, the greater the number of productivity-augmenting variables that are included in the model the lower the derived estimate of discrimination is likely to be, because most often, with the notable exception of Asian Americans, minority workers have lower levels of most forms of human capital. Second, the lower the level of disaggregation the lower the likely estimate of discrimination.[2] Several studies find, for example, that when men's and women's earnings are compared in the same establishment, as well as within detailed job classifications, the earnings differential is greatly reduced (Ferber and Spaeth, 1984). Caution is required in interpreting these results since there is a potentially serious sample selection problem. Workers facing the most discrimination will be excluded from these establishments and job classifications, and hence will not feature in the sample.

Studies of internal labour markets are particularly germane to the discrimination legislation which is intra- rather than inter-firm or organizations-based. Recent examples of internal labour market studies are Kelley (1982), who found that segregated systems continued to operate against women and blacks in the promotion process as indicated by significant sex and race differences in the experience–earnings profiles of workers in the same plant; Olson and Becker (1983), who found that standards for promotions were set at a higher level for women than for men, so that women were less likely to be promoted than men of equal ability; and Killingsworth and Reimers (1983), who found that in a US army base differences in pay were accompanied by differences in ranking, with women and blacks more likely than comparable white men to be in blue-collar than white-collar jobs. We cannot, therefore, necessarily conclude that discrimination would entirely disappear if the level of disaggregation was taken to its furthest degree.

Estimates of the extent of discrimination also tend to differ according to whether a dummy variable is inserted into the above equation to represent the minority group concerned rather than separate equations estimated for each of the groups. The former approach will produce biased estimates if significant interactions exist between membership of that minority group and various other characteristics which are not themselves a function of discrimination. For example, if one group invested less per year worked in enhancing their productivity, because they expected to spend less time in market work, there would be a reason to expect the slope of the earnings experience profile to differ between groups for reasons that have little or nothing to do with discrimination. Thus,

Borjas (1983), analysing wage differentials in the federal bureaucracy, finds that the use of a simple dummy for race or gender leads to downward biased estimates of the standardized wage differential (i.e. an under-estimate of discrimination). Estimating separate equations for each group which is subject to comparison overcomes this problem, although other problems remain. Thus, Greenhalgh (1980), Dolton and Makepeace (1985b) and Joshi and Newell (1986) examined male–female differentials in Britain by comparing the earnings equations of single and married women with single and married men; Zabalza and Arrufat in Zabalza and Tzannatos (1985a) compared married men and women. Stewart (1983) compared British blacks and whites earnings functions as derived from their occupations. All found evidence of discrimination in the differentials. Alternatively, models with sets of interaction dummies on a subset of independent variables could be tried (Dolton and Makepeace, 1985b). Ultimately, the best model will need to be found from specification testing of the alternatives.

2.2. *The residual approach and omitted variable bias*

The conventional direct regression or residual approach decomposes earnings into differences resulting from different endowments of human capital and differences in coefficients. Thus comparing black (B) and white (W) workers the crude earnings differential can be decomposed, as follows.

$$\log \bar{E}_W - \log \bar{E}_B = (a_W - a_B) + (\bar{X}_W - \bar{X}_B)b_W + \bar{X}_B(b_W - b_B) \tag{2}$$

where E = mean of earnings
X = vector of means of characteristics variables
a = intercept terms
b = vector of coefficients on personal characteristics variables
W, B = subscripts referring to Whites and Blacks respectively.

Discrimination is frequently measured as the sum of the difference in intercepts and coefficients. However, it has been argued (Jones 1983) that the decomposition of the intercept difference is in most cases arbitrary and uninterpretable, since its value is not independent of measurement decisions relating to the independent variables in the model. This is a matter of some import as in a number of data sets differences in the values of the intercept have been substantial and in some the whole of the difference is found to lie in the intercepts (e.g. Aldrich and Buchele, 1986). As Filer (1983) notes, it is sensible to avoid referring to differences in constant terms as 'discrimination' whilst uncertainty remains as to whether they contain any further unidentified differences in productivity-related characteristics. Omitted variable bias can have unpredictable effects on the estimates of discrimination.[3]

In addition, there is the well-known index number problem, that different measures of discrimination are obtained according to whether the earnings function of the minority or majority group is taken as the basis for estimation, provided that the slopes of the two functions differ. The assumption normally made, that the majority earnings function is the one that would prevail in the absence of discrimination, implies the use of a partial equilibrium approach and ignores the possibility of favouritism towards the majority group predominating over discrimination against the minority group. The conventional procedure also places the whole weight on the means of the earnings functions being compared. It has recently been suggested that an improvement could be made if the whole of the observed distribution of the log of earnings were compared with the whole distribution in the absence of discrimination. This could be achieved by determining the appropriate form for the density of the log of earnings from the observed density and then using the moments described to find the density where there is no discrimination (Dolton and Makepeace, 1985a). However, using higher moments rather than the first moment may serve to reduce even further confidence in the estimates.

This is, however, perhaps a less serious problem than that of errors in variables. For example, particularly in relation to male and female employment, differences in wages may reflect compensating differentials for the relative attractiveness of work. A recent study (Filer, 1985) shows that on average men and women hold jobs with substantially different working conditions and these are, on the whole, such as to require higher payment to jobs held predominantly by men. This study found that the mean of the values of job characteristics in a 1977 Quality of Employment Survey differed significantly between men and women in 12 out of 28 cases. When such differences were incorporated into the decomposition of male and female wages the proportion of variance explained by differences in characteristics increased by approximately one-third.[4] It must not be assumed, however, that women always receive appropriate compensation for the non-pecuniary disadvantages of their work. One study found that whilst hazardous work brings forth a positive compensating differential in the case of men, in the case of women the variable is significant and negatively related, perhaps reflecting differences in bargaining power (Barry, 1985).[5] Another variable that is omitted in most studies is information. Bartlett and Miller (1985) found in a study of female executives that information networks (who you know) were as important as performance variables in helping women climb the corporate ladder. We must also acknowledge that average earnings are themselves only part of the total remuneration package received by workers and it is possible that fringe benefits vary systematically among groups. Under such circumstances errors in variables are highly likely to occur.

It may be necessary to modify the measures used in this approach not only in the light of the possibility of omitted variables but also of sample-selection bias and endogeneity problems, by methods described in Killingsworth (1983). Studies are increasingly recognizing and correcting for sample selection bias effects on women's earnings functions in particular (Joshi and Newell, 1986; Dolton and Makepeace, 1985b; Berger and Glenn, 1986), and we return to this question below in discussing discrimination measurement in legal cases.

2.3. *Demand or supply effects?*

Even supposing that problems of errors in variables are insignificant, the use of a reduced-form equation in the decomposition exercise does not appear to be wholly appropriate as the basis of the measurement of discrimination, which is a demand-side phenomenon. This is reinforced by the fact that many important demand variables such as firm size, output and prices of non-labour inputs are not included in the model. Further, it has been demonstrated that even the decomposition of an appropriately specified demand function will not yield an estimate of discrimination of the Becker type (Butler, 1982). Whilst a structural demand equation would be a considerable improvement over a reduced-form equation for isolating employer discrimination, it itself yields estimates which are based both on direct discrimination and indirect discrimination which will influence the relative marginal productivities of the favoured and discriminated-against groups. In order to isolate Becker's discrimination coefficient it is first necessary to estimate a production function.

Discrimination as conventionally measured will be influenced, in particular, by differences in supply elasticities; in the case of male/female comparisons there is every reason to expect such differences.[6] Filer (1983) shows, for example, that tastes for market work differ substantially between men and women and that these can account for up to 10% of the unexplained gap between male and female earnings. Another study by Daymont and Andresani (1984) analysing the gender differential in earnings among recent college graduates found a tendency for young men and women to prefer different occupational roles and to major in different fields of study. Together these differences accounted for two-thirds of the gender gap in earnings three years after graduation. Dolton and Makepeace (1985b) consider the possibility of female participation and earnings being influenced by a family role specialization effect, using a sample of British graduates. They suggest, therefore, that it makes little sense to talk of a well-defined residual discrimination effect. Thus, it would seem that earlier studies have overestimated labour market discrimination against young female college graduates.[7] However, we should bear in mind that it is by no means certain that the use of reduced-form equations is inappropriate in the context of the law, which does not generally allow employers to pay men and women differently for the same work on account of supply (taste) differences.

2.4. *Reverse regression approach*

Recently a new approach to the measurement of discrimination, known as reverse regression, has been advocated by an American statistician, H. Roberts. This method compares job qualifications of members of different race or gender groups who are earning the same wage. If discrimination is present it seems, at first sight, reasonable to expect not only that minority workers with given qualifications will earn less than majority workers, but also that at any given wage minority workers will be better qualified than the remainder of the workforce.

In the reverse regression approach, equation (1) above is replaced for each minority group, i, by an equation such as the following, which has personal characteristics as the dependent variable, and earnings as an explanatory variable:

$$\bar{X}_i = a_i + b_i \log \bar{E}_i + \varepsilon_2. \tag{3}$$

It might be supposed that this would give the same qualitative answer as the traditional approach – that if one group, say the majority, is paid more on average than an equally qualified minority group, so will an equally paid minority group be more qualified than the remainder of the labour force. In fact, this is by no means certain, as a number of empirical studies reveal.[8] For example, Hashimoto and Kochin (1980) provide an example of non-whites having low median levels of income for given levels of schooling, whilst at the same time having lower levels of schooling for given incomes (i.e. reverse discrimination), and similar findings for other data sets were revealed by Birnbaum (1979), Kamalich and Polacheck (1982) and Conway and Roberts (1983) amongst others. Goldberger (1984) summarizes these results as suggesting that 'reverse regression points to a lower estimate of salary discrimination than does direct regression. Indeed, it often suggests reverse discrimination... If so, the new approach has obvious attractions for defendants (employers) in discrimination suits and, indeed, has already been used in that context.'

Yet this approach itself is not without its critics. Solon (1983) objected that shifting the productivity proxies to the left hand side of the equation and the wage to the right hand side creates another problem, since the latter will be correlated with the error term thereby biasing the result against discrimination. Hojman (1984) noted that reverse regression had the effect of excluding the constant term from the wage regressions as confirmed in his own empirical results for the sex differential in Australia. Using a univariate model, Goldberger also finds that the reverse regression estimate of discrimination may be biased downward and may even be negative in the presence of discrimination. In only one case, using multivariate models, where each observed qualification is merely an indicator of the employer's productivity assessment subject to a gender-free disturbance, does the reverse regression yield a valid estimator. Blau and Kahn (1985) point out that there are other reasons for preferring direct regressions. They suggest that errors in the salary variable (e.g. the omission of fringe benefits) may give rise to an errors-in-variable problem; that with more than one proxy for productivity we cannot be sure of the relative weighting of the reverse regression coefficient; and finally, we cannot infer hiring standards merely by regressing qualifications on the wages of incumbents as opposed to applicants. In view of these problems they express a preference for direct regression provided there are accurate measures of performance and instrumental variables or grouped data are used.[9] Conway and Roberts (1983) suggest that both direct and reverse regression approaches should be utilized, but the above criticisms suggest that reverse regression results should be treated with a degree of caution.

2.5. *Discrimination measurement in legal cases*

The complexity of the measurement problem does not assist the work of the courts in attempting to decide whether or not a defendant is guilty of discrimination, yet statistical analysis has played an increasing part in US legal cases in two main respects – determining the populations amongst which comparisons are to be made and estimating the presence or absence of discrimination by means of regression analysis. Gastwirth (1984) notes that statistical testing has been used since 1977 to determine the significance of any difference between the observed and expected number of minorities or women hired or promoted, but in many cases the courts have not used as powerful statistical tests as are available.

One problem of applying statistical techniques to legal cases is that the current distribution of wages and employment for any given employer is a consequence of decisions made over a long period of time. It is quite possible that an analysis of the current distribution may suggest discrimination, when the employer's current practices are discrimination free. Under US law an employer may be prosecuted if he can be shown to have discriminated at any time after 1964 when the legislation first came into effect. If, however, we are interested in the extent to which discrimination currently manifests itself, it would be appropriate to concentrate on *current* hiring and promotion decisions. These will be reflected in the employer's offer curve which measures the probability of receiving a job offer or promotion given characteristics, irrespective of whether that job offer is accepted (Chiplin, 1979; Dolton, 1984). The employee's acceptance curve, which measures the probability of an employee accepting new or continued employment in a given occupation by a particular employer, is also of relevance. Since the outcome will be determined by the choices of the two parties there is an identification problem. That is, we do not normally observe the potential employees to whom employment may have been offered or the potential employers for whom employees may have chosen to work. Data on current employees in actual firms are doubly truncated therefore (Abowd, 1983).

In order to assess whether discrimination has occurred, one also needs a measure of the potential available workforce in a particular group. In measuring this availability, attention is directed to the numbers of minority workers in the locality or Standard Metropolitan Area. An alternative, not without its own problems, is to limit attention to the qualified applicant pool (Knopff, 1986). This obscures the fact that, for any firm, the size of the area of recruitment is a function of the wage and that the propensity of workers to travel long distances to work is influenced by personal characteristics such as sex, age, marital status and other factors. As Ehrenberg and Smith (1985) note in relation to US legal experience,

> to date the courts appear to have overlooked the fact that willingness to commute differs by race and sex. There is much evidence that females tend to live closer to their jobs than males and some evidence that non-whites commute shorter distances than whites. Thus, availability ratios might reasonably be expected to differ by gender or race.

However, not only willingness to commute, but ability to do so, may vary. If firms are unable to discriminate by offering different wages for the same job, they may set higher job rejection rates for minority workers. Thus one British study found that both Asian and West Indian manual workers travelled on average about 35% further to work than did economically similar (same wage) white workers living in the same area of Birmingham (McCormick, 1986).

In many cases with which the courts deal, sample sizes will be small and this may lead to the adoption of arbitrary standards in terms of expected hiring rates. Further, if samples from which comparisons are to be made are restricted to particular occupational levels to ensure homogeneity, the problem of selection bias arises. This will occur whenever unmeasured variables, which determine whether an individual is in the restricted sample or not, are correlated with the unmeasured variables influencing earnings in the restricted sample. The same selection bias will also occur whenever inclusion in the restricted sample is affected by particular demographic characteristics. A good example of the latter occurs with female labour force participants at any one time who may not be a random sub-set of those women who could work. If one wishes to detect the degree of discrimination against women in general it is necessary following Heckman (1979) to formulate a sample selection model of earnings determination using two-step and maximum likelihood procedures.[10]

As far as regression analysis is concerned, the use of such techniques in the courts has now become so well accepted that the argument is no longer that of whether regression analysis is an appropriate way of detecting the presence of discrimination, but rather whether it has been applied correctly to the particular case in question (see Bloom and Killingsworth, 1982).[11] The use of economic analysis in determining employee availability leaves scope for advocacy or the use of economists to support the case of either party as well as use as expert witnesses in legal cases. There can be few areas of law in which such complex and disputatious methods of economic analysis have been applied. Some have questioned the appropriateness of such legal intervention in a market economy. The case for legal intervention could be ultimately argued to depend on its success in isolating and eliminating discrimination, and it is to this issue that we must now turn.

3. The impact of the legislation

Since the enactment of anti-discriminatory legislation in the USA and in Britain, policy makers and academics have had a strong interest in testing its effectiveness.[12] In particular, research has sought to address the question of whether legislation is one factor which can prevent sex and racial discrimination from persisting. Obviously, attempts to answer this question rely upon the existence of accurate and unambiguous measures of discrimination, as described above in Section 2. But there are other questions of method which such research must face.

Analysing the impact of the anti-discriminatory legislation is no easy matter, given the influence of other labour market policy measures and the fact that there is not one single policy to consider but several, each of which has varied over time either in terms of the content or the intensity with which it has been applied. Most of the empirical work is North American and reflects its legislative framework, including provisions for affirmative action which are not matched elsewhere. On the whole, two approaches have been used to capture the effects of legislation: time series analysis, which uses dummy variables and time trends to capture the effect in the post-legislative period, and cross-sectional analysis, which focuses on those firms which are subject to affirmative action relative to those which are not. It is necessary to consider each of these separately below, as they are analysing different aspects of policy. Finally, it is necessary to examine the recent policy shift towards equal pay for work of equal value which is reflected both in the USA (under the comparable worth banner) and in Europe and Australia in terms of a redefinition of equal pay legislation.

3.1. *Time series analysis*

An early attempt to take into account the effect of cyclical and trend factors on black/white income ratios was that of Masters (1975). Analysing annual data over the period 1964–71 he found that the black/white income ratio had increased by nine percentage points, though he also recognized that some of this improvement may have occurred for reasons other than the Civil Rights Act. Beller (1979) went a stage further in attempting to assess the effect of the strengthening of Title VII of the Civil Rights Act in 1972, this time on the male/female earnings differentials, finding that the legislative provisions had reduced this differential by about seven percentage points between 1967 and 1974. Although official statistics show no narrowing of the actual differential during this period, her results allowed for the fact that the increased entry of inexperienced women into the labour force would have had a depressing effect on women's earnings. In a further study (1980), Beller found that these results were influenced by the level of economic activity. That is, women's earnings would have been higher in 1974 and the sex differential smaller had the unemployment rate been lower. Also the downward influence on male earnings would have been reduced. This in turn suggests that a sufficiently low employment rate will reduce the costs to male employees of the implementation of equality of opportunities policies. However, Beller's results have been questioned on the grounds that the variables used to measure the impact of these policies (a vector of enforcement variables assigned to each individual on the basis of geographical area, class of worker, and industry of employment) are inadequate and that the demonstration effect of legal cases may alter behaviour in some firms and industries that are not directly affected – a criticism which poses a problem for most of the cross-section studies to which reference is made below.

We must also allow for the fact that equal opportunity policies may require some time before they begin to take substantial effect. Thus Smith and Welch (1984) point out that the resources available to the EEOC and the OFCC in the early years of the policies were inadequate for ensuring even minimal detection of discriminatory firms or for providing effective sanctions for altering behaviour. There were, too, substantial time lags before the enforcement machinery was put into place. It is, therefore, instructive to consider those studies which incorporate more recent time periods. Brown (1982) finds, using data up to 1977, that both black males and black females have experienced increasing earnings relative to whites of the same sex. However, the distribution of gains in the period since 1964 needs some explanation. Whilst 60% of all EEOC complaints were filed by black males, relative gains were much greater for black *females*, and whilst theoretical models suggest that greater gains will accrue to those in the middle of the skill distribution, gains in practice have been concentrated among the most educated and advantaged, a point with which Smith and Welch (1984) concur. However, Golbe (1985) offers a theoretical explanation for the latter outcome. Affirmative action quotas increase the probability of employers being sued for dismissals. This will have the effect of raising the demand for minority workers with above average credentials and lowering it for those with below average credentials.

Several studies have focused on relative employment gains rather than or as well as income gains. This has been examined most comprehensively by Leonard (1984), who models affirmative action as a tax on the employment of white males in the government contractor sector which is subject to such regulation. Over 68 000 establishments over the period 1974 to 1980 were analysed, with dummy variables for whether the establishment was a government contractor and whether it had experienced a compliance review over the years 1975–79. He found that black and female employment increased significantly faster in government contractor establishments, with compliance reviews playing an important role over and above that of contractor status. The more sizeable effects in the case of black women support the two birds with one stone hypothesis, namely that, by fulfilling two quotas for the price of one, black women are especially favoured by affirmative action.[13] Leonard concludes

> Members of protected groups have enjoyed improved employment opportunities at contractor establishments, and compliance reviews appear to have been an effective tool in changing employment patterns. The evidence here is that a process that has frequently been criticised as largely an exercise in paper pushing has actually been of material importance in prompting companies to increase their employment of minorities and females.

In contrast to findings for earlier periods, Beller (1985) finds that occupational segregation of men and women declined substantially in the 1970s, most of it reflecting the entry of women into traditionally male occupations, including managerial posts. She suggests tentatively that this improvement could be the result of equal opportunities policies.

In Britain the paucity of data has deterred serious attempts to estimate the effect of equal opportunities legislation on racial differentials, but some studies have attempted to estimate the effect of the legislation on the sex differential, which narrowed appreciably in the mid 1970s when the legislation became fully operational. However, in Britain the impact of the Equal Pay Act (1970) was complicated by the simultaneous use of flat rate incomes policies during much of the period which, by narrowing the skill differential, might have been expected to raise female relative pay also. A study by Chiplin, Curran and Parsley (1980) suggested that incomes policy might have been the predominant factor in raising female relative pay, given that the policy was observed in practice, but their regression analysis examined the period up to 1976 only, when the new legislation had perhaps not had its full effect.[14] Zabalza and Tzannatos (1985b) analysed the period up to 1980, utilizing a two-stage least-squares model which incorporated incomes policy dummies as well as legislation dummies and a relative-hours variable. Given that we expect the relative demand curve for men and women to be downward sloping the inclusion of this last variable is a considerable improvement on earlier work which considered the wage and employment effect separately, or ignored the latter altogether. Zabalza and Tzannatos's results suggest that the overall effect of the legislation has been to increase the relative earnings of women by 19% – a figure much greater than that detected in the USA, whereas the gains attributed to incomes policies are transitory and amount to less than 2%. However, these results should be treated with a degree of caution for a number of reasons. First Zabalza and Tzannatos's incomes policy dummies do not appear to conform to those periods which are most equalizing.[15] Second, the New Earnings Survey (a one per cent sample survey of the employee British labour force) on which the analysis is based is undertaken in one week in April and does not tell us when the annual pay adjustment takes place for each bargaining unit. Ideally we require a continuous earnings series to capture the precise effects of the above policy measures. Third, standard dummies do not enable us to account fully for incomes policies of varying degrees of equalization. Further, there is a degree of overlapping of the incomes policy and equal pay dummies with the time trend which itself could be picking up some of these effects and which may give rise to problems of multi-collinearity. Fifth, incomes policies prior to 1975 laid down exclusion clauses allowing for the implementation of equal pay, so that the policies were not distinct. It is a matter of conjecture how effective the one policy would have been without the other in raising female relative pay. Finally, it should be borne in mind that the period when female relative pay improved markedly was one of unprecedented inflation. Thus, for instance, between April 1974 and April 1975 the index of average earnings rose by 30.7%. From an employer's perspective the cost of raising female relative pay might have appeared slight in relation to the general upward trend in earnings. It can be seen, then, that there were particular circumstances pertaining in Britain which makes generalization concerning the efficacy of equal pay policy somewhat difficult.

Support for the conclusion that the Equal Pay Act has improved women's earnings relative to men's earnings comes from Joshi and Newell (1986). Their work is not time series, strictly speaking, since they analyse the 1946 birth cohort data which allowed them to compare the cohorts men's and women's earnings functions before and after the legislation. It is an interesting study because of the novel approach through having cohort data.

What of the impact of the legislation on relative female employment? Zabalza and Tzannatos show that although the total number of hours worked by women increased by 17.6% relative to those of men between 1970 and 1980, there was a slowdown in the annual growth rate from 2.7% during 1970–75 to 0.6% during 1975–80. Further, a substantial part of this increase in female employment occurred in the public sector. In the private sector relative employment grew by only 1.9% over the period 1970–75 and actually fell by 0.4% per annum over the period 1975–80. Still, this is a much smaller decline than one might have anticipated in the light of the very large increase in relative earnings which actually occurred.

Another study using a different data set, the Department of Employment's sample survey of manufacturing industry 1948–1982 (Pike, 1985) found that over this period the ratio of female to male employment fell from about 40% to 29%, the rate of decline accelerating in the period coinciding with the implementation of equal pay. Her translog cost function suggests that men and women are substitutable in production with elasticities of substitution close to unity which leads her to conclude that there is little evidence of a segmented labour market between male and female workers in British manufacturing industry. Her study is consistent with the suggestion also that the effects of equal pay legislation may differ significantly between public and private sectors.

Interpretation of time series results such as the above can be problematic, including problems of disentangling short-term and life-time effects, censoring and sample composition change. On the issue of life-time effects Lazear (1979) argued, for instance, that trends in observed relative earnings in the USA substantially overstated the improvement in the position of black workers, since it reflected a reduction in the amount of on-the-job training, whilst for women the reverse was the case. However, it has been argued that the evidence for this proposition is not convincing (Brown, 1982). Statistically one cannot reject the hypothesis that the difference in human capital investments between men and women and blacks and whites had remained constant over the period examined; also Smith and Welch's (1977) analysis does not point to any erosion of black gains as cohorts age, which we would expect if Lazear's hypothesis were correct. Further, account must be taken of the decline in black labour force participation rates relative to white, especially since 1964; these would produce post-1964 trends similar to those observed, to the extent that marginal labour force participants are drawn from the lower end of the earnings distribution.[16] As Brown (1982) notes, under such circumstances identifying equal opportunity, supply and truncation effects imposes extreme demands upon time series data; collinearity among the variables and the relative absence of strong supply side variables to act as instruments are the two main problems. However, in his 1984 paper Brown presents a new method for correcting published median earnings for such censoring. After taking the correction factor into account but not the employment effects, he finds that 60% of the male post-1964 trend and half the corresponding trends for females remains after such correction over the period 1953–78.

The related but broader problem of sample composition change was considered by Duncan and Hoffman (1983), who noted that trends in the aggregate earnings ratio reflect both the experience of age cohorts with continuing labour force participation and the effects of the replacement of the departing cohort by the entering cohort. Analysing the period 1967/70 to 1975/80 the wage gap fell moderately for the continuing cohort. It was the wage gap differences between the entering and departing cohorts which were substantial, with higher relative earnings for black workers in the entering cohort. Almost 60% of the increase in the aggregate earnings ratio in this study was attributable to changing sample composition.

Despite the rapid increase in female labour force participation, it appears that sample composition is less important in explaining the failure of female earnings to rise than it is in explaining the improvement in relative black earnings. Mallan (1982) finds that the rise in female labour force participation ratio between 1956 and 1975 did not depress the overall level of experience, as some authors had suggested; rather the reverse was true for the whole sample. Overall, then, censoring or sample selection does not explain away either the improvement in black relative pay or the failure of female relative pay to increase.

3.2. *Cross-section analysis*

Zabalza and Tzannatos (1985a,b) suggest that the Equal Pay Act in Britain did have a favourable effect on women's earnings. The early US cross-sectional studies of the enforcement of racial equality laws produced mixed results. Various analyses (Hildebrand *et al.*, 1976) suggested that there had been a significant increase in minority employment in contract compliance firms, but the size of the effect was relatively small and the impact on occupational advancement negligible. These results were confirmed by Beller (1978), using data on the ratio of the number of charges of discrimination to employees in covered firms 1968–70. Though the enforcement of the employment provisions of Title VII of the Civil Rights Act appeared to increase both relative black employment and wage rates, this was more than offset by the negative effects of enforcing the wage provisions.[17] Thus these studies suggested that legislation had made little impact by the end of the sixties.[18]

Brown (1982), reviewing studies of the impact of the OFCC, suggests a positive, though hardly revolutionary, effect from legislation of possibly 10% on relative black male employment in contractor firms, but very little effect on black females. In reaching this conclusion he acknowledged problems like that of including demonstration effects on non-contractor firms referred to earlier and the possible attempts by non-contractor firms to gain contractor status by minority hiring. But he goes on to ask, what is the lever by which the OFCC has achieved these gains? Do worthy contractors have a higher probability of gaining government contracts or less worthy ones suffer compliance reviews? These issues have been examined by Leonard. In one of his 1985 papers he develops a model which suggests that the OFCC should target those firms at the lower end of the distribution in respect to compliance review. Yet the evidence is quite the reverse. Completely segregated firms are amongst the least likely to be reviewed. However, a strategy of focusing on firms with greater proportions of females and black workers is consistent with a policy of equality of outcome or income re-distribution (as opposed to opportunity). To be effective such a strategy needs to shift the demand curve where the supply of labour is relatively inelastic, such as in the case of non-clerical white-collar labour forces.

In a second paper, Leonard (1985b) asks a rather different question, namely, do promises exacted from employers during the review process actually lead to changes in behaviour? In fact the regression estimates do suggest a measurable and significant improvement in the employment of minorities and women at reviewed establishments, though such establishments display a tendency to exaggerate the overall growth in employment of labour of all types.

A rather different approach is adopted by Osterman (1982) who focuses not on changes in relative wages or employment, but on quit rates as indicators of worker's perceptions of their opportunities at work. Thus the assumption is that an effective affirmative action programme will lead to a reduction in quits. In addition, rather than using a dummy variable for whether a firm is a government contractor or not, he includes variables measuring enforcement patterns, namely the number of compliance reviews per industry divided by industry employment and the fraction of the industry's output sold to the federal government. Each of these turn out to be significant in explaining the propensity to quit, both being inversely related to quits. A number of important implications follow from this study. High female quit rates are possibly a function of opportunities (as well as life style); increased opportunities leading to reduced quits will eventually reduce the wage differential between men and women, and finally lower quit rates will reduce firms' losses in investments in human capital, thereby raising profitability in covered firms.

We would expect that the strengthening of the affirmative action programme with its centralization in the Labor Department in 1978 would lead to an improvement in the relative position of minorities and women in the 1980s compared with the earlier period. Few if any studies have extended far enough into the 1980s to test this proposition adequately, but in general it does appear that later studies detect more substantial effects than earlier ones. Yet, some puzzles still remain. For example, as Smith and Welch (1984) point out, most of the wage gains for black workers occurred prior to 1974 before an effective monitoring structure for affirmative action had been put into place, and in the later period, when such powers had been enhanced, the wage effects for young black workers were in fact perverse. Finally, it should be noted that there had been no attempt to estimate rates of return (social or private) to affirmative action policies, let along to compare these with the potential rates of return to alternative policies. This seems an important omission given the size of the expenditures involved; these administrative costs have been variously put (Leonard 1985a) at somewhere between $50 million and $1 billion a year, depending on what is included in the estimate.

3.3. *Equal value or comparable worth* (CW)

The perceived relative failure to close the wage gap for minorities and women has led to calls for extensions to existing legislation, amongst which equal pay for work of equal value or comparable worth, have been prominent.[19] In Europe this has followed an Equal Pay Directive issued by the European Commission in 1975 and subsequently confirmed by the European Court of Justice as applying to all member states. In the USA it stems from the belief that occupational segregation has resulted in a situation in which women's work is undervalued relative to that of men (Hartmann, 1985). Pressure has been brought to bear in a number of states therefore, to see upward adjustments in women's pay where this appeared to be warranted on account of points awarded under job evaluation exercises.

These policies raise fundamental issues as to the nature of the operation of labour markets (Killingsworth, 1985), of job evaluation and of the meaning of equitable payment. It is suggested by the proponents of CW, such as Treiman and Hartmann (1981), that a percentage female variable should be included in a human capital model, together with both the characteristic of the worker and of the job, in order to eliminate the depressing effect on female pay of occupational segregation. Hence, we have

$$\log \bar{E}_i = a' + \Sigma b_i' \bar{R}_i + \Sigma c_j' \bar{X}_{ij} + d' F_i + \varepsilon' \qquad (4)$$

where E_i = mean earnings in occupation i

R_i = mean rating of occupation i under a job evaluation scheme (e.g. points score)

X_{ij} = mean characteristics (e.g. education, experience) of incumbents j in occupation i.

F_i = females as a percentage of total employment in occupation i.

This technique adjusts the coefficients b' and c' to estimate the contribution of each factor to earnings amongst jobs that have the same sex ratio. A second possibility referred to by Treiman and Hartmann is to use the factor weights derived from equations relating to white males in predominantly male jobs as the standard to be applied to all jobs including predominantly female jobs.

As Ehrenberg and Smith (1984) point out, we need to establish the sensitivity to functional form of estimates drawn from equations such as the above. A consideration also needs to be made of whether or not it is reasonable to sum individual factor scores under a job evaluation scheme to obtain a total score. But a more fundamental question is to what extent should a negative relationship between the wage and the degree to which an occupation is dominated by females be taken to reflect an undervaluation of women's work relative to that of males? As we have seen earlier, there is every reason to expect that this relationship may at least in part reflect sex differences in tastes for different types of work, or monopsony power, as well as occupational exclusion. As Johnson and Solon (1986) point out, implementing CW where tastes differ is not only inefficient but also inequitable, whilst CW legislation is inappropriate for dealing with occupational exclusion or monopsony. In any event, the evidence is far from clear that occupational exclusion or job segregation explains a major part of the earnings differential between men and women. Polachek (1984) points out that the earnings gap attributable to percentage female in any occupation is typically small (between four and six per cent), whilst O'Neill (1984) finds that a 10% points increase in the percentage female in an occupation is associated with only a 1.5% decline in pay. Even Aldrich and Buchele (1986), who are sympathetic to the concept of comparable work, find that job segregation accounts for only 15% of the wage gap between the sexes, a result very close to that found in Britain (see Miller 1987). Further, job evaluation itself is a subjective means of valuing a job and may itself reflect market forces rather than equitable payment.

Accepting these difficulties, what would be the likely effect of introducing CW or equal pay for work of equal value? Bergmann (1985) reviews some of the effects, but specific results of enacting this policy are available from the Australian experience. Equal pay for work of equal value was adopted in 1972 and introduced in three uniform steps over the period to June 1975, following the introduction of 'equal pay for equal work' in 1969. In fact, between 1969 and 1975 the pay of women relative to that of men in Australia increased by about 30%. Gregory and Duncan (1981) show that during those years when the relative wages of females rose most (i.e. 1973 and 1974) the largest increase in the rate of unemployment for women in response to the relative wage change was 10% or a mere 0.2% of the labour force. They conclude therefore that 'measured female unemployment was remarkably unresponsive to the equal pay decisions'. However, McGavin (1983), using hours data, demonstrates that the use of aggregate employment data conceals shifts in the composition of employment. He points out that much of the growth of female employment was concentrated in the public sector, and in his view the Australian experience does not refute the neo-classical proposition that a rise in the relative price of a factor will lead to a reduction in its use. Also we should perhaps make some allowance for the effect of the particular Australian institutional arrangements for settling pay before using Australian experience as a guide to likely effects of this type of legislation in other countries.

Several attempts have been made to simulate the potential impact of introducing CW more generally throughout the USA. Thus, Ehrenberg and Smith (1984) estimate that full implementation of CW in the government sector for three states would raise pay in predominantly female jobs by between 15% and 20%. If fixed budgets are assumed the result would be a decline in female employment of up to 6%. For the whole economy, Johnson and Solon (1986) estimate that CW would reduce the existing difference between male and female pay by between 3.4% and 8.0% assuming complete coverage of such legislation and ignoring general equilibrium effects.[20] Buchele and Aldrich (1985) develop an institutional model of employment and wage determination which they believe is implicit in the principle of CW. They use the model to estimate the likely impact of the introduction of CW. Defining CW in terms of equal returns to job requirements, they find that the earnings gap would be reduced by 63% if CW were to be applied generally. There are, however, a number of caveats. Their sample is not representative of the entire workforce; their results depend on their particular model of wage determination; and there are minimal controls for industry and region. Further, it should also be noted that whilst the coefficient on their education-based measure of job requirements is significant for men, it is insignificant for women. In contrast, the coefficient on the other experience-based measure is significant for women, but insignificant for men. This makes interpretation difficult, especially in the light of the fact that the coefficient of determination is only in the range 0.16 to 0.23. More problematically, their estimates lump in the constant term which, as suggested above, may represent lack of knowledge of the determinants of pay as much as discrimination. In their later 1986 study, Aldrich and Buchele remove the constant-term effect both for the above reason and because it includes inter-firm effects which would not be corrected by comparable worth. They then find that 'women's' jobs pay *higher* returns to schooling, experience and job tenure than do 'men's' jobs, which they regard as implausible and which suggests that part of the constant term may well be discriminatory. Their solution to this dilemma is to add in a percentage female variable to both female and male equations, finding that comparable worth would raise women's wages by 5.4% and male wages by 2.5%, and thereby reducing the overall female/male wage gap by 2.8%. Higher estimates are obtained if the male equation is used to estimate the female wage adjustment. They argue (somewhat dubiously) that differences in preferences should not cause differential returns to job traits, and also find that differences in working conditions, following Filer, do not make a major contribution. However, their results do seem to be based on strong and questionable assumptions concerning the potential mobility of female workers among jobs and are very sensitive to the assumptions on which they are based.

In practice the impact of CW will depend on how extensively it is implemented and it may well have different effects in the public and private sectors. It should also be noted that most advocates argue for introducing CW within organizations rather than across them or over the whole economy. Further, unlike equal opportunity policies such as affirmative action which attempt to increase the costs of those who discriminate, CW itself will raise the costs of those who comply. Thus organizations have every incentive to minimize its impact.

4. Conclusions

There is no consensus on the extent to which discrimination now manifests itself in the labour market. This arises partly from disagreements as to which of the available methods is most appropriate for measuring its extent and to problems with the data which leave open a number of different interpretations of the results of estimating the extent of discrimination in different segments of the labour market.

Attempts to isolate the effects of policy are confounded by problems of identifying appropriate variables for capturing the precise policy impact and of removing the contaminatory effects of other policy initiatives and changes emanating from elsewhere in the labour market. Despite such uncertainties there has been an attempt in many countries to tighten up anti-discrimination legislation or to implement new forms of policy such as comparable worth.

Therefore, despite the vast literature on discrimination and increasingly sophisticated measurement techniques, our ability to detect its incidence at all precisely is still rudimentary. That in turn makes it much more likely that policies adopted will lower rather than increase efficiency of labour utilization. It also follows that it is difficult to make precise estimates of the degree to which equal opportunity policies have been successful in eliminating discrimination, which in turn complicates the search for the optimal form of policy. Further, we still lack knowledge of the relative efficiency of equality of opportunity policies in relation to alternatives. Would manpower policies, for example, raise the level of human capital of minority groups and women more than equal opportunity policies? How effective would be measures to increase labour force participation for such groups (such as the provision of child care facilities) or even subsidies to encourage employers to overcome their aversion to hiring such workers? These questions need to be addressed if policy makers are genuinely concerned to alter the prospect of certain groups, and do it most efficiently.

Acknowledgements

We are grateful to John Pencavel and two anonymous referees for helpful comments. The usual disclaimers apply.

Notes

1. Rampton (1981) claims that pre-entry discrimination is an important aspect of the experience of young West Indians in Britain.
2. Asher and Popkin (1984), for example, argue that aggregate specifications often used to examine wage differentials fail to control for important demographic variations in wage patterns. In their study of postal workers they introduce interaction terms to control for gender and race differentials by industry.
2. The effects of omitted variable bias can be seen in Hashimoto and Kochin (1980). Generally, however, there appears to be a presumption that the bias will operate in the direction of providing an exaggerated estimate of the effect of discrimination. Hashimoto and Kochin suggest that one method of evaluating the bias in the estimates of the coefficient of the minority group dummy variable is that of grouping on a basis which can be reasonably expected to be independent of measurement errors. In their case they group observations according to state of residence at age 16, which greatly reduces the effect of race on earnings.

4. This study also finds that discrimination is much less apparent for women with college degrees compared with those who ceased their education after high school, but in their case the omission of a tastes variable makes little difference to the estimate of discrimination.
5. Ferber and Spaeth also find that the earnings of women are related to the sex of the supervisor. That is, having a male supervisor raises female earnings by almost 25%, whilst responsibility for financial control raises the earnings of both sexes substantially. Both of these factors might possibly be taken as an indication of discrimination illustrating the problem of determining which variables are to be regarded as legitimate productivity capturing variables in the analysis.
6. Butler shows that if blacks have a less elastic supply (or demand) curve in any given market, the reduced form is likely to underestimate the amount of racial discrimination.
7. Corcoran and Courant (1985) have recently attempted to develop a model which explicitly takes tastes (or socialization) into account. This assumes that individual workers have utility functions which are defined to include income, leisure and attributes of job described in terms of traditional sex appropriateness.
8. These two measures are in fact quite distinct. Conway and Roberts refer to a situation in which the conditional distributions of income given job qualifications are the same for both groups as Fairness 1 and that in which the conditional distributions of job qualifications given income are the same for both groups as Fairness 2.
9. Similarly, Green and Ferber (1984) conclude, after conducting an empirical test of whether reverse regression is appropriate for measuring salary discrimination (using data on faculty salaries in a large university), that reverse regression will not yield unbiased estimates of salary discrimination.
10. It could be argued that it is more sensible to compare the earnings of men and women who have enjoyed continuous participation in the labour force than use the Heckman procedure, which in this respect might be considered as a solution looking for a problem. For an example of the use of this procedure see Killingsworth (1983) and P. J. Dolton and G. H. Makepeace (1986).
11. They point out that some court decisions have erred in assuming that unmeasured variables *must* produce biased results, whilst others have in contrast rejected claims that omitted variables necessarily invalidate regression analysis where such claims were not backed up with evidence of the magnitude of the alleged statistical bias.
12. For a review of the legislation in the USA and Britain see Chiplin and Sloane (1982) or Meehan (1984).
13. Smith and Welch (1984) also report a 'startling' growth in black employment in reporting firms over the period 1970–80, contrasting with a decline in the percentage of this group in non-reporting firms.
14. The Equal Pay Act 1970 started so that there was no legal requirement to remove discriminatory differentials until the end of 1975.
15. These are April 1973 to November 1973 when the incomes policy limit was 4% plus £1 with £5 maximum; April 1974 to October 1974 when £4.40 was paid out for threshold increases and August 1975 to August 1976 when there was a £6 limit. These correspond fairly closely to the period of substantial upward movement in the female/male earnings differential. In addition to the above, there were two periods when income policies were proportional but also laid down minima and maxima. These are the period November 1973 to August 1974 when the minimum was £2.25 and the maximum £7, and August 1977 when the minimum was £2.50 and the maximum £4.
16. Such a possibility had been noted by Butler and Heckman (1977) who suggested the reduction in labour supply resulted from the expansion of transfer programmes such as the anti-poverty programme for those who would receive low wages if they remained in the labour force.

17. Brown (1982) suggests Beller's results are suspect because the frequency of charges as a measure of the intensity of EEOC efforts is complicated by the growing backlog of charges at this time, the lack of improvement in the relative position of the minority group may feed back into the number of charges, and the use of a geographical variable (the state) as a unit of observation seems less satisfactory than that of the industry in which an employee works.
18. In addition to studies of affirmative action programmes, an attempt has been made by Medoff (1980) to test for the effect of ratification or non-ratification by various states of the Equal Rights Amendment. He finds that women in states that have ratified the ERA are most likely to work in jobs commensurate with their abilities, but to receive less pay than their male equivalents in comparison with women in non-ratified states. These findings have, however, been disputed by Hunt (1983) on the grounds that it is not legitimate to use a single regression equation as Medoff did to estimate discrimination coefficients in the two categories of state. Using a different data set and using separate regressions for men and women he finds, contrary to Medoff that, after controlling for workforce characteristics, the discrimination coefficient is lower in ratifying states.
19. Different terminology is used in different countries. In the USA it has become the norm to refer to comparable worth and in other countries to equal pay for work of equal value.
20. Killingsworth (1984) has criticized Johnson and Solon's estimation procedure in an earlier 1984 paper. He claims it underestimates the likely impact, since it assumes that CW will have an impact only on that part of the wage differential associated with the proportion female in a particular occupation, thus ignoring the potential impact on uniformly lower wages for all women relative to all comparable men. Ehrenberg and Smith (1987) have attempted to assess the effects of a comparable worth policy on female employment in state and local sectors. Even a 20% wage adjustment would only reduce female employment by 2 or 3%, because of the low degree of substitutability between men and women across major occupation groups. However, there are a number of caveats regarding their statistical estimates.

References

Abowd, J. M. (1983) Economic and statistical analysis of discrimination in job assignment. *Industrial Relations Research Association, Proceedings of the 38th Annual Meeting, December 28–30, San Francisco, 1983.*

Abowd, J. M. and Killingsworth, M. R. (1983) Sex discrimination, atrophy and the male–female wage differential. *Industrial Relations* 22, 387–402.

Akin, J. S. and Garfinkel, I. (1980) The quality of education and cohort variation in black–white earnings differentials: comment. *American Economic Review* 70, 186–91.

Aldrich, M. and Buchele, R. (1986) *The Economics of Comparable Worth*. Cambridge, Mass.: Ballinger Publishing Company.

Asher, M. and Popkin, J. (1984) The effect of gender and race differentials on public–private wage comparisons: a study of postal workers. *Industrial and Labor Relations Review* 38, 16–25.

Barry, J. (1985) Women production workers: low pay and hazardous work. *American Economic Review* 75, 262–5.

Bartel, A. P. (1981) Wage growth and job turnover: an empirical analysis. In S. Rosen (ed.) *Studies in Labor Markets*. Chicago: Chicago University Press.

Bartlett, R. L. and Miller, T. I. (1985) Executive compensation female executives and networking. *American Economic Review* 75, 266–70.

Becker, G. S. (1957) *The Economics of Discrimination*. London and Chicago: University of Chicago Press.

—— (1964) *Human Capital*. New York: National Bureau of Economic Research.

Beller, A. H. (1978) The economics of enforcement of an anti-discrimination law: Title VII of the Civil Rights Act of 1964. *Journal of Law and Economics* 21, 359–80.

—— (1979) The impact of equal opportunity laws on the male/female earnings differential. In C. B. Lloyd, *et al.* (eds) *Women in the Labor Market*. New York and Guildford: Columbia University Press.

—— (1980) The effects of economic conditions on the success of equal opportunity laws: an application to the sex differential in earnings. *Review of Economics and Statistics* LXII, 379–87.

—— (1985) Changes in the sex composition of US occupations, 1960–1981. *Journal of Human Resources* XX, 235–50.

Berger, M. C. and Glenn, D. E. (1986) Selectivity bias and earnings differences by gender and race. *Economics Letters* 21, 291–6.

Bergmann, B. R. (1985) The economic case for comparable worth. In Hartmann (1985).

Birnbaum, M. H. (1979) Procedures for the detection of the correction of salary inequities. In T. R. Pezzullo and B. E. Brittingham (eds) *Salary Equity*. Lexington, Mass.: Lexington Books.

Blakemore, A. E. and Low, S. A. (1983) Race and the acquisition of and returns to OJT for youth. *Industrial Relations* 22, 374–86.

—— (1984) Sex differences in occupational selection: the case of college majors. *Review of Economics and Statistics* 66, 157–62.

Blau, Francine, D., (1984) Discrimination against women: theory and evidence. In W. Darity Jr. *Labor Economics: Modern Views*. Boston: Klewer & Nijhoff Publishing.

Blau, F. D. and Kahn, L. M. (1985) On estimating discrimination in the economy: comment. *Southern Economic Journal* 51, 1221–6.

Bloom, D. E. and Killingsworth, M. R. (1982) Pay discrimination research and litigation: the use of regression. *Industrial Relations* 21, 318–39.

Borjas, G. J. (1980) *Race, Labor Turnover and Male Earnings,* Final Report to the US Department of Labor, December 1980.

—— (1983) The measurement of race and gender wage differentials: evidence from the federal sector. *Industrial and Labor Relations Review* 37, 79–91.

—— (1984) Race, turnover and male earnings. *Industrial Relations* 23, 73–89.

Brown, C. (1982) The federal attack on labor market discrimination: the mouse that roared. In R. G. Ehrenberg *Research in Labor Economics* Vol. 5, pp 33–68.

—— (1984) Black–White earnings ratios since the Civil Rights Act: the importance of labour market drop-outs. *Quarterly Journal of Economics* 99, 31–44.

Buchele, R. and Aldrich, M. (1985) How much difference would comparable worth make? *Industrial Relations* 24, 222–33.

Butler, R. J. (1982) Estimating wage discrimination in the labor market. *Journal of Human Resources* 17, 606–21.

Butler, R. J. and Heckman, J. (1977) The government's impact on the labor market status of black Americans: a critical review. In F. E. Bloch *et al. Equal Rights and Industrial Relations.* Industrial Relations Research Association.

Cain, G. C. (1976) The challenges of segmented labor market theories to orthodox theory: a survey. *Journal of Economic Literature* December 1976, Vol. XIV, No. 4.

Chiplin, B. (1979) On evaluation of sex discrimination: some problems and a suggested solution. In C. B. Lloyd, R. S. Andrews and C. L. Gilroy (eds) *Women in the Labor Market*. New York: Columbia University Press.

Chiplin, B., Curran, M. and Parsley, C. J. (1980) Relative female earnings in Great Britain and the impact of legislation. In P. J. Sloane (ed.) *Women and Low Pay*. London: Macmillan.

Chiplin, B. and Sloane, P. J. (1976) *Sex Discrimination in the Labour Market*. London: Macmillan.

Chiplin, B. and Sloane, P. J. (1982) *Tackling discrimination at the workplace: An analysis of sex discrimination in Britain*. Cambridge: Cambridge University Press.

Chiswick, B. R. (1983a) The earnings and human capital of American Jews. *Journal of Human Resources* 18, 313–36.

—— (1983b) 'An analysis of the earnings and employment of Asian-American men. *Journal of Labor Economics* 2, 197–214.

Conway, D. A. and Roberts, H. V. (1983) Reverse regression, fairness and employment discrimination. *Journal of Business Economics and Statistics* 1, 75–85.

Corcoran, M. E. and Courant, P. N. (1985) Sex role socialisation and labor market outcomes. *American Economic Review, Papers and Proceedings* 75, 275–8.

Darity, W. A. and Williams, R. M. (1985) Peddlers forever? Culture, competition and discrimination. *American Economic Review, Papers and Proceedings* 75, 256–61.

Daymont, T. N. and Andresani, P. J. (1984) Job preferences, college major and the gender gap in earnings. *Journal of Human Resources* XIX, 408–28.

Dex, S. (1979) Economists' theories of the economics of discrimination. *Ethnic and Racial Studies*, 2, 90–108.

—— (1986) *The costs of discriminating: a review of the literature*, Research and Planning Unit Paper 39. London: The Home Office.

Dolton, P. (1984) Testing for sex discrimination in maximum likelihood models. *Applied Economics* 16, 225–35.

Dolton, P. J. and Makepeace, G. (1985a) The statistical measurement of discrimination. *Economic Letters* 18, 391–3.

—— (1985b) Marital status, child rearing and earnings differentials in the graduate labour market. *Economic Journal* 97, 897–922.

—— (1986) Sample selection and male–female earnings differentials in the graduate labour markets. *Oxford Economic Papers* 38, 317–41.

Duncan, G. J. and Hoffman, S. D. (1979) On-the-job training and earnings differences by race and sex. *Review of Economics and Statistics* 61, 594–603.

—— (1983) A new look at the causes of the improved economic status of black workers. *Journal of Human Resources* 18, 268–81.

Ehrenberg, R. and Smith, R. S. (1984) Comparable worth in the public sector. National Bureau of Economic Research, Working Paper.

—— (1985) Economic and statistical analysis in employment discrimination cases. *Industrial Relations Research Association Proceedings of the 36th Annual Meeting, December 28–30, San Francisco, 1983.*

—— (1987) Comparable worth wage adjustments and female employment in the state and local sector. *Journal of Labour Economics* 5, 43–62.

Ferber, M. A. and Spaeth, J. L. (1984) Work characteristics and the male–female earnings gap. *American Economic Review, Papers and Proceedings* 74, 260–4.

Filer, R. K. (1983) Sexual difference in earnings: the role of individual personalities and tastes. *Journal of Human Resources* 18, 82–9.

Filer, R. K. (1985) Male–female wage differences: the importance of compensating differentials. *Industrial and Labor Relations Review* 38, 426–37.

Flanagan, R. J. (1974) Labor force experience, job turnover and racial wage differentials. *Review of Economics and Statistics* 56, 521–9.

Gastwirth, J. L. (1984) Statistical methods for analysing claims of employment discrimination. *Industrial and Labor Relations Review* 38, 75–86.

Golbe, D. L. (1985) Imperfect signalling, affirmative action and black–white wage differentials. *Southern Economic Journal* 51, 842–8.

Goldberger, A. S. (1984) Reverse regression and salary discrimination. *Journal of Human Resources* XIX, 293–318.

Green, C. A. and Ferber, M. A. (1984) Employment discrimination: an empirical test of forward versus reverse regressions. *Journal of Human Resources* XIX, 557–69.

Greenhalgh, C. (1980) Male–female wage differentials in Great Britain: is marriage an equal opportunity? *Economic Journal* 90, 751–75.

Gregory, R. G. and Duncan, R. C. (1981) Segmented labour markets and the Australian experience of equal pay for women. *Journal of Post-Keynesian Economics* 3(3), 403–28.

Hartmann, H. I. (ed.)(1985) *Comparable Worth: New Directions for Research*. Washington, D.C.: National Academy Press.

Hashimoto, M. and Kochin, L. (1980) A bias in the statistical estimation of the effects of discrimination. *Economic Inquiry* 18, 478–86.

Heckman, J. J. (1979) Sample selection bias as a specification error. *Econometrica* XLVII, 153–62.

Hildebrand, G. H. *et al.* (1976) A symposium: evaluating the impact of affirmative action: a look at the Federal Contract compliance programme. In *Industrial and Labor Relations Review* 29 (4), 485.

Hoffman, S. D. (1979) Black/white life cycle earnings differences and the vintage hypothesis: a longitudinal analysis. *American Economic Review* 69, 855–67.

Hojman, D. E. (1984) Downward bias in the new measure of wage discrimination. *Economic Letters* 14, 87–91.

Hunt, J. C. (1983) Discrimination in ERA states. *Economic Enquiry* 21, 140–5.

Johnson, G. and Solon, G. (1986) Estimates of the direct effects of comparable worth policy. *American Economic Review* 76, 1117–25.

Jones, F. L. (1983) On decomposing the wage gap: a critical comment on Blinder's method. *Journal of Human Resources* 18, 126–30.

Joshi, H. E. and Newell, M. L. (1986) *Pay Differentials and Parenthood: Analysis of Men and Woman Born in 1946*. Report to the Department of Employment.

Kamalich, R. E. and Polachek, S. W. (1982) Discrimination: fact or fiction? An examination using an alternative approach. *Southern Economic Journal* 49, 450–61.

Kelley, M. R. (1982) Discrimination in seniority systems: a case study. *Industrial and Labor Relations Review* 36, 40–55.

Killingsworth, M. R. (1983) *Labor Supply*. Cambridge: Cambridge University Press.

—— (1984) Economic analysis of comparable worth and its consequences. *Industrial Relations Research Association Proceedings*, Dallas, Texas, December 29.

—— (1985) The economics of comparable worth: analytical, empirical and policy questions. In Hartmann (1985).

Killingsworth, M. R. and Reimers, C. W. (1983) Race ranking promotions and pay at a federal facility: a logit analysis. *Industrial and Labor Relations Review* 37, 92–107.

Knopff, R. (1986) On proving discrimination: statistical methods and unfolding policy logics. *Canadian Public Policy* XII, 573–83.

Lazear, E. (1979) Male–female wage differentials: has the Government had any effect? In C. B. Lloyd *et al.* (eds.) *Women in the Labour Market*. New York and Guildford: Columbia University Press.

Leigh, J. P. (1983) Sex differences in absenteeism. *Industrial Relations* 22, 349–61.

Leonard, J. S. (1984) The impact of affirmative action on employment. *Journal of Labor Economics* 439–63.

—— (1985a) Affirmative action as earnings redistribution: the targeting of compliance reviews. *Journal of Labor Economics* 3, 363–84.

—— (1985b) What are promises worth? The impact of affirmative action goals. *Journal of Human Resources*, XX, 3–20.

Link, C., Rutledge, E. and Lewis, K. (1976) Black–white, differences in returns to schooling: some new evidence. *American Economic Review* 66, 221–3.

—— (1980) The quality of education of cohort variation in black–white earnings differentials: a reply. *American Economic Review* 70, 196–203.

McCormick, B. (1986) Employment opportunities, earnings and the journey to work of minority workers in Britain. *Economic Journal* 96, 375–82.
McGavin, P. A. (1983) Equal pay for women: a reassessment of the Australian experience. *Australian Economic Papers* 22, 48–59.
Mallan, L. B. (1982) Labor force participation, work experience and the human pay gap between men and women. *Journal of Human Resources* XVII, 437–48.
Masters, S. H. (1975) *Black–White Income Differences: Empirical Studies and Policy Implications*. New York: Academic Press.
Medoff, M. H. (1980) The equal rights amendment: an empirical analysis of sexual discrimination. *Economic Inquiry* 18, 367–79.
Medoff, J. L. and Abraham, K. G. (1980) Experience, performance and earnings. *Quarterly Journal of Economics* 95, 703–36.
—— (1981) Are those paid more really more productive? The case of experience. *Journal of Human Resources* XVI, 186–216.
Meehan, E. H. (1984) *Women's Rights at Work: Campaigns and Policy in Britain and the United States*. London: MacMillan.
Miller, P. W. (1987) The wage effect of the occupational segregation of women in Britain. *Economic Journal* 97(388), 885–96.
Mincer, J. (1974) *Schooling, Experience and Earnings*. New York: Columbia University Press.
Olson, C. A. and Becker, B. E. (1983) Sex discrimination in the promotion process. *Industrial and Labor Relations Review* 36, 624–41.
O'Neill, June (1984) Earnings differentials: empirical evidence and causes. In G. Schmid and R. Weitzel (eds) *Sex Discrimination and Equal Opportunity: The Labor Market and Employment Policy*. London: Gower.
Osterman, P. (1982) Affirmative action and opportunities: a study of female quit rates. *Review of Economics and Statistics* LXIV, 604–12.
Pike, M. (1985) The employment response to equal pay legislation. *Oxford Economic Papers* 37, 304–18.
Polachek, S. (1981) Occupational self-selection: a human capital approach to sex differences in occupational structure. *Review of Economics and Statistics* LXIII, 60–69.
Polachek, S. (1984) Women in the economy: perspectives on gender inequality. Paper for U.S. Commission on Civil Rights Conference on Comparable Worth, 6–7 June, 1984.
Rampton, A. (1981) *West Indian children in our schools*. Cmnd. 8273. London: HMSO.
Shorey, J. (1983) An analysis of sex differences in quits. *Oxford Economic Papers* 35, 213–27.
Siebert, W. S. (1985) Development in the economics of human capital. In D. Carline *et al. Labour Economics*. London and New York: Longman.
Sloane, P. J. (1985) Discrimination in the labour market. In D. Carline *et al.* (eds) *Labour Economics*. London and New York: Longman.
Smith, J. P. and Welch, F. R. (1977) Black–white male wages ratios in 1960–1970. *American Economic Review* 67, 323–38.
Smith, J. P. and Welch, F. R. (1984) Affirmative action and labour markets. *Journal of Labor Economics* 2, 269–301.
Solon, G. (1983) Errors in variables and reverse regression in the management of wage discrimination. *Economic Letters* 13, 393–6.
Sowell, T. (1981) *Ethnic America*. New York: Basic Books.
—— (1983) *The Economics and Politics of Race*. New York: Morrow.
—— (1984) *Civil Rights, Rhetoric or Reality?* New York: Morrow.
Stewart, M. (1983) Racial discrimination and occupational attainment in Britain. *Economic Journal* 93, 521–41.
Szymanski, A. (1976) Racial discrimination and white gain. *American Sociological Review* 41, 403–14.

Treiman, D. and Hartmann, H. (1981) *Women, Work and Wages: Equal Pay for Jobs of Equal Value*. Washington, D.C.: National Academy Press.

Zabalza, A. and Tzannatos, Z. (1985a) *Women and Equal Pay*. Cambridge: Cambridge University Press.

—— (1985b) The effect of Britain's anti-discrimination legislation on relative pay and employment. *Economic Journal* 95, 679–99.

[26]

OCCUPATIONAL MOBILITY OF BLACK WOMEN, 1958–1981: THE IMPACT OF POST-1964 ANTIDISCRIMINATION MEASURES

AUGUSTIN KWASI FOSU*

This study finds that between 1965 and 1981, black women's occupational mobility rose relative to that of white women and white men by about 20% and 24%, respectively, and that more than half of these gains remain even after controlling for pre-existing trends, cyclical economic conditions, education, and factors potentially influencing the labor supply. No evidence is found to support the null hypothesis that this pattern is explained in significant measure by a decline in the labor supply of black women. The author argues, instead, that the results reflect the effects of Title VII of the 1964 Civil Rights Act and, by the mid-1970s, affirmative action laws.

TITLE VII of the 1964 U.S. Civil Rights Act outlawed employment discrimination based on race, gender, and other defined attributes. In 1965, "affirmative action" was established upon the creation of the Office of Federal Contract-Compliance Programs (OFCCP) by Executive Order 11246 to monitor the hiring and promotion practices of federal contractors with specific regard to blacks. Employers were required to adopt formal goals and a timetable for achievement of those goals in 1968, and the program was extended to women as a class in 1972.

Previous studies analyzing firms covered by federal contracts (contract firms) and those not covered (noncontract firms) have concluded that affirmative action failed to appreciably raise the occupational status of blacks in the 1960s or early 1970s. (Burman 1973; Ashenfelter and Heckman 1976; Goldstein and Smith 1976; Heckman and Wolpin 1976.) A more recent study by Leonard (1984), however, suggests that affirmative action had a significant positive impact on blacks' occupational status between 1974 and 1980, measured both absolutely and in relation to whites.

The above studies are unlikely to reveal *economywide* effects of the various post-1964 antidiscrimination measures, however, since most of these studies are based on comparisons between contract and noncontract firms. After all, Title VII applied to both types of firms, and noncontract firms aspiring to obtain federal contracts might conceivably adopt

* Augustin Kwasi Fosu is Associate Professor of Economics at the School of Business Administration, Oakland University. This research was supported by grants from the Oakland University Research Committee and School of Business Administration. The author thanks the Center for Urban Studies, Wayne State University, where an earlier version of the paper was revised while he served as Visiting Associate Professor from May to August 1989.

A data appendix containing additional results, together with copies of the computer program used to generate the results presented in the paper, is available from the author at the Department of Economics, School of Business Administration, Oakland University, Rochester, Michigan 48309–4401.

Industrial and Labor Relations Review, Vol. 45, No. 2 (January 1992). © by Cornell University.
0019-7939/92/4502 $01.00

affirmative action. Thus, although these studies found no *differential* effect of affirmative action on black occupational mobility in (for example) the mid-1960s and early 1970s, Title VII, and possibly affirmative action, might have had a significant impact on the economy as a whole during that period.

Albelda (1986) examined occupational mobility with respect to race and gender by analyzing the annual index of occupational dissimilarity using economywide data for the 1958–81 period. Unfortunately, as I argue below, the index by itself may not indicate the direction of occupational mobility. Furthermore, the post-1964 period is not isolated in Albelda's study.

Medoff (1985) employed a decennial index reflecting the relative occupational mobility of blacks and observed an acceleration in the index over the 1960–80 period. Because of the decennial nature of the data, however, it was not possible to distinguish among the influences of post-1964 antidiscrimination measures, human capital factors, and supply and cyclical economic conditions. Medoff's study was also limited to black men, so it shed no evidence on black women.

The present study employs economywide data to investigate the occupational mobility of black women for the 1958–81 period by first developing an annual index of their mobility and then comparing it with the indexes for white women and white men. The focus on black women is intended to help offset the emphasis on black men by many previous studies (for example, Smith and Welch 1989; Medoff 1985; Smith 1984). Furthermore, even though the post-1964 antidiscrimination measures applied to both men and women, the two groups have differed greatly in occupational distribution, with black women mostly in clerical and service jobs and black men primarily in blue-collar jobs.

I control for educational, cyclical, and censoring supply factors in a structural regression model that isolates the post-1964 period, in order to test the hypothesis that the relative occupational position of black women has improved since the mid-1960s, probably in response to the antidiscrimination measures of the era. Additional hypotheses regarding trends and censoring supply effects are also examined.

Theoretical Framework

Occupational distribution is governed by individual characteristics as well as institutional characteristics. The former include human capital factors (such as education), and may also include such attributes as race and gender when the labor market is segmented or segregated with respect to those demographic variables. Institutional factors entail supply and demand conditions of the relevant labor market, as well as the segmentation or segregation of the particular occupation. For example, over one-third of all employed black women in 1960 were in the Private Household category[1] and fewer than 10% were in Clerical, compared with corresponding figures of about 5% and 33% for employed white women. Although some of these disparities may be explained by human capital differences between black and white women,[2] there is ample evidence that a substantial portion might be attributable to occupational discrimination (Doeringer and Piore 1971; Marshall 1974; Cain 1976).

The picture of black female occupational structure had changed by 1980, however, when less than 10% of employed black women were in Private Household, and roughly 30% were in Clerical, a proportion nearly equal to the 36% figure for white women. Human capital factors might explain some of this mobility; years of schooling of black women relative to white women, for example, increased from about .80 to near unity between 1960

[1] The data cited here are derived from sources indicated in Table 2.

[2] As an example of the impotence of the human capital model in explaining occupational gender segregation, see England (1982). Regarding racial differences, see Darity (1982).

and 1980. Still, might a significant portion of the mobility be attributable to post-1964 antidiscrimination measures? To understand fully the relative roles of the various factors at work, an occupational index reflecting mobility across all occupations must be constructed.

Consider the following occupational index for the ith demographic group at a given point in time:

$$(1) \qquad I_i = \sum_{j=1}^{N} w_j(L_{ij}/L_i),$$

$$\text{with} \sum_{j=1}^{N} w_j = 1,$$

where L_{ij} = the number of the ith group employed in occupation j; L_i = the total number of the ith group employed; w_j = the relative "status" weight of occupation j; and N = the number of occupations. To simplify the analysis, let $N = 2$, and $w_2 > w_1$, and define s_{ij} as equal to L_{ij}/L_i. Thus (dropping the i index):

$$(2) \qquad I = w_1 s_1 + w_2 s_2,$$
$$\text{with } w_1 + w_2 = 1,$$
$$\text{and } s_1 + s_2 = 1.$$

Therefore,

$$(3) \qquad \partial I/s_1 = (w_1 - w_2) < 0$$
$$\text{and } \partial I/\partial s_2 = (w_2 - w_1) > 0$$

Similarly,

$$(4) \qquad \partial I/\partial w_1 = (s_1 - s_2),$$
$$\text{and } \partial I/\partial w_2 = (s_2 - s_1)$$

Thus, according to (3), the index will rise as a result of increasing the share of the group in the high-status occupation or decreasing the share in the low-status occupation. By (4), increases (decreases) in the relative status of the occupation with a greater concentration of the demographic group will raise (lower) the group's index.[3]

Since factors other than antidiscrimination programs, such as technological changes, may influence the relative status of occupations,[4] however, and the success of such programs in reducing occupational discrimination is measured by their effect on mobility from the low-status Occupation 1 to the high-status Occupation 2, the index should not be sensitive to changes in the weights w_i. Hence, I adopt a fixed-weighted index; that is, $dw_1/dt = 0$, and $dw_2/dt = 0$ (with t denoting time).

The relative share of black female employment in the low- or high-status occupation, s_1 or s_2, thus is an indicator of black female occupational mobility. It is important, therefore, to consider factors that may influence s_1 or, alternately, s_2. (Note that $s_1 + s_2 = 1$, by definition.)

Two types of barriers to black female entry into the high-status Occupation 2 are considered here: human capital, and institutional constraints imposed by labor market discrimination. For example, I expect s_2 to increase with black female education (both quantity and quality), as a higher level of education is expected to raise the probability that black women will

---

[3] An alternative index, the occupational segregation index, is usually used to measure the occupational progress of a disadvantaged group (Duncan and Duncan 1955; Beller 1982, 1984; Albelda 1986). This index is defined for the ith group relative to the kth reference group as:

$$S^{ik} = 1/2 \sum_j |\gamma_{kj} - \gamma_{ij}|$$

where γ_{kj} = the share of the kth group's employment in occupation j and γ_{ij} = the share of the ith group's employment in occupation j.

I prefer the index developed in the present paper, however. First, the segregation index fails to distinguish upward occupational mobility from downward mobility. For example, if the disadvantaged group were to move downward into a lower-valued occupation dominated by the reference group, the segregation index would indicate greater equality; and if, conversely, the movement were into a high-valued occupation in which the disadvantaged group was already over-represented, a higher level of segregation might be indicated by the segregation index, even though such a movement would, *ceteris paribus*, imply upward mobility.

[4] If discrimination exists, however, minority mobility into a given occupation may, at a certain threshold, begin to lower the status of that occupation. I assume here that, given the relatively small population of black women in the economy, that threshold is not reached.

satisfy the human capital requirements of Occupation 2. On the other hand, experience, another important human capital variable within the earnings equation, would probably have little or no influence on s_2, since the resulting human capital is likely to be primarily job-specific.

The existence of institutional barriers would understate s_2, since for such barriers to be effective there must exist a nonempty subset of black women in Occupation 1 who meet the human capital requirements of Occupation 2. As the institutional constraints to entry ease, however, perhaps due to the antidiscrimination measures of Title VII and the Contract Compliance Programs of the 1960s, those black women satisfying the human capital requirements will likely locate in Occupation 2. Due to mobility costs, most women entering Occupation 2 would be new entrants into the labor force. In any case, s_2, and hence the index of black female occupational mobility I_{BF}, should rise over time with the easing of institutional barriers, which, I postulate, was accelerated by the antidiscrimination measures of the 1960s.

Other supply factors may influence s_2 as well. For example, expanded government and other social welfare programs of the 1960s may have induced low earners to drop out of the labor force. Such a result should reduce employment in the low-wage Occupation 1, which, by assumption, has a disproportionate number of black female workers. In that case, s_1 will decrease (and s_2 increase), raising I_{BF}, even though there is no black female occupational mobility. This phenomenon is akin to the "censoring hypothesis" advanced by Butler and Heckman (1977) regarding earnings. According to Butler and Heckman, these supply censoring variables would exaggerate relative black wages. Similarly, such factors would artificially raise I_{BF}. Additionally, an economic downturn (upturn) that results in a fall (rise) in the low-wage occupational employment share s_1 will spuriously raise (lower) I_{BF}. The index must, therefore, be purged of these censoring influences incongruent with occupational mobility.

Table 1. Index of Occupational Mobility for Black Women: 1960, 1970, and 1980.

Year	*Absolute Index*	*Index Relative to White Women*	*Index Relative to White Men*
1960	.079	.737	.750
1970	.094	.861	.875
1980	.109	.954	1.000

The absolute index is the weighted arithmetic mean of black female occupational employment, with female occupational median earnings as weights. The relative indices are the respective ratios of the black female absolute index to the white female index and the white male index, each calculated similarly, with the female and white male occupational median earnings serving as respective weights (see text for details). Note that since the weights differ between men and women, columns 3 and 4 are not comparable. In particular, the relative index value of 1.000 in column 4 does not indicate occupational equality between black women and white men, whereas such a value in column 3 would suggest occupational equality between black and white women.

Source: U.S. BLS (1982, 1978).

Empirical Specification and Results

Table 1 presents the absolute and relative fixed-weighted indexes for black female occupational employment in 1960, 1970, and 1980, based on U.S. Bureau of Labor Statistics (BLS) occupational employment data.[5] The weights used are the

[5] U.S. BLS (1978, 1982). The occupational categories are Professional and Technical; Managerial and Administration; Sales; Clerical; Craft and Kindred; Nontransport Operatives; Transport Operatives; Nonfarm Labor; Private Household Service; Other Service; and Private Farm Labor. Thus, the index used here does not reflect mobility within these broad occupations. Existing data, however, show that the occupational standing of black women relative to white women has remained virtually unchanged between 1960 and 1981 in clerical and service occupations, which contain the bulk of black and white female workers. For example, the ratio of occupational indexes of black women to white women at the three-digit SIC level was .965 and 1.01 for clerical and service, respectively, in 1960, and 1.00 and 1.01 in 1981. (These indexes are calculated as in equation 1 using census and BLS data, with respective female occupational job median earnings serving as weights for each year. Details are available from the author on request.)

Due to changes in the occupational classification system introduced into the CPS in January 1971 and again in 1972, occupational data for these years are

respective occupational median earnings.[6] The female indexes employ the female occupational median wages, and the white male index is based on white male occupational median wages.[7] The absolute index shows an increase of 38% between 1960 and 1980. The growth rates are 19% and 16%, respectively, between 1960 and 1970 and between 1970 and 1980.

Compared with the index for white women, the index for black women increased by 29% from 1960 to 1980, and rose significantly over both decennial periods. A similar pattern emerges for black women relative to white men. Note, however, that the weights of the black female and white male indices differ, so the value of the relative index of 1.000 for 1980 in column 4 of Table 1, for example, does *not* indicate occupational equality between black women and white men. By comparison, a relative index value of 1.0 for black versus white women would suggest equality between them, since the weights are the same.

To separate out various influences on the index, the following structural model is estimated:

$$y_t = x_{1t}b_1 + x_{2t}b_2 + e_t, \quad t = 1, 2, \ldots, T \tag{5}$$

$$x_{2t} = x_{1t}g_1 + x_{4t}g_2 + v_t, \quad t = 1, 2, \ldots, T, \tag{6}$$

where y_t = relative black female fixed-weighted occupational index in period t; x_{1t} and x_{2t} are the row vectors of values in period t for the pre-determined and endogenous regressors of the structural equation (5), respectively; x_{4t} is the row vector of values of exogenous censoring variables influencing black female relative labor supply in period t; b_1 and b_2 are the respective regression coefficient vectors of the structural equation to be estimated; g_1 and g_2 denote the coefficient vectors of the auxiliary equation; e_t and v_t are the perturbation terms of the structural and auxiliary equations, respectively; and T is the sample period.

All specifications of the structural equation (5) contain the constant term, with the fully specified model incorporating the following as the predetermined variables: a post-1964 time trend LT65, an overall time trend LTIME, a cyclical economic condition variable GNPD1, and relative education LED as the human capital variable.[8] LT65 is intended to capture post-1964 antidiscrimination measures, and LTIME reflects pre-existing underlying trends unrelated to these measures. For example, occupational barriers could have been easing even prior to the mid-1960s due to changing sociopolitical conditions. In addition, migration of blacks to the North probably resulted in increases in

not strictly comparable with those for the earlier years. The changes, however, affected mostly Managers and Administrators (U.S. BLS 1979:207), which represented very small proportions of both black and white women. For example, the proportion of employed white women in Managers and Administrators ranged from 4.7% to 7.8% between 1958 and 1981, and that for black women ranged from 1.5% to 4.2%. Thus, the occupational index used here would be little affected.

[6] Using the Census Bureau's index of socioeconomic status (reflecting both income and skill requirements) in place of median earnings does not alter any of the basic results. (The results of that trial are available from the author on request.) One reason for preferring the results based on median earnings is that the socioeconomic status scores are based on men's educational and income characteristics, and men and women are generally located in different jobs even in the same occupation.

[7] Since women tend to be segregated into "female" jobs, the overall occupational medians were considered to be inappropriate weights. A similar argument could be made for black women relative to white women if these two groups are delineated by job segregation, as Malveaux (1985), for example, suggested. Unfortunately, there were too few black women in some occupations to obtain separate occupational medians for them. For those occupations with separate data, however, there were virtually no differences between black and white female median earnings.

Regarding the more recent period, consistent occupational earnings data by race and gender were available for the years 1973–78, so the averages for these years were used as the fixed weights. As note 6 indicates, however, the basic results are not sensitive to the precise choice of these weights. In fact, using 1959 occupational earnings as weights produced virtually the same occupational indexes.

[8] The present formulation is akin to the earnings model employed by Freeman (1978), for example. Precise definitions of all variables employed here, as well as data sources, are given in Table 2.

Table 2. Variable Definitions.

Variable Name	*Definition*
LT65	Log(1 + T65), where T65 is a post-1964 linear trend equaling 1 in 1965, 2 in 1966, etc.
LT75	Same as LT65, but trend begins in 1975.
LTIME	Log (TIME), where TIME is a linear trend equaling 1 in 1947, 2 in 1948, etc.
GNPDI	Deviation of the logarithm of real GNP (1972 $) from a linear trend.
LOCIND	Logarithm of relative black female (BF) occupational index.
LED	Logarithm of relative BF median years of schooling.
LEMP	Logarithm of relative BF civilian employment.
LPOP	Logarithm of relative BF civilian population.
LRAFDC	Logarithm of real average benefit per family of Aid to Families with Dependent Children, December each year (1972 $).
LRUI	Logarithm of real average weekly benefit under state Unemployment Insurance programs (1972 $).

Sources: GNPDI, LED, LEMP, and LPOP are based on data from *Employment and Training Report of the President;* LOCIND is calculated using data from U.S. BLS (1982, 1978); and data for LRAFDC and LRUI are from the *Social Security Bulletin* and *Historical Statistics of the United States.*

their educational quality not reflected in the quantity measure, LED (Smith 1984). Both LT65 and LTIME are, therefore, expected to exhibit positive coefficients.

The cyclical economic condition variable GNPDI should reflect cyclical censoring factors discussed above. If so, its coefficient will be negative. Similarly, the right-hand endogenous variable, relative employment (LEMP), is intended to purge the occupational index of possible changes in it that are unrelated to occupational mobility. This purge is expressed in the auxiliary equation (6), where the censoring variables x_{4t}, as in the earnings equations of Freeman (1978), are measured by the real average benefit per family of Aid to Families with Dependent Children (LRAFDC), real average weekly unemployment benefits (LRUI), and relative population (LPOP). As mentioned above, LRAFDC, LRUI, and LPOP may influence the relative supply of black women, which may in turn affect their distribution across occupations in a manner unrelated to occupational mobility. The inclusion of these variables in the auxiliary equation is intended to screen them from the index. (See Table 2 for a list of variables with definitions.)

The error term e_t was found to be generally serially correlated, and the Beach-MacKinnon maximum likelihood technique was employed as the estimating procedure. Because of the small-sample nature of the problem, this technique was judged preferable to the alternative Cochrane-Orcutt method.[9] (Beach and MacKinnon 1978.) Following Freeman's (1978) earnings specification, the double-log equation was used. Compared with other functional forms (such as the linear and exponential), the double-log specification exhibited consistently high values of its likelihood function at the maximum.

Results from the above estimation for the 1958–81 period are reported in Table 3 for restricted and fully specified versions of the structural equation. Equation (1A) of Table 3 reveals that with the cyclical nature of the economy controlled for, there was a significant positive overall trend in

[9] Beach and MacKinnon (1978) found that for small samples the full maximum likelihood estimator was more efficient than the estimator based on the Cochrane-Orcutt method, especially when the data are trended. Park and Mitchell (1980) confirmed this finding, but they also observed that OLS and *all* the various procedures normally used to correct for autocorrelation tend to underestimate the standard errors of the coefficients when data are trended, so that one must "apply a more stringent confidence level for hypothesis testing" (p. 199). Fortunately, the t-ratios associated with the key variable LT65 all exceed 5.0 (see Table 3), so even if Park and Mitchell's claim that the probability of a type I error was "about 26% in a test done at the 5% level" is granted, simple extrapolation shows that the LT65 coefficient is still significant at a two-tailed level better than .005. See the appendix for additional diagnostic results.

Table 3. Regression Results: Relative Black Female Occupational Mobility, 1958–1981. (t-Ratios in Parentheses)

Eqn.	*Const.*	LT65	LT75	LTIME	GNPDI	LED	LEMP	DW	SEE	$\overline{R}^2$	LLFTN
Relative to White Women:											
(1A)	−.638***	.055***	—	.120***	−.178***	—	—	2.07	.0084	.994	82.79
	(−11.78)	(9.62)		(5.98)	(−3.30)						
(2A)	−.763***	.054***	—	.157***	−.109*	−.137*	—	2.07	.0079	.995	84.86
	(−9.13)	(10.25)		(5.78)	(−1.74)	(−1.90)					
(3A)	−1.32**	.048***	—	.218***	−.080	−.287*	−.186	2.15	.0079	2SLS	85.43
	(−2.37)	(5.85)		(3.24)	(−1.15)	(−1.74)	(−1.02)				
(3A′)	.455**	.071***	—	—	−.206**	.288***	.374***	2.02	.0100	2SLS	79.34
	(2.40)	(15.32)			(−2.80)	(3.54)	(3.90)				
(4A)	−3.62***	—	−.000	.554***	.057	−.917***	−.847***	1.95	.0140	2SLS	71.78
	(−5.90)		(−0.36)	(8.30)	(0.44)	(−4.04)	(−3.31)				
(5A)	−1.19**	.049***	−.001	.235***	−.115	−.325*	−.092	2.22	.0077	2SLS	86.79
	(−2.22)	(6.32)	(−1.40)	(3.64)	(−1.65)	(−2.06)	(−0.49)				
Relative to White Men:											
(1B)	−.695***	.054***	—	.146***	−.282***	—	—	1.87	.0112	.983	75.97
	(−7.59)	(5.51)		(4.29)	(−3.18)						
(2B)	−.958***	.057***	—	.220***	−.150**	−.391***	—	2.13	.0082	.996	84.13
	(−12.62)	(11.30)		(8.89)	(−2.43)	(−5.04)					
(3B)	−9.71*	.057***	—	.222**	−.149**	−.395*	−.002	2.13	.0084	2SLS	84.14
	(−1.90)	(10.96)		(2.66)	(−2.30)	(−2.09)	(−.02)	—			
(3B′)	.396***	.058***	—	—	−.187**	.084	.255***	1.98	.0098	2SLS	79.89
	(3.53)	(8.17)			(−2.31)	(1.08)	(6.15)				
(4B)	−.331	—	−.000	.242**	−.069	−.178	.237	1.58	.0125	2SLS	74.02
	(−.48)		(−0.24)	(2.24)	(−0.55)	(−0.66)	(1.51)				
(5B)	−1.04**	.056***	−.001	.259***	−.169**	−.513**	.019	2.29	.0080	2SLS	85.89
	(−2.24)	(11.46)	(−1.64)	(3.41)	(−2.76)	(−2.92)	(0.20)				

Note: The dependent variable is the logarithm of the relative occupational index, LOCIND. All variables are defined in Table 2. DW, SEE, and $\overline{R}^2$ are the usual regression statistics. LLFTN is the logarithm of the likelihood function at its maximum.

* Statistically significant at the .10 level; ** at the .05 level; *** at the .01 level (two-tailed tests).

black female relative occupational mobility over the 1958–81 period, and an additional positive trend during the post-1964 era. The negative and statistically significant coefficient of GNPDI also suggests that economic downturns would *increase* the index by reducing the proportions of those black women located in low-wage occupations; the reverse would occur during upswings. This finding is consistent with the neoclassical hypothesis that disadvantaged and low-skilled workers constitute a disproportionate number of those laid off during recessions and added to the work force during upswings. Thus, the censoring hypothesis that the observed occupational mobility of black women would increase as a result of labor force withdrawals of the relatively low-skilled is confirmed cyclically.[10] This finding also underscores the need to use an occupational index based on annual rather than decennial data embodied in previous studies (for example, Medoff 1985), and to control for cyclical factors.

Equations (2A) and (3A) of Table 3 essentially tell the same story as (1A) with respect to the significance of both the overall and post-1964 time trends, although the coefficient of LT65 falls slightly and that of LTIME increases upon inclusion of the education and predicted employment variables. Also, the significance of the cyclical variable GNPDI is reduced, as is to be expected when educational and supply conditions are controlled for, since GNPDI presumably reflects cyclical components of these variables.

Unexpectedly, the coefficient of the educational variable LED is negative and statistically significant in both equation (2A) and equation (3A) of Table 3. A

[10] In an earlier study (Fosu 1987), I found a similar pattern for black female earnings gains.

closer inspection of the data shows that black women's median years of schooling were increasing steadily even before the mid-1960s, so that LED is highly correlated with the overall time trend LTIME (r = .95). This result suggests that LTIME probably incorporates education.

To gauge the extent to which LED might be a substitute for LTIME, equation (5) is re-estimated with LTIME omitted. The results, reported as (3A′) of Table 3, show a positive impact of education and an increase in the coefficient of the post-1964 trend LT65. Equation (3A′) represents a poor fit as compared with (3A), however, with SEE increasing and the null hypothesis that (3A′) is the "correct" specification being easily rejected.[11] This outcome suggests that although it may incorporate the time trend of black female education, as measured by the median years of schooling, LTIME probably also reflects additional important factors related to black female occupational mobility. Among these factors may be an improvement in the quality of black female education (Smith 1984) and easing of occupational barriers even prior to the antidiscrimination measures of the mid-1960s.[12] It is important to stress, however, that the post-1964 trend's coefficient is especially robust, irrespective of the exclusion status of the educational variable.

The addition of the employment variable LEMP, intended to reflect labor supply conditions, slightly raises the pre-existing underlying trend in the index of black female relative occupational mobility (compare equations 2A and 3A in Table 3). Although not statistically significant, the coefficient of LEMP exhibits a negative sign, as expected under the censoring hypothesis. That is, increases (decreases) in relative black female employment due to population and welfare program changes would augment (reduce) the relative representation in the labor force of low-skilled black women and would thus decrease (increase) the black female relative occupational index. Nevertheless, the entry of LEMP results in only a slight reduction in the coefficient of LT65, suggesting that the censoring hypothesis is not very potent for the post-1964 era, consistent with previous findings for black female earnings (Fosu 1987).

The results for black women relative to white men (equations 1B to 3B′ of Table 3) are similar to those discussed above. The educational variable still exhibits a significant negative coefficient, which becomes positive when LTIME is excluded (equation 3B versus 3B′ of Table 3). The impact of the cyclical variable GNPD1 continues to be negative, but it is even more significant here, suggesting the more "secondary" nature of black women's labor relative to white men's. In addition, the overall trend is shown to be significant. Above all, however, the post-1964 variable exhibits a robustly positive coefficient. Entering the employment variable intended to reflect supply censoring does not even reduce this coefficient.

Now consider the post-1964 trend's share of the contribution to the growth in the relative occupational mobility of black

---

[11] The likelihood ratio test statistic for the null hypothesis (H_0) that LTIME is excludable equals 12.18 for (3A) compared with (3A′). With χ^2 (1, .005) = 7.88, H_0 is easily refuted.

[12] Research on the impact of relative median years of schooling on relative earnings, for instance, has produced mixed results. For example, Freeman (1978) reported both negative and positive (but statistically insignificant) effects. Also, Brown's (1984) earnings equations yielded positive educational coefficients and negative LTIME coefficients together, suggesting a statistical tradeoff between the two variables.

In the separate black and white female equations, not reported here, the coefficient of LED is negative for black women but positive and significant for white women, lending some credence to the notion that LED reflects a deterioration in the quality of education for black but not white women. This hypothesis is particularly plausible with respect to the period since the mid-1960s, when black migration from the South was complete and the quality of black schools in the central cities of the North may have begun deteriorating as resources emigrated with white flight into the suburbs. (In a test with a possible bearing on this question, an interactive variable involving LED and a dummy variable for the post-1964 period exhibits a negative sign while the coefficient of LED becomes positive in an augmented equation involving equation 3A of Table 3. These results are not reported here, since the robustness of the LT65 coefficient is apparently invariant to the exclusion status of LED.)

women, as measured by the index constructed herein. The coefficient of LT65 from equation (3A) of Table 3 is .048, and the mean annual change in the logarithm of the relative black female/white female occupational index over the 1965–81 sample period is .012. Therefore, with a mean annual change in LT65 of .137, I estimate that roughly 55% of the 1965–81 growth in the occupational mobility of black women relative to that of white women may be attributable to independent effects of post-1964 trends. Similarly, those residual effects appear to account for about 52% of black women's gains relative to white men's.[13]

Previously reported evidence indicates that affirmative action raised the occupational mobility of black women in contract firms, both absolutely and relative to whites, between 1974 and 1980 (Leonard 1984). Might this finding imply an additional economywide trend during the post-1974 period? To test this hypothesis, a post-1974 time trend LT75 was introduced into the model. First, LT65 was replaced with LT75 (in the fully specified model). The results are reported as equations (4A) and (4B) in Table 3. Second, the fully specified model was augmented with LT75, and the estimates are presented as equations (5A) and (5B), Table 3.

Equations (4A) and (4B) of Table 3 show that replacing LT65 with LT75 yields a negative but very small and insignificant coefficient for the post-1974 trend. In addition, there appears to be a substantial reduction in the goodness of fit, with the standard error of estimate (SEE) rising, and the log of the likelihood function at its maximum (LLFTN) falling rather substantially. Augmenting the model with LT75 similarly shows a negative but statistically insignificant coefficient for LT75. SEE falls slightly, however, and LLFTN increases minimally. Employing a likelihood ratio test, the null hypothesis that LT75 does not belong in the model is not rejected; but the null hypothesis that LT65 is excludable from the model is easily refuted.[14]

Thus, the economywide improvement in the relative occupational mobility of black women, presumably attributable to post-1964 antidiscrimination measures, appears to have occurred much earlier than the time when affirmative action was found to be effective. It appears, therefore, that the observed post-1964 trend was probably attributable to Title VII.[15] On the other hand, the finding here of no further upward trend as of the mid-1970s, coupled with Leonard's (1984:378) report

[13] The mean annual logarithmic change in the relative black female/white male occupational index over the 1965–81 period is .015, and the coefficient of LT65 from equation (3B) of Table 3 is .057.

[14] The likelihood ratio test statistic for the null hypothesis that the coefficient of LT75 equals zero is 2.72 for (3A) compared with (5A); and it equals $-2(84.14-85.89) = 3.50$ for (3B) with (5B). Hence, the null hypothesis is not rejected at the .05 level, since $\chi^2(1, .05) = 3.84$. On the other hand, the test statistic equals 30.02 and 23.74 for (4A) with (5A) and (4B) with (5B), respectively, so that the null hypothesis that the coefficient of LT65 equals zero is easily rejected even at the .005 level, for $\chi^2(1, .005) = 7.88$.

[15] Given the imprecision with which such factors as human capital are measured, the exact magnitude of the contribution of antidiscrimination efforts to the above finding of a significant independent post-1964 impact cannot be inferred with certainty.

As is usual in the labor economics literature, measurement of the quality of education, for example, is extremely difficult. To some extent, however, educational quality should be reflected in the overall time trend LTIME. Smith (1984), for example, has argued that the quality of black education increased with black migration to the North. This migration appears to have ended by the 1960s, however (*ibid.*), and probably the improvement in the quality of black education tapered off at that time too. Indeed, given the increasing resource depletion arising from white emigration from the central cities, it would be difficult to argue that the relative quality of black female education has been increasing since the mid-1960s, and that this improvement is responsible for gains in black women's occupational mobility after 1964.

Furthermore, the length and quality of black female on-the-job training could have increased over the post-1964 period. If so, then LT65 would reflect these factors as well. To the extent that such improvements promoted occupational mobility and derived from sources other than antidiscrimination measures, LT65 would overstate the impact of the measures. On the other hand, if antidiscrimination programs also aided the relative educational attainment of black women, then LT65 might actually understate the effect of the programs when education is controlled for.

for the same period of a "differential impact of affirmative action over and above the effects of general policies," suggests that the impact of Title VII on black female occupational mobility waned as of the mid-1970s, and that declines in the pre-existing trend might have been observed in the absence of affirmative action.[16]

Conclusion

I have presented evidence showing increases in the occupational mobility of black women over the 1958–81 period, both in absolute terms and relative to the mobility of white women and white men. Positive trends are observed even prior to the antidiscrimination measures of the mid-1960s. On the other hand, an estimation that controls for prior trends as well as cyclical conditions of the economy, education, and even censoring supply factors reveals a significant post-1964 positive impact. Slightly over half of the increase in black women's relative occupational mobility over the 1965–81 period reflects this independent impact.

In the light of previous findings suggesting that increases in the occupational mobility of racial minorities might have occurred in contract firms as a result of affirmative action and not earlier than the mid-1970s (Burman 1973; Ashenfelter and Heckman 1976; Goldstein and Smith 1976; Heckman and Wolpin 1976; Leonard 1984), I tested the hypothesis of an economywide trend beginning in the mid-1970s. The results do not reveal an additional upward trend as of that period. The trend presumably attributable to post-1964 antidiscrimination measures is found to have begun much earlier than the mid-1970s.

Two conclusions seem to emerge. First, given the finding of previous studies that affirmative action was ineffective in the 1960s or early 1970s, the observed residual post-1964 trend is likely attributable to Title VII. Second, in the light of my finding of no further economywide trend as of the mid-1970s and Leonard's (1984) finding of a net positive effect of affirmative action over the same period, affirmative action may have picked up a slackening in the impact of Title VII as of the mid-1970s.

This study sheds light on the censoring hypothesis that the observed acceleration in the relative upward occupational mobility of black women after 1964 is attributable to labor supply decreases of the low-skilled rather than demand shifts. Some cyclical evidence is found to confirm this hypothesis, as proportionately more low-skilled black female workers presumably leave the labor force during downturns and enter it during upswings. The observed increase in black female upward occupational mobility after 1964, however, appears to be little influenced by these censoring supply factors.

Given the small sample in this time-series study, caution must be observed in judging to what extent the above finding of a substantial independent post-1964 impact can be ascribed to antidiscrimination efforts. As remarked, for instance, such factors as human capital are imprecisely measured. Thus, the present findings should be regarded as suggestive. Nevertheless, the results are consistent with, for example, Heckman and Payner's (1989:138) conclusion that in South Carolina, "human capital stories, supply shift stories, and tight market stories do not account for the black breakthrough," and there has been a "significant contribution of federal antidiscrimination programs" to gains in the occupational mobility of black Americans.

[16] Both Title VII and affirmative action (with application to blacks) were in effect as of the mid-1960s. Since the latter measure was found to be ineffective before the mid-1970s (see, for example, Ashenfelter and Heckman 1976; Goldstein and Smith 1976), the finding of an independent post-1964 upward trend is probably attributable to Title VII. Given Leonard's finding of a positive net effect of affirmative action as of the mid-1970s, however, one would expect an additional post-1974 upward trend if Title VII continued to exert an undiminished effect.

Appendix

Robustness of Results: A Further Assessment

This appendix further assesses the extent to which the validity of the main finding of the paper—a positive additional trend in black female occupational mobility beginning in the mid-1960s rather than in the mid-1970s—might be vitiated by problems of multicollinearity usually present in time series or by the use of the Beach-MacKinnon (BM) maximum likelihood estimation procedure. Reported in Table A1 (equations 1–6) are OLS results of the basic specifications of the black female/white female model; results of the black female/white male model equations are similar and are not reported here. I have chosen to use the more basic equations involving the three relevant trend variables—LTIME, LT65, and LT75—so that problems of multicollinearity can be more easily detected.

Also reported in Table A1 (equations 1–6) are variance inflation factors VIF (VIF $= (1 - R_j^2)^{-1}$, where R_j^2 is the R^2 from regressing the jth regressor on the remaining regressors in the equation) measuring the degree of multicollinearity. There is no general agreement in the econometric literature concerning what values of VIF are harmful, but as a rule of thumb, a value below 10 might generally be considered safe (Kennedy 1985:153). More important, these VIFs should provide some information on the *relative* collinearity of the regressors and thus on the relative precision of their respective estimated coefficients.

Equation (1) of Table A1 is the most basic version of the model. It employs the post-1964 and post-1974 trend variables, LT65 and LT75, as the only regressors other than the constant. Although the coefficients of both variables are positive and statistically significant, the LT75 coefficient is smaller and less significant, representing only about one-sixth of the value of the LT65 coefficient. Furthermore, the VIFs are rather low for this equation (1.81, i.e., $R_j^2 = .45$), so multicollinearity should not be a major concern. When the cyclical variable GNPDI is

Table A1. Additional Regression Results and VIF (Absolute t-Ratios in Parentheses)

									VIF		
Eqn.	*Const.*	LT65	LT75	LTIME	GNPDI	DW	SEE	$\bar{R}^2$	LT65	LT75	LTIME
(1)	−.311	.081	.013	—	—	1.35	.012	.986	1.81	1.81	—
		(26.94)	(2.85)								
(2)	−.312	.083	.011	—	−.071	1.42	.012	.987	2.15	2.28	—
		(24.73)	(2.17)		(0.75)						
(3)	−.590	.056	.007	.103	—	1.63	.009	.993	15.60	2.08	17.70
		(8.27)	(2.04)	(4.11)							
(4)	−.645	.054	—	.123	−.170	2.15	.008	.994	15.40	—	15.40
		(8.84)		(5.71)	(2.95)						
(5)	−1.41	—	−.0014	.309	−.175	0.48	.019	.969	—	2.70	2.55
			(0.16)	(15.96)	(1.20)						
(6)	−.621	.055	.003	.114	−.141	2.17	.008	.994	15.70	2.75	18.59
		(8.82)	(0.87)	(4.81)	(2.11)						
(6i)	−.617	.055	.003	.113	−.150	—	.008	.995	—	—	—
		(9.31)	(0.89)	(4.93)	(2.34)						
(6ii)	−.616	.055	.003	.112	−.152	2.06	.008	.995	—	—	—
		(9.41)	(0.89)	(4.97)	(2.31)						
(6iii)	−.615	.056	.003	.112	−.152	2.06	.008	.995	—	—	—
		(9.45)	(0.89)	(4.98)	(2.32)						
(7i)	.010	.029	−.009	—	—	—	.010	.312	—	—	—
		(2.58)	(0.84)								
(7ii)	.010	.031	−.009	—	—	2.18	.010	.369	—	—	—
		(2.81)	(0.92)								
(7iii)	.010	.032	−.009	—	—	2.16	.010	.378	—	—	—
		(2.88)	(.93)								

The dependent variable is the logarithm of the relative black female/white female occupational index LOCIND. All variables are defined in Table 2. First differences are used in (7i)–(7iii). DW, SEE, and $\bar{R}^2$ are the usual regreession statistics. Equations (1)–(6) are estimated using OLS; (6i)–(6iii) are estimated using the Prais-Winsten, Maximum Likelihood, and Nonlinear Least Squares procedures, respectively; (7i)–(7iii) are estimated using the same procedures as (6i)–(6iii).

VIF is the variance inflated factor, defined as $(1\text{-}R^2_j)^{-1}$, *where* R^2_j is the resulting coefficient of determination when the jth independent variable is regressed on the remaining explanatory variables in the regression equation.

added as a regressor in equation (2), the results are similar to those of equation (1).

In equation (3), the overall time trend LTIME is included in addition to LT65 and LT75. The goodness of fit of the model improves slightly, as SEE is lowered. The coefficient of LTIME is positive and significant, whereas the coefficients of LT65 and LT75 are reduced in magnitude, suggesting that the larger values of the coefficients for these two time trends in equation (1) were probably reflecting preexisting time trends as well. The LT75 coefficient continues to be small in both magnitude and statistical significance as compared with the LT65 coefficient. The VIF also remains small for LT75 (2.1, i.e., $R_j^2 = .52$), further confirming that its estimated coefficient is probably not subject to much imprecision. On the other hand, the relatively high VIF values for LT65 and LTIME (17.7 max, i.e., $R_j^2 = .94$), not unusual for time-series studies, suggest a tradeoff between the coefficients of these two variables (LT65 and LTIME are positively correlated). The .056 estimate for the coefficient of LT65 in equation (3) may actually be on the low end, with the possibility that its "true" value resides between .056 and .081. Apparently, whereas there is relatively little (positive) correlation between LT75 and LT65 or between LT75 and LTIME, LT65 and LTIME are relatively highly (positively) correlated. The important point, however, is that equations (1) and (3) appear to produce similar estimates of the LT65 coefficient.

The remaining equations (4–6) together suggest that LT75 is superfluous, but that LT65 is not. These results are identical to those based on the more complicated equations of Table 3. In particular, including LT75 does not improve the fit of the model, nor does it appreciably alter the other coefficients (compare equation 6 to equation 4). The VIF values for LT65 and LTIME are still relatively large, while that for LT75 remains low (equation 6), again suggesting that the estimated coefficient for LT75 is reasonably precise and that there may be a tradeoff between the LT65 and LTIME coefficient estimates. On the other hand, excluding LT65 from the model results in a substantial reduction in the goodness of fit (equation 5 versus equation 6). Indeed, the very low DW value of equation (5) suggests a missing variable, namely, LT65. The coefficient of LT75 remains small and insignificant whether or not LT65 is in the equation, and the VIF for LT75 is still rather low, suggesting that multicollinearity is unlikely to be responsible for this result.

As a further test of the invariance of the paper's main findings to the estimating method, the fully specified basic model (equation 6, Table A1) was reestimated using the Prais-Winsten (Yule-Walker) procedure, the maximum likelihood method, and nonlinear (unconditional) least squares. The respective results are reported as equations (6i)–(6iii) in Table A1. Not only are all three sets of results alike, but they are similar to the OLS results (equation 6 of Table A1) and the BM results in the text. In particular, these results confirm that whereas the post-1964 trend variable exhibits a highly significant positive coefficient, the post-1974 trend variable does not.

A key finding of this study is that an additional positive trend in black female occupational mobility began in the mid-1960s rather than the mid-1970s. To further establish that this finding is not attributable simply to the inclusion of the overall time trend LTIME as an independent variable, LTIME was omitted from the equation, and the dependent variable LOCIND as well as both independent variables LT65 and LT75 were detrended using first differencing. (Nelson and Kang 1984; Nelson and Plosser 1982; Plosser and Schwert 1978.) The results based on the Prais-Winsten, maximum likelihood, and nonlinear least squares procedures are reported in equations (7i)–(7iii) of Table A1, respectively. Again, the coefficient of (differenced) LT65 is positive and statistically significant, whereas that of (differenced) LT75 is negative, though insignificant. Furthermore, a graphical depiction of the relationship in Figure A1 shows that an acceleration in the economywide black female/white female relative occupational mobility index began in 1964 rather than in the mid-1970s.

In summary, the results reported here conform with those in the text and suggest that the main findings of the paper are not attributable to the use of the BM procedure to correct for autocorrelation or to problems of multicollinearity. In particular, as the VIF values indicate, the finding of little or no additional black female occupational mobility trend as of the mid-1970s does not appear to result from severe multicollinearity. Furthermore, although the important point here is that the coefficient of LT65 seems rather robust, the relative positive collinearity between LT65 and LTIME indicates a possible tradeoff between the coefficients of these two variables, so that the "true" coefficient of LT65 may actually be slightly larger than the one used in the paper (.048). Most important, LT75 is found to be extraneous in the mobility equation, contrary to the finding for LT65, and the degree of collinearity between LT75 and LT65, as well as between LT75 and LTIME, is rather low. Finally, this pattern of results persists despite the use of various estimating methods and a detrending of the relevant series, and it is evident in a graphical depiction of the relationship. Thus, the primary finding of the paper that there was probably an additional upward trend in black female occupational mobility beginning in the mid-1960s rather than in the mid-1970s appears to withstand additional scrutiny.

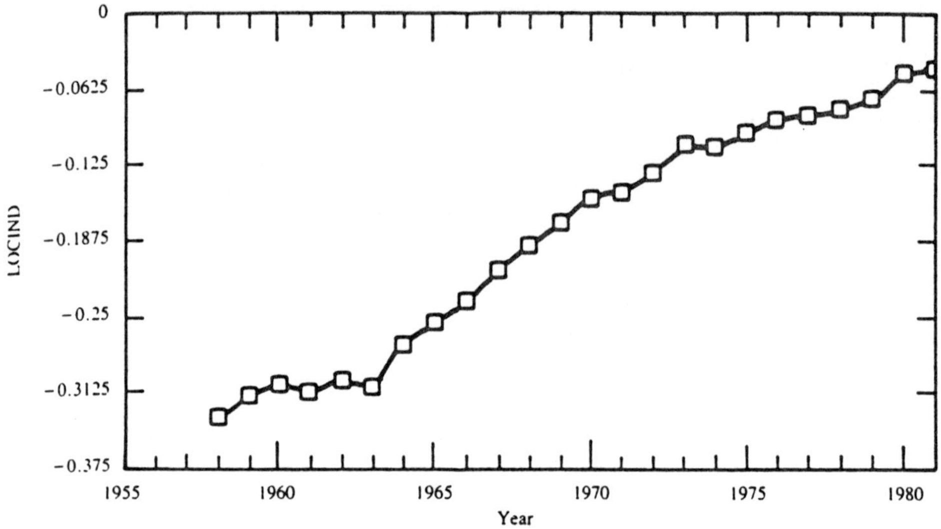

LOCIND is the logarithm of the black female/white female relative occupational index; see Table 2 for details.

Figure A1. LOCIND vs. Time.

REFERENCES

Albelda, Randy P. 1986. "Occupational Segregation by Race and Gender, 1958–1981." *Industrial and Labor Relations Review*, Vol. 39, No. 3 (April), pp. 404–11.

Ashenfelter, Orley, and James Heckman. 1976. "Measuring the Effect of an Antidiscrimination Program." In Orley Ashenfelter and James Blum, eds., *Evaluating the Labor Market Effects of Social Programs*. Princeton, N.J.: Industrial Relations Section, Princeton University, pp. 46–84.

Beach, Charles M., and James G. MacKinnon. 1978. "A Maximum Likelihood Procedure for Regression with Autocorrelated Errors." *Econometrica*, Vol. 46, No. 1 (January), pp. 51–58.

Beller, Andrea H. 1982. "Trends in Occupational Segregation by Sex: 1960–1990." Working Paper PS #8203, School of Social Sciences, University of Illinois–Urbana-Champaign, October.

———. 1984. "Trends in Occupational Segregation by Sex and Race, 1960–1981." In Barbara F. Reskin, ed., *Sex Segregation in the Workplace: Trends, Explanations, Remedies*. Washington, D.C.: National Academic Press, pp. 11–26.

Brown, Charles. 1984. "Black-White Earnings Ratios Since the Civil Rights Act of 1964: The Importance of Labor Market Dropouts." *Quarterly Journal of Economics*, Vol. 99, No. 1 (February), pp. 379–87.

Burman, George. 1973. "The Economics of Discrimination: The Impact of Public Policy." Ph.D. thesis, Graduate School of Business, University of Chicago.

Butler, Richard, and James J. Heckman. 1977. "The Government's Impact on the Labor Market Status of Black Americans: A Critical Review." In Leonard J. Hausman et al., eds., *Equal Rights and Industrial Relations*. Madison, Wis.: Industrial Relations Research Association, pp. 235–81.

Cain, Glen. 1976. "The Challenge of Segmented Labor Market Theories to Orthodox Theory: A Survey." *Journal of Economic Literature*, Vol. 14, No. 4 (December), pp. 1215–57.

Darity, William. 1982. "The Human Capital Approach to Black–White Earnings Inequality: Some Unsettled Questions." *Journal of Human Resources*, Vol. 17, No. 1 (Winter), pp. 72–93.

Doeringer, Peter B., and Michael J. Piore. 1971. *Internal Labor Markets and Manpower Analysis*. Lexington, Mass.: Lexington Books.

Duncan, Gus Dudley, and Beverly Duncan. 1955. "A Methodological Analysis of Segregation Indexes." *American Sociological Review*, Vol. 20 (April), pp. 210–17.

England, Paula. 1982. "The Failure of Human Capital Theory to Explain Occupational Sex Segregation." *Journal of Human Resources*, Vol. 17, No. 3 (Summer), pp. 358–70.

Fosu, Augustin Kwasi. 1987. "Explaining Post-1964 Earnings Gains by Black Women: Race or Sex?" *Review of Black Political Economy*, Vol. 15, No. 3 (Winter), pp. 41–55.

Freeman, Richard B. 1978. "Time Series Evidence on Black Economic Progress: Shifts in Demand or in Supply." Discussion Paper No. 632, Harvard University (July).

Goldstein, Morris, and Robert S. Smith. 1976. "The Estimated Impact of the Antidiscrimination Program Aimed at Federal Contractors." *Industrial and*

Labor Relations Review, Vol. 29, No. 4 (July), pp. 523–43.

Heckman, James J., and Brook S. Payner. 1989. "Determining the Impact of Federal Antidiscrimination Policy on the Economic Status of Blacks: A Study of South Carolina." *American Economic Review*, Vol. 79, No. 1 (March), pp. 138–77.

Heckman, James J., and Kenneth I. Wolpin. 1976. "Does the Contract Compliance Program Work? An Analysis of Chicago Data." *Industrial and Labor Relations Review*, Vol. 29, No. 4 (July), pp. 544–64.

Kennedy, Peter. 1985. *A Guide to Econometrics*, 2nd ed. Cambridge: MIT Press.

Leonard, Jonathan S. 1984. "Employment and Occupational Advance Under Affirmative Action." *Review of Economics and Statistics*, Vol. 66, No. 3 (August), pp. 377–85.

Malveaux, Julianne. 1985. "The Economic Interests of Black and White Women: Are They Similar?" *Review of Black Political Economy*, Vol. 14, No. 1 (Summer), pp. 5–27.

Marshall, Ray. 1974. "The Economics of Racial Discrimination: A Survey." *Journal of Economic Literature*, Vol. 12, No. 3 (September), pp. 849–71.

Medoff, Marshall H. 1985. "Discrimination and the Occupational Progress of Blacks Since 1950." *American Journal of Economics and Sociology*, Vol. 44, No. 3 (July), pp. 294–303.

Nelson, C. R., and H. Kang. 1984. "Pitfalls in the Use of Time as an Explanatory Variable in Regression." *Journal of Business and Economic Statistics*, Vol. 2, No. 1 (January), pp. 73–82.

Nelson, C. R., and C. I. Plosser. 1982. "Trends and Random Walks in Macroeconomic Time Series: Some Evidence and Implications." *Journal of Monetary Economics*, Vol. 10, No. 2 (September), pp. 139–62.

Park, Rolla Edward, and Bridger M. Mitchell. 1980. "Estimating the Autocorrelated Error Model with Trended Data." *Journal of Econometrics*, Vol. 13, No. 2 (June), pp. 185–201.

Plosser, C. I. and G. W. Schwert. 1978. "Money, Income and Sunspots: Measuring Economic Relationships and the Effects of Differencing." *Journal of Monetary Economics*, Vol. 4, No. 4 (November), pp. 637–60.

Smith, James P. 1984. "Race and Human Capital." *American Economic Review*, Vol. 74, No. 4 (September), pp. 685–98.

Smith, James P., and Finis R. Welch. 1989. "Black Economic Progress After Myrdal." *Journal of Economic Literature*, Vol. 27, No. 2 (June), pp. 519–64.

Social Security Administration. 1958–82. *Social Security Bulletin*. Washington, D.C.: GPO.

U.S. Bureau of Labor Statistics. 1978. *Handbook of Labor Statistics*. Washington, D.C.: GPO.

______. 1979. *Employment and Earnings*. Washington, D.C.: GPO.

______. 1982. *Labor Force Statistics Derived from the Current Population Survey: A Databook*, Vol. 1. Washington, D.C.: GPO.

U.S. Bureau of the Census. 1975. *Historical Statistics of the United States, Colonial Times to 1970*. Bicentennial edition, Part 2. Washington, D.C.: GPO.

U.S. Department of Labor. 1976–82. *Employment and Training Report of the President*. Washington, D.C.: GPO.

[27]

BLACK-WHITE EARNINGS RATIOS SINCE THE CIVIL RIGHTS ACT OF 1964: THE IMPORTANCE OF LABOR MARKET DROPOUTS*

CHARLES BROWN

Published median earnings of wage and salary workers by race and sex are based on distributions that exclude those without earnings and those not employed as wage and salary workers at the time of the survey. It has been argued that the changing importance of these exclusions, rather than any improvement in the distribution of offered wages for blacks, accounts for the apparent increase in black-white relative median earnings. This paper presents a new method for correcting the published medians for such censoring. The apparent improvement in relative earnings is reduced but not eliminated by the correction.

Have the federal equal employment opportunity regulations that took effect in 1965[1] had the desired effect of raising relative minority earnings? While cross-section studies have given conflicting indications, time series studies have generally suggested an affirmative conclusion. Early studies [Freeman, 1973; Vroman, 1974 and 1975] found increases in relative black-white earnings in the post-1964 period after controlling for cyclical conditions, relative education, and previous trends. While the improved situation of the late 1960s was sometimes attributed instead to the unusually prolonged tight labor markets of the period (see the "Discussion" following Freeman's 1973 paper), rising relative earnings during the 1974–1975 recession seriously eroded the credibility of this view [Butler-Heckman, 1977].

In two recent papers Butler and Heckman [1977, 1978] have proposed an alternative interpretation of the time-series evidence on relative earnings of blacks and whites. While Freeman argued

*The research reported here is part of the NBER's research program in Labor Studies, funded by the Ford Foundation, Grant No. 795-0225. The views expressed are my own, and not those of the NBER. I have benefited from the comments of seminar participants at the NBER and the University of Chicago, and Jerome Culp, Frank Levy, Kathy Swartz, Wayne Vroman, and two referees on earlier drafts of this paper. Norman Bowers, Mary Henson, George Patterson, Paul Ryscavage, and Sylvia Terry provided unpublished data; their help was essential to the paper's completion.

1. Title VII of the Civil Rights Act of 1964 became effective July 2, 1965. It originally covered employers with 100 or more employees, but the cutoff was reduced to 25 in 1968. In 1972, Title VII was amended to extend to all employers with 15 or more employees. Executive Order 11246 was issued in 1965 and amended by Executive Order 11375 in 1968. These orders required that firms adopt nondiscriminatory hiring policies as a condition for federal contracts. In 1968, regulations implementing these orders added the requirement that firms develop affirmative action plans, "including where there are deficiencies, the development of specific goals and timetables for the prompt achievement of full and equal employment opportunity."

The Quarterly Journal of Economics, February 1984 CCC 0033-5533/84/010031-14$04.00

that rising black-white earnings ratios since 1964 were evidence of the effectiveness of Federal antidiscrimination efforts in increasing the relative demand for blacks, Butler-Heckman argued that they are largely a reflection of supply-side forces that resulted from the expansion of transfer programs. Their interpretation actually encompasses two separate responses—the economic response of the price of labor to changes in supply, and the effect of sample censoring on median earnings as low earners withdraw from the labor market and the median (which is based on those with earnings) rises. Not surprisingly, attempts to distinguish on the basis of time series data among three competing forces (antidiscrimination policies, supply shifts, and censoring effects), which are to some extent concentrated in the same (post-1964) period, have been inconclusive.

The purpose of this paper is to consider a different approach to disentangling these forces. The key is to attempt to correct for the censoring effect by using information on earnings distributions to assess its impact. After reviewing the earlier papers in greater detail (Section I), the alternative approach to handling the censoring problem is outlined in Section II. The impacts of demand- and supply-side forces on relative black-white earnings are then considered in Section III. Conclusions are presented in Section IV.

I. Summary of Previous Work

Freeman's finding of post-1964 improvements in the relative position of blacks was based on regressing the logarithm of the ratio of black-white median wage and salary earnings[2] on a measure of antidiscrimination policy (logarithm of per capita cumulative EEOC expenditures, or a post-1964 time trend) and other variables (such as a simple trend, a measure of cyclical factors, and the median-education ratio). The finding of significant positive coefficients for the antidiscrimination policy variable is taken as evidence of the success of these policies.

While others have challenged this interpretation of the post-1964 improvement (attributing it to changing attitudes or to improvements in black education not captured by relative median education), Butler and Heckman [1977] argued that the time series evidence does not show that any real improvement occurred. They noted that the creation of federal antidiscrimination programs coin-

2. Following other authors, we shall use "black" where "nonwhites" would be more precise. In 1978, 85 percent of the nonwhites who appear in the median earnings series used below were black.

cided with the expansion of antipoverty programs, especially transfer programs. Such programs would be expected to reduce labor force participation among those who would otherwise receive low wages. Withdrawal from the labor market has two effects: (1) the supply of labor is reduced; (2) holding the distribution of offered wages constant, the withdrawal of low earners increases published median earnings, because the medians are based on those with earnings. Given that on average blacks face lower offered wages than whites, increasing transfers would have a relatively larger effect on black labor market participation. This would lead to a reduction in the relative supply of black labor (and assuming that blacks and whites were not perfect substitutes, an increase in relative offered wages); relative median earnings would increase further due to the more severely censored distributions. Consequently, relative median earnings of blacks could have risen in the post-1964 period even in the absence of the demand-side factors emphasized by Freeman. While Butler and Heckman [1977, p. 267] concede that antidiscrimination policies *may* have improved the position of young blacks, they conclude that there is no evidence that blacks as a group have benefited from such policies, once the supply-side factors are properly taken into account.

Freeman [1978, p. 9] observed that the relative supply of black males and females did not decline since 1964—falling relative labor force participation was just offset by the increasing black share of labor force age population. A backward shift in the supply curve would have raised relative black earnings, but, unless the demand curve also shifted, relative employment would have fallen. Butler and Heckman [1978] reemphasize the censoring issue, noting that this effect depends on the fraction of potential labor market participants who do not in fact participate, not on relative supplies per se.

Three observations about the censoring issue seem important:

1. Censoring effects do depend on the fraction of the potential distribution that is nonparticipant, so they are worrisome even if relative supplies are not shifting. Moreover, because (unlike relative supplies) censoring appears to show the "right" time pattern (i.e., predict rising black-white earnings ratios since 1964), this is likely to be the more important half of the Butler-Heckman argument.

2. Neither Butler-Heckman nor Freeman has discussed the "universe" for which the published median wage and salary earnings series is calculated, and the series they use to account for censoring are somewhat loosely related to that universe. Butler-Heckman correctly note that those who have no wage and salary earnings in year

t are ignored in computing median earnings in year *t*. However, the published series include only those with wage and salary earnings in year *t who are employed as wage and salary workers in March* (the survey month) *of the following year.*[3] The italicized restriction is considerably more important in practice than the positive wage and salary earnings condition. In 1968–1979, 95 to 99 percent of white and black males, and 94 to 96 percent of white and black females employed as wage and salary workers in March had wage and salary earnings in the previous year. However, only 73 to 84 percent of white and black males, and 70 to 79 percent of white and black females who had wage and salary earnings during the year were employed as wage and salary workers the following March.[4] Since wage and salary employment in March of the following year is the key factor in determining whether an individual "appears" in the median earnings calculation, it is the correct series for dealing with censoring. Butler-Heckman and Freeman, in contrast, use annual averages of monthly employment or labor force participation data (for year *t*).[5]

3. With twenty-five or thirty time-series observations, one is unlikely to be able to estimate accurately Freeman's demand-side effects *and* the Butler-Heckman relative supply *and* censoring effects, especially when a time trend is included as a "nuisance" variable [Butler and Heckman, 1978, pp. 33–34 and 45; Freeman, 1978, pp. 16 and 19]. Consequently, it seems desirable to estimate the impact of one of these factors with outside information, in order to estimate the importance of the remaining influences with greater precision from the time series data.

3. The table in question is headed "... Median Wage or Salary Income [in year *t*] of Wage and Salary Workers." A head note indicated that "figures are restricted to persons who were wage and salary workers at the time of the survey" from 1958–1962. From 1967–1978 (except 1975), the head note indicates that the table "excludes those with no wage or salary income in [year *t*]." However, Appendix notes make it clear that both restrictions apply. For example, the 1974 volume states "medians for wage and salary income... are based on the distribution of persons ... having [this] type of income.... The data on ... class of worker... in [the median wage and salary income table] refers to the job held during the survey week."

4. The number of wage and salary workers with wage and salary earnings in the previous year by race and sex are from unpublished Census Bureau tabulations. The numbers of wage and salary workers by race and sex are from unpublished Bureau of Labor Statistics tabulations. Numbers of persons with wage and salary earnings are taken from published Current Population Survey tables. These and other data appear in an Appendix to this paper, available from the author.

5. Even as a measure of the number of persons with positive earnings, these annual averages of monthly values are appropriate only to the extent that employment or nonemployment is quite permanent throughout the year.

II. Dealing with Censoring

The solution to the censoring problem outlined below accepts median wage and salary earnings in the untruncated distributions as the "correct" measure of labor market position, and attempts to adjust the published medians to approximate the correct values based on knowledge about the distribution of wage and salary earnings.

Define

y = logarithm of wage and salary earnings
$F(y)$ = cumulative distribution function for the uncensored distribution of y
x = fraction of potential workers who are employed as wage and salary workers.

The "uncensored" distribution includes all those who would have had positive earnings in the absence of the supply-side effects discussed above. Median ln-earnings in this hypothetical distribution y_M is defined by $F(y_M) = 0.50$. Now *assume* that *all* of the induced non-participation involves individuals in the low-earning portion of this hypothetical distribution. Then the median of the observed distribution y_0 is defined by

(1) $$F(y_0) = (1 - x) + (x/2) = 0.50 + (1 - x)/2.$$

Because median ln-earnings equals ln (median earnings), y_0 is simply the logarithm of the published median earnings value.

This is illustrated in Figure I. The shaded area represents the $100(1 - x)$ percent of potential earners who are not included in the wage and salary earnings distribution. The assumption that all of these nonearners would be in the lower tail of the distribution if they were included is reflected in the figure. The logarithm of the published median y_0 divides the unshaded area into two equal por-

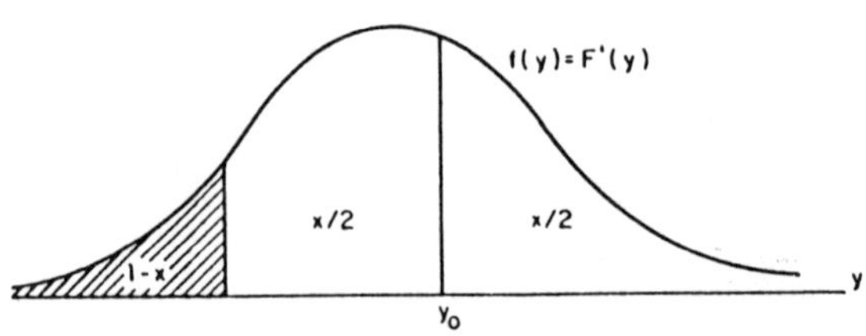

FIGURE I

tions, each representing $100(x/2)$ percent. Consequently, in terms of the untruncated distribution, $F(y_0)$ equals $(1-x)+x/2$ or $0.50+(1-x)/2$.

Figure I shows all $100(1-x)$ percent of potential workers being assigned to the left-hand tail of the distribution. This is for diagrammatic convenience; any assignment to the left of y_M would produce the same result.[6] It is clear from the figure that this assumption produces the largest possible correction in median ln-earnings, given x.[7]

If $F'(y)$ is relatively constant in the range between y_0 and y_M, we can use the first-order Taylor series approximation:

$$F(y_0) \approx F(y_M) + (y_0 - y_M) \cdot F'(y_M). \tag{2}$$

Substituting $F(y_0) = 0.50 + (1-x)/2$ and $F(y_M) = 0.50$, and solving for y_M gives

$$y_M = y_0 - (1-x)/[2F'(y_M)]. \tag{3}$$

The assumption that F' is nearly constant between y_0 and y_M (so that a first-order approximation will be accurate) is quite reasonable.[8] It will also be assumed that $F'(y_M)$ is constant over time for each group. (While this is less certain, previous studies, which estimated truncation effects from a time-invariant regression coefficient, have implicitly made this assumption.) Letting C^W and C^B equal $1/[2F'(y_M)]$ for whites and blacks, respectively, we can write the "corrected" log-earnings ratio in terms of the published data as

6. Those not included in the distributions underlying the published medians can be divided into two groups: Those without earnings, and those with earnings who were not employed as wage and salary workers the following March. For the second group, wage and salary earnings distributions are available for 1966–1978. For all four race-sex groups, in both 1966 and 1978, roughly one eighth of these individuals had earnings that exceeded the published median. *If* one eighth of *all* those who are censored from the distribution would appear above the median in the uncensored distribution, then the correction used in this paper is one *fourth* too large.

7. Levy [1980] and Darity and Myers [1980] make a similar assumption when they recompute medians [Levy] or means [Darity-Myers] counting zero earnings as "true" zeros. The analogous problem of dealing with nonearners in micro-data earnings equations is considered by Kneiser, Padilla, and Polachek [1978, pp. 267–70] and Jencks [1979, pp. 283–84].

8. This assumption requires that F' be constant as one moves to the left of y_0. This is only weakly related to whether y is symmetrically distributed. Symmetry (of the censored distribution) means that $F'=0$ at y_0, but does not prevent F' from declining rapidly to the left of y_0. On the other hand, an asymmetric distribution can be relatively flat around y_0. A rough sense of the appropriateness of this assumption can be reached by calculating the average value of F' over the interval containing y_0, and then over that and the next-lowest interval. If F' is constant in this region, the ratio of these two average values would be 1.0. Using 1978 data for the distributions described below, the ratio was 0.94 for white and black males, 0.88 for white females, and 0.85 for black females.

$$y_M^B - y_M^W = y_0^B - y_0^W - [C^B(1 - x^B) - C^W(1 - x^W)]. \quad (4)$$

In the calculations below, x_t is measured by the fraction of the population employed as wage and salary workers in March of year $t + 1$, relative to the year in which that fraction was highest. If r_t is the wage and salary employment-population ratio in year $t + 1$, and r^* the highest value of r_t over the sample period, then $x_t = r_t/r^*$. Because wage and salary employment by race and sex are available (from unpublished BLS tabulations of CPS data) for 1954–1979, x_t can be calculated for 1953–1978. Over this period, x_t ranged from a maximum of 1.0 for each race-sex group to a minimum of 0.92 for white males, 0.80 for black males, 0.63 for white females, and 0.80 for black females. For white males, the series displays no overall or post-1964 trend, while a post-1964 decline is evident for black males. Rising female labor force participation is reflected in an upward overall trend for white and black females; white (but not black) females also show a positive post-1964 trend. Thus, a comparison of relative participation (as measured by this series) for blacks and whites of either sex reveals the pattern described by Butler-Heckman in the post-1964 period.

Unpublished distributions from which the published wage-and-salary earnings medians were calculated are available for 1966–1978. If p is the relative frequency for the censored distribution in the interval y_a to y_b that includes both y_M and y_0, then xp is the corresponding frequency in the uncensored distribution. F' can then be calculated as $xp/(y_b - y_a)$. The resulting values of F' were used to calculate values of the correction factor C, which is shown in Table I. On average, C is larger for black males than for white males, while white female and black female values are quite similar.

The mean values of C in Table I and the wage salary employment series x_t were used to calculate "corrected" median earnings ratios, based on equation (4). These are shown in Table II, along with the "uncorrected" ratios based on the published median wage and salary earnings series.

III. Trends in Corrected Median Earnings Ratios

The logarithms of these uncorrected and corrected ratios were used to estimate time series equations similar to those used by Freeman and Butler-Heckman (Table III). Odd-numbered columns present results with uncorrected dependent variables, and even-numbered columns use the corrected earnings ratios.

TABLE I

VALUES OF C, THE TRUNCATION CORRECTION FACTOR

Year	White males	Black males	White females	Black females
1966	0.576	1.000	1.399	1.675
1967	0.609	0.904	1.372	1.245
1968	0.549	0.905	1.274	1.124
1969	0.620	0.891	1.419	1.453
1970	0.646	0.995	1.360	1.215
1971	0.689	1.018	1.232	1.245
1972	0.758	1.058	1.320	1.125
1973	0.837	1.069	1.392	1.187
1974	0.714	1.141	1.259	1.366
1975	0.806	1.224	1.229	1.167
1976	0.795	1.260	1.116	0.996
1977	0.786	1.183	1.157	0.981
1978	0.884	1.271	0.974	0.873
Mean, 1966–1978	0.713	1.071	1.269	1.204

Columns 1 and 3 update Freeman's original [1973, 1977] regressions, which controlled for trend, cyclical effects, and (in column 3) relative median years of schooling. *DGNP* is the cyclical variable, defined as the deviation of the logarithm of real GNP from trend. A trend that begins in 1965 is included to capture the effect of the Civil Rights Act and the Contract Compliance program.[9] In column 1, relative black earnings rise by an additional 1.6 percent per year for males, and 2.2 percent for females, in the post-1964 period. In column 2, where the dependent variable is corrected for censoring, this post-1964 trend falls to 1.0 percent for males, and 1.1 percent for females. Thus, *60 percent of the male post-1964 trend and half of the corresponding trend for females survives correction for censoring.* The estimated importance of cyclical fluctuations also increases when censoring is accounted for, especially for males. This is expected, since black employment is more cyclically sensitive, and we assigned those not employed (in March $t + 1$) to the lower tail of the distribution.

Relative median education is added in columns 3 and 4. While the additional variable has the anticipated positive effect, it has little effect on the estimated post-1964 trend for males. The post-1964

9. The post-1964 trend is easier to interpret than Freeman's EEOC expenditure variable. It also avoids the arbitrariness of defining the logarithm of zero for the pre-1965 period.

TABLE II

BLACK-WHITE EARNINGS RATIOS

Year	Males		Females	
	Published	"Corrected"	Published	"Corrected"
1953	0.594	0.576	0.485	0.626
1954	0.568	0.567	0.447	0.562
1955	0.588	0.596	0.433	0.552
1956	0.562	0.575	0.445	0.571
1957	0.554	0.528	0.455	0.568
1958	0.580	0.559	0.446	0.566
1959	0.580	0.542	0.532	0.642
1960	0.599	0.563	0.503	0.626
1961	0.570	0.543	0.513	0.626
1962	0.553	0.523	0.531	0.638
1963	0.568	0.552	0.532	0.634
1964	0.585	0.564	0.581	0.709
1965	0.576	0.558	0.575	0.708
1966	0.594	0.562	0.643	0.777
1967	0.639	0.612	0.703	0.830
1968	0.664	0.627	0.721	0.838
1969	0.666	0.625	0.792	0.904
1970	0.665	0.612	0.849	0.957
1971	0.673	0.595	0.860	0.928
1972	0.681	0.614	0.935	1.015
1973	0.695	0.615	0.896	0.934
1974	0.709	0.594	0.977	0.992
1975	0.734	0.614	0.973	1.011
1976	0.700	0.591	1.014	1.002
1977	0.705	0.605	1.009	1.016
1978	0.715	0.616	1.010	1.010

trend increases to 6.4 percent for females in the uncorrected equation, and to 5.0 percent when censoring is taken into account. The "overall" trend in relative earnings for females swings from positive to negative when relative education is added.

Columns 1–4 do not include relative employment as an explanatory variable. Following Freeman, we add predicted values of relative employment[10] (from an auxiliary reduced-form equation) as an explanatory variable. The auxiliary equation uses the logarithm of relative population, real AFDC benefits per family, and real weekly unemployment benefits,[11] in addition to the independent

10. The employment variable used here is the annual average of monthly values in year t.

11. Data on number of Unemployment Insurance recipients by race are available only back to the late 1960s; benefits by race are unavailable.

TABLE III

TRENDS IN BLACK-WHITE EARNINGS RATIOS: 1953–1978

	Males								Females							
	(1)	(2)	(3)	(4)	(5)	(6)	(7)	(8)	(1)	(2)	(3)	(4)	(5)	(6)	(7)	(8)
Earnings ratio "corrected?"	No	Yes	No	Yes	No	Yes	No	Yes	No	Yes	No	Yes	No	Yes	No	Yes
Constant	−0.557	−0.564	−0.280	−0.369	−2.133	−2.146	−1.493	−1.698	−0.873	−0.622	0.192	0.360	−5.730	−5.373	−1.919	−2.004
	(30.8)	(30.4)	(1.88)	(2.31)	(1.22)	(1.23)	(0.88)	(0.95)	(25.8)	(19.3)	(0.65)	(1.25)	(2.60)	(2.51)	(0.80)	(0.85)
Time trend	0.002	−0.001	−0.009	−0.009	0.004	0.001	−0.006	−0.006	0.027	0.022	−0.038	−0.038	0.023	0.018	−0.029	−0.027
(1953 = 1)	(0.72)	(0.67)	(1.50)	(1.39)	(1.13)	(0.31)	(0.87)	(0.79)	(6.72)	(5.84)	(2.09)	(2.13)	(5.10)	(4.21)	(1.35)	(1.29)
Post-1964	0.016	0.010	0.015	0.009	0.016	0.009	0.015	0.009	0.022	0.011	0.064	0.050	0.021	0.011	0.057	0.042
time trend	(4.84)	(2.94)	(4.59)	(2.64)	(4.32)	(2.62)	(4.18)	(2.41)	(3.48)	(1.90)	(5.05)	(4.07)	(3.36)	(1.75)	(3.67)	(2.76)
DGNP	0.356	0.810	0.075	0.612	0.630	1.085	0.301	0.859	0.936	1.169	0.274	0.559	0.823	1.058	0.341	0.634
	(1.72)	(3.81)	(0.31)	(2.32)	(1.69)	(2.90)	(0.74)	(2.01)	(2.42)	(3.17)	(0.76)	(1.59)	(2.11)	(2.79)	(0.91)	(1.71)
ln(relative			0.627	0.441			0.588	0.399			2.556	2.354			2.123	1.870
schooling)			(1.87)	(1.23)			(1.65)	(1.07)			(3.62)	(3.43)			(2.44)	(2.18)
Predicted ln(rel.					−0.687	−0.689	−0.521	−0.571					−2.518	−2.464	−1.001	−1.121
employment)					(0.90)	(0.90)	(0.72)	(0.75)					(2.20)	(2.22)	(0.88)	(1.00)
R^2	0.91	0.69	0.92	0.71	0.90	0.69	0.91	0.71	0.97	0.95	0.98	0.97	0.97	0.95	0.98	0.97
S.E.	0.031	0.032	0.029	0.031	0.033	0.033	0.031	0.032	0.058	0.055	0.047	0.045	0.058	0.056	0.048	0.047
Durbin-Watson	1.22	1.98	1.37	2.00	1.39	2.08	1.48	2.06	1.12	1.23	2.20	2.08	1.37	1.33	2.01	1.80

T-statistics appear in parentheses below coefficients.

variables in Table III, as explanatory variables. These are the same variables used by Butler-Heckman and Freeman. Columns 5–8 should be interpreted as structural relative-demand equations.[12] Thus, in principle, they provide a more accurate test of the view that government pressure has improved blacks' relative position by increasing the (relative) demand for their services.

The effect of relative employment on relative earnings is consistently negative and sometimes "significant." However, comparing columns 5–8 with columns 1–4 makes it clear that the addition of relative employment as an explanatory variable does not significantly alter previous findings. The post-1964 trend estimate for males remains at about 1.5 percent in uncorrected equations, and at about 1.0 percent in corrected versions. The female relative-earnings equations that exclude relative education are essentially unaffected by adding relative employment (compare columns 5–6 with 1–2), while the post-1964 trend is reduced slightly in both corrected and uncorrected equations that included relative education. The main effect of adding relative employment is to increase the importance of the cyclical variable *DGNP*.

The reduced-form equation for relative employment is itself of interest, in light of Butler-Heckman's assertion that transfer programs were responsible for declining relative employment. For males, while relative population is, as expected, a significant positive determinant of relative employment, neither transfer variable is significant, and the *AFDC* variable is positive. For females, both transfer variables were negative, though only the Unemployment Insurance variable was significant (and then only when relative education was omitted). (The elasticity of relative employment of females with respect to relative population was only 0.3, and was not significant.) Thus, the instrumental variables suggested by Butler-Heckman are not very strong, which is in turn reflected in the relatively large standard errors for the relative employment variable in Table III.[13]

Three further experiments, not reported in Table III, were also considered. First, examination of Table I suggested that the correction factors themselves might be trended, especially for males. To deal with this possibility, the correction factor C for each race-sex

12. The addition of relative employment to the equation assumes, as seems reasonable, that blacks and whites of a given sex are not perfect substitutes [Butler and Heckman, 1977, pp. 252–53]. Of course, the specification is far short of a "complete" system in which male-female, and capital-labor substitutions are modeled.

13. Neither Levy [1980] nor Darity and Myers [1980] find transfers very helpful in explaining changing relative employment probabilities in their comparisons of two years' cross-section data. Leonard [1979] reports that expansion of Social Security *disability* benefits explains a significant proportion of the decline in labor force participation among men 45–54, but this expansion began in the mid 1950s and does not appear concentrated in the post-1964 period. Indeed, his Figure I suggests that the proportion of nonwhites in this age group receiving such benefits increased quite smoothly in the 1957–1974 period.

group was regressed on a linear time trend and *DGNP*, using the thirteen available observations (1966–1978). The fitted values of the correction factors (for the entire 1953–1978 period) were then used to correct the published earnings ratios. The post-1964 trends estimated with these corrected dependent variables were somewhat reduced for males (0.007 and 0.006, for the equations comparable with columns 2 and 4 in Table III), but were virtually unaffected for females.

A second experiment was based on the realization that relative median education is a less than ideal summary measure of the relative schooling levels of blacks and whites. Because high school graduation is so common a completed schooling level, median years of education "moves" very little once it is "trapped" in the twelve-year interval. Differences in average schooling levels, and the logarithm of the ratio of average years of schooling, were therefore considered as alternative measures of relative schooling. They produced marginally larger post-1964 trends for males, 60 percent of which survived when the dependent variable was corrected. Estimated post-1964 trends were 0.03 for females based on an uncorrected dependent variable, and slightly less than half of this level with the corrected version. The average schooling variables consistently fit the data less well than Freeman's original ln-median form.

Finally, as a check on the correcting procedure, the correction term from equation (4), $C^B(1 - x^B) - C^W(1 - x^W)$ was included as an explanatory variable (using the $t + 1$ values of *DGNP* and of the logarithms of relative population, real *AFDC*, and unemployment benefits as instruments) in equations (1) and (3) in Table III. If the correction is appropriate, the coefficient of the correction term should be 1.0, or at least not significantly different from this value. In fact, it was always within one standard error of the hypothesized value, the point estimates being 0.69 and 0.47 (males) and 1.92 and 1.17 (females), respectively. The post-1964 trends differed little from those in the corresponding "corrected" equations (columns 2 and 4 of Table III), except for the female equation when relative education is not included (where it fell to 0.002 as its standard error more than doubled).

IV. Conclusions

Attempting to estimate simultaneously demand, supply, and censoring effects on black-white relative earnings places an extreme burden on postwar time-series data. The approach taken in this paper is to "correct" the published median wage and salary earnings figures for censoring, and then estimate demand and supply effects much as earlier studies have done.

The corrected estimates support the view that while censoring has exaggerated the relative improvement in black male and female earnings, it has not singlehandedly produced the improvement. For males, about half of the post-1964 trend as conventionally measured remains after correcting for censoring. For females, the results are more sensitive to the specification of the relative earnings equation: between half and four fifths of the conventionally estimated post-1964 trend survives.

The correction for censoring makes the fairly strong assumption that all of the changes in wage and salary employment to population ratios has occurred in the lower tail of the distribution. If the fraction of these changes that are drawn from above the median is constant over time and equal for both races, our correction procedure overstates the portion of the post-1964 improvement in relative earnings that is due to censoring, and understates the true improvement. It is, however, possible that the "censoring rules" differ significantly by race or over time; in this case, the direction of the errors from our assumed censoring rule is uncertain. On balance, it seems likely that the importance of the censoring correction would be overstated, so the conclusion that the relative earnings improvement is "real" seems secure.

UNIVERSITY OF MARYLAND

REFERENCES

Butler, Richard, and James J. Heckman, "The Government's Impact on the Labor Market Status of Black Americans: A Critical Review," in Leonard J. Hausman *et al.*, eds., *Equal Rights and Industrial Relations* (Madison, WI: Industrial Relations Research Association, 1977), pp. 235–81.

——, and ——, "A New Look at the Empirical Evidence on the Assertion that Government Policy Has Shifted the Aggregate Relative Demand Function in Favor of Blacks," unpublished paper, 1978.

Darity, William, and Samuel L. Myers, "Changes in Black-White Income Inequality, 1968–78: A Decade of Progress?" *Review of Black Political Economy*, X (Summer 1980), 365–79.

Freeman, Richard B., "Changes in the Labor Market for Black Americans, 1948–72," *Brookings Papers on Economic Activity*, 1 (1973), 67–131.

——, *Black Elite* (New York: McGraw-Hill, 1977).

——, "Time Series Evidence on Black Economic Progress: Shifts in Demand or in Supply?" unpublished paper, Harvard University, May 1978.

Leonard, Jonathan S., "The Social Security Disability Program and Labor Force Participation," NBER Working Paper No. 392, 1979.

Jencks, Christopher, *et. al.*, *Who Gets Ahead?* (New York: Basic Books, 1979).

Kneiser, Thomas J., Arthur H. Padilla, and Solomon W. Polachek, "The Rate of Return to Schooling and the Business Cycle," *Journal of Human Resources*, XIII (Spring 1978), 264–77.

Levy, Frank, "Changes in Employment Prospects of Black Males," *Brookings Papers on Economic Activity*, 2 (1980), 513–38.

Vroman, Wayne, "Changes in Black Workers' Relative Earnings: Evidence from the 1960's," in George M. von Furstenberg, Ann R. Horowitz, and Bennett Harrison, eds., *Patterns of Racial Discrimination*, vol. 2 (Lexington, MA: Lexington Books, 1974), 167–96.

——, "Changes in the Labor Market Position of Black Men Since 1964," *Industrial Relations Research Association, Proceedings of the Twenty-Seventh Annual Winter Meeting*, 1975, pp. 294–301.

[28]

EMPLOYMENT AND OCCUPATIONAL ADVANCE UNDER AFFIRMATIVE ACTION

Jonathan S. Leonard*

Abstract—Affirmative action is not only supposed to help move minorities and females into employment, it is also supposed to help move them up the job ladder, and it is this second goal that is perhaps the more controversial. Studies of affirmative action during the late 1960s and early 1970s found it generally ineffective in the white-collar and skilled occupations. Using disaggregated employment data in a new sample of nearly 70,000 establishments, this study finds that affirmative action was generally successful during the late 1970s in increasing minority employment in skilled white-collar occupations as well as in unskilled jobs.

ONE of the major affirmative action battlefields lies in the white-collar and craft occupations. It is in these skilled positions that employers are most sensitive to productivity differences and have complained the most about the burden of goals for minority and female employment. It is also in this region of relatively inelastic supply that the potential wage gains to members of protected groups are the greatest. The handful of past studies in this area have unanimously concluded that affirmative action has been ineffective in occupational upgrading and that the employment gains it has engendered for minorities have been concentrated in low skill positions. For the late 1970s this paper shall argue the opposite, using a new detailed set of data on changes in establishment level demographics covering more than 16 million employees between 1974 and 1980.

Previous studies of affirmative action between 1966 and 1973 are reviewed in section I, which then develops a model of affirmative action as a tax on white male employment. Section II presents evidence of the impact of the contract compliance program on total employment by race and sex. Section III discusses the main findings on occupational advance under affirmative action. To show the impact of affirmative action on occupational upgrading, two tests are presented. First, a summary measure of occupational status, an occupational index, is constructed for each demographic group and its growth compared across contractor and non-contractor establishments. If affirmative action is effective, the relative occupational index for minorities and females should increase faster at the contractor establishments that bear the affirmative action obligation. Second, to support the summary evidence on occupational status, employment changes within detailed occupations are analyzed. The conclusions of this study are presented in the final section.

Received for publication January 27, 1983. Revision accepted for publication January 17, 1984.

* University of California, Berkeley.

I thank Richard Freeman, Zvi Griliches, Finis Welch, and Jim Smith for their comments. This research was supported in part by the Office of the Assistant Secretary for Policy Evaluation of the U.S. Department of Labor, and by the School of Business Administration, University of California at Berkeley. Points of view or opinions stated here do not necessarily represent the official position or policy of the Department of Labor or of the University of California.

I. The Framework for Analysis

All four past studies of the impact of affirmative action on occupational advance have found that while affirmative action increases total black male employment among federal contractors, it does not increase their employment share in the skilled occupations. Burman (1973) found the employment impact of affirmative action to be largest in clerical and operative occupations, and negative, though insignificant, for managers between 1967 and 1970. He also found that affirmative action had an insignificant impact on an index of occupational status. Ashenfelter and Heckman (1976) extended these results, finding that affirmative action led to increases in black males' employment share, but that this was largest and most significant among operatives between 1966 and 1970. At the tops of occupational ladders, black males' share was estimated to fall relative to that of white males in the contractor sector, sometimes significantly. Overall, Ashenfelter and Heckman found no significant impact of contractor status on the relative occupational position of black workers. Goldstein and Smith (1976) found similar results between 1970 and 1972. Heckman and Wolpin (1976) found that black male employment gains were concentrated in blue-collar occupations between 1972 and 1973. They also found that contractors utilized a greater proportion of white males, and fewer blacks and females than did non-contractors in some white-collar occupations.

These studies suggest that contractors have been able to fulfill their obligations by hiring into relatively unskilled positions. Before 1974, affirmative action appears to have been more effective in increasing employment than in promoting occupational advancement. Some might argue that such a result is only to be expected given a short supply of skilled minorities or females. The presumption behind affirmative action, however, is that trainable members of protected groups will be considered for skilled employment. Even in the case of a small fixed supply, in its initial years affirmative action should induce a reshuffling of skilled blacks and women from non-contractor to contractor firms, without any upgrading of individuals necessary. I shall present evidence that by the late 1970s affirmative action was no longer as ineffective as it may have been in its early years in increasing minority employment in skilled occupations. This difference may reflect the increasing supply of highly educated blacks, as well as a more aggressive enforcement program, in particular the consolidation of enforcement activities into the Office of Federal Contract Compliance Programs (OFCCP) in 1978.

A Model of Affirmative Action as a Tax

Affirmative action may be thought of as a tax on the employment of white males in the contractor sector. If they are immobile, white male workers bear the tax burden and their relative wages fall.

Assume the owner of the firm maximizes utility:

$$\max U = T(F(m)) - T(W_M)m - T(W_F) \times (1 - m) - t(m - \bar{m}) - d(1 - m) \quad (1)$$

where

T = total employment
m = proportion of white males in T
$\bar{m}$ = average proportion of white males employed in given industry and geographic area
W_M = wage of white males
W_F = wage of other workers
t = tax on proportion male employment
d = taste for discrimination against females and non-whites
$F(\cdot)$ = a production function with $F' > 0$, $F'' < 0$.

Abstracting from the scale effect by fixing $T = 1$, the first order condition is

$$F' = W_M - W_F + t - d \quad (2)$$

from which we find

$$m = g(W_M, W_F, t, d). \quad (3)$$

Intuitively, an increase in the affirmative action "tax" shifts the demand curve for white male labor down.

I assume fixed tastes for discrimination and fixed technology, or less restrictively, technological change that is neither male nor female saving so that the change in demand is a function only of wages and the tax. All firms are assumed to be wage takers in the same labor market, with the wage elasticity of labor demand the same in the contractor and non-contractor sectors. Empirically, contractor and non-contractor establishments show similar growth rates, so scale effects are likely to be similar. The difference between the change in the employment of white males at contractor firms, Δm_C, and at non-contractor firms, Δm_{NC}, is then simply a function of affirmative action pressure.

$$\Delta m_C - \Delta m_{NC} = g(t). \quad (4)$$

This is the central equation to be tested, comparing shifts in the proportional employment of members of protected groups across contractor and non-contractor establishments across time. If affirmative action has been effective, these employment shifts will be greater among contractors. This measures the differential impact of affirmative action over and above the effects of general policies, or changes in tastes. Also, since any general supply shift will affect contractors and non-contractors alike, this should isolate the impact of affirmative action on labor demand.

II. The Employment Effect of Affirmative Action

Before examining the impact of affirmative action on occupational advance, it is helpful to analyze changes in total employment by demographic group. This section presents the results of weighted least squares regressions of the change in share of total employment by demographic group as a function of contractor status ($C74$), review status ($REVIEW$), establishment size, growth rate, corporate structure, percentage non-clerical white-collar, industry, and region. The dependent variable is the change in the employment share of the given demographic group.[1] These equations are estimated on a longitudinal sample of 68,690 establishments in 1974 and 1980. This study developed a new and detailed data set based on establishment level demographic data from EEO-1 reports matched with internal OFCCP records of compliance reviews made available by the OFCCP's Division of Program Analysis.

Table 1 shows that between 1974 and 1980, black males' employment share grew significantly more by 0.11 percentage points at establishments that were contractors in 1974 than at non-contractors. This is an increase of 1.4% of black males' initial 1974 employment share in the contractor sector of 7.3%, after six years under affirmative action. For black females, contractor status was associated with a significant 0.14 percentage point increase in employment share, or 3.6% of their initial 3.8% share of employment. For white females, the increase was 0.25 percentage points, or 1.0% of their initial 24.4% share. Contractor establishments did not increase non-black minority employment significantly faster than non-contractors. White males, a summary measure, did significantly worse at contractor establishments.

Table 1 also measures the impact of compliance reviews, conditional on contractor status. These are almost exclusively Department of Defense reviews, which account for nearly half of all reviews. Compliance reviews contributed to significant percentage point increases of 0.32 for black males, 0.23 for non-black minority males and 0.15 for black females, and significantly retarded the growth in white male and white female representation. Judging by the significant relative decline in white males' employment share at reviewed establishments, compliance reviews have been effective in promoting blacks and minority males, though at the same time they appear to have reduced white females' share of employment.[2]

These estimates suggest an affirmative action program that works for blacks, more so than for

[1] Heckman and Wolpin (1976) report significant evidence of positive serial correlation of errors on the order of 0.9 in a similar data set. This is expected to bias downwards the short-run impact of contractor status in the case of black males. The first-difference specification used here should reduce potential bias from serial correlation of such magnitude. The point estimates reported here change in other specifications reported at length in other work, particularly in the case of females, but these do not alter the main conclusions drawn here.

[2] This does not mean that female employment is not improving among the reviewed, but rather that it is improving faster among non-reviewed. A weaker result for females than for minorities is consistent with compliance reviews that ask for more than last year, rather than more than average, during a period of rapidly increasing female labor supply.

TABLE 1.—WEIGHTED LEAST SQUARES REGRESSIONS OF THE EFFECT OF CONTRACTOR AND REVIEW STATUS ON THE CHANGE IN THE PERCENTAGE EMPLOYED BY DEMOGRAPHIC GROUP, 1974–1980

$N = 68{,}690$

Demographic Group: Equation:	Mean	White Males 1	Black Males 2	Other Males 3	White Females 4	Black Females 5
C74	.601	−.0061	.0011	.0002	.0025	.0014
		(.0009)	(.0004)	(.0004)	(.0008)	(.0004)
REVIEW	.041	−.0032	.0032	.0023	−.0035	.0015
		(.0011)	(.0005)	(.0005)	(.0010)	(.0005)
SIZE	.237	.00095	−.0001	−.00066	−.0005	.0003
		(.0003)	(.0001)	(.0001)	(.0002)	(.0001)
SIZE^2	.409	−.00006	.000006	.00003	.00003	-6.46×10^{-7}
		(.000017)	(.000006)	(.000006)	(.00001)	(5.8×10^{-6})
GROWTH	.197	−.0073	.0018	.0007	.0019	.0019
		(.0004)	(.0002)	(.0002)	(.0004)	(.0002)
SINGLE	.183	.0094	−.0014	.0031	−.0081	−.0042
		(.0010)	(.0005)	(.0004)	(.0009)	(.0005)
PWC	.381	−.039	.0067	.00024	.028	.0026
		(.002)	(.0008)	(.0008)	(.0015)	(.0008)
MSE		1.63	.37	.35	1.41	.36

Note: All equations include 27 industry and 4 region dummies, and are weighted by establishment size in 1974. *C74* is set to one if the establishment was part of contractor company in 1974. *REVIEW* is set to one if the establishment completed a compliance review between 1974 and 1980. *SIZE* is thousands of 1974 employees. *GROWTH* is the rate of total employment growth. *SINGLE* is set to one if the establishment was not part of a multi-establishment company. *PWC* is the proportion of non-clerical white-collar employees. Standard errors are in parentheses.

other protected groups.[3] Both male and female black employment shares have increased faster at contractor establishments than at non-contractors, and faster at contractors that have completed a compliance review than at non-reviewed contractors.

III. Occupational Detail

The goal of affirmative action is not merely to increase the employment of members of protected groups, but to promote their advancement up the job ladder. The distribution of minorities and females across occupations can be summarized with an index of occupational status. This index weights the proportion of members of a given demographic group in an occupation by the 1969 mean earnings by occupation of full-year employed males from the 1970 Census of Population. If the within occupation variance of wages is small then changes in the occupational index should explain a good deal of overall wage changes. If affirmative action has led to blacks or females being employed in higher paying jobs, then this index should increase faster at contractor firms, under conditions derived below.

The advance of black males under affirmative action does show up in net occupational upgrading. In table 2, black males' occupational index relative to its 1974 value increases 2% more in contractor establishments than in non-contractors, and an additional 1% in reviewed establishments. Relative to white males, black males' occupational index has increased 1% during six years of affirma-

[3] To determine the within industry, within region impact of affirmative action all of the equations in table 1 include 27 industry dummy variables and 4 region dummy variables. Some of these variables have significant and large effects, details of which are reported in the author's *The Impact of Affirmative Action*. Establishments that were part of larger corporations had significantly larger increases in female and black male employment. Establishment size itself works in the opposite direction; black males experienced significantly slower growth in representation at larger establishments. Establishments that are growing and so have many job openings showed significant increases in minority and female representation. White females, but not other groups, experienced significantly and substantially greater employment growth at establishments that were white-collar intensive.

Other specifications not shown here tested for interactions of contractor and review status with size, growth and initial minority or female representation. The data give no clear answer to the question of how the impact of contractor status varies by the establishment's initial employment of minorities and females. There is evidence that affirmative action for black males has been more effective at male intensive establishments.

TABLE 2.—INDEX OF OCCUPATIONAL STATUS; OLS EQUATIONS OF THE EFFECT OF CONTRACTOR AND REVIEW STATUS ON OCCUPATIONAL INDEX BY DEMOGRAPHIC GROUP
$N = 13{,}936$

Demographic Group: Equation:	White Males 1	Black Males 2	Other Males 3	White Females 4	Black Females 5
C74	50.9	120.6	204.4	41.3	84.3
	(12.8)	(18.6)	(24.1)	(11.5)	(15.7)
REVIEW	60.4	98.9	102.1	54.6	26.5
	(19.0)	(27.6)	(35.9)	(17.1)	(23.3)
O74[a]	0.82	0.62	0.60	0.83	0.63
	(0.005)	(0.006)	(0.006)	(0.006)	(0.007)
SIZE	0.0011	−0.010	0.022	0.006	0.005
	(0.005)	(0.007)	(0.009)	(0.004)	(0.006)
G[b]	−8.50	−16.9	−21.3	−26.5	−6.90
	(1.40)	(2.0)	(2.5)	(2.5)	(1.3)
SINGLE	30.88	−150.7	−42.9	12.8	−53.4
	(14.40)	(21.0)	(27.2)	(13.0)	(17.7)
R^2	0.71	0.50	0.47	0.69	0.49
MSE	338,731	713,418	1,203,759	273,348	509,357
Mean of the Dependent Variable	9258	8152	8663	8510	7977

Note: All equations include 27 industry and 4 regional dummies. Sample limited to establishments with at least one employee in each demographic group. Standard errors are in parentheses.
[a] *O74* is the lagged dependent variable: the index of occupational status for the given demographic group in 1974.
[b] *G* is the rate of growth of total employment of the given demographic group between 1974 and 1980.

tive action.[4] In the equations for occupational index, employment growth by demographic group is controlled for, along with establishment size, corporate structure, industry, region, and lagged employment share. As expected, the higher the employment growth, the lower the rate of occupational advance, since many new entrants are at the bottom of occupational ladders.[5]

Between 1974 and 1980, the ratio of black male to white male mean employment income for full-time, full-year workers increased by 2.3%, from 0.684 to 0.700 according to Census Current Population Reports for full-time full-year workers. Since 69% of all employment in the study sample is in contractor establishments, our results imply that about 30% of the increase in the relative economic position of black males may be due to occupational advance induced by affirmative action. While this does not include the effect of promotion within the broad occupational categories used here, it is still likely to be an overestimate both because the study sample probably overstates the proportion of total employment that is in the contractor sector, and because part of the increase in the relative occupational index is probably due to the movement of skilled blacks into the contractor sector, rather than to the advance of blacks within the sector.

Occupational Detail and Occupational Indexes

While an occupational index provides a dramatic and succinct summary measure, it can be misleading in isolation. Consider just three examples. First, the occupational index would increase if firms laid off unskilled blacks or women. Second, affirmative action could cause massive promotions, but only within job classifications, causing no change at all in an index of occupational status. Third, even if affirmative action induces an increase in the employment of minorities and females at the top of the job ladder, the occupational index may still decline due to a composition effect. To guard against such misinterpretations, the occupational index should be used in conjunction with detailed employment data.

To clarify these issues consider the following formalization of the relationship between an occupational index and growth rates within occupations. An occupational index is

$$Z_t = \sum_i W_i \alpha_{it} \tag{5}$$

where

Z_t is the occupational index in year t

W_i is earnings in occupation i in a fixed year

α_{ijt} is the proportion of all workers of a given demographic group j who are employed in occupation i in year t, $\Sigma_i \alpha_{it} = 1$.

Taking the derivative with respect to time:

$$\frac{dZ_t}{dt} = \sum_i W_i \frac{d\alpha_{it}}{dt}. \tag{6}$$

But the side condition on the shares is that

$$\sum_i \frac{d\alpha_{it}}{dt} = 0. \tag{7}$$

So the occupational index can only increase over time if α_{it} increases in high wage occupations. However, the occupational index of blacks can decline even though black representation is growing in every occupation. Formally,

$$Z = \sum W_i \frac{N_{ij}}{N_j} \tag{8}$$

and

$$P_i = \frac{N_{ij}}{N_i} \tag{9}$$

where

N_{ij} = number of demographic group j employed in occupation i

N_j = number of employees in demographic group j

N_i = number of employees in occupation i

$\alpha_i = N_{ij}/N_j$.

[4] This does not include within occupation promotions, which are substantial within such broadly defined occupations. It also refers to the changing net position of black males at the average establishment, not to the average career transition of the average black male. In particular, since our unit of observation is the establishment, no individual black male need move to a higher occupation for the index at the average contractor establishment to increase, if many highly skilled blacks migrate into the contractor sector.

[5] For all groups, the faster the growth in total employment, the lower the occupational status. This effect appears strongest for white females and for non-black minority males, while it is weaker and less significant for white males and black females. This coefficient measures the difference in occupational status of members of a given demographic group across establishments with fast and slow growth of that group. As such, attempts to use it for cross-group comparisons must be interpreted with care. In particular the coefficient tells us only how the occupational status differs from that of the average worker of the same group.

To see how Z_t changes with changes in P_i, first totally differentiate:

$$dZ_t = \sum W_i \alpha_i \left[d \ln N_{ij} - d \ln N_j \right] \quad (10)$$

Or in terms of P_i:

$$dZ_t = \sum_i W_i \alpha_i \left[d \ln N_i + d \ln P_i - d \ln N_j \right]. \quad (11)$$

The condition for no change in the occupational index is then that

$$\sum_i W_i \alpha_i [d \ln N_i + d \ln P_i] = Z_t d \ln N_j. \quad (12)$$

If $d \ln P_i > 0$ across all occupations, then this condition is more likely to hold if:

(1) $d \ln N_i$ is negative
(2) the covariances of W_i and α_i with $d \ln P_i$ are negative
(3) $d \ln N_j$ is large and positive.

The occupational index is more likely to remain unchanged even though minority representation is increasing in all occupations if (1) total employment is declining; (2) earnings and share of minority employment are low where the proportional increases in minority share of employment are high (composition effect); and (3) total employment of minorities is increasing.

Employment Shifts within Occupations

The full story of the impact of affirmative action requires an analysis of employment data within disaggregated occupations. To test this I regress the change in employment share on contractor and review status, establishment size, corporate structure, industry, region, and growth of total employment for the given demographic group, in samples of establishments reporting employment in nine occupations and two trainee positions. These regressions are weighted by total initial period employment within the given occupation. The key results from this mass of information are condensed in a set of summary tables by demographic group, tables 3 to 6. In these tables the coefficients on contractor and review status are expressed as a percentage of initial 1974 employment share. The evidence is most striking in the case of black males in table 3. In every occupation except laborers and white-collar trainees, black males' share of employment has increased faster in contractor than in non-contractor establishments, and except for operatives and professionals these differences are significant. This impact is found in both the proportionate change in black males' share of total employment, and in the proportionate change in the ratio of black male to white male share.

The marginal impact of a compliance review, conditional on contractor status, is also shown. The relative importance of being a contractor and of being a reviewed contractor is mixed across occupations, but in every case, except blue-collar trainees and clerks, reviewed establishments have increased black males' employment share more than non-reviewed contractors.

The total impact of the contract compliance program, the weighted sum of contractor and review effects, shows some evidence of a twist in demand toward more highly skilled black males. Since 17.4% of all contractor employment is in reviewed establishments, the total impact is calculated as the sum of the contractor effect and 0.174 times the review effect. The contract compliance program has not reduced the demand for black males in low skilled occupations, except for laborers. It has raised the demand for black males more in the highly skilled white-collar and craft jobs than in the blue-collar operative, laborer, and service occupations. While this may help explain why highly skilled black males have been better off than their less skilled brethren, it does not help explain why low skilled black males should be having greater difficulty over the years in finding and holding jobs.

Affirmative action has also helped non-black minority males, although to a lesser extent. Table 4 shows evidence of a twist in demand toward Hispanic, Asian, and American Indian males in white-collar occupations, particularly in sales and clerical positions, and away from this group in operative and laborer positions. Compliance reviews have had a strong and significant additional impact in the professional, managerial, and craft occupations. The total impact of the contract compliance program on non-black minority males is positive in the white-collar, craft, and service occupations, and in training programs. Relative to white males, affirmative action has increased the occupational status of non-black minority males by 2%.

The evidence in table 5 suggests that the contract compliance program has had a mixed, and often negative impact on white females. For tech-

TABLE 3.—SUMMARY OF THE IMPACT OF CONTRACTOR AND REVIEW STATUS ON THE CHANGE IN BLACK MALE EMPLOYMENT BY OCCUPATION

Occupation	% of All Black Males in Occupation in 1974	Elasticity of Black Males' Share with Respect to Contractor Status	Elasticity of Black Males' Share with Respect to Review Status	Total	Elasticity of Ratio of Black Male to White Male Share with Respect to Contractor Status	Elasticity of Ratio of Black Male to White Male Share with Respect to Review Status	Total
1. Officials and Managers	.030	.09[b]	.08[a]	.10	.10	.08	.11
2. Professionals	.015	.08	.07	.09	.12	.07	.13
3. Technicians	.020	.08[a]	.05	.09	.08	.05	.09
4. Sales	.032	.19[b]	.14	.21	.20	.20	.23
5. Clerical	.032	.10[b]	−.04	.09	.11	−.04	.10
6. Craft	.119	.11[b]	.06[b]	.12	.11	.07	.12
7. Operatives	.418	.004	.008	.005	.016	.017	.019
8. Laborers	.198	−.016	.03	−.011	−.005	.003	−.004
9. Service	.137	.02[a]	.007	.02	.06	.13	.08
10. Trainees—White Collar	.003	−.08	.45[a]	−.002	−.09	.45	−.003
11. Trainees—Blue Collar	.106	.04	−.07	.03	.05	−.08	.04
12. Occupational Index	—	.02[b]	.01[b]	.02	.01	.006	.01

Note: Significance levels indicated only for elasticity of black males' share.
[a]Significant at the 0.05 level.
[b]Significant at the 0.01 level.

TABLE 4.—SUMMARY OF THE IMPACT OF CONTRACTOR AND REVIEW STATUS ON NON-BLACK MINORITY MALE EMPLOYMENT BY OCCUPATION

Occupation	% of All Other Males in Occupation in 1974	Elasticity of Other Males' Share with Respect to Contractor Status	Elasticity of Other Males' Share with Respect to Review Status	Total	Elasticity of Ratio of Other Male to White Male Share with Respect to Contractor Status	Elasticity of Ratio of Other Male to White Male Share with Respect to Review Status	Total
1. Officials and Managers	.048	.05[a]	.10[b]	.07	.06	.10	.08
2. Professionals	.057	.14[b]	.17[b]	.17	.18	.17	.21
3. Technicians	.035	.06	−.04	.05	.06	−.04	.05
4. Sales	.052	.15[b]	.22[a]	.19	.16	.28	.21
5. Clerical	.044	.14[b]	.16[a]	.17	.15	.15	.18
6. Craft	.159	.03	.08[b]	.04	.03	.09	.05
7. Operatives	.300	−.04	.03	−.03	−.03	.04	−.02
8. Laborers	.193	−.08[b]	−.03	−.09	−.07	−.06	−.08
9. Service	.110	.02	.08	.03	.01	.21	.05
10. Trainees—White Collar	.002	.92[b]	−.88[b]	.78	.90	−.99	.73
11. Trainees—Blue Collar	.006	.23	.04	.24	.25	.02	.25
12. Occupational Index	—	.02[b]	.01[b]	.02	.02	.01	.02

Note: Significance levels indicated only for elasticity of other males' share.
[a]Significant at the 0.05 level.
[b]Significant at the 0.01 level.

TABLE 5.—SUMMARY OF THE IMPACT OF CONTRACTOR AND REVIEW STATUS ON WHITE FEMALE EMPLOYMENT BY OCCUPATION

Occupation	% of All White Females in Occupation in 1974	Elasticity of White Females' Share with Respect to: Contractor Status	Review Status	Total	Elasticity of Ratio of White Female to White Male Share with Respect to: Contractor Status	Review Status	Total
1. Officials and Managers	.037	.06[a]	.008	.06	.06	.01	.06
2. Professionals	.083	.06[b]	−.01	.06	.09	−.01	.09
3. Technicians	.049	−.003	.006	−.002	−.004	.01	−.002
4. Sales	.133	−.04[b]	.11[b]	−.02	−.03	.16	−.002
5. Clerical	.299	−.007[b]	−.008[a]	−.008	.0002	−.013	−.002
6. Craft	.024	−.04	−.007	−.04	−.04	−.001	−.04
7. Operatives	.195	.03[b]	−.03[b]	.02	.05	−.02	.05
8. Laborers	.069	.06[b]	−.23[b]	.02	.07	−.26	.02
9. Service	.111	.03[b]	.13[b]	.05	.06	.26	.11
10. Trainees—White Collar	.002	−.03	−.05	−.04	−.05	−.06	−.06
11. Trainees—Blue Collar	.002	−.13	−.13	−.15	−.12	−.14	−.14
12. Occupational Index	—	.01[b]	.01[b]	.01	−.00	.00	−.00

Note: Significance levels indicated only for elasticity of white females' share.
[a]Significant at the 0.05 level.
[b]Significant at the 0.01 level.

nical, sales, clerical, craft, and trainee workers, contractor status is associated with a significant decline in white females' employment share. Compliance reviews have also often had a negative impact. While both contracts and reviews produce a significant 1% increase in white females' occupational status, this positive impact disappears when changes in white females' occupational status are compared to the relatively greater gains of white males.

Table 6 shows that in contrast to whites, black females in contractor establishments have increased their employment share in all occupations except technical, craft, and white-collar trainee. Compliance reviews have had a mixed effect across occupations. The positive impact of the contract compliance program is even more marked when the position of black females is compared with that of white females. Overall, black females' index of occupational status has increased 1% relative to that of white females under affirmative action. With the same qualifications as in the male case, this net movement across broad occupations may account for 20% of the 3.2% increase from 0.917 in 1974 to 0.946 in 1980 in the ratio of black female to white female earnings observed in Bureau of the Census data.

The conclusion drawn from this detailed analysis of employment by occupation is that with the exception of white females, affirmative action appears to have contributed to the occupational advance of members of protected groups. In particular, for non-white males affirmative action has increased demand relatively more in the more highly skilled occupations. The finding of occupational advance for non-white males is reinforced by evidence from CPS wage equations that affirmative action has narrowed the difference in earnings between the races by raising the occupational level of non-white males.[6]

IV. Conclusion

If minorities and females do not share the skills and interests of white males, then perhaps the best one can expect from an affirmative action program

[6] These wage equations are reported at greater length in other work (Leonard, 1983b). To the extent that contractors may have selectively reclassified upwards black and female intensive detailed occupations at a faster rate than did non-contractors, this study and its predecessors will overstate the actual occupational advance due to affirmative action. Of course pure reclassification would cause black losses in the lower occupations, which is generally not observed.

TABLE 6.—SUMMARY OF THE IMPACT OF CONTRACTOR AND REVIEW STATUS ON BLACK FEMALE EMPLOYMENT BY OCCUPATION

Occupation	% of All Black Females in Occupation in 1974	Elasticity of Black Females' Share with Respect to Contractor Status	Elasticity of Black Females' Share with Respect to Review Status	Total	Elasticity of Ratio of Black Female to White Female Share with Respect to Contractor Status	Elasticity of Ratio of Black Female to White Female Share with Respect to Review Status	Total
1. Officials and Managers	.015	.07	−.13	.05	.007	−.14	−.017
2. Professionals	.026	.18[b]	−.16[a]	.15	.11	−.15	.08
3. Technicians	.051	−.13[b]	.12[a]	−.11	−.13	.11	−.11
4. Sales	.061	.19[b]	−.27	.14	.24	−.34	.18
5. Clerical	.190	.05[a]	.05	.06	.05	.05	.06
6. Craft	.024	−.29[b]	−.19[a]	−.32	−.27	−.18	−.30
7. Operatives	.276	.08[b]	.17[b]	.11	.05	.21	.09
8. Laborers	.112	.24[b]	.19[b]	.27	.18	.55	.28
9. Service	.245	.08[b]	.17[b]	.11	.05	.16	.08
10. Trainees—White Collar	.003	−1.01[b]	.32	−.94	−1.05	.39	−.98
11. Trainees—Blue Collar	.004	.08	.02	.08	.24	.18	.27
12. Occupational Index	—	.01[b]	.00	.01	.01	−.00	.01

Note: Significance levels indicated only for elasticity of black females' share.
[a]Significant at the 0.05 level.
[b]Significant at the 0.01 level.

is to increase their employment. But to the extent that minorities and females share the qualifications and interests of white males, an effective affirmative action program should improve their chances of sharing the same occupations too.

This policy works despite generating considerable resistance. But just as no policy works in isolation, so none can be evaluated in isolation. The major finding here is that affirmative action has not only increased minority employment among contractors, it has also increased the demand for minorities in skilled jobs in the contractor sector. The relative demand shift has been greater for skilled than unskilled workers. The success of this program in skilled occupations after 1974, where none had been observed before, is probably due in part to the increasing supply of skilled minorities in many fields, as well as to the more aggressive use of sanctions after the early 1970s. The weaker results for white females must be considered in light of the massive increase in female labor supply that has led to increased female employment throughout the economy, and which may have obscured the contractor effect. We have also seen minorities and females enjoying the greatest gains at growing establishments, both contractor and non-contractor. The lesson drawn is that affirmative action programs work best when they are vigorously enforced, when they work with other policies that augment the skills of members of protected groups, and when they work with growing employers.

REFERENCES

Ashenfelter, Orley, and James Heckman, "Measuring the Effect of an Antidiscrimination Program," in Orley Ashenfelter and James Blum (eds.), *Evaluating the Labor Market Effects of Social Programs* (Princeton: Industrial Relations Section, Princeton University, 1976), 46–84.

Burman, George, *The Economics of Discrimination: The Impact of Public Policy*, unpublished Ph.D. thesis, Graduate School of Business, University of Chicago, 1973.

Freeman, Richard B., "Changes in the Labor Market for Black Americans, 1948–1970," *Brookings Papers* (1, 1973), 67–120.

Goldstein, Morris, and Robert S. Smith, "The Estimated Impact of the Antidiscrimination Program Aimed at Federal Contractors," *Industrial and Labor Relations Review* 29 (July 1976), 523–543.

Heckman, James J., and Kenneth I. Wolpin, "Does the Contract Compliance Program Work? An Analysis of Chicago Data," *Industrial and Labor Relations Review* 29 (July 1976), 544–564.

Leonard, Jonathan, "The Impact of Affirmative Action," U.S. Department of Labor report, July 1983.

———, "Splitting Blacks? Affirmative Action and Earnings Inequality within and across Races," unpublished paper, University of California (1983b).

[29]

Determining the Impact of Federal Antidiscrimination Policy on the Economic Status of Blacks: A Study of South Carolina

By James J. Heckman and Brook S. Payner*

This paper assesses the contribution of federal antidiscrimination policy to the dramatic improvement of black economic status in manufacturing that occurred in South Carolina in the mid-1960s. Using a unique data source for South Carolina on wages and employment by race, sex, and industry we evaluate competing explanations. Human capital stories, supply shift stories, and tight labor market stories do not account for the black breakthrough. Our study documents a significant contribution of federal antidiscrimination programs.

Two decades of research have failed to produce professional consensus on the contribution of federal government civil rights activity to the economic progress of black Americans. There are several reasons why this is so. In part it is due to the lack of convincing measures of federal civil rights activity. In part it is due to the reliance of much of the literature on notoriously fragile macro-time-series in which numerous plausible explanations compete for scarce degrees of freedom. Highly aggregated time-series or cross-section studies do not isolate well-defined labor markets in which supply and demand factors can be meaningfully separated, although it is the separation of these factors that is essential to the resolution of the debate on federal impact. Much valuable institutional detail may be lost in the process of data aggregation or in the fitting of "general-purpose" wage equations which constrain equality in coefficient estimates across diverse sectors.

This paper takes a new look at this old question using a unique body of data on employment and wages by race and sex for the manufacturing sector of South Carolina. Some of the data are available at the disaggregated county level affording useful cross-sectional variation. By focusing attention on well-defined labor markets, it is easier to separate out supply- and demand-side impacts on black status. Unlike most previous studies of the topic that focus exclusively on black wages, our study analyzes both black wages and employment.

Trends in black economic progress in South Carolina are typical of trends for the South as a whole. As noted by Richard Butler (1985), James Smith and Finis Welch (1986), and the U.S. Commission on Civil Rights, a sizable component of the post-1960 U.S. aggregate relative wage and occupational improvement for blacks arises from

*Heckman is the A. Whitney Griswold Professor of Economics, Yale University, New Haven, CT 06520-1972. Payner is a Vice-President of Citicorp, New York, New York, 10043. This paper draws on research reported in a longer paper "The Impact of the Economy and the State on the Economic Status of Blacks: A Study of South Carolina" written jointly with Richard Butler. This research was supported by the National Science Foundation under grant nos. SES-7711231, SES-814225, DAR-792594, SES-8411246, and SES-8739151. This research was originated at the University of Wisconsin, Fall 1977, and has been assisted at various stages by Richard Butler, Chris Flinn, Jon Moen, and Guilherme Sedlacek. Steve Cameron provided first-class research assistance for the work reported here. Margaret Watson, formerly of the South Carolina Department of Labor, provided valuable advice on the South Carolina data used here. We have benefited from comments received from Steve Cameron, V. Joseph Hotz, Rick Levin, Tom Mroz, Theodore W. Schultz, T. N. Srinivasan, Glyn Williams, David Weir, Gavin Wright, and participants in seminars at Yale, Stanford, The Hoover Institution, Sloan School, MIT, University of South Carolina, NBER, Cambridge, Penn, Princeton, and the Economic History Workshop at the University of Chicago.

improvements in the South. Thus a study of black economic progress in the South is likely to illuminate the sources of southern and hence U.S. black economic progress. A study of black progress in southern manufacturing is of particular interest. Butler shows that a substantial portion of the gain in black economic status in the South (more than three-eighths) arises from the movement of blacks from traditional sectors into operative and craftsman jobs concentrated in manufacturing. Relative wage growth within these occupations accounts for an additional one-quarter of black gains in the South.

Three major—and not necessarily mutually exclusive—explanations have been advanced to explain the growth in aggregate black male relative (to white male) earnings found in the post-1964 U.S. data. 1) Some authors, seizing on the coincidence in timing between the passage of Title VII and other related federal antidiscrimination activity and the relative improvement in black wages, assign a central role to federal antidiscrimination activity. (Richard Freeman, 1973, 1981; Wayne Vroman, 1974, and Charles Brown, 1984.) Other scholars deny this claim (see, for example, Smith and Welch, 1986.) 2) Welch, 1973; Smith, 1984; and Smith and Welch, 1986, assign a central, but not necessarily exclusive, role to human capital formation and the importance of previous state government discrimination in the provision of schooling. 3) Still others (James Tobin, 1965; William Wilson, 1986; Milton Friedman, 1962) assign an important role to the rising cost of discrimination in tight labor markets associated with industrialization, the emergence of competitive markets, or demand management policies.

Few scholars dispute the importance of schooling in raising black incomes. Most acknowledge that tight labor markets favor employment of blacks although there is considerable controversy surrounding the effect of tight labor markets on racial wage differentials. Most of the disagreement in the literature centers on the contribution of federal antidiscrimination activity—the focus of this paper.

We address this question by using empirical proof by elimination. Using a variety of data sources and measures of federal activity and eliminating other plausible explanations, we conclude that federal policy benefited black economic status in South Carolina.

Ours is a tale of two sectors. The strongest evidence of federal impact is found in the traditional manufacturing sectors of the state that were already thriving when Jim Crow laws formalized racial segregation in employment in 1915. Human capital stories cannot explain the timing of black improvement in these sectors.

There is little evidence of federal impact on black status in the more modern sectors of the state that emerged after 1945. Somewhat surprisingly, we also find no evidence of employment discrimination in state, local, or federal government hiring after accounting for individual qualifications. The growth in black employment and wages in these sectors appears to be market- or supply-side driven.

Our analysis establishes the value of more disaggregated industrial and institutional analyses in assessing the contribution of federal activity to black status. We demonstrate the importance of accounting for the relevant economic and institutional histories of industries in understanding black economic progress. Our evidence confirms the wisdom of Gavin Wright's (1986) emphasis on the role of institutions in explaining southern economic history. Our analysis also provides evidence against the widely held belief espoused by Charles Murray (1984) and other conservatives that federal government policy has not contributed to the elevation of black economic status.

We develop our argument in the following way. In Section I, we present salient features of the South Carolina labor market experience of blacks. Five striking graphs suggest that the federal government may have played an important role in improving black status. Although we sound cautionary notes against first impressions, in the remainder of the paper we demonstrate that they are correct.

Section II establishes that trends in South Carolina are like those in the U.S. South. Thus our analysis of South Carolina data contains important lessons for understanding the progress of blacks in the South and

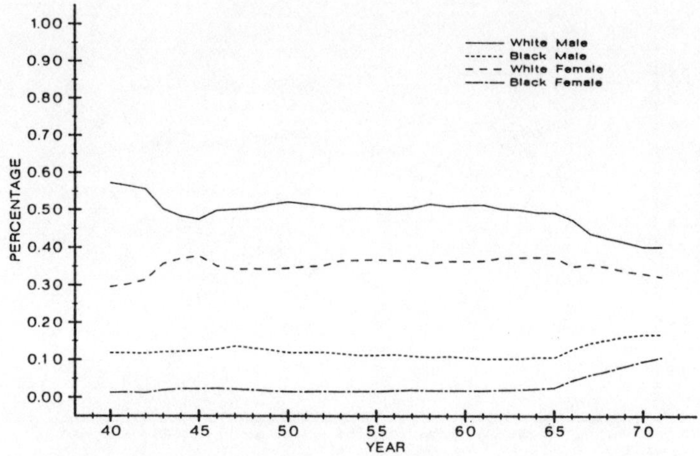

FIGURE 1. AGGREGATE EMPLOYMENT SHARES IN SOUTH CAROLINA MANUFACTURING

hence their progress in the United States as a whole.

Section III states and Section IV evaluates competing arguments using detailed analyses of the data. The paper concludes with a summary of the evidence.

I. The Black Breakthrough in South Carolina Manufacturing

Figures 1 and 2 plot South Carolina industrial data on employment and wages by race and sex for the period 1940–80. The data are from the Annual Reports of the South Carolina Department of Labor. Below, and in a companion paper (the authors and Butler), we establish the validity of this self-reported data collected from firms.

Black employment is a stable fraction of total employment between 1940 and 1965 (Figure 1). Suddenly, in 1965, the proportion of black employment begins to grow at a time when total manufacturing employment is growing. The relative wage series for black workers shows an upturn at the same time although it is less dramatic (Figure 2).

Textiles are the major industry in the state employing 80 percent of all manufacturing employment in 1940 and a still sizable 40 percent in 1980. Most of the breakthrough in black employment occurs in this industry and the related apparel industry. There is much less evidence of any dramatic breakthrough in the non-textile, non-apparel sector of manufacturing. Although there is visible growth in the share of black *female* employment after 1965 (see Figure 3), the rise in relative wages for black females starts long before 1965 (see Figure 4). The decline in the black male share in this sector and the rise in the female share for both races is largely due to the entry on a large scale of the female-intensive electrical machinery industry into the state in 1964 and the entry into the food industry of new firms employing women of both races in equal proportions. (See the authors and Butler for further evidence on this point.)

Figure 5 presents employment shares by race and sex in textiles between 1910 and 1977.[1] It confirms the impression conveyed by Figure 1. Through two World Wars, the Great Depression, and the booms of the

[1] Data on wages were not collected before 1940. There are no consistent time-series data on employment in non-textile industries before that date.

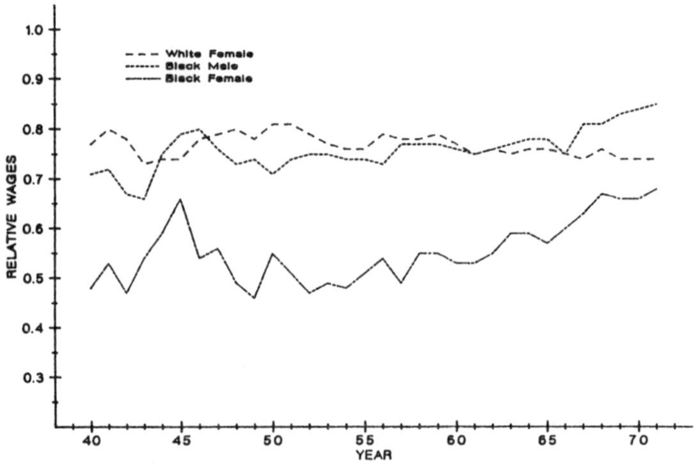

FIGURE 2. SOUTH CAROLINA MANUFACTURING' WAGES RELATIVE TO WHITE MALES

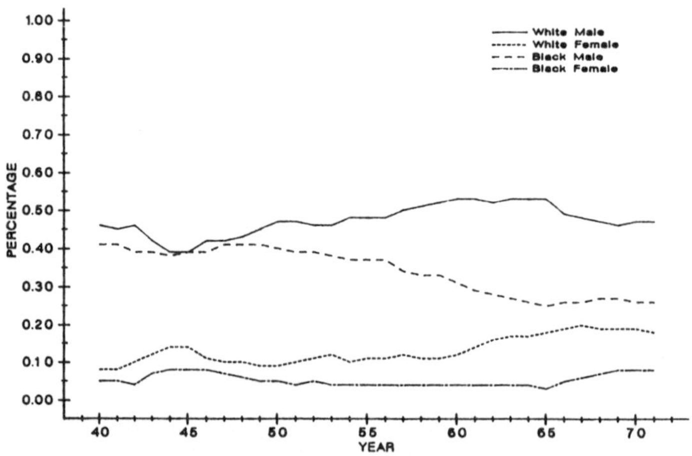

FIGURE 3. AGGREGATE EMPLOYMENT SHARES IN SOUTH CAROLINA NON-TEXTILE NON-APPAREL MANUFACTURING

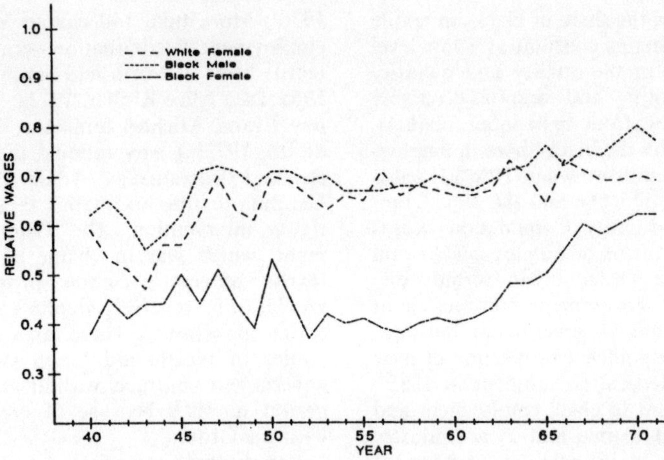

FIGURE 4. SOUTH CAROLINA NON-TEXTILE NON-APPAREL MANUFACTURING WAGES RELATIVE TO WHITE MALES

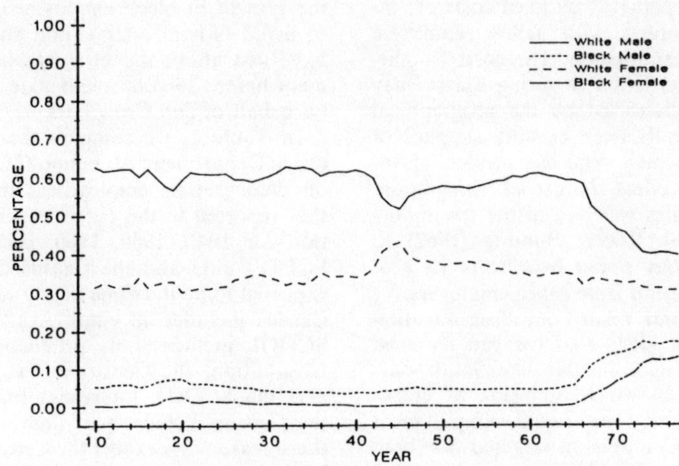

FIGURE 5. AGGREGATE EMPLOYMENT SHARES IN THE SOUTH CAROLINA TEXTILE INDUSTRY

1950s and 1920s the share of blacks in textile employment remains constant at a low level despite growth in the quality and quantity of black schooling and despite economic scarcity resulting from tight labor markets. Suddenly in 1965 the black share in employment begins to improve when Title VII legislation becomes effective and the Equal Employment Opportunity Commission begins to press textile firms to employ blacks and when Executive Order 11246 forbids discrimination by government contractors at the risk of forfeit of government business. Textiles sold a significant proportion of their output to the federal government in 1965.[2] The improvement in black employment and wages occurs at a time and in an industry that suggests a major role for government activity.

This evidence supporting government impact is reinforced by some additional background information on South Carolina textiles. That industry may well have been an ideal example of Kenneth Arrow's 1974 model of discrimination. Initial racial exclusion ratified by a 1915 Jim Crow law may have been perpetuated by fixed costs of employment coupled with fellow employee tastes for discrimination. The costs to marginal experimentation in hiring blacks may well have been raised by the geographical isolation of mills from existing supplies of black labor which required residential integration to effect industrial integration. Southern textiles was one of the few industries found by Robert Bunting (1962) to have monopsony power because of its geographical isolation from other employers.

Title VII and related antidiscrimination activity seems likely to have had its most visible effect in industries like South Carolina textiles in which exclusion of blacks was so blatant. The Equal Employment Opportunity Commission targeted Southern textiles and conducted hearings on employment discrimination in that industry in late 1966 and early 1967. These hearings were widely publicized. (See Richard Rowan, 1970.) More than 140 charges of wage and employment discrimination were filed against textile firms in North and South Carolina in 1965. (See Alice Kidder, 1972a; Kidder, Sidney Evans, Michael Simmons, and Dupont Smith, 1972b.) Any rational theory of government bureaucracy would make South Carolina textiles an inviting target for equal rights intervention. The Defense Department, which was in charge of monitoring textile affirmative-action programs, was known to be relatively vigorous in pursuit of equal opportunity. Three large textile companies in North and South Carolina had government contracts withdrawn for a brief period in 1968 because of noncompliance with the Order.

Before any conclusion about the efficacy of federal policy is embraced, however, it is important to raise some cautionary questions, the answers to which constitute the remainder of this paper.

The first argument against the obvious is that the data are suspect. Since textile and apparel firms report the basic data underlying Figures 1–5, they may have lied about the growth in black employment after 1965 to avoid federal intervention and they may have lied about the level of black employment before 1965 to avoid state intervention on behalf of Jim Crow laws.

In Table 1, we compare the South Carolina Department of Labor (SCDOL) data on demographic employment in textiles to that reported in the U.S. Census of Population for 1940, 1950, 1960, and 1970. The SCDOL data and the Census data are not expected to be the same in any year since the Census includes all employees, whereas the SCDOL includes only production workers. In addition, the Census interviews workers and the SCDOL interviews firms. Finally, the Census includes part-time workers. For these reasons we expect the Census figures to be larger except perhaps in 1970. SCDOL includes chemical industry workers with textile workers. The chemical industry expanded rapidly in the state during the 1960s, although it is a much smaller employer than textiles. Despite these numerical discrepancies, the same pattern of dramatic black improvement is found in both data sources.

[2] About 5 percent—120 million—1965 dollars.

TABLE 1—TEXTILE EMPLOYMENT

Year	Total	White Males	White Females	Black Males	Black Females
	(Percentage Share of Demographic Group in Parentheses)				
	Total Textile Employment from United States Census				
1970	143779	68977	48642	16585	9575
		(47.8)	(33.8)	(11.5)	(6.5)
1960	132166	78951	44601	6513	401
		(59.5)	(35.3)	(5.0)	(0.3)
1950	131558	75613	49326	6113	506
		(57.5)	(37.5)	(4.7)	(0.4)
1940	100461	61701	34355	5128	277
		(61.4)	(34.2)	(4.1)	(0.3)
	Production Worker Textile Employment from SCDOL				
1970	145108	68992	48548	19488	8080
		(47.6)	(33.5)	(13.4)	(5.6)
1960	120665	72122	42903	5448	192
		(59.8)	(35.6)	(4.5)	(0.2)
1950	124379	71065	42903	5987	311
		(57.1)	(37.8)	(4.8)	(0.3)
1940	92725	57517	31484	3555	168
		(62.2)	(34.0)	(3.8)	(0.2)

Sources: 1940 Census data from U.S. Bureau of the Census (1943, p. 370); 1950 Census data from U.S. Bureau of the Census (1953, p. 183); 1960 Census data from U.S. Bureau of the Census (1964, p. 346); 1970 Census data from U.S. Bureau of the Census (1973b, p. 680); SCDOL data from the Department of Labor of the State of South Carolina as described in the Appendix.

In a companion paper (the authors and Butler), we extensively document the accuracy of the data so that the faulty data argument can be dismissed.

The second argument against the obvious is harder to refute. The South Carolina labor market was unusually tight after 1964. Tightness arose from the 1960s national boom coupled with the growth in real manufacturing output (see Figure 6, in 1967 dollars), entry of firms and investment. Textile output was expanding during the period of the black breakthrough. The growth in demand for textile labor coupled with a dramatic contraction in the traditional sources of white labor supply due to the secular decline in South Carolina agriculture may have created unusual pressure for integration of the industry as a means of keeping down labor costs. Federal antidiscrimination activity may have simply facilitated the inevitable by giving employers an excuse for doing what they wanted to do anyway. Most economists who have analyzed the desegregation of southern textiles claim that the primary source of black improvement was the tight labor market. (Rowan, 1970, and Donald Osborne, 1966).[3]

Other arguments can also be advanced against the obvious explanation. The first is a supply shift argument that focuses on the decline in South Carolina (and southern) agriculture as a source of growth in black industrial employment. The second argument is the "human capital" argument. One version of this argument mirrors Smith's explanation of black aggregate relative wage growth in the 1960s and claims that growth in the quality and quantity of black school-

[3]An exception is Kidder (1972a) who assigns a central role to changes in community mores.

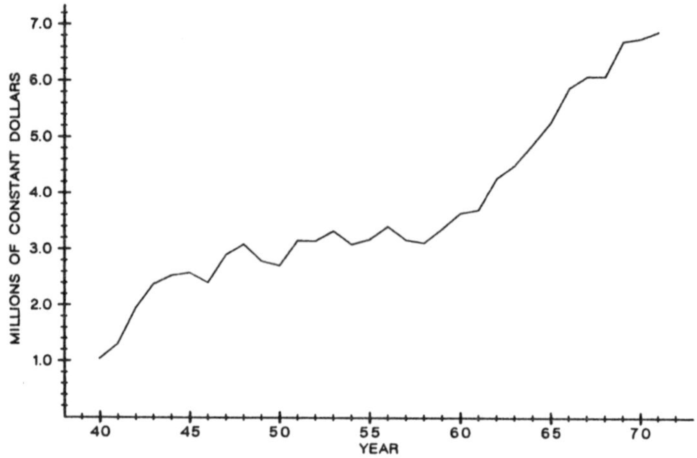

FIGURE 6. SOUTH CAROLINA MANUFACTURING TOTAL REAL OUTPUT

ing may have accounted for the black breakthrough in textiles and related industries.

We address these arguments in the remainder of the paper. We first document that trends in the status of blacks in South Carolina are typical of those in the South.

II. South Carolina in Context

Butler establishes that for the period 1960–70 more than two-thirds of the growth in the aggregate occupational index of black males relative to white males is due to improvement in relative wages or occupational standing in the South. He goes on to note that much of this improvement comes in the operative and craftsman categories that are concentrated in manufacturing. Scholars at the U.S. Commission on Civil Rights (Table 8.1) document that the rate of convergence of black male wages to white male wages in percentage terms was almost twice as fast in the South as in the non-South over the period 1960–80 for males age 25–54. Since roughly half of the black population lives in the South, these estimates imply that two-thirds of the growth in relative black status over the period in attributable to developments in the South. If it can be established that trends in black relative status in South Carolina resemble those in the rest of the South, our study of that state acquires a more general character.

The dramatic breakthrough in black employment in South Carolina textiles was also experienced in other major southern textile states. Table 2 documents this claim using U.S. Census data. Annual data are not available for these contiguous states so it is not possible to compare the exact timing of the black breakthroughs. But we can be sure that the breakthrough in all states occurred in the same decade. It is likely that lessons learned about South Carolina textiles apply to these states as well.

South Carolina is not a microcosm of the South but the state and the region share many common trends. The proportion of the population that is black in 1940 is higher in South Carolina (44 percent) than for the South as a whole (26 percent). The black proportion declines in both geographic entities until 1970. Both South Carolina and the South experienced a substantial decline in agricultural employment between 1940 and 1980 and a substantial growth in manufacturing employment. Due to the presence of the textile industry in the state, the fraction of the work force employed in manufacturing is higher in South Carolina than in the

TABLE 2—EMPLOYMENT OF BLACKS AND WHITES IN TEXTILES IN OTHER SOUTHERN TEXTILE STATES

	1950	1960	1970	1980
		North Carolina		
Whites	206,383	213,161	282,935	267,207
Blacks	8,746	8,565	46,910	76,620
		Georgia		
Whites	95,254	88,659	143,175	145,015
Blacks	7,029	5,955	27,361	46,778
		Virginia		
Whites	38,249	34,804	68,702	68,195
Blacks	2,189	1,783	11,969	18,188

Source: U.S. Census, Employment by Industry, 1950, 1960, 1970, and 1980.

South as a whole. The breakout of blacks from traditional sectors was similar in the South and in South Carolina. Tables 3 and 4 reveal that trends in employment by race and sex are also similar. The convergence of the industrial distribution of black employment to that of white employment is similar in both. Employment in domestic service (personal services) and agriculture declines for black women and employment in manufacturing and professional services increases in South Carolina and in the South. The pattern of educational improvement is the same in the South as in South Carolina. (See the paper by the authors and Butler.)

Trends in southern labor markets are undeniably reflected in the labor market of South Carolina. Lessons learned about black progress in South Carolina seem likely to apply to the South as a whole.

III. The Causes of the Improvement in Black Economic Status in South Carolina Manufacturing

Various demand-side and supply-side explanations have been offered as causes of the black breakthrough in manufacturing in South Carolina. On the supply side, one explanation relates to the decline of agricultural employment in the South which was a consequence of technology and government policy and which led to shifts in the supply of blacks available to manufacturing. In South Carolina, black employment in agriculture declined by about 98,000 workers between 1950 and 1970. Over the same decades, black employment in manufacturing increased by about 40,000 workers. The timing of these changes suggests a possible causal role with the decline of agriculture releasing supplies of black labor to the manufacturing sector.

A second supply-side explanation relates to the increasing quantity and quality of black education during the 1940s and 1950s that made blacks better qualified to compete with whites in the labor market. In South Carolina, there is considerable evidence of black educational gains relative to whites during the years leading up to 1965. Figure 7 shows the average highest grade completed by 5-year birth cohorts from 1900 to 1954.[4] The figure shows steady convergence over the period. As documented by Welch, one year of schooling for a black student was not equivalent to one year of schooling for a white student in the system of segregated schools that existed in the south and in South Carolina prior to 1960. Measured con-

[4]These figures were calculated using the 1950 Public Use Sample for the cohorts born between 1900 and 1924 and the 1980 Public Use Sample for the cohorts born between 1925 and 1954.

TABLE 3—IN SOUTH CAROLINA INDUSTRIAL DISTRIBUTION OF EMPLOYED PERSONS (21–65) BY PERCENTAGE

Industry	1980	1970	1960	1950	1940
			Black Females		
Agriculture	2.6	8.7	24.2	39.2	39.2
Business Services	3.5	1.0	0.2	0.5	0.0
Government	3.5	0.9	0.2	0.2	0.2
Manufacturing	32.5	19.9	4.1	2.4	2.0
Mining/Construction	0.6	0.3	0.2	0.1	0.0
Personal Services	13.9	36.9	51.2	43.8	51.4
Professional Services	29.7	22.7	14.5	9.3	5.7
Trade	11.3	8.3	4.6	4.0	1.4
Other	2.3	1.2	0.7	0.6	0.1
			Black Males		
Agriculture	6.4	12.6	27.2	50.6	58.3
Business Services	3.8	2.6	1.7	1.6	1.0
Government	4.5	3.7	1.8	1.3	0.7
Manufacturing	38.2	33.0	24.2	19.7	14.5
Mining/Construction	15.6	16.1	14.7	8.6	10.5
Personal Services	1.9	3.7	4.6	2.9	4.1
Professional Services	8.9	8.3	6.3	3.2	2.3
Trade	12.0	11.9	12.2	6.5	4.4
Other	8.8	8.1	7.2	5.6	4.3
			White Females		
Agriculture	1.1	1.0	2.8	7.6	9.6
Business Services	8.9	6.3	5.8	2.7	1.0
Government	3.9	3.6	3.7	2.6	3.3
Manufacturing	28.8	39.3	43.3	51.9	48.2
Mining/Construction	1.7	1.3	0.6	0.9	0.9
Personal Services	3.8	4.8	4.7	4.9	7.9
Professional Services	27.8	21.8	17.1	12.9	14.7
Trade	20.3	18.8	18.5	14.4	12.4
Other	3.8	3.2	3.6	2.0	1.9
			White Males		
Agriculture	3.6	4.5	8.2	20.8	26.4
Business Services	7.9	6.6	6.1	4.6	2.9
Government	5.0	6.2	4.8	5.0	4.3
Manufacturing	33.5	36.6	40.5	34.7	30.5
Mining/Construction	12.5	12.4	9.8	8.5	11.6
Personal Services	1.3	1.6	1.7	1.5	2.5
Professional Services	9.8	7.5	4.9	3.0	3.3
Trade	17.1	17.4	17.5	15.9	12.5
Other	9.2	7.1	6.4	5.9	6.0

Sources: Computed from 1940, 1950, 1960, 1970, and 1980 Public Use Samples, U.S. Census of Population.

vergence understates the true convergence because the quality of black schooling was increasing over time. Elsewhere (the authors and Butler) we document that in South Carolina, as in many southern states, elementary school expenditure per student began to converge in the 1930s while high school expenditure per student began to converge in the mid-to-late 1940s.

One demand-side argument is that as the demand for labor increased, the costs of discrimination increased. Since the period of

TABLE 4—INDUSTRIAL DISTRIBUTION OF EMPLOYED PERSONS (21–65) IN THE CENSUS SOUTH BY PERCENTAGE

Industry	1980	1970	1960	1950	1940
	Black Females				
Agriculture	1.6	3.8	15.6	16.5	17.7
Business Services	7.0	3.0	2.4	1.4	0.9
Government	8.1	4.4	2.3	1.9	0.7
Manufacturing	17.2	12.0	4.4	5.1	3.5
Mining/Construction	0.9	0.4	0.0	0.2	0.3
Personal Services	13.7	34.7	48.9	53.1	65.8
Professional Services	33.0	27.3	15.0	10.4	6.6
Trade	14.3	12.3	10.0	10.4	4.0
Other	4.2	2.1	1.3	1.0	0.5
	Black Males				
Agriculture	4.9	10.1	18.8	33.2	43.6
Business Services	5.9	3.8	2.7	2.8	2.5
Government	6.4	7.5	5.4	3.6	1.5
Manufacturing	26.9	27.1	23.4	20.9	14.2
Mining/Construction	13.6	12.6	12.5	10.8	12.6
Personal Services	2.5	4.5	6.3	5.3	7.5
Professional Services	12.9	10.3	7.3	3.6	2.8
Trade	14.5	12.9	14.1	10.8	8.2
Other	1.2	11.3	9.5	9.0	7.1
	White Females				
Agriculture	1.5	1.5	3.0	6.3	5.0
Business Services	12.0	8.6	7.9	5.0	4.1
Government	5.7	5.2	5.7	6.7	6.3
Manufacturing	16.7	19.7	21.6	23.0	22.9
Mining/Construction	2.2	1.7	1.4	1.1	0.9
Personal Services	4.9	6.9	8.6	9.3	16.1
Professional Services	30.0	27.0	20.7	17.0	18.8
Trade	22.2	25.0	25.9	26.7	21.7
Other	4.8	4.4	5.3	5.0	4.3
	White Males				
Agriculture	4.4	5.8	11.2	22.2	30.0
Business Services	9.1	7.9	6.5	5.1	4.4
Government	7.0	7.8	6.3	6.8	5.0
Manufacturing	22.6	23.9	25.8	20.0	16.7
Mining/Construction	15.6	14.7	15.0	14.7	15.5
Personal Services	1.3	1.9	2.2	2.0	2.3
Professional Services	10.7	9.1	5.9	3.8	3.6
Trade	17.7	18.9	17.4	15.9	14.4
Other	11.6	10.0	9.7	9.4	8.3

Sources: Computed from 1940, 1950, 1960, 1970, and 1980 Public Use Samples from U.S. Census of Population

the mid-to-late 1960s was characterized by strong economic growth and low unemployment, the argument may be correct for the South Carolina market. Another demand-side explanation assigns a central role to federal government affirmative action and civil rights activity.

IV. The Evidence

A. *Supply Shifts*

In this section, we examine the evidence in support of each of the major hypotheses beginning with the supply shift hypothesis.

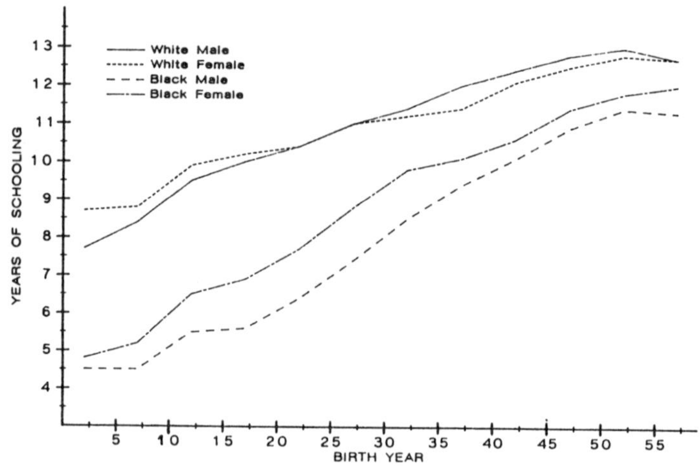

FIGURE 7. AVERAGE HIGHEST GRADE COMPLETED BY YEAR OF BIRTH

TABLE 5—MANUFACTURING AND AGRICULTURE EMPLOYMENT

Year	White Males	White Females	Black Males	Black Females
		Manufacturing		
1950	110182	63883	34020	2663
1960	137357	82251	34097	3798
1970	162652	106437	50515	25819
		Agriculture		
1950	72773	7730	89882	27794
1960	33318	4304	43724	14290
1970	18305	2333	15403	3737

Sources: 1950 from U.S. Bureau of the Census (1953, p. 183); 1960 from U.S. Bureau of the Census (1964, p. 346); 1970 from U.S. Bureau of the Census (1973b, p. 680).

Table 5 shows agriculture and manufacturing employment in South Carolina in 1950, 1960, and 1970 by race and sex. The numbers indicate that although black agricultural employment declined by 60,000 during the 1950s, black manufacturing employment increased by only 1,200 in the decade suggesting virtually no effect of the decline in agriculture during the 1950s on manufacturing employment. During the 1960s, black agricultural employment decreased by about 38,000 and black manufacturing employment increased by a similar amount. However, the changes by sex demonstrate that black males accounted for most of the decline in agricultural employment (28,000), but for less than half of the increase in black manufacturing employment (10,000). Most of the increase in black manufacturing employment was accounted for by females (22,000) whereas black female agricultural employment declined by only 10,000. In a companion paper (the authors and Butler) we document that only a tiny fraction of black entrants into industry came from agriculture. A simple supply shift argument can-

TABLE 6—AVERAGE AND ADJUSTED YEARS OF SCHOOL COMPLETED BY WHITE WORKERS IN TEXTILES IN 1960

Cohort	White Males		White Females	
	Average	Adjusted	Average	Adjusted
21–25	9.3	11	10.6	12
26–30	8.7	11	9.6	12
31–35	8.6	11	9.6	12
36–40	8.1	10	9.0	11
41–45	8.1	10	8.0	10
46–50	7.3	9	7.7	10
51–55	6.8	9	6.7	9
56–60	6.0	8	6.4	8

Source: Computed from 1960 Public Use Sample, U.S. Census of Population.

not account for the growth in black manufacturing employment during the 1960s or the 1950s.

B. *Schooling Quality and Quantity*

We next consider the schooling quality and quantity hypothesis. Table 6 gives the average education, by 5-year age cohort, of white males and white females employed in the textile industry in 1960. These averages are indicative of the education required for employment in the textile industry in 1960. Since the quality of black schooling is lower than that of whites, Table 6 also reports quality corrected or adjusted years of education. The adjusted figures are formed by adding two years to the white average and rounding to the nearest complete year or 12, whichever is greater. The purpose of this admittedly *ad hoc* adjustment is to correct for the difference in schooling quality by race to see if blacks are qualified to work in textiles on the basis of their educational attainment.

In Table 7 we show the percentage of black males and females in South Carolina with years of schooling completed greater than or equal to the white male and female adjusted averages given in Table 6 above. Already by 1960, over 25 percent of all blacks in South Carolina between the ages of 21 and 30 had sufficient education to be employed in textiles as measured by skill levels presented in Table 6. In the older cohorts, about 20 percent of black females and 15 percent of black males had sufficient education. Yet less than 1 percent of employed black females and less than 5 percent of employed black males between the ages of 21 and 65 worked in the textile industry in 1960. About 25 percent of all employed whites in the same age range worked in textiles in 1960. Lack of education is not keeping blacks out of textiles in 1960.

TABLE 7—PERCENT OF BLACKS WITH AVERAGE EDUCATION LEVEL OF WHITES IN TEXTILES IN 1960

Cohort	Black Males	Black Females
21–25	25.9	31.7
26–30	25.4	22.4
31–35	17.7	18.2
36–40	15.3	20.9
41–45	8.4	21.6
46–50	14.2	20.4
51–55	10.2	11.4
56–60	16.2	18.8

Source: Computed from 1960 Public Use Sample, U.S. Census of Population.

One implication of a pure form of the educational improvements hypothesis is that controlling for education and other individual characteristics, blacks should not be underrepresented in the textile industry in 1960 relative to 1970. Table 8 gives the coefficients on a race dummy variable from a series of linear probability regression models for males. The sample of all employed persons is

TABLE 8—RACE COEFFICIENTS FROM MALE EMPLOYMENT LINEAR PROBABILITY MODELS (*T*-STATISTICS IN PARENTHESES)

	Agriculture, Forestry, Fisheries				
Year	1940	1950	1960	1970	1980
Age					
21–25	0.19	0.08	0.16	0.03	0.01
	(4.73)	(1.16)	(5.74)	(2.69)	(2.55)
26–30	0.22	0.28	0.11	0.05	0.00
	(5.66)	(4.26)	(3.95)	(4.03)	(0.88)
31–35	0.19	0.18	0.08	0.04	0.01
	(3.98)	(2.47)	(3.06)	(2.83)	(2.06)
36–40	0.30	0.17	0.16	0.02	0.01
	(6.63)	(2.33)	(4.92)	(1.59)	(1.7)
41–45	0.24	−0.11	0.16	0.04	0.03
	(4.33)	(1.09)	(4.27)	(2.34)	(3.14)
46–50	0.22	0.26	0.12	0.03	0.02
	(4.04)	(2.56)	(3.14)	(1.61)	(2.49)
51–55	0.23	0.45	0.12	0.06	0.03
	(3.7)	(4.26)	(2.4)	(2.46)	(2.85)
56–60	0.12	0.24	0.20	0.06	0.02
	(1.73)	(1.68)	(3.83)	(2.4)	(1.69)
61–65	0.20	0.25	0.24	0.00	0.01
	(2.53)	(1.66)	(2.5)	(0.04)	(0.71)

	Mining and Construction				
Year	1940	1950	1960	1970	1980
Age					
21–25	−0.03	0.02	0.07	−0.04	−0.02
	(1.23)	(0.47)	(2.5)	(1.99)	(2.3)
26–30	−0.02	−0.05	0.09	0.01	−0.04
	(0.59)	(0.99)	(2.54)	(0.7)	(3.39)
31–35	−0.06	0.07	0.03	−0.04	−0.01
	(1.59)	(1.15)	(0.94)	(1.41)	(1.32)
36–40	0.01	0.03	−0.04	−0.03	−0.00
	(0.24)	(0.54)	(1.25)	(1.36)	(0.37)
41–45	−0.04	0.06	0.02	0.06	0.01
	(1.01)	(1)	(0.61)	(2.29)	(0.93)
46–50	−0.01	0.09	0.06	0.06	0.01
	(0.24)	(1.26)	(1.9)	(2.5)	(0.87)
51–55	−0.05	−0.08	0.07	0.02	0.02
	(1.15)	(1.42)	(1.55)	(0.62)	(1.51)
56–60	−0.01	−0.05	−0.05	−0.04	0.05
	(0.38)	(1.05)	(1.1)	(1.41)	(2.64)
61–65	−0.08	0.08	−0.04	0.01	0.04
	(1.45)	(0.66)	(0.69)	(0.29)	(1.71)

	Transportation, Communication, and Utilities				
Year	1940	1950	1960	1970	1980
Age					
21–25	0.01	0.00	0.01	−0.02	−0.02
	(0.68)	(0.16)	(0.25)	(1.07)	(2.7)
26–30	−0.02	−0.02	0.02	0.00	−0.02
	(0.8)	(0.5)	(0.76)	(0.19)	(2.27)
31–35	0.00	0.01	0.01	0.02	−0.01
	(0.00)	(0.14)	(0.47)	(1.05)	(1.05)
36–40	0.01	0.10	0.04	−0.01	−0.00
	(0.39)	(2.04)	(1.4)	(0.69)	(0.25)

TABLE 8—CONTINUED

	Transportation, Communication, and Utilities				
Year	1940	1950	1960	1970	1980
41–45	−0.03	0.14	0.04	−0.00	−0.00
	(1.17)	(2.03)	(1.48)	(0.17)	(0.22)
46–50	0.03	−0.03	−0.00	0.02	0.00
	(1.46)	(0.71)	(0.04)	(1.02)	(0.07)
51–55	−0.03	−0.03	0.03	0.06	0.01
	(1.1)	(1.31)	(0.83)	(2.79)	(0.81)
56–60	−0.04	−0.04	0	0.02	0.02
	(1.21)	(1.21)	(0.01)	(1.21)	(1.38)
61–65	0.01	−0.04	−0.02	−0.00	0.03
	(0.59)	(0.48)	(0.52)	(0.04)	(1.4)

	Wholesale and Retail Trade				
Year	1940	1950	1960	1970	1980
Age					
21–25	0.03	−0.08	−0.01	−0.05	−0.05
	(1.31)	(1.39)	(0.23)	(2.11)	(3.85)
26–30	−0.03	−0.13	0.02	−0.05	−0.07
	(1.43)	(2.24)	(0.47)	(2)	(5.81)
31–35	0.03	−0.09	−0.03	0.00	−0.06
	(1.03)	(1.4)	(0.73)	(0.03)	(4.9)
36–40	−0.05	−0.06	−0.03	0.04	−0.05
	(1.56)	(1.02)	(0.84)	(1.32)	(3.42)
41–45	−0.03	−0.02	0.02	−0.01	−0.05
	(0.75)	(0.3)	(0.42)	(0.27)	(3.09)
46–50	−0.10	−0.01	−0.03	−0.04	−0.05
	(2.9)	(0.16)	(0.97)	(1.54)	(2.83)
51–55	−0.04	−0.11	0.02	−0.06	−0.04
	(0.93)	(1.12)	(0.33)	(1.91)	(2.31)
56–60	−0.06	−0.14	−0.07	−0.05	−0.05
	(1.8)	(1.52)	(1.48)	(1.64)	(2.24)
61–65	−0.02	−0.14	−0.07	−0.05	−0.11
	(0.5)	(0.95)	(0.8)	(1.2)	(3.61)

	Federal Government				
Year	1940	1950	1960	1970	1980
Age					
21–25	−0.04	.[a]	0.00	0.00	0.00
	(2.86)	.[a]	(0.01)	(0.04)	(0.88)
26–30	−0.01	−0.01	−0.00	0.00	0.00
	(0.90)	(0.44)	(0.10)	(0.16)	(0.30)
31–35	0.01	−0.00	0.02	−0.00	−0.00
	(0.52)	(0.24)	(1.00)	(0.27)	(0.56)
36–40	−0.01	0.03	−0.01	0.00	−0.00
	(0.88)	(1.90)	(0.54)	(0.20)	(0.58)
41–45	0.00	−0.01	−0.01	−0.01	0.00
	(0.05)	(0.19)	(0.66)	(0.67)	(0.24)
46–50	0.01	−0.00	−0.01	−0.01	0.00
	(0.31)	(0.06)	(0.65)	(0.67)	(0.55)
51–55	0.01	−0.03	−0.01	0.00	0.01
	(0.76)	(0.57)	(0.41)	(0.15)	(0.82)
56–60	−0.01	.	0.01	0.03	0.01
	(0.73)	.	(0.26)	(1.45)	(0.57)
61–65	0.01	.	−0.03	0.01	0.01
	(0.35)	.	(0.82)	(0.52)	(0.63)

TABLE 8—CONTINUED

Year	1940	1950	1960	1970	1980
	State Government (Excluding School Teachers)				
Age					
21–25	−0.00	.[a]	.	−0.00	0.01
	(0.63)	.	.	(0.18)	(2.20)
26–30	−0.00	−0.00	−0.00	−0.01	0.01
	(0.25)	(0.38)	(0.42)	(0.91)	(1.13)
31–35	−0.01	.	−0.00	−0.00	0.00
	(0.61)	.	(0.52)	(0.48)	(0.36)
36–40	−0.01	.	−0.00	−0.00	0.00
	(0.50)	.	(0.25)	(0.61)	(0.89)
41–45	−0.01	.	0.00	−0.00	0.00
	(0.61)	.	(0.04)	(0.65)	(0.45)
46–50	−0.01	.	−0.00	0.00	0.02
	(0.90)	.	(0.42)	(0.75)	(2.75)
51–55	−0.03	−0.02	−0.00	−0.00	−0.01
	(1.33)	(0.54)	(0.21)	(0.42)	(1.19)
56–60	−0.02	.	−0.00	−0.01	0.01
	(1.01)	.	(0.17)	(0.98)	(1.00)
61–65	−0.01	.	−0.01	−0.00	−0.00
	(0.59)	.	(0.41)	(0.35)	(0.32)
	Local Government (Excluding School Teachers)				
Year	1940	1950	1960	1970	1980
Age					
21–25	.	−0.00	0.01	−0.01	−0.00
	.	(0.13)	(0.81)	(1.08)	(0.59)
26–30	.	.	−0.01	−0.01	−0.00
	.	.	(0.60)	(0.76)	(0.23)
31–35	.	0.07	−0.00	−0.00	0.00
	.	(3.29)	(0.35)	(0.10)	(0.40)
36–40	.	−0.01	0.00	0.01	0.00
	.	(0.46)	(0.08)	(1.30)	(0.24)
41–45	.	−0.04	0.01	0.01	−0.00
	.	(1.05)	(0.48)	(1.43)	(0.12)
46–50	.	−0.04	−0.03	−0.01	−0.01
	.	(1.96)	(1.92)	(1.28)	(1.41)
51–55	.	−0.02	0.01	−0.03	0.01
	.	(0.65)	(0.82)	(2.28)	(1.84)
56–60	.	.	−0.04	−0.01	−0.01
	.	.	(1.61)	(0.76)	(0.52)
61–65	.	−0.03	−0.03	−0.03	−0.01
	.	(0.48)	(1.03)	(1.80)	(0.50)
	Personal Services				
Year	1940	1950	1960	1970	1980
Age					
21–25	0.02	0.04	0.02	0.01	−0.00
	(1.41)	(1.42)	(1.87)	(1.4)	(0.53)
26–30	0.03	−0.01	0.02	0.01	−0.00
	(1.58)	(0.54)	(1.15)	(0.84)	(1.41)
31–35	0.07	0.08	0.03	0.00	0.00
	(3.08)	(2.68)	(2.29)	(0.32)	(0.76)
36–40	0.04	0.02	0.01	0.02	0.01
	(2.02)	(1.11)	(0.69)	(2.02)	(2.01)
41–45	0.01	0.07	0.04	0.01	0.00
	(0.38)	(2.05)	(2.99)	(1.12)	(0.96)

TABLE 8—CONTINUED

	Personal Services				
Year	1940	1950	1960	1970	1980
46–50	0.01	0.05	0.05	0.04	0.02
	(0.81)	(0.95)	(3.17)	(3.21)	(3.14)
51–55	0.07	.	−0.02	0.02	0.00
	(3.04)	.	(0.9)	(1.24)	(0.07)
56–60	0.06	0.03	0.10	0.05	0.02
	(2.2)	(0.46)	(3.06)	(2.73)	(2.28)
61–65	0.02	.	0.01	0.05	0.04
	(1.67)	.	(0.34)	(2.24)	(3.72)

	Professional Services				
Year	1940	1950	1960	1970	1980
Age					
21–25	0.01	0.05	0.08	0.03	0.02
	(0.49)	(1.82)	(3.97)	(2.00)	(2.63)
26–30	0.04	0.03	0.07	0.04	0.04
	(2.87)	(1.2)	(3.18)	(2.55)	(4.01)
31–35	0.04	0.01	0.08	0.05	0.04
	(2.19)	(0.22)	(3.81)	(3.07)	(4.09)
36–40	0.03	0.07	0.05	0.07	0.03
	(1.62)	(2.16)	(2.3)	(3.92)	(2.72)
41–45	0.05	0.03	0.02	0.04	0.05
	(2.39)	(0.55)	(0.9)	(2.13)	(4.58)
46–50	0.03	0.04	0.05	0.06	0.06
	(1.65)	(0.88)	(2.22)	(3.04)	(4.63)
51–55	0.04	0.09	0.10	0.08	0.06
	(2.25)	(1.64)	(3.26)	(3.9)	(4.7)
56–60	0.04	0.00	0.02	0.10	0.05
	(2.00)	(0.05)	(0.7)	(4.26)	(3.27)
61–65	0.00	−0.01	0.12	0.16	0.11
	(0.12)	(0.25)	(2.13)	(4.18)	(4.95)

	Recreation Services				
Year	1940	1950	1960	1970	1980
Age					
21–25	0.01	−0.02	−0.01	0.01	−0.01
	(1.03)	(0.94)	(1.13)	(2.28)	(1.54)
26–30	0.00	0.01	0.01	−0.00	−0.00
	(0.11)	(0.54)	(1.97)	(0.54)	(0.6)
31–35	0.01	.	−0.00	0.00	0.00
	(2.24)	.	(0.25)	(0.76)	(1.46)
36–40	0.00	.	0.00	0.00	0.00
	(0.03)	.	(0.55)	(0.44)	(0.01)
41–45	−0.004	.	.	0.00	0.00
	(0.42)	.	.	(0.01)	(1.27)
46–50	−0.01	−0.01	0.01	0.01	0.01
	(0.77)	(0.23)	(1.27)	(2.02)	(1.77)
51–55	0.01	−0.01	−0.00	0.00	0.00
	(1.23)	(0.33)	(0.51)	(0.41)	(0.99)
56–60	−0.01	.	0.03	0.01	0.00
	(0.63)	.	(2.54)	(1.16)	(0.48)
61–65	−0.00	.	−0.01	−0.00	0.01
	(0.2)	.	(0.55)	(0.44)	(0.82)

TABLE 8—CONTINUED

	Financial and Business Services				
Year	1940	1950	1960	1970	1980
Age					
21–25	−0.00	0.01	−0.04	−0.03	−0.02
	(0.37)	(0.24)	(2.34)	(2.18)	(2.45)
26–30	0.01	−0.01	−0.04	−0.02	−0.02
	(0.39)	(0.28)	(1.49)	(1.2)	(2.66)
31–35	−0.01	−0.04	−0.04	−0.01	−0.04
	(0.76)	(1.14)	(1.8)	(0.38)	(4.38)
36–40	−0.01	−0.05	−0.04	−0.05	−0.03
	(0.44)	(1.11)	(1.54)	(2.7)	(3.28)
41–45	0.02	0.01	−0.01	−0.05	−0.02
	(1.39)	(0.26)	(0.27)	(2.64)	(2.03)
46–50	0.00	0.03	−0.03	−0.04	−0.04
	(0.25)	(0.53)	(1.57)	(2.37)	(3.08)
51–55	−0.01	−0.05	0.01	−0.01	−0.03
	(0.34)	(0.83)	(0.21)	(0.67)	(2.76)
56–60	0.05	0.03	−0.01	0.01	−0.04
	(1.95)	(0.85)	(0.21)	(0.33)	(2.46)
61–65	−0.01	−0.01	0.05	−0.01	−0.05
	(0.31)	(0.24)	(0.94)	(0.32)	(2.34)

	Traditional Manufacturing (Non-Textile)				
Year	1940	1950	1960	1970	1980
Age					
21–25	0.04	0.14	0.06	0.05	0.02
	(1.47)	(2.30)	(1.79)	(2.91)	(1.78)
26–30	0.03	0.14	0.02	−0.00	0.03
	(0.93)	(2.79)	(0.53)	(0.17)	(4.07)
31–35	0.09	−0.00	0.03	0.02	0.03
	(2.85)	(0.02)	(1.06)	(1.05)	(3.68)
36–40	0.03	0.08	0.14	0.06	0.01
	(0.86)	(1.51)	(4.16)	(2.70)	(1.26)
41–45	0.01	0.03	−0.01	0.06	0.02
	(0.18)	(0.36)	(0.29)	(2.58)	(1.48)
46–50	.	0.03	0.01	0.06	0.04
	(0.04)	(0.40)	(0.35)	(2.78)	(3.11)
51–55	.	0.02	0.02	0.07	0.05
	(0.28)	(0.33)	(0.36)	(2.63)	(3.51)
56–60	0.02	0.20	0.08	0.02	0.03
	(0.50)	(2.42)	(2.02)	(0.92)	(1.96)
61–65	−0.00	0.06	−0.03	0.07	0.06
	(0.16)	(0.66)	(0.52)	(2.35)	(2.93)

	Nontraditional Manufacturing (Non-Textile)				
Year	1940	1950	1960	1970	1980
Age					
21–25	−0.00	−0.01	−0.02	0.03	0.01
	(0.10)	(0.72)	(1.00)	(1.58)	(1.42)
26–30	−0.01	−0.01	−0.03	−0.03	0.01
	(0.99)	(0.40)	(1.20)	(1.43)	(1.15)
31–35	−0.02	−0.03	−0.02	−0.04	0.01
	(1.46)	(0.98)	(0.80)	(1.76)	(0.89)
36–40	−0.02	0.01	−0.01	−0.02	−0.00
	(1.68)	(0.43)	(0.30)	(1.01)	(0.15)
41–45	0.02	0.02	−0.01	−0.03	−0.01
	(1.41)	(0.39)	(0.59)	(1.50)	(0.62)

TABLE 8—CONTINUED

	Nontraditional Manufacturing (Non-Textile)				
Year	1940	1950	1960	1970	1980
46–50	0.00	−0.05	0.02	−0.03	−0.01
	(0.26)	(1.57)	(0.79)	(1.53)	(0.78)
51–55	.[a]	−0.05	−0.01	0.02	−0.01
	.	(1.05)	(0.44)	(0.77)	(0.59)
56–60	−0.01	−0.04	−0.03	0.02	0.01
	(0.74)	(0.74)	(1.07)	(0.94)	(0.94)
61–65	−0.01	.[a]	−0.03	0.01	−0.01
	(0.43)	.	(0.57)	(0.28)	(0.26)

	Chemicals				
Year	1940	1950	1960	1970	1980
Age					
21–25	0.03	0.00	−0.01	−0.02	−0.01
	(3.11)	(0.08)	(0.76)	(1.60)	(1.81)
26–30	0.03	0.00	−0.00	−0.02	0.00
	(2.58)	(0.18)	(0.08)	(1.28)	(0.12)
31–35	0.02	0.05	−0.01	−0.01	0.00
	(1.68)	(1.92)	(0.36)	(0.69)	(0.10)
36–40	0.01	−0.01	−0.03	0.01	0.01
	(1.76)	(0.36)	(1.78)	(0.52)	(1.08)
41–45	−0.00	0.03	0.02	−0.02	0.01
	(0.25)	(0.87)	(0.98)	(1.43)	(0.80)
46–50	0.00	−0.00	0.01	0.01	−0.01
	(0.75)	(0.11)	(0.56)	(0.53)	(0.82)
51–55	.[a]	.[a]	−0.03	0.01	−0.02
	(0.48)	.	(1.35)	(0.49)	(2.35)
56–60	0.01	0.04	0.02	0.01	−0.00
	(0.60)	(1.18)	(0.94)	(0.63)	(0.41)
61–65	0.01	.[a]	−0.00	−0.00	0.01
	(0.57)	.	(0.08)	(0.24)	(0.43)

	Apparel				
Year	1940	1950	1960	1970	1980
Age					
21–25	−0.00	.	−0.01	−0.01	0.01
	(0.29)	.	(0.90)	(1.21)	(2.83)
26–30	.[a]	.	−0.02	0.01	0.00
	.	.	(1.45)	(2.34)	(1.24)
31–35	.	.	0.00	0.01	0.00
	.	.	(0.99)	(0.53)	(0.24)
36–40	−0.00	−0.01	−0.00	−0.01	0.00
	(0.53)	(0.74)	(0.31)	(0.93)	(0.09)
41–45	−0.00	−0.02	−0.01	−0.01	−0.00
	(0.11)	(0.91)	(0.80)	(1.05)	(0.28)
46–50	.	.	−0.00	−0.01	−0.01
	.	.	(0.20)	(0.73)	(1.04)
51–55	.	.	0.00	−0.01	−0.01
	.	.	(0.15)	(0.71)	(0.99)
56–60	.	.	−0.02	−0.00	−0.01
	.	.	(1.10)	(0.38)	(1.38)
61–65	.	.	−0.00	−0.00	0.00
	.	.	(0.08)	(0.09)	(0.11)

TABLE 8—CONTINUED

	Textiles				
Year	1940	1950	1960	1970	1980
Age					
21–25	−0.26	−0.23	−0.31	0.02	0.05
	(8.89)	(4.04)	(8.49)	(0.63)	(4.95)
26–30	−0.30	−0.22	−0.24	−0.02	0.05
	(9.14)	(3.75)	(5.87)	(0.95)	(5.39)
31–35	−0.35	−0.29	−0.20	−0.06	0.02
	(8.76)	(4.28)	(5.78)	(2.16)	(1.49)
36–40	−0.34	−0.38	−0.23	−0.11	0.01
	(9.73)	(5.68)	(6.13)	(4.03)	(0.78)
41–45	−0.22	−0.18	−0.27	−0.07	−0.03
	(5.93)	(2.64)	(5.93)	(2.75)	(1.89)
46–50	−0.18	−0.34	−0.22	−0.14	−0.07
	(5.24)	(3.93)	(5.88)	(4.80)	(4.17)
51–55	−0.22	−0.18	−0.29	−0.21	−0.08
	(5.34)	(2.17)	(5.04)	(6.97)	(4.53)
56–60	−0.13	−0.26	−0.25	−0.20	−0.11
	(3.41)	(2.89)	(5.01)	(5.92)	(5.16)
61–65	−0.14	−0.15	−0.16	−0.20	−0.13
	(2.93)	(1.52)	(2.30)	(5.21)	(4.87)

[a] "." indicates insufficient data to compute estimate.

broken down by sex and 5-year cohorts.[5] The left-hand side variable is equal to one if the individual is employed in a given industry and zero otherwise. The right-hand side variables include an intercept, years of schooling, years of schooling squared, and a race dummy equal to one for blacks and zero for whites. The regressions are performed for each Census year from 1940 to 1980.[6] A full report of these regressions is given in Heckman, Payner, and Butler (1989). The industry categories, based on SIC codes, are:

1. Agriculture, forestry, and fisheries
2. Mining and construction
3. Transportation, communication, and utilities
4. Wholesale and retail trade
5. Federal government
6. State government
7. Local government
8. Personal services
9. Professional services
10. Recreation services
11. Finance and business services
12. Traditional manufacturing—paper, printing, publishing, food products, stone, clay, miscellaneous manufactures, lumber, and furniture
13. Nontraditional manufacturing—transportation equipment, electrical and nonelectrical machinery, metal industries and founderies and machine shops—industries that enter the state on a large scale after 1945
14. Chemicals
15. Apparel
16. Textiles.

A nonzero coefficient on the race dummy may be interpreted as arising from discrimination on the demand side. Controlling for individual characteristics, the coefficient on the dummy variable indicates whether blacks are more or less likely than whites to be employed in a given industry. Alternatively, and less plausibly, the coefficient on the dummy may be interpreted as the outcome of racial sectoral preferences on the supply

[5]The regressions were also run using civilian labor force and total population as the sample instead of employed persons. The results described in the text are unaffected by these changes in the sample.

[6]Selected regressions were repeated using a probit specification to correct for heteroscedasticity. The results were qualitatively similar to those reported here.

side. In either case, the coefficient tells the relative likelihood of finding a black worker in a given industry, controlling for individual characteristics.

The race dummy coefficients are reported for these industries along with the least squares t-statistics in parentheses. Prior to 1960, we find that adjusting for qualifications black males are not underrepresented in *any* industry except textiles. In fact, black males are overrepresented in agriculture and professional services as of 1960. It is important to note that in 1960 blacks are underrepresented in the nontraditional manufacturing industries in relation to their share in the population and the labor force. However, controlling for individual characteristics, Table 8 shows that black males are not underrepresented in these industries.

For black females compared to white females the story is quite similar. (See the authors and Butler). Besides being underrepresented in textiles, black females are also underrepresented in the closely allied apparel industry. Also, in 1960 black females are overrepresented in most industries, including nontraditional manufacturing, chemicals, government, services, and trade.

The 1970 regressions show little change from 1960 for black males except in textiles. In the younger cohorts of textile workers, blacks are no longer underrepresented and in the older cohorts, they are much less so than in 1960. For black females, the 1960 to 1970 comparison yields similar results. The younger cohorts are no longer underrepresented in textiles by 1970, and the older cohorts are less underrepresented. Also, a similar story is true for apparel workers. (See the authors and Butler). These improvements for younger workers are consistent with theories that stress the incentives of making firm-specific investments in younger workers with longer expected working lives rather than in older workers.

The regressions show that, controlling for education and other individual characteristics, blacks are significantly underrepresented in the textile industry in 1960 and before. In 1970, however, the underrepresentation disappears for the younger cohorts and diminishes considerably for the older cohorts. If educational improvement led to the black gains in textile employment, the regressions controlling for education would have shown no underrepresentation of blacks in 1960, and no change in underrepresentation from 1960 to 1970.

In a companion paper (the authors and Butler) we examine the effect of accounting for improvements in black schooling quality on our analysis. We run regressions using quality-corrected education variables formed using data on educational expenditure by race. The qualitative results are the same as those obtained without adjusting for quality of education.

As a final test, we ask the question: what happens to the probability of finding a black employed in the textile industry as the average level of black education rises from its 1960 to its 1970 level? The results for black males are shown in Table 9 for selected industries using the 1970 linear probability model regression coefficients.[7] For black males in most industries, including nontraditional manufacturing, chemicals, different levels of government, financial and business services and wholesale and retail trade, the effect of increasing education is to increase the probability of employment. In textiles, as well as agriculture, the effect is to actually *decrease* the probability of employment. Textiles is a low skill industry. Increasing education has the effect of decreasing the probability of employment in low skill industries.

Although blacks had already made gains in education relative to whites in the years leading up to 1965, the evidence presented here does not support the claim that educational improvements led to increased black employment and wages in the textile industry. First, the gains in schooling measured by years completed and expenditure per student per year came gradually. Second, by 1960, between one-fifth and one-fourth of the adult blacks in South Carolina had sufficient education to work in the textile industry. How-

[7] This analysis was repeated using the 1960 regression coefficients with qualitatively similar results.

TABLE 9—THE EFFECT OF INCREASING BLACK MALE EDUCATION FROM ITS 1960 TO ITS 1970 LEVEL ON THE PROBABILITY OF EMPLOYMENT (in Percents) SELECTED INDUSTRIES

	Age				
Industry	21–25	26–30	31–35	36–40	41–45
Agriculture, Forestry, and Fisheries	−3.1	−2.6	−2.2	−2.1	−6.9
Transportation, Communication, and Utilities	−.1	1.2	1.2	1.0	2.5
Wholesale and Retail Trade	1.8	1.4	2.7	2.2	4.7
Federal Government	.5	.1	.1	.1	.5
State Government (Excluding School Teachers)	.3	.2	.1	.1	−.4
Local Government (Excluding School Teachers)	6.2	.2	−.1	.2	−.4
Professional Services	2.7	1.4	.3	2.7	−3.7
Financial and Business Services	−.3	.5	1.2	.3	1.4
Nontraditional Manufacturing	9.0	1.0	1.5	0.7	1.0
Chemicals	.8	.7	.4	.5	1.0
Textiles	−1.7	−2.2	−1.5	−2.8	.1

	Age			
Industry	46–50	51–55	56–60	61–65
Agriculture, Forestry, and Fisheries	−1.9	−.6	−1.2	−1.2
Transportation, Communication, and Utilities	1.0	.5	.6	.2
Wholesale and Retail Trade	2.3	1.2	1.1	.8
Federal Government	.2	.0	.0	.0
State Government (Excluding School Teachers)	.2	.0	.0	.0
Local Government (Excluding School Teachers)	−.3	.1	.3	.1
Professional Services	−.8	−.4	.0	−.3
Financial and Business Services	.6	.3	.4	.0
Nontraditional Manufacturing	1.8	.6	.2	1.0
Chemicals	.2	.1	.1	.1
Textiles	−2.0	−.7	−1.2	−.2

Source: Based on regressions reported in Heckman, Payner, and Butler (1988). For Education, Public Use Samples, U.S. Census of Population, for 1960 and 1970.

ever, black females were practically excluded and black males were employed in very small numbers in textiles. Third, even controlling for education, blacks were found to be severely underrepresented in textiles in 1960, but much less so in 1970. Also, in all other industries with the exception of apparel, blacks were not found to be underrepresented when educational background is taken into account. Finally, if years of schooling of blacks are increased, the probability of blacks being employed in textiles actually decreases.

The evidence presented here confirms the powerful role of education in elevating black employment in other sectors of the economy, especially government and the emerging new industrial sector of the state that apparently never discriminated against blacks (or at least black qualifications) on a statistically or numerically significant scale. As black skills improved, so did their representation in these sectors.

C. *The Tight Labor Market Hypothesis*

With statewide aggregate data, the tight labor market hypothesis is not testable. The black breakthrough in textiles is an event that occurs only once. Many other events

TABLE 10—SOUTH CAROLINA POPULATION AND POPULATION SHARES IN SELECTED COUNTIES IN 1960

County	Percentage White	Percentage Black	Size of Population (Thousands)
Abbeville	68	32	21.4
Anderson	80	20	98.5
Cherokee	79	21	35.2
Chester	60	40	30.9
Greenville	82	18	209.8
Lancaster	73	27	39.4
Laurens	70	30	47.6
Oconee	89	11	40.2
Orangeburg	40	60	68.6
Pickens	90	10	46.0
Spartanburg	78	22	156.8

Source: U.S. Bureau of the Census (1964, p. 42)

that occur contemporaneously with the black breakthrough are equally plausible candidates for being the cause. Without more variation in the data one cannot discriminate among the possibilities. Although we do not have evidence from other comparably tight labor market episodes in South Carolina, we do have a time-series of cross sections on the black breakthrough as it occurs in different counties of South Carolina. Even with these data, the labor market hypothesis is not testable if one believes that South Carolina is a single labor market or that all counties are identical. In that case, a tight labor market could cause simultaneous effects across counties just as uniformly applied government policy could. However, if the counties of South Carolina do not form a single labor market, the two hypotheses can be differentiated. A tight labor market would affect the various counties differently, whereas uniformly applied government policy would plausibly affect all counties simultaneously. We argue that the counties of South Carolina are different labor markets and that the simultaneous breakthrough of blacks in textiles across those counties is evidence against the labor market hypothesis and in favor of the government activity hypothesis. We begin by examining data from 11 South Carolina counties for which we can form a consistent time-series on textile employment by race and sex for the period 1910–77. Most of the 11 counties are in the Piedmont region in the northeast portion of the state. However, the south central and central portions of the state are also represented.

Table 10 shows population levels and shares respectively by race and sex for these 11 counties in 1960. The counties vary greatly in racial composition. They also vary greatly in size of the population.

Table 11 shows total employment and employment in selected industries in 1960. The county population employed varies from 34 percent to 41 percent. The proportion of the employed working in manufacturing varies from 55 percent to 20 percent. The counties vary substantially in the size of the manufacturing work force. To the extent that regional labor markets exist, we expect the effect of changing labor market conditions to be different across counties. Anthony Tang (1958) documents sharp differences among contiguous Piedmont counties in South Carolina in many indicators of economic development.

Figures 8 to 18 show employment shares by race and sex in the textile industry for these 11 counties from 1910 to 1977. In 7 of the 11 counties, the textile breakthrough for black females occurs in the fiscal-year 1965. The textile industry data are collected on a fiscal-year basis. Therefore fiscal 1966 covers July 1965 through June 1966. In the four remaining counties, the black female break-

TABLE 11—SOUTH CAROLINA COUNTY-LEVEL EMPLOYMENT BY INDUSTRY IN 1960

County	Total Employment	Percent Employed in: Manufacturing	Textiles	Agriculture	Percent of Manufacturing Employees in Textiles	Percent of Population Employed
Abbeville	7763	45	27	9	59	36
Anderson	40401	47	33	6	69	41
Cherokee	12980	46	26	7	57	37
Chester	11232	44	35	10	79	36
Greenville	80944	39	20	2	51	39
Lancaster	14898	55	46	4	84	38
Laurens	17647	47	26	8	54	37
Oconee	15199	47	34	8	71	38
Orangeburg	23427	20	2	25	10	34
Pickens	18313	53	21	4	40	40
Spartanburg	61762	44	29	5	65	39

Source: All variables except textile employment from U.S. Bureau of the Census (1964, p. 42); Textile employment data from Department of Labor of the State of South Carolina as described in the Data Appendix.
Note: South Carolina Department of Labor data are average annual employment during the fiscal year July 1959 to June 1960. Census data are at a point in time during the Census survey.

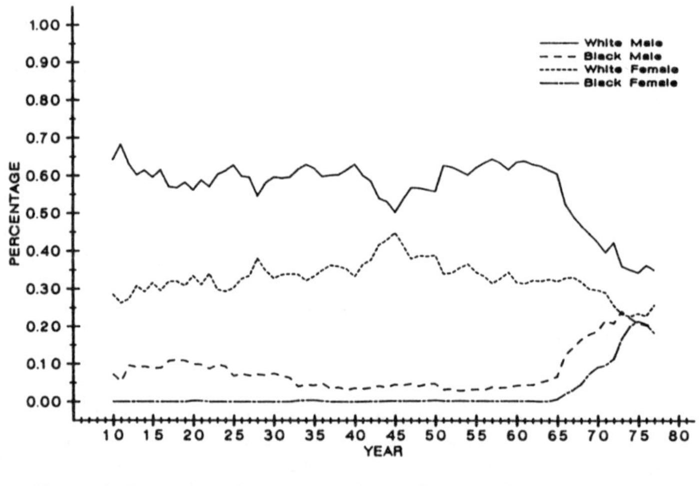

FIGURE 8. EMPLOYMENT SHARES IN THE SOUTH CAROLINA TEXTILE INDUSTRY, ABBEVILLE COUNTY

through in textiles occurs in fiscal-year 1966. Since these are fiscal years, we cannot rule out the possibility that the breakthrough occurs in calendar year 1965 in all counties.

After 55 years of near total exclusion from the industry, black females became employed in significant numbers for the first time in the mid-1960s in each county. Similarly, after constant but low utilization in the industry prior to the mid-1960s, black males significantly increase their employment in textiles in fiscal years 1965 or 1966 in each county. If the state of South Carolina were a single homogeneous labor market with no

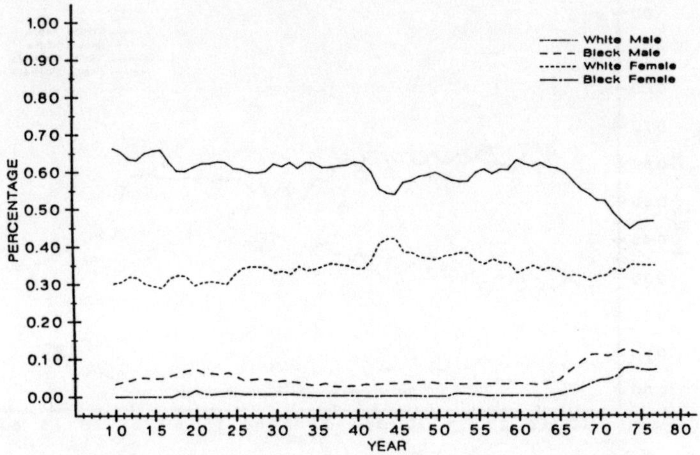

FIGURE 9. EMPLOYMENT SHARES IN THE SOUTH CAROLINA TEXTILE INDUSTRY, ANDERSON COUNTY

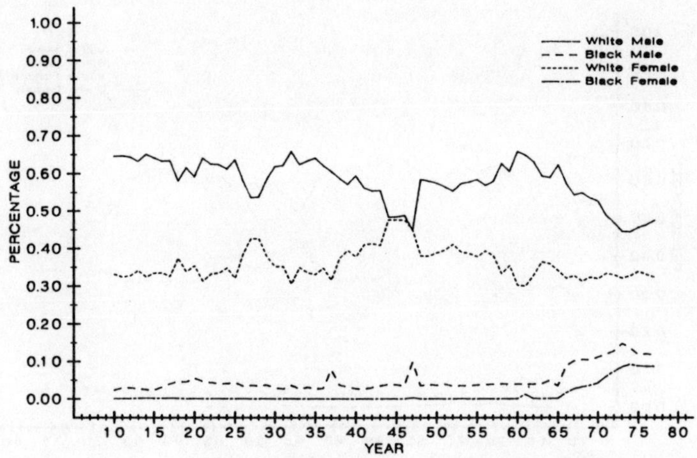

FIGURE 10. EMPLOYMENT SHARES IN THE SOUTH CAROLINA TEXTILE INDUSTRY, CHEROKEE COUNTY

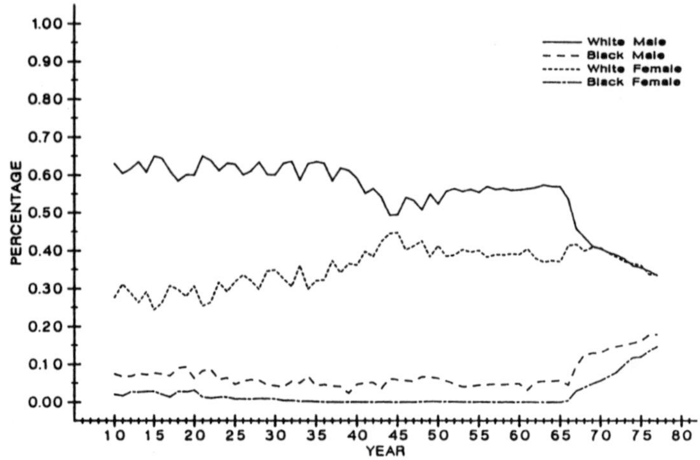

FIGURE 11. EMPLOYMENT SHARES IN THE SOUTH CAROLINA TEXTILE INDUSTRY, CHESTER COUNTY

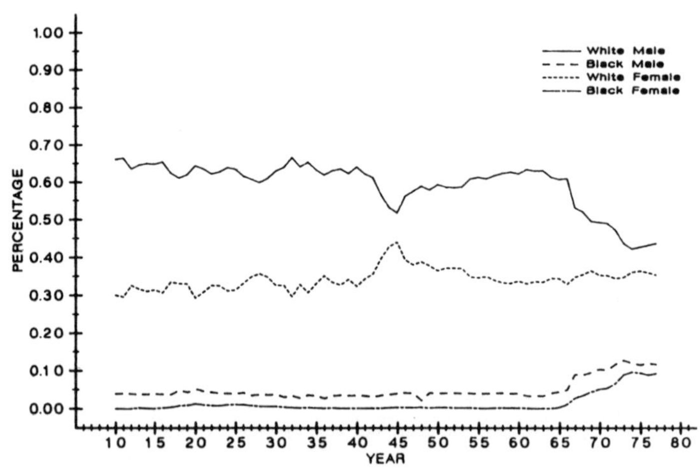

FIGURE 12. EMPLOYMENT SHARES IN THE SOUTH CAROLINA TEXTILE INDUSTRY, GREENVILLE COUNTY

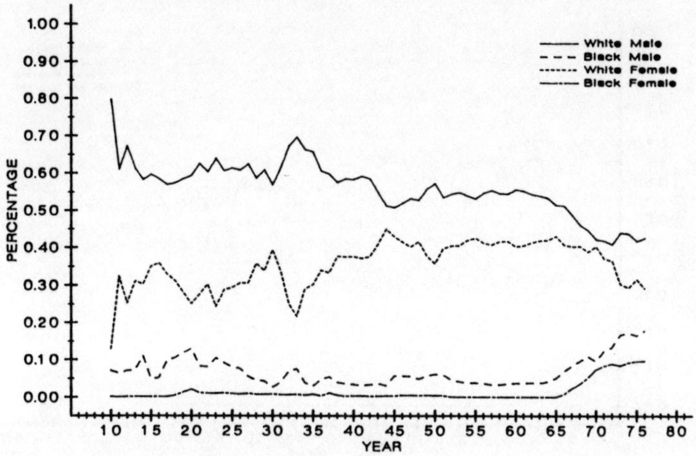

FIGURE 13. EMPLOYMENT SHARES IN THE SOUTH CAROLINA TEXTILE INDUSTRY, LANCASTER COUNTY

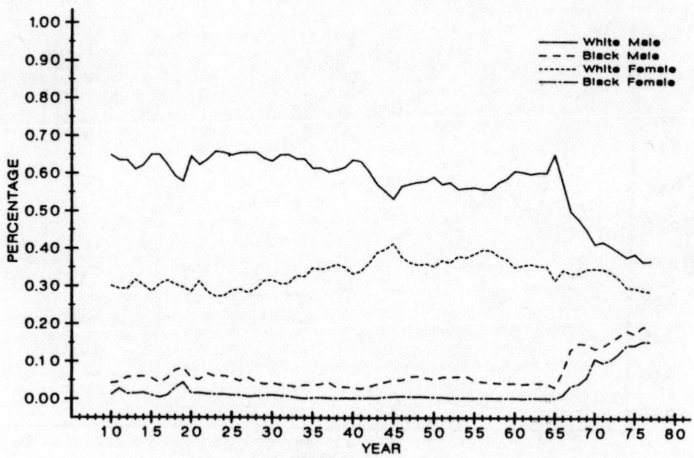

FIGURE 14. EMPLOYMENT SHARES IN THE SOUTH CAROLINA TEXTILE INDUSTRY, LAURENS COUNTY

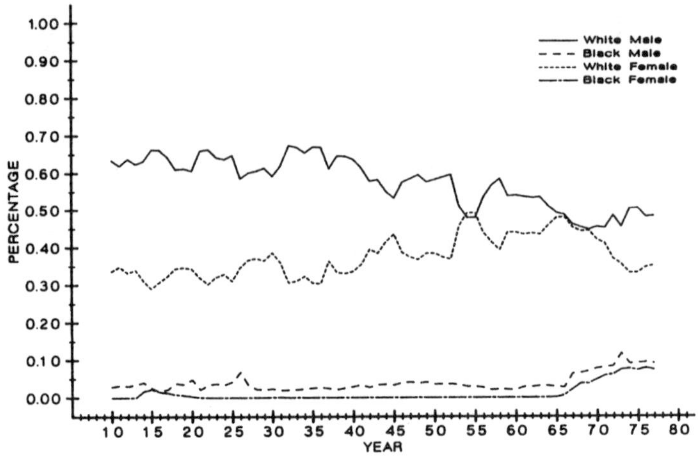

FIGURE 15. EMPLOYMENT SHARES IN THE SOUTH CAROLINA TEXTILE INDUSTRY, OCONEE COUNTY

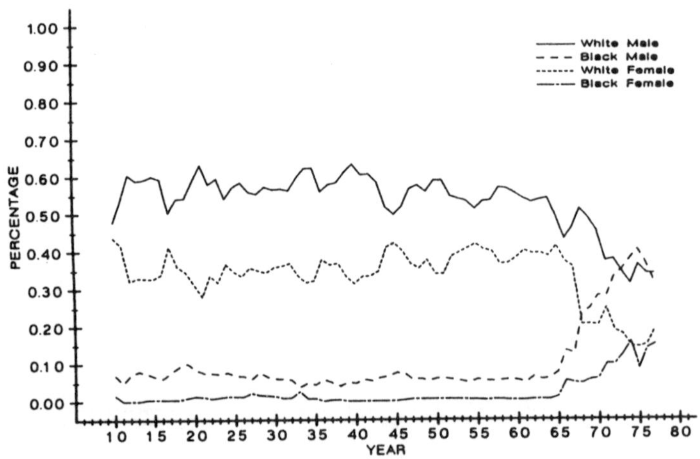

FIGURE 16. EMPLOYMENT SHARES IN THE SOUTH CAROLINA TEXTILE INDUSTRY, ORANGEBURG COUNTY

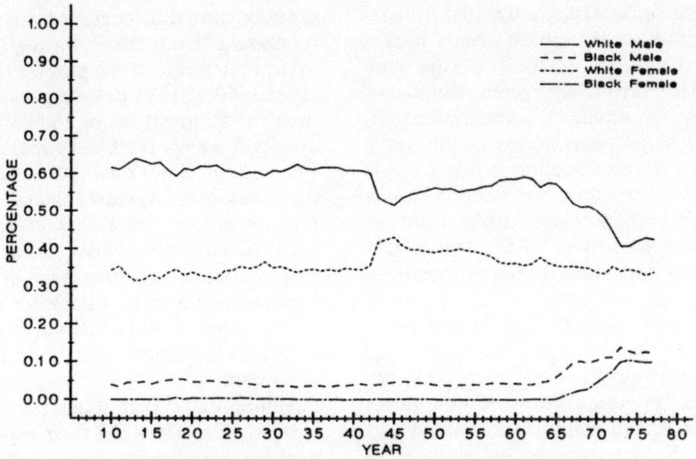

FIGURE 17. EMPLOYMENT SHARES IN THE SOUTH CAROLINA TEXTILE INDUSTRY, PICKENS COUNTY

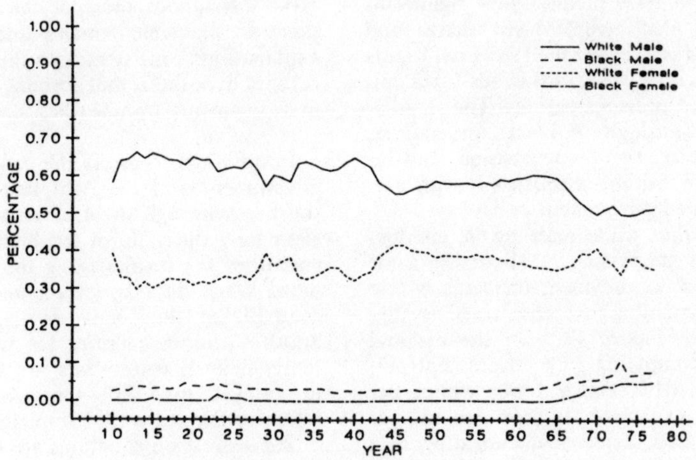

FIGURE 18. EMPLOYMENT SHARES IN THE SOUTH CAROLINA TEXTILE INDUSTRY, SPARTANBURG COUNTY

mobility costs for workers, a tight labor market might produce the simultaneous breakthrough of black employment of the type exhibited here. However, given significant differences in employment, industrialization, and racial demographics across counties, we conclude that South Carolina is not a single labor market. Therefore, we do not expect changing labor market conditions alone to have the same impact on black textile employment simultaneously across all counties.

D. *The Government Activity Hypothesis*

Evidence supporting the government activity hypothesis comes from the time-series on statewide textile employment and wages by demographic group presented above. The share of black textile employment was virtually unaffected by events that occurred from 1910 to 1965. This is especially true for black female employment. Under the tight labor market hypothesis we might expect some changes in black employment shares in the upswings of the numerous business cycles that occur prior to 1965. The government activity hypothesis predicts that significant changes in black employment shares and wages would occur after the 1964 Civil Rights Acts but has no prediction about black improvement in previous periods. The simultaneous breakthrough of blacks in counties varying in size, racial composition, and industrial composition is consistent with uniformly applied government policy.

The fact that white male textile employment begins decreasing at about the same time as black employment increases is also consistent with the government activity hypothesis. See Figure 19.[8] On the demand side, firms complying with government policy would likely employ fewer whites per unit output expansion as their demand for blacks increased. Evidence documenting that this occurred is given below. Examination of the wage data gives a supply-side explanation for the decrease in white male textile employment that occurred after 1965. After increasing from 1959 through 1965, white male real wages were practically unchanged from 1966 to 1971 despite growth in employment and output in the industry. See Figure 20. Real wages for blacks increased through the end of the 1960s. If textile firms were discriminating against blacks before 1965, but not in later years, then under the government activity hypothesis, white wages would stop rising as a large pool of black labor became available to textiles for the first time. Black wages would continue to rise over time as blacks become employed in higher paying occupations.

White male real wages stop growing in textiles after 1966. As their wages in textiles declined relative to those in other industries, white males left textiles for other industries. The slowing of wage growth for white males does not occur in all industries. Figure 21 shows real wages in non-textile manufacturing. For white males, real wages continue to grow after 1965 at a rate similar to that experienced prior to 1965. Wages for other demographic groups in these industries also grew throughout most of the 1960s. Thus there are plausible demand- and supply-side explanations consistent with the government activity hypothesis that account for the white male departure from textiles.

In an effort to assess the contributions of government and the tight labor market to the breakthrough in black employment, we estimate reduced form employment by race equations for textiles using the county-level data. Wage data by race and sex are not available at the county level. For the 11 South Carolina counties for which consistently defined textile data are available, we fit pooled time-series–cross-section equations for the years 1947 through 1971.

The regression equations are of the form

$$(1)\qquad Y_{ijt} = X_{it}a_j + f_{ij} + g_{jt} + \eta_{ijt},$$

where i refers to the county, j refers to the demographic group, and t refers to time. The fixed-effects f_{ij} and g_{jt}, are, respectively, county-specific and year-specific inter-

[8]This decline occurs in the 11 counties analyzed in the preceding section and for the state as a whole.

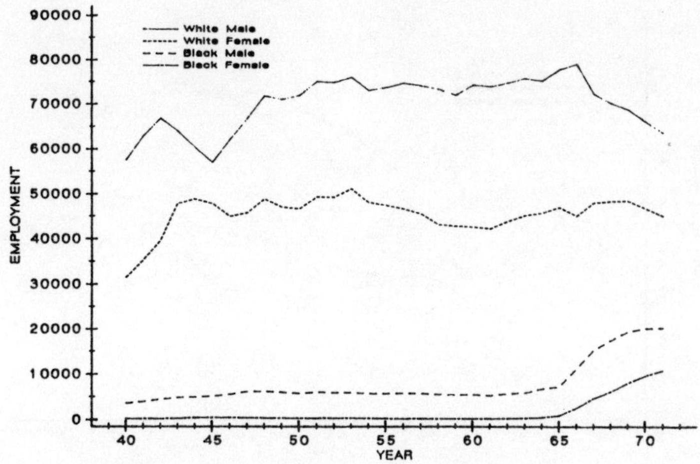

FIGURE 19. AGGREGATE EMPLOYMENT IN THE SOUTH CAROLINA TEXTILE MANUFACTURING INDUSTRY

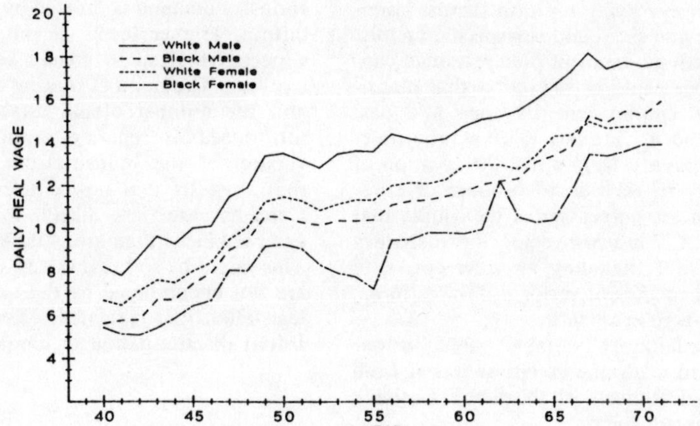

FIGURE 20. SOUTH CAROLINA TEXTILE INDUSTRY AVERAGE DAILY REAL WAGES

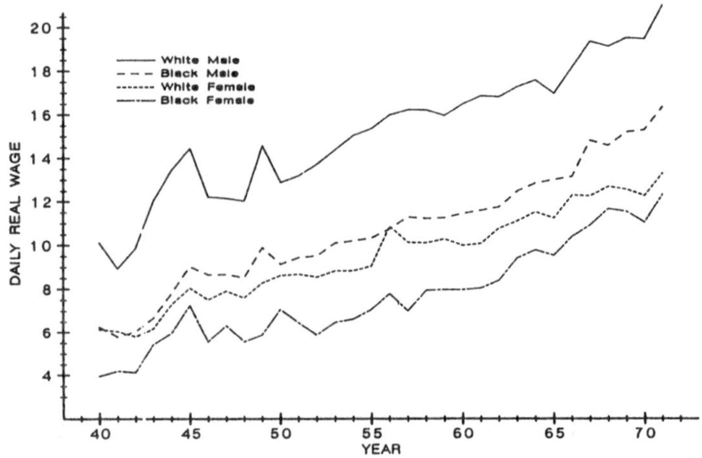

FIGURE 21. SOUTH CAROLINA NON-TEXTILE MANUFACTURING INDUSTRY AVERAGE DAILY REAL WAGES

cepts for each demographic group. These estimated fixed effects control for a variety of omitted variables that are likely to affect demographic employment. Absorbed in g_{jt} are any time-varying uniform (across counties) statewide race- and sex-specific factors, like uniform government policy, human capital improvements or migration that plausibly affect employment by race and sex. Absorbed in f_{ij} are any idiosyncratic time-invariant county factors like the location of the county in relation to product or labor markets or the percentage of the county that is black. "X_{it}" is a row vector of explanatory variables, not including an intercept, with associated coefficient vector a_j. The term η_{ijt} is a mean-zero error term.

The explanatory variables used in our analysis are, with one exception, taken from the Annual Reports of the South Carolina Department of Labor:

Textile Output = Real textile output in millions of dollars.

New Establishments = Number of establishments which entered the county after 1957.

Old Establishments = Number of establishments which entered the county before 1958.

Non-Textile Output = Real non-textile manufacturing output in million dollars.

Defense Contracts = Real cumulative defense contracts in million dollars.[9]

Industry demand is proxied by county textile output. Higher levels of output would be expected to lead to greater employment of workers. The number of new establishments and the number of old establishments are introduced as separate variables to test a version of the industrialization hypothesis that suggests that new entrants into South Carolina are less likely to discriminate against blacks than are older establishments. This might be so because new establishments are not encumbered by the restrictive racial legislation that regulated old establishments. Initial discrimination in employment might

[9]Defense contracts data by establishment were available after 1965. The Department of Defense gave us data on Prime Contract Awards over $10,000 by county for South Carolina over the period 1966–71. Cumulative contracts were used because a contract award received in one year was not necessarily only for that year alone. For instance, some firms had negative values for defense contracts in years when previous contracts were canceled. A similar variable, cumulative EEOC expenditures, was used by Freeman (1973).

persist due to fixed costs of hiring and due to fellow employee discrimination. Many new establishments were northern-owned and it is possible that their owners had lower tastes for discrimination. Joan Hoffman (1975) reports evidence favoring this hypothesis. Even in the absence of an old establishment—new establishment differential, the total number of establishments is a plausible regressor which (since output is being held fixed in the regression) measures the effect of establishment size on demographic employment.

Non-textile manufacturing output in the county is the best available proxy for the tightness of the non-textile labor market. Manufacturing employed over one-third of all workers in South Carolina between 1960 and 1970. Textile workers have more mobility into non-textile manufacturing than out of manufacturing altogether.[10]

County-level defense contract expenditure provides a good measure of government activity for the textile industry because the office of Federal Contract Compliance and the Defense Department monitored the compliance of textile firms with the affirmative action and nondiscrimination provisions of Executive Order 11246. Orley Ashenfelter and Heckman (1976) present evidence that the presence of a government contract makes it more likely for a firm to integrate its work force and employ more blacks.

Cumulative rather than current expenditure is used to measure the long-term impact of contracts. Estimation with a distributed lag version of this variable does not affect any inference. The effects of uniform government antidiscrimination policies which cannot be directly measured are absorbed into the estimated year effects.

We also estimate an interactive version of the preceding model which permits the a_j coefficients to assume different values after 1964. This interactive specification enables us to test for the presence of structural shift in demographic employment equations which would result from effective government antidiscrimination and affirmative action measures.

In order to determine the appropriate transformation of the dependent variable for the employment equations, we follow Takeshi Amemiya (1985) and James Powell (1981) as described in Amemiya and estimate a non-normal Box-Cox model that uses

$$\left(Y_{ijt}^{\lambda j}-1\right)/\lambda_j,$$

rather than Y_{ijt} as the dependent variable. The main inferences from using linear Y_{ijt} are preserved in the Box-Cox regressions but the latter fit the data better. "λ_j" is estimated along with the other coefficients of the model using nonlinear least squares. Both log and linear versions of X produce the same inference. To simplify the presentation of these results, we report only the linear X version of these estimates in Table 12. The slope coefficients are for the stated dependent variable. The sign of the estimated effect on Y_{ijt} is the same as the sign of the coefficient reported in the table. Durbin-Watson statistics for each county (reported in a companion paper by the authors and Butler) indicate few problems with serial correlation in the estimated county residuals. Corrections for heteroscedasticity using Halbert White's method do not overturn any inference obtained using least squares standard errors. For the sake of brevity we only report the results of tests based on the conventional least squares standard errors.

There is evidence of statistically significant positive effects of defense contracts on black employment and statistically significant negative effects of this variable on white male employment. Increased textile output raises employment for all demographic groups. The interacted output variables reveal a post-1964 shift in the output-employment coefficient in favor of black workers. For black females, there is little evidence of any textile output expansion effect before 1965—a result that should be obvious from inspecting Figures 8 to 18. In the noninteractive specification, higher non-textile output in a county is associated with

[10] From the 1970 Public Use Sample, we calculate that of all textile workers in 1965, about 90 percent were employed in a manufacturing industry in 1970.

TABLE 12—BOX-COX DEMOGRAPHIC EMPLOYMENT EQUATIONS FIT USING THE AMEMIYA-POWELL PROCEDURE[a]
(*t*-statistics shown in parentheses)

	Black Males	Black Females	White Females	White Males
λ_j	.4 (35.46)	.45 (25.5)	.50 (7.79)	.60 (11.15)
Textile Output	.0018 (16.0)	.00304 (5.98)	.0025 (15.2)	.0018 (16.89)
New Establishments	.0217 (12.4)	.0857 (12.64)	−.0180 (−8.22)	−.0108 (−7.51)
Old Establishments	.0208 (13.8)	.0422 (6.16)	−.0038 (−1.74)	.0040 (2.70)
Non-Textile Output	−.0008 (−9.28)	−.0011 (−2.74)	−.0015 (−10.70)	−.0009 (−10.65)
Defense Contracts	.0013 (3.21)	.0159 (8.81)	.0007 (1.23)	−.0035 (−10.23)
		Model with Interactions		
	Black Males	Black Females	White Females	White Males
λ_j	.45 (24.14)	.45 (39.73)	.775 (13.3)	.80 (20.56)
Textile Output	.0008 (5.51)	−.0007 (−1.58)	.0036 (18.97)	.0027 (35.3)
New Establishments	.0154 (6.18)	.0631 (7.78)	−.0014 (−3.31)	−.0035 (−2.25)
Old Establishments	.0231 (15.67)	.0566 (11.94)	.0027 (1.32)	.0080 (8.415)
Non-Textile Output	−.0010 (−8.61)	−.0003 (−.654)	−.0024 (−11.57)	−.0014 (−17.82)
Defense Contracts	.0010 (2.32)	.0107 (8.67)	.0006 (1.15)	−.0034 (−15.2)
Δ Textile Output	.0014 (9.21)	.0081 (18.1)	−.0010 (−5.33)	−.0013 (−16.5)
Δ New Firms	.0025 (.912)	.0103 (1.16)	.0078 (2.07)	.0018 (1.09)
Δ Old Firms	−.0034 (−3.43)	−.0429 (−13.69)	−.0066 (−4.92)	-3.04×10^{-6} (−.005)
Δ Non-Textile Output	−.0002 (−1.69)	−.0019 (−5.46)	.0016 (8.83)	.0009 (13.72)

[a]The instruments used to fit these models are X, squares of X, and all interactions. The Y_{ijt} are divided by the grand mean employment (over time and county) for each demographic group. These are 4,082 for white males, 2,687 for white females, 396 for black males, and 78 for black females.

less employment in textiles for each demographic group. The pattern is preserved in the interactive model but the effect strengthens for blacks and weakens for whites in the post-1964 period.

In the model without interactions there is a clear effect of establishment size on employment by race. Smaller establishments (measured by output per establishment) tend to hire more blacks. Larger establishments tend to hire more white females while the estimated scale effect for white males is ambiguous. The only pronounced new establishment–old establishment effect is for black females. There is evidence that new establishments hire more black women and fewer whites than do old establishments. The interactive specifications reveal that new establishments tend to hire more blacks and fewer white males.

The estimated models show a steady increase in estimated year effects for black workers in the post-1964 period. (These estimates are reported in our companion paper with Butler, 1989.) Further evidence of structural shift in the labor market is revealed by simulating the best-fitting models over the crucial period 1965–70. Such simulations allow examination of the change in employment attributable to changes in each X variable and the change not explained by the regression. The results of such a simulation are presented in Table 13, which presents results for both the interactive and the noninteractive models.

The most striking feature of Table 13 is the failure of each fitted model to account for most of the observed employment change. Much of the improvement in black status is accounted for by unexplained post-1964 year effects. The importance of such year effects is consistent with the operation of unmeasured government antidiscrimination policy. Although the estimated defense coefficient is statistically significant, the contribution of defense contracts to black employment is

TABLE 13—EFFECTS OF CHANGING VARIABLES ON TEXTILE EMPLOYMENT 1965–1970[a]

	Black Males	Black Females	White Females	White Males
	From Model Without Interactions			
Actual Change	5041	4215	565	−6778
Change from All Sources	747	823	−319	−3045
From Output	307	116	2179	2131
From New Establishments	489	448	−2256	−2045
From Old Establishments	−64	−29	61	−103
From Non-Textile Output	−75	−21	−651	−608
Defense Contracts	90	310	347	−2420
	From Model With Interactions			
Change from All Sources	1241	820	1412	−1399
Change from Defense Contracts and Structural Shift	903	562	1151	−2743
From Output	126	−26	2590	2946
From New Establishments	365	329	−1292	−601
From Old Establishments	−68	−40	−38	−174
From Non-Textile Output	−85	−5	−994	−827
Defense Contracts	100	208	257	−2177
From Interaction Output	223	306	−720	−1418
From Interaction New Establishments	588	54	884	309
From Interaction Old Establishments	9	30	94	0
From Interaction Non-Textile Output	−17	−36	636	543

[a]For county i and demographic group j the effect of changing the lth component of X_{it} at time t, X_{itl} to $X_{i,t+k,l}$ is estimated by

$$\Delta Y_{jt} = Y_{j,t+k} - Y_{j,t}$$

$$= \lambda_j a_{jl} \sum_{i=1}^{I} (Y_{ijt})^{(1-\lambda_j)} \left\{ \left[\frac{Y_{ij,t+k}}{Y_{ijt}} - 1 \right] \Big/ \left[\left(\frac{Y_{ij,tk}}{Y_{ijt}} \right)^{\lambda_j} - 1 \right] \right\} \Delta X_{itl},$$

where I is the number of counties, $t = 1965$, $t + k = 1970$. The coefficients from Table 12 are used.

numerically weak.[11] If all post-1964 interaction effects are attributed to government policy, between 70 to 80 percent of the predicted change in black employment is attributable to this source. In any case, unmeasured components account for most of the

[11]There are conditions under which we underestimate the contribution of defense contracts to the increase in black employment. The contract data refer to work done in the county but firms were required to comply with Executive Order 11246 in all plants, even those not producing goods for sale to the government. There are many textile firms with plants in different counties and different states. County textile defense expenditure is thus an error-ridden measure of the appropriate variable. In a simple demographic model of demand which regresses employment solely on the measured contract variable, the estimated contract effect is downward biased if the variable indicating whether the *plant* has a contract is independent of the disturbance term in the equation. If the demographic demand equation contains additional explanatory variables which are correlated with the indicator variable, the sign of the bias is ambiguous.

observed change. Such dramatic structural shift seems inconsistent with pure forms of the tight labor market or industrialization hypotheses. Government activity—residually defined—seems to be the most plausible source of this change.

V. Summary and Conclusions

This paper examines the sources of black economic progress in South Carolina. Lessons from that state are of general interest because trends in black progress in South Carolina resemble trends in the South as a whole and black improvement in the South accounts for a substantial component of aggregate U.S. black improvement over the period 1960–80. We focus on the manufacturing sector. Butler documents that much of the southern black progress comes through entry of black workers into craftsmen and operative occupations and improvement in relative black wages in those occupations which are concentrated in manufacturing.

Using a unique body of time-series–cross-section data on employment and wages by race and sex supplemented by a variety of U.S. government sources, we examine a number of competing explanations for the breakthrough in black employment and wages in the manufacturing sector that occurred after 1964. We demonstrate the value of disaggregating the data and establish that different factors account for black progress in different sectors.

The principal manufacturing employer in the state is the textile industry. This industry was already a substantial employer by 1915 when Jim Crow laws formalized a preexisting exclusion of blacks from the main operative and craftsman occupations of that industry. We document that over the period 1910–64, the share of black employment was low and stable despite a variety of economic circumstances in the state. Suddenly, in 1965, blacks of both sexes become employed on a large scale. That year witnessed the implementation of Title VII of the 1964 Civil Rights Act which forbade employment discrimination. Executive Order 11246 was also issued in that year. The Order forbade discrimination by government contractors and required the establishment of affirmative-action programs. The South Carolina textile industry sold 5 percent of its output to the U.S. government in 1965. The Equal Employment Opportunity Commission targeted southern textiles and held hearings on the industry in 1966. The improvement in black status after 1964 is uniform across geographically diverse local labor markets. Regression analyses of black employment reveal a structural shift in employment equations that cannot be accounted for by conventional measures of output or the growth in alternative opportunities. There is some evidence of greater black employment in counties that sold more goods to the U.S. government. Both the timing evidence and the regression evidence suggest that government activity played an important role in integrating textiles. As a large new supply of black workers became available to the industry, the real wages of white workers—which had been rising for six consecutive years before 1965—suddenly flattened. A similar but less well-documented story can be told for black female progress in the closely related apparel industry.

Alternative explanations of the black breakthrough in textiles appear to be much less cogent. A supply shift story attributing the black improvement to the decline in agriculture cannot account for the timing of the black breakthrough in textiles. The human capital story of improvement in black skill also cannot account for the timing. Increases in black human capital between 1960 and 1970 should have reduced black employment because textiles is a low skill industry. By 1960, there were plenty of blacks with skill levels adequate to perform textile jobs.

The only viable alternative to the story of government as the agent of change in textiles is the story that assigns a central role to the tightness of the labor market. By the mid-1960s, South Carolina had a booming economy. New industries entered the state and the traditional reservoir of white farm labor had disappeared. Real wages in textiles increased making competition with low wage foreign firms more difficult. The incentives to draw on a new source of low wage labor were great.[12]

What cannot be dismissed and indeed seems quite plausible is that in 1965 entrepreneurs seized on the new federal legislation and decrees to do what they wanted to do anyway. One could argue that the federal antidiscrimination and affirmative-action laws came into existence in 1964 precisely because the U.S. labor market was tight to an unprecedented degree and discrimination was becoming costly. This study cannot reject the hypothesis that it was the confluence of tight labor markets and new laws that made integration in textiles occur so rapidly. Separating these factors requires information from another episode in which comparable laws are put in place in a slack labor market.

We do not claim that federal activity accounts for black progress in other sectors of the state. A major finding of our analysis is that once skill levels are accounted for blacks were not excluded from other sectors even in 1960. Newer industries entering the state long after the institution of Jim Crow laws tended to be color-blind in their employment practices. Surprisingly, so were state and local governments by 1960. Blacks were underrepresented in these sectors only because they lacked skills. As their skill levels expanded, so did their employment in those sectors.

DATA APPENDIX

We have combined data from U.S. government sources with data published by the state of South Carolina. Three types of data were combined to form the South Carolina data base: annual county-level data, annual state-level data, and census-year data. For the period 1910–35, the data come from *Reports and Resolutions of South Carolina to the General Assembly of the State of South Carolina*. For the period 1936–71, the data come from the *Annual Report of the Department of Labor to the State of South Carolina*. In addition to the South Carolina data we collected U.S. Population Census data for the Census South and selected southern states.

We obtain the following data, by county for each fiscal year (July 1 to June 30).

For the textile industry, the variables are: value of annual product (dollars); average number of days plants operated; total wages of production workers (dollars); by sex, average employment of production workers, by race and sex; and number of establishments.

From a listing of all textile plants by name in each county are formed: number of establishments started after 1957, number of establishments started before 1958.

Establishments are counted at the plant level, although individual plants may belong to the same firm. For total manufacturing, we collect annual data on value of annual product (dollars). Total manufacturing excludes lumber, timber, and turpentine. Non-textile output (annual product) by county is formed by subtracting textile output from total manufacturing output. The county textile data exclude totals for knitting mills and synthetics mills for the period 1910–69. In 1970 and 1971 the totals include knitting mills and synthetics. Unlike the county-level data, statewide aggregate data for the textile industry include the knitting and synthetics mills over the entire sample period.

From the U.S. Census of Population reports for 1960 for South Carolina, we obtain population, total employment, manufacturing employment, textile employment, and agriculture employment for selected counties.

We obtained defense contract data from *Prime Contract Awards Over $10,000 by State, County, Contractor and Place* for South Carolina from 1966 to 1971. Total defense contracts for textile establishments by county by year are formed by matching firm or plant names listed in this data source with firm or plant names listed in the *Annual Reports of the South Carolina Department of Labor*.

In addition to the county data, we use aggregate statewide industry data from the South Carolina Department of Labor reports. These data are for every manufacturing industry except lumber, timber, and turpentine. The available data include: value of annual product (dollars); average number of days plants operated; average number of production workers, by race and sex; total wages, by race and sex (dollars).

Average daily wages by race and sex are computed by dividing total wages (deflated by the CPI) for each race and sex group by the product of the number of production workers in that group and the number of days plants operated.

Statewide data on employment in textiles, manufacturing total and agriculture by race and sex were obtained from the U.S. Bureau of the Census, Census of Population for 1940, 1950, 1960, and 1970. Statewide textile industry employment by race and sex were collected for 1950, 1960, 1970, and 1980 for the states of North Carolina, Georgia, and Virginia from U.S. Bureau of the Census, Census of Population: Vol. 2, for those states.

U.S. Census public use micro-data computer tapes are another source of data. The 1940, 1950, and 1960 tapes each contain a 1 percent sample, the 1970 tape

[12] However it should be noted that many employers feared that blacks were more likely to join unions. (Rowan, 1970.) In the nonunionized textile labor market this would be a serious negative consideration.

contains a 2 percent sample, and the 1980 tape contains a 5 percent sample. We use the following variables from each Census tape for South Carolina:

occupation, industry, race, sex, age, annual wage income (dollars) last year, hours worked last week, weeks worked last year, highest grade completed, and labor force status (civilian, employed, unemployed, out of labor force).

From the U.S. Bureau of the Census Public Use Samples we also obtain data for the Census South. We use 1 percent samples for 1940 and 1950, 0.1 percent samples for 1960 and 1970, and a 0.5 percent for 1980. Data on race, sex, age, industry, and labor force were obtained for each Census year.

For certain analyses, we form the following five categories of manufacturing industries: textiles, chemicals, apparel, nontraditional manufacturing, and traditional manufacturing. Chemicals and apparel were isolated because of their similarity to textiles. The other two categories were formed on the basis of a ranking of the percentage change in employment from 1960 to 1970 in the remaining manufacturing industries. The five nontraditional high growth industries are: transportation equipment, electrical machinery, nonelectrical machinery, metal working, and foundries and machine shops. The six traditional low growth industries are: food products, paper and pulp, stone and clay, lumber and furniture, printing and publishing, and miscellaneous manufacturing.

The data from the South Carolina reports are available for the fiscal year beginning July 1. The Census and Department of Defense data are available for the calendar year. We chose the following convention for matching data from the various sources. The fiscal year is defined to correspond to the calendar year in which the fiscal year ends.

A copy of the South Carolina data is available from ICPSR at the University of Michigan.

REFERENCES

Amemiya, Takeshi, *Advanced Econometrics*, Cambridge: Harvard University Press, 1985.

______ **and Powell, James L.,** "A Comparison of the Box-Cox Maximum Likelihood Estimator and the Non-Linear Two-Stage Least Squares Estimator," *Journal of Econometrics*, December 1981, *17*, 351–81.

Arrow, Kenneth J., "Models of Job Discrimination," in A. H. Pascal, ed., *Racial Discrimination in Economic Life*, Lexington, MA: Lexington: D. C. Heath, 1974, ch. 1.

Ashenfelter, Orley and Heckman, James, "Measuring the Effect of an Antidiscrimination Program," in Orley Ashenfelter and James Blum, eds., *Evaluating the Labor-Market Effects of Social Programs*, Princeton Industrial Relations Section, Princeton: Princeton University Press; 1976, ch. 2, 46–84.

Brown, Charles, "Black-White Earnings Ratios Since the Civil Rights Act of 1964: The Importance of Labor Market Dropouts," *Quarterly Journal of Economics*, May 1984, *99*, 31–44.

Bunting, Robert L., *Employer Concentration in Local Labor Markets*, Chapel Hill: University of North Carolina Press, 1962.

Butler, Richard J., "Demand Side Changes and Relative Black Wage Growth in the 1960's," mimeo., Brigham Young University, 1985.

Directorate for Information, Operations and Reports (DIOR), *DOD Prime Contract Awards over $10,000 by State, County, Contractor and Place, Fiscal Years 1966 through 1980*. Washington: The Pentagon, 1980.

Freeman, Richard B., "Changes in the Labor Market for Black Americans," *Brookings Papers on Economic Activity*, 1: Spring 1973, 67–120.

______, "Black Economic Progress after 1964: Who has Gained and Why?," in S. Rosen, ed., *Studies in Labor Markets*, Chicago: 1981, ch. 8.

Friedman, Milton *Capitalism and Freedom*, Chicago: University of Chicago Press, 1962.

Heckman, James, Payner, Brook and Butler, Richard, "The Impact of the Economy and the State on the Economic Status of Blacks," forthcoming in D. Galenson, ed., *Markets in History: Economic Studies of the Past*, Cambridge, England: Cambridge University Press, 1989, ch. 6.

Hoffman, Joan, *Racial Discrimination and Economic Development*, Lexington, MA: D. C. Heath, 1975.

Kidder, Alice, (1972a) "Federal Compliance Efforts in the Carolina Textile Industry: A Summary Report," *Proceedings of the 25th Annual Meeting of the Industrial Relations Research Association*, Madison, WI: Industrial Relations Research Association, 1972, 353–61.

______, **Sidney Evans, Simons, Michael and Smith, Dupont,** (1972b) "Changes in Minority Participation in the Textile Industry of

North Carolina and South Carolina 1966 to 1969," Department of Economics, North Carolina A&T-Greensboro, NC, 1972.

Murray, Charles, *Losing Ground*, New York: Basic Books, 1984.

Osborne, Donald, "Negro Employment in the Textile Industries of North and South Carolina," Research Report, 1966–70, Equal Employment Opportunity Commission, Washington: November 21, 1966.

Rowan, Richard L., "The Negro in the Textile Industry," in H. Northrup, R. Rowan, D. Barnum, and J. Howard, eds., Part 5, *Negro Employment in Southern Industry*, Philadelphia: University of Pennsylvania Press, 1970, ch. 5.

Smith, James, "Race and Human Capital," *American Economic Review*, September 1984, 74, 685–98.

______ **and Welch, Finis,** *Closing the Gap: Forty Years of Economic Progress for Blacks*, Santa Monica, CA: Rand, 1986.

Tang, Anthony M., *Economic Development in the Southern Piedmont*, University of North Carolina Press, Chapel Hill: University of North Carolina Press, 1958.

Tobin, James, "On Improving the Economic Status of the Negro," *Daedalus*, Fall 1965, *94*, 878–98.

Vroman, Wayne, "Changes in Black Worker's Relative Earnings: Evidence for the 1960's," in G. Von Furstenberg, ed., *Patterns of Racial Discrimination*, Vol. II, Lexington, MA: D. C. Heath, 1974.

Welch, Finis, "Black-White Differences in the Return to Schooling," *American Economic Review*, December 1973, *63*, 893–907.

White, Halbert, "A Heteroskedasticity-Consistent Covariance Matrix Estimator and a Direct Test for Heteroskedasticity," *Econometrica*, May 1980, *48*, 817–38.

Wilson, William, *The Truly Disadvantaged: Inner City, The Under Class and Public Policy*, Chicago: University of Chicago Press, 1986.

Wright, Gavin, *Old South, New South*, New York: Basic Books, 1986.

South Carolina Department of Education, *Annual Report of the State Superintendant of Education of the State of South Carolina*. Columbia, SC: Printed under the Direction of the State Budget and Control Board, 1931–1957.

______, *Reports and Resolutions of South Carolina to the General Assembly of the State of South Carolina*, Columbia, SC: Printed under the Direction of the State Budget and Control Board, 1910–1936.

______, *South Carolina Department of Labor Annual Report*, Columbia, SC: Printed under the Direction of the State Budget and Control Board, 1936–1977.

United States Commission on Civil Rights, *The Economic Progress of Black Men in America*, Washington: U.S. Government Clearinghouse Publication 91, 1986.

U.S. Bureau of the Census, *Census of Population: 1940*, Vol. 2, *Characteristics of the Population*, part 6, Washington: USGPO, 1943.

______, *Census of Population: 1950*, Vol. 2, *Characteristics of the Population*, part 40, Washington: USGPO, 1953.

______, *Census of Population: 1960*, Vol. 2, *Characteristics of the Population*, part 42, South Carolina, Washington: USGPO, 1964.

______, *Census of Manufacturers: 1967*, Vol. 3, *Area Statistics*, part 2, Washington: USGPO, 1971.

______, (1973a) *Census of the Population: 1970*, Vol. 1, *Characteristics of the Population*, part 1, United States Summary—Section 1, Washington: USGPO, 1973.

______, (1973b) *Census of Population: 1970*, Vol. 1, *Characteristics of the Population*, part 42, South Carolina, Washington: USGPO, 1973.

______, (1973c) *Census of Population: 1960*, Public Use Microdata Sample, (machine-readable data file)/prepared by the Bureau of the Census, Washington: The Bureau (producer and distributor), 1973.

______, (1973d) *Census of Population: 1970*, Public Use Microdata Sample, (machine-readable data file)/prepared by the Bureau of the Census, Washington: The Bureau (producer and distributor), 1973.

______, (1973e) *Annual Survey of Manufacturers: 1970 and 1971*, Washington: USGPO, 1973.

______, (1983a) *1980 Census of Population*, Vol. 1, ch. C, "General Social and Economic Characteristics," part 1, U.S. Summary, Washington: USGPO, 1983.

______, (1983b) *1980 Census of Population*, Vol. 1, ch. C, "General Social and Economic Characteristics," part 42, South Carolina, Washington: USGPO, 1983.

______, (1983c) *Census of Population and Housing: 1980*, Public Use Microdata Sample (A and B Samples), (machine-readable data file)/prepared by the Bureau of the Census, Washington: The Bureau (producer and distributor), 1983.

______, (1984a) *Census of Population: 1940*, Public Use Microdata Sample, (machine-readable data file)/prepared by the Bureau of the Census, Washington: The Bureau (producer and distributor), 1984.

______, (1984b) *Census of Population: 1950*, Public Use Microdata Sample, (machine-readable data file)/prepared by the Bureau of the Census, Washington: The Bureau (producer and distributor), 1984.

[30]

THE MALAYSIAN ECONOMY IN PERSPECTIVE

The origins of the contemporary (Peninsular) Malaysian economy can be traced to the economy built by its population under British colonial auspices. The initial motive for British hegemony in the region from the late eighteenth century was the need to break the mercantilist stranglehold over trade with East and Southeast Asia by opening up new free ports around the strategic Malacca Straits. The banner of free trade was initially sufficient to ensure British superiority in international commerce. The changing requirements dictated by the consolidation of oligopoly in Western Europe in the latter half of the last century precipitated the scramble for colonies, to which Malaya fell victim. Beginning from 1874 with the tin-rich central portion of the West Coast of the peninsula, the British eventually asserted control over the entire area now known as Peninsular Malaysia by the outbreak of the First World War four decades later. The main target of this initial stage of the second phase of British colonial expansion in Malaya was control over the lucrative tin-mining industry, then already thriving in Perak, and to a lesser extent, Selangor. The attractive natural environment suitable for rubber cultivation and the availability of cheap immigrant labour from India, China and the neighbouring islands of what is now Indonesia soon gave rise to a thriving plantation section. Hence, the modern capitalist sector developed most on the West Coast, with its naturally endowed tin deposits and artificially-created infrastructure, which was later extended to serve the growing plantation sector. Meanwhile, the British – perhaps fearing the possibility of peasant revolt – initially sought to insulate the indigenous population from capitalist developments by consolidating them as a yeoman peasantry, and later tried to restrict them to rice cultivation against their own rational preferences in order to reduce the foreign exchange bill for imported rice to feed the rest of the population. While the majority of the Chinese population become workers (as did the bulk of the Indian population), many Chinese entrepreneurs seized the commercial opportunities engendered by the rapidly growing market economy, while others developed productive enterprises, most of which remained subordinate to the hegemony of British capital and the colonial state.

While admittedly cursory, the preceding outline of some key

aspects of economic development under colonial auspices offers important insights into the inherited structure of the Peninsular Malaysian economy. For instance, the regional imbalances between the East Coast and the West Coast have their origin in the more advanced growth in the latter due to the location of the early tin mines, the consequent pattern of colonial annexation and infrastructural development, as well as the subsequent growth process involving the typical capitalistic strategy of "building upon the best." Similarly, the differences between the rice growing North and the rest of the peninsula are related to the history of colonial territorial expansion on the peninsula, as well as the British desire to preserve Malay peasants as rice farmers, despite the clear peasant preference for the consistently more lucrative alternative of rubber cultivation, which threatened British plantation interests.[1] The typical urban-rural gap is, of course, related to the usual roles of town and country in the capital accumulation process, exacerbated by the relative backwardness of the peasant sector compared, for example, to the plantation sector. Ethnic differences – which dominate most discussions of contemporary Malaysian society – often refer, to "the identification of race with economic function" in official parlance, or the relationship of ethnicity to class and occupation, which has its origins in the formation of the colonial economy.

With the effective suppression of radical nationalist challenge to colonial authority following the Japanese Occupation 'moderate' post-colonial rule by the Alliance (of the English-educated elites of the three major ethnic groups) was assured. For instance, the Alliance's program for the first general elections in 1955 faithfully incorporated the main proposals of the World Bank mission dispatched earlier to advise on post-colonial economic policy. Considerably aided by favourable world market conditions for its primary commodity exports and some early success in its import-substituting industrialization program, the Malayan and then (from 1963) the Malaysian economy sustained a high growth rate with a low inflation rate until 1973.

Other forces, however, were also at work. As can be seen in Table 1, the statistical evidence on income distribution patterns

[1] See Jomo (1985: Chapter 3)

TABLE 1
RURAL-URBAN SIZE DISTRIBUTION OF HOUSEHOLD INCOME, PENINSULAR MALAYSIA

	ALL HOUSEHOLDS					RURAL HOUSEHOLDS					URBAN HOUSEHOLDS				
Year	1957/8	1967/8	1970	1973	1976	1957/8	1967/8	1970	1973	1976	1957/8	1967/8	1970	1973	1976
Income Share of															
Top 5%	22.1	23.6	28.1	26.4	n.a	19.0	19.2	23.9	n.a	n.a	20.7	23.4	27.5	n.a	n.a
Top 20%	48.6	51.3	55.9	53.7	61.9	44.5	46.8	51.0	n.a	n.a	49.6	51.8	55.0	n.a	n.a
Middle 40%	35.5	34.4	32.5	34.0	27.8	37.3	36.7	35.9	n.a	n.a	33.2	34.0	32.8	n.a	n.a
Bottom 40%	15.9	14.3	11.6	12.3	10.3	18.2	16.5	13.1	n.a	n.a	17.2	14.2	12.2	n.a	n.a
Mean Household Income (M$)	215	240	264	324	801	172	185	201	n.a	n.a	307	360	407	n.a	n.a
Median Household Income (M$)	156	154	167	n.a	319	131	134	145	n.a	n.a	216	246	283	n.a	n.a
Gini Ratio	.41	.44	.50	.50	.57	.38	.40	.46	.46	.50	.42	.45	.50	.48	.57
Theil Index	.29	n.a.	.48	.43	.71	.25	n.a	.40	n.a	.55	.30	n.a	.45	n.a	.70
Sample size	2,760	6,696	26,310	7,285	1,064	–	–	–	–	–	–	–	–	–	–

n . a. : not available

Sources : 1. D.R. Snodgrass (1980) : 79, Table 4.8
2. Ishak Shari & Rogayah M. Zain (1978a) : 241 & 246, Tables 5 & 8.
3. M. W. Kusnic & J. Da Vanzo (1980): 117, Table 4.3

in 1957 and 1970 – though strictly non-comparable for methodological reasons – does point to a worsening distribution of income over the sixties. The data also suggest a growing gap between town and country over the same period. Interestingly, as shown in Table 2, this phenomenon was true for all the major ethnic groups, with the Gini coefficient for the Malay community increasing most – from a situation of least intra-ethnic inequality in 1957 to one of greatest inequality in 1970. This may have been primarily due to the relatively rapid growth of the Malay-dominated bureaucracy (with the 'Malayanization' of the civil service after independence) and the miniscule Malay capital-owning class.

This growing inequality – on overall as well as intra-ethnic lines – did not only result in growing inter-class tensions, but more importantly, was perceived primarily in racial terms, not least because of officially-encouraged political and social mobilization and expression along ethnic lines. Hence, Malay opposition to domination by capital was primarily expressed in terms of resentment against ethnic Chinese (who comprised the bulk of small businessmen), while non-Malay frustrations were directed against the state, widely identified with UMNO (the dominant partner in the ruling Alliance party) and the Malay-dominated post-colonial state machinery. These warped, but nevertheless common perceptions culminated in widespread ethnic-inspired opposition to the order of the sixties – a period marked by an import-substituting industrialization strategy, which generated little employment and had run out of steam by the mid-sixties, and a rural development strategy which emphasized productivity increases, while skirting the more difficult, but fundamental problems of redistribution in favour of the land-hungry peasantry. The post-general elections 'race riots' of May 1969 were in a sense then a consequence of the post-colonial state's exacerbation of the ethnic dimensions of the socio-economic class structure inherited, largely intact, from the colonial period. This tinder box was fuelled by the frustrated ambitions of the emerging Malay middle class who, though enjoying nominal political control over the country, saw the gradual decline of British economic hegemony giving way to Chinese capital. This 'political-bureaucratic' stratum became more assertive from the mid-sixties, establishing hegemony after the tragic events of May

TABLE 2
SIZE DISTRIBUTION OF HOUSEHOLD INCOME BY ETHNIC GROUP, PENINSULAR MALAYSIA

	MALAY HOUSEHOLDS					CHINESE HOUSEHOLDS					INDIAN HOUSEHOLDS				
Income Share of	1957/8	1967/8	1970	1973	1976	1957/8	1967/8	1970	1973	1976	1957/8	1967/8	1970	1973	1976
Top 5%	18.1	22.2	24.6	22.7	n.a	19.2	19.9	25.4	18.8	n.a	19.4	22.3	28.4	25.6	n.a
Top 20%	42.5	48.2	52.5	50.8	n.a	46.0	46.7	52.6	48.6	n.a	43.6	48.1	54.2	51.3	n.a
Middle 40%	37.9	34.8	34.8	35.5	n.a	35.9	36.3	33.5	35.5	n.a	36.6	35.6	31.5	33.7	n.a
Bottom 40%	19.6	17.0	12.7	13.7	n.a	18.1	17.0	13.9	15.9	n.a	19.8	16.3	14.3	15.0	n.a
Mean Income	140	63	177	222	529	302	349	399	444	1247	243	260	310	365	519
Median Income	112	120	122	n.a	357	223	261	269	n.a	623	188	191	195	n.a	232
Gini Ratio	.34	.40	.47	.45	.47	.38	.39	.45	.42	.58	.35	.40	.46	.44	.49
Theil Index	.21	n.a	.40	.36	.44	.23	n.a	.39	.31	.73	.25	n.a	.39	.35	.50

n.a. : not available

Sources : 1. D.R. Snodgrass (1980 : 76 – Table 4.7)
2. Ishak Shari & Rogayah M. Zain (1978: 21 – Table 5)
3. M.W. Kusnic & J. Da Vanzo (1980 : 52 – Table 15)

13, 1969.[2]

The New Economic Policy (NEP) declared in 1970 marked the political ascendance of these interests. The first of the NEP's two main prongs is committed to eradicating 'absolute' poverty – defined largely in terms of raising the real income, and presumably the economic welfare of the population above a certain "poverty line", officially defined with reference to the equivalent of M$33 per capita per month, or M$396 per annum in 1970. According to official estimates, about 49.3% of all households in Peninsular Malaysia in 1970 received incomes below the poverty line. The incidence of poverty is said to be particularly high among padi growers, rubber smallholders, coconut small-holders, fishermen, estate workers, residents of New Villages, agricultural labourers and the urban poor. A key element in government anti-poverty programs is supposed to be greater access of the poor to productive assests and inputs, training, credit, processing and marketing facilities and basic social services. Official projections claim that the overall incidence of poverty for Peninsular Malaysia has been declining since 1970 to 43.9% in 1975 and 29.2% in 1980. Using data from the 1977 Agricultural Census, the government estimated the incidence of poverty in 1976 at 35.1% for Peninsular Malaysia alone and 37.7% for the whole country (including Sabah and Sarawak). Despite the government's avowed commitment to poverty eradication, it should be emphasized that there is no official commitment to reducing economic inequality between the rich and the poor. On the contrary, there have even been pronouncements by prominent government leaders on the need to maintain economic inequality as an incentive for stimulating private enterprise. For example, Dr. Mahathir Mohamed (the present Prime Minister of Malaysia) once said that ". . . . in trying to redress the imbalance it will be necessary to concentrate your effort on the Malays, to bring out more Malay entrepreneurs and to make Malay millionaires, if you like, so that the number of Malays who are rich equals the number of Chinese who are rich, the number of Malays who are poor, equals the number of Chinese who are poor and the number of unemployed Malays equals the

[2] For a more detailed discussion of the background, nature and causes of this important episode in Malaysian history, see Van Vorys, 1975).

number of unemployed Chinese, then you can say that parity has been achieved". (Quoted in Patrick Low, 1971).

The other major prong of the NEP is somewhat euphemistically referred to as "restructuring society". This involves a broad commitment to eliminating the identification of ethnicity with 'economic function', which has been largely achieved at the lower echelons of the labour force, especially in the industrial sector. Roughly speaking, success in restructuring employment tends to decline as one goes up the occupational pyramid, with considerable difficulty at the level of credentialed and technical professionals. The primary mechanism used by the government in this area is 'preferential treatment', 'affirmative action' or 'ethnic discrimination' (depending on how one sees it) in training (e.g., through admissions policies or educational aid disbursement) and recruitment (especially into the state sector). Such policies are criticized, by those who argue that not enough is being done for the Bumiputeras to rectify inter-ethnic inequalities as well as others who emphasize government discrimination and oppression along ethnic lines as well as violation of meritocratic principles (which still is the rationale for the present hierarchical socio-economic order).

Even more contentious is the key component of the 'restructuring' prong which is committed to the creation of an indigenous (Bumiputera) 'commercial and entrepreneurial' class owning at least 30% of the corporate sector by 1990. Although it was originally projected that only a quarter of this 30% (i.e. 7.5%) would be in the hands of Bumiputera individuals, with the rest held by public enterprises ostensibly representing the interests of the entire Bumiputera community, in view of the current official commitment to privatization, there is a strong likelihood that the proportions will be revised for Bumiputera individuals to hold 10%, or a third of the total Bumiputera quota for 1990.

Changes in the Malaysian economy over the past quarter century, especially rapid economic growth, can no longer be denied: the annual growth rate of the Gross Domestic Product (GDP) in Peninsular Malaysia was on average, 5.8% during 1957-70 (Rao, 1976), while the GDP for the whole of Malaysia rose by 7.8% per year, on average, between 1971 and 1980 (Malaysia, 1981). There have been several especially important changes. Post-colonial industrial development has involved two main stages so far, namely import substitution from the late fifties to the mid-sixties, and export-oriented industrialization since the late sixties. Rural development efforts, mainly directed at the peasantry, contrast with British colonial neglect. Initially, such efforts were aimed at strengthening the yeoman peasantry, but since the late seventies, more attention has been given to the development of capitalist agriculture. The government's efforts to diversify the economy have not only involved efforts to diversify agriculture (through the introduction of oil palm, cocoa, etc.), but also the growth of various kinds of industries – import substituting, as well as export-oriented, including industries based on local primary resources.

However, this pattern of economic development – considered laudable in several respects, e.g., growth – has not only maintained existing gaps in income distribution between the rich and the poor, but also increased the openness or dependence of the Malaysian economy. As Table 3 shows, the export share of the GDP rose from 34.9% in 1947 (right after the economic disruption due to the Second World War) to 47.1% in 1957, dropped to 43.8% in 1970 – after some import-substitution industrialization during the sixties – and then rose again to 59.2% in 1980 after the switch to export-oriented industrialization and the general re-emphasis on production for export. Similarly, imports calculated as a percentage of the GDP rose from 25.1% in 1947 to 37.5% in 1957, 39.6% in 1970 and 56.6% in 1980. Gross domestic capital formation as a share of the GDP rose from 10.8% in 1947 to 11.6% in 1957 and 20.7% in 1970, reflecting increasing investments, especially in manufacturing, after independence, 28.4% in 1980, reflecting increased government investments after announcement of the NEP, and 31.6% in 1983, suggesting that capital accumulation and investments were hardly affected by the recession.

Since public sector consumption's share of the GDP has also risen from 9.0% in 1947 to 14.2% in 1957, 15.6% in 1970, 17.0% in 1980 and 18.7% in 1983, private sector consumption's share fell from 70.4% in 1947 to 64.6% in 1957, 59.4% in 1970, 52.0% in 1980, rising slightly to 54.3% in 1983. These trends may suggest that economic growth has not only given rise to a relatively higher rate of capital accumulation and investment at

TABLE 3
PERCENTAGE COMPOSITION OF GDP AT CURRENT PRICES BY AGGREGATE DEMAND COMPONENTS, 1947, 1957, 1980, AND 1983

	1947[1]	1957[1]	1970[2]	1980[2]	1983[3]
Private consumption	70.4	64.6	59.4	52.0	54.3
Public consumption	9.0	14.2	15.6	17.0	18.7
Gross Domestic Capital Formation	10.8	11.6	20.7	28.4	31.6
Export of goods and services	34.9	47.1	43.8	59.2	54.4
Imports of goods and services	25.1	37.5	39.6	56.6	59.0
GDP at market prices (million ringgit)	2,601	4,985	12,308	51,838	67,480

Sources: 1. V.V. Bhanoji Rao (1976 : 97 — Table A')
2. Malaysia (1981 : 17 — Table 2.2)
3. Malaysia (1984 : 44 — Table 2.2)

the expense of consumption, but also that the decline of private consumption's share may suggest a relative decline in wage and salary earnings (as opposed to earnings from capital investment, which are far more likely to be reinvested).

Hence, though the openness of the economy contributed to rapid economic growth in the late seventies, Malaysia's export commodity prices generally took a tumble in the early eighties. Rubber prices fell by 17.3% in 1981 and 23.0% in 1982 from 302.6 sen per kilogram in 1980 to 192.7 sen in 1982, before picking up again in 1983. Crude petroleum prices dropped from $682.00 per tonne in 1981 to $553.40 in 1983 and continue to slip, while petroleum production has grown from 258,000 U.S. barrels per day in 1981 to 440,000 barrels in 1984. Oil exports rose from 10,143,000 tonnes in 1981 to 14,223,900 tonnes in 1983, though oil export revenue only grew by 13.7% from $6,918 million in 1981 to $7,871 million in 1983, as export unit values fell by 19%.

Tin prices dropped from $36,040 per tonne in 1980 to $30,093 in 1983, while export volume also declined from 69,500 tonnes in 1980 to 57,100 tonnes in 1983. The average price of saw logs fluctuated from $173 per cubic meter in 1980 to $156 in 1981, $175 in 1982 and $149 in1983, while the price of sawn timber dropped from $393 in 1980 to $360 in 1981 and $351 in 1982, before picking up to $371 in 1983. Even the price of palm oil dropped from $1,176 per tonne in 1980 and $1,153 in 1981 by 14.7% to $984 in 1982, before picking up to $1,022 in 1983.

LNG (liquefied natural gas), touted as the great hope for the future, came on stream in 1983, and was exported at a price of $578 per tonne, much below the $821 anticipated by the Fourth Malaysia Plan. Needless to say, selling all Malaysia's LNG at indexed contract prices to a couple of Japanese buyers does not enhance Malaysian bargaining power. Only manufactured exports made an impressive recovery in 1983, increasing by 31.6% in that year alone, thus helping to push up total export value by 17.0% in 1983 to $32,923 million.

To sum up, the unit value of Malaysian agricultural export commodities declined at an average of 6.8% per annum during 1981-83, reaching only 70.7% of 1980 price levels in 1982. Forest product export prices dropped by 3.9% annually to only

88.7% of 1980 prices in 1983, while mineral product prices declined by 3.4% yearly to only 90.1% of 1980 prices in 1983 (Malaysia, 1984 : 50 – Table 2.5).

Despite the global economic recession of the early 1980s, the Malaysian economy continued to grow at an average annual GDP growth rate of 6.2% (at constant prices) during 1981-83. During this period, construction grew at 13.1% yearly, while transport, storage and communications expanded at a creditable average annual rate of 11.6%. The mainly export-oriented primary sector lagged behind, with an annual growth rate of only 4.2%, despite a 16.2% jump in 1983 alone in mining and quarrying, largely accounted for by increased petroleum output. Even more ominously, imputed banking service charges rose at an average rate of 20.4% over this period, largely due to increased government borrowing (Malaysia, 1984: 39 – Table 2.1)

Despite experiencing setbacks due to its heavy dependence on the world economy, the Malaysian economy became increasingly open during 1981-83. Exports grew at an annual rate of 6.2% in current price terms, and 7.5% in 1970 price terms during 1981-83, while imports grew at 10.7% in current price terms, and by 9.6% in 1970 price terms, compared to the average annual GDP growth rate of 9.2% at current prices and 6.2% at 1970 prices. In current price terms, the export share of the GDP dropped from 59.2% in 1980 to 54.1% in 1983, while imports as a proportion of the GDP rose from 56.6% in 1980 to 58.7% in 1983. However in terms of 1970 prices, the export share of the GDP only rose from 43.3% in 1980 to 45.0% in 1983, while the proportion of imports rose from 48.4% in 1980 to 53.2% in 1983. (See Table 2).

The significant discrepancy between trends at current prices and trends in 1970 price terms underscores the considerable influence of shifts in the terms of trade. Using 1970 as a base year, the export price index fell from 270.2 in 1980 to 260.1 in 1983, while the import price index rose from 231.0 in 1980 to 238.2 in 1983; hence, the terms of trade fell by 2.2% per annum during 1980-83. Hence, although the GDP grew during 1980-83 at an annual average of 9.2% in current prices, and 6.2% in 1970 prices terms, real purchasing power only grew at 5.1% per annum (Malaysia, 1984: 54 – Table 2.8).

Despite the recession and the adverse change in the terms of trade in the early 1980s, Malaysian imports grew at an average rate of 9.1% yearly, i.e. faster than the real GDP growth rate. The import of consumption goods grew slightly faster, by 9.4% per annum, while the food share rose from $1,185 million in 1980 to $1,745 million in 1983, i.e. by an average of 13.8% per annum.

Balance of payments trends in recent years have caused great concern. Although the unprecedented deficit of $1,199 million in the merchandise account in 1982 was reversed in 1983, it does not seem likely that Malaysia can expect to enjoy the healthy trade balances of the past in the near future.

More ominously, the services deficit continued to grow; from $6,021 million in 1982 to $8,295 million in 1983, of which freight and insurance alone accounted for $2,243 million. Even more alarming has been the outflow of investment income,[3] which rose by 60.4% in 1983 to $3,592 million. Meanwhile, the net inflow of foreign loans grew from $310 million in 1980 to $2,909 million in 1981 and $4,622 million in 1982 before dropping to $3,824 million in 1983. Commercial credit too has risen dramatically in recent years, from $101 million in 1981 to $581 million in 1982 and $1,095 million in 1983. Needless to say, these loans will have to be repaid with interest, and hence their current positive contribution to the balance of payments is only temporary and will eventually be reversed.

Hence, while the recent jump in the foreign debt has helped offset the two economic crises faced by Malaysia recently, i.e. the balance of payments problem and the fiscal deficit, this role is really only temporary and will inextricably draw the economy into a debt spiral unless this tendency is checked as soon as possible.

One of the root causes of this problem is clear, namely the openness or dependence of the Malaysian economy vis-a-vis the global economy, especially the industrial powers of the North. There is, of course, no easy solution, though a strong, sustained commitment to greater national economic self-reliance (not autarchy) on the basis of a more nationally-oriented and integrated economic structure would be a fundamental step in this direction.

---

[3]This apparently includes debt servicing, though this inclusion is not standard IMF usage. See Andrew Sheng "Balance of Payments Issues in the Fourth Malaysia Plan" Jomo (ed.) *Malaysia's New Economic Policies* Kuala Lumpur : Malaysian Economic Association, 1985.

In this connection, it is unfortunate that national policymakers have not seized the golden opportunity provided by the recession of the early 1980s to steer the economy more firmly in this direction since it is relatively less painful to undertake such fundamental economic restructuring in times of weakened relations with the North.

In principle, the Malaysian government's recent commitment to heavy industrialization can provide the balance and basis for a more coherent and integrated national economic structure capable of 'walking on two legs'. Unfortunately, however, the choice of industries announced so far (e.g. steel, cement, petrochemicals, motorcar) may actually deepen technological dependence in some cases, while loading Malaysia with dubiously viable industries, which are losing money or are otherwise unacceptable elsewhere.

Similarly, the recently renewed commitment to developing agriculture is welcome, especially if it is committed to achieving greater food (as opposed to merely rice) self-sufficiency, and also if it is coupled with greater efforts to develop resource-based industries. To be meaningful, this commitment should not merely respond to the World Bank's recently revived encouragement of agricultural production by developing nations, after the heady days of the New International Economic Order and rapid industrialization in the seventies.

The real lesson from Japan's economic success – which has recently become a model for Malaysian emulation – is, of course, the national roots and orientation for independent economic growth established from the Meiji period, which involved limiting foreign involvement to highly selective activities. Hence, if the current official 'Look East' policy captures this basic aspect of the Japanese phenomenon, this and other aspects of the government's new policy initiatives can re-orient the economy towards achieving greater self-reliance. For example, recent pronouncements about a second round of import substitution, though limited, would nonetheless be a positive step in this direction.

For such initiatives to succeed and be sustained, it will be necessary to further expand the domestic market. Consistent with the equitable objectives of the New Economic Policy – to eradicate poverty and to eliminate the identification of race with economic function – this can be achieved by redistribution in favour of the poor (who have a higher propensity to spend), thus increasing effective demand, rather than by indiscriminate population increase (as currently advocated), which would not necessarily deepen the market, since it would tend to increase the problem of generating employment opportunities and to keep wages low.

INCOME DISTRIBUTION – ESTIMATION EXERCISES

This section provides an empirical survey of income distribution trends and patterns after independence. Besides presenting the overall picture in the economy, an analysis of ethnic and rural-urban differentiation is also carried out.

Tables 1 and 3 present income data from the 1957/58 Household Budget Survey (HBS), the 1967/68 Survey Research Malaysia-Ford Social and Economic Survey (SES), Post-Enumeration Survey (PES) of the 1970 National Population Census, the 1973 Household Expenditure Survey (HES) and the 1976/77 Malaysian Family Life Survey (MFLS) which excluded single-member households. The 1957/58 HBS, the 1970 PES and the 1973 HES were all conducted by the Statistics Department of Malaysia, while the 1967/68 SES and the 1976/77 MFLS were conducted by private research organisations. (Details of these surveys are found in Appendix 1).

It should be pointed out that these surveys were not primarily intended as income distribution surveys. The income distribution data that was generated were by-products of surveys intended for other purposes. It must also be stressed that the income data are not strictly comparable because of the different sources and designs, differing coverage, concepts used, response rate, errors, etc. For example, the 1957/58 HBS and the 1967/68 SES omitted zero-income households. Snodgrass (1974) considers this omission as a possible – though minor – source of bias towards increased inequality. By assuming the existence of uncounted zero-income households in both the surveys in a proportion equal to that found in the 1970 PES, he only obtained a small rise in the Gini ratio – from .412 to .419 in 1957/8, and from .444 to .450 in 1967/68.

However, since three of the five surveys considered here were undertaken directly by the Statistics Department, while another (the 1976/77 MFLS) was conducted in collaboration with personnel from the Statistics Department, these surveys share some basic consistency in the central concepts and methodologies used (see Appendix). Therefore, despite their shortcomings, the data can still provide us with some useful insights into the problem, since there are no better alternative sources.

Development & Inequality

The income inequality situation in Peninsular Malaysia, as measured by the Gini Ratio (GR) and Theil Index (TI), seems to have worsened since 1957, except for a slight, but probably insignificant improvement around 1973. The GR have been estimated to be 0.41 in 1957/8, 0.44 in 1967/68, 0.50 in 1970, 0.50 in 1973 and 0.57 in 1976/77. The brevity of the periods under consideration suggests that short-term fluctuations may be at play, though the apparent long-term trend is one of growing income disparities.

Changes in income inequality between 1957 and 1976 are – predictably – also reflected in changes in the income shares going to the various income groups over the period. The income share of the top 20% of households increased from 48.6% of total income in 1957/8 to 55.9% in 1970, and 61.9% in 1976. The share going to the top 5% rose from 22.1% in 1957/8 to 28.1% in 1970. In contrast, the income share of the bottom 40% of households declined from 15.9% in 1957/8 to 11.6% in 1970 and 10.3% in 1976. Mean household income grew from $215 in 1957/8 to $264 in 1970, $324 in 1973 and $801 in 1976.

Table 1 also shows the pattern of changes in income inequality in rural and urban areas of Peninsular Malaysia over the same period. For all the years mentioned, income disparities appear to be greater in urban areas than in rural areas, though the difference for 1973 may be considered negligible. The changes in income inequality in both areas appear to follow the overall trend of generally growing inequality. Between 1957 and 1976, income inequality in both areas generally worsened, again with a slight quirk for the 1973 survey.

Table 2 seeks to show the extent of income inequality and changes over time for major ethnic groups in Peninsular Malaysia. Mean incomes of non-Malay households increased more than average incomes of Malay households, but Malay households have generally enjoyed relatively higher income growth rates. Kusnic and Da Vanzo (1980) suggest that broadening the definition of incpme to include 'non-market income' – an idea fraught with serious methodological issues surrounding the assumptions involved – would reduce the relative difference in incomes between Chinese and non-Chinese households because relatively more Chinese income is obtained from market activities. While there exist inter-ethnic differences in terms of mean income, income disparities have risen for all ethnic groups. The increase in income inequality seems to be most serious among the Malays, followed by the Indians and the Chinese. In 1957/8, intra-ethnic inequality was highest for the Chinese and lowest for the Malays, but by 1970 and 1973, this ranking was reversed (though the 1976 data suggest yet another reversal).

In this connection, it is relevant to note that Anand (1973) and Ishak & Rogayah (1978) found that nearly 90 percent of overall income inequality in Peninsular Malaysia in 1970 was due to differences **within** ethnic groups, rather than between them. Similarly, Kusnic and Da Vanzo (1980) found that between 80% to 90% of overall income inequality in Peninsular Malaysia was due to differences within ethnic or even urban/rural sub-groups rather than between them.

Kusnick & Da Vanzo (1980) have also argued that by broadening the definition of income to include 'total observable income' (defined as the sum of a household's monetary and non-monetary receipts, i.e. by including transfer income, the value of living in one's own home, in-kind income and cottage-industry income was 17% higher than the mean 1976/77 household 'market income' (defined as the sum of a household's "money income receipts from formal market transactions") of $8219 for their sample of 1068 households. Including their estimate of the value of housework activities, other than cooking and childcare ('total actual income I'), increased the mean by another 17 percent, while including the value of time devoted to childcare and cooking ('total actual income II') increased the mean by another 16 percent. Total actual (household) income II' for the poorest decile of the population was over 3.6 times the corresponding figure for 'market income', while the income share of the poorest 20 per cent more than doubled. "Indeed, broadening the definition of income has the greatest impact on the poorest segments of the population", while inequality (by all indicators) fell as the definition of income was broadened.

The authors argue that "the poor in Malaysia appear to attempt to compensate for their relatively low market income by producing many foods and services for their own consumption", which explains the rise in their income share when the definition of income is broadened to include non-market activities. But the poor tend to work relatively long hours at these productive household activities and hence forego relatively more leisure time. Hence, failure to adjust for 'leisure consumption' results in overestimation of the relative economic welfare of the poor. They also find that 'broadening the definition of income' considerably changes the ranking of households in terms of income distribution.

It is pertinent to remind ourselves here of the official conception of poverty. Simply put, the government views poverty in absolute rather than relative terms and claims to monitor the incidence of poverty in relation to a (publicly undisclosed) poverty line. With such a conception of poverty operative, it is conceivable that income inequality could grow while the poverty rate goes down, if economic growth rates are sufficiently high. Evidence from the Fourth Malaysia Plan (4MP) suggests that this may have been the case during the 1970s. Unlike the period 1957-70, when income inequality grew as the lower income groups suffered declining real incomes (Treasury, 1974) – i.e. a situation of the rich getting richer and the poor getting poorer – during the 1970s, it appears that the real income of the bottom forty per cent increased while overall income inequality continued to grow (Malaysia, 1981: 37 – Table 3.3).

In the absence of definitive indicators, the growing ratios between mean and median incomes between 1970 and 1979 for the Peninsular Malaysian Malay, Chinese, urban and rural subgroupings – shown in Table 4 – suggest growing income inequality in all these communities over the last decade especially when taken into consideration with the income distribution situation in 1970 and trends since then, as suggested by various other studies. Table 4 also shows that the average annual growth rate of mean income between 1971 and 1979 for the lowest four income deciles was lower than that for all households; this was also true for Malay Chinese and Indian households separately considered. In other words, rising incomes all around and poverty eradication in the 1970s have apparently been accompanied by continued high income inequality. It is noteworthy (see Table 4) that the official Gini coefficient went down very slightly from 0.513 in 1970 to 0.508 in 1979, a decline imperceptible at the second decimal point. However, other calculations have yielded a Gini coefficient of 0.502 for 1970 (Ishak & Rogayah, 1978, Snodgrass,

**TABLE 4 : PENINSULAR MALAYSIA
RATIO OF MEAN AND MEDIAN INCOMES, 1970-79
($ per household per month)**

		in constant 1970 prices					*in current prices*				
		1970	1973	1976	1979	Annual growth rate, 1971-79 (%)	1973	1976	1979	Annual growth rate, 1971-79 (%)	Annual growth rate (1971-79) of mean income of bottom 40% (%)
Malay	mean	172	209	237	296	6.2	242	345	492	12.4	10.5
	median	120	141	160	197	5.7	163	233	327	11.8	
	(ratio)	(1.43)	(1.48)	(1.48)	(1.50)	(1.09)			(1.50)	(1.05)	
Chinese	mean	394	461	540	565	4.1	534	787	938	10.1	8.4
	median	268	298	329	373	3.7	343	480	620	9.8	
	(ratio)	(1.47)	(1.55)	(1.64)	(1.51)	(1.11)			(1.51)	(1.03)	
Indian	mean	304	352	369	455	4.6	408	538	756	10.6	9.9
	median	194	239	247	314	5.5	277	360	521	11.6	
	(ratio)	(1.57)	(1.47)	(1.49)	(1.45)	(0.84)			(1.45)	(0.91)	
Others	mean	813	1,121	870	1147	3.9	1,299	1,268	1904	9.9	14.8
	median	250	306	270	331	3.2	355	394	550	9.1	
	(ratio)	(3.25)	(3.06)	(3.22)	(3.47)	(1.22)			(3.46)	(1.09)	
All	mean	264	313	353	417	5.2	362	514	693	11.3	10.5
	median	166	196	215	263	5.2	227	313	436	11.3	
	(ratio)	(1.59)	(1.60)	(1.64)	(1.59)	(1.00)			(1.59)	(1.00)	
Urban	mean	428	492	569	587	3.6	570	830	975	9.6	
	median	265	297	340	361	3.5	345	495	600	9.5	
	(ratio)	(1.62)	(1.66)	(1.67)	(1.63)	(1.03)			(1.63)	(1.01)	
Rural	mean	200	233	269	331	5.7	269	392	550	11.9	
	median	139	159	180	222	5.3	184	262	369	11.4	
	(ratio)	(1.44)	(1.47)	(1.49)	(1.49)	(1.08)			(1.49)	(1.04)	

Sources : Malaysia (1981 : 37 – Table 3.3; 56 – Table 3.9)
Malaysia (1984 : 94 – Table 3.8)

1970). again pointing to an increase in the Gini coefficient during the seventies.

Since the uneven distribution of ownership of productive assets is an important factor explaining different income streams, and hence inequality, it is useful to observe the pattern of wealth ownership in Peninsular Malaysia. Relevant statistics relating to ownership and control of wealth are sparse and far from comprehensive. Nonetheless, it is clear that wealth in Peninsular Malaysia is held very unequally.

Some recent studies (Lim, 1980; Lim & Anderson, 1979; Sieh, 1977; Tan, 1982) of the concentration of wealth in large companies provide interesting insights into the extent of inequality in wealth ownership in the country. In their study of 34 large corporations in Malaysia, Lim and Anderson (1979) found that "ownership of stocks in these firms is highly concentrated in the hands of a small number of investors . . . . the largest 25 shareholders own more than 51% of the ordinary stock". They also pointed out that "despite the large number of shareholders in all companies, the majority of shares is still concentrated in the hands of the top 25 investors". Sieh (1977), conducted a study of the official shareholders list of the 98 largest Malaysian-incorporated companies engaged in manufacturing in 1974-75 and found an extremely high degree of concentration of equity capital in a small number of large holdings with an overall Gini ratio of 0.91. Her study also showed that 1% of the more than 100,000 shareholders accounted for almost 80% of all shareholdings. In his study of the pattern of ownership and control of some of the largest corporations in Malaysia, Tan Tat Wai (1982) concluded that there is a "great concentration of the wealth and resources of the leading companies in the country in the hands of a very few . . . (and) . . . no more than a few scores of family share in the fruit of this!".

REFERENCES

Ishak Shari & Rogayah M. Zain (1978) "Some Aspects of Income Inequality in Peninsular Malaysia, 1957–70", in H.T. Oshima & T. Mizoguchi, (eds), *Income Distribution by Sectors and Over Time in East And Southeast Asian Countries*, (Manila: Council of Asian Manpower Studies)

Jomo K.S. (1985) *A Question of Class: Capital, the State and Uneven Development in Malaysia* (Kuala Lumpur: Oxford University Press)

Kusnic, Michael W. & Da Vanzo, Julie (1980) *Income Inequality And The Definition of Income* (Santa Monica: The Rand Corporation for the Agency for International Development)

Lim Mah Hui (1980) *Ownership and Control of the One Hundred Largest Corporations in Malaysia* (Kuala Lumpur: Oxford University Press)

Lim Mah Hui & Mary Anderson (1979) "Concentration of Wealth and Power in the Top Corporations in Malaysia', in Cheong Kee Check *et al.* (ed) *Malaysia: Some Contemporary Issues in Socioeconomic Development* (Kuala Lumpur: Malaysian Economic Association)

Low, Patrick (1971) *Trends in Malaysia I* (Singapore: Institute of Southeast Asian Studies).

Malaysia, Government of (1981) *Fourth Malaysia Plan, 1981–85* (Kuala Lumpur: Government Printer)

Malaysia, Government of (1984) *Mid-Term Review of the Fourth Malaysia Plant* (Kuala Lumpur: Government Printer)

Sich Mei Ling (1977) "Size Distribution of Shareholdings in Manufacturing: Case of Malaysia, 1974–5". Paper presented at a Malaysian Economic Association Seminar, Kuala Lumpur (May)

Snodgrass, Donald R. (1980) *Inequality and Economic Development in Malaysia* (Kuala Lumpur: Oxford University Press)

Tan Tat-Wai (1982) *Income Distribution and Determination in West Malaysia* (Kuala Lumpur: Oxford University Press)

Van Vorys, Karl (1975) *Democracy Without Consensus* (Princeton: Princeton University Press)

Name Index

Abowd, J.M. 507, 513
Abraham, K.G. 507
Akin, J.S. 507
Albelda, R.P. 533
Aldrich, M. 509, 522, 523
Althausser, R.P. 241
Amaker, N.C. 359
Amemiya, T. 601
Anand 625
Anderson 628
Anderson, R.G. 341
Andresani, P.J. 511
Arrow, K. 113, 439, 574
Ashenfelter, O. 195, 338, 342, 344, 465, 473, 474, 532, 541, 560, 601
Ayres, I. 369

Ballen, J. 376
Barbezat, D.A. 342
Barry, J. 510
Bartel, A.P. 507
Bartlett, R.L. 510
Batchelder, A. 194
Bates, D. 488
Beach, C.M. 537
Becker, B.E. 507, 508
Becker, G.S. 4, 65, 74, 241, 243, 439, 447, 474, 505, 507
Beller, A.H. 68, 515, 516, 519
Bendick, M. 400
Berg, I. 72
Berger, M.C. 510
Bergmann, B.R. 72, 522
Berndt, E.R. 99
Bianchi, S. 331
Birnbaum, M.H. 512
Blackburn, M.L. 230
Blakemore, A.E. 507
Blau, F.D. 67, 338, 339, 507, 512
Blinder, A.S. 4, 65, 66, 241
Bloom, D.E. 230, 514
Bobo, L. 331
Bok, S. 384
Bonacich, E. 488
Bond, H. 199
Borjas, G.J. 507, 509
Bowsher, C.A. 381
Bratt, R. 325
Brown, C. 68, 341, 516, 518, 519, 570
Buchele, R. 509, 522, 523
Bunting, R. 574
Burman, G. 532, 541, 560
Butler, R.J. 242, 511, 535, 546–9, 552, 556, 569, 571, 576–8, 588, 589, 601, 602, 604

Cain, G. 65, 67, 348, 506, 533
Card, D. 227
Carter, S. 341
Chiplin, B. 339, 506, 513, 517
Chiswick, B.R. 507
Christensen, L.R. 99
Cloward, R. 457
Cohen, M.S. 4
Colosanto, D. 331
Conway, D.A. 512
Cross, H. 350, 369, 386, 390, 392
Culp, J. 349, 350
Curran, M. 517

Daniel, W.W. 340
Darity, W.A. 195, 488, 506, 507
Da Vanzo 624, 625
Daymont, T.N. 511
DelCastillo, S.W. 356, 357, 398, 399, 401, 403
Dewald, W.G. 341
Dex, S. 506
Doeringer, P.B. 83, 439, 533
Dolton, P.J. 509–11, 513
Donahue, J.J. 377, 412
Douglas, P. 461
Douty, H. 462
Downs, A. 83
Duncan, G.J. 507, 519
Duncan, O.D. 31, 75, 241
Duncan, R.C. 522
Dunson, B.H. 349, 350

Edgeworth, F.Y. 116
Edley, C. 385
Edwards, R. 439
Ehrenberg, R. 513, 521, 522
Ellwood, D. 347
Evans, S. 574

Farley, R. 331
Feins, J. 325, 329
Ferber, M.A. 68, 338, 339, 508
Filer, R.K. 507, 509, 510, 511, 523
Fix, M. 369, 383, 386, 390, 392
Flanagan, R.J. 507
Fomby, T. 336
Fosu, A.K. 539
Freeman, R.B. 95, 196, 230, 237, 376, 537, 546–9, 552–4, 556, 557, 570
Friedman, M. 458, 570
Fuchs, V.R. 3
Fusfield, D. 488

Galster, G. 378, 379, 398, 405
Garfinkel, I. 507
Garstwirth, J.L. 513
Gay, P. 341
Getty, J.P. 44
Giansello, J. 404
Glenn, D.E. 510
Golbe, D.L. 516
Goldberger, A.S. 512
Goldstein, M. 532, 541, 560
Gordon, D. 439
Grant, J.H. 95
Greenhalgh, C. 509
Gregory, R.G. 522

Hamermesh, D.S. 95
Hanoch, G. 194
Hansen, R. 68
Hanushek, E.A. 227, 234
Harrison, B. 72, 81
Hartmann, H.I. 521
Hashimoto, M. 512
Heckman, J.J. 377, 395, 398, 403, 514, 532, 535, 541, 546–9, 552, 556, 560, 571, 577, 578, 588, 589, 601, 602
Hicks, J. 90
Hildebrand, G.H. 519
Hill, H. 488
Hill, R.C. 336
Hoffman, J. 601
Hoffman, S.D. 507, 519
Hojman, D.E. 512
Holzer, H. 376
Hubbock, J. 341
Hughes, J.W. 342

Ihlanfeldt, K.R. 376
Ishak 625, 626

James, F.J. 356, 357, 398, 399, 400, 403
Jaynes, J.D. 376, 377
Jerdee, T.H. 68
Johnson, G. 522
Johnson, H.G. 467
Johnson, S. 336–7
Johnston, J. 326
Jones, F.L. 509
Joshi, H.E. 186, 510, 517
Joshi, V. 186
Jowell, R. 101–3, 107, 273, 291, 294, 300, 301, 340, 341
Juhn, C. 233

Kahn, L.M. 512
Kamalich, R.E. 512
Karpinos, B. 212
Kasarda, J.D. 347
Keeney, W.M. 405, 406, 410, 411
Kelley, M.R. 508
Kenney, G.M. 392
Kidder, A. 574
Killingsworth, M. 507, 508, 510, 514, 521
King, T. 378
Kirschenman, J. 381
Kitagawa, E.M. 241
Knopff, R. 513
Kochlin, L. 512
Kosters, M.H. 230
Krueger, A. 227
Kuhn, P.J. 339
Kusnic 624, 625

Ladd, H. 378
Lazear, E. 518
Leigh, D. 473, 474
Leigh, J.P. 507
Leonard, J.S. 360, 516, 520, 521, 532, 540
Leontief, W. 89, 90, 99
Levin, H. 195
Lieberson, S. 189
Lim 628
Link, C. 507
Low, P. 615
Low, S.A. 507
Lyle, G. 72

MacKinnon, J.G. 537
Maher, J. 462
Main, E. 72
Makepeace, G. 509–11
Malkiel, B.G. 4
Malkiel, J.A. 4
Mallan, L.B. 519
Marshall, R. 533
Mashaw, J. 404

Masters, S.H. 515
McCormick, B. 514
McGavin, P.A. 522
McIntosh, N. 101–2, 107, 340, 341, 349
McIntyre, S. 400
Meade, L.M. 347, 359
Medoff, J.L. 507
Medoff, M.H. 533, 538
Michelson, S. 72, 84
Mieszkowski, P. 467
Miller, P.W. 522
Miller, T.I. 510
Mills, E. 376
Millspaugh 399
Mincer, J. 66, 507
Miyazaki, H. 439
Mohamed, M. 614
Munnell, A. 378
Murphy, K. 230, 233
Murray, C. 570
Myrdal, G. 194

Neckerman, K. 381
Newell, M.L. 510, 517

Oaxaca, R. 142, 241–5, 338, 342, 344
O'Leary, V. 68
O'Neill, J. 68, 522
Olsen, C.A. 507, 508
Osborne, D. 575
Osterman, P. 520

Parsley, C.J. 517
Payner, B.S. 541, 571, 577, 578, 588, 589, 601, 602
Pierce, B. 233
Pike, M. 518
Piore, M.J. 439, 533
Piven, F. 457
Polachek, S. 67, 507, 512, 522
Powell, J. 601
Prescott-Clarke, P. 101–3, 107, 273, 291, 294, 300, 301, 340, 341
Price, R. 376

Rees, A. 376
Reich, M. 439, 488, 489, 492, 493, 499
Reimers, C.W. 508
Reynolds, L. 465
Riach, P.A. 341–3
Ribich, T. 72
Rich, J. 341–3
Ridley, S.E. 369
Roberts, H. 511, 512
Rogayah 625, 626
Rosen, B. 68
Rosen, S. 465
Rowan, R. 574, 575
Ryscavage, P. 459

Sanborn, H. 3
Schafer, R. 378
Schiller, B. 72
Schuman, H. 331, 371
Schumpeter, J. 62
Shorey, J. 507
Siebert, W.S. 507
Siegelman, P. 377, 395, 398, 403, 412
Sieh 628
Simiscalco, G. 404
Simmons, M. 574
Simonson, J. 330
Simpson, A. 401, 402
Simpson, G. 330, 331
Sjoquist, D.L. 376
Sloane, P.J. 339, 506
Smith, D.J. 101–2, 107, 340, 341, 349, 574
Smith, J.P. 68, 226, 233, 360, 515, 516, 518, 520, 533, 537, 539, 569, 570
Smith, R.S. 513, 521, 522, 532, 541, 560
Snipp, C.M. 189
Snodgrass 623, 626
Solon, G. 512, 522
Sowell, T. 507
Spaeth, J.L. 508
Spandau, A. 121
Spence, A.M. 439
Squires, G. 369
Stafford, F. 29
Stanley 387
Steed, C. 331
Stewart, M. 509
Strauss, D.A. 377
Struyk, R. 369, 383, 386, 390, 392
Swinton, D.H. 115

Takaki, R. 192
Tan, T.W. 628
Tang, A. 591
Teiman, M. 68
Thomas, J. 404
Throop, A. 459
Thurow, L. 72, 194, 439
Thursby, J.G. 341
Tobin, J. 570
Treiman, D. 521
Turner, M. 350, 369, 383, 386, 390, 392
Tzannatos, Z. 509, 517–9

Velez, W. 369
Vietorisz, T. 81
Vroman, W. 546, 570

Wallace, J. 406
Wallace, P.A. 361, 362
Ward, M. 68
Ward, R. 340
Waters, M. 189
Weiss, R. 72, 74
Welch, F. 85, 195, 197, 210, 217, 226, 230, 233, 360, 439, 515, 516, 518, 520, 533, 569, 570, 577
Wienk, R. 325, 330, 339, 369, 378, 397
Wigler, M. 241
Williams, R.M. 376, 377, 506
Wilson, W.J. 347, 570
Wissoker, D.A. 392
Wolpin, K.I. 532, 541, 560
Wright, E.O. 488
Wright, G. 570

Yinger, M. 330, 331, 339, 340, 343, 394, 397, 401

Zabalza, A. 509, 517–9
Zeman, M. 194

The International Library of Critical Writings in Economics

1. Multinational Corporations
   Mark Casson

2. The Economics of Innovation
   Christopher Freeman

3. Entrepreneurship
   Mark Casson

4. International Investment
   Peter J. Buckley

5. Game Theory in Economics
   Ariel Rubinstein

6. The History of Economic Thought
   Mark Blaug

7. Monetary Theory
   Thomas Mayer

8. Joint Production of Commodities
   Neri Salvadori and Ian Steedman

9. Industrial Organization
   Oliver E. Williamson

10. Growth Theory (Volumes I, II and III)
    R. Becker and E. Burmeister

11. Microeconomics: Theoretical and Applied (Volumes I, II and III)
    Robert E. Kuenne

12. The Economics of Health (Volumes I and II)
    A.J. Culyer

13. Recent Developments in Macroeconomics (Volumes I, II and III)
    Edmund S. Phelps

14. Urban and Regional Economics
    Paul C. Cheshire and Alan W. Evans

15. Modern Public Finance (Volumes I and II)
    A.B. Atkinson

16. Exchange Rate Economics (Volumes I and II)
    Ronald MacDonald and Mark P. Taylor

17. The Economic Value of Education: Studies in the Economics of Education
Mark Blaug

18. Development Economics (Volumes I, II, III and IV)
Deepak Lal

19. The New Classical Macroeconomics (Volumes I, II and III)
Kevin D. Hoover

20. The Economics of the Environment
Wallace E. Oates

21. Post Keynesian Theory of Growth and Distribution
Carlo Panico and Neri Salvadori

22. Dynamic Labor Demand and Adjustment Costs
Giorgio Galeazzi and Daniel S. Hamermesh

23. The Philosophy and Methodology of Economics (Volumes I, II and III)
Bruce J. Caldwell

24. Public Choice Theory (Volumes I, II and III)
Charles K. Rowley

25. Evolutionary Economics
Ulrich Witt

26. Economics and Psychology
Shlomo Maital and Sharone L. Maital

27. Social Choice Theory (Volumes I, II and III)
Charles K. Rowley

28. Non-Linear Dynamics in Economic Theory
Marc Jarsulic

29. Recent Developments in Experimental Economics (Volumes I and II)
John D. Hey and Graham Loomes

30. Monopoly and Competition Policy (Volumes I and II)
F.M. Scherer

31. The Economics of Technical Change
Edwin Mansfield and Elizabeth Mansfield

32. The Economics of Exhaustible Resources
Geoffrey Heal

33. The Economics of Institutions
Geoffrey M. Hodgson

34. The Economics of Transport (Volumes I and II)
Herbert Mohring

35. Implicit Contract Theory
Sherwin Rosen

36. Foundations of Analytical Marxism (Volumes I and II)
John E. Roemer

37. The Economics of Product Differentiation (Volumes I and II)
Jacques-François Thisse and George Norman

38. Economic Growth in Theory and Practice: A Kaldorian Perspective
John E. King

39. Markets and Socialism
Alec Nove and Ian D. Thatcher

40. Recent Developments in the Economics of Education
Elchanan Cohn and Geraint Johnes

41. The Theory of Inflation
Michael Parkin

42. The Economics of Location (Volumes I, II and III)
Melvin L. Greenhut and George Norman

43. Financial Intermediaries
Mervyn K. Lewis

44. The Political Economy of Privatization and Deregulation
Elizabeth E. Bailey and Janet Rothenberg Pack

45. Gender and Economics
Jane Humphries

46. Macroeconomics and Imperfect Competition
Jean-Pascal Bénassy

47. Labor Economics (Volumes I, II, III and IV)
Orley C. Ashenfelter and Kevin F. Hallock

48. The Economics of Altruism
Stefano Zamagni

49. The Economic Analysis of Rent Seeking
Robert D. Tollison and Roger D. Congleton

50. Economics and Biology
Geoffrey M. Hodgson

51. The Economics of Ageing
John Creedy

52. Fiscal and Monetary Policy (Volumes I and II)
Thomas Mayer and Steven M. Sheffrin

53. The Economics of Information (Volumes I and II)
David K. Levine and Steven A. Lippman

54. Transaction Cost Economics (Volumes I and II)
Oliver E. Williamson and Scott E. Masten

55. Agricultural Economics
George H. Peters

56. International Debt (Volumes I and II)
Graham Bird and P. Nicholas Snowden

57. Economics and Discrimination (Volumes I and II)
William A. Darity, Jr

58. Business Cycle Theory
Finn E. Kydland

59. International Trade (Volumes I and II)
J. Peter Neary

60. The Money Supply in the Economic Process
Marco Musella and Carlo Panico

Future titles will include:

Long Wave Theory
Christopher Freeman

Small Firms and Economic Growth
Zoltan Acs

General Equilibrium Theory
Gerard Debreu

Producer Cooperatives and Labor-Managed Systems
David L. Prychitko and Jaroslav Vanek

The Foundations of Public Finance
Peter Jackson

Ethics and Economics
Alan Hamlin

The Economics of Training
Robert J. LaLonde and Orley Ashenfelter

The Economics of the Family
Nancy Folbre

The New Growth Theory
Gene M. Grossman

Chaotic Dynamics in Economics
W. Davis Dechert

The Economics of Communication and Innovation
Donald M. Lamberton

The Economics of Uncertainty
John D. Hey

International Finance
Robert Z. Aliber

Welfare Economics
William J. Baumol and Janusz A. Ordover

The Theory of the Firm
Mark Casson

The Economics of Inequality and Poverty
A.B. Atkinson

The Economics of Housing
John M. Quigley

Population Economics
Julian L. Simon

The Economics of Crime
Isaac Ehrlich

The Economics of Integration
Willem Molle

The Rhetoric of Economics
Donald McCloskey

Migration
Oded Stark

Economic Forecasting
Paul Ormerod

The Economics of Defence
Keith Hartley and Nicholas Hooper

Consumer Theory
Kelvin Lancaster

Law and Economics
Richard A. Posner and Francesco Parisi

The Economics of Business Policy
John Kay

Microeconomic Theories of Imperfect Competition
Jacques Thisse and Jean Gabszewicz

The Economics of Increasing Returns
Geoffrey Heal

The Balance of Payments
Michael J. Artis

Cost-Benefit Analysis
Arnold Harberger and Glenn P. Jenkins

The Economics of Unemployment
P.N. Junankar

Mathematical Economics
Graciela Chichilnisky

Economic Growth in the Long Run
Bart van Ark

Gender in Economic and Social History
K.J. Humphries and J. Lewis

The Economics of Local Finance and Fiscal Federalism
Wallace Oates

Privatization in Developing and Transitional Economies
Colin Kirkpatrick and Paul Cook

Input-Output Analysis
Heinz Kurz and Christian Lager

The Economics of Global Warming
Tom Tietenberg